The American Journey

GREYSCALE

BIN TRAVELER FORM

Cut By Willyy   Qty 18   Date 23.01.25

Scanned By _____ Qty _____ Date _____

Scanned Batch IDs

_____ _____ _____

Notes / Exception

_____

_____

_____

_____

_____

The American Journey
A History of the United States

SEVENTH EDITION
Volume 1 (To 1877)

David Goldfield
University of North Carolina, Charlotte

Jo Ann E. Argersinger
Southern Illinois University

Carl Abbott
Portland State University

Peter H. Argersinger
Southern Illinois University

Virginia DeJohn Anderson
University of Colorado, Boulder

William L. Barney
University of North Carolina, Chapel Hill

PEARSON

Boston   Columbus   Indianapolis   New York   San Francisco   Upper Saddle River
Amsterdam   Cape Town   Dubai   London   Madrid   Milan   Munich   Paris   Montréal   Toronto
Delhi   Mexico City   São Paulo   Sydney   Hong Kong   Seoul   Singapore   Taipei   Tokyo

Editor in Chief: Dickson Musslewhite
Executive Editor: Ed Parsons
Editorial Program Manager: Seanna Breen
Director of Marketing: Brandy Dawson
Executive Marketing Manager: Wendy Albert
Senior Managing Editor: Ann Marie McCarthy
Production Project Manager: Debra A. Wechsler
Senior Operations Supervisor: Mary Fischer
Operations Specialist: Mary Ann Gloriande
Art Director: Maria Lange
Interior Design: Red Kite Project
Cover Design: Maria Lange/Red Kite Project
Cover Illustration: Paul Chung

Cover: Sam Houston's life was a wild journey that saw him become an adopted citizen of the Cherokee Nation, win elections as the governor of Tennessee and then Texas, emerge as a hero of the Texas War for Independence, and defy his fellow Texans with his Unionist stance during the secession crisis. Photo © Archive Images/Alamy.
Digital Media Editor: Michael Halas
Digital Media Project Manager: Elizabeth Roden Hall
Full-Service Project Management and Composition: PreMedia Global USA Inc.
Printer/Binder: R. R. Donnelley / Williard
Cover Printer: Lehigh-Phoenix Color/Hagerstown
Text Font: Minion Pro 10.5 pts

Credits and acknowledgments borrowed from other sources and reproduced, with permission, in this textbook appear on appropriate page within text (or beginning on page C-1).

Library of Congress Cataloging-in-Publication Data
Goldfield, David R.
    The American journey : a history of the United States / David Goldfield, University of North Carolina, Charlotte; Carl Abbott, Portland State University; Virginia DeJohn Anderson, University of Colorado, Boulder; Jo Ann E. Argersinger, Southern Illinois University; Peter H. Argersinger, Southern Illinois University; William L. Barney, University of North Carolina, Chapel Hill; — Seventh edition; combined volume.
        pages cm
    ISBN 978-0-205-95852-8 (pbk. : combined) — ISBN 978-0-205-96096-5 (pbk. : v. 1) — ISBN 978-0-205-96095-8 (pbk. : v. 2)
    1. United States—History—Textbooks. I. Title.
    E178.1.G614 2013
    973—dc23

2013013884

10 9 8 7 6 5 4 3 2 1

Combined Volume:
ISBN 10: 0-205-95852-4
ISBN 13: 978-0-205-95852-8

Volume 1:
ISBN 10: 0-205-96096-0
ISBN 13: 978-0-205-96096-5

Volume 1 à la carte:
ISBN 10: 0-205-96246-7
ISBN 13: 978-0-205-96246-4

Volume 2:
ISBN 10: 0-205-96095-2
ISBN 13: 978-0-205-96095-8

Volume 2 à la carte:
ISBN 10: 0-205-96245-9
ISBN 13: 978-0-205-96245-7

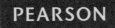

Brief Contents

Contents

Special Features

From Then to Now

Video Series

Explore . . .

Maps

Figures

Tables

Preface

New to This Edition

Every chapter in the seventh edition of *The American Journey* has been carefully revised to present a briefer, more accessible approach to the material while continuing to emphasize its unique features—chronological organization, geographical literacy, regional balance, and religion.

Personalize Learning with New MyHistoryLab

This text features full **integration with the new MyHistoryLab**—a rich resource that delivers proven results in helping students succeed, provides engaging experiences that personalize learning, and comes from a trusted partner with educational expertise and a deep commitment to helping students and instructors achieve their goals.

- The **Pearson eText**, with a new streamlined design for tablet devices, lets students access *The American Journey* anytime, anywhere, and any way they want—and they can listen to and download every chapter. Section tabs on the margin of every page make the text much easier to navigate. The new Pearson eText is now fully interactive and links to all the learning resources in the MyLab.
- **Chapter launcher videos** introduce students to the material, helping to engage them even before they begin reading the chapter. Each chapter has a 15-minute segment, comprised of a three-minute overview and three four-minute videos on specific topics. The videos are featured on the second page, directly after the chapter opener.
- In the new **MyHistoryLibrary with audio**, students can read, listen to, annotate, download, and print over 200 of the most commonly assigned primary source documents. These documents can also be annotated by instructors.
- With the new **History Explorer**, students visualize and analyze historical evidence in a powerful mapping resource. The modules cover topics from English Colonization to the Civil Rights Movement, and each contains an assignable exercise with automated assessment. They are also featured in every chapter of the text in a special box.
- The new **automated writing assessment engine** allows students to further explore key topics by responding to them in essay form. The system offers ten formal prompts on standard topics like the American Revolution, the Lewis and Clark expedition, and the New Deal. Each assignment is based on one of MyHistoryLab's engaging **Author Video Lectures**.
- A **personalized study plan** for each student, based on Bloom's Taxonomy, promotes critical thinking skills and helps students succeed in the course and beyond.
- **Assessment** tied to videos, applications, and chapters enables instructors and students to track progress and get immediate feedback. Instructors will be able to find the best resources for teaching their students.

- **MyHistoryLab icons** are paired with images in the text for more thorough integration between the book and online resources.
- The new **Instructor's eText** makes it easier than ever for instructors to access subject-specific resources for class preparation. Housed within MyHistoryLab, it serves as the hub for all available instructor resources—including the new MyHistoryLab Instructor's Guide.
- The new **MyHistoryLab Instructor's Guide** outlines the basic steps for registering and building a course in MyHistoryLab and describes the key resources and assignments available for each chapter of *The American Journey*.
- The **Class Preparation Tool** collects the best class presentation resources in one convenient online destination. Resources include PowerPoint slides, streaming audio and video, audio clips for class tests and quizzes, and all illustrations for creating interactive lectures.

Engage Students and Improve Critical Thinking

- **Chapter introductory vignettes** provide brief firsthand accounts from individuals who powerfully recount the personal journeys they took in their lives. Each of these "voices" relates to the themes that follow in the chapter.
- **Chapter images** are bigger, visually interesting, and informative. Photographs and pieces of fine art encapsulate emotional and historical meaning. Captions provide valuable information that allows for a fuller understanding of the people who lived the American journey.
- **From Then to Now** relates important issues and events in each chapter to the issues and events of today, letting students see the relevance of history to their lives. This feature also provides thought-provoking visuals to support and enhance the narrative.

Support Instructors

- **Learning Objective questions** highlight the important issues and themes. Each is linked to one of the chapter's main sections, and they are all emphasized in the chapter overview.
- The **Chapter Review** on the last page addresses all four Learning Objective questions from the beginning of each chapter in brief 50-word answers, summarizing the important issues and themes.
- The **thematic timeline** ending each chapter reinforces the essential points of the narrative, as events are tied to key terms from the text.

About the Authors

David Goldfield is the Robert Lee Bailey Professor of History at the University of North Carolina, Charlotte. A native of Memphis, he grew up in Brooklyn, New York, and attended the University of Maryland. He is the author or editor of sixteen books dealing with the history of the American South, including two works, *Cotton Fields and Skyscrapers: Southern City and Region* (1982) and *Black, White, and Southern: Race Relations and Southern Culture* (1991), nominated for the Pulitzer Prize in history, and both received the Mayflower Award for Non-Fiction. *Still Fighting the Civil War: The American South and Southern History* appeared in 2002 and received the Jules and Frances Landry Prize and was named by *Choice* as an Outstanding Non-fiction Book. His most recent book is *America Aflame: How the Civil War Created a* Nation (2011). Goldfield is the President of the Southern Historical Association (2012–13) and is also the editor of the *Journal of Urban History*. He serves as an expert witness in voting rights and death penalty cases, as a consultant on the urban South to museums and public television and radio, and as an Academic Specialist for the U.S. State Department, leading workshops on American history and culture in foreign countries. He also serves on the Advisory Board of the Lincoln Prize.

Carl Abbott is a professor of Urban Studies and Planning at Portland State University. He taught previously in the history departments at the University of Denver and Old Dominion University, and held visiting appointments at Mesa College in Colorado, George Washington University, and the University of Oregon. He holds degrees in history from Swarthmore College and the University of Chicago. He specializes in the history of cities and the American West and serves as co-editor of the *Pacific Historical Review*. His books include *The New Urban America: Growth and Politics in Sunbelt Cities* (1981, 1987), *The Metropolitan Frontier: Cities in the Modern American West* (1993), *Political Terrain: Washington, D. C. from Tidewater Town to Global Metropolis* (1999), *Frontiers Past and Future: Science Fiction and the American West* (2006), and *How Cities Won the West: Four Centuries of Urban Change in Western North America* (2008).

Virginia DeJohn Anderson is Professor of History at the University of Colorado at Boulder. She received her B.A. from the University of Connecticut and as a Marshall Scholar earned an M.A. degree at the University of East Anglia in Norwich, England. Returning to the United States, she received her A.M. and Ph.D. degrees from Harvard University. A recipient of fellowships from the American Council of Learned Societies and the National Endowment for the Humanities, she is the author of *New England's Generation* (1991) and *Creatures of Empire: People and Animals in Early America* (2004). She has also published several articles on colonial history, which have appeared in such journals as the *William and Mary Quarterly* and the *New England Quarterly*. Her current book project is tentatively entitled *The Martyr and the Traitor: The Perilous Lives of Moses Dunbar and Nathan Hale in the American Revolution.*

Jo Ann E. Argersinger received her Ph.D. from George Washington University and is Professor of History at Southern Illinois University, where she won the George S. and Gladys W. Queen Award for Outstanding Teacher in History. A recipient of fellowships from the Rockefeller Foundation and the National Endowment for the Humanities, she is a historian of U.S. women, labor, and transnational history. Her publications include *Toward a New Deal in Baltimore: People and Government in the Great Depression* (1988), *Making the Amalgamated: Gender, Ethnicity, and Class in the Baltimore Clothing Industry* (1999), and *The Triangle Fire: A Brief History with Documents* (2009). She is currently writing a book entitled *Contested Visions of American Democracy: Public Housing and Citizenship in the International Arena* and working on a video project entitled *Women in America*.

Peter H. Argersinger is Professor of History at Southern Illinois University, where he was named Outstanding Scholar by the College of Liberal Arts. He received his B.A. from the University of Kansas and his M.A. and Ph.D. from the University of Wisconsin. He has been a Fellow of the Woodrow Wilson International Center for Scholars in Washington, D.C., and he has received fellowships, grants, and awards from the National Endowment for the Humanities, the American Historical Association, the Organization of American Historians, the Massachusetts Historical Society, and other organizations. Among his books on American political and rural history are *Populism and Politics* (1974), *Structure, Process, and Party* (1992), and *The Limits of Agrarian Radicalism* (1995). His most recent book, integrating legal and political history, is *Representation and Inequality in Late Nineteenth-Century America: The Politics of Apportionment* (2012). His current research focuses on the political crisis of the 1890s.

William L. Barney is Professor of History at the University of North Carolina at Chapel Hill. A native of Pennsylvania, he received his B.A. from Cornell University and his M.A. and Ph.D. from Columbia University. He has published extensively on nineteenth-century U.S. history and has a particular interest in the Old South and the coming of the Civil War. Among his publications are *The Road to Secession* (1972), *The Secessionist Impulse* (1974), *Flawed Victory* (1975), *The Passage of the Republic* (1987), *Battleground for the Union* (1989) and *The Making of a Confederate: Walter Lenoir's Civil War* (1997). He is currently finishing an edited collection of essays on nineteenth-century America and a book on the Civil War. Most recently, he has edited *A Companion to 19th-Century America* (2001) and finished *The Civil War and Reconstruction: A Student Companion* (2001).

Acknowledgments

All of us are grateful to our families, friends, and colleagues for their support and encouragement. Jo Ann Argersinger and Peter Argersinger would like in particular to thank Margaret L. Aust, Rody Conant, Lizzie Gilman, and Ann Zinn; William Barney thanks Pamela Fesmire and Rosalie Radcliffe; Virginia Anderson thanks Fred Anderson, Kim Gruenwald, Ruth Helm, Eric Hinderaker, and Chidiebere Nwaubani; and David Goldfield thanks Frances Glenn and Jason Moscato.

Supplementary Instructional Materials

FOR INSTRUCTORS	FOR STUDENTS
MyHistoryLab www.myhistorylab.com **Save Time. Improve Results.** MyHistoryLab is a dynamic website that provides a wealth of resources geared to meet the diverse teaching and learning needs of today's instructors and students. MyHistoryLab's many accessible tools will encourage students to read their text and help them improve their grade in their course.	**MyHistoryLab** www.myhistorylab.com **Save Time. Improve Results.** MyHistoryLab is a dynamic website that provides a wealth of resources geared to meet the diverse teaching and learning needs of today's instructors and students. MyHistoryLab's many accessible tools will encourage you to read your text and help you improve your grade in your course.
Instructor's Resource Center www.pearsonhighered.com/irc This website provides instructors with additional text-specific resources that can be downloaded for classroom use. Resources include the Instructor's Resource Manual, PowerPoint presentations and the test item file. Register online for access to the resources for *The American Journey*.	**www.coursemart.com** CourseSmart eTextbooks offer the same content as the printed text in a convenient online format—with highlighting, online search, and printing capabilities. You **save 60% over the list price** of the traditional book.
Instructor's Resource Manual Available for download at www.pearsonhighered.com/irc, the Instructor's Resource Manual contains chapter outlines, detailed chapter overviews, lecture outlines, topics for discussion, and information about audio-visual resources.	**Books à la Carte** These editions feature the exact same content as the traditional printed text in a convenient, three-hole-punched, loose-leaf version at a discounted price—allowing you to take only what you need to class. You'll **save 35% over the net price** of the traditional book.
Test Item File Available for download at www.pearsonhighered .com/irc, the Test Item File contains more than 1,500 multiple-choice, identification, matching, true-false, and essay test questions and 10–15 questions per chapter on the maps found in each chapter.	**Library of American Biography Series** www.pearsonhighered. com/educator/series/Library-of-American-Biography/10493.page Pearson's renowned series of biographies spotlighting figures who had a significant impact on American history. Included in the series are Edmund Morgan's *The Puritan Dilemma: The Story of John Winthrop*, B. Davis Edmund's *Tecumseh and the Quest for Indian Leadership*, J. William T. Youngs, *Eleanor Roosevelt: A Personal and Public Life*, and John R. M. Wilson's *Jackie Robinson and the American Dilemma*.
PowerPoint Presentations Available for download at www.pearsonhighered.com/irc, the PowerPoints contain chapter outlines and full-color images of maps, figures, and images.	**American Stories: Biographies in United States History** This two-volume collection of sixty-two biographies provides insight into the lives and contributions of key figures as well as ordinary citizens to American history. Introductions, pre-reading questions, and suggested resources helps students connect the relevance of these individuals to historical events. Volume 1 **ISBN-10: 0131826549 ISBN-13: 9780131826540**; Volume 2 **ISBN-10: 0131826530 ISBN-13: 9780131826533**

(continued)

FOR INSTRUCTORS	FOR STUDENTS
MyTest www.pearsonmytest.com MyTest is a powerful assessment generation program that helps instructors easily create and print quizzes and exams. Questions and tests can be authored online, allowing instructors ultimate flexibility and the ability to efficiently manage assessments anytime, anywhere! Instructors can easily access existing questions and edit, create, and store using simple drag-and-drop and Word-like controls.	**Penguin Valuepacks** www.pearsonhighered.com/penguin A variety of Penguin-Putnam texts is available at discounted prices when bundled with *The American Journey, 5/e*. Texts include Benjamin Franklin's *Autobiography and Other Writings*, Nathaniel Hawthorne's *The Scarlet Letter*, Thomas Jefferson's *Notes on the State of Virginia*, and George Orwell's *1984*.
Retrieving the American Past (www.pearsoncustom.com, **keyword search | rtap**) Available through the Pearson Custom Library, the *Retrieving the American Past* (RTAP) program lets you create a textbook or reader that meets your needs and the needs of your course. RTAP gives you the freedom and flexibility to add chapters from several best-selling Pearson textbooks, in addition to *The American Journey, 5/e* and/or 100 topical reading units written by the History Department of Ohio State University, all under one cover. Choose the content you want to teach in depth, in the sequence you want, at the price you want your students to pay.	**A Short Guide to Writing About History, 7/e** Written by Richard Marius, late of Harvard University, and Melvin E. Page, Eastern Tennessee State University, this engaging and practical text helps students get beyond merely compiling dates and facts. Covering brief essays and the documented resource paper, the text explores the writing and researching processes, identifies different modes of historical writing, including argument, and concludes with guidelines for improving style. **ISBN-10: 0205673708; ISBN-13: 9780205673704**
	Longman American History Atlas This full-color historical atlas designed especially for college students is a valuable reference tool and visual guide to American history. This atlas includes maps covering the scope of American history from the lives of the Native Americans to the 1990s. Produced by a renowned cartographic firm and a team of respected historians, the Longman American History Atlas will enhance any American history survey course. **ISBN: 0321004868; ISBN-13: 9780321004864**

MyHistoryLab

An online homework, tutorial, and assessment program, MyHistoryLab offers immersive content, tools, and experiences to engage students and help them succeed.

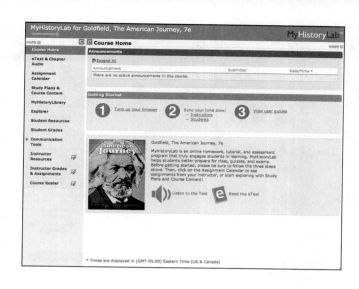

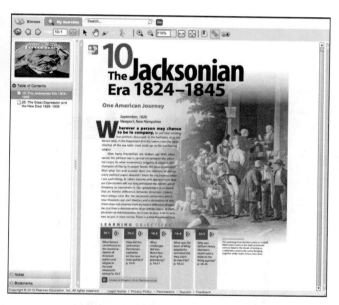

Pearson eText with Audio

Contained within MyHistoryLab, the Pearson eText enables students to access their textbook online—through laptops, iPads, and tablets. Download the free Pearson eText app to use on tablets. Students may also listen to their text with the Audio eText.

New MyHistoryLibrary

A new release of Pearson's MyHistoryLibrary contains more than 200 of the most commonly assigned primary source documents, delivered through Pearson's powerful eText platform. Each reading may also be listened to in the Audio eText companion.

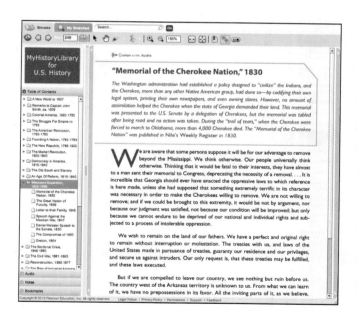

MyHistoryLab Video Series:
Key Topics in US History

This comprehensive video series helps students get up-to-speed on key topics. Correlated to the chapters of *The American Journey*, each video unit reviews key topics of the period, readying students to get the most from the text narrative. The videos feature seasoned historians reviewing the pivotal stories of our past, in a lively format designed to engage and inform.

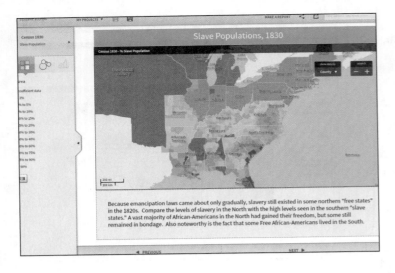

Explorer

This path-breaking new application in MyHistoryLab enables students to use dynamic maps to understand pivotal events and topics. A unique Explorer application is correlated to each chapter of *The American Journey*.

Writing Space

MyHistoryLab Writing Space provides the best way to develop and assess concept mastery and critical thinking through writing. Use Writing Space to create, track, and grade writing assignments, access writing resources, and exchange meaningful, personalized feedback quickly and easily. Plus, Writing Space includes integrated access to Turnitin, the global leader in plagiarism prevention.

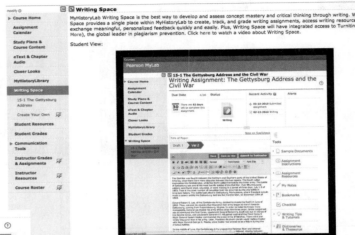

Key Supplements & Customer Support

Annotated Instructor's eText

Contained within MyHistoryLab, the *Annotated Instructor's eText* for your Pearson textbook leverages the powerful Pearson eText platform to make it easier than ever for you to access subject-specific resources for class preparation. The *AI eText* serves as the hub for all instructor resources, with chapter-by-chapter links to PowerPoint slides, content from the Instructor's Manual, and to *MyHistoryLab's* ClassPrep engine, which contains a wealth of history content organized for classroom use.

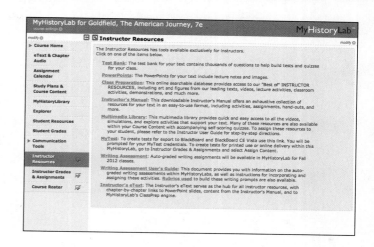

Instructor's Manual

The Instructor's Manual for your Pearson textbook contains chapter overviews, discussion questions, and suggested assignments for each chapter, including both general and text-specific content. It also contains a MyHistoryLab syllabus and suggestions for integrating MyHistoryLab into your course.

PowerPoint Presentations

Strong PowerPoint presentations make lectures more engaging for students. Correlated to the chapters of your Pearson textbook, each presentation includes a full lecture script, discussion questions, a wealth of images and maps, and links to the full array of MyHistoryLab media.

MyTest Test Bank

Containing a diverse set of multiple choice and essay questions, the MyTest test bank supports a variety of assessment strategies. The large pool of multiple choice questions for each chapter includes factual, conceptual, and analytical questions, so that instructors may assess students on basic information as well as critical thinking.

Customer Support

Pearson's dedicated team of local representatives will work with you not only to choose course materials but also to integrate them into your class and assess their effectiveness. Moreover, live support for MyHistoryLab users, both educators and students, is available 24/7.

1 Worlds Apart

One American Journey

Report from an Aztec messenger

A fter a difficult journey of over two hundred miles, the exhausted man arrived at the royal palace in the grand city of Tenochtitlán. He had hurried all the way from the Gulf Coast with important news for the Aztec leader, Moctezuma.

Our lord and king, forgive my boldness. I am from Mictlancuauhtla. When I went to the shores of the great sea, there was a mountain range or small mountain floating in the midst of the water, and moving here and there without touching the shore. My lord, we have never seen the like of this, although we guard the coast and are always on watch.

[When Moctezuma sent some officials to check on the messenger's story, they confirmed his report.]

Our lord and king, it is true that strange people have come to the shores of the great sea. They were fishing from a small boat, some with rods and others with a net. They fished until late and then they went back to their two great towers and climbed up into them. . . . They have very light skin, much lighter than ours. They all have long beards, and their hair comes only to their ears.

From *The Broken Spears* by Miguel León-Portilla.
Copyright © 1962, 1990 by Miguel León-Portilla. Expanded
and updated edition © 1992 by Miguel León-Portilla.
Reprinted by permission of Beacon Press, Boston.

Mexico: Hernán Cortés is greeted by Moctezuma's messenger in 1519: Mexican Indian painting, sixteenth century.

LEARNING OBJECTIVES

1.1	1.2	1.3	1.4	1.5
How did the precontact histories of Native Americans, especially in the centuries just before 1492, shape their encounters with Europeans? p. 3	What were the key characteristics of West African society? p. 8	How did events in Europe both shape and inspire exploration of the Americas? p. 13	What were the biological consequences of contact between Europeans and Native Americans? p. 14	Why did early French and English efforts at colonization falter? p. 23

((· Listen to Chapter I on MyHistoryLab

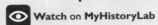 Watch the Video Series on MyHistoryLab

Learn about some key topics related to this chapter with the *MyHistoryLab Video Series: Key Topics in U.S. History.*

1 A New World: To 1607 Prior to its discovery by Europeans, the First Peoples had lived in the Americas for millennia. This video surveys the history of the Native Americans from their migrations across the Bering Straits, their adaptation to a range of environmental conditions, and the various cultures they developed, from hunter-gatherers to empires based on sophisticated methods of agriculture. The video also describes the first hundred years of European exploration that had an unprecedented impact on Native American cultures.

Watch on MyHistoryLab

The First Americans Prior to 1492, the pre-Columbian and Mesoamerican cultures of Central America and Mexico, notably the Mayans and Aztecs, developed distinctive cultures and built great empires. This video describes their civilizations as well as other Native American societies in North America, such as the Puebloan peoples, the Plains Indians, and the Mississippian mound-building cultures.

Watch on MyHistoryLab

3 The Expansion of Europe What motivated the European voyages of discovery in the fifteenth and sixteenth centuries? This video discusses Columbus and other explorers whose search and competition for a passage to the Indies led them to the New World, which, instead of spices, offered unimaginable wealth, converts to Christianity, and land and resources that would launch a vast trade in African slaves to exploit.

Watch on MyHistoryLab

The Protestant Reformation Many early European settlers who came to North America were religious refugees. This video explores the Protestant Reformation, beginning with Martin Luther, a German monk, who "protested" against the practices of the Catholic Church. This resulted in many new Protestant denominations that spread through Europe and England. Protestantism ultimately became a driving force for English colonization.

Watch on MyHistoryLab

Personal Journeys Online

- Christopher Columbus, *Journal of the First Voyage*, October 12, 1492. Account of his first meeting with Caribbean islanders.
- Martin Frobisher, *Account of First Voyage to the New World*, 1576. Description of his arrival in Canada and his encounter with native people.

Moctezuma was filled with foreboding when he received the messenger's initial report. Aztec religion placed great emphasis on omens and prophecies, which were thought to foreshadow coming events. Several unusual omens had recently occurred—blazing lights in the sky, one temple struck by lightning, and another that spontaneously burst into flames. Now light-skinned strangers appeared offshore. Aztec spiritual leaders regarded these signs as unfavorable and warned that trouble lay ahead.

The messenger's journey to Tenochtitlán occurred in 1519. The "mountains" he saw were in fact the sails of European ships, and the strange men were Spanish soldiers under the command of Hernán Cortés. Before long, a variety of peoples—Native Americans, Africans, and Europeans—who had previously lived worlds apart would come together to create a world that was new to all of them.

This new world reflected the diverse experiences of the many peoples who built it. Improving economic conditions in the fifteenth and early sixteenth centuries propelled Europeans overseas to seek new opportunities for trade and settlement. Spain, Portugal, France, and England competed for political, economic, and religious domination within Europe, and their conflict carried over into the Americas. Native Americans drew upon their familiarity with the land and its resources, patterns of political and religious authority, and systems of trade and warfare to deal with the European newcomers. Africans did not come voluntarily to the Americas but were brought by the Europeans to work as slaves. They too would draw on their cultural heritage to cope with a new land and a new, harsh condition of life.

Native American Societies before 1492

1.1 How did the precontact histories of Native Americans, especially in the centuries just before 1492, shape their encounters with Europeans?

In 1492, the year Columbus landed on a tiny Caribbean island, perhaps 70 million people—nearly equal to the population of Europe at that time—lived on the continents of North and South America, most of them south of the present border between the United States and Mexico. They belonged to hundreds of groups, each with its own language or dialect, history, and way of life.

From the start, the original inhabitants of the Americas were peoples in motion. The first migrants arrived at least 15,000 years ago, traveling from central and northern Siberia and slowly making their way to southern South America. These people, and subsequent migrants from Eurasia, probably traveled across a land bridge that emerged across what is now the Bering Strait. During the last Ice Age, much of the earth's water was frozen in huge glaciers. This process lowered ocean levels, exposing a 600-mile-wide land bridge between Asia and America. Recent research examining genetic and linguistic similarities between Asian and Native American populations suggests that there may also have been later migrations.

Hunters, Harvesters, and Traders

The earliest Americans adapted to an amazing range of environmental conditions, from the frozen Arctic to southwestern deserts to dense eastern woodlands. At first, they mainly subsisted by hunting the mammoths, bison, and other large game that roamed throughout North America. Archaeologists working near present-day Clovis, New Mexico, have found carefully crafted spear points—some of which may be more than 13,000 years old. Such efficient tools possibly contributed to overhunting, which, along with climate change, led to the extinction of many large game species. By about 9000 B.C.E., the world's climate began to grow warmer, turning grasslands into deserts and reducing the animals' food supply. Humans too had to find other food sources.

Between roughly 8000 B.C.E. and 1500 B.C.E., Native American societies changed in important ways. Native populations steadily increased, and men and women assumed more specialized roles in their villages. Men did most of the hunting and fishing, activities that required travel. Women remained closer to home, harvesting and preparing wild plant foods and caring for children.

Across the continent, native communities also developed complex networks of trade. They not only exchanged material goods, but also marriage partners, laborers, ideas, and religious practices. Trade networks sometimes extended over great distances.

Women were the principal farmers in most Native American societies, growing corn, beans, and other crops in fields cleared by Indian men. Many of these New World foods would be transported across the Atlantic to become important to Old World diets.

Ideas about death and the afterlife also passed between groups. So too did certain burial practices, such as the placing of valued possessions in the grave along with the deceased person's body. In some areas, the increasing complexity of exchange networks, as well as competition for resources, encouraged concentrations of political power. Chiefs might manage trade relations and conduct diplomacy for groups of villages rather than for a single community.

The Development of Agriculture

No Native American adaptation was more momentous than the domestication of certain plants and the development of farming. Native Americans may have turned to farming when population growth threatened to outrun the wild food supply. Women, with their knowledge of wild plants, probably discovered how to save seeds and cultivate them, becoming the world's first farmers.

Wherever agriculture took hold, important social changes followed. Populations grew, because farming produced a more secure food supply than did hunting and gathering. Permanent villages appeared as farmers settled near their fields. In central Mexico, agriculture eventually sustained the populations of large cities. Trade in agricultural surpluses flowed through networks of exchange. In many Indian societies, women's status improved because of their role as the principal farmers. Even religious beliefs adapted to the increasing importance of farming.

The adoption of agriculture further enhanced the diversity of Native American societies that developed over centuries within broad regions, or **culture areas** (see Map 1.1). Within each area, inhabitants shared basic patterns of subsistence and social organization, largely reflecting the natural environment to which they had adapted. Most, but not all, of them eventually relied upon farming.

culture areas Geographical regions inhabited by peoples who share similar basic patterns of subsistence and social organization.

Nonfarming Societies

Agriculture was impossible in the challenging environment of the Arctic and subarctic. There, nomadic bands of Inuits and Aleuts moved seasonally to fish or hunt whales, seals, and other sea animals and, in the brief summers, to gather wild berries.

📖 **Read the Document** Álvar Núñez Cabeza de Vaca, "Indians of the Rio Grande" (1530s)

1.1

1.2

1.3

1.4

1.5

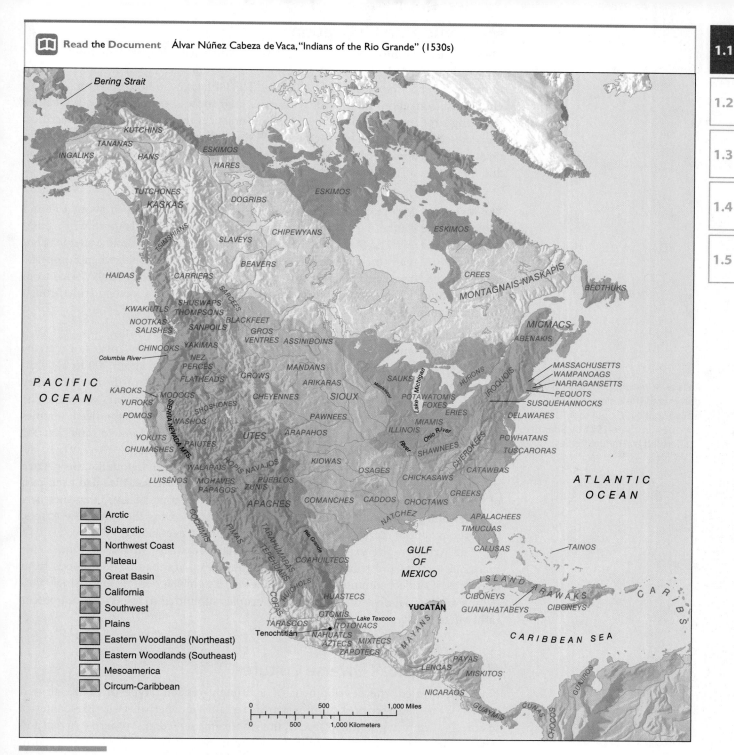

MAP 1.1 NORTH AMERICAN CULTURE AREAS, c. 1500 Over the course of centuries, Indian peoples in North America developed distinctive cultures suited to the environments in which they lived. Inhabitants of each culture area shared basic patterns of subsistence, craft work, and social organization. Most, but not all, Indian peoples combined farming with hunting and gathering.

Along the Northwest Coast and the Columbia River Plateau, one of the most densely populated areas of North America, abundant natural resources permitted native peoples to prosper without farming. Local rivers and forests supplied fish, game, and edible plants.

Farther south, in present-day California, hunter-gatherers once lived in smaller villages, which usually adjoined oak groves where Indians gathered acorns as an important food source. Nomadic hunting bands in the Great Basin, where the climate was warm and dry, learned to survive on the region's limited resources.

5

Mesoamerican Civilizations

Mesoamerica, the birthplace of agriculture in North America, extends from central Mexico into Central America. A series of complex, literate, urban cultures emerged in this region beginning around 1200 B.C.E. The Olmecs, who flourished on Mexico's Gulf Coast from about 1200 to 400 B.C.E., and their successors in the region built cities featuring large pyramids, developed religious practices that included human sacrifice, and devised calendars and writing systems. Two of the most prominent Mesoamerican civilizations that followed the Olmecs were the Mayans in the Yucatán and Guatemala and the Aztecs of Teotihuacán in central Mexico.

The Mayans.   Mayan civilization reached its greatest glory between about 150 and 900 C.E. in the southern Yucatán, creating Mesoamerica's most advanced writing and calendrical systems. The Mayans of the southern Yucatán suffered a decline after 900, but there were still many thriving Mayan centers in the northern Yucatán when Europeans arrived in the Americas. The great city of Teotihuacán dominated central Mexico from the first century to the eighth century C.E., and influenced much of Mesoamerica through trade and conquest.

The Aztecs.   Some 200 years after the fall of Teotihuacán, the Toltecs, a warrior people, rose to prominence, dominating central Mexico from about 900 to 1100. In the wake of the Toltec collapse, the **Aztecs** migrated from the north into the Valley of Mexico and built a great empire that soon controlled much of Mesoamerica. The magnificent Aztec capital, Tenochtitlán, was a city of great plazas, magnificent temples and palaces, and busy marketplaces. In 1492, Tenochtitlán was home to some 200,000 people, making it one of the largest cities in the world at the time.

The great pyramid in Tenochtitlán was the center of Aztec religious life. Here Aztec priests sacrificed human victims to offer to the gods. Human sacrifice had been part of Mesoamerican religion since the time of the Olmecs. People believed that such ceremonies pleased the gods and prevented them from destroying the earth. The Aztecs, however, practiced sacrifice on a much larger scale than ever before.

The Aztec empire expanded through military conquest, driven by a quest for sacrificial victims and tribute payments of gold, food, and handcrafted goods from hundreds of subject communities. But as the empire grew, it became increasingly vulnerable to internal division. Neighboring peoples submitted to the Aztecs out of fear rather than loyalty.

Aztecs A warrior people who dominated the Valley of Mexico from about 1100 until their conquest in 1519–1521 by Spanish soldiers led by Hernán Cortés.

North America's Diverse Cultures

North of Mexico, the development of a drought-resistant type of maize around 400 B.C.E. enabled a series of cultures sharing certain characteristics with Mesoamerica to emerge. Beginning about 300 B.C.E., the Hohokams settled in southern Arizona and devised elaborate irrigation systems that allowed them to harvest two crops of corn, beans, and squash each year. Trade networks linked the Hohokams to people living as far away as California and Mexico. Their culture endured for over a thousand years but mysteriously disappeared by 1450.

Ancestral Puebloans.   Early in the first century C.E., Ancestral Puebloan peoples (sometimes called Anasazis) began to settle in farming communities where the borders of present-day Colorado, Utah, Arizona, and New Mexico meet. Scarce rainfall, routed through dams and hillside terraces, watered the crops. Ancestral Puebloans originally lived in villages, or pueblos (*pueblo* is the Spanish word for "village") built on mesas and canyon floors. In New Mexico's Chaco Canyon, perhaps as many as 15,000 people dwelled in a dozen large towns and hundreds of outlying villages. But after about

1200, villagers began carving multistoried stone houses into canyon walls, dwellings that could only be reached by difficult climbs up steep cliffs and along narrow ledges. Warfare and climate change may have worked together to force the Puebloans into these precarious homes.

Around 1200, the climate of the Southwest grew colder, making it more difficult to grow enough to feed the large population. Food scarcity may have set village against village and encouraged attacks by outsiders. Villagers probably resorted to cliff dwellings for protection as violence spread in the region. By 1300, survivors abandoned the cliff dwellings and dispersed into smaller villages along the Rio Grande. Their descendants include the Hopis and Zunis, as well as other Puebloan peoples in the desert Southwest.

Plains Indians. The Great Plains of the continent's interior were much less densely settled than the desert Southwest. Mandans, Pawnees, and other groups settled along river valleys, where women farmed and men hunted bison. Plains Indians moved frequently, seeking more fertile land or better hunting. Wherever they went, they traded skins, food, and obsidian (a volcanic glass used for tools and weapons) with other native peoples.

Mound-Building Cultures. As agriculture spread to the Eastern Woodlands, a vast territory extending from the Mississippi Valley to the Atlantic seaboard, several "mound-building" societies—named for the large earthworks their members constructed—developed in the Ohio and Mississippi valleys. These peoples built hundreds of mounds, often in the shapes of humans, birds, and serpents. Most were grave sites, where people were buried with valuable goods, including objects made from materials obtained through long-distance trade.

The last mound-building culture, the Mississippian, emerged between 1000 and 1500 in the Mississippi Valley. Mississippian farmers raised enough food to support sizable populations and major urban centers. The largest city by far was **Cahokia**, located near present-day St. Louis in a fertile floodplain with access to the major river systems of the continent's interior. By 1250, Cahokia had perhaps 20,000 residents, making it nearly as large as medieval London and the largest American city north of Mexico. Cahokia dominated the Mississippi Valley, linked by trade to dozens of villages in the midwestern region. Mississippian culture began to decline in the thirteenth century, perhaps due to an ecological crisis where population outstripped food supply.

What followed in the Eastern Woodlands region was a century or more of warfare and political instability. In the Northeast, the Iroquois and Hurons moved from dispersed settlements into fortified villages. Both the Hurons and the Iroquois formed confederacies that were intended to diminish internal conflicts and increase their collective spiritual strength. Among the Iroquois, five separate nations—the Mohawks, Oneidas, Onondagas, Cayugas, and Senecas—joined to create the **Great League of Peace and Power** around the year 1450. Similar developments occurred in the Southeast, where chronic instability led to regional alliances and shifting centers of trade and political power.

Eastern Woodlands peoples were the first to encounter English explorers, and later, English settlers, at the start of the seventeenth century. By that point these native peoples relied on a mixture of agriculture and hunting, fishing, and gathering for their subsistence. They lived in villages with a few hundred residents, with greater densities of settlement in the South (where a warmer climate and longer growing season prevailed) than in the North.

Cahokia Located near modern St. Louis, this was one of the largest urban centers created by Mississippian peoples, containing perhaps 30,000 residents in 1250.

Great League of Peace and Power Confederation of five Iroquois nations— the Mohawks, Oneidas, Onondagas, Cayugas, and Senecas—formed in the fifteenth century to diminish internal conflict and increase collective strength against their enemies.

The Caribbean Islanders

The Caribbean islands were peopled by mainland dwellers who began moving to the islands around 5000 B.C.E. Surviving at first by hunting and gathering, island peoples

This artist's rendering, based on archaeological evidence, suggests the size and magnificence of the Mississippian city of Cahokia. By the thirteenth century, it was as populous as medieval London and served as a center of trade for the vast interior of North America.

began farming perhaps in the first century C.E. Canoes carried trade goods throughout the Caribbean, as well as to Mesoamerica and coastal South America.

By 1492, as many as 4 million people may have inhabited the Caribbean islands. Powerful chiefs ruled over villages, conducted war and diplomacy, and controlled the distribution of food and other goods obtained as tribute from villagers.

Long before Europeans reached North America, the continent's inhabitants had witnessed centuries of dynamic change. Empires rose and fell, and new ones took their place. Large cities flourished and disappeared. Periods of warfare occasionally disrupted the lives of thousands of individuals. The Europeans' arrival, at the end of the fifteenth century, coincided with a period of particular instability, as various Native American groups competed for dominance in the wake of the collapse of the centralized societies at Cahokia and Chaco Canyon. Yet Native American societies also experienced important continuities. These included an ability to adapt to widely varying environmental conditions, the preservation of religious and ceremonial traditions, and an eagerness to forge relationships of exchange with neighboring peoples. Both continuities with past experience and more recent political changes would shape the ways native peoples responded to the European newcomers.

West African Societies

1.2   What were the key characteristics of West African society?

n the three centuries after 1492, six out of every seven people who crossed the Atlantic to the Americas were not Europeans but Africans. Like the Americas, Africa had witnessed the rise of many ancient and diverse cultures (see Map 1.2). They ranged from the sophisticated Egyptian civilization that developed in the Nile Valley more than 5,000 years ago to the powerful twelfth-century chiefdoms of Zimbabwe to the West African empires that flourished in the time of Columbus and Cortés. The vast majority of Africans who came to the Americas after 1492 arrived as slaves, transported by Europeans eager to exploit their labor.

📖 **Read the Document** Askia Muhammad al-Turi, Reform in Songhai (1500)

1.1

1.2

1.3

1.4

1.5

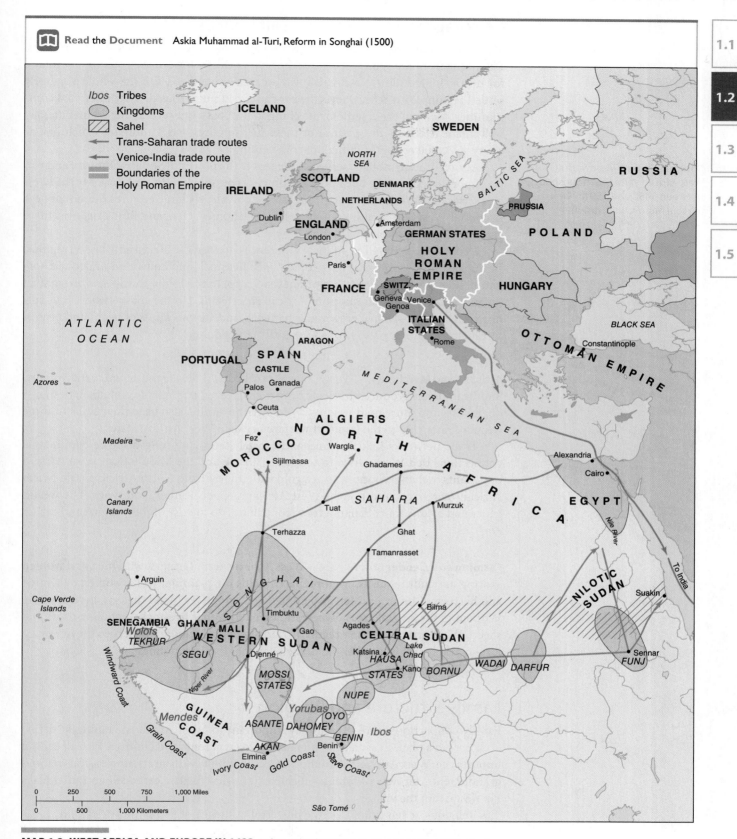

MAP 1.2 WEST AFRICA AND EUROPE IN 1492 Before Columbus's voyage, Europeans knew little about the world beyond the Mediterranean basin and the coast of West Africa. Muslim merchants from North Africa largely controlled European traders' access to African gold and other materials.

Songhai Empire A powerful West African state that flourished between 1450 and 1591, when it fell to a Moroccan invasion.

Geographical and Political Differences

Most African immigrants to the Americas came from the continent's western regions. Extending from the southern edge of the Sahara Desert toward the equator and inland for nearly 1,000 miles, West Africa was an area of contrasts. On the whole a sparsely settled region, West Africa nevertheless contained numerous densely inhabited communities. Many of these settlements clung to the coast, but several important cities lay well inland. Perhaps the greatest of these metropolises was Timbuktu, which had as many as 70,000 residents in the fifteenth century.

At that time, Timbuktu served as the seat of the powerful **Songhai Empire** and was an important center of trade and government. The Songhai Empire was only the latest in a series of powerful West African states. Equivalently large empires did not appear in coastal West Africa, although the Asante, Dahomey, Oyo, and Bini kingdoms there grew to be quite powerful.

Geographical as well as political differences marked the inland and coastal regions. In the vast interior grasslands, people raised livestock and cultivated millet and sorghum. Rice also served as an important food crop. In the 1500s, Europeans brought an Asian variety to add to indigenous African rice strains. On the coast—where rain falls nearly every day—people grew yams, bananas, and various kinds of beans and peas in forest clearings. They also kept sheep, goats, and poultry.

Artisans and Merchants.   West Africans excelled as skilled artisans and metalworkers. Smiths in Benin produced intricate bronze sculptures, and Asante craftsmen designed distinctive miniature gold weights. West African smiths also used their skills to forge weapons, attesting to the frequent warfare between West African states.

Trade networks linked inland and coastal states, and long-distance commercial connections tied West Africa to southern Europe and the Middle East. West African merchants exchanged locally mined gold with traders from North Africa for salt. North African merchants also bought West African pepper, leather, and ivory. The wealth generated by this trans-Saharan trade contributed to the rise of the Songhai and earlier empires.

Farming and Gender Roles.   Most West Africans were farmers, with men and women sharing agricultural tasks. Men prepared fields for planting, while women cultivated and harvested the crops. Men also hunted and, in the grassland regions, herded cattle. Women in the coastal areas owned and cared for other livestock, including goats and sheep. West African women regularly traded goods, including the crops they grew, in local markets and were essential to the vitality of local economies.

Family Structure and Religion

Family connections were exceedingly important to West Africans, helping to define each person's place in society. While ties between parents and children were of central importance, West Africans also emphasized their links with aunts, uncles, cousins, and grandparents. Groups of families formed clans that further extended an individual's kin ties within the village.

Religious beliefs magnified the powerful influence of family on African life. Ideas and practices focused on themes of fertility, prosperity, health, and social harmony. Because many West Africans believed that their ancestors acted as mediators between the worlds of the living and the dead, they held elaborate funerals for deceased members and performed public rituals at their grave sites. Such rituals helped keep the memory of ancestors alive for younger generations.

West Africans believed that spiritual forces suffused the natural world. They performed ceremonies to ensure the spirits' goodwill and protect people from evil

Craftsmen from the West African kingdom of Benin were renowned for their remarkable bronze sculptures. This intricate bronze plaque depicts four African warriors in full military dress. The two tiny figures in the background may be Portuguese soldiers, who first arrived in Benin in the late fifteenth century.

spirits and sorcerers. West Africans preserved their faith through oral traditions, not written texts.

Islam began to take root in West Africa as early as the tenth century, introduced by Muslim traders and soldiers from North Africa. Urban dwellers, especially merchants, were more likely to convert to the new religion, as were some rulers. Farmers, accustomed to religious rituals that focused on agricultural fertility, tended to resist Islamic influence more strongly or adopt religious practices that mingled Islamic and traditional beliefs.

European Merchants in West Africa and the Slave Trade

Before the fifteenth century, Europeans knew little about Africa beyond its Mediterranean coast. But many Christian merchants had traded for centuries with Muslims in the North

African ports. When stories of West African gold reached European traders, they tried to move deeper into the continent. But they encountered powerful Muslim merchants intent on monopolizing the gold trade.

The kingdom of Portugal sought to circumvent this Muslim monopoly. Portuguese forces conquered Ceuta in Morocco and gained a foothold on the continent in 1415. Because this outpost did not provide direct access to gold, Portuguese mariners began exploring the West African coast and establishing trading posts along the way.

By the 1430s, the Portuguese had discovered perhaps the greatest source of wealth they could extract from Africa—slaves. A vigorous market in African slaves had existed in southern Europe since the middle of the fourteenth century, and within West Africa itself for centuries. Chronic underpopulation in many parts of West Africa had led to the development of slavery as a way to maintain control over scarce and valuable laborers. Most slaves within Africa lost their freedom because they were captured in war, but others had been kidnapped or were enslaved as punishment for a crime. First the Portuguese, and later other Europeans, exploited rivalries among various West African states to encourage them to take war captives who could be sold into an expanding transatlantic slave trade. Virtually all of the African slaves who ended up in the New World had first been enslaved by fellow Africans.

European visitors who observed African slaves in their homeland often described them as "slaves in name only" because they were subject to so little coercion. Also, slavery in Africa was not necessarily a permanent status and did not automatically apply to the slaves' children. African merchants who sold slaves to European purchasers had no reason to suspect that those slaves would be treated any differently by their new owners.

Africans caught in the web of the transatlantic slave trade, however, entered a much harsher world. Separated from beloved kinfolk, removed from a familiar landscape, and hard-pressed to sustain spiritual and cultural traditions in a new environment, Africans faced daunting challenges as they journeyed across the ocean and entered into the history of the New World.

Elmina Castle, located on the coast of what is now Ghana, was founded by the Portuguese in 1482 as a trading post. In 1637, the Dutch West India Company seized the castle and converted it for use in the slave trade.

Western Europe on the Eve of Exploration

1.3 How did events in Europe both shape and inspire exploration of the Americas?

When Columbus sailed from Spain in 1492, he left a continent that was recovering from the devastating warfare and disease of the fourteenth century and was about to embark on the devastating religious conflicts of the sixteenth century. Between 1337 and 1453, England and France had fought a series of conflicts known as the Hundred Years' War. And between 1347 and 1351, an epidemic known as the Black Death wreaked havoc on a European population already suffering from persistent malnutrition. Perhaps a third of all Europeans died, with results that were felt for more than a century.

The plague left Europe with far fewer workers, a result that contributed to southern Europeans' interest in the African slave trade. To help the economy recover, the survivors learned to be more efficient and rely on technological improvements. Innovations in banking, accounting, and insurance also fostered economic recovery. Although prosperity was distributed unevenly among social classes, on the whole, Europe had a stronger, more productive economy in 1500 than ever before.

In much of Western Europe, economic improvement encouraged an extraordinary cultural movement known as the Renaissance, a "rebirth" of interest in the classical civilizations of ancient Greece and Rome. The Renaissance originated in the city-states of Italy, where a prosperous and educated urban class promoted learning and artistic expression.

The daily lives of most Europeans, however, remained untouched by intellectual and artistic developments. Most Europeans resided in agricultural communities that differed in important ways from Native American and West African societies. In European societies, men performed most of the heavy work of farming, while women focused on household production of such goods as butter, cheese, and cloth, and cared for their families. Europeans lived in states organized into more rigid hierarchies than could be found in most parts of North America or West Africa, with the population divided into distinct classes. European society was also patriarchal, with men dominating political and economic life.

The Consolidation of Political and Military Authority

By the end of the fifteenth century, a measure of stability returned to the countries about to embark on overseas expansion. The monarchs of Spain, France, and England successfully asserted royal authority over their previously fragmented realms, creating strong state bureaucracies to control political rivals. They gave special trading privileges to merchants to gain their support, creating links that would later prove important in financing overseas expeditions.

The consolidation of military power went hand in hand with the strengthening of political authority. Before overseas expansion began, European monarchs exerted military force to extend their authority closer to home. Louis XI and his successors used warfare and intermarriage with the ruling families of nearby provinces to extend French influence. In the early sixteenth century, England's Henry VIII sent soldiers to conquer Ireland. And the Spain of 1492 was forged from the successful conclusion of the *reconquista* ("reconquest") of territory from Muslim control.

Muslim invaders from North Africa first entered Spain in 711 and their descendants ruled much of the Iberian Peninsula (which includes Spain and Portugal) for centuries. Beginning in the mid-eleventh century, Christian armies embarked on a long effort to reclaim the region. By 1450, only the southern tip of Spain remained under Muslim control. After the marriage of Ferdinand of Aragon and Isabella of Castile in 1469 united Spain's two principal kingdoms, their combined forces completed the *reconquista*. Granada, the last Muslim stronghold, fell in 1492, shortly before Columbus set out on his first voyage.

reconquista The long struggle (ending in 1492) during which Spanish Christians reconquered the Iberian Peninsula from Muslim occupiers, who first invaded in the eighth century.

Religious Conflict and the Protestant Reformation

Even as these rulers sought to unify their realms, religious conflicts began to tear Europe apart. For more than 1,000 years, Catholic Christianity had united Western Europeans in one faith. By the sixteenth century, the Catholic Church, headed by the pope, had accumulated enormous wealth and power. In reaction to this growing influence, many Christians, especially in northern Europe, began to criticize the popes and the church itself for worldliness and abuse of power.

In 1517, a German monk, Martin Luther, invited open debate on a set of propositions critical of church practices and doctrines. Luther believed that the church had become too insistent on the performance of good works, such as charitable donations or other actions intended to please God. He called for a return to what he understood to be the purer beliefs of the early church, emphasizing that salvation came not by good deeds but only by faith in God. With the help of the newly invented printing press, his ideas spread widely, inspiring a challenge to the Catholic Church that came to be known as the **Reformation**.

When the Catholic Church refused to compromise, Luther and other critics formed their own religious organizations. Luther urged people to foster their own spiritual growth by reading the Bible, which he translated for the first time into German. What started as a religious movement, however, quickly acquired an important political dimension.

Sixteenth-century Germany was a fragmented region of small kingdoms and principalities. They were officially part of a larger Catholic political entity known as the Holy Roman Empire, but many German princes were discontented with imperial authority. Many of these princes also supported Luther. When the Holy Roman Empire under Charles V (who was also king of Spain) tried to silence them, the reformist princes protested. From that point on, these princes—and all Europeans who supported religious reform—became known as **Protestants**.

The Protestant movement took a more radical turn under the influence of the French reformer John Calvin, who emphasized the doctrine of **predestination**. Calvin maintained that an all-powerful and all-knowing God chose at the moment of Creation which humans would be saved and which would be damned. Nothing a person could do would alter that spiritual destiny. Once the ideas of Luther and Calvin began to spread in Europe, no one could contain the powerful Protestant impulse. In succeeding years, other groups formed, split, and split again, increasing Europe's religious fragmentation.

The Reformation fractured the religious unity of Western Europe and spawned a century of bloody warfare. Protestants fought Catholics in France and the German states. Popes initiated a "Counter-Reformation" to strengthen the Catholic Church—in part by internal reform and in part by persecuting its opponents and reimposing religious conformity. Europe thus fragmented into warring camps just when Europeans were coming to terms with their discovery of America. Some of the key participants in exploration, such as Spain and Portugal, rejected Protestantism, while others, including England and the Netherlands, embraced religious reform.

Reformation Sixteenth-century movement to reform the Catholic Church that ultimately led to the founding of new Protestant Christian religious groups.

Protestants Europeans who supported reform of the Catholic Church in the wake of Martin Luther's critique of church practices and doctrines.

predestination The belief that God decided at the moment of Creation which humans would achieve salvation.

Contact

1.4 What were the biological consequences of contact between Europeans and Native Americans?

eligious fervor, political ambition, and the desire for wealth propelled European nations into overseas expansion as well as conflict at home. Portugal, Spain, France, and England competed to establish footholds on other continents in an intense scramble for riches and dominance.

The Lure of Discovery

The potential rewards of overseas exploration captured the imaginations of a small but powerful segment of European society. Most people, busy making a living, cared little about distant lands. But certain princes and merchants anticipated spiritual and material benefits from voyages of discovery. The spiritual advantages included making new Christian converts and blocking Islam's expansion. On the material side, the voyages would contribute to Europe's prosperity by increasing trade.

Merchants especially sought access to Asian spices like pepper, cinnamon, ginger, and nutmeg that added interest to an otherwise monotonous diet and helped preserve foods. But the overland spice trade—and the trade in other luxury goods such as silk and furs—spanned thousands of miles, involved many middlemen, and was controlled at key points by Muslim merchants. One critical center was Constantinople, the bastion of Christianity in the eastern Mediterranean. When that city fell to the Ottomans— Muslim rulers of Turkey—in 1453, Europeans feared that caravan routes to Asia would be disrupted. This encouraged merchants to turn westward. Mariners ventured farther into ocean waters, seeking direct access to the African gold trade and, eventually, a sea route around Africa to Asia.

Advances in Navigation and Shipbuilding. Ocean voyages required sturdier ships than those that plied the Mediterranean. Because oceangoing mariners traveled beyond sight of coastal features, they also needed reliable navigational tools. In the early fifteenth century, Prince Henry of Portugal sponsored the efforts of shipbuilders and mapmakers to solve these practical problems. By 1500, Iberian shipbuilders had perfected the caravel, a ship whose narrow shape and steering rudder suited it for ocean travel. European mariners adopted two important navigational devices—the magnetic compass (first developed in China) and the astrolabe (introduced to Europe by Muslims from Spain)—that allowed mariners to determine their position in relation to a star's known location in the sky.

Portuguese mariners slowly worked their way along Africa's western coast, establishing trading posts where they exchanged European goods for gold, ivory, and slaves (see Map 1.3). Bartolomeu Días reached the southern tip of Africa in 1488. Eleven years later, Vasco da Gama brought a Portuguese fleet around Africa to India, opening a sea route to Asia. These initiatives gave Portugal a virtual monopoly on Far Eastern trade for some time.

Christopher Columbus and the Westward Route to Asia

Christopher Columbus was one of many European mariners excited by the prospect of tapping into the wealth of Asia. Born in Genoa in 1451, he later lived in Portugal and Spain, where he read widely in geographical treatises and listened closely to the stories and rumors that circulated among mariners.

Columbus was not the first European to reach the New World. Several centuries earlier, Norse explorers from Scandinavia sailed and raided around the North Atlantic. These Vikings, as they were known, occupied Iceland by the late ninth century C.E. and later moved on to Greenland. Between 1001 and 1014, Leif Erikson made several voyages to the northern coast of Newfoundland, where he helped to establish a short-lived Viking colony at Vinland and became one of the first Europeans to encounter Native Americans. After the Viking colony disappeared, European fishermen continued to make seasonal voyages to the area, but it would be several centuries before Columbus initiated another attempt at settlement.

Neither was Columbus the first European to believe that he could reach Asia by sailing westward. The idea developed logically during the fifteenth century as mariners gained knowledge and experience. Most Europeans knew that the world was round, but scoffed at the idea of a westward voyage to Asia in the belief that no ship could carry enough provisions for such a long trip. Columbus's confidence that he could succeed grew from a mathematical error. He mistakenly calculated the earth's circumference as

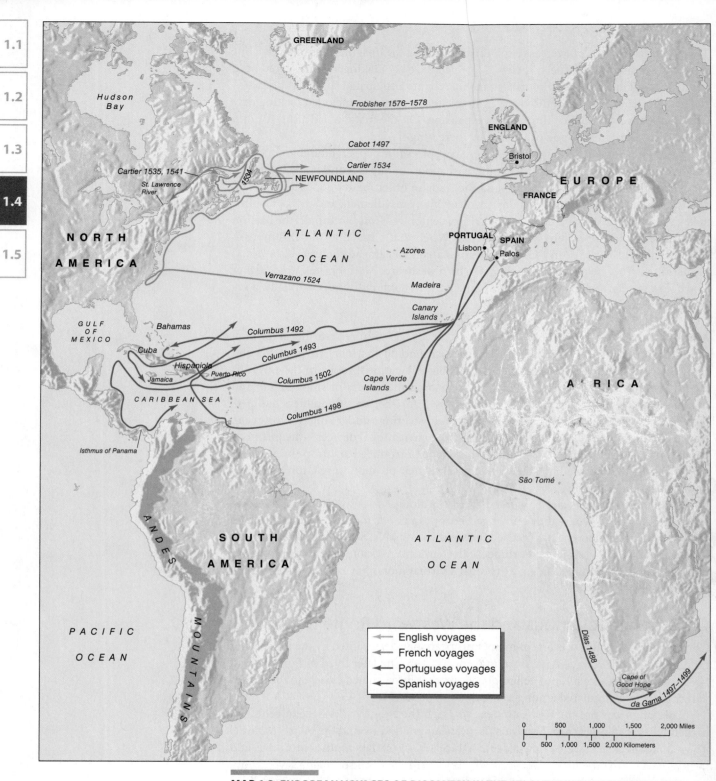

MAP 1.3 EUROPEAN VOYAGES OF DISCOVERY IN THE ATLANTIC IN THE FIFTEENTH AND SIXTEENTH CENTURIES During the fifteenth and sixteenth centuries, Europeans embarked on voyages of discovery that carried them to both Asia and the Americas. Portugal dominated the ocean trade with Asia for most of this period.

18,000 (rather than 24,000) miles and so concluded that Asia lay just 3,500 miles west of the Canary Islands. Columbus first sought financial support for a westward voyage from the king of Portugal, whose advisers disputed his calculations and warned him that he would starve at sea before reaching Asia. Undaunted, he turned to Portugal's rival, Spain.

Columbus tried to convince Ferdinand and Isabella that his plan suited Spain's national goals. If he succeeded, Spain could grow rich from Asian trade, send Christian missionaries to Asia (a goal in keeping with the religious ideals of the *reconquista*), and perhaps enlist the Great Khan of China as an ally in the long struggle with Islam. The Spanish monarchs nonetheless kept Columbus waiting nearly seven years—until 1492, when the last Muslim stronghold at Granada fell to Spanish forces—before they gave him their support.

After thirty-three days at sea, Columbus and his men were carried by prevailing ocean currents to the Bahamas, probably landing on what is now called Watling Island. They spent four months exploring the Caribbean and visiting several islands. Although puzzled by his failure to find the fabled cities of China and Japan, Columbus believed that he had reached Asia. Three more voyages between 1493 and 1504, however, failed to yield clear evidence of an Asian landfall or Asian riches.

Frustrated in their search for wealth, Columbus and his men turned violent, sacking native villages and demanding tribute in gold. They forced gangs of Indians to pan rivers for the precious nuggets. But Caribbean gold reserves, found mainly on Hispaniola, Puerto Rico, and Cuba, were not extensive. Dissatisfied with the meager results, Columbus sought to transform the Indians themselves into a source of wealth.

In 1494, Columbus suggested to the Spanish monarchs that the Indies could yield a profit if islanders were sold as slaves. In succeeding decades, the Spanish government periodically called for fair treatment of Indians and prohibited their enslavement, but such measures were ignored by colonists on the other side of the Atlantic.

Columbus died in Spain in 1506, still convinced he had found Asia. What he had done was to set in motion a process that would transform both sides of the Atlantic. It would eventually bring wealth to many Europeans and immense suffering to Native Americans and Africans.

Watch **the** Video   What Is Columbus's Legacy?

A decidedly European view of Columbus's landing appears in this late-sixteenth-century print. Columbus and his men, armed with guns and swords, are resplendent in European attire, while nearly naked Indians offer them gifts. To the left, Spaniards erect a cross to claim the land for Christianity. In the upper right, frightened natives flee into the woods.

The Spanish Conquest and Colonization

Of all European nations, Spain was best suited to take advantage of Columbus's discovery. Its experience with the *reconquista* gave it a religious justification for conquest (bringing Christianity to nonbelievers) and an army of seasoned soldiers—*conquistadores*—eager to seek their fortunes in America now that the last Muslims had been expelled from Spain. In addition, during the *reconquista*, Spain's rulers developed efficient techniques for controlling newly conquered lands that could be applied to New World colonies.

The Spanish first consolidated their control of the Caribbean, establishing outposts on Cuba, Puerto Rico, and Jamaica (see Map 1.4). The *conquistadores* were more interested in finding gold and slaves than in creating permanent settlements. Leaving a trail of destruction, they attacked native villages and killed or captured the inhabitants.

The End of the Aztec Empire. In 1519, Hernán Cortés and 600 soldiers—the light-skinned strangers who inspired the Indian messenger to rush to Moctezuma—landed

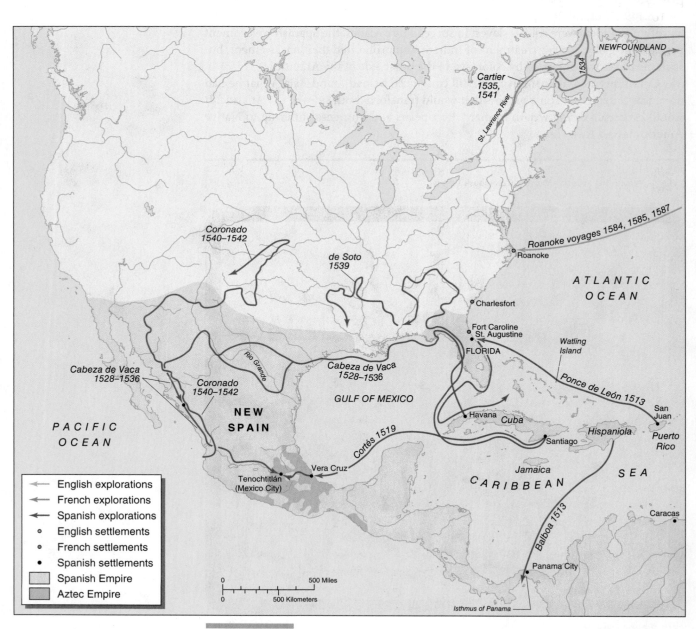

MAP 1.4 SPANISH, ENGLISH, AND FRENCH SETTLEMENTS IN NORTH AMERICA IN THE SIXTEENTH CENTURY By the end of the sixteenth century, only Spain had established permanent settlements in North America. French outposts in Canada and at Fort Caroline, as well as the English settlement at Roanoke, failed to thrive. European rivalries for North America, however, would intensify after 1600.

on the coast of Mexico. Their subsequent actions more than fulfilled the Aztec king's belief that the Spaniards' arrival was an evil omen. By 1521, Cortés and his men had conquered the powerful Aztec empire, discovering riches beyond their wildest dreams. They "picked up the gold and fingered it like monkeys," reported one Aztec witness.

The swift, decisive Spanish victory depended on several factors. In part, the Spanish enjoyed certain technological advantages. Their guns and horses often enabled them to overwhelm larger groups of Aztec foot soldiers armed with spears and swords. But technology alone cannot account for the conquest of a vastly more numerous enemy.

Cortés benefited from two other factors. First, he exploited divisions within the Aztec empire. The Spanish acquired indispensable allies among subject Indians who resented Aztec domination, tribute demands, and seizure of captives for religious sacrifice.

A second and more important factor was disease. One of Cortés's men was infected with smallpox, which soon devastated the native population. European diseases were unknown in the Americas before 1492, and Indians lacked resistance to them. Historians estimate that nearly 40 percent of the inhabitants of central Mexico died of smallpox within a year. Other diseases followed, including typhus, measles, and influenza. By 1600, the population of Mexico may have declined from more than 15 million to less than a million people.

The Fall of the Inca Empire. In 1532, Francisco Pizarro and 180 men discovered the Inca empire high in the Peruvian Andes. It was the largest empire in the Americas, stretching more than 2,000 miles from what is now Ecuador to Chile. An excellent network of roads and bridges linked this extensive territory to the imperial capital of Cuzco. Prosperous from trade and agriculture based on complex irrigation systems, the empire was also prone to political division. The Spaniards arrived at a moment of weakness for the empire. A few years before, the Inca ruler had died, probably from smallpox, and civil war had broken out between two of his sons. Pizarro captured the victor, Atahualpa, but despite receiving a colossal ransom had Atahualpa killed. The Spaniards then captured Cuzco, eventually extended control over the whole empire, and established a new capital at Lima.

By 1550, Spain's New World empire stretched from the Caribbean through Mexico to Peru. It was administered from Spain by the Council of the Indies, which enacted laws for the empire and supervised an elaborate bureaucracy charged with their enforcement. The council aimed to project royal authority into every village in New Spain in order to maintain political control and extract as much wealth as possible from the land and its people. Its power, however, was never as complete as Spanish officials wished.

For more than a century, Spanish ships crossed the Atlantic carrying seemingly limitless amounts of treasure from the colonies. To extract this wealth, the colonial rulers subjected the native inhabitants of New Spain to compulsory tribute payments and forced labor. Tens of thousands of Indians toiled in silver mines in Peru and Bolivia and on sugar plantations in the Caribbean. When necessary, Spaniards imported African slaves to supplement a native labor force ravaged by disease and exhaustion.

Spanish Incursions to the North. The desire for gold lured Spaniards farther into North America. In 1528, an expedition to Florida ended in disaster when the Spanish intruders provoked an attack by Apalachee Indians. Most of the Spaniards perished, but Álvar Núñez Cabeza de Vaca and three other men (including an African slave) escaped from their captors and managed to reach Mexico after a grueling eight-year journey. In a published account of his ordeal, Cabeza de Vaca insisted that the interior of North America contained a fabulously wealthy empire.

This report inspired other Spaniards to seek such treasures. In 1539, Hernán de Soto led an expedition from Florida to the Mississippi River. Along the way, the Spaniards harassed the native peoples, demanding provisions, burning villages, and capturing women to be servants and concubines. In these same years, Francisco Vásquez de Coronado led three hundred troops on an equally destructive expedition through present-day Arizona, New Mexico, and Colorado on a futile search for the mythical Seven Cities of Cíbola, rumored to contain hoards of gold and precious stones.

The failure to find gold and silver halted Spain's attempt to extend its empire to the north. So, too, did the lack of densely settled Indian communities, whose inhabitants could be exploited for tribute and labor. By the end of the sixteenth century, the Spanish maintained just two precarious footholds north of Mexico. One was a fortified naval base at St. Augustine, on Florida's Atlantic coast. The other settlement was located far to the west in what is now New Mexico.

Almost from the start of the conquest, the bloody tactics of the Spanish conquerors aroused protest back in Spain. The Indians' most eloquent advocate was Bartolomé de Las Casas, a Dominican priest shamed by his own role (as a layman) in the conquest of Hispaniola. In 1516, the Spanish king appointed him to the newly created office of Protector of the Indians, but his efforts had little effect.

The Seeds of Economic Decline. Between 1500 and 1650, an estimated 181 tons of gold and 16,000 tons of silver were shipped from the New World to Spain, making it the richest and most powerful state in Europe (see Figure 1.1). But this influx of American treasure had unforeseen consequences that would soon undermine Spanish predominance.

In 1492, the Spanish crown, determined to impose religious conformity after the *reconquista,* expelled from Spain all Jews who refused to become Christians. The refugees included many leading merchants who had contributed significantly to Spain's economy. The remaining Christian merchants, awash in American riches, saw little reason to invest in new trade or productive enterprises that might have sustained the economy once the flow of New World treasure diminished. As a result, Spain's economy eventually stagnated.

Compounding the problem, the flood of American gold and silver contributed to what historians have called a "price revolution" in Europe. Beginning in the late fifteenth century, as Europe's population recovered from the Black Death, demographic

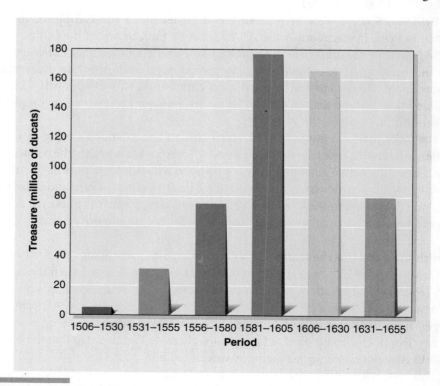

FIGURE 1.1 VALUE OF NEW WORLD TREASURE IMPORTED INTO SPAIN, 1506–1655 During the sixteenth and early seventeenth centuries, Spain was the only European power to reap great wealth from North America. The influx of New World treasure, however, slowed the development of Spain's economy in the long run. [Note: A ducat was a gold coin.]

SOURCE: Adapted from J. H. Elliott, *Imperial Spain, 1469–1716.* (1964 Hodder & Stroughton).

and economic factors led to a rise in prices. This inflationary cycle was made worse by the influx of New World gold and silver.

The Columbian Exchange

Spain's long-term economic decline was just one of many consequences of the conquest of the New World. In the long run, the biological consequences of contact—what one historian has called the **Columbian Exchange**—proved to be the most momentous (see Table 1.1, The Columbian Exchange).

The most catastrophic result of the exchange was the exposure of Native Americans to Old World diseases. Europeans and Africans, long exposed to these diseases, had developed some immunity to them. Native Americans, lacking such contact, had not. The Black Death of 1347–1351, Europe's worst epidemic, killed perhaps a third of its population. Epidemics of smallpox, measles, typhus, and influenza struck Native Americans with far greater force, killing anywhere from 50 to 90 percent of the people in communities exposed to them.

Another important aspect of the Columbian Exchange was the introduction of Old World livestock to the New World, which began when Columbus brought horses, sheep, cattle, pigs, and goats with him on his second voyage in 1493. The large European beasts created problems as well as opportunities for native peoples. With few natural predators to limit their numbers, livestock populations boomed in the New World, competing with native mammals. At least at first, the Indians' unfamiliarity with the use of horses in warfare often gave mounted European soldiers a decisive military advantage. But some native groups adopted these animals for their own purposes. Yaquis, Pueblos, and other peoples in the Southwest began to raise cattle and sheep. By the eighteenth century, Plains Indians had reoriented their culture around the use of horses, which had become essential for travel and hunting buffalo. Horses also became a primary object for trading and raiding among Plains peoples.

European ships carried unintentional passengers too. The black rat, a carrier of disease, arrived on the first voyages. So did insects, including honeybees, previously unknown in the New World. Ships also brought weeds such as thistles and dandelions, whose seeds were embedded in hay for animal fodder.

Foods were another important item of exchange. Columbus transported such European crops as wheat, chickpeas, melons, onions, and fruit trees to the Caribbean. Native Americans, in turn, introduced Europeans to corn, tomatoes, squash, beans, cacao, peppers, and potatoes, as well as nonfood plants such as tobacco and cotton. Spaniards learned from Indians how to process cacao beans into chocolate beverages, which became very popular in Europe. Lacking some of the other ingredients New World peoples used to flavor their drinks, Spaniards back in Europe substituted Asian spices, making chocolate truly a global beverage. New World food crops in general enriched Old World diets and, due to their nutritional benefits, eventually contributed to a sharp rise in Europe's population.

Columbian Exchange The transatlantic exchange of plants, animals, and diseases that occurred after the first European contact with the Americas.

 Read the Document   José de Acosta, The Columbian Exchange (1590)

TABLE 1.1 THE COLUMBIAN EXCHANGE

	From Old World to New World	From New World to Old World
Diseases	Smallpox, measles, plague, typhus, influenza, yellow fever, diphtheria, scarlet fever, whooping cough	Sexually transmitted strain of syphilis
Animals	Horses, cattle, pigs, sheep, goats, donkeys, mules, black rats, honeybees, cockroaches	Turkeys
Plants	Wheat, sugar, barley, apples, pears, peaches, plums, cherries, coffee, rice, dandelions, and other weeds	Maize, beans, peanuts, potatoes, sweet potatoes, manioc, squash, papayas, guavas, tomatoes, avocados, pineapple, chili pepper, cacao

✳ Explore Global Exploration on MyHistoryLab

HOW DID GLOBAL EXPLORATION CHANGE THE OLD AND NEW WORLDS?

Beginning in the 1400s, explorers left Europe and headed west in search of faster trade routes to Asia to keep up with the growing European demand for luxury goods such as silk and spices. In the process, they encountered huge civilizations in the Americas: complex societies that often had high levels of economic and social interconnectedness. Over the next two centuries, Europeans attempted to conquer these Native American societies by force, set up colonies, and establish trade ties, connecting the Old World (Europe, Asia, and Africa) with the New World (the Americas). This Age of Global Exploration had a profound impact on world history and was especially destructive to societies in the Americas, as vast numbers of people in the New World succumbed to Old World diseases.

Note: Each figure represents a million people.

*Colonial Powers: England, Spain, Portugal, France

Titled "Custom of the Indians," this woodcut of Italian origin and dating from about 1500 is believed to be the first European depiction of Native Americans in the New World.

POPULATIONS OF PRECONTACT NATIVE AMERICAN AND COLONIAL POWERS (c. 1500)

The Americas
(60–70 million)

Colonial Powers*
(29.7 million)

The Americas
(60–70 million)

Colonial Powers
(29.7 million)

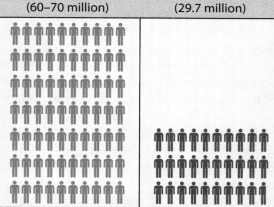

KEY QUESTIONS   Use MyHistoryLab *Explorer* to answer these questions:

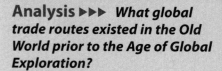

Analysis ▶▶▶ *What global trade routes existed in the Old World prior to the Age of Global Exploration?*

Map the late medieval trade contacts between Europe, Asia, and North Africa.

Comparison ▶▶▶ *In what ways were societies in the Americas interrelated before the arrival of the Europeans?*

Map the economic interconnectedness of the New World.

Consequence ▶▶▶ *How did the new trans-Atlantic trade connect different parts of the world?*

Map the integration of the Old and New Worlds into a single trading network.

Cultural Perceptions and Misperceptions

Curiosity and confusion often marked early encounters between Europeans and Native Americans. The first Indians whom Cortés allowed aboard a Spanish ship fainted at the sound of a large cannon being fired. French explorers were similarly taken by surprise when they choked while smoking Iroquois tobacco, which they thought tasted like "powdered pepper". These relatively minor mishaps were soon overshadowed by more substantial interactions that highlighted cultural differences between Indians and Europeans.

Most Indians believed that the universe contained friendly and hostile spiritual forces in human and other-than-human forms (such as plants, animals, and stars). People interacted with the spirit world through ceremonies that often involved exchanging gifts. North of Mexico, Indians (like West Africans) passed on religious beliefs through oral traditions, not in writing. To Europeans accustomed to worshiping one God in an organized church and preserving their beliefs in a written Bible, Indian spiritual traditions were incomprehensible. Many Europeans assumed that Indians worshiped the Devil. Indians, in turn, often found Christianity confusing and at first rejected European pressure to convert. As some Iroquois explained to colonists, "We do not know that God, we have never seen him, we know not who he is."

Different understandings of gender roles provided another source of confusion. Europeans regarded men as superior to women and thus the natural rulers of society. They disapproved of the less restrictive gender divisions among Native Americans. Europeans, accustomed to societies in which men did most agricultural work, objected to Indian women's dominant role in farming and assumed that men's hunting was more for recreation than subsistence. They concluded that Indian women lived "a most slavish life." Indians, in turn, thought that European men failed to make good use of their wives.

In order for Indians and Europeans to get along peaceably, each side would have to look past these and other cultural differences and adapt to the new circumstances under which both groups now lived. At first, such harmony seemed possible. But it soon became clear that Europeans intended to dominate the lands they discovered, sparking a vigorous resistance from native peoples who strove to maintain their autonomy in a changed world.

Competition for a Continent

1.5 Why did early French and English efforts at colonization falter?

Spain's New World bonanza attracted the attention of other European states eager to share in the wealth. Portugal soon acquired its own profitable piece of South America. In 1494, the conflicting claims of Portugal and Spain were resolved by the **Treaty of Tordesillas**. The treaty drew a north–south line approximately 1,100 miles west of the Cape Verde Islands. Spain received all lands west of the line, while Portugal held sway to the east. This limited Portugal's New World empire to Brazil, where settlers established sugar plantations worked by slave labor. But the treaty also protected Portugal's claims in Africa and Asia, which lay east of the line.

France and England rejected this division of the Western Hemisphere between Spain and Portugal. Their initial challenges to Spanish dominance in the New World, however, proved quite feeble. Domestic troubles—largely sparked by the Protestant Reformation—distracted the two countries from the pursuit of empire. By the close of the sixteenth century, both France and England insisted on their rights to New World lands, but neither had created a permanent settlement to support its claim.

Treaty of Tordesillas Treaty negotiated by the pope in 1494 to resolve the territorial claims of Spain and Portugal. It drew a north–south line approximately 1,100 miles west of the Cape Verde Islands, granting all lands west of the line to Spain and all lands east of the line to Portugal. This limited Portugal's New World empire to Brazil but confirmed its claims in Africa and Asia.

Early French Efforts in North America

France was a relative latecomer to New World exploration. In 1494, French troops invaded Italy, beginning a long and ultimately unsuccessful war with the Holy Roman Empire. Preoccupied with European affairs, France's rulers paid little attention to America. But when news of Cortés's exploits in Mexico arrived in the 1520s, King Francis I wanted his own New World empire to enrich France and block further Spanish expansion. In 1524, Francis sponsored a voyage by Giovanni da Verrazano, an Italian navigator, who mapped the North American coast from present-day South Carolina to Maine. During the 1530s and 1540s, the French mariner Jacques Cartier made three voyages in search of rich mines to rival those of Mexico and Peru. He explored the St. Lawrence River up to what is now Montreal, hoping to discover a water route through the continent to Asia (the so-called Northwest Passage).

On his third voyage, in 1541, Cartier was to serve under the command of a nobleman, Jean-François de la Rocque, Sieur de Roberval, who was commissioned by the king to establish a permanent settlement in Canada. This first attempt to found a French colony failed miserably. The Iroquois inhabitants of the region, suspicious of repeated French intrusions on their lands, saw no reason to help them. A year after they arrived in Canada, Roberval and the surviving colonists were back in France.

Disappointed with their Canadian expeditions, the French made a few forays to the south, establishing outposts in what is now South Carolina in 1562, and Florida in 1564. They soon abandoned the Carolina colony, and Spanish forces captured the Florida fort. Then, back in France, a prolonged civil war broke out between Catholics and Protestants. Renewed interest in colonization would have to await the return of peace at home.

English Attempts in the New World

The English were quicker than the French to stake a claim to the New World but no more successful at colonization. In 1497, King Henry VII sent John Cabot, an Italian mariner, to explore eastern Canada on England's behalf. But neither Henry nor any of his wealthy subjects would invest the funds necessary to follow up on Cabot's discoveries.

The lapse in English activity in the New World stemmed from religious troubles at home. Between 1534 and 1558, England changed its official religion several times. King Henry VIII, who had once defended the Catholic Church against its critics, took up the Protestant cause when the pope refused to annul his marriage to Catherine of Aragon. In 1534, Henry declared himself the head of a separate Church of England and seized the Catholic Church's English property. Because many English people sympathized with the Protestant cause, there was relatively little opposition to Henry's actions. But in 1553, Mary—daughter of the spurned Catherine of Aragon—became queen and tried to bring England back to Catholicism. She had nearly 300 Protestants burned at the stake for their beliefs (earning her the nickname "Bloody Mary"), and many others went into exile in Europe.

Mary's brief but destructive reign ended in 1558, and her half-sister Elizabeth, a committed Protestant, became queen. Elizabeth ruled for forty-five years (1558–1603), restoring Protestantism as the state religion, bringing stability to the nation, and renewing England's interest in the New World. She and her subjects saw colonization not only as a way to gain wealth and political advantage but also as a Protestant crusade against Catholic domination.

The Colonization of Ireland. England's first target for colonization, however, was not America but Ireland. Henry VIII had tried, with limited success, to bring the island under English control in the 1530s and 1540s. Elizabeth renewed the attempt in the 1560s with a series of brutal expeditions that destroyed Irish villages and slaughtered the inhabitants. Several veterans of these campaigns later took part in New World colonization and drew on their Irish experience for guidance.

Two aspects of that experience were particularly important. First, the English transferred their assumptions about Irish "savages" to Native Americans. Englishmen in America frequently observed similarities between Indians and the Irish. Because the English held the "wild Irish" in contempt, these observations encouraged them to scorn the Indians. When Indians resisted their attempts at conquest, the English recalled the Irish example, claiming that native "savagery" required brutal suppression.

Second, the Irish experience influenced English ideas about colonial settlement. English conquerors set up "plantations" surrounded by palisades on seized Irish lands. These plantations were meant to be civilized outposts in a savage land. Their aristocratic owners imported Protestant tenants from England and Scotland to farm the land. Native Irish people, considered too wild to join proper Christian communities, were excluded. English colonists in America followed this precedent when they established plantations that separated English and native peoples.

Expeditions to the New World. Sir Humphrey Gilbert, a notoriously cruel veteran of the Irish campaigns, became fascinated with the idea of New World colonization. He composed a treatise to persuade Queen Elizabeth to support such an endeavor. The queen, who counted Gilbert among her favorite courtiers, authorized several exploratory voyages, including Martin Frobisher's three trips in 1576–1578 in search of the Northwest Passage to Asia. Frobisher failed to find the elusive passage and sent back shiploads of glittering ore that proved to be fool's gold. Elizabeth had better luck in allowing privateers, such as John Hawkins and Francis Drake, to raid Spanish ships and New World ports for gold and silver.

Meanwhile, Gilbert continued to promote New World settlement, arguing that it would increase England's trade and provide a place to send unemployed Englishmen. Gilbert suggested offering free land in America to English families willing to emigrate.

Read the Document   Thomas Harriot, The Algonquian Peoples of the Atlantic Coast (1588)

In one of his many portraits of Roanoke Indians, John White offered front and back images of a dignified Native leader in a fringed deerskin skirt. In the background, Roanoke Indians fish from canoes; to the left is a fish weir and trap.

From Then to Now

The Disappearance of Cod from the Grand Banks

N ot long after John Cabot returned from his voyage to America in 1497, rumors circulated that he had found astonishingly rich fishing grounds off the coast of Newfoundland. As it happened, Basque fishermen sailing from ports in northern Spain and southwestern France already knew about this bonanza. But Cabot's discovery spread the news, and by the 1550s, more than a hundred ships a year traveled from Europe to fish in the waters of the Grand Banks in the northern Atlantic. By the early sixteenth century, 60 percent

By the twentieth century, commercial fishermen using enormous nets and motorized boats helped to shrink cod stocks to an all-time low.

Hand-lining for cod, the fishing method depicted in this eighteenth-century engraving, produced ample catches but did not reduce cod populations to dangerously low levels.

of the fish eaten in Europe was cod, and most of it came from the Grand Banks.

Now, 500 years later, cod stocks are at an all-time low due in part to ocean warming and in part to overfishing. Until the early nineteenth century, most fishermen used handlines—single baited hooks fastened to a weight— dropped in the water from sailing vessels. Now commercial fishermen use enormous nets, harvesting their catch from motorized vessels. Experts differ on whether cod populations can recover. Canadian officials have established a moratorium on fishing in the area in order to see if recovery is possible. The long-term legacy of John Cabot's voyage may well be the disappearance of the resource that drew him and many other European adventurers to North America in the first place.

Question for Discussion

- What does the story of the Grand Banks tell us about the long-run environmental consequences of Europeans' contact with the New World?

In 1578, he received permission to set up a colony along the North American coast. It took him five years to organize an expedition to Newfoundland, which he claimed for England. After sailing southward seeking a more favorable site for a colony, Gilbert headed home, only to be lost at sea during an Atlantic storm. The impetus for English colonization did not die with him, however, for his half-brother, Sir Walter Raleigh (another veteran of the Irish wars), took up the cause.

The Roanoke Colony. In 1584, Raleigh sent an expedition to find a suitable location for a colony. The Carolina coast seemed promising, so Raleigh sent men in 1585 to build a settlement on Roanoke Island. Most of the colonists were soldiers fresh from Ireland who refused to grow their own food, insisting that the Roanoke Indians should feed them. When the local chief, Wingina, organized native resistance, they killed him. Eventually, the colonists, disappointed not to have found any treasure and exhausted by a harsh winter, returned to England in 1586.

Two members of these early expeditions, however, left a more positive legacy. Thomas Hariot studied the Roanoke and Croatoan Indians and identified local plants and animals, hoping that some might prove to be profitable commodities. John White drew maps and painted a series of watercolors depicting the natives and the coastal landscape. When Raleigh tried once more, in 1587, to found a colony, he chose White to be its leader. This attempt also failed. The ship captain dumped the settlers—who, for the first time, included women and children—on Roanoke Island so that he could pursue Spanish treasure ships. White waited until his granddaughter, Virginia Dare (the first English child born in America), was born and then sailed to England for supplies. But the outbreak of war with Spain delayed his return for three years. Spain had gathered an immense fleet to invade England, and all English ships were needed for defense. Although England defeated the Armada in 1588, White could not obtain a relief ship for Roanoke until 1590. When he finally returned, he found the settlement deserted.

At this point, Raleigh gave up on North America and turned his attention to his Irish plantations. But England's interest in colonization did not wane. In 1584, Richard Hakluyt had aroused enthusiasm for America by writing the *Discourse on the Western Planting* for the queen and her advisers. He argued that England would prosper from trade and the sale of New World commodities. Once the Indians were civilized, Hakluyt added, they would eagerly purchase English goods. Equally important, England could plant "sincere religion" (that is, Protestant Christianity) in the New World and block Spanish expansion. Hakluyt's arguments fired the imaginations of many people, and the defeat of the Spanish Armada emboldened England to challenge Spain's New World dominance. The experience of Roanoke should have demonstrated the difficulty of establishing colonies. But the English were slow to learn; when they resumed colonization efforts in 1607, once again there were disastrous results for the people involved. As it was, the sixteenth century ended with no permanent English settlement in the New World.

Conclusion

Dramatic changes occurred in North America during the century after the Aztec messenger spotted Spanish ships off the Mexican coast and made his journey to tell Moctezuma about his discovery. The conquistadores were only the first trickle in what became a flood of Old World immigrants. Europeans, eager for wealth and power, set out to claim a continent that just a hundred years earlier they had not dreamed existed. African slaves were brought to the Caribbean, Mexico, and Brazil, and forced to labor under extremely harsh conditions for white masters. The Aztec and Incan empires collapsed in the wake of the Spanish conquest. In the Caribbean and parts of Mexico and Peru, untold numbers of native peoples succumbed to European diseases they had never before encountered.

And yet, conditions in 1600 bore clearer witness to the past than to the future. Despite all that had happened, North America was still Indian country. Only Spain had established North American colonies, and even its soldiers struggled to expand north of Mexico. Spain's outposts in Florida and New Mexico staked claims to territory that it did not really control. Except in Mexico and the Caribbean, Europeans had merely touched the continent's shores. In 1600, despite the virulent epidemics, native peoples (even in Mexico) still greatly outnumbered European and African immigrants. The next century, however, brought many powerful challenges both to native control and to the Spanish monopoly of settlement.

For Suggested Readings go to MyHistoryLab.

Chapter Review

Native American Societies before 1492

1.1 How did the precontact histories of Native Americans, especially in the centuries just before 1492, shape their encounters with Europeans? p. 3

Prior to European contact, North America contained a large and diverse Native American population, with different cultures, subsistence practices, and political organizations. Over the course of centuries, various native societies had flourished, but by the time Europeans arrived, some of the most powerful empires were in decline.

West African Societies

1.2 What were the key characteristics of West African society? p. 8

West African societies varied in size from small kingdoms to large empires. Most people lived by farming, but there were also many skilled artisans. Religion and family ties were central to West African life. Although contact with Europe was limited, Europeans were aware of the African gold trade.

Western Europe on the Eve of Exploration

1.3 How did events in Europe both shape and inspire exploration of the Americas? p. 13

By the end of the fifteenth century, Western Europe had recovered from the warfare and epidemics of earlier years. But it would soon be fragmented by religious divisions stemming from the Protestant Reformation. Such divisions led to renewed conflict and competition among European states that would affect New World exploration.

Contact

1.4 What were the biological consequences of contact between Europeans and Native Americans? p. 14

Columbus's effort to reach Asia via a westward voyage across the Atlantic led to the European discovery of America. Spanish soldiers quickly conquered the Aztec and Incan empires, aided by the deaths of Native Americans lacking immunity to European diseases. The transmission of germs was one of many biological consequences of contact.

Competition for a Continent

1.5 Why did early French and English efforts at colonization falter? p. 23

Learning of Spain's access to New World gold and silver, France and England desired their own empires. The French attempted to establish permanent settlements in Canada and the English at Roanoke. Yet neither effort was successful, in part because French and English rulers were preoccupied with religious conflicts at home.

Timeline

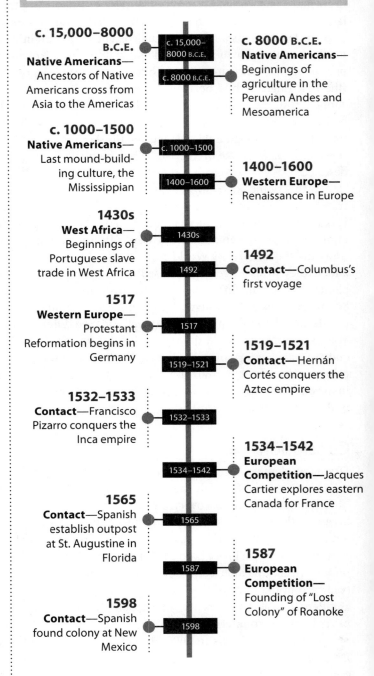

c. 15,000–8000 B.C.E.
Native Americans— Ancestors of Native Americans cross from Asia to the Americas

c. 15,000–8000 B.C.E.

c. 8000 B.C.E.
Native Americans— Beginnings of agriculture in the Peruvian Andes and Mesoamerica

c. 8000 B.C.E.

c. 1000–1500
Native Americans— Last mound-building culture, the Mississippian

c. 1000–1500

1400–1600
Western Europe— Renaissance in Europe

1400–1600

1430s
West Africa— Beginnings of Portuguese slave trade in West Africa

1430s

1492
Contact—Columbus's first voyage

1492

1517
Western Europe— Protestant Reformation begins in Germany

1517

1519–1521
Contact—Hernán Cortés conquers the Aztec empire

1519–1521

1532–1533
Contact—Francisco Pizarro conquers the Inca empire

1532–1533

1534–1542
European Competition—Jacques Cartier explores eastern Canada for France

1534–1542

1565
Contact—Spanish establish outpost at St. Augustine in Florida

1565

1587
European Competition— Founding of "Lost Colony" of Roanoke

1587

1598
Contact—Spanish found colony at New Mexico

1598

2 Transplantation and Adaptation 1600–1685

One American Journey

Letter from Richard Frethorne
to His Parents

Martin's Hundred in Virginia, 1623

Loving and kind father and mother:

My most humble duty remembered to you, . . . This is to let you understand that I your child am in a most heavy case by reason of the nature of the country, [which] is such that it causeth much sickness, as the scurvy and the bloody flux and diverse other diseases, which maketh the body very poor and weak. . . . [Since] I came out of the ship I never ate anything but peas, and loblollie (that is water gruel). . . . A mouthful of bread for a penny loaf must serve for four men which is most pitiful. . . . [We] live in fear of the enemy every hour . . . for our plantation is very weak by reason of the death and sickness of our company. . . .

But I am not half a quarter so strong as I was in England, and all is for want of

LEARNING OBJECTIVES

2.1	2.2	2.3	2.4	2.5	2.6
How did the French use Indian alliances to create their North American empire? p. 31	How significant was New Netherland as part of the Dutch global empire? p. 34	Why did the English have such difficulties establishing colonies in the Chesapeake? p. 35	Why were the English colonies in New England so different from those in the Chesapeake? p. 42	Why did the first biracial colonial societies appear in the Caribbean? p. 48	How influential were the ideas of the different proprietors of the Restoration colonies in shaping the development of their settlements? p. 50

Pocahontas's marriage to John Rolfe in 1614 ushered in a brief period of peace between the Powhatan Indians and English colonists. This engraving shows her in English-style dress. Around the image is engraved her native name, Matoaka, as well as the English name, Rebecca, she assumed upon her conversion to Christianity.

(((Listen to **Chapter 2** on **MyHistoryLab**

2.1

2.2

2.3

2.4

2.5

2.6

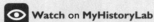 Watch the Video Series on MyHistoryLab

Learn about some key topics related to this chapter with the *MyHistoryLab Video Series: Key Topics in U.S. History.*

1 **Beginnings of English Colonial Societies: 1607–1660** Because the Crown claimed ownership of all English colonial possessions, merchants and gentlemen who wished to establish settlements in the New World had to petition King James I and his successors for royal charters. This video describes the companies that established colonies, such as the Virginia Company and the Plymouth Company, and shows how difficult life could be for the first settlers—and dangerous; in one case, an entire colony mysteriously disappeared.

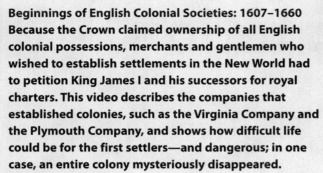 Watch on MyHistoryLab

Jamestown The important colony of Jamestown, founded in the lower Chesapeake Bay by the Virginia Company in 1607, is the subject of this video. Captain John Smith, Chief Powhatan, and his daughter Pocahontas are all important figures in its early history, as is the tobacco plant, which changed the entire economy of the colony and made it one of the richest in the New World. **2**

Watch on MyHistoryLab

3 **The Chesapeake** Unlike the colonies of New England, the Chesapeake colonies differed both in how they were formed, as this video illustrates, and in how people lived. Maryland was a proprietary colony, that is, the sole possession of George Calvert, Lord Baltimore. Calvert's intention was for Baltimore to become a refuge for Catholic people persecuted in England. The colonists of Maryland had a better relationship with the Indians than the Protestant settlers of Virginia.

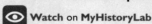 Watch on MyHistoryLab

New England This video surveys the founding of the New England colonies, primarily the Pilgrims and Puritans in Massachusetts, Rhode Island, and Connecticut. In achieving religious freedom from England, however, the colonists found a new antagonist in the Native Americans. Both groups tried and failed to coexist; the breakdown in their relationships is examined in light of the conflicts between the Wampanoag and Pequot peoples. **4**

Watch on MyHistoryLab

victuals, for I do protest unto you that I have eaten more in [one] day at home than I have allowed me here for a week. . . .

[I] saith that if you love me you will redeem me suddenly, for which I do entreat and beg.... Good father, do not forget me, but have mercy and pity my miserable case. I know if you did but see me, you would weep to see me....

Richard Frethorne

Susan M. Kingsbury, ed., *The Records of the Virginia Company of London,* 4 vols. (Washington, DC, 1935), 4:58–62.

Personal Journeys Online

- Rev. Francis Higginson, July 1629. Letter from Massachusetts to His Friends in Leicester, England.

- Father Isaac Jogues, Novum Belgium, 1646. Description of New Amsterdam.
- Hans Sloan, A Voyage to the Islands, 1707. Description of early eighteenth-century Jamaica.

2.1

2.2

2.3

2.4

2.5

2.6

R ichard Frethorne had journeyed across the Atlantic to seek his fortune in the new colony of Virginia. Like many emigrants, he hoped that one day he would become a prosperous landowner, a status beyond his reach in England. Instead of health and prosperity, Frethorne found sickness and starvation. Fears of an attack by enemy Indians compounded his misery. Yet the starving young Englishman could not simply board the next ship for England. He was under contract to work for the Virginia Company and could not leave until he had completed his term of service; hence Frethorne's anguished plea to his father to "redeem" him, or buy out the remainder of his contract so that he could return home sooner.

Frethorne's experience reveals several important aspects of European colonization in the New World. Although his distress was not shared by all colonists, it was sadly typical of many English emigrants to early Virginia. Colonization offered opportunities for advancement, to be sure, but often at the price of sickness, suffering, and danger. Virginia turned out to be England's first permanent colony in the New World, but from Frethorne's perspective in 1623, it was a fragile settlement teetering on the brink of disaster.

Virginia's eventual success, and that of other English colonies, depended upon the willingness of thousands of individuals like Richard Frethorne to face the challenges posed by overseas settlement. Even as their emigration was inspired by hopes of improvement, their quest also reflected England's desire to claim a portion of the New World for itself. In this scramble for American colonies, England's greatest adversaries were France and the Netherlands. If ordinary colonists were often preoccupied with their own tribulations, their leaders could never forget the high stakes involved in the international race for overseas possessions.

The French in North America

2.1 How did the French use Indian alliances to create their North American empire?

I n the mid-sixteenth century, religious warfare between Catholics and Protestants at home had interrupted France's efforts to establish a foothold in North America. So long as this conflict divided the nation, the only French subjects who maintained regular contact with the New World were fishermen making seasonal voyages to the waters off the coast of Newfoundland. But in the early seventeenth century, after King Henry IV restored civil order in France, the situation changed. With the creation of permanent settlements first along the St. Lawrence River and later in the continent's interior, France staked its claim to a New World empire.

The Quest for Furs and Converts

French fishermen who dried their catch along the Newfoundland shore often encountered Indians interested in trading beaver pelts for European goods. There was a ready market for these furs in Europe, where beaver hats had become very fashionable. Thus furs joined fish as a source of wealth, and a reason for French explorers and entrepreneurs to establish the colony of New France.

In 1608, Samuel de Champlain led an expedition up the St. Lawrence River to found a permanent settlement at Quebec. This village was eventually joined by two others—Trois-Rivières (founded 1634) and Montreal (1642)—located farther up the river (see Map 2.1). For several decades, the colony was managed by the Company of New France, a private corporation working on its own behalf as well as in France's imperial

2.1

2.2

2.3

2.4

2.5

2.6

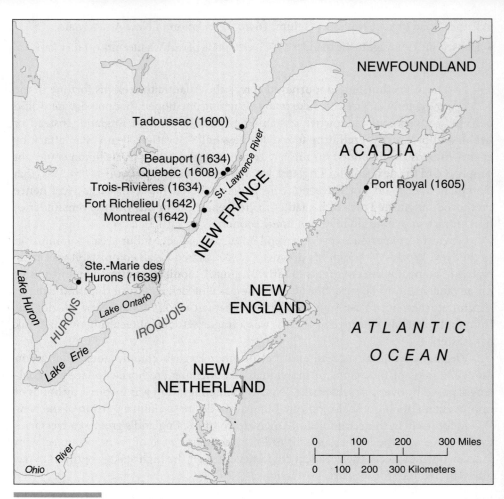

MAP 2.1 NEW FRANCE, c. 1650 By 1650, New France contained a number of thinly populated settlements along the St. Lawrence River Valley and the eastern shore of Lake Huron. Most colonists lived in Quebec and Montreal; other sites served mainly as fur-trading posts and Jesuit missions to the Huron Indians.

interests. New France grew slowly; by the 1660s, there were only 3,200 colonists clustered in and around the three main villages.

The fur trade supporting the colony's development functioned as a partnership between Indians and Europeans. At first, some colonists anticipated that economic ties between the two peoples would be supplemented by marital ones as French traders took Indian wives. Intermarriage, however, was never widespread, occurring mainly among ***coureurs de bois*** (**"woods runners"**), independent fur traders who ventured into the forests to live and trade among native peoples.

Indian peoples such as the Montagnais and Hurons welcomed the French not only as trading partners, but also as military allies, making sure that the newcomers understood that the two roles had to be linked. As a result, the fur trade entangled the French in rivalries among Indian groups that long predated European contact.

Some French colonists regarded saving Indian souls as more important than profiting from furs. Beginning in the 1630s, Jesuit missionaries—members of a Catholic religious order founded during the Counter-Reformation—tried to convince Indians to come to the French settlements to hear Christian preaching and learn European ways. When that tactic failed, Jesuits traveled to native villages and learned native languages, bringing Christianity directly to Indian populations.

The Development of New France

After 1663, New France underwent several important changes. King Louis XIV disbanded the Company of New France and assumed direct control of the colony. The French government also vastly improved Canada's military defenses, investing money

coureurs de bois French for "woods runners," independent fur traders in New France.

Read the **Document** Iroquois Chiefs Address the Governors of New York and Virginia (1684)

2.1

2.2

2.3

2.4

2.5

2.6

Because Indians expected their trading partners also to be military allies, Europeans were often drawn into native conflicts. This illustration, from Samuel de Champlain's 1613 description of the founding of New France, shows him joining his Huron allies in an attack on the Iroquois.

in the construction of forts and sending over professional soldiers. This was a greater investment in defense than English kings would provide for their colonies until the middle of the eighteenth century.

French officials launched a massive campaign to increase migration to the colony. They sent more than 700 orphaned girls and widows—called *filles du roi,* or "king's daughters"—to provide wives in a colony where there were six men of marriageable age for every unmarried French woman. Many male immigrants were *engagés,* or **indentured servants,** who agreed to work for three years in return for food, lodging, a small salary, and a return passage to France.

Despite these efforts, only about 250 French immigrants arrived each year. Several factors discouraged prospective colonists. Rumors circulated about frigid Canadian winters and surprise Indian attacks. In addition, the government required settlers to be Catholic (although Protestants often resided in Canada temporarily), reducing the pool from which colonists could be recruited. In the end, nearly three out of four immigrants who went to Canada returned home. By 1700, the population had grown to about 15,000 (less than 7 percent of the English population in the mainland colonies that year; see Figure 2.1), mostly due to a remarkable level of natural increase.

French officials sought to restrict settlement to the St. Lawrence Valley, fearing that further expansion would render the empire impossible to defend. The impetus to move inland, however, could not be restrained. By the 1670s, French traders and missionaries had reached the Mississippi River. In 1681–1682, René-Robert Cavelier, Sieur de La Salle, followed the Mississippi to the Gulf of Mexico, claiming the entire valley (which he named Louisiana in honor of the king) for France. When officials tried to restrict the direct trade between Indians and the *coureurs de bois,* many of these Frenchmen drifted off to settle in what became known as the *pays des Illinois* along the Mississippi. This expansion of French influence alarmed the English, who had founded colonies along the Atlantic seaboard and feared a growing French presence in the west.

Prosperous and expansive, Canada provided France with a secure foothold on the North American mainland. Its successful establishment contributed to an escalating European competition for land and trade in the New World. Soon new rivals entered the scene.

indentured servant An individual—usually male but occasionally female—who contracted to serve a master for a period of four to seven years in return for payment of the servant's passage to America. Indentured servitude was the primary labor system in the Chesapeake colonies for most of the seventeenth century.

2.1

2.2

2.3

2.4

2.5

2.6

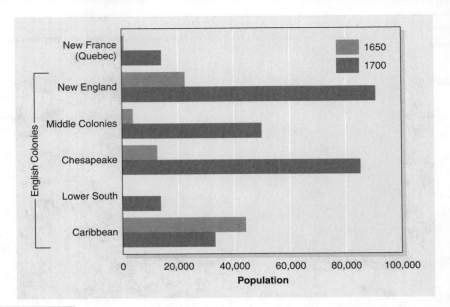

FIGURE 2.1 EUROPEAN POPULATIONS OF NEW FRANCE (QUEBEC) AND ENGLISH COLONIES IN 1650 AND 1700 Although New France's population grew rapidly between 1650 and 1700, it remained only a tiny fraction of the population of England's North American colonies. By 1700, English colonists on the mainland outnumbered New France's inhabitants by a factor of about 16 to 1.

SOURCE: From THE ECONOMY OF BRITISH AMERICA, 1607–1789 by John J. McClusker and Russell R. Menard. Published for the Omohundro Institute of Early American History and Culture. Copyright © 1985 by the University of North Carolina Press. www.uncpress.unc.edu.

The Dutch Overseas Empire

2.2 How significant was New Netherland as part of the Dutch global empire?

The Dutch Republic joined the scramble for empire in the early seventeenth century. The Northern Provinces, sometimes known as Holland, had in 1581 declared their independence from Spain (whose kings ruled the region as part of the Holy Roman Empire), although sporadic fighting continued for another half century. The new republic, dominated by Protestants, was intent on challenging Catholic Spain's power in the New World as well as the Old. More than any other factor, however, the desire for profit drove the Dutch quest for colonies.

The Dutch East India Company

By 1600, the Dutch emerged as the leading economic power in Europe. The republic earned considerable wealth from manufacturing such goods as textiles, jewelry, and glass, and Amsterdam soon became Europe's financial capital. The centerpiece of Dutch prosperity, however, was commerce, which expanded dramatically in the early seventeenth century. This commercial vitality provided the context for overseas expansion into both the Atlantic and Pacific.

The instrument of colonial dominance was the Dutch East India Company, founded in 1602 to challenge what had until then been a virtual Portuguese monopoly of Asian trade. Its first success was the capture of the Spice Islands (now Indonesia and East Timor), followed by the takeover of Batavia (Jakarta), Ceylon (Sri Lanka), and Sumatra. The company established slave-trading posts on the Gold Coast of West Africa, where it competed with the Portuguese, and at the Cape of Good Hope on Africa's southern tip. Its far-flung commercial net eventually encompassed parts of India and Formosa (Taiwan).

The West India Company and New Netherland

The Dutch next set their sights on the Americas, creating the West India Company in 1621. After taking control of West African slave-trading posts and temporarily occupying part of Brazil, the West India Company moved into the Caribbean (acquiring four islands by the 1640s) and North America. Its claim to the Connecticut, Hudson, and Delaware valleys stemmed from the 1609 voyage of Henry Hudson, an Englishman sailing for the Dutch, who discovered the river that bears his name.

The first permanent Dutch settlers on mainland North America arrived in 1624 to set up a fur-trading post at Fort Orange (now Albany). Two years later, Peter Minuit and a company of Protestant refugees established New Amsterdam on Manhattan Island, which Minuit had purchased from the Indians. The Hudson River corridor between these two settlements became the heart of the New Netherland colony. Like New France, its economic focus was the fur trade. Dutch merchants forged ties with the Iroquois, who exchanged furs for European tools and weapons.

At its peak, New Netherland's colonists only numbered about 10,000. What they lacked in numbers the colonists made up for in divisiveness. New Netherland became a magnet for religious refugees from Europe, as well as a destination for Africans acquired through the slave trade. (In 1638, about 100 Africans—free and slave—lived in New Amsterdam, constituting nearly a third of that city's population.) Ethnic and religious differences hindered a sense of community. Among the colony's Dutch, German, French, English, Swedish, Portuguese, and African settlers were Calvinists, Lutherans, **Quakers,** Catholics, and Muslims. In addition, twenty-three Jews arrived in New Amsterdam in 1654 to establish the first permanent Jewish community in North America. Many of them had lived in Brazil while it was briefly under Dutch rule, but when the Portuguese reclaimed the colony, the Jewish settlers were forced to move yet again, this time to New Netherland.

The West India Company dispatched several inept but aggressive governors who made an unstable situation worse by provoking conflict with Indians. Although the colonists maintained good relations with their Iroquois trading partners on the upper Hudson River, they had far less friendly dealings with the Algonquian peoples around New Amsterdam. In one particularly gruesome incident in 1645, Governor Willem Kieft ordered a massacre at an encampment of Indian refugees who had refused to pay him tribute. Ten years later, Governor Peter Stuyvesant antagonized Susquehannock Indians along the Delaware River by seizing a small Swedish colony where the Susquehannocks had traded.

Such actions provoked retaliatory raids by the Indians, further weakening the colony. Though profitable, the fur trade did not generate the riches to be found in other parts of the Dutch empire. By the 1650s, New Netherland increasingly looked like a poor investment to company officials back in Europe.

Quakers Members of the Society of Friends, a radical religious group that arose in the mid-seventeenth century. Quakers rejected formal theology and an educated ministry, focusing instead on the importance of the "Inner Light," or Holy Spirit that dwelt within them. Quakers were important in the founding of Pennsylvania.

English Settlement in the Chesapeake

2.3 Why did the English have such difficulties establishing colonies in the Chesapeake?

Following the Roanoke colony's disappearance after 1587 (see Chapter 1), twenty years passed before the English again attempted to settle in America. When they did, in 1607, it was in the lower Chesapeake Bay region. The new settlement, Jamestown, at first seemed likely to share Roanoke's dismal fate. But it endured, eventually developing into the prosperous colony of Virginia. The reason for Virginia's success was an American plant—tobacco—that commanded good prices from European consumers. Tobacco also underlay the economy of a neighboring colony, Maryland, and had a profound influence on the development of Chesapeake society.

2.1

2.2

2.3

2.4

2.5

2.6

2.1

2.2

2.3

2.4

2.5

2.6

joint-stock company Business enterprise in which a group of stockholders pooled their money to engage in trade or to fund colonizing expeditions. Joint-stock companies participated in the founding of the Virginia, Plymouth, and Massachusetts Bay colonies.

The Ordeal of Early Virginia

In 1606, several English merchants petitioned King James I for a charter incorporating two companies to attempt New World settlement. One, the London, or Virginia, Company, included merchants from the city of London; the other, the Plymouth Company, included merchants from England's western ports. James I issued a charter granting the companies two tracts of land along the mid-Atlantic coast. These **joint-stock companies** sold shares to investors (who expected a profit in return) to raise money for colonization.

The Jamestown Colony. Three small ships carried 104 settlers, all men, to the mouth of Chesapeake Bay in May 1607 (see Map 2.2). On a peninsula about 50 miles up a river they named the James in honor of their king, the colonists built a fortified settlement they called Jamestown. Hoping to earn quick profits for Virginia Company investors, they began hunting for gold and searching for the Northwest Passage to Asia. But the swampy region was a breeding area for malarial mosquitoes and parasites carrying other diseases. Spending all their time searching for riches, the settlers neglected to plant crops, and their food supplies dwindled. By January 1608, only thirty-eight colonists were still alive.

After the disastrous first year, the colony's governing council turned to Captain John Smith for leadership. He imposed military discipline on Jamestown, organizing settlers into work gangs and decreeing that "he that will not worke shall not eate." His high-handed methods revived the colony but antagonized certain settlers who believed that their social status exempted them from manual labor. When a gunpowder

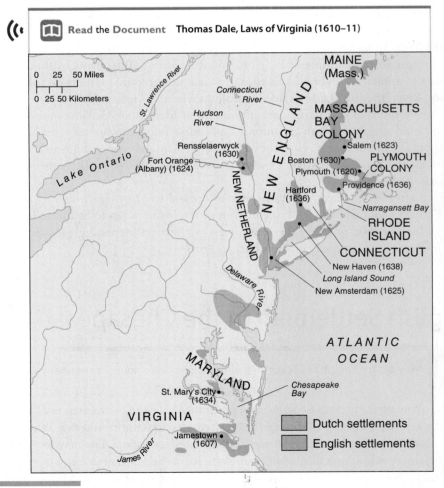

Read the Document Thomas Dale, Laws of Virginia (1610–11)

MAP 2.2 ENGLISH AND DUTCH MAINLAND COLONIES IN NORTH AMERICA, c. 1655 Early English colonies clustered in two areas of the Atlantic seaboard—New England and the Chesapeake Bay. Between them lay Dutch New Netherland, with settlements stretching up the Hudson River. The Dutch also acquired territory at the mouth of the Delaware River in 1655 when they seized a short-lived Swedish colony located there.

explosion wounded Smith in 1609 and forced him to return to England, his enemies had him replaced as leader.

Once again, the colony nearly disintegrated. More settlers arrived, only to starve or die of disease. Of the 500 people in Jamestown in the autumn of 1609, just 60 remained alive by the spring of 1610. Facing financial ruin, company officials back in England tried to conceal the state of the colony. They reorganized the company twice and sent more settlers, including glassmakers, winegrowers, and silkmakers, in a desperate effort to find a marketable colonial product. They experimented with harsh military discipline. When it became clear that such severity discouraged immigration, the company tried more positive inducements.

The first settlers had been expected to work in return for food and other necessities; only company stockholders were to share in the colony's profits. But settlers wanted land, so governors began assigning small plots to those who finished their terms of service to the company. In 1616, the company instituted the **headright system,** giving 50 acres to anyone who paid his own way to Virginia and an additional 50 acres for each person (or "head") he brought with him.

In 1619, three other important developments occurred. That year, the company began transporting women to become wives for planters and induce them to stay in the colony. It was also the year in which the first Africans arrived in Virginia. In addition, the company created the first legislative body in English America, the **House of Burgesses,** setting a precedent for the establishment of self-government in other English colonies. Landowners elected representatives to the House of Burgesses, which, subject to the approval of the company, made laws for Virginia.

Despite these changes, the settlers were still unable to earn the company a profit. To make matters worse, the headright system expanded English settlement beyond Jamestown. This strained the already tense relations between the English and the Indians onto whose lands they had intruded.

The Powhatan Confederacy and the Colonists.   When the English arrived in 1607, they planted their settlement in the heart of territory ruled by the powerful Indian leader Powhatan. Chief of a confederacy of about thirty tribes with some 14,000 people, Powhatan had little to fear at first from the struggling English outpost. After an initial skirmish with English soldiers, he sent gifts of food, assuming that by accepting the gifts, the colonists acknowledged their dependence on him. Further action against the settlers seemed unnecessary, because they appeared fully capable of destroying themselves.

This conclusion was premature. Armed colonists began seizing corn from Indian villages whenever native people refused to supply it voluntarily. In retaliation, Powhatan besieged Jamestown and tried to starve the colony to extinction. The colony was saved by the arrival of reinforcements from England, but war with the Indians continued until 1614.

The marriage of the colonist John Rolfe to Pocahontas, Powhatan's daughter, helped seal the peace in 1614. Pocahontas had briefly been held captive by the English during the war and had been instructed in English manners and religion by Rolfe. Sent to negotiate with Powhatan in the spring of 1614, Rolfe asked the chief for his daughter's hand. Powhatan gave his consent, and Pocahontas—baptized in the Church of England and renamed Rebecca—became Rolfe's wife.

Powhatan died in 1618, and his brother Opechancanough succeeded him as chief. The new chief made plans for retaliation against growing numbers of settlers. Early in the morning on March 22, 1622, hundreds of Indian men traveled to the English settlements, as if they meant to visit or trade. Instead, they attacked the unsuspecting colonists, killing 347 by the end of the day—more than one-fourth of the English population.

The surviving colonists almost immediately plotted revenge. English forces struck at native villages, killing the inhabitants and burning cornfields. During the ensuing nine years of war, the English treated the Indians with a ferocity that recalled their earlier subjugation of the Irish.

Although Opechancanough's attack failed to restrain the colonists, it destroyed the Virginia Company. Economic activity ceased as settlers retreated to fortified garrisons.

2.1

2.2

2.3

2.4

2.5

2.6

headright system A system of land distribution during the early colonial era that granted settlers 50 acres for themselves and another 50 acres for each "head" (or person) they brought to the colony.

House of Burgesses The legislature of colonial Virginia. First organized in 1619, it was the first institution of representative government in the English colonies.

2.1

2.2

2.3

2.4

2.5

2.6

((∙   📖 Read the Document   Chief Powhatan, Remarks to Captain John Smith
(c. 1609)

C.Smith taketh the King of Pamaunkee prisoner 1608

This illustration shows John Smith seizing the scalplock of Opechancanough, Chief Powhatan's brother, during an English raid on an Indian village. Smith released his prisoner only after Indians ransomed him with corn. Thirteen years later, Opechancanough led a surprise attack against the colonists.

The company went bankrupt, and a royal commission investigating the 1622 attack was shocked to discover that nearly ten times more colonists had died from starvation and disease than at the hands of Indians. King James dissolved the company in 1624, and Virginia became a royal colony the following year. The settlers continued to enjoy self-government through the House of Burgesses, but now the king chose the colony's governor and council, and royal advisers monitored its affairs.

The Importance of Tobacco

Ironically, the demise of the Virginia Company helped the colony succeed. In their search for a marketable product, settlers had begun growing tobacco after 1610. The first cargo of Virginia-grown tobacco arrived in England in 1617 and sold at a profitable 3 shillings per pound. Company officials, unwilling to base the colony's economy on a single crop, tried to restrict annual production to 100 pounds per person. Colonists ignored these restrictions, and tobacco production really surged after the company dissolved.

2.1

2.2

2.3

2.4

2.5

2.6

Between 1627 and 1669, annual tobacco exports climbed from 250,000 pounds to more than 15 million pounds. As the supply grew, the price per pound plunged from 13 pence in 1624 to a mere penny in the late 1660s, where it remained for the next half century. Now thoroughly dependent on tobacco for their livelihood, the only way colonists could compensate for falling prices was to grow even more, pushing exports to England to more than 20 million pounds per year by about 1680 (see Figure 2.2).

Tobacco shaped nearly every aspect of Virginia society, from the recruitment of colonists to patterns of settlement. Planters scrambled to claim lands near navigable rivers so that ships could reach their plantations and carry their crops to market. As a result, the colonists dispersed into plantations located along waterways instead of settling in compact communities. Settlers competed to produce the biggest and best crop and get it to market the fastest, hoping to enjoy even a small price advantage over everyone else.

Tobacco kept workers busy nine months of the year. Planters sowed seeds in the early spring, transplanted seedlings a few weeks later, and spent the summer pinching off the tops of the plants (to produce larger leaves) and removing worms. After the harvest, the leaves were "cured"—dried in ventilated sheds—and packed in large barrels. During the winter, planters cleared and fenced more land and made barrels for next year's crop. Working on his own, one planter could tend 2,000 plants, which yielded about 500 pounds of cured tobacco. When the price was high, this supplied a comfortable income. But as the price plummeted, planters could keep up only by producing more tobacco, and to do that they needed a large labor force.

The planters turned to England, importing thousands of indentured servants, or contract workers, who (like Richard Frethorne) agreed to a fixed term of labor, usually four to seven years, in exchange for free passage to Virginia. The master provided food, shelter, clothing, and, at the end of the term of service, "freedom dues" paid in corn and clothing. Between 1625 and 1640, 1,000 or more indentured servants arrived each year. The vast majority came from the ranks of England's unemployed, who emigrated in hopes of "bettering their condition in a Growing Country."

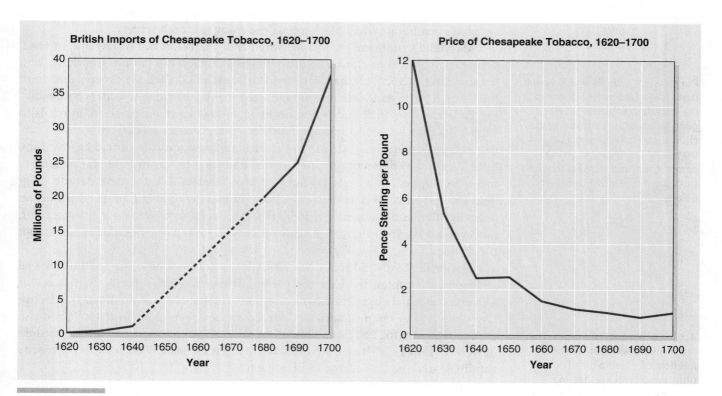

FIGURE 2.2 THE SUPPLY AND PRICE OF CHESAPEAKE TOBACCO, 1620–1700 Tobacco cultivation dominated the economy of the Chesapeake region throughout the seventeenth century. As planters brought more and more land under cultivation, the amount of tobacco exported to Britain shot up and the price plummeted. (As the dashed line indicates, no data available for the years 1640–1680.)

SOURCE: Russell R. Menard, "The Tobacco Industry in the Chesapeake Colonies, 1617–1730: An Interpretation," *Research in Economic History,* 5 (1980).

2.1

2.2

2.3

2.4

2.5

2.6

Most found such hopes quickly dashed. Servants died in alarming numbers from disease, and those who survived faced years of backbreaking labor. Masters squeezed as much work out of them as possible with long hours and harsh discipline. New obstacles faced servants who managed to survive their terms of indenture. For every ex-servant who became a landholder, dozens died in poverty. To prevent freed servants from becoming economic rivals, established planters avoided selling them good land, particularly after tobacco prices hit bottom in the 1660s. Many ex-servants found land only in places less suitable for tobacco cultivation and more vulnerable to Indian attack. As a result, they became a discontented group. In 1675, their discontent would flare into rebellion (discussed in Chapter 3).

Maryland: A Refuge for Catholics

The success of tobacco in Virginia encouraged further English colonization in the Chesapeake region. In 1632, King Charles I granted 10 million acres of land north of the bay to the nobleman George Calvert, Lord Baltimore. Unlike Virginia, which was founded by a joint-stock company, Maryland was a **proprietary colony**—the sole possession of Calvert and his heirs. They owned all the land, which they could divide up as they pleased, and had the right to set up the colony's government.

Calvert, who was Catholic, intended Maryland to be a refuge for others of his faith. When Queen Elizabeth's accession made England a Protestant nation, Catholics became a disadvantaged minority. In Maryland, Calvert wanted Catholic colonists to enjoy economic and political power. He intended to divide the land into manors—large private estates like those of medieval England—and distribute them to wealthy Catholic friends. These manorial lords would live on rents collected from tenant farmers and hold the most important governmental offices.

Calvert died before settlement began, and it was the sad fate of his son, Cecilius, to see his father's plans unravel. The majority of colonists, who began arriving in 1634, were Protestants who despised Catholics. Refusing to live as tenants on Catholic estates, they claimed land of their own—a process that accelerated after 1640, when Maryland adopted a headright system like Virginia's as a way to recruit settlers.

Maryland's problems intensified when civil war broke out in England in 1642. For years, political and religious disputes had divided the nation. Charles I, who became king in 1625, clashed with the **Puritans,** who called for further reform of the Church of England. He also antagonized many government leaders by dissolving Parliament in 1629 and ruling on his own for eleven years. Needing funds to suppress a rebellion in Scotland in 1640, however, Charles was forced to recall Parliament. Its leaders, sympathetic to the Puritan cause, quickly turned against him. Both king and Parliament recruited armies and went to war in 1642. Parliamentary forces triumphed, and in 1649 they executed Charles. For the next decade, England was governed as a protectorate, not a monarchy. Oliver Cromwell, a Puritan general, ruled until his death in 1658. His son, Richard, proved an inept successor, however, and in 1660 a group of army officers invited Charles's exiled son to accept the throne.

During the 1640s and 1650s, Maryland Protestants took advantage of the upheaval in England to contest the Calverts' control of the colony. To pacify them, Cecilius Calvert established a legislature, assuming that Protestants would dominate the elective lower house while he could appoint Catholics to the upper house. In 1649, Calvert also approved the **Act for Religious Toleration,** the first law in America to call for freedom of worship for all Christians, but even this brought no peace. The Protestant majority continued to resist Catholic political influence.

Instead of a peaceful Catholic refuge, Maryland soon resembled neighboring Virginia. Its settlers raised tobacco and imported as many indentured servants as possible. Throughout the seventeenth century, Protestants kept up their opposition to the proprietor's control and resisted Catholic efforts to govern the colony that was supposed to have been theirs.

proprietary colony A colony created when the English monarch granted a huge tract of land to an individual or group of individuals, who became "lords proprietor." Many lords proprietor had distinct social visions for their colonies, but these plans were hardly ever implemented. Examples of proprietary colonies are Maryland, Carolina, New York (after it was seized from the Dutch), and Pennsylvania.

Puritans Individuals who believed that Queen Elizabeth's reforms of the Church of England had not gone far enough in improving the church, particularly in ensuring that church members were among the saved. Puritans led the settlement of Massachusetts Bay Colony.

Act for Religious Toleration The first law in America to call for freedom of worship for all Christians. It was enacted in Maryland in 1649 to quell disputes between Catholics and Protestants, but it failed to bring peace.

2.1

2.2

2.3

2.4

2.5

2.6

From Then to Now
Tobacco and the American Economy

A ccording to a legal settlement reached in 1998, the American tobacco industry agreed to pay $206 billion to forty-six state governments as compensation for the medical costs of treating smoke-related illnesses. Health issues dominated the debates leading to the agreement, but economic questions also influenced the discussion. This was hardly surprising, for tobacco is the oldest commercial crop produced in what is now the United States. The healthfulness of tobacco was debated even in the seventeenth century, but that did not deter Virginia's colonists from growing the crop.

The first shipment of Virginia tobacco reached London in 1617, and by the turn of the eighteenth century, colonists exported more than 30 million pounds of it annually. High levels of production led to falling prices, but colonists responded by growing even more. After the Revolution, tobacco became a fixture of the agricultural economies in the new states of Kentucky, Tennessee, Missouri, and Ohio. Down to the twentieth century, tobacco remained so vital to the U.S. economy that the federal government subsidized its production—the only non-food crop (besides cotton) to benefit from high price supports.

In 2004, Congress passed a law ending the price support program, which had set production quotas and kept prices high. Since then, American tobacco production has actually increased, but without price supports, the market is riskier. Since it is difficult for farmers who have invested heavily in tobacco production to shift to other crops, it is unclear what the long-term effect of Congressional action will be. Thus, four centuries after the founding of Jamestown, economic decisions made by early Virginia colonists continue to affect an American nation in ways they could never have imagined.

Question for Discussion

- In what ways have long-term economic issues complicated the task of dealing with tobacco-related health problems?

This seventeenth-century engraving shows a fashionable European woman indulging in a pipe of tobacco.

Modern-day tobacco fields such as this one in North Carolina testify to the continuing economic importance of the crop.

Life in the Chesapeake Colonies

Few people could have predicted how much life in the Chesapeake colonies would differ from England. Many differences stemmed from the region's distinctive population. Because of their labor needs, masters preferred to recruit young men in their teens and twenties as indentured servants, importing three or four times as many of them as women. As a result, the populations of Virginia and Maryland were overwhelmingly young and male. Even as late as 1700, Virginia had three English men for every two women. As a consequence of this gender imbalance, many male ex-servants found that marriage was as remote a possibility as landownership.

Malaria and other diseases inflicted hardship on nearly everyone. Few colonists lived past 50, and women's susceptibility to disease during pregnancy meant that

2.1

2.2

2.3

2.4

2.5

2.6

many of them barely made it to 40. Such high mortality, combined with late marriages (because servants could not wed until their terms were up), limited the size of families and slowed population growth. As many as one out of four children died in their first year, and more died before age 20.

Under such conditions, the only way the populations of the Chesapeake colonies could grow during most of the seventeenth century was through immigration. The number of English settlers rose from about 8,000 in 1640 to 24,000 in 1660. Still mostly young and mostly male, the immigrants helped the region's distinctive demographic patterns persist until the end of the century.

These conditions hindered colonists from reproducing customary patterns of family life. The frequency of early death produced unusual households, containing various combinations of step-parents and children from different marriages. Many women would be widows at some point in their lives, which gave them temporary control over the family property. Husbands often arranged for their widows to manage their estates until the eldest son reached age 21. Few women received land outright, and if widows remarried, their new spouses usually took control of the estates left by their first husbands. As in England itself, the Chesapeake colonies accorded women little formal authority within society.

The precariousness of life encouraged settlers to invest every penny of profit in land and labor, postponing investment in goods that would bring a more comfortable existence. Poor settlers slept on the floor on straw mattresses and had few other furnishings, often not even a chair or bench to sit on. Rich planters owned more goods, but often of poor quality. Nearly everyone subsisted on a rude diet of pork and corn. Servants and poor colonists had no choice but to accept crude living conditions. Their more fortunate neighbors tolerated discomfort in order to invest in family estates where their descendants might live in greater luxury.

Rough as these conditions were, they far surpassed the circumstances of most native peoples in the Chesapeake. The English population may have been growing slowly, but it still overwhelmed the Indian population, which suffered high mortality from European diseases. By 1685, there were more than ten colonists for every Indian living in eastern Virginia. By that point, many Native Americans in the Chesapeake had retreated to isolated towns, in hopes of preserving control over dwindling lands and maintaining some independence from English domination.

The Founding of New England

2.4 Why were the English colonies in New England so different from those in the Chesapeake?

Six colonies appeared in the New England region between 1620 and 1640, settled by thousands of people troubled by religious, political, and economic upheavals in England. Even before permanent colonists arrived, New England's native population felt the effects of European contact. Between 1616 and 1618, a terrible epidemic swept through coastal New England, killing up to 90 percent of the Indians living there. The devastated survivors were struggling to cope with the consequences of this disaster just as the colonists began to arrive.

The Pilgrims and Plymouth Colony

Plymouth Colony, the first of the New England settlements, was founded in 1620. Its origins lay in religious disputes that had plagued England since the late sixteenth century. Most of Queen Elizabeth's subjects approved of her efforts to keep England a Protestant nation, but some reformers believed that she had not rid the Church of England of all Catholic practices. The enemies of these reformers, ridiculing them for wanting to purify the Church of England (or **Anglican** Church) of all corruption, called them Puritans.

English Puritans believed in an all-powerful God who, at the moment of Creation, determined which humans would be saved and which would be damned. They held that salvation came through faith alone, not good works, and urged believers to seek a direct, personal relationship with God. The centerpiece of their spiritual life was conversion: the transforming experience that occurred when individuals felt the stirrings of grace in their souls and began to hope that they were among the saved. Those who experienced conversion were considered saints and acquired new strength to live godly lives.

Puritans believed that certain Anglican practices interfered with conversion and the believer's relationship with God. But what they hated most about the Anglican Church was that anyone could be a member. Puritans believed that everyone should attend church services, but they wanted church membership, which conferred the right to partake in the Lord's Supper, or communion, to be limited to saints who had experienced conversion.

Elizabeth and the rulers who followed her—who as monarchs were the "supreme heads" of the Church of England—tried to silence the Puritans. Some Puritans, known as **separatists,** concluded that the Church of England would never change and left it to form their own congregations. One such group, mainly artisans and middling farmers from the village of Scrooby, in Nottinghamshire, became the core of Plymouth Colony.

The Scrooby separatists left England in 1607–1608 for Holland, where they stayed for more than a decade. Although they could worship in peace there, many struggled to make a living. Some Scrooby separatists contemplated moving to America and contacted the Plymouth Company. Called **Pilgrims** because they thought of themselves as spiritual wanderers, they were joined by other separatists and by nonseparatist "strangers" hired to help get the colony started. In all, 102 men, women, and children set sail on the *Mayflower* in September 1620.

After a long and miserable voyage, they landed near Massachusetts Bay. To prevent the colony from disintegrating into factions before their ship had even landed, the leaders drafted the Mayflower Compact. This document bound all signers to abide by the decisions of the majority.

The Pilgrims settled at Plymouth, the site of a Wampanoag village recently depopulated by disease. William Bradford, Plymouth's governor for many years, described finding abandoned cornfields, Indian graves, and baskets of corn buried underground. Although it helped feed them for a while, this corn was not enough to prevent the Pilgrims from suffering their first winter through a terrible "starving time" that left nearly half of them dead.

When two English-speaking natives, Squanto and Samoset, emerged from the woods the next spring, the surviving Pilgrims marveled at them as "special instruments sent of God." Samoset had learned English from traders, and Squanto had learned it in England, where he lived for a time after being kidnapped by a sea captain. Squanto was the sole survivor of the Patuxets, who had succumbed to disease while he had been away. The two native men approached the Pilgrims on behalf of Massasoit, the Wampanoag leader. Although suspicious of the newcomers, the Wampanoags thought the Pilgrims might be useful allies against their enemies, the Narragansetts. In 1621, the Wampanoags and the Pilgrims signed a treaty of alliance, although each side understood its terms differently. The Pilgrims assumed that Massasoit had submitted to the superior authority of King James, whereas Massasoit assumed that he and the English king were equal partners.

Plymouth remained small, poor, and weak, never exceeding about 7,000 settlers. Although its families achieved a modest prosperity, the colony as a whole never produced more than small shipments of furs, fish, and timber to sell in England. After 1630, the first New England colony was overshadowed by a new and more powerful neighbor, Massachusetts Bay.

Anglican Of or belonging to the Church of England, a Protestant denomination.

2.1

2.2

2.3

2.4

2.5

2.6

separatists Members of an offshoot branch of Puritanism. Separatists believed that the Church of England was too corrupt to be reformed and hence were convinced that they must "separate" from it to save their souls. Separatists helped found Plymouth Colony.

Pilgrims Settlers of Plymouth Colony, who viewed themselves as spiritual wanderers.

2.1

2.2

2.3

2.4

2.5

2.6

Massachusetts Bay Colony and Its Offshoots

The Puritans who founded Massachusetts shared many beliefs with the Pilgrims of Plymouth Colony—with one important exception. Unlike the Pilgrims, most Massachusetts settlers rejected separatism, insisting that the Anglican Church could be reformed. Their goal was to create godly churches to serve as models for the English church. Charles I, who became king in 1625, opposed the Puritans more forcefully than his father had. England at the time also suffered from economic troubles—including crop failures and a depression in the wool industry—that many Puritans saw as signs of God's displeasure with their country. These ominous events at home encouraged them to move to the New World.

In 1629, a group of Puritan merchants and gentlemen received a royal charter for a joint-stock enterprise, the Massachusetts Bay Company, to set up a colony north of Plymouth. John Winthrop, a prosperous lawyer, was selected as the colony's governor. In the spring of 1630, a fleet of eleven ships carried Winthrop and about 1,000 men, women, and children across the Atlantic.

Stability, Conformity, and Intolerance.   Winthrop described the settlers' mission in New England as a **covenant,** or contract, with God, binding them to meet their religious obligations in return for God's favor. The settlers also created covenants to define their duties to one another. When they founded towns, colonists signed covenants agreeing

covenant A formal agreement or contract.

((•)) 📖 **Read** the **Document**   **John Winthrop, "A Model of Christian Charity" (1630)**

John Winthrop (1588–1649) served as the Massachusetts Bay Colony's governor for most of its first two decades. Throughout his life, Winthrop—like many fellow Puritans—struggled to live a godly life in a corrupt world.

to live together in peace. Worshipers in each town's church likewise wrote covenants binding themselves to live in harmony.

The desire for peace and purity could breed intolerance. Settlers scrutinized their neighbors for signs of unacceptable behavior. Standards for church membership were strict; only those who could convincingly describe their conversion experiences were admitted. But the insistence on covenants and conformity also created a remarkably stable society.

That stability was enhanced by the development of representative government. By 1634, colony leaders had converted the charter of the Massachusetts Bay Company into a plan of government. The General Court, which initially included only the shareholders of the joint-stock company, was transformed into a two-house legislature. Freemen—adult males who held property and were church members—elected representatives to the lower house, as well as eighteen members (called "assistants") to the upper house. They also chose a governor and deputy governor.

2.1
2.2
2.3
2.4
2.5
2.6

The Connecticut Valley and the Pequot War. At least 13,000 settlers came to New England and established dozens of towns between 1630 and 1642, when the outbreak of the English Civil War halted emigration. The progress of settlement was generally untroubled in coastal Massachusetts, but when colonists moved into the Connecticut River Valley, tensions with Indians developed. These erupted in 1637 in the brief, tragic conflict called the **Pequot War.**

English settlers from Massachusetts first arrived in the Connecticut Valley in the mid-1630s. The local Pequot Indians resented their recent loss of special trading rights with a Dutch outpost in the area, and approached Massachusetts Bay as an ally. But when English settlers demanded Pequot submission to English authority, the Pequots turned against them too. A struggle for control over the land and trade of eastern Connecticut began.

Pequot War Conflict between English settlers (who had Narragansett and Mohegan allies) and Pequot Indians over control of land and trade in eastern Connecticut. The Pequots were nearly destroyed in a set of bloody confrontations, including a deadly English attack on a Mystic River village in May 1637.

The colonists allied with the Pequots' enemies, the Narragansetts and Mohegans. Together they overwhelmed the Pequots in an astonishingly bloody war. More settlers moved to Connecticut, which soon declared itself a separate colony. In 1639, the settlers adopted the Fundamental Orders, creating a government similar to that of Massachusetts, and the English government granted them a charter in 1662.

Roger Williams and the Founding of Rhode Island. Massachusetts spun off other colonies as its population expanded in the 1630s and dissenters ran afoul of its intolerant government. Roger Williams, who founded Rhode Island, was one of these religious dissenters. Williams was a separatist minister who declared that because Massachusetts churches had not rejected the Church of England, they shared its corruption. He opposed government interference in religious affairs—such as laws requiring settlers to attend worship services—and argued for the separation of church and state. Williams even attacked the Massachusetts charter, insisting that the king had no right to grant Indian lands to English settlers.

When Williams refused to be silenced, the General Court banished him, intending to ship him back to England. But in the winter of 1635, Williams slipped away. He and a few followers found refuge among the Narragansett Indians, from whom he purchased land for the village of Providence, founded in 1636. More towns sprang up nearby when a new religious challenge sent additional refugees to Rhode Island from Massachusetts.

Anne Hutchinson's Challenge to the Bay Colony. Anne Hutchinson arrived in Boston from England with her family in 1634. Welcomed by the town's women for her talents as a midwife, she began to hold religious meetings in her house. During these meetings, she denounced several ministers, who had taught worshippers that there were spiritual exercises they could perform that might prepare them for sainthood. Hutchinson insisted that there was nothing humans could do to encourage God to make them saints.

2.1
2.2
2.3
2.4
2.5
2.6

✳ Explore English Colonization on MyHistoryLab

HOW DID ENGLISH COLONIZATION TRANSFORM EASTERN NORTH AMERICA?

The early 1600s brought major changes to the eastern portion of North America. Prior to that time, Native Americans made up the overwhelming majority of the population and controlled virtually the entire region. However, as the seventeenth century began, European powers began staking claims in the region and establishing settlements up and down the coast over the following decades. Such changes shook historical Native American trading and settlement patterns as members of some of these nations lost their land to the newcomers and others entered successful alliances with Europeans to navigate their changing world. As the seventeenth century closed, the English in particular—having absorbed competing European colonial claims of the Dutch and Swedish and expanding ever deeper into the continent—had created a powerful presence.

The Jethro Coffin House, a saltbox house built in 1686, is the oldest surviving structure in Nantucket, Massachusetts.

NON-INDIAN POPULATION OF THE THIRTEEN COLONIES TO 1750

Colony	1650	1700	1750
New Hampshire	1,300	5,000	27,500
Massachusetts (includes Plymouth and Maine)	16,600	55,900	188,000
Rhode Island	800	5,900	33,200
Connecticut	4,100	26,000	111,300
New York	4,100	19,100	76,700
New Jersey		14,000	71,400
Pennsylvania		18,000	119,700
Delaware	200	2,500	287,00
Maryland	4,500	29,600	141,100
Virginia	18,700	58,600	231,000
North Carolina		10,700	73,000
South Carolina		5,700	64,000
Georgia			5,200

SOURCE: "Population, by race and by colony or locality: 1610–1780." Table Eg1-59 in *Historical Statistics of the United States, Earliest Times to the Present: Millennial Edition*, edited by Susan B. Carter et al. New York: Cambridge University Press, 2006. http://dx.doi.org/10.1017/ISBN-9780511132971.Eg1-193

KEY QUESTIONS   Use **MyHistoryLab *Explorer*** to **answer** these **questions:**

Cause ▶▶▶ *Where did English settlers expand—and Native Americans suffer territorial losses—in North America during this period?*

Chart the growth of English colonization.

Comparison ▶▶▶ *In what ways did English expansion face competition from its European rivals?*

Map the claims of other European nations in eastern North America.

Analysis ▶▶▶ *How did the Iroquois Confederacy change over this time?*

Trace the expansion of Iroquois control of new territories along its borders.

2.1

2.2

2.3

2.4

2.5

2.6

Many people flocked to Hutchinson's meetings. But her critics believed her to be a dangerous antinomian (someone who claimed to be free from obedience to moral law), because she seemed to maintain that saints were accountable only to God and not to any worldly authority. Her opponents also objected to her teaching of mixed groups of men and women. Colony magistrates arrested her and tried her for sedition—that is, for advocating the overthrow of the government.

The court found her guilty and banished her. With many of her followers, she moved to Rhode Island, where Roger Williams had proclaimed a policy of religious toleration. Other followers returned to England or moved north to what became in 1679 the colony of New Hampshire.

Families, Farms, and Communities in Early New England

"This plantation and that of Virginia went not forth upon the same reasons," declared one of Massachusetts's founders. Virginians came "for profit," whereas New Englanders emigrated to bear witness to their Puritan faith. Unlike the unmarried young men who moved in great numbers to Virginia, most New Englanders settled with their families. This had important implications for the development of New England society.

Even though emigration from England slowed to a trickle after 1642, New England's population continued to grow. By 1660, the number of colonists exceeded 33,000. This demographic expansion stemmed from the initial emigration of families. With a more balanced sex ratio (about three men to two women) than there was in the early Chesapeake, marriage and childbearing were more common.

Settling in a region with a healthier climate, New Englanders were largely spared early deaths from malaria and other diseases that ravaged the Chesapeake settlers. Most children survived to reach adulthood and form families of their own. Many New Englanders enjoyed unusually long lives for the seventeenth century, reaching their seventies and even eighties.

Women in Early New England. In New England, as in other colonies and England itself, women were assumed to be legally and economically dependent on the men in their families. Since fewer New England marriages were shortened by the early death of a spouse, fewer New England women experienced widowhood, the one time in their lives when they might enjoy legal independence and exercise control over property.

Women's economic contributions were central to the family's success. In addition to caring for children, cooking, sewing, gardening, and cleaning, most women engaged in household production and traded the fruits of their labor with other families. They sold eggs, made butter and cheese, brewed beer, and wove cloth. Wives of shopkeepers and craftsmen occasionally managed their husbands' businesses when the men had to travel or became ill.

Community and Economic Life. New Englanders' lives were shaped not only by their families but also by their towns. Unlike Chesapeake colonists, who tended to disperse into separate plantations, New Englanders clustered into communities that might contain fifty or a hundred families. The Massachusetts government strongly encouraged town formation by granting land to groups of families who promised to settle together. Once they found a town they liked, families tended to stay in place. Grown children, inheriting parental estates and finding spouses nearby, often settled in the same community as their parents.

At the center of each town stood the meetinghouse. Every Sunday, townspeople gathered there to listen to the minister preach God's word. At other times, the meetinghouse served as a town hall, where men assembled to discuss matters ranging from local taxes to making sure everyone's fences were mended. Massachusetts law required towns with at least fifty families to support a school (so children could learn to read the Bible), and men often wrangled at town meetings over the choice and salary of a schoolmaster. Townsmen tried, not always successfully, to reach decisions by consensus. To

2.1

2.2

2.3

2.4

2.5

2.6

oversee day-to-day local affairs, they chose five to seven trusted neighbors to serve as selectmen. Each town could also elect two men to represent it in the colony legislature.

New England's stony soil and short growing season offered few ways to get rich, but most people achieved a modest prosperity. They grew corn and other foods and raised livestock to feed their families, selling or trading what they could not use. Their goal was to achieve a competency—enough property to ensure the family's economic independence. Without the income generated by a staple crop like tobacco, New England farmers could not hire large numbers of indentured servants and so relied on family labor.

New Englanders regularly traded goods and services with their neighbors. A carpenter might erect a house in return for barrels of salted beef. Men with teenaged sons sent them to help neighbors whose children were still small. Midwives delivered babies in return for cheese or eggs. Women nursed sick neighbors, whom they might later call on for similar help. These transactions allowed most New Englanders to enjoy a comfortable life, one that many Virginians might have envied.

New England prospered by developing a diversified economy less vulnerable to depression than Virginia's. Farmers sent livestock and meat to merchants to be marketed abroad. Fishermen caught cod and other fish to be sold in Europe. New Englanders became such skilled shipbuilders and seafaring merchants that by the 1670s, London merchants complained about competition from them. England itself had little use for the dried fish, livestock, salted meat, and wood products that New England vessels carried, but enterprising merchants found exactly the market they needed in the West Indies.

Competition in the Caribbean

2.5 Why did the first biracial colonial societies appear in the Caribbean?

The Spanish claimed all Caribbean islands by right of Columbus's discovery, but during the seventeenth century, France, the Netherlands, and England acquired their own island colonies. Europeans competed for these islands in the hope that they would yield precious metals and provide bases for privateering expeditions. It eventually became clear that the islands would produce treasure of another sort—sugar, which was in great demand in Europe. In order to reap the enormous profits that sugar could bring, Caribbean planters of all nationalities imported enormous numbers of African people to work as slaves under the harshest conditions to be found in the New World.

Sugar and Slaves

Europeans prized sugar as a sweetener, preservative, decoration—even a medicine—and paid high prices for it. Columbus accordingly brought sugar canes to the New World on his second voyage, in 1493. Soon after the Spanish began growing sugar on Santo Domingo, they began importing African slaves as workers, because Indian slaves were dying in great numbers. The Spanish brought sugar to the South American mainland, as did the Portuguese, who turned Brazil into one of the world's major producers. Everywhere that sugar flourished, African slaves could be found.

At first, English colonists who came to the West Indies in the 1620s and 1630s raised tobacco and imported indentured servants to work their fields. By that time, however, tobacco prices were dropping. Moreover, the disease environment of the West Indies proved even harsher than in the Chesapeake, and settlers died in great numbers.

By the 1640s, a planter in the English colony of Barbados boasted of "a great change on this island of late from the worse to the better, praised be God." That change was a shift from tobacco to sugar cane. Sugar rapidly transformed the West Indies. Planters

African slaves working at a sugar mill in the West Indies, probably on a Dutch-owned island: line engraving, seventeenth century.

2.1

2.2

2.3

2.4

2.5

2.6

deforested whole islands to raise sugar cane. They stopped planting food crops and raising livestock—thereby creating a demand for lumber and provisions that boosted New England's economy.

For some years after the transition to sugar, English planters continued to import white indentured servants. Due to the islands' unhealthy environment and harsh working conditions, however, servants died in great numbers. Given the example of prosperous Spanish and Portuguese plantations using slave labor, and the willingness of the Dutch to supply them with slaves, the English switched to African laborers, whom they considered better suited to agricultural work in a tropical climate. The planters' decision had an enormous impact on English colonial life, first in the islands and then on the mainland, where slavery would develop later in the seventeenth century (see Chapter 3).

A Biracial Society

As happened on virtually all the Caribbean islands, the English West Indies developed a biracial plantation society—the first in the English colonial world. By 1700, more than 250,000 slaves had been brought to the English islands, and they soon constituted a majority of the population. Slaves lived in wretched conditions, underfed, poorly dressed, and housed in rough huts. They labored six days a week from sunrise to sunset—except at harvest time, when they toiled seven days a week in round-the-clock shifts. Masters considered them property, often branding them like livestock and hunting them with bloodhounds when they ran away.

Laws, sometimes called **slave codes,** declared slavery to be a lifelong condition that passed from slave parents to their children. Slaves had no legal rights and were under the complete control of their masters. Only rarely would masters who killed slaves face prosecution, and those found guilty were subject only to fines. Slaves, in contrast, faced appalling punishments even for minor offenses. Slaves who rebelled were burned to death.

Astonishingly, slaves maintained some elements of normal life even under these brutal conditions. When masters began to import African women as well as men—hoping to create a self-reproducing labor force—slaves formed families and preserved

slave codes Sometimes known as "black codes." A series of laws passed mainly in the southern colonies in the late seventeenth and early eighteenth centuries to define the status of slaves and codify the denial of basic civil rights to them. Also, after American independence and before the Civil War, state laws in the South defining slaves as property and specifying the legal powers of masters over slaves.

2.1

2.2

2.3

2.4

2.5

2.6

at least some African traditions. They gave their children African names. They celebrated and worked to the rhythms of African music. And slaves drew on their West African heritage to perform elaborate funeral rituals, often burying their dead with food and other goods to accompany them on the journey to the afterlife.

White planters, profiting handsomely from their slaves' toil, lived better than many English gentlemen. But sugar made relatively few white colonists wealthy. Its production required a heavy investment in land, slaves, mills, and equipment. As great planters took vast amounts of land for themselves, freed servants and small farmers struggled to survive. After 1650, many of these poor men, looking for other places to live, headed for the mainland.

The Restoration Colonies

2.6 How influential were the ideas of the different proprietors of the Restoration colonies in shaping the development of their settlements?

T he initial burst of English colonization ended in 1640 when England tottered on the brink of civil war. With the restoration of Charles II to the throne in 1660, however, interest in North America revived. During his reign (1660–1685), four new colonies—Carolina, Pennsylvania, New Jersey, and New York—were created (see Map 2.3). All were proprietary colonies, essentially the private property of the people to whom they had been given. Two of them—Carolina and Pennsylvania—like the earlier proprietary colony of Maryland, provided their owners the chance to test idealistic social visions. The origins of New York and New Jersey as English colonies, by contrast, lay not in visions of social harmony but in the stern reality of military conquest (see Table 2.1).

Early Carolina: Colonial Aristocracy and Slave Labor

In 1663, Charles II granted a group of supporters an enormous tract of land stretching from southern Virginia to northern Florida. The proprietors, who included several Barbados planters, called their colony Carolina, after *Carolus,* the Latin form of the king's name. One of the proprietors, Anthony Ashley Cooper, worked closely with his secretary, John Locke, to devise the **Fundamental Constitutions of Carolina.** This plan to ensure the colony's stability linked property ownership and political rights to a hierarchical social order. It called for the creation of a colonial aristocracy, who would own two-fifths of the land and wield extensive political power. Below them, a large class of freeholders would own small farms and elect representatives to an assembly. At the bottom of the social order would be slaves.

This plan never went into effect. People moved in from Virginia and the West Indies and settled where they pleased. They even voted in the assembly to reject the Fundamental Constitutions. They antagonized the local Indians, who had initially welcomed English traders eager to buy deerskins but grew hostile when colonists sold guns to some tribes in exchange for Indian captives. The captives were later sold as slaves, principally to the West Indies. Native resentments deepened as settlers moved onto their lands. The result was a deadly cycle of violence.

The colonists at first raised livestock to be sold to the West Indies. But the introduction of rice in the 1690s transformed the settlers' economy, making it, as one planter noted, "as much their staple Commodity, as Sugar is to Barbados and Jamaica, or Tobacco to Virginia and Maryland." The English had never grown rice, but West Africans had. Rice cultivation in Carolina coincided with an increase in the number of African slaves there, who probably introduced the crop. Ironically, the profits earned from rice persuaded Carolina planters to invest even more heavily in slave labor.

Fundamental Constitutions of Carolina A complex plan for organizing the colony of Carolina, drafted in 1669 by Anthony Ashley Cooper and John Locke. Its provisions included a scheme for creating a hierarchy of nobles who would own vast amounts of land and wield political power; below them would be a class of freedmen and slaves. The provisions were never implemented by the Carolina colonists.

2.1

2.2

2.3

2.4

2.5

2.6

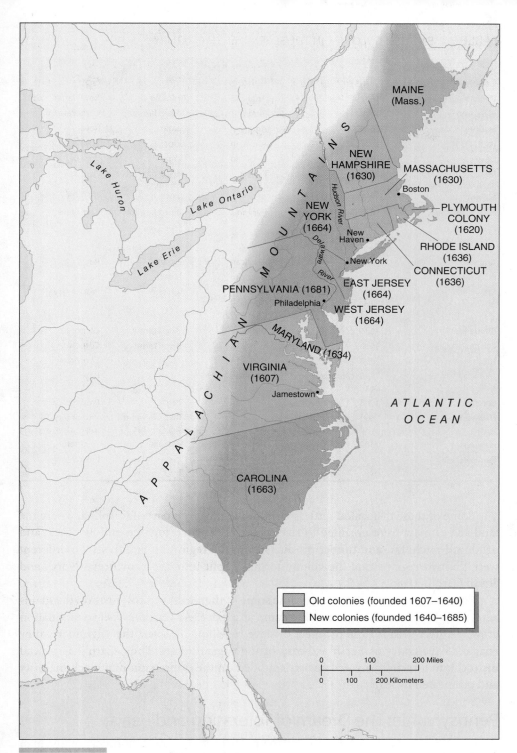

MAP 2.3 ENGLISH NORTH AMERICAN COLONIES, c. 1685 After the restoration of Charles II in 1660, several large proprietary colonies joined earlier English settlements in New England and the Chesapeake. By 1685, a growing number of English settlers solidified England's claim to the Atlantic coast from Maine (then part of Massachusetts Bay Colony) to the southern edge of Carolina.

Carolina society soon resembled the sugar islands from which many of its founders had come. By 1708, there were more black slaves than white settlers; two decades after that, black people outnumbered white people by two to one. Rice farming required a substantial investment in land, labor, and equipment, including dikes and dams for flooding fields. Those who could afford such an investment set themselves up as planters in Carolina's coastal rice district, acquiring large estates and forcing poorer settlers to move elsewhere.

2.1

2.2

2.3

2.4

2.5

2.6

TABLE 2.1 ENGLISH COLONIES IN THE SEVENTEENTH CENTURY

Colony	Date of Founding	Established Religion	Economy	Government
Virginia	1607	Anglican	Tobacco	Royal (after 1625)
Plymouth	1620	Puritan	Mixed farming	Corporate
St. Christopher	1624	Anglican	Sugar	Royal
Barbados	1627	Anglican	Sugar	Royal
Nevis	1628	Anglican	Sugar	Royal
Massachusetts (including present-day Maine)	1630	Puritan	Mixed farming, fishing, shipbuilding	Corporate
New Hampshire	1630 (first settlement, annexed to Massachusetts 1643–1679)	Puritan	Mixed farming	Corporate (royal after 1679)
Antigua	1632	Anglican	Sugar	Royal
Montserrat	1632	Anglican	Sugar	Royal
Maryland	1634	None (Anglican after 1692)	Tobacco	Proprietary
Rhode Island	1636	None	Mixed farming	Corporate
Connecticut	1636	Puritan	Mixed farming	Corporate
New Haven	1638	Puritan	Mixed farming	Corporate
Jamaica	1655 (captured from Spanish)	Anglican	Sugar	Royal
Carolina	1663	Anglican	Rice	Proprietary
New York	1664 (captured from Dutch)	None	Mixed farming, furs	Proprietary (royal after 1685)
New Jersey	1664	None	Mixed farming	Proprietary
Pennsylvania	1681	None	Wheat, mixed farming	Proprietary

Some of these dislocated settlers went to the northern part of Carolina, where the land and climate were unsuited to rice. There they raised tobacco and livestock, and produced pitch, tar, and timber products from the region's pine forests. So different were the two regions that the colony formally split into two provinces—North and South Carolina—in 1729.

South Carolina rice planters became some of the wealthiest colonists on the mainland. But their luxurious style of life came at a price. As Carolina's slave population grew, planters dreaded the prospect of slave rebellion. To avert this nightmare, they enacted slave codes as harsh as those of the sugar islands. Thus, Carolina evolved instead into a racially divided society founded on the oppression of a black majority and permeated by fear.

Pennsylvania: The Dream of Toleration and Peace

Even as early Carolina diverged from the plans of its founders, another Englishman dreamed of creating a colonial utopia. William Penn put his plans into action in 1681, when Charles II granted him a huge tract of land north of Maryland. Penn intended his colony to be a model of justice and peace, as well as a refuge for members of the Society of Friends, or Quakers, a persecuted religious sect to which Penn belonged.

The Society of Friends was one of many radical religious groups that emerged in England during the civil war. Rejecting predestination, they maintained that every soul had a spark of grace and that salvation was possible for all who heeded that "Inner Light." They rejected trained clergy and church rituals as unnecessary to salvation. Instead of formal religious services, Quakers held meetings at which silence reigned until someone, inspired by the Inner Light, rose to speak.

Quaker beliefs had disturbing social and political implications. Although they did not advocate complete equality of the sexes, Quakers granted women spiritual

2.1

2.2

2.3

2.4

2.5

2.6

equality with men, allowing them to preach, hold separate prayer meetings, and exercise authority over "women's matters." Arguing that social distinctions were not the work of God, Quakers refused to defer to their "betters." Because their faith required them to renounce the use of force, Quakers refused to perform military service, which their enemies considered tantamount to treason.

When English authorities began harassing Quakers, William Penn, who was himself jailed briefly, conceived his plan for a New World refuge. He aimed to launch a "holy experiment," a harmonious society governed by brotherly love. Using his father's connection with the king, he acquired the land that became Pennsylvania ("Penn's Woods") and recruited settlers from among Europe's oppressed peoples and persecuted religious sects. By 1700, 18,000 emigrants had left England, Wales, Scotland, Ireland, and various German provinces for the new colony.

Many came in families and settled in an area occupied by the Delaware Indians, whose numbers, though still substantial, had recently been reduced by disease and warfare. The "holy experiment" required colonists to live "as Neighbours and friends" with the Indians as well as with one another. Penn aimed to accomplish this by paying Indians for land and regulating trade. As long as Penn controlled his colony, relations between the settlers and the Indians were generally peaceful—so much so that refugee Indians from nearby colonies moved into Pennsylvania. Relations between Penn and the settlers, however, were less cordial.

In the **Frame of Government** he devised for Pennsylvania, Penn remained true to his Quaker principles with a provision allowing for religious freedom. But true to his aristocratic origins, he designed a legislature with limited powers and reserved considerable authority for himself. When Penn returned to England after a brief stay in the colony (1682–1684), the settlers began squabbling among themselves. The governor and council, both appointed by Penn, fought with elected members of the assembly. Penn's opponents—many of whom were fellow Quakers—objected to his proprietary privileges, including his control of foreign trade and his collection of fees from landholders.

By 1720, Pennsylvania's ethnically and religiously diverse colonists numbered more than 30,000. The colony, with some of the richest farmland along the Atlantic coast, was widely known as the "best poor man's country in the world." Growing wheat and other crops, the settlers lived mostly on scattered farms rather than in towns. From the busy port of Philadelphia, ships carried much of the harvest to markets in the West Indies and southern Europe. Penn's "holy experiment" in social harmony may have failed, but, as a thriving colony, Pennsylvania succeeded handsomely.

Frame of Government William Penn's 1682 plan for the government of Pennsylvania, which created a relatively weak legislature and strong executive. It also contained a provision for religious freedom.

New Netherland Becomes New York

The proprietary colonies of New York and New Jersey were carved out of the Dutch colony of New Netherland. Competition between the English and the Dutch intensified in the mid-seventeenth century as the two peoples struggled for trade supremacy on the high seas. Their antagonism generated two Anglo-Dutch wars in 1652–1654 and 1665–1667. In the New World, tensions were heightened by the presence of English colonists on Long Island, which the Dutch claimed for themselves.

In 1664, Charles II brought matters to a head by claiming that since the site of New Netherland lay within the bounds of the original charter of Virginia, the land belonged to England. He granted the territory to his brother James, duke of York, who sent ships to back up England's claim. Their arrival provoked a rebellion by Long Island's English colonists, leading the Dutch governor, Peter Stuyvesant—who commanded just 150 soldiers—to surrender without firing a shot.

The duke of York became proprietor of this new English possession, which was renamed New York. James immediately created another colony, New Jersey, which he granted to his supporters. New York, which James retained for himself, was the most valuable part of the former Dutch colony. It included the port of New York City (the

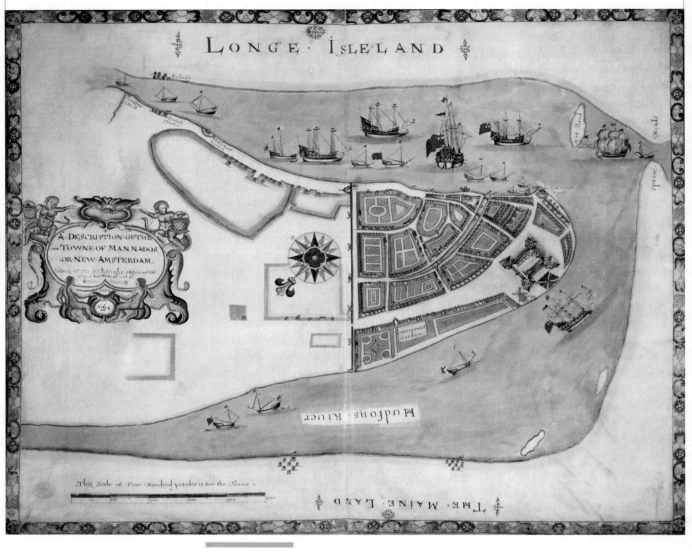

James, duke of York, received this map of New Amsterdam in 1664, when England seized New Netherland from the Dutch and the duke became proprietor of the new colony of New York. The top of the map is oriented to the east, with the lower tip of Manhattan Island facing to the right.

former New Amsterdam) and the Hudson Valley with its fur trade. James encouraged Dutch colonists to remain and promoted immigration from England to strengthen the colony and gain income from land sales. By 1700, the settlers numbered 20,000.

For nearly twenty years after its takeover by the English, New York lacked something all other English colonies had—a representative assembly. After neighboring New Jersey and Pennsylvania created their own assemblies, however, New Yorkers pressed their proprietor to follow suit. Only in 1683, when it became clear that New York might lose population to Pennsylvania, did James relent and create the assembly that brought New York in line with other English colonies.

Conclusion

Even as England gained a permanent foothold in North America, it faced vigorous competition from France and the Netherlands. A new Atlantic world was beginning to emerge as the migration of people and goods across the ocean linked the Old and New Worlds as never before.

2.1

2.2

2.3

2.4

2.5

2.6

Commerce was the main focus of the short-lived New Netherland colony and a more durable New France. Profits from the fur trade encouraged the French to maintain friendly relations with their Indian allies and ensured that French kings would closely monitor the colony's affairs. English colonization was a more haphazard process. English kings granted charters—sometimes to joint-stock companies (Virginia, Plymouth, Massachusetts), sometimes to proprietors (Maryland, Carolina, New York, New Jersey, Pennsylvania)—and let the colonies develop more or less on their own.

The result was a highly diverse set of English colonies stretching from the Maine coast to the Caribbean. Settlers adjusted to different environments, developed different economies and labor systems, and worshiped in different churches. In South Carolina, New York, Pennsylvania, and the West Indies, most colonists were not even of English origin. What held these colonies together—besides their establishment under English charters and their enmity toward the Spanish and French—was an overlay of common English institutions of government. By the mid-1680s, all the colonies had legislatures that provided for self-government and laws and judicial institutions based on English models.

The planting of French, Dutch, and English colonies not only ended Spain's monopoly of settlement in North America but also challenged the Indians' hold on the continent. Forced to deal with a rising tide of settlers and often to choose sides between European rivals, native peoples adapted to rapidly changing circumstances. Transplanted Europeans adapted too, not only in their dealings with native peoples but also in finding and controlling the laborers they needed to make their colonies prosper. For English colonists this meant the widespread adoption of slavery, an institution that did not exist in England itself. For millions of Africans, the result was forced migration to the New World.

For Suggested Readings go to MyHistoryLab.

Chapter Review

The French in North America

2.1 How did the French use Indian alliances to create their North American empire? p. 31

France's New World empire primarily lay along the St. Lawrence River valley in Canada. Its economic focus was the fur trade, carried out in partnership with local Indians. This economic tie also required the French to form military alliances with their Native American trading partners.

The Dutch Overseas Empire

2.2 How significant was New Netherland as part of the Dutch global empire? p. 34

By the early seventeenth century, the Dutch had become the pre-eminent commercial power in Europe, with an overseas empire extending from the New World to Asia. In North America, the Dutch colony of New Netherland relied mainly on the fur trade conducted by the colonists' Iroquois allies.

English Settlement in the Chesapeake

2.3 Why did the English have such difficulties establishing colonies in the Chesapeake? p. 35

In 1607, Virginia became England's first permanent colony in North America. Its first settlers struggled with endemic disease and conflict with Indians. Tobacco production became its lifeline, and led to massive importations of young, male indentured servants. In 1634, Maryland joined Virginia as another tobacco-growing Chesapeake colony.

The Founding of New England

2.4 Why were the English colonies in New England so different from those in the Chesapeake? p. 42

The New England colonies were founded by Puritans, who sought refuge from persecution by English authorities. The settlers established close-knit communities governed by their religious principles. Lacking a cash crop like tobacco, New Englanders grew food crops and raised livestock, relying on their families for labor.

Competition in the Caribbean

2.5 Why did the first biracial colonial societies appear in the Caribbean? p. 48

Many European nations competed for control of Caribbean islands, where sugar soon became a lucrative cash crop. Everywhere, planters imported African slaves to labor on sugar plantations under harsh conditions. Africans, subject to restrictive slave codes, soon outnumbered white settlers on the islands.

The Restoration Colonies

2.6 How influential were the ideas of the different proprietors of the Restoration colonies in shaping the development of their settlements? p. 50

After 1660, Carolina and Pennsylvania were founded by proprietors with grand visions. Carolina's founders hoped to create an orderly, hierarchical society, while William Penn envisioned his colony as a harmonious Quaker refuge. In neither case did the founders' plans work out as they had hoped.

Timeline

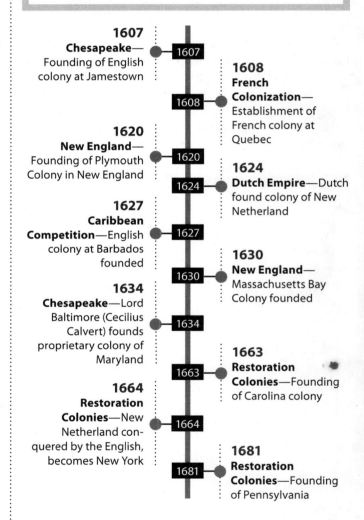

1607
Chesapeake— Founding of English colony at Jamestown

1607

1608
1608
French Colonization— Establishment of French colony at Quebec

1620
New England— Founding of Plymouth Colony in New England

1620

1624
1624
Dutch Empire—Dutch found colony of New Netherland

1627
Caribbean Competition—English colony at Barbados founded

1627

1630
1630
New England— Massachusetts Bay Colony founded

1634
Chesapeake—Lord Baltimore (Cecilius Calvert) founds proprietary colony of Maryland

1634

1663
1663
Restoration Colonies—Founding of Carolina colony

1664
Restoration Colonies—New Netherland conquered by the English, becomes New York

1664

1681
1681
Restoration Colonies—Founding of Pennsylvania

3 A Meeting of Cultures

One American Journey

Narrative by Olaudah Equiano

One day [in 1756], when all our people were gone out to their work as usual, and only I and my sister were left to mind the house, two men and a woman got over our walls, and in a moment seized us both; and without giving us time to cry out, or to make any resistance, they stopped our mouths and ran off with us into the nearest wood. Here they tied our hands, and continued to carry us as far as they could. . . . Thus I continued to travel, both by land and by water, through different countries and various nations, till at the end of six or seven months after I had been kidnapped, I arrived at the sea coast. . . .

The first object that saluted my eyes when I arrived on the coast was the sea, and a slave ship, which was then riding at anchor, and waiting for its cargo. These filled me with astonishment, that was soon converted into terror, which I am yet at a loss to describe. . . . I was immediately handled and tossed up to see if I was sound, by some of the crew; and I was now persuaded that I had got into a world of bad spirits, and that they were going to kill me. Their complexions too, differing so much from ours, their long hair, and the language they spoke, which was very different from any I had ever heard, united to confirm me in this belief. . . . I asked . . . if we were not to be eaten by those white men with horrible looks, red faces, and long hair. . . .

In a little time after, amongst the poor chained men, I found some of my own nation. . . . They gave me to understand we were to be carried to these white people's country

The horrors of slavery began as soon as Africans were torn from their families and marched to ships anchored off the coast.

LEARNING OBJECTIVES

3.1 (((•
How did the different patterns of interaction between Europeans and native peoples shape colonial development in the Spanish borderlands, New France, and the English colonies? p. 59

3.2 (((•
How and why did race-based slavery develop in British North America? p. 68

3.3 (((•
What methods did Europeans employ to acquire and manage labor in colonial America? p. 78

 Listen to Chapter 3 on MyHistoryLab

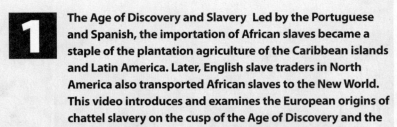

Watch the Video Series on MyHistoryLab

Learn about some key topics related to this chapter with the *MyHistoryLab Video Series: Key Topics in U.S. History.*

1 **The Age of Discovery and Slavery** Led by the Portuguese and Spanish, the importation of African slaves became a staple of the plantation agriculture of the Caribbean islands and Latin America. Later, English slave traders in North America also transported African slaves to the New World. This video introduces and examines the European origins of chattel slavery on the cusp of the Age of Discovery and the slave economy that developed in the American colonies.

 Watch on MyHistoryLab

Race Slavery Profits and the economic considerations that drove slavery in the Americas are discussed in this video. Slave owners and traders were primarily concerned with the wealth generated by slave labor. For that reason, brutal practices aimed at producing the most profit were practiced often at the expense of the health, safety, and humanity of the slaves themselves. **2**

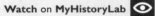 Watch on MyHistoryLab

3 **The Evolution of Slavery in North America** The first Africans in North America were treated more like the white indentured servants of the Virginia plantations. This video surveys the progression and development of slavery in the North American colonies from its almost accidental beginnings to the perpetual, race-based slavery that would typify the British American colonies.

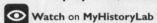 Watch on MyHistoryLab

Slavery in the Colonies Most Africans who were brought to the Americas stayed in the Caribbean. Others, after a period of "seasoning," continued on to North America and were sold throughout the British colonies. This video examines how slavery differed from colony to colony and the ways, although limited, that slaves had to influence their lives and destinies in the New World. **4**

 Watch on MyHistoryLab

to work for them. . . . [Many weeks later] we were landed up a river a good way from the sea, about Virginia county, where we saw few of our native Africans, and not one soul who could talk to me.

The Interesting Narrative of the Life of Olaudah Equiano, or Gustavus Vassa, The African (Longman Publication).

Personal Journeys Online

- Pedro Naranjol, *Indian Account of the Pueblo Revolt*, 1680.
- Job Ben Solomon, *Some Memoirs of the Life of Job*, 1734. Description of Job's capture and sale into slavery.
- Gottlieb Mittelberger, *Journey to Pennsylvania*, 1756. Description of the arrival of German redemptioners to Pennsylvania.

Olaudah Equiano, born in 1745 in the African kingdom of Benin, was only a boy when his terrifying journey to America began. The son of an Igbo chief, he was caught in the web of an expanding transatlantic slave trade that reached from the

African interior to nearly every port town in the Americas and the Caribbean. From modest beginnings in the sixteenth century, the slave trade had expanded dramatically, transforming every society it touched. Equiano's Virginia scarcely resembled that of John Smith. Tobacco still reigned supreme, but by the mid-eighteenth century, more workers were black than white. Slavery had spread from England's Caribbean colonies to dominate the Chesapeake settlements as well.

At the same time, in Virginia and elsewhere in North America, Indian peoples faced new challenges as they endeavored to maintain their independence despite a flood of immigrants from Europe and Africa. Indians employed different tactics—adaptation, coexistence, diplomacy, resistance—to assert their claims to land and their right to participate in the events and deliberations that affected their lives. The America to which Olaudah Equiano had been forcibly transported remained a place where Indian voices had to be heeded.

Equiano's journey did not end in Virginia. Over the next quarter-century, he traveled to other mainland colonies, the West Indies, England, Turkey, Portugal, and Spain. He worked as the servant of a naval officer, a barber, a laborer, an overseer—saving money to purchase his freedom. Such an extraordinary career testified to Equiano's resilience and determination. It also bore witness to the emergence of an international market for laborers, which—like slavery and Indian relations—shaped the development of North America. Thousands of people from England, Scotland, Ireland, and Germany attempted to take advantage of that market and seek their fortunes in America, increasing the white population and expanding onto new lands. The interactions of Indians, Africans, and Europeans created not one but many New Worlds.

Indians and Europeans

3.1 How did the different patterns of interaction between Europeans and native peoples shape colonial development in the Spanish borderlands, New France, and the English colonies?

Although, by 1750, European colonists and African slaves together outnumbered Indians north of the Rio Grande, Native Americans still dominated much of the continent. Colonists remained clustered along the coasts, and some native peoples had scarcely seen any Europeans.

The character of the relationship between Indians and Europeans depended on more than relative population size and the length of time they had been in contact. It was also shaped by the intentions of the newcomers—whether they came to extract resources, to trade, to settle, or to gain converts—and by the actions of Native American groups intent on preserving their cultures. The result was a variety of regionally distinctive New World communities.

Indian Workers in the Spanish Borderlands

More than any other European colonists, the Spanish sought direct control over Indian laborers. Their success in doing so depended on two factors: the existence of sizable Indian communities and Spanish military force. North of the Rio Grande, these conditions could be found in New Mexico and, to a lesser extent, in Florida. Native villages provided workers and existing structures of government that the Spanish converted to their own uses. At the same time, Spanish soldiers ensured that the Indians obeyed orders even though they greatly outnumbered the colonists.

One important method of labor control was the *encomienda*. *Encomiendas*, granted to influential Spaniards in New Mexico, gave these colonists the right to collect tribute from the native peoples living on a specific piece of land. The tribute usually took the form of corn, blankets, and animal hides. It was not supposed to include forced labor, but often it did.

 encomienda In the Spanish colonies, the grant to a Spanish settler of a certain number of Indian subjects, who would pay him tribute in goods and labor.

repartimiento In the Spanish colonies, the assignment of Indian workers to labor on public works projects.

The Spanish also relied on the **repartimiento**, a mandatory draft of Indian labor for public projects, such as building forts, bridges, and roads. Laws stated that native workers should be paid and limited the length of their service, but the Spanish often ignored these provisions and sometimes compelled Indians to work on private estates.

The native peoples strongly resented these practices. Spanish demands for labor and tribute remained constant, even when Indian populations declined from disease or crops failed, and workers who resisted were severely punished. Resentments simmered beneath a surface of cooperation until late in the seventeenth century, when long-standing native anger burst forth in rebellion.

The Web of Trade

Not all economic exchanges between Indians and Europeans were directly coercive. Indians sometimes used trade relations to exert influence over Europeans. Native Americans thought of trade as one aspect of a broader alliance between peoples. Europeans who wished to trade with Indians had to prove their friendship by offering gifts such as wampum (shell beads used as a kind of currency) and military aid as well as manufactured goods.

The French readily adapted to the Native American understanding of trade, realizing that good relations were essential to keeping New France's fur trade operating smoothly. The fur trade benefited Indians too. "The Beaver does everything perfectly well," noted one native leader, "it makes kettles, hatchets, swords, knives, bread; and, in short, it makes everything."

The benefits of trade were immediate and obvious; the problems were slower to appear. The one exception was the problem of disease, which followed almost immediately from Indians' contacts with European traders. The Huron population declined by half in just six years between 1634 and 1640. Indians trading with the Dutch in New Netherland in the 1650s reported that their once sizable population "had been melted down" by smallpox.

Although Indian hunters enjoyed considerable autonomy in their work, French merchants began to use economic pressure to control them. By supplying Indians with

This illustration depicts an encounter between a French trader and an Indian hunter in the Canadian wilderness. The exchange of European goods for furs was central to the economy of New France.

trade goods in advance, merchants obligated them to bring in furs as payment. One year's hunting thus paid the previous year's debts. Hunters who tried to avoid payment would lose access to more trade goods. Extending credit in this way allowed the French to control native workers without having to subjugate them.

The French could control the Indians through credit because over time native peoples grew dependent on European manufactures. In many communities, Indians abandoned native crafts and instead relied on imported goods. As a result, they had no alternative but to increase their hunting in order to have furs to trade for what they needed. "The Cloaths we wear, we cannot make ourselves," a Carolina Cherokee observed in 1753. "We cannot make our Guns. . . . Every necessary Thing in Life we must have from the white People." One consequence of this predicament was over-hunting; as early as the 1640s, beaver could no longer be found in much of New England, New York, and Pennsylvania.

Trade with Europeans eventually encouraged violence and warfare. Indians had fought one another before European colonization, but these wars were generally limited in scope and destructiveness. In much of eastern North America, "mourning wars" predominated. Warriors conducted raids mainly to seize captives rather than to kill large numbers of their enemies. The captives would either be ritually killed to avenge the deaths of individuals lost in earlier conflicts or adopted into the captors' group to replace the dead. After Europeans arrived, Indians adapted the mourning-war tradition to new circumstances. Warriors raided their enemies to replace family members lost to disease and fought to avenge losses resulting from the fierce competition for a diminishing supply of fur-bearing animals. The proliferation of firearms made the conflicts deadlier, and more casualties led to further mourning wars.

The **Beaver Wars**, a long struggle between the Hurons and the Iroquois that began in the 1640s, illustrated the ferocity of such contests. The Hurons were trading partners and allies with the French, and the Iroquois had forged ties with Dutch merchants in the Hudson River Valley. To satisfy the European demand for furs, the Hurons and Iroquois both hunted beaver at an unsustainable rate. By the 1630s, they had killed nearly all the beavers on their own lands and began to look elsewhere. The Hurons raised more corn to trade for furs with Indians living north of the Great Lakes, where beavers were still abundant. The Iroquois, however, began to raid Huron trading parties and attack Huron villages.

The Iroquois triumphed in this struggle largely because the Dutch supplied them with guns, whereas the French were reluctant to arm the Hurons. In the end, thousands of Hurons were killed or captured, and many others fled westward. The cycle of warfare did not end with the Hurons' destruction. The victorious Iroquois went on to challenge Indian nations near the Great Lakes and in the Ohio Valley.

Beaver Wars Series of bloody conflicts, occurring between the 1640s and 1680s, during which the Iroquois fought the Hurons and French for control of the fur trade in the east and the Great Lakes region.

Displacing Native Americans in the English Colonies

In New France and New Netherland, where the fur trade took precedence over farming, Indians outnumbered Europeans. This numerical superiority and their key role as suppliers of furs allowed native peoples to negotiate with settlers from a position of strength. The situation was different in the English colonies, in which increasingly numerous settlers came to farm and thus competed directly with Indians for land.

Land Use and Property Rights. English settlers who thought that there was enough territory for everyone misunderstood how Indians used land. Eastern Algonquian peoples cleared areas for villages and planting fields, which native women farmed until the soil grew less fertile. Then they moved to a new location, allowing the former village site to return to forest. In ten to twenty years, they or their descendants might return to that site to clear and farm it again. In the winter, village communities broke up into small hunting bands. Thus what the colonists considered "vacant" lands were either being used for nonfarming activities such as hunting or regaining fertility in order to be farmed in years to come. Settlers who built towns on abandoned native village sites deprived the Indians of access to these areas.

Disputes also arose from misunderstandings about the definition of land ownership and property rights. Indian villages claimed sovereignty over a certain territory, which their members collectively used for farming, fishing, hunting, and gathering. No Indian claimed individual ownership of a specific tract of land. Europeans, of course, did, and for them ownership conferred on an individual the exclusive right to use or sell a piece of land. These differences created problems whenever Indians transferred land to settlers. The settlers assumed that they had obtained complete rights to the land, whereas the Indians assumed that they had given the settlers not the land itself but only the right to use it. The English understanding of what was meant by a land sale prevailed, however, enforced in the colonists' courts under the colonists' laws.

Colonial agricultural practices also strained relations with the Indians. Cutting down forests destroyed Indian hunting lands. When colonists dammed rivers, they disturbed Indian fishing. When they surrounded their fields with fences, colonists made trespassers of natives who crossed them. Yet the colonists let their cattle and pigs loose to graze in the woods and meadows, where they could wander into unfenced Indian cornfields and damage the crops.

Colonial Land Acquisition.   As their numbers grew, the colonists acquired Indian lands and displaced native inhabitants. Because Indians owned land collectively, only their leaders had the authority to negotiate sales. Settlers, however, sometimes bought land from individual Indians who had no right to sell it. Because land transfers were usually arranged through interpreters and recorded in English, Indians were not always fully informed of the terms of sale. Even Indians who willingly sold land grew resentful as colonists approached them for more. Native peoples could also be forced to sell land to settle debts to English creditors.

Settlers occasionally obtained land by fraud. Some colonists simply settled on Indian lands and appealed to colonial governments for help when the Indians objected. Land speculators amplified this kind of unrest as they sought to acquire land as cheaply as possible and sell it for as much as they could.

Finally, colonists often seized Indian lands in the aftermath of war, as befell, among many others, the Pequots in 1637 in Connecticut, and in Carolina, the Tuscaroras in 1713 and the Yamasees in 1715. In each case, settlers moved onto land left vacant after colonial forces killed, captured, and dispersed native peoples. This hunger for land by the colonists generated relentless pressure on native peoples, and the pattern of mutual suspicion and territorial competition that developed would be difficult to alter.

Bringing Christianity to Native Peoples

In addition to trade and settlement, religion played a powerful role in shaping relations between Native Americans and Europeans. The three major New World empires of Spain, France, and England competed for Indians' souls as well as their lands and riches.

Catholic Missionaries in Spanish Colonies.   Franciscan priests were the driving force behind Spain's efforts to control New Mexico and Florida (see Map 3.1). Spain valued both regions for strategic reasons. Neither colony attracted many settlers, however, because neither offered much opportunity for wealth. When Franciscan missionaries proposed to move in, Spanish officials, eager to back up their claims with a more visible Spanish presence, provided financial support.

Franciscans settled near native villages in New Mexico and Florida in order to convert their inhabitants to Catholicism. The priests wore their finest vestments and displayed

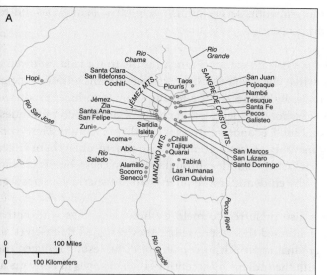

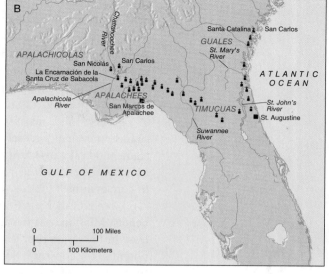

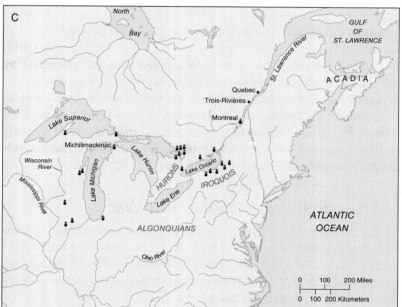

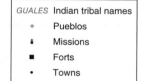

GUALES	Indian tribal names
●	Pueblos
⛪	Missions
■	Forts
•	Towns

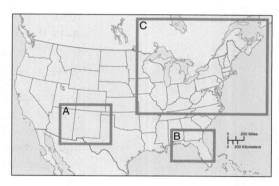

MAP 3.1 SPANISH AND FRENCH MISSIONS IN SEVENTEENTH-CENTURY NORTH AMERICA
Spanish Franciscans in New Mexico (A) and Florida (B) and French Jesuits in New France (C) devoted considerable
effort to converting native peoples to Catholic Christianity.

religious paintings and statues, trying to impress the Indians. They gave away bells, knives,
cloth, and food. The natives believed that accepting these gifts obliged them to listen to the
priests' Christian message and help the Franciscans build houses and churches.

After brief religious instruction, the missionaries convinced many Indians to
accept baptism into the Catholic Church. Many of these conversions were doubtless
genuine, but they also had practical motivations. Conversions often followed epidemics that devastated native villages but spared the Spanish, leading Indians to wonder
if the Christian God might be more powerful than their own gods. In New Mexico,
the Spanish promised Pueblo converts protection against Apache raids and access to
Franciscan storehouses in times of famine. Ironically, the corn in the storehouses often
came from the Indians' own fields, collected by the Spanish as tribute.

The Franciscans insisted that converts abandon their former ways of life and adopt
Spanish food, clothing, gender relations, and work routines along with Catholicism.
Their efforts met with mixed success. Many Indians preferred to supplement native
beliefs and practices with the new teachings. Because the missionaries reacted to this

spiritual mixture with horror, inflicting severe punishments that sometimes led to death, native peoples often practiced their own rituals in secret.

French Jesuits in Canada.   To a certain extent, French Jesuits in Canada followed a similar strategy, moving to native villages and seeking to awe Indians with European technology and Catholic rituals. By the 1650s, the Jesuits claimed to have produced thousands of converts, some of whom formed separate native Christian communities.

French missionaries combined economic pressure with preaching. They persuaded merchants to sell guns only to converted Indians and to offer them other trade goods at a discount. Such tactics doubtless brought some success, but as in New Mexico, the crises engendered by epidemics more often than not sparked an upsurge in conversions.

Converts in New France also preferred to meld Catholic teachings with native beliefs. Missionaries hardly condoned this response but they resigned themselves, at least in the short run, to a gradual approach to conversion. The Jesuits reduced the potential for confrontation with the Indians by accepting small changes in converts at first in hopes of a wholesale transformation to follow.

Missionaries in English Colonies.   The Protestant English were less successful at attracting Native American converts. Puritans frowned on the rituals and religious objects that drew Indians to Catholicism, but Protestant practices, including lengthy sermons and Bible study, held little allure for Indians accustomed to a more ritualistic spiritual life. Even so, Protestant missionaries achieved some success, principally in New England. Beginning in the 1650s and 1660s, Puritan ministers such as John Eliot and Thomas Mayhew, Jr., attracted converts. Eliot helped to establish several "praying towns," where Indians received instruction in Protestant Christianity and English ways. By 1674, about 2,300 Indians resided in these towns.

After the First Hundred Years: Conflict and War

After nearly a century of European settlement, violence between colonists and Indians erupted in all three North American empires. Each deadly encounter—King Philip's War in New England, Bacon's Rebellion in Virginia, the Pueblo Revolt in New Mexico, and the resumption of the Beaver Wars in New France—reflected distinctive features of English, Spanish, and French patterns of colonization.

King Philip's War.   The growing frustration of the Wampanoags, who had befriended the Pilgrims more than a half century earlier, with the land-hungry settlers whose towns now surrounded them, sparked **King Philip's War**, which broke out in 1675. Massasoit's younger son, Metacom—called King Philip by the English—led the Wampanoags in the struggle to preserve their independence. He had little reason to trust English settlers.

In the spring of 1675, a colonial court found three Wampanoags guilty of murdering a Christian Indian who had warned the English of Wampanoag preparations for war. Despite Philip's protest that the evidence against the men was tainted, the court sentenced them to be hanged. This act convinced the Wampanoags that they had to strike back against the English before it was too late. Only "a small part of the dominion of my ancestors remains," declared Philip. "I am determined not to live until I have no country." The final blow occurred in June 1675, when colonists killed an Indian they found in an abandoned house and then ignored the Indians' outrage at the murder.

Native warriors attacked outlying villages in Plymouth Colony, moved into the Connecticut River Valley, and then turned eastward to strike towns within 20 miles of Boston. As the Narragansetts and other groups joined the uprising, Philip successfully eluded the combined forces of Massachusetts, Connecticut, and Plymouth. By early 1676, however, the Indians were exhausted, weakened by disease and food shortages.

King Philip's War Conflict in New England (1675–1676) between Wampanoags, Narragansetts, and other Indian peoples against English settlers; sparked by English encroachments on native lands.

Philip moved into western New England, where his men clashed with the powerful Mohawks, long-standing enemies of the Wampanoags and allies of English fur traders in New York. Philip died in an ambush in August 1676, and the war ended soon after.

At least 1,000 colonists and perhaps 3,000 Indians died in King Philip's War. One out of every sixteen male colonists of military age was killed, making this the deadliest conflict in American history in terms of the proportion of casualties to total population. The Indians forced back the line of settlement but lost what remained of their independence in New England. Philip's head, impaled on a stake, was left for decades just outside Plymouth as a grisly warning of the price to be paid for resisting colonial expansion.

Bacon's Rebellion.   As King Philip's War raged in New England, **Bacon's Rebellion** erupted in Virginia and had a similarly devastating effect on that colony's native population. Frustrated by shrinking economic opportunities in eastern Virginia, where established planters controlled the best land, many settlers, including new arrivals and recently freed indentured servants, moved to Virginia's western frontier. There they came into conflict with the region's resident Indians. In the summer of

Bacon's Rebellion Violent conflict in Virginia (1675–1676), beginning with settler attacks on Indians but culminating in a rebellion led by Nathaniel Bacon against Virginia's government.

This eighteenth-century image depicts King Philip, Wampanoag leader of the conflict against New England colonists. Note that he is shown with English goods, including musket, powder horn, and clothing, as well as with a Native-style beaded belt.

1675, a group of frontier settlers attacked the Susquehannocks to seize their lands. The Indians struck back, prompting Nathaniel Bacon, a wealthy young planter who had only recently arrived in Virginia, to lead a violent campaign against all Indians, even those at peace with the colonial government. Governor William Berkeley ordered Bacon and his men to stop their attacks. They defied him and marched on Jamestown, turning a war between settlers and Indians into a rebellion of settlers against the colonial authorities.

The rebels believed that Berkeley and the colonial government represented the interests of established tobacco planters who wanted to keep men like themselves from emerging as potential competitors. Desperate because of the low price of tobacco, the rebels demanded voting rights, lower taxes, and easier access to land—meaning, in effect, the right to take land from the Indians. Berkeley offered to build forts along the frontier, but the rebels were not interested in defensive measures. What they wanted was help in exterminating the Indians. They captured and burned the colonial capital at Jamestown, forcing Berkeley to flee. Directing their aggression against Indians once more, they burned Indian villages and massacred the inhabitants.

By the time troops arrived from England to put down the rebellion, Bacon had died of dysentery and most of his men had drifted home. Berkeley hanged twenty-three rebels, but the real victims of the rebellion were Virginia's Indians. The remnants of the once-powerful Powhatans lost their remaining lands and either moved west or lived in poverty on the edges of English settlement. Hatred of Indians became a permanent feature of frontier life in Virginia, and government officials appeared more eager to spend money "for extirpating all Indians" than for maintaining peaceful relations.

Pueblo Revolt Rebellion in 1680 of Pueblo Indians in New Mexico against their Spanish overlords, sparked by religious conflict and excessive Spanish demands for tribute.

The Pueblo Revolt.   In 1680, the **Pueblo Revolt** against the Spanish in New Mexico had a very different outcome than did the conflicts in Virginia and New England. Nearly 20,000 Pueblo Indians had grown restless under the harsh rule of only 2,500 Spaniards. The spark that ignited the revolt was an act of religious persecution. Spanish officials unwisely chose this troubled time to stamp out the Pueblo religion. In 1675, the governor arrested forty-seven native religious leaders on charges of sorcery. The court ordered most of them to be publicly whipped and released but sentenced four to death.

Led by Popé, one of the freed leaders, the outraged Pueblos organized for revenge. A growing network of rebels emerged as Spanish soldiers marched into Pueblo villages and destroyed *kivas,* the chambers that Indians used for religious ceremonies. Working from the village of Taos in northern New Mexico, by the summer of 1680, Popé commanded an enormous force of rebels drawn from twenty Pueblo villages. On August 10, they attacked the Spanish settlements. Popé urged them to destroy "everything pertaining to Christianity." By October, all the surviving Spaniards had fled New Mexico.

They did not return for thirteen years. By then, internal rivalries had split the victorious Pueblo coalition, and Popé had been overthrown as leader. Few Pueblo villages offered much resistance to the new Spanish intrusion. Even so, the Spanish now understood the folly of pushing the Indians too far. Officials reduced demands for tribute and ended the *encomienda* system. The Franciscans eased their attacks on Pueblo religion. New Spanish governors, backed by military force, kept the peace as best they could in a place where Indians still outnumbered Europeans.

Resumption of the Beaver Wars.   The Iroquois experience in the last phase of the Beaver Wars threatened to parallel that of the Indians of New England and Virginia. What began as a struggle between the Iroquois and western native peoples for control of the fur trade blossomed into a larger conflict that was absorbed into the imperial rivalry between England and France. Although the Iroquois suffered devastating losses, they did not lose their independence. The key to Iroquois survival in the war's aftermath was the adoption of a position of neutrality between the European powers.

One of the many pueblos scattered along the Rio Grande Valley, Taos served as Popé's headquarters at the start of the Pueblo Revolt in August 1680. Within a few weeks, the Indians drove the Spanish from New Mexico and destroyed most of their settlements. The Spanish did not return until 1693.

Looking for new trading partners to replace the Hurons, the French turned in the 1680s to various Indian peoples living near the Great Lakes. But the Iroquois had begun to raid these same peoples for furs and captives, much as they had attacked the Hurons in the first phase of the Beaver Wars in the 1640s. They exchanged the furs for European goods with English traders, who had replaced the Dutch as their partners after the conquest of New Netherland. Many of the captives were adopted into Iroquois families.

The French attacked the Iroquois to prevent them and their English allies from extending their influence in the west. In June 1687, a combined force of French and Christian Indian soldiers invaded the lands of the Senecas, the westernmost of the five nations of the Iroquois League. The Iroquois retaliated by besieging a French garrison at Niagara, where nearly 200 soldiers starved to death, and killing hundreds of colonists in attacks on French villages along the St. Lawrence River.

The French participated much more directly and suffered greater losses in this renewal of the Beaver Wars than they had in the earlier fighting. In 1688, France and England went to war in Europe, and the struggle between them and their Indian allies for control of the fur trade in North America became part of a larger imperial contest. The European powers made peace in 1697, but calm did not immediately return to the Great Lakes region.

The conflict was even more devastating for the Iroquois. The English, still solidifying their control over their new colony of New York, provided minimal military assistance, and the Iroquois suffered heavy casualties. Perhaps a quarter of their population died from disease and warfare by 1689. The devastation encouraged Iroquois diplomats to find a way to extricate themselves from future English-French conflicts. The result, in 1701, was a pair of treaties, negotiated separately with Albany and Montreal, which recognized Iroquois neutrality and, at least for several decades, prevented either the English or the French from dominating the western lands.

Africans and Europeans

3.2 How and why did race-based slavery develop in British North America?

The movement of Africans to the Americas was one of the largest forced migrations in world history. By the time New World slavery finally ended, with its abolition in Brazil in 1888, more than 12 million Africans had arrived on American shores. From a relatively small stream in the sixteenth century, African migration accelerated to a great flood by the 1700s.

Virtually all Africans arrived as slaves, making the history of the African experience in the Americas inseparable from the history of slavery and the slave trade. As one eighteenth-century Englishman noted, Africans were "the strength and sinews of this western world," performing much of the labor of colonization. The vast majority of African slaves ended up in Brazil, the West Indies, or New Spain. Only one out of twenty Africans came to the British mainland colonies, but this still amounted to nearly 350,000 individuals (see Figure 3.1). Their presence transformed English colonial societies everywhere, but particularly in the South. At the same time, Africans were themselves transformed. Out of their diverse African ethnic backgrounds and the experience of slavery itself they forged new identities as African American peoples.

Labor Needs and the Turn to Slavery

Europeans in the New World were thrilled to find that land was abundant and quite cheap by European standards. They were perplexed, however, by the unexpectedly high

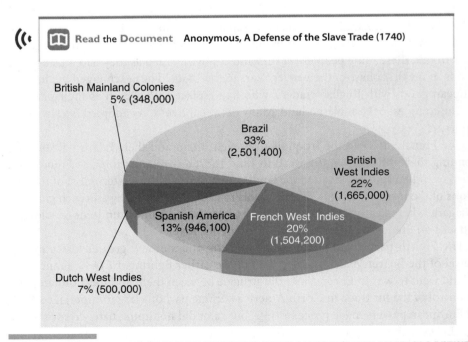

((• 📖 **Read the Document** **Anonymous, A Defense of the Slave Trade (1740)**

British Mainland Colonies
5% (348,000)

Brazil
33%
(2,501,400)

British
West Indies
22%
(1,665,000)

French West Indies
20%
(1,504,200)

Spanish America
13% (946,100)

Dutch West Indies
7% (500,000)

FIGURE 3.1 DESTINATION OF SLAVES IMPORTED FROM AFRICA TO THE AMERICAS BETWEEN 1451 AND 1810 Approximately 7.5 million Africans were brought as slaves to the Americas before 1810. The vast majority went to the Caribbean, Mexico, and South America, where they toiled in mines and on sugar plantations.

SOURCE: Philip Curtin, *The Atlantic Slave Trade: A Census*, p. 268 (1969 University of Wisconsin Press).

cost of labor. In Europe, the reverse had been true. There land was expensive but labor cheap, because competition for jobs among large numbers of workers pushed wages down. Colonial workers commanded high wages because there were so few of them compared to the supply of land to be developed. In addition, few settlers wanted to work for others when they could get farms of their own. The scarcity and high cost of labor led some colonial employers to turn to enslaved Africans as a solution.

The development of slavery in the colonies was not inevitable. Europeans had owned slaves (both white and black) long before the beginning of American colonization, but slaves formed a small—and shrinking—minority of European laborers. By the fifteenth century, slavery had all but disappeared in northern Europe except as punishment for serious crimes. English laws in particular protected the personal freedom of the king's subjects.

Slavery persisted longer in southern Europe and the Middle East. In both regions, religion influenced the choice of who was enslaved. Because neither Christians nor Muslims would hold as slaves members of their own faiths, Arab traders turned to sub-Saharan Africa to find slaves. Eventually, the Arabic word for slave—'*abd*—became a synonym for "black man." By the fifteenth century, a durable link between slave status and black skin had been forged in European minds.

Europeans in the New World, beginning with Columbus, first enslaved Indians as a way of addressing the labor shortage. Spaniards held Indian slaves in all their New World colonies, as did the Portuguese in Brazil. French Canadians enslaved Fox and other Great Lakes area Indians captured in wars in the North American interior. English colonists condemned Indian war captives to slavery as punishment for their opposition to English rule.

In early Carolina, English traders saw the traffic in Indian slaves as an irresistible opportunity for profit. They encouraged their native allies to raid Spanish missions in Florida and to make smaller incursions into French Louisiana. Between 1670 and 1715, as many as 51,000 Indian slaves were shipped out of Carolina to Caribbean and other markets. The profits gained in this violent trade were then invested in the development of Carolina's colonial economy. Native American slaves, however, could not fill the colonists' labor needs. Everywhere disease and harsh working conditions reduced their numbers. English colonists also discovered problems with enslaving Indians. When traders incited Indian wars to gain slaves, bloodshed often spread to English settlements. Enslaved Indian men refused to perform agricultural labor, which they considered women's work. And because they knew the land so well, Indians could easily escape. As a result, although the Indian slave trade persisted in the English colonies through the eighteenth century (and into the nineteenth century), by 1700 it had given way to a much larger traffic in Africans.

The Shock of Enslavement

European traders did not themselves enslave Africans. Instead, they relied on other Africans to capture slaves for them, tapping into and expanding a preexisting internal African slave trade. With the permission of local rulers, Europeans built forts and trading posts on the West African coast and bought slaves from African traders. African rulers occasionally enslaved and sold their own people as punishment for crimes, but most slaves were seized in raids on neighboring peoples. Attracted by European cloth, liquor, guns, and other goods, West Africans fought among themselves to secure captives and began kidnapping individuals from the interior.

Once captured, slaves marched in chains to the coast, to be confined in cages until there were enough to fill a ship. Captains examined them to ensure their fitness and branded them like cattle with a hot iron. The slaves then boarded canoes to be ferried to the ships. Desperation overwhelmed some of them, who jumped overboard and drowned rather than be carried off to an unknown destination. Even before the ships left African shores, slaves sometimes mutinied, though such rebellions rarely succeeded.

✳ Explore the Trans-Atlantic Slave Trade on MyHistoryLab

IN WHAT WAYS WAS BRITISH NORTH AMERICA INVOLVED IN THE TRANS-ATLANTIC SLAVE TRADE?

For some three centuries, the trans-Atlantic slave trade brought a total of more than 10 million Africans to the shores of the Americas where they provided an unpaid, bond-servant labor force primarily in agriculture, especially in the southern Thirteen Colonies. However, slavery was not contained to the southern colonies (and later states), as Africans found themselves enslaved up and down the Eastern Seaboard. Americans bought slaves and further participated in the slave trade as sailors, captains, shipbuilders, traders, and financiers. Slavery influenced the economy, politics, and society that provided the foundations for the United States.

Handbills such as these alerted buyers when and where they could purchase chattel slaves, who were sold, traded, and auctioned as commodities just like livestock, corn, tobacco, and the like.

ORIGINS OF AFRICANS IN NORTH AMERICA, 1700–1800

Region
Angola
Bight of Benin
Bight of Biafra
Gold Coast
Senegambia
Sierra Leone

NATIONS PARTICIPATING IN THE SLAVE TRADE, 1700–1800

Nation*
Britain
Portugal
France
The Netherlands
Denmark
British Colonies/North America

*In order of most to fewest number of slaves traded
SOURCE: Prentice Hall American History Atlas, 1998, p. 13.

KEY QUESTIONS   Use **MyHistoryLab *Explorer*** to **answer** these **questions:**

Comparison ▶▶▶ *Which colonies, later states, imported the most slaves?*

Map the differences among the regions of North America.

Analysis ▶▶▶ *How did the ratio of male to female slaves differ across the Thirteen Colonies?*

Hypothesize the explanations for this distribution.

Consequence ▶▶▶ *What were the major economic activities for different regions of mainland British America and the early United States?*

Consider the connections between slavery and regional economic production.

Slaves who could not escape while still in Africa suffered through a horrendous six- to eight-week-long ocean voyage known as the **Middle Passage**. Captains wedged men below decks into spaces about 6 feet long, 16 inches wide, and 30 inches high. Women and children were packed even more tightly. Except for brief excursions on deck for forced exercise, slaves remained below decks, where the air grew foul from the vomit, blood, and excrement in which the terrified victims lay. "The shrieks of the women, and the groans of the dying," recalled Olaudah Equiano, "rendered it a scene of horror almost inconceivable." Some slaves went insane; others refused to eat. On many voyages, between 5 and 20 percent of the slaves perished from disease and other causes, but captains had usually packed the ships tightly enough to make a profit from selling the rest.

Those who survived the dreadful voyage endured the fear and humiliation of sale. Planters generally preferred males and often sought slaves from particular African ethnic groups, in the belief that some Africans would work harder than others. Ship captains sometimes sold slaves at public auctions, where purchasers poked them, looking for signs of disease. Many terrified Africans, like Equiano, thought they were going to be eaten.

African Slaves in the New World

The Spanish and Portuguese first brought Africans to the Americas to replace or supplement the dwindling numbers of Indian slaves toiling in silver mines and on sugar plantations. The Dutch, who scrambled for a share of the lucrative slave trade, quickly followed suit. English colonists, less familiar with slavery, adopted it more slowly. West Indian planters were the first English settlers to do so on a large scale in the 1640s. In most other English colonies, however, different economic conditions either postponed or prevented slavery's widespread adoption.

Slavery in the Southern Colonies. The first African immigrants arrived in Virginia in 1619. Brought by a Dutch merchant ship, most—if not all—were probably slaves. Yet slavery did not fully take hold in Virginia until the end of the seventeenth century, at which point Africans comprised a significant portion of the population (see Figure 3.2). For decades, tobacco planters saw no reason to stop using white indentured servants. Servants (because they worked for masters only for a period of years rather than for life) cost less than slaves, were readily available, and were familiar. For most of the seventeenth century, by contrast, slaves were expensive, difficult to obtain, and exotic. By the 1680s, however, planters in Virginia and Maryland began to shift from servants to slaves.

Two related developments caused this change. First, white indentured servants became harder to find. Fewer English men and women chose to emigrate as servants after 1660 because an improving economy in England provided jobs at home. At the same time, Virginia's white population tripled between 1650 and 1700, increasing the number of planters competing for a shrinking supply of laborers. Planters also faced competition from newer colonies such as Pennsylvania and New Jersey, which had more generous land policies for immigrants.

Second, as white servants grew scarcer, changes in the slave trade made African slaves more available. Before the 1660s, the Dutch and Portuguese merchants who dominated the trade mainly supplied their own colonies and the profitable West Indian market. But beginning in 1674, England's Royal African Company began shipping slaves directly to English buyers. The supply of slaves surged after 1698, when the Royal African Company lost its special trading rights, and many English merchants and New Englanders entered the fiercely competitive trade.

Chesapeake planters eventually found reasons besides availability to prefer slaves to servants. Slaves were a better long-term investment. Because slave status passed from slave mothers to their children, buying both men and women gave planters a self-reproducing labor force. Runaway black slaves were more easily recaptured than

Middle Passage The voyage between West Africa and the New World slave colonies.

escaped servants, who blended into the white population. And unlike indentured servants, slaves were slaves for life. They would never compete as planters with their former masters or, like Nathaniel Bacon's followers, pose a threat to order if they failed to prosper.

Chesapeake planters had already come to see white servants as possessions, people whose labor could be bought and sold like any other commodity. This attitude

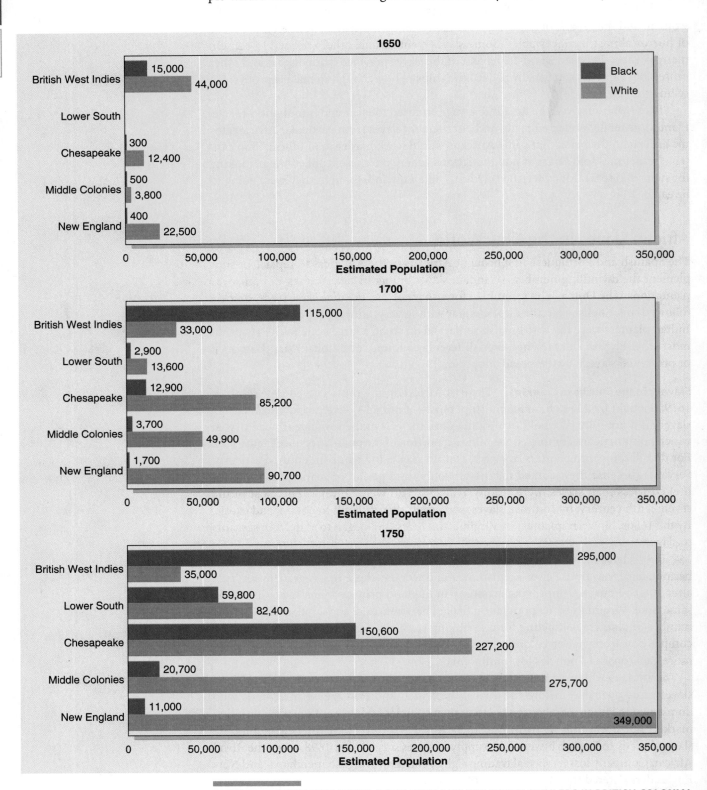

FIGURE 3.2 ESTIMATED POPULATION OF BLACK AND WHITE SETTLERS IN BRITISH COLONIAL REGIONS, 1650–1750 Settler populations increased rapidly in all colonial regions, but the racial composition varied. By 1750, black people overwhelmingly predominated in the West Indies and were quite numerous in the southern colonies; north of Maryland, however, their numbers remained small.

SOURCE: From THE ECONOMY OF BRITISH AMERICA, 1607–1789 by John J. McClusker and Russell R. Menard. Published for the Omohundro Institute of Early American History and Culture. Copyright © 1985 by the University of North Carolina Press. www.uncpress.unc.edu.

The freed slave Olaudah Equiano appears in this 1780 portrait by an unknown artist. After purchasing his freedom, Equiano wrote a vivid account of his capture in Africa and his life in slavery. One of the first such accounts to be published (in 1789), this narrative testified to slavery's injustice and Equiano's own fortitude and talents.

doubtless eased the transition in the 1680s and 1690s to the much harsher system of slavery. In Carolina, of course, slaves were there from the start, brought in the 1670s by colony founders accustomed to slavery in Barbados. By 1720, slavery was firmly embedded in all the southern colonies except sparsely settled North Carolina. In that year, one-third of Virginia's settler population, and nearly three-quarters of South Carolina's, were black.

Slavery grew rapidly in the southern colonies because it answered the labor needs of planters engaged in the commercial production of tobacco and rice. The demand for slaves became so powerful that it destroyed James Oglethorpe's plan to keep them out of Georgia, the last of England's mainland colonies, founded in 1732. Oglethorpe intended Georgia to be a refuge for English debtors, who normally were jailed until they could repay their creditors. His idea was to send debtors to Georgia to work at producing marketable goods such as silk and wine. Slaves were initially prohibited not only to prevent them from competing with the debtors, but also to make it difficult for fugitive slaves from South Carolina to escape there. With slavery forbidden, any black person seen in Georgia would be immediately recognizable as a runaway. But when Georgia's colonists began to grow rice, they demanded the right to have slaves. In 1750, the colony's founders reluctantly legalized slavery; by 1770, slaves made up nearly half of the colony's population.

Slavery in the Northern Colonies.   Far fewer slaves lived north of the Chesapeake, although they were present in every British colony. They were too expensive for most northern farmers—who mainly produced food for their families, not staple crops for an international market—to use profitably. This was not true, however, for farmers with larger properties in parts of Long Island, the Hudson Valley, Rhode Island, northern New Jersey, and southeastern Pennsylvania, where commercial wheat farming and livestock raising prevailed. In the eighteenth century, these landowners acquired significant numbers of slaves.

Northern slaves could often be found in cities, especially ports such as Newport, Rhode Island, where newly arrived Africans landed. At the start of the eighteenth century, one out of six Philadelphia residents was a slave; by 1740, slaves made up 15 percent of the city's workingmen. In mid-eighteenth-century New York City, slaves comprised between 12 and 14 percent of the population. Many urban slaves were domestic servants in the homes of rich merchants and professionals. Substantial numbers also labored as artisans.

Changing Race Relations in the Colonies.   Race relations in the mainland colonies were less rigid in the seventeenth century than they would later become. Before 1700, slaves did not form a majority of the population in any colony, a situation that may have made them seem less threatening to white people. In some areas, free black people—often slaves who had bought their own freedom—prospered in an atmosphere of racial tolerance that would be unthinkable by the eighteenth century.

The career of an ambitious black Virginian named Anthony Johnson, for example, resembled that of many white settlers—a remarkable achievement, given that he arrived in the colony in 1621 as a slave. Johnson's master allowed him to marry and start a family while he was still a slave and may even have allowed Anthony to purchase his and

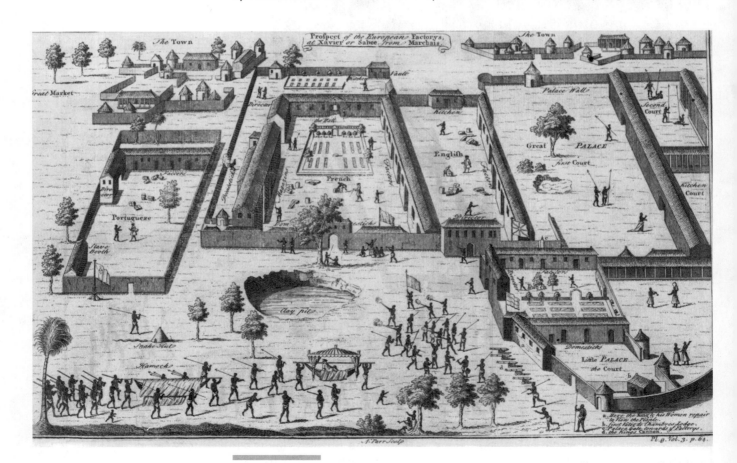

This 1730 image depicts a European slave trading settlement on the Guinea coast of Africa. Merchants from Portugal, France, England, and the Netherlands gathered here to purchase laborers for their colonial plantations.

his family's liberty. Once free, the Johnsons settled in eastern Virginia, where Anthony and his sons eventually acquired substantial plantations. Like white settlers, Johnson occasionally took his neighbors to court and even successfully sued them. He and his sons also owned slaves. Anthony Johnson belonged to the first of what one historian has called the "charter" generation of American slaves, and his experience reveals how much slavery changed over time. This generation of slaves mainly came from African port towns, where Europeans and Africans had mingled for generations, or by way of the West Indies or New Netherland. Familiar with European ways, often fluent in European languages, they acquired skills and knowledge that enabled them to bargain with their masters in ways their descendants would not be able to replicate. They came in small groups, cultivated their masters as patrons, negotiated for their own property, and often gained their freedom. They enjoyed such advantages because they came to colonies where slavery had not yet become firmly embedded, where the meaning of bondage was still being worked out.

Repressive Laws and Slave Codes.   But Johnson's descendants, and the generations of slaves and free black people who came after them, encountered much harsher conditions. Once slavery became the dominant labor system in the Chesapeake, tobacco planters no longer welcomed free black people, fearing that they might encourage slaves to escape. In 1691, Virginia's legislature prohibited individual masters from freeing their slaves. Lawmakers passed another measure in 1699 requiring newly freed black people to leave the colony altogether. Black families like the Johnsons, who were already free, suffered under increasing discrimination.

Bad as the situation of free black people had grown, the condition of slaves was far worse. Slave codes, laws governing slavery, essentially reduced an entire class of human beings to property. In Virginia, from the middle of the seventeenth century on, new laws added to slaves' oppression. A 1662 measure defined slavery as a lifelong and inherited status that passed from slave mothers to their children—even children with white fathers. Masters who might have felt uneasy about holding fellow Christians as slaves were relieved in 1667 when another law stated that baptism would not release slaves from bondage. Two years later, the House of Burgesses gave masters the power of life and death over their slaves, decreeing that masters would not be charged with a felony if their slaves died during punishment. These and other measures were gathered into a comprehensive slave code in Virginia in 1705.

Slave codes appeared virtually everywhere, North and South, but were particularly harsh in the southern colonies. White colonists in the Tidewater Chesapeake and South Carolina feared the consequences of a growing black population. One South Carolina planter predicted in 1720 that slaves would soon rise up against their masters because black people were "too numerous in proportion to the White Men there."

African American Families and Communities

The harshness of the slaves' condition could be relieved somewhat by the formation of close ties with others who shared their circumstances. For such ties to be created, however, several developments had to occur. Slaves had to become sufficiently numerous in specific localities so that black people could have regular contact with one another. Ethnic and language barriers carried over from Africa had to erode so that slaves could communicate. And for families to be formed, there had to be enough slave women as well as men. Because these conditions were slow to develop, occurring at different rates in different colonies, the formation of African American families and communities was delayed until well into the eighteenth century.

The Rise of the Creole Slave Population.   Slaves were far more numerous in the southern colonies, and it was there that African American families and communities emerged with greater success. This was especially true in South Carolina and parts of the Tidewater Chesapeake, where in certain localities slaves formed a majority of the population. Even more significant, these regions witnessed the rise of a creole, or American-born, slave population by about the 1750s. This development distinguished slavery in the mainland British colonies from that in the West Indies, where disease and overwork killed so many slaves that the black population grew only because of the constant importation of Africans.

The rise of a creole slave population in the Chesapeake and in Carolina set off a chain of related events that fostered family and community life. Creoles lived longer than African immigrants, and creole women usually bore twice as many children as African-born mothers. This circumstance allowed the slave population to grow by natural increase and more closely resemble a normal population of men and women, children and elders. At the same time, creole slaves grew up without personal memories of Africa, and thus African ethnic differences receded in importance.

Work and Family Life.   Most of a slave's life was structured by work. The vast majority of southern slaves were field hands. On large plantations, masters selected some slave men to be trained as shoemakers, weavers, or tailors and chose others as drivers or leaders of work gangs. With the exception of nurses and cooks, few slave women avoided the drudgery of field labor. If they had families, the end of the day's work in the fields only marked the start of domestic duties back in the slave quarters. But no matter how onerous, work did not absorb every minute of the slaves' lives, and in the intervals around their assigned duties many slaves nurtured ties of family and community that combined African traditions with New World experience.

By the late eighteenth century, more than half of Chesapeake and Carolina slaves lived in family groups. These were fragile units, subject to the whims of masters who did not recognize slave marriages as legal, broke up families by sale, and could take slave women as sexual partners at will. Many slave husbands and wives resided on different plantations, although on larger Carolina estates two-parent slave households grew increasingly common. Over time, dense kinship networks formed, reflecting

((Read the Document   James Oglethorpe, The Stono Rebellion (1739)

This eighteenth-century painting from South Carolina records the preservation of certain African traditions in American slave communities. The dance may be Yoruba in origin, while the stringed instrument and drum were probably modeled on African instruments.

West African influences. Slaves placed great emphasis on kin connections, even using familiar terms such as "aunt" and "uncle" to address friends. Some slave husbands, as was customary in West Africa, took more than one wife. In naming their children, slaves mingled old and new practices, sometimes giving them the African names of distant kin and sometimes using English names.

Community Life and Religion.   Community life forged ties between slave families and single slaves on the plantations and offered further opportunities to preserve elements of African heritage. Since Christianity offered little competition to African religious practices during most of the colonial period, and few masters showed much interest in converting their slaves before the Revolution, traces of African religious practices endured in America. Magical charms and amulets have been found buried in slave quarters, indicating that spiritual ceremonies may have been conducted out of sight of white masters. Reflecting their West African background, slaves placed great emphasis on funerals, in the belief that relatives remained members of kin communities even after death.

African influences shaped aspects of slaves' recreational activity and material life. Slave musicians used African-style instruments, including drums and banjos, to accompany traditional songs and dances. Where slaves were allowed to build their own houses, they incorporated African elements into the designs—for instance, by using mud walls and roofs thatched with palmetto leaves. Their gardens frequently contained African foods, such as millet, yams, peppers, and sesame seeds, along with European and Native American crops.

Resistance and Rebellion

Even as family ties made a life in bondage more tolerable, they made it more difficult for slaves to attempt escape or contemplate rebellion. Slaves who resisted their oppression ran the risk of endangering families and friends as well as themselves. But the powerful desire for freedom was not easily suppressed, and slaves found ways to defy the dehumanization that slavery entailed.

Running away from a master was a desperate act, but thousands of slaves did just that. Deciding where to go posed a problem. Escape out of the South did not bring freedom, because slavery was legal in every colony. After 1733, some runaways went to Florida, where Spanish officials promised them freedom. Others tried to survive on their own in the woods or join the Indians—a choice that carried the risk of capture or death. Perilous as it was, escape proved irresistible to some slaves, especially young males. In a few isolated areas on the South Carolina frontier, runaways formed outlaw "maroon" settlements.

Many slaves chose less perilous ways to resist their bondage. Slaves worked slowly, broke tools, and pretended to be ill in order to exert some control over their working lives. When provoked, they also took more direct action, damaging crops, stealing goods, and setting fires. Slaves with knowledge of poisonous plants occasionally tried to kill their owners, although the penalty for being caught was to be burned to death.

The most serious, as well as the rarest, form of resistance was organized rebellion. South Carolinians and coastal Virginians, who lived in regions with slave majorities, had a particular dread of slave revolt. But because rebellions required complete secrecy, careful planning, and access to weapons, they were extremely hard to organize. No slave rebellion succeeded in the British colonies. Rumors usually leaked out before any action had been taken, prompting severe reprisals against the alleged conspirators.

Three major slave revolts did occur, and they instilled lasting fear in white colonists. In 1712 in New York City, where black people made up 20 percent of the population, about twenty slaves set a building on fire and killed nine white men who came to put it out. The revolt was quickly suppressed, with twenty-four rebels sentenced

Stono Rebellion Uprising in 1739 of South Carolina slaves against whites; inspired in part by Spanish officials' promise of freedom for American slaves who escaped to Florida.

to death. Another slave insurrection occurred in Virginia in 1730, sparked by a false rumor that local officials had suppressed a royal edict calling for the emancipation of Christian slaves. More than 300 rebels escaped into the Dismal Swamp along the border with North Carolina, attacking white settlers in the area. Using Indians to hunt down the fugitives, Virginia authorities captured and executed twenty-four of the rebellion's leaders. Another major revolt, the **Stono Rebellion**, struck South Carolina in 1739. About twenty slaves—including several recently arrived Angolans—broke into a store and armed themselves with stolen guns. Marching southward along the Stono River, their ranks grew to perhaps a hundred. Heading for freedom in Spanish Florida, they attacked white settlements along the way. White troops (with Indian help) defeated the rebels within a week, but tensions remained high for months. The death toll, in the end, was about two dozen white people and perhaps twice as many black rebels.

In the wake of these rebellions, colonial assemblies passed laws requiring stricter supervision of slave activities. In South Carolina, other measures encouraged more white immigration to offset the colony's black majority. Planters in the southern colonies in particular considered slavery indispensable to their economic survival, even though this labor system generated so much fear and brutality. Their slaves, in turn, obeyed when necessary, resisted when possible, and kept alive the hope that freedom would one day be theirs.

European Laborers in Early America

3.3   What methods did Europeans employ to acquire and manage labor in colonial America?

Slavery was one of several responses to the scarcity of labor in the New World. It took hold mainly in areas where the profits from export crops such as sugar, rice, and tobacco offset the high purchase price of slaves and where a warm climate permitted year-round work. Elsewhere European masters and employers found various ways to acquire and manage European laborers.

A Spectrum of Control

Slavery was the most oppressive extreme in a spectrum of practices designed to exert control over workers and relieve the problems caused by the easy availability of land and the high cost of labor. Most colonial laborers were, in some measure, unfree (see Table 3.1). One-half to two-thirds of all white immigrants to the English colonies arrived as indentured servants, bound by contract to serve masters for a period of years. But indentured servants, though less costly than slaves, carried too high a price for farmers who raised crops mainly for subsistence. Servants could be found in every colony, but were most common in the Chesapeake and, to a lesser extent, in Pennsylvania, where they worked for farmers producing export crops.

Slaves replaced white indentured servants in Chesapeake tobacco fields during the eighteenth century. Masters continued to import servants for a while to fill skilled jobs but in time trained slaves to fill those positions. Thus, by the middle of the eighteenth century, white servitude, although it still flourished in some places, was in decline as a dominant labor system.

Eighteenth-century Chesapeake planters also availed themselves of another unfree labor source: transported English convicts. Lawmakers in England saw transportation as a way of getting rid of criminals who might otherwise be executed. Between 1718 and 1775, nearly 50,000 convicts were sent to the colonies, 80 percent of whom ended up in the Chesapeake. Most were young, lower-class males forced by economic hardship to

Read the **Document**   **Robert Beverly, A Virginian Describes the Difference between Servants and Slaves from *The History of Virginia in Four Parts* (1722)**

TABLE 3.1   PREDOMINANT COLONIAL LABOR SYSTEMS, 1750

	Colony	Labor System
New England	Massachusetts	Family farms
	Connecticut	Family farms
	New Hampshire	Family farms
	Rhode Island	Family farms
Middle Colonies	New York	Family farms, tenancy
	Pennsylvania and Delaware	Indentured servitude, tenancy, family farms
	New Jersey	Family farms, tenancy
South	Maryland	Slavery
	Virginia	Slavery
	North Carolina	Family farms, slavery
	South Carolina	Slavery

turn to crime. A few convicts eventually prospered in America, but most faced lives as miserable as those they had known in England.

An arrangement similar to indentured servitude—the **redemptioner** system—brought many families, especially from German provinces, to the colonies in the eighteenth century. Instead of negotiating contracts for service before leaving Europe, as indentured servants did, redemptioners promised to redeem, or pay, the costs of passage on arrival in America. They often paid part of the fare before sailing. If they could not raise the rest soon after landing, the ship captain who brought them sold them into servitude. The length of their service depended on how much they still owed.

Purchasing slaves, servants, or convicts did not make sense for everyone. Colonists who owned undeveloped land faced many tasks—cutting trees, clearing fields, building fences and barns—that brought no immediate profit. Rather than buy expensive laborers to accomplish these ends, landowners rented undeveloped tracts to families without property. Both tenants and landlords benefited from this arrangement. Tenants enjoyed greater independence than servants and could save toward the purchase of their own farms. The landlord secured the labor necessary to transform his property into a working farm, thus increasing the land's value. He also received an annual rent payment and eventually profited from selling the land, often to the tenant family who had rented it.

Merchants eager to develop New England's fisheries devised other means to fill their labor needs. Because it was fairly easy to get a farm, few New Englanders took on the risky job of fishing. Moreover, few could afford the necessary equipment, including boats, provisions, and salt (used for preserving fish). Merchants recruited fishermen by advancing credit to coastal villagers so that they could outfit their own boats. Many fishermen ran up such large debts that they were obliged to continue supplying fish to their creditors, whether they wanted to or not.

In the northern colonies, the same conditions that made men reluctant to become fishermen deterred them from becoming farm laborers, except perhaps for high wages. Paying high wages, however, or the high cost of servants or slaves was difficult for New Englanders with farms that produced no export crops and could not be worked during cold winter months. So northern farmers turned to the cheapest and most dependable workers they could find—their children.

Children as young as 5 or 6 years old began with simple tasks and moved on to more complex work as they grew older. By the time they were in their late teens, girls knew how to run households, and boys knew how to farm. Fathers used their ownership of property to prolong the time their sons worked for them. Young men could

redemptioner Similar to an indentured servant, except that a redemptioner signed a labor contract in America rather than in Europe.

From Then to Now
Slavery and Human Trafficking

A frican slavery first became part of American history in 1619, when twenty slaves arrived in Virginia. By 1770, slaves could be found in every colony, and their numbers had grown to half a million people. The American Revolution, with its rhetoric of freedom, challenged slavery but did not end it. It took almost another century, the Civil War, and the passage of the Thirteenth Amendment in 1865 to make slavery unconstitutional. When Brazil emancipated its slaves in 1888, it seemed as though this oppressive institution had finally disappeared from the Americas.

But that was not the case. In 2012, the International Labour Office estimated that 20.9 million people around the world were victims of human trafficking, or modern-day slavery. Coerced into jobs they cannot leave without facing financial or even physical hardships, many are compelled to work for little or no pay in agriculture, construction, domestic work, and manufacturing. Nearly a quarter of the victims suffer from sexual exploitation. Over half of the people enmeshed in this modern forced-labor system are female, and nearly a quarter of them are children. Victims of human trafficking can be found in every part of the world, including the United States.

In March 2012, President Barack Obama created an interagency task force to address the problem of human trafficking. In so doing, he cited the passage of the Emancipation Proclamation in 1863 as a key example of America's commitment to the cause of freedom. It will, however, take a concerted effort on a global scale to end a practice that for centuries has proven to be so difficult to eradicate.

Question for Discussion

- Why has it been so hard for societies to end the practice of human trafficking?

Marchand d'Esclaves de Gorée

Slave merchants such as this Frenchman often negotiated with African traders to acquire slaves to ship to the New World.

In 2012, Secretary of State Hillary Clinton and other members of the government task force met to coordinate U.S. efforts to combat human trafficking.

not marry until they could set up their own households and relied on their fathers to provide them with land to do so. Fathers often waited until their sons were in their mid-twenties, compelling them until then to invest their labor in the paternal estate.

New European Immigrants

European immigrants flooded into America in the seventeenth and eighteenth centuries. Nearly 250,000 Scots-Irish people—descendants of Protestant Scots who had settled in northern Ireland in the sixteenth and seventeenth centuries—came to the colonies after 1718, when their landlords raised rents to intolerable levels. Tens of thousands of immigrants arrived from Scotland during the same period, some seeking

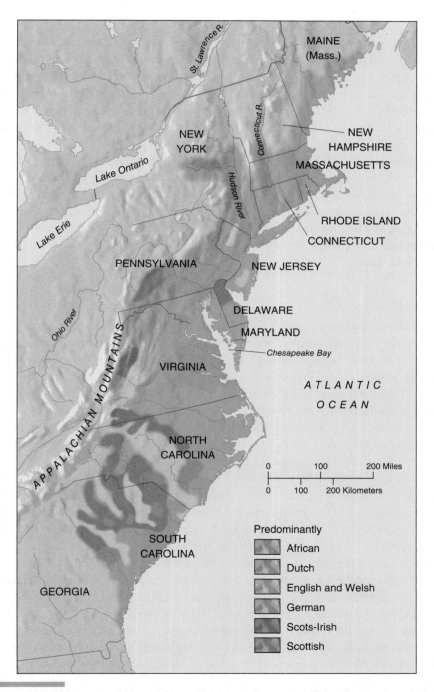

MAP 3.2 ETHNIC DISTRIBUTION OF SETTLER POPULATION IN BRITISH MAINLAND COLONIES, c. 1755 Settlers of different ethnic backgrounds tended to concentrate in certain areas. Only New Englanders were predominantly English, while Africans dominated in the Chesapeake Tidewater and South Carolina. German, Scottish, and Scots-Irish immigrants often settled in the backcountry.

economic improvement and some sent as punishment for rebellions against the king in 1715 and 1745. Thousands of Irish Catholics arrived as servants, redemptioners, and convicts.

Continental Europe contributed another stream of emigrants. Many German Protestants left the Rhine Valley, where war, economic hardship, and religious persecution had brought misery. Most traveled eastward, to Russia and Prussia, but perhaps as many as 100,000 journeyed to the colonies. French Protestants (known as Huguenots) began emigrating after 1685, when their faith was made illegal in France. Swiss Protestants likewise fled religious persecution. Even a few Poles, Greeks, Italians, and Jews reached the colonies in the eighteenth century.

Many emigrants responded to pamphlets and newspaper articles that exaggerated the bright prospects of life in America. Others studied more realistic accounts from friends and relatives who had already emigrated. Landowners sent agents to port towns to recruit new arrivals to become tenants, often on generous terms.

Streams of emigrants flowed to places where land was cheap and labor most in demand (see Map 3.2). Few went to New England, where descendants of the first settlers occupied the best land. They also avoided areas where slavery predominated—the Chesapeake Tidewater and lowland South Carolina—in favor of the foothills of the Appalachian Mountains, from western Pennsylvania to the Carolinas. There, one emigrant declared, a "poor man that will incline to work may have the value of his labour."

This observation, though partly true, did not tell the whole story. Any person who came as a servant, redemptioner, or tenant learned that his master or landlord received much of "the value of his labour." Not all emigrants realized their dreams of becoming independent landowners. The scarcity of labor in the colonies led as easily to the exploitation of white workers as of slaves and Indians. Even so, for many people facing bleak prospects in Europe, the chance that emigration might bring prosperity was too tempting to ignore.

Conclusion

The ocean voyage that brought Olaudah Equiano across the Atlantic carried him to a land containing a strikingly diverse mosaic of peoples and communities. Along the St. Lawrence River lay Kahnawake, a village of Mohawks and Abenakis who had adopted Catholicism and French ways under Jesuit instruction. In New England towns, farmers tilled fields that their Puritan grandparents had cleared. German immigrants populated the isolated Pennsylvania settlement of Ephrata. The hundred or so slaves on Robert Carter's Virginia plantation gathered on Sunday evenings to nurture ties of community with songs and dances, while the master cultivated his very different sense of community with the neighboring planters. In North Carolina, Swiss settlers rebuilt the coastal town of New Bern, destroyed during the Tuscarora War, while 100 miles farther west, Scottish emigrants cleared land for farms near present-day Fayetteville. In Mose, Florida, near St. Augustine, runaway slaves built a town under the protection of Spanish soldiers. Far to the west, the Spanish, *mestizo,* and Pueblo residents of Santa Fe warily reestablished ties broken during the Pueblo Revolt.

For some of the people in these communities, emigration and settlement had brought opportunity; for others, including Equiano and his fellow Africans, it brought oppression. English and other European settlers became landowners in unprecedented numbers and adopted new ways to control laborers. For many, though not all, European immigrants, the colonies offered the chance for economic improvement. Yet at the same time, millions of African slaves suffered under the most repressive colonial labor regime, fighting its grip whenever possible. Slave communities testified to African Americans' assertion of their humanity in the face of a system that sought to deny it. And even as Europeans and Africans adapted to different New World circumstances, Indians struggled with the consequences of disease, trade, religious conversion, settlement, and warfare resulting from European immigration.

As the eighteenth century wore on, the North American colonies attracted more attention from their home countries. Spain, France, and England recognized the colonies' growing economic power and strove to harness it to block the expansion of their rivals. Everywhere the effort to strengthen imperial ties created ambivalence among colonists. Because the English settlers were by far the most numerous, their responses were the most pronounced. As they saw more clearly the differences between themselves and England itself, some colonists began to defend their distinctive habits, while others tried more insistently than ever to imitate English ways. The tension between new and old had characterized colonial development from the start. What made the eighteenth century distinctive were the many ways in which the tensions worked themselves out.

For Suggested Readings go to MyHistoryLab.

Chapter Review

Indians and Europeans

3.1 How did the different patterns of interaction between Europeans and native peoples shape colonial development in the Spanish borderlands, New France, and the English colonies? p. 59

Where Europeans mainly sought to trade with Indians, as in New France, intercultural relations were fairly peaceful. Spanish efforts to convert Indians to Catholicism produced more contention. The greatest conflict occurred in the English colonies, where settlers soon outnumbered Indians and proceeded to dispossess them of their land.

Africans and Europeans

3.2 How and why did race-based slavery develop in British North America? p. 68

A tremendous need for labor, especially to produce staple crops such as sugar, tobacco, and rice, led English colonists to acquire African slaves. Appearing first in the West Indies, slavery spread to Carolina and the Chesapeake. White colonists' racial prejudice led to a system that deprived slaves of the most basic human rights.

European Laborers in Early America

3.3 What methods did Europeans employ to acquire and manage labor in colonial America? p. 78

Slavery was the most oppressive extreme in a spectrum of labor practices. Colonists also used legal contracts to control indentured servants, redemptioners, and English convict laborers. Some landowners rented land to tenant farmers. Especially in New England, fathers used their control of land to compel their sons to work for them.

Timeline

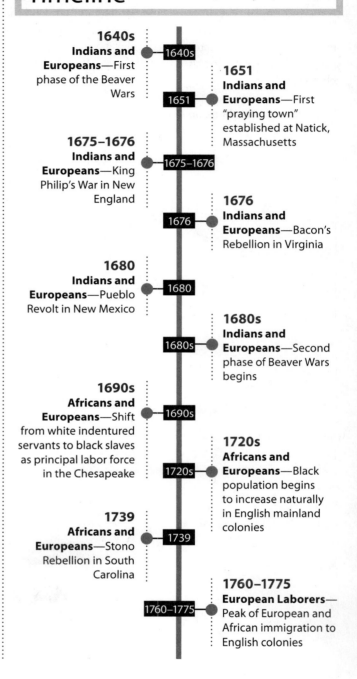

1640s
Indians and Europeans—First phase of the Beaver Wars
`1640s`

`1651`
1651
Indians and Europeans—First "praying town" established at Natick, Massachusetts

1675–1676
Indians and Europeans—King Philip's War in New England
`1675–1676`

`1676`
1676
Indians and Europeans—Bacon's Rebellion in Virginia

1680
Indians and Europeans—Pueblo Revolt in New Mexico
`1680`

`1680s`
1680s
Indians and Europeans—Second phase of Beaver Wars begins

1690s
Africans and Europeans—Shift from white indentured servants to black slaves as principal labor force in the Chesapeake
`1690s`

`1720s`
1720s
Africans and Europeans—Black population begins to increase naturally in English mainland colonies

1739
Africans and Europeans—Stono Rebellion in South Carolina
`1739`

`1760–1775`
1760–1775
European Laborers—Peak of European and African immigration to English colonies

4 English Colonies in an Age of Empire
1660s–1763

One American Journey

A Letter from George Washington

Virginia 26th April 1763

Mr. Lawrence

Be pleased to send me a genteel sute of Cloaths made of superfine broad Cloth handsomely chosen; I shou[l]d have Inclosed [for] you my measure but in a general way they are so badly taken here that I am convinced it wou[l]d be of very little service; I wou[l]d have you therefore take measure of a Gentleman who wears well made Cloaths of the following size—to wit—Six feet high & proportionably made; if any thing rather Slender than thick for a Person of that highth with pretty long arms & thighs—You will take care to make the Breeches longer than those you sent me last, & I wou[l]d have you keep the measure of the Cloaths you now make by you and if any alteration is required, in my next [letter] it shall be pointed out. Mr Cary will pay your Bill—& I am Sir Yr Very H[um]ble Serv[an]t . . .

George Washington

W. W. Abbot and Dorothy Twohig, eds., *The Papers of George Washington,* Colonial Series, vol. 7 (Charlottesville, 1990).

Susanna Truax, the subject of this 1730 portrait, was evidently a member of a prosperous colonial family eager to display its imported English wares. Note the tea table at the left of the picture, topped with a teapot, cup and saucer, and sugar bowl—symbols of the Truax family's genteel style of life.

LEARNING OBJECTIVES

4.1 ((How did trade policy shape the relationship between Britain and the colonies? p. 87

4.2 ((In what ways did colonial culture change in the eighteenth century? p. 93

4.3 ((How did the Glorious Revolution affect colonial politics? p. 99

4.4 ((In what ways did British, Spanish, and French expansion into new territories reflect patterns established earlier? p. 103

4.5 ((How significant were imperial wars in shaping colonial society? Which one had the most important impact on North America? p. 107

((**Listen to Chapter 4 on MyHistoryLab**

Learn about some key topics related to this chapter with the *MyHistoryLab Video Series: Key Topics in U.S. History.*

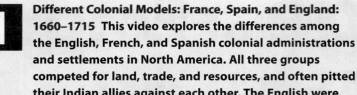

1 **Different Colonial Models: France, Spain, and England: 1660–1715** This video explores the differences among the English, French, and Spanish colonial administrations and settlements in North America. All three groups competed for land, trade, and resources, and often pitted their Indian allies against each other. The English were most successful in establishing a facsimile of English society in the New World. Spain and France focused on extracting natural resources and relied on missionaries, soldiers, and traders rather than settlers to stake their claims. These differences, in turn, shaped the interactions of all three groups with Native American peoples.

 Watch on **MyHistoryLab**

France and the American Interior New France, which, at its height, encompassed Canada and much of the interior of North America, is the focus of this video. The French established their principal settlements along such waterways as the St. Lawrence River, the Great Lakes, and the Mississippi River. The French sought trade, mainly in furs, rather than extensive settlement. The French formed alliances with Native American partners and coexisted with them to ensure the safety of French missionaries and traders.

Watch on **MyHistoryLab**

3 **The Spanish Empire on the Defensive** Although the Kingdom of Spain was the first to establish a vast empire in the New World, it found itself competing with other European powers, especially as England and France displaced it as the leading power in Europe. This video charts the decline of New Spain, which lacked a mercantile tradition and focused on extracting precious metals and enslaving the Native American populations under its control rather than developing a more sustainable form of colonization.

 Watch on **MyHistoryLab**

England's Empire Takes Shape After Charles II and his successors ascended the throne, England adopted a somewhat more centralized colonial policy that focused on trade regulation. This video examines this sea change in imperial policy, as Britain's navy increasingly dominated the Atlantic. It also examines other changes, including the rapid population growth of eighteenth-century British North America and the frontier settlement pressures that displaced Native Americans and put Great Britain in conflict with its rival, France. **4**

Watch on **MyHistoryLab**

Personal Journeys Online

- Eliza Lucas Pinckney, *Letterbook,* 1742. Description of a South Carolina plantation mistress's day.

- Alexander Hamilton, *Itinerarium,* 1744. Description of sociability in eighteenth-century Philadelphia.

- Nathan Cole, "Spiritual Travels," October 23, 1740. A Connecticut farmer hears George Whitefield preach.

George Washington, along with a few dozen other privileged Virginians, had traveled to Williamsburg for a visit that mixed politics, business, and pleasure. Like Washington, these men had come to the capital to represent their respective counties in the House of Burgesses. When not engaged in government business, they attended to private affairs. Washington was surely not the only one to take the opportunity to write to his London tailor and order the fashionable clothing that advertised his status as a gentleman.

April 1763 marked the fourth time Washington had gone to Williamsburg to take his seat in the legislature. Just 31 years old in that year, he had recently married Martha Custis, a wealthy widow, and inherited his older brother's plantation at Mount Vernon. Washington already owned more land than most English gentlemen. With land and wealth to support his ambitions, he wanted to live, look, and behave like an English country gentleman.

Throughout British America, colonists who had achieved wealth and power tried, like Washington, to imitate the habits and manners of the English gentry. Their aspirations testified to important developments in the eighteenth century. Prosperity and the demand of a growing population for English products tied the colonies ever more tightly into a trade network centered on the imperial metropolis, London. The flow of goods and information between Britain and America fueled the desires of Washington and other successful colonists for acceptance as transatlantic members of the British elite.

These developments in Great Britain's American colonies brought them to the attention of European statesmen, who increasingly factored North America into their calculations. Parliament devised legislation to channel colonial products into British ports and away from European competitors. Spain and France viewed the economic growth and geographic expansion of British North America as a threat to their own colonial possessions, and responded by augmenting their own territorial claims. With expansion came conflict, and with conflict, war: a series of four imperial wars, which themselves became powerful engines of change in the New World.

Economic Development and Imperial Trade in the British Colonies

4.1 How did trade policy shape the relationship between Britain and the colonies?

England's greatest assets in its competition with other European nations were a dynamic economy and a sophisticated financial system that put commerce at the service of the state. British leaders came to see colonies as indispensable to the nation's economic welfare. Colonies supplied raw materials unavailable in the mother country, and colonists and Indians provided a healthy market for British manufactured goods.

As the eighteenth century progressed, colonial economies grew in tandem with the economy of Great Britain. Parliament knitted the colonies into an empire with commercial legislation, while British merchants traded with and extended credit to growing numbers of colonial merchants and planters. Over time, these developments joined the economies of the colonies and the mother country into a vast transatlantic system.

The Regulation of Trade

To improve its competitive position in transatlantic trade, England adopted a policy of **mercantilism**. The goal was to achieve a favorable balance of trade within the empire as a whole, with exports exceeding imports. Colonies played a crucial role, since they supplied commodities that British consumers would otherwise have to purchase from foreign competitors. Certain colonial products, such as tobacco or rice, could also be exported to foreign markets, further improving the balance of trade. Between 1651 and 1733, Parliament passed four types of mercantilist regulations to put this policy into action (see Table 4.1).

The first type of regulation aimed at ending Dutch dominance in overseas trade. Beginning with the Navigation Act of 1651, all trade in the empire had to be conducted in English or colonial ships, with crews of which at least half were Englishmen

mercantilism Economic system whereby the government intervenes in the economy for the purpose of increasing national wealth.

TABLE 4.1 BRITISH IMPERIAL TRADE REGULATIONS, 1651–1733

Name of Act	Key Features
Navigation Act of 1651	Aimed to eliminate Dutch competition in overseas trade
	Required most goods to be carried in English or colonial ships
	Required crews to be at least half English
Navigation Act of 1660	Required all colonial trade to be carried in English ships
	Required master and three-quarters of crew to be English
	Created list of enumerated goods, such as tobacco and sugar, that could be shipped only to England or another English colony
Staple Act of 1663	Required products from Europe, Asia, and Africa to be landed in England before being shipped to the colonies
Plantation Duty Act of 1673	Attempted to reduce smuggling
	Required captains of colonial ships to post bond that they would deliver enumerated goods to England or pay the "plantation duty" that would be owed in England
Navigation Act of 1696	Plugged loopholes in earlier laws
	Created vice-admiralty courts in colonies to enforce trade regulations
Woolens Act of 1699	Forbade export of woolen cloth made in the colonies, to prevent competition with English producers
Hat Act of 1732	Prohibited export of colony-made hats
Molasses Act of 1733	Placed high tax on French West Indian and other foreign molasses imported into colonies to encourage importation of British West Indian molasses

or colonists. The act stimulated rapid growth in England's merchant marine and New England's shipping industry, which soon became the most profitable sector of New England's economy.

The second type of legislation stipulated that certain colonial goods, called **enumerated products**, could be shipped only to England or to another English colony. These goods initially included tobacco, sugar, and indigo; other products, such as rice, were added later. These laws also required European goods to pass through England before they could be shipped to the colonies. When these goods entered English ports, they were taxed, making them more expensive and encouraging colonists to buy English-made items.

The third and fourth types of regulations further enhanced the advantage of English manufacturers who produced for the colonial market. Parliament subsidized certain goods, including linen and gunpowder, to allow manufacturers to undersell European competitors in the colonies. Other laws protected English manufacturers from colonial competition by prohibiting colonists from manufacturing wool, felt hats, and iron on a large scale.

England's commercial goals were largely achieved. The Dutch eventually lost their preeminence in the Atlantic trade. Colonial trade helped the English economy to grow and contributed to London's emergence as Western Europe's largest city. Colonists enjoyed protected markets for their staple crops and low prices on English imports. Colonial merchants took full advantage of commercial opportunities within the empire.

Occasionally, merchants evaded these laws by smuggling. Customs officials, sent over from England beginning in the 1670s, were hard-pressed to stop them. Smuggling tended to increase in wartime; the risks may have been higher, but so too were profits. Without the support of colonial authorities (some of whom might have been involved in illicit trade themselves), customs officials struggled to enforce parliamentary regulations.

The Colonial Export Trade and the Spirit of Enterprise

By the eighteenth century, the Atlantic had become a busy thoroughfare of international commerce (see Map 4.1). British and colonial vessels carried goods and people from Great Britain, continental Europe, and West Africa to the colonies and returned tons of raw materials to the Old World. At the heart of Anglo-American trade lay the highly profitable commerce in staple crops, most of which were produced by slave labor.

enumerated products Items produced in the colonies and enumerated in acts of Parliament that could be legally shipped from the colony of origin only to specified locations.

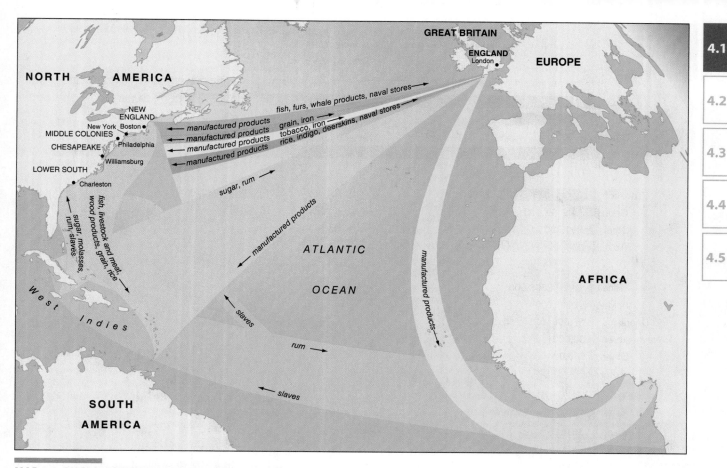

MAP 4.1 ANGLO-AMERICAN TRANSATLANTIC COMMERCE By the eighteenth century, Great Britain and its colonies were enmeshed in a complex web of trade. Britain exchanged manufactured goods for colonial raw materials, while Africa provided the enslaved laborers who produced the most valuable colonial crops.

West Indian sugar far surpassed all other colonial products in importance (see Figure 4.1). By the late 1760s, the value of sugar exports reached almost £4 million per year—nearly 50 percent more than the total value of all other exports from British American colonies.

Tobacco from the Chesapeake colonies was the second most valuable staple crop. Nearly 90 percent of the crop was re-exported to continental Europe. Persistent low prices, however, led many tobacco planters to sow some of their land with wheat after about 1750. This change lessened their dependence on tobacco and allowed them to take advantage of the strong demand for flour in southern Europe and the West Indies.

Exports of rice and indigo (a plant that produced a blue dye used in cloth manufacture) enriched many South Carolina planters. Parliament encouraged indigo production by granting subsidies to growers and placing stiff taxes on foreign indigo. It also subsidized colonial production of naval stores—such as tar, pitch, and turpentine—to reduce England's dependence on Swedish suppliers. The export of these items made up an important part of the North and South Carolina economies.

Wheat exports from the Middle Colonies boomed in the eighteenth century. Since farmers in Great Britain grew enough wheat to supply the domestic market, there was little demand there for colonial flour. But there was a strong market for it in the West Indies and Europe, particularly when poor harvests and warfare disrupted European supplies.

New England had no staple crop and produced little for export. The region's merchants nevertheless prospered by carrying other colonies' goods to market. By 1770, New England's earnings from shipping fees, freight charges, and insurance exceeded the total value of its own exports.

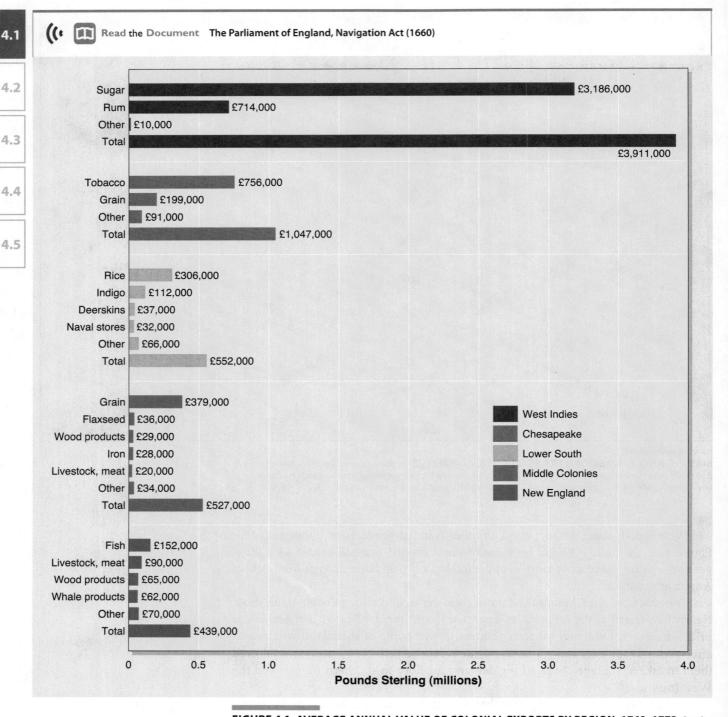

FIGURE 4.1 AVERAGE ANNUAL VALUE OF COLONIAL EXPORTS BY REGION, 1768–1772 Staple crops—especially sugar—produced by slave labor were the most valuable items exported from Britain's North American colonies.

SOURCE: From THE ECONOMY OF BRITISH AMERICA, 1607–1789 by John J. McClusker and Russell R. Menard. Published for the Omohundro Institute of Early American History and Culture. Copyright © 1985 by the University of North Carolina Press. www.uncpress.unc.edu.

New England merchants also strengthened trade links to the West Indies that had first been forged in the 1650s. By the mid-eighteenth century, more than half of all New England exports went to the islands. Merchants accepted molasses and other sugar by-products in payment, bringing them back to New England to be distilled into cheap rum. Traders then carried rum to Africa to exchange for slaves. Although British merchants dominated the African slave trade, New Englanders also profited. Fewer than 10 percent of New England's population were slaves, but because New Englanders trafficked in human cargo and provisioned the West Indies, their commercial economy nonetheless depended on slavery.

Scenes like this were common in the dockyards at Deptford and other parts of eighteenth-century London. Boxes and barrels of English goods were loaded aboard sailing ships that returned months later with sugar, tobacco, rice, and other products from every part of England's worldwide empire.

The Import Trade and Ties of Credit

By the late 1760s, more than £4 million worth of British manufactured goods flowed into the colonies each year. This import trade satisfied a demand for items that could not be produced—at least not cheaply—in North America.

Imported weapons, woolen cloth, knives, and jewelry often made their way into Indian villages. Indians were discerning customers and rejected goods not made to their liking. Native leaders sometimes acquired imported goods for exchange with allies as well as for their own use.

The colonists' even heavier consumption of manufactures was vital to British overseas commerce. In terms of value, colonists imported more goods than they exported. This imbalance was remedied in good part by colonial earnings from shipping fees and payments from the British government for colonial military expenses.

British merchants extended credit to colonists on generous terms so they could buy British products. Major tobacco planters welcomed the easy credit that British merchants provided. These merchants marketed the planters' tobacco and supplied them with English goods, charging the costs of purchase and transportation against the profits they expected the next year's crop to bring.

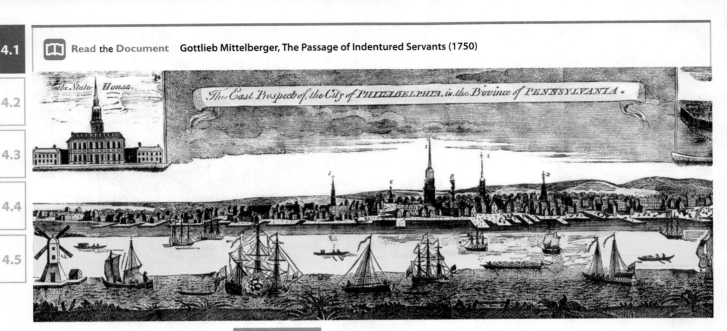

The East Prospect of the City of PHILADELPHIA, in the Province of PENNSYLVANIA.

By the 1750s, Philadelphia had become one of colonial America's most populous cities and a thriving center of trade.

Easy credit let planters indulge themselves with English goods, and many sank into debt. When trade was brisk and tobacco prices high, no one worried. But when tobacco prices dropped or an international crisis made overseas trading risky, creditors called in the debts owed to them. At such times, colonial debtors realized how much they (like the Indians involved in European trade) depended on goods and credit supplied by distant merchants.

Becoming More Like Britain: The Growth of Cities and Inequality

As colonial commerce grew, so did colonial cities—the connecting points in the economic network tying the colonies to London and other British ports. Boston, New York, Philadelphia, and Charleston were as large as many British provincial towns. Only about 5 percent of all mainland colonists lived in cities, but the influence of urban centers far outweighed their size.

All colonial cities (like Britain's major ones) were seaports. New York, then as now, had one of the world's finest harbors, from which it conducted a profitable commerce. Cities provided such amenities as inns, taverns, coffeehouses, theaters, and social clubs. Their populations were diverse in ethnic origin and religion. In addition, the African American population in the northern colonies tended to live in cities. By 1750, slaves made up 20 percent of New York City's population, about 10 percent of Philadelphia's, and nearly 9 percent of Boston's.

Artisans in Colonial Cities.   Colonial cities had higher proportions of artisans than did rural villages. Many of them labored at trades directly related to overseas commerce, such as shipbuilding or ropemaking. Others produced pottery, furniture, paper, glassware, and iron tools.

Colonial manufacturing took place in workshops often attached to artisans' houses. Artisans managed a workforce consisting of their wives and children, along with journeymen or apprentices. Usually teenage boys, apprentices contracted to work for a master for four to seven years in order to learn the "mysteries" of his craft. Like indentured servants, they received no wages but worked for food, clothing, shelter, and a small payment at the end of their service. Once an apprentice finished his training, he became a journeyman, working for a master but now earning wages and saving to set up his own shop.

Many artisans flourished in colonial cities, but prosperity was by no means guaranteed. In Philadelphia, skilled artisans typically earned enough for a modest subsistence. Yet workers at less skilled crafts often made only a bare living, and ordinary laborers faced seasonal unemployment.

Cities like Philadelphia, New York, and Charleston provided opportunities for some women to support themselves with craft work. Mary Wallace and Clementia Ferguson, for instance, stitched fashionable hats and dresses for New York customers. Nonetheless, even in cities, women's options were limited. Most employed women were widows striving to maintain a family business until sons grew old enough to take over.

The Growing Gap between Rich and Poor. Wherever colonists engaged heavily in commerce—in cities or on plantations—the gap between rich and poor widened during the eighteenth century. In 1687, the richest 10 percent of Boston's residents owned 46 percent of the taxable property in the town; by 1771, the top tenth held 63 percent of the taxable wealth. Similar changes occurred in Philadelphia. In South Carolina and the Chesapeake, many planters added to the already substantial holdings in land and slaves that they had inherited. It became increasingly difficult for newcomers to enter their ranks. At the same time, the colonies' growing reliance on slave labor—especially in the South—created a sizable class of impoverished people denied the chance to better their condition. By 1770, slaves, for whom America was anything but a land of opportunity, constituted one out of five residents of the British colonies.

To address the growing problem of poverty among white colonists, cities built workhouses, and towns collected funds for poor relief in greater amounts than ever before. Many poor people were aged or ill, without families to help them. Able-bodied workers forced to accept public relief usually owed their misfortune to temporary downturns in the economy.

Even in the worst of times, no more than one out of ten white colonists (mainly city dwellers) depended on public assistance. For free black people who were unemployed and denied public relief, conditions were far worse. A Pennsylvania law went so far as to allow them to be enslaved. Bad as it was, the problem of poverty among white colonists had not reached anything like the levels seen in Britain. As much as one-third of England's population regularly received relief, and the numbers swelled during hard times. Eighteenth-century white colonists, on average, enjoyed a higher standard of living than most British residents or other Europeans. So long as land was available—even if one had to move to the edges of settlement to get it—colonists could at least eke out a bare subsistence, and many did much better.

The Transformation of Culture

4.2   In what ways did colonial culture change in the eighteenth century?

Despite the convergence of British and colonial society, many influential settlers worried that America remained culturally inferior to Great Britain. During the eighteenth century, some prosperous colonists strove to overcome this provincial sense of inferiority. They built grand houses and filled them with imported goods, cultivated what they took to be the manners of the British gentry, and followed British and European intellectual developments. Some colonial gentlemen even reshaped their religious beliefs to reflect European notions that God played only an indirect role in human affairs.

These elite aspirations, however, were not shared by all settlers. Most colonists, although they might purchase a few imported goods, had little interest in copying the manners of the British elite, and few of them altered their spiritual beliefs to fit European

The Governor's Palace in Williamsburg, Virginia, completed in 1722, was one of the grandest and most expensive dwellings in the colony.

patterns. Indeed, familiar religious practices flourished in eighteenth-century America, and when a tremendous revival swept through the colonies beginning in the 1730s, religion occupied center stage in American life.

Goods and Houses

Eighteenth-century Americans imported more manufactured products from England with every passing year. This practice did not simply reflect the growth of the colonial population, for the rate at which Americans bought British goods exceeded the rate of population increase. Colonists owned more goods, often of better quality, than their parents and grandparents had possessed.

In the less secure economic climate of the seventeenth century, colonists had limited their purchases of goods, investing instead in land to pass on to their children. But by the eighteenth century, prosperous colonists felt secure enough to buy goods to make their lives more comfortable. Tea drinking became more common, and colonial women in particular might host tea parties as a sign of their status and genteel manners. Colonists acquired goods to advertise their more refined style of life.

Prosperous colonists built grand houses where they lived in greater comfort than ever before. By the 1730s, numerous southern planters had built "great houses" while others transformed older houses into more stylish residences. Washington extensively remodeled Mount Vernon, adding a second story and extra wings to create a home fit for a gentleman. In the northern colonies, merchants built the most impressive houses, often following architectural pattern books imported from England.

These houses were not only larger but also different in design from the homes of less affluent colonists. Most settlers lived in one- or two-room dwellings and thus cooked, ate, and slept in the same chamber. But the owners of great houses could devote rooms to specialized uses, such as kitchens and private bedrooms.

Prosperous colonists did not build such homes merely to advertise their wealth. They wanted to create the proper setting for a refined way of life, emulating the English gentry in their country estates and London townhouses. But they knew that the true measure of their gentility lay not just in where they lived and what they owned but in how they behaved.

Shaping Minds and Manners

Colonists knew that the manners of British gentlefolk set them apart from ordinary people. Many Americans therefore imported "courtesy books" containing the rules of polite behavior. These publications advised would-be gentlemen on how to show regard for social rank, practice personal cleanliness, and respect other people's feelings. Many colonists subscribed to English journals such as the *Tatler* and the *Spectator* that printed articles describing good manners.

Women, too, cultivated genteel manners. In Charleston, South Carolina, and other colonial cities, girls' boarding schools advertised instruction in "Polite Education." Female pupils received only the rudiments of intellectual training in reading, writing, and arithmetic, for it was assumed that women had little need of such accomplishments. The private schools' curricula instead focused on French, music, dancing, and fancy needlework. These were skills that advertised girls' genteel status and prepared them for married lives as elite ladies.

Some people expressed their gentility through more intellectual pursuits, taking advantage of the relatively high literacy rates among white colonists. In New England, where settlers placed great emphasis on Bible study, about 70 percent of men and 45 percent of women could read and write. Only a third of men in the southern colonies, and even fewer women, could read and write, but even these literacy rates were higher than among Britain's general population. Eighteenth-century colonists enjoyed greater access to printed material than ever before. In 1704, the *Boston News-Letter* became the first continuously published newspaper in British America. By the 1760s nearly every colony had a regularly published newspaper, and booksellers opened shops in several cities. Prominent colonists began to participate in a transatlantic world of ideas.

Educated colonists were especially interested in the new ideas that characterized what has been called the **Age of Enlightenment**. The European thinkers of the Enlightenment drew inspiration from recent advances in science that suggested that the universe operated according to natural laws that human reason could discover. The hallmark of Enlightenment thought was a belief in the power of human reason to improve the human condition.

This optimistic worldview marked a profound intellectual shift. Enlightenment thinkers rejected earlier ideas about God's unknowable will and continued intervention in human and natural events. They instead assigned God a less active role as the creator of the universe, who had set the world running according to predictable laws, and then let nature and humans shape events. Such ideas inspired a growing international community of scholars to try to discover the laws of nature and to work toward human progress.

Colonial intellectuals sought membership in this scholarly community. A few of them—the Reverend Cotton Mather of Massachusetts, William Byrd, Benjamin Franklin—gained election to the Royal Society, the most prestigious learned society in England. Most of their scholarly contributions were unimpressive, but Franklin achieved genuine intellectual prominence. His experiments with a kite proved that lightning was electricity (a natural force whose properties were poorly understood at the time) and gained him an international reputation.

If Franklin's career embodied the Enlightenment ideal of the rational exploration of nature's laws, it also revealed the limited impact of Enlightenment thought in colonial America. Only a few prosperous and educated colonists could afford such intellectual pursuits. Franklin came from humble origins—his father was a maker of candles and soap—but his success as a printer allowed him to retire from business at the age of 42. Only then did he purchase the equipment for his electrical discoveries and have the leisure time to begin his scientific work. Franklin's equipment—and leisure—were as much badges of gentlemanly status as George Washington's London-made suit.

Most colonists remained ignorant of scientific advances and Enlightenment ideas, having little leisure to devote to literature and polite conversation. When they found

Age of Enlightenment Major intellectual movement occurring in Western Europe in the late seventeenth and early eighteenth centuries.

Read the Document Benjamin Franklin, Observations Concerning the Increase
of Mankind, Peopling Countries, etc. (1751)

By the time he was in his forties, Benjamin Franklin had already achieved considerable fame as an author, scientist, and inventor.

time to read, they picked up not a courtesy book or the *Spectator* but the Bible, which was the best-selling book of the colonial era. Religion principally shaped the way in which they viewed the world and explained human and natural events.

Colonial Religion and the Great Awakening

Church steeples dominated the skylines of colonial cities. By the 1750s, Boston and New York each had eighteen churches, and Philadelphia boasted twenty. Churches and meetinghouses likewise dominated country towns. Often the largest and finest buildings in the community, they bore witness to the diverse and thriving condition of religion in America.

In every New England colony except Rhode Island, the Puritan (or Congregationalist) faith was the established religion. Congregational churches in the region, headed by ministers trained at Harvard College and Yale (founded in 1701), served the majority of colonists, who were required to pay taxes to support them. Though proud of the Puritan tradition that had inspired New England's origins, ministers and believers nonetheless had to adapt to changing social and religious conditions.

The principal adaptation consisted of a move away from strict requirements for church membership. In order to keep their churches pure, New England's founders had required prospective members to give convincing evidence that they had experienced a spiritual conversion before they could receive communion and have their children baptized. By the 1660s, however, fewer colonists sought admission under such strict standards, which left them and their unbaptized children outside the church. To address this problem, the clergy in 1662 adopted the **Halfway Covenant**. This allowed adults who had been baptized (because their parents were church members), but who had not themselves experienced conversion, to have their own children baptized.

Halfway Covenant Plan adopted in 1662 by New England clergy to deal with problem of declining church membership, allowing children of baptized parents to be baptized whether or not their parents had experienced conversion.

Congregational churches also had to accept a measure of religious toleration in New England. In 1691, Massachusetts received a royal charter granting "liberty of Conscience" to all Protestants, bringing the colony in line with England's religious policy. At the same time, some Congregationalist preachers began emphasizing personal piety and good works in their sermons, ideas usually associated with Anglicanism. These changes indicated a shift away from the Puritan exclusiveness of New England's early years.

In the South, the established Church of England consolidated its authority in the early eighteenth century but never exerted effective control over spiritual life. Many a parson in England could ride from one side of his parish to the other in an hour, but Anglican clergymen in the southern colonies served parishes that were vast and sparsely settled. Ministers also found that influential planters, accustomed to running parishes when preachers were unavailable, resisted their efforts to take control of churches. Aware that the planters' taxes paid their salaries, many ministers found it easiest simply to preach and behave in ways that offered the least offense. Frontier regions often lacked Anglican churches and clergymen altogether. In such places, dissenting religious groups, such as Presbyterians, Quakers, and Baptists, gained followers among people neglected by the Anglican establishment.

No established church dominated in the Middle Colonies of New York, New Jersey, and Pennsylvania. The region's ethnically diverse population and William Penn's policy of religious toleration guaranteed that a multitude of groups would compete for followers. Yet religion flourished in the Middle Colonies. By the middle of the eighteenth century, the region had more congregations per capita than even New England.

Groups such as the Quakers and the Mennonites, who did not have specially trained ministers, easily formed new congregations in response to local demand. Lutheran and German Reformed churches, however, required European-educated clergy, who were always scarce. Pious laymen held worship services in their homes even as they sent urgent letters overseas begging for ordained ministers. When more Lutheran and Reformed clergy arrived in the 1740s and 1750s, they sometimes discovered, as Anglican preachers did in the South, that laymen balked at relinquishing control of the churches.

Bewildering spiritual diversity, relentless religious competition, and a comparatively weak Anglican Church all distinguished the colonies from Britain. Yet in one important way, religious developments during the middle third of the eighteenth century drew the colonies closer to Britain. A great transatlantic religious revival, originating in Scotland and England, first touched the Middle Colonies in the 1730s. In 1740–1745, it struck the northern colonies with the force of a hurricane, and in the 1760s, the last phase of the revival spread through the South. America had never seen anything like this immense revival, which came to be called the **Great Awakening**.

By 1730, Presbyterians in Pennsylvania had split into factions over such issues as the disciplining of church members and the requirement that licensed ministers have university degrees. What began as a dispute among clergymen eventually blossomed into a broader challenge to religious authority. That challenge gained momentum in late 1739, when one of the most charismatic evangelists of the century, George Whitefield, arrived in the colonies from England.

Great Awakening Tremendous religious revival in colonial America striking first in the Middle Colonies and New England in the 1740s and then spreading to the southern colonies.

Read the Document   Jonathan Edwards, "Some Thoughts Concerning the Present Revival of Religion in New England" (1742)

During George Whitefield's tour of the American colonies in 1739–1741, the famous revivalist minister often preached to large crowds gathered outdoors to hear one of his powerful sermons.

Whitefield, an Anglican minister, had experienced an intense religious conversion while he was still a university student. Already famous in Britain as a preacher of great emotional fervor, he embarked on a tour of the colonies in the winter of 1739–1740. As soon as Whitefield landed in Delaware, his admirers whipped up local enthusiasm, ensuring that he would preach to huge crowds in Pennsylvania and New Jersey. Whitefield then moved on to New England, where some communities had already experienced local awakenings. In 1734–1735, for instance, the Congregationalist minister Jonathan Edwards had led a revival in Northampton, Massachusetts, urging his parishioners to recognize their sinfulness and describing hell in such a terrifying way that many despaired of salvation.

Whitefield's tour through the colonies knitted these scattered local revivals into the Great Awakening. Crowds gathered in city squares and open fields to listen to his sermons. Whitefield exhorted his audiences to examine their souls for evidence of the "indwelling of Christ" that would indicate that they were saved. He criticized other ministers for emphasizing good works and "head-knowledge" instead of the emotional side of religion.

Whitefield's open-air sermons scarcely resembled the colonists' accustomed form of worship. Settlers normally gathered with family and neighbors in church for formal, structured services. They sat in pews assigned on the basis of social status, reinforcing standards of order and community hierarchy. But Whitefield's sermons were highly dramatic performances. He preached for hours in a booming voice, gesturing wildly and sometimes even dissolving in tears. Thousands of strangers, jostling in crowds that often outnumbered the populations of several villages put together, wept along with him.

In the wake of Whitefield's visits, Benjamin Franklin noted, "it seem'd as if all the World were growing Religious." Revivals and mass conversions often followed his appearances, to the happy astonishment of local clergy. But their approval evaporated when more extreme revivalists appeared. Officials who valued civic order tried to silence such extremists by passing laws that prohibited them from preaching in a town without the local minister's permission.

Disputes between individuals converted in the revivals—called **New Lights**—and those who were not (Old Lights) split churches. New Lights insisted, as the separatist founders of Plymouth once had, that they could not remain in churches with sinful members and unconverted ministers and so left to form new churches.

The Awakening came late to the southern colonies, but it was there, in the 1760s, that it produced perhaps its greatest controversy. Many southern converts became Baptists, combining religious criticism of the Anglicans with condemnation of the wealthy planters' way of life. Plainly dressed Baptists criticized the rich clothes, drinking, gambling, and pride of Virginia's gentry. The planters, in turn, viewed the Baptists as dangerous people who could not "meet a man upon the road, but they must ram a text of Scripture down his throat." Most of all, they hated the Baptists for their willingness to preach to slaves.

Although the revivals themselves gradually waned, the Great Awakening had a lasting impact on colonial society. In addition to introducing colonists to a fervent evangelicalism, it forged new links between Great Britain and the colonies. Evangelical ministers on both sides of the Atlantic exchanged correspondence. Periodicals such as the *Christian History* informed British and American subscribers of advances in true religion throughout the empire.

The revivals also brought newcomers into Christian congregations. Chesapeake slaves responded to the evangelists' message and—often contrary to the intent of the white preachers—drew lessons about the equality of humankind. A few black preachers circulated in the slave quarters, spreading the message of salvation and freedom. The impact of revivalism on Indians was less dramatic, but still significant. Evangelicals enjoyed their greatest success in small Native American communities, whose inhabitants were attracted to a less formal style of preaching, particularly in New England. Native converts often urged fellow Indians to heed the Christian message of self-discipline, not to emulate English colonists, but to revitalize villages beset by alcoholism and other problems linked to European domination.

The Awakening did not greatly increase women's church membership, since women already constituted majorities in many congregations. But by emphasizing the emotional power of Christianity, revivals accorded greater legitimacy to what was thought to be women's more sensitive temperament.

Everywhere, the New Light challenge to established ministers and churches undermined habits of deference to authority. Revivalists urged colonists to think for themselves in choosing which church to join, and not just to conform to what the rest of the community did. As their churches fractured, colonists faced more choices than ever before in their religious lives.

The exercise of religious choice also influenced political behavior. Voters noticed whether candidates for office were New or Old Lights and cast their ballots for men on their own side. Tactics first used to mobilize religious groups—such as organizing committees and writing petitions and letters—also proved useful for political activities. The Awakening thus fostered greater political awareness and participation among colonists.

New Lights People who experienced conversion during the revivals of the Great Awakening.

4.1

4.2

4.3

4.4

4.5

The Colonial Political World

4.3   How did the Glorious Revolution affect colonial politics?

The political legacy of the Great Awakening—particularly the emphasis on individual choice and resistance to authority—corresponded to developments in the colonial political world. For most of the seventeenth century, ties within the empire developed from trade rather than governance. But as America grew in wealth and population, king and Parliament sought to manage colonial affairs more directly.

The Dominion of New England and the Limits of British Control

Before 1650, England made little attempt to exert centralized control in North America. Each colony more or less governed itself, and most political activity occurred at the town or county level. Busy with the routines of daily life, most colonists devoted little time, and even less interest, to politics.

When Charles II became king in 1660, he initially showed little interest in the colonies except as sources of land and government offices with which he could reward his supporters. Charles's brother James, the duke of York, envisioned a more tightly controlled empire. He encouraged Charles to appoint military officers with strong ties of loyalty to him as royal governors. In 1675, James convinced Charles to create the Lords of Trade, a committee of the Privy Council (the group of nobles who served as royal advisers), to oversee colonial affairs.

When James II became king in 1685, the whole character of the empire abruptly changed. Seeking to transform it into something much more susceptible to England's control, James set out to reorganize it along the lines of Spain's empire, combining the colonies into three or four large provinces. He appointed powerful governors to carry out policies that he himself would formulate.

James began in the north, creating the **Dominion of New England** out of eight previously separate colonies stretching from Maine (then part of Massachusetts) to New Jersey. He chose Sir Edmund Andros, a former army officer, to govern the vast region with an appointive council but no elective assembly.

Events in England ultimately sealed the fate of the Dominion. For years, English Protestants had worried about James's absolutist governing style and his conversion to Catholicism. Their fears increased in 1688, when the queen bore a son to carry on a Catholic line of succession. Parliament's leaders invited Mary, James's Protestant daughter from his first marriage, and her husband, William of Orange, the stadtholder of the Netherlands, to take over the throne. In November 1688, William landed in England and gained the support of most of the English army. In December, James fled to France, ending a bloodless coup known as the **Glorious Revolution**.

Bostonians overthrew Andros the following April and shipped him back to England. Massachusetts colonists hoped that their original charter of 1629 would be reinstated, but a new one was issued in 1691. It made several important changes. Massachusetts now included the formerly separate Plymouth Colony as well as Maine. Its colonists no longer elected their governor, who would instead be appointed by the monarch. Voters no longer had to be church members, and religious toleration was extended to all Protestants. The new charter ended exclusive Puritan control in Massachusetts but also restored political stability.

The impact of the Glorious Revolution in other colonies likewise reflected local conditions. In New York, after Andros's deputy left, Jacob Leisler, a rich merchant and militia captain, gained power and ruled in a dictatorial fashion. Too slow in relinquishing power to the new royal governor in 1691, Leisler was arrested for treason and executed. In Maryland, Protestants used the occasion of William and Mary's accession to the throne to lobby for the end of the Catholic proprietorship. They were partly successful. The Calvert family lost its governing powers but retained rights to vast quantities of land. The Anglican Church became the established faith, and Catholics were barred from public office.

Salem Witchcraft

In Massachusetts, during the three years between Andros's overthrow and the arrival of a royal governor in 1692, the colony lacked a legally established government. In this atmosphere of uncertainty, an outbreak of accusations of witchcraft in Salem grew to unprecedented proportions. Over the years, New Englanders had executed a dozen or

Dominion of New England James II's failed plan of 1686 to combine eight northern colonies into a single large province, to be governed by a royal appointee with no elective assembly.

Glorious Revolution Bloodless revolt that occurred in England in 1688 when parliamentary leaders invited William of Orange, a Protestant, to assume the English throne.

From Then to Now
The Diversity of American Religious Life

I n 2007, researchers contacted more than 35,000 Americans, asking them to describe themselves in terms of their religious identification. The resulting data revealed the astonishing diversity of the religious environment in the modern United States. While just over three-quarters of the respondents identified themselves as Christians, they claimed affiliation with more than twenty-five different denominations. The non-Christians comprised an equally diverse group, including about twenty additional faiths. These data reflect the enduring religious diversity that has characterized American life. Such diversity dated from the earliest years of colonization and increased during the eighteenth century when the Great Awakening sparked factional splits in churches and the creation of new congregations. The influx of Irish, Scots, and German immigrants also added new faiths to the colonial religious mixture.

By the time of the Revolution, religious diversity had become so firmly entrenched in American life that people feared the establishment of a single state church far more than the consequences of having a multiplicity of faiths within a single nation. This fear helped inspire the First Amendment to the Constitution, with its guarantee of the "free exercise" of religion and its prohibition of any national religious establishment. The First Amendment, in turn, created the conditions under which religious diversity could flourish in America from the founding era to the present day.

Question for Discussion

- How have immigration patterns in America shaped religious diversity?

The construction of a Hindu temple in Malibu, California, testifies to the persistence of religious diversity in modern America.

The predominance of church steeples in this engraving of colonial New York's skyline testifies to the religious vitality of the city.

so accused witches, usually older women. But in the winter of 1691–1692, when several young girls of Salem experienced fits and other strange behavior, hundreds of settlers were accused of witchcraft and nineteen were hanged.

Salem's crisis occurred against a backdrop of local economic change, which created friction between agrarian and more commercial parts of the town. Recent conflicts with Indians on the nearby frontier also made many colonists worry that God was punishing them for their sins. Moreover, the town had recently experienced bitter controversy over the appointment of a minister. All of these tensions contributed to the frenzy of witchcraft accusations.

The Legacy of the Glorious Revolution

At the time of the Glorious Revolution, colonists rejected James II, not English authority in general. Their motives largely reflected powerful anti-Catholic sentiment. William's firm Protestantism reassured them, and most colonists assumed that life would return to normal. But the Glorious Revolution in England and the demise of the Dominion had long-lasting effects that shaped political life in England and America for years to come.

In England, the Glorious Revolution signaled a return to political stability after years of upheaval. English people celebrated the preservation of their rights from the threat of a tyrannical king. In 1689, Parliament passed the Bill of Rights, which justified James's ouster and bound future monarchs to abide by the rule of law. They could not suspend statutes, collect taxes, or engage in foreign wars without Parliament's consent, or maintain a standing army in peacetime. Parliamentary elections and meetings would follow a regular schedule. In sum, Parliament claimed to be the Crown's equal partner in governing England.

Colonists, too, celebrated the vindication of their rights as Englishmen. They believed that their successful resistance to Andros confirmed that their membership in the empire was founded on voluntary allegiance, not forced submission to the mother country. Observing the similarity between Parliament and the colonial assemblies, they concluded that their own legislatures had a critical role in governance and in the protection of their rights and liberties. On both sides of the Atlantic, representative government had triumphed.

In fact, Parliament claimed full authority over the colonies and did not recognize their assemblies as its equal. For more than a half century, however, it did not vigorously assert that authority. In addition, William and his immediate successors lacked James's compulsion to control the colonies.

During the early eighteenth century, Parliament and royal ministers confined their attention to matters of trade and military defense and otherwise left the colonies on their own. This mild imperial rule, later called the era of "salutary neglect," allowed the colonies to grow in wealth, population, and self-government. It also encouraged colonists to assume equality with the English as members of the empire.

Diverging Politics in the Colonies and Great Britain

British people on both sides of the Atlantic believed that politics ought to reflect social organization. They often compared the state to a family. Just as fathers naturally headed families, adult men led societies. In particular, adult male property holders, who enjoyed economic independence, claimed the right to vote and hold office. Women (who generally could not own property), propertyless men, and slaves had no political role because they, like children, were subordinate to the authority of others. Their dependence on husbands, fathers, masters, or employers—who could influence their political decisions—rendered them incapable of exercising freedom of choice.

Eighteenth-century people also believed that government should reflect society's hierarchical organization. In Britain, this idea was embodied in the monarchy and Parliament. The Crown, of course, represented the interests of the royal family. Parliament represented society's two main divisions: the aristocracy in the House of Lords and the common people in the House of Commons. Americans shared the view that government should mirror social hierarchies but found it much more difficult to put the idea into practice.

American society grew closer to the British model during the eighteenth century but was never identical to it. Thus, its political structure would never fully mirror that of Britain. One obvious difference was that America lacked an aristocracy. Elite colonists were often just two or three generations removed from humble beginnings. Hence the acute anxiety that inspired George Washington and other colonial gentlemen to seek refinement, to gain the automatic recognition that Britain's elites enjoyed.

In both Britain and America, land ownership was the prerequisite for political participation, because it freed people from dependence on others and gave them a stake in society. In Britain, this requirement sharply limited participation. By the mid-eighteenth century, one-tenth of all English heads of households owned all the country's land, and thus only a correspondingly tiny proportion of men could vote. Landholding in America, however, was much more widespread. A majority of white male farmers eventually owned the land they tilled, and in most colonies, 50 to 75 percent of white men were eligible to vote.

Distinctive social conditions in Britain and America also gave rise to different notions of political representation. Electoral districts for Parliament came in a confusing mixture of shapes, reflecting their status in past centuries. Once-important towns sent representatives on the basis of their former prominence. At the same time, rapidly growing cities, such as Manchester, lacked any representation at all. Most people in Britain, however, accepted the idea of **virtual representation**, which held that representatives served the interests of the nation as a whole, not just the locality from which they came. They maintained that since the colonists held interests in common with British people at home, they were virtually represented in Parliament, just like Manchester's residents.

Since the founding of their colonies, however, Americans had experienced **actual representation** and believed that elected representatives should be directly responsive to local interests. The Americans' experience with actual representation made them extremely skeptical of Parliament's claims to virtual representation. For the first half of the eighteenth century, however, Parliament did not press this claim, and the tensions between the two ideas remained latent.

The most direct political confrontations between Britain and the colonies instead focused on the role of colonial governors. In every colony except Connecticut and Rhode Island (where voters chose the executive), either the king or the proprietor appointed the governor. The governors' interests thus lay with their British patrons and not the colonies. More important, governors exercised great power over the colonial assemblies. Governors could veto laws passed by the assemblies, delay legislative sessions, and dissolve the assemblies at will.

In practice, several conditions hampered governors' efforts to exercise their legal authority. Many arrived with detailed instructions on how to govern, which limited their ability to negotiate with colonists over sensitive issues. Governors controlled few offices or other prizes to use as patronage to buy the allegiance of their opponents. And in several colonies, including Massachusetts and New York, governors relied on the assemblies to appropriate the money for their salaries.

Despite concerns about the power of governors, most colonists accepted the loose and sometimes contradictory political ties of empire. They saw their connections to Britain as voluntary, based on common identity and rights. So long as Parliament treated them as partners in empire and refrained from ruling by coercion, colonists could celebrate British government as "the most perfect combination of human powers in society . . . for the preservation of liberty and the production of happiness."

By the middle of the eighteenth century, the blessings of British government extended to more colonists than ever before. The population of British America grew rapidly and spread out over vast amounts of land. The expansion of British settlement, in turn, alarmed other European powers. Both Spain and France launched new settlements as the competition for the continent entered a new and volatile phase.

virtual representation The notion that parliamentary members represented the interests of the nation as a whole, not those of the particular district that elected them.

actual representation The practice whereby elected representatives normally reside in their districts and are directly responsive to local interests.

4.1

4.2

4.3

4.4

4.5

Expanding Empires

4.4 In what ways did British, Spanish, and French expansion into new territories reflect patterns established earlier?

During the first half of the eighteenth century, England, Spain, and France enlarged their North American holdings according to patterns established during the previous century. England's empire expanded in tandem with the unrelenting growth of its colonial population. Spain and France still relied on missionaries, soldiers, and traders to stake their claims to American territory. Over time, these empires came into closer contact with one another, intensifying the competition for land, trade, resources, and Indian allies (see Map 4.2).

📖 **Read the Document**   Jean Baptiste Colbert, "Mercantilism: Dissertation on Alliances" (1669)

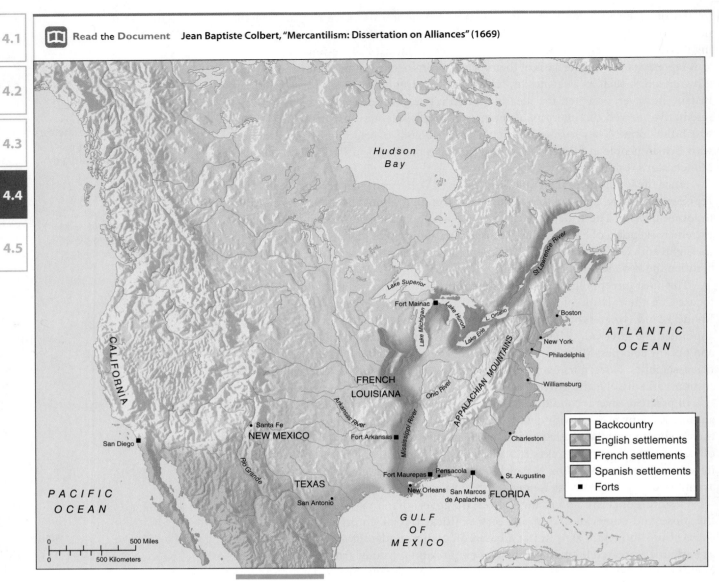

MAP 4.2 EXPANDING SETTLEMENT, c. 1750 Imperial rivalries drove Spain, France, and England to expand their North American empires in the mid-eighteenth century. Once again, this sparked conflict with native peoples as well as with European competitors.

British Colonists in the Backcountry

Population growth in eighteenth-century British North America was truly astonishing. The non-Indian population in the mainland colonies numbered about 260,000 in 1700; by 1760, it had increased to more than 1.5 million (see Figure 4.2). Much of this growth stemmed from natural increase.

Immigration also boosted the population. Thousands of Scots-Irish and German settlers, in addition to thousands of African slaves, helped the population of the Lower South increase at nearly twice the rate of New England, which attracted few immigrants (and therefore remained the most thoroughly English of all colonial regions). By 1770, Pennsylvania had 240,000 settlers, ten times the number it had in 1710.

Most of the coast from Maine to Georgia was settled by 1760, forcing new immigrants to move inland. The most dramatic expansion occurred in the foothills and valleys of the Appalachian Mountains from Pennsylvania to Georgia, a region known as the backcountry.

Between 1730 and 1770, nearly a quarter of a million German, Scots-Irish, and English colonists entered the backcountry. They mainly raised crops and livestock for

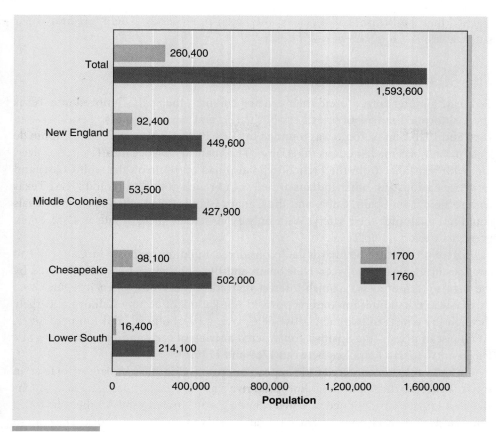

FIGURE 4.2 POPULATION GROWTH IN BRITISH MAINLAND COLONIES, 1700–1760 Both natural increase and immigration contributed to a staggering rate of population growth in British North America. Some colonists predicted that Americans would soon outnumber Britain's inhabitants—a possibility that greatly concerned British officials.

SOURCE: From THE ECONOMY OF BRITISH AMERICA, 1607–1789 by John J. McClusker and Russell R. Menard. Published for the Omohundro Institute of Early American History and Culture. Copyright © 1985 by the University of North Carolina Press. www.uncpress.unc.edu.

subsistence on small, isolated farms. Community life developed slowly, because many backcountry settlers moved frequently and a surplus of men among the first settlers delayed the formation of families.

Contemporary observers, especially eastern elites, derided the crudeness of frontier life. Their disparaging comments reflected emerging tensions between backcountry settlements and older seacoast communities. Many eastern planters acquired vast tracts of western land with the intent of selling it to these "crude" settlers. Their interests collided with those of many backcountry settlers, including squatters who occupied the land without acquiring legal title in the hope that their labor in clearing farms would establish their property rights.

Backcountry settlers often complained that the rich eastern planters who dominated the colonial legislatures ignored western demands for adequate representation. They also argued that the crudeness of frontier life was only temporary. Perhaps the best measure of their desire to resemble eastern planters was the spread of slaveholding in the backcountry.

Tensions grew throughout the backcountry as colonists encroached on Indian lands. Indians moving to avoid friction with whites frequently encroached on lands claimed by other tribes—particularly those of the Iroquois Confederacy—leading to conflict among native peoples.

Even where British settlers had not yet appeared, English and Scottish traders could often be found aggressively pursuing trade with the Indians. Spanish and French observers feared this commercial expansion even more than the movement of settlers. Knowing that the Indians viewed trade as a counterpart to military alliance, they worried that the British, with cheaper and better trade goods, would lure away their native allies.

The Spanish in Texas and California

To create a buffer zone around their existing colonies, the Spanish moved into Texas and California. Franciscan priests established several missions in east Texas between 1690 and 1720. San Antonio was founded in 1718; its fortified chapel, San Antonio de Valero, later became famous as the Alamo. The Spanish advance into Texas, however, met with resistance from the French (who also had outposts on the Gulf Coast) and from the Caddos and other Indians armed with French guns. Efforts to fill east Texas with settlers from Spain, Cuba, and the Canary Islands failed when Spanish officials could not guarantee their safety. With only 1,800 settlers there as late as 1742, Spain exerted a weak hold on Texas.

Sixteenth-century Spaniards had considered building outposts in California to supply ships traveling between New Spain and the Philippines but were deterred by the region's remoteness. Spanish interest revived in the 1760s, when it seemed that Russia, which had built fur-trading posts in Alaska, might occupy California. Largely through the efforts of two men—José de Gálvez, a royal official, and Junípero Serra, a Franciscan priest—the Spanish constructed a string of forts and missions from San Diego north to San Francisco between 1769 and 1776.

Initially they encountered little opposition from California's Indians, who lived in small, scattered villages. With no European rivals nearby, the Spanish erected an extensive mission system designed to convert and educate Indians and set them to work. Thousands of native laborers farmed irrigated fields and tended livestock. They did so under extremely harsh conditions. According to one observer, Christian Indians who settled at the missions endured a fate "worse than that of slaves." The Spanish worked them hard and maintained them in overcrowded, unsanitary dwellings. Native women suffered from sexual exploitation by Spanish soldiers. Epidemics of European diseases swept through the Indian population. Signs of native resistance met with quick and cruel punishment.

Spain's empire grew, even as it weakened, during the eighteenth century. Its scattered holdings north of the Rio Grande functioned as colonies of another colony—New Spain—shielding it from foreign incursions. From the beginning, Spain's vision of empire had rested not on extensive settlement but on subjugation of native peoples in order to control their labor. After 1700, the limitations of this coercive approach to empire became apparent.

The French along the Mississippi and in Louisiana

French expansion followed the major waterways of the St. Lawrence River, the Great Lakes, and the Mississippi. Concerned about defending scattered settlements, French officials forbade colonists to move into the interior. But colonists went anyway, building six villages along the Mississippi in a place they called the *pays des Illinois.*

The first Illinois settlers were independent fur traders (*coureurs de bois,* or "woods runners"). Many found Christian Indian wives and farmed the rich lands along the river. The settlers, using the labor of their families and of black and Indian slaves, produced surpluses of wheat, corn, and livestock to feed the growing population of New Orleans and the lower Mississippi Valley.

French Louisiana contained a remarkably diverse population of Indian peoples, French soldiers and settlers, and German immigrants, as well as African slaves, who by the 1730s outnumbered the European colonists. Discouraged by the lack of profits, French officials and merchants neglected Louisiana, and even Catholic missionaries failed to establish a strong presence. Significant European emigration to Louisiana essentially ceased after the 1720s.

But the French approach to empire in Louisiana as in Canada depended more on Indian alliances than on settlement. Louisiana's principal allies were the Choctaws, whom one military official called "the bulwark of the colony." The Choctaws and other native allies offered trade and military assistance in return for guns, trade goods, French help in fighting British raiders seeking Indian slaves, and occasional French mediation of Indian disputes.

French expansion along the Mississippi Valley drove a wedge between Florida and Spain's other mainland colonies; it also blocked the westward movement of English settlers. But France's enlarged empire was only as strong as the Indian alliances on which it rested. Preserving good relations was expensive, however, requiring the constant exchange of diplomatic gifts and trade goods. When France ordered Louisiana officials to limit expenses and reduce Indian gifts in 1745, the officials objected that the Choctaws "would ask for nothing better than to have such pretexts in order to resort to the English."

The fear of losing Indian favor preoccupied officials in 1745 because at that moment France's empire in America consisted of two disconnected pieces: New France, centered in the St. Lawrence Valley and the Great Lakes basin, and Louisiana, stretching from New Orleans to the *pays des Illinois*. Between them lay 1,000 miles of wilderness, through which only one thoroughfare passed—the Ohio River. For decades, communication between the two parts of France's North American empire had posed no problem because Indians in the Ohio Valley allowed the French free passage through their lands. If that policy ended, however, France's New World empire would be dangerously divided.

A Century of Warfare

4.5 How significant were imperial wars in shaping colonial society? Which one had the most important impact on North America?

The expansion of empires in North America reflected the policies of European states locked in a relentless competition for power and wealth. From the time of the Glorious Revolution, English foreign policy aimed at limiting the expansion of French influence. This, in turn, resulted in a series of four wars. As the eighteenth century wore on, the conflicts between the two countries increasingly involved their American colonies as well as Spain and its colonies. The outcome of each of the wars in America depended no less on the participation of colonists and Indians than on the policies and strategies of the European powers. The conclusion of the final conflict signaled a dramatic shift in North American history (see Table 4.2).

TABLE 4.2 THE COLONIAL WARS, 1689–1763

Name in the Colonies	European Name and Dates	Dates in America	Results for Britain
King William's War	War of the League of Augsburg, 1688–1697	1689–1697	Reestablished balance of power between England and France
Queen Anne's War	War of the Spanish Succession, 1702–1714	1702–1713	Britain acquired Nova Scotia
King George's War	War of the Austrian Succession, 1739–1748	1744–1748	Britain returned Louisbourg to France British settlers began moving westward Weakening of Iroquois neutrality
French and Indian War	Seven Years' War, 1756–1763	1754–1763	Britain acquired Canada and all French territory east of Mississippi Britain gained Florida from Spain

King William's War The first Anglo-French conflict in North America (1689–1697), the American phase of Europe's War of the League of Augsburg.

Queen Anne's War American phase (1702–1713) of Europe's War of the Spanish Succession.

Country, or "Real Whig," ideology Strain of thought first appearing in England in the late seventeenth century in response to the growth of governmental power and a national debt. Main ideas stressed the threat to personal liberty posed by a standing army and high taxes and emphasized the need for property holders to retain the right to consent to taxation.

Grand Settlement of 1701 Separate peace treaties negotiated by Iroquois diplomats at Montreal and Albany that marked the beginning of Iroquois neutrality in conflicts between the French and the British in North America.

Imperial Conflict and the Establishment of an American Balance of Power, 1689–1738

When he became king of England in 1688, the Dutch Protestant William of Orange was already fighting the War of the League of Augsburg against France's Catholic king, Louis XIV. Almost immediately, William brought England into the conflict. The war lasted until 1697 and ended, as most European wars of this period did, in a negotiated peace that reestablished the balance of power. Little territory changed hands, either in this war or in the War of the Spanish Succession (1702–1714), which followed it.

In America, these two imperial wars—known to British colonists as **King William's War** and **Queen Anne's War**, after the monarchs on the throne at the time—ended with equal indecisiveness. Neither war caused more than marginal changes for the colonies in North America. Both had profound effects, however, on the English state and the Iroquois League.

All European states of the eighteenth century financed their wars by borrowing. But the English were the first to realize that wartime debts did not necessarily have to be repaid during the following peace. The government instead created a funded debt. Having borrowed heavily from large joint-stock corporations, the government used tax revenues to pay the interest on the loans but not to pay off the loans themselves.

As the debt grew larger, more taxes were necessary to pay interest on it. Taxes also rose to pay for a powerful navy and standing army. When the treasury created a larger bureaucracy to collect taxes, many Englishmen grew nervous. Their anxiety emerged as a strain of thought known as **Country, or "Real Whig," ideology**. Country ideology stressed the threats that a standing army and a powerful state posed to personal liberty. It also emphasized the dangers of taxation to property rights and the need for property holders to retain their right to consent to taxation. Real Whig politicians publicized their fears but could not stop the growth of the state.

In America, the first two imperial wars transformed the role of the Iroquois League. During King William's War, the Iroquois allied with the English, but received little help from them when the French and their Indian allies attacked Iroquois villages. By 1700, the Iroquois League had suffered such horrendous losses—perhaps a quarter of the population had died from causes related to the war—that its leaders sought an alternative to direct alliance with the English.

With the **Grand Settlement of 1701**, the Iroquois adopted a policy of neutrality with regard to the French and British empires. Their goal was to refrain from alliances with either European power and instead maneuver between them. The strategic location of the Iroquois between New France and the English colonies allowed them to serve as a geographical and diplomatic buffer. Neutral Iroquois diplomats could play the English against the French, gaining favors from one side in return for promises not to ally with the other. This neutralist policy ensured that for nearly fifty years, neither Britain nor France could gain ascendancy in North America.

Iroquois neutrality offered benefits to the Europeans as well as the Indians. The British began to negotiate with them for land. The Iroquois claimed sovereignty over much of the country west of the Middle and Chesapeake colonies. To smooth relations with the British, the Iroquois sold them land formerly occupied by Delawares and Susquehannocks. These transactions helped to satisfy the colonists' land hunger and to enrich the Iroquois League.

Meanwhile a neutral Iroquois League claiming control over the Ohio Valley and blocking British access across the Appalachian Mountains helped the French protect the strategic corridor that linked Canada and Louisiana. If the British ever established a permanent presence in the Ohio Valley, however, the Iroquois would cease to be of use to the French. The Iroquois remained reasonably effective at keeping the British out of the valley until the late 1740s. The next European war, however, altered these circumstances.

King George's War Shifts the Balance, 1744–1748

The third confrontation between Britain and France in Europe, the War of the Austrian Succession—**King George's War** to the British colonists—began as a small war between Britain and Spain in 1739. Its immediate cause was British attempts to poach on trade to Spain's Caribbean colonies. But in 1744, France joined in the war against Britain and conflict once again erupted in North America.

New Englanders saw a chance to attack Canada. Their target was the great fortress of Louisbourg on Cape Breton Island, a naval base that dominated the Gulf of St. Lawrence. An expedition from Massachusetts and Connecticut, supported by a squadron of Royal Navy warships, captured Louisbourg in 1745. This success cut Canada off from French reinforcement. English forces should now have been able to conquer New France.

Instead, politically influential merchants in Albany, New York, chose to continue their profitable trade with the enemy across Lake Champlain, enabling Canada to hold out until the end of the war. When the peace treaty was signed in 1748, Britain, which had fared badly in the European fighting, returned Louisbourg to France. This diplomatic adjustment, routine by European standards, shocked New Englanders. At the same time, New York's illegal trade with the enemy appalled British administrators. They began thinking of ways to prevent such independent behavior in any future war.

King George's War furnished an equal share of shocks for New France, which had suffered more than in any previous conflict. Even before the war's end, traders from Pennsylvania began moving west to buy furs from Indians who had once traded with the French. The movements of these traders, along with the appearance of Virginians in the Ohio Valley after 1748, gravely concerned the French.

In 1749, the governor general of New France set out to assert direct control over the region by building a series of forts from Lake Erie to the Forks of the Ohio (where the Monongahela and Allegheny rivers meet to form the Ohio River). This decision signaled the end of France's commitment to Iroquois neutrality. The Iroquois now found themselves trapped between empires edging closer to confrontation in the Ohio Valley.

The Iroquois, in fact, had never exerted direct power in the Ohio Country. Their control instead depended on their ability to dominate the peoples who actually lived there—western Senecas, as well as Delawares and Shawnees, in theory Iroquois dependents. The appearance of English traders in the valley offering goods on better terms than the French or the Iroquois had ever provided undermined Iroquois dominance.

The Ohio Valley Indians increasingly pursued their own independent course. One spur to their disaffection from the Iroquois was the 1744 **Treaty of Lancaster**, by which Iroquois chiefs had sold the rights to trade at the Forks of the Ohio to Virginia land speculators. The Virginians assumed that these trading rights included the right to acquire land for eventual sale to settlers. The Ohio Valley Indians found this situation intolerable, as did the French. When, in 1754, the government of Virginia sent out a small body of soldiers under Lieutenant Colonel George Washington to protect Virginia's claim to the Forks of the Ohio, the French struck back.

The French and Indian War, 1754–1763: A Decisive Victory

In April 1754, French soldiers overwhelmed a group of Virginians who had been building a small fort at the Forks of the Ohio. They erected a much larger fort of their own, Fort Duquesne, on the spot. The French intended to follow up by similarly ousting Washington's weak, untrained troops, who had encamped farther up the Monongahela River. However, at the end of May, Washington's men killed or captured all but one member of a small French reconnaissance party. The French decided to teach the

King George's War The third Anglo-French war in North America (1744–1748), part of the European conflict known as the War of the Austrian Succession.

Treaty of Lancaster Negotiation in 1744 whereby Iroquois chiefs sold Virginia land speculators the right to trade at the Forks of the Ohio.

Albany Plan of Union Plan put forward in 1754 calling for an intercolonial union to manage defense and Indian affairs. The plan was rejected by participants at the Albany Congress.

French and Indian War The last of the Anglo-French colonial wars (1754–1763) and the first in which fighting began in North America. The war ended with France's defeat.

Virginians a lesson. On July 3, they attacked Washington at Fort Necessity, forcing him to surrender.

Even before this news reached Britain, imperial officials worried that the Iroquois might ally with the French. Britain ordered New York's governor to convene an intercolonial meeting in Albany—known as the Albany Congress—to discuss matters with the Iroquois. Several prominent colonists, including Governor William Shirley of Massachusetts and Benjamin Franklin, took advantage of the occasion to put forward the **Albany Plan of Union**, which called for an intercolonial union to coordinate defense, levy taxes, and regulate Indian affairs. But the colonies, too suspicious of one another to see their common interests, rejected the Albany Plan, which British officials also disliked. Meanwhile, events in the west took a turn for the worse.

The French expulsion of the Virginians left the Indians of the region, Delawares and Shawnees, with no choice but to ally with the French in what came to be called the **French and Indian War** (see Map 4.3). Soon French and Indian attacks fell like hammer blows on backcountry settlements from Pennsylvania to the Carolinas. The Iroquois tried to remain neutral, but their neutrality no longer mattered. Europeans were at last contending directly for control of the Ohio Country.

The French and Indian War blazed in America for two years before it erupted as a fourth Anglo-French war in Europe in 1756. Known in Europe as the Seven Years' War (1756–1763), it involved fighting in the Caribbean, Africa, India, and the Philippine Islands as well as in Europe and North America. It was unlike any other eighteenth-century conflict, not only in its immense scope and expense but also in its decisive outcome.

The war had two phases in North America—1754 to 1758 and 1758 through 1760. During the first phase, the French enjoyed a string of successes as they followed their proven strategy—guerrilla war conducted by Indian allies acting with Canadian soldiers.

The first full campaign of the war, in 1755, saw not only the British colonial frontiers collapsing in terror but also a notable defeat inflicted on the troops Britain had dispatched under the command of Major General Edward Braddock to attack Fort Duquesne. Braddock's defeat set the tone for virtually every military engagement of the next three years and opened a period of demoralization and internal conflict in the British colonies.

Britain responded to Braddock's defeat by sending a new commander in chief with more trained British soldiers. The new commander, Lord Loudoun, insisted on managing every aspect of the war effort, not only directing the campaigns but also dictating the amount of support, in men and money, that each colony would provide. Colonial soldiers, who had volunteered to serve under their own officers, objected to Loudoun's command. By the end of 1757, a year of disastrous military campaigns, colonial assemblies were also refusing to cooperate.

Britain's aim had been to "rationalize" the war by making it conform to European professional military standards. This approach required soldiers to advance in formation in the face of massed musket fire without breaking rank. Few colonial volunteers met professional standards, and few colonists thought them necessary, especially when British soldiers suffered defeat after defeat at the hands of French and Indian guerrillas. British officers assumed that colonial soldiers were simply lazy cowards. But colonial volunteers saw British officers as brutal taskmasters.

Despite the astonishing success of their guerrilla tactics, the French, too, began moving toward a more European style of warfare. In the process, they destroyed their strategic and tactical advantages. In 1756, the Marquis de Montcalm assumed command of French forces. In his first battle, the successful siege of Fort Oswego, New York, Montcalm was horrified by the behavior of his Indian allies, who killed wounded prisoners, took personal captives, and collected scalps as trophies. He came to regard the Indians—so essential to the defense of New France—as mere savages.

Following his next victory, the capture of Fort William Henry, New York, Montcalm conformed to European practice by allowing the defeated garrison to go home in return

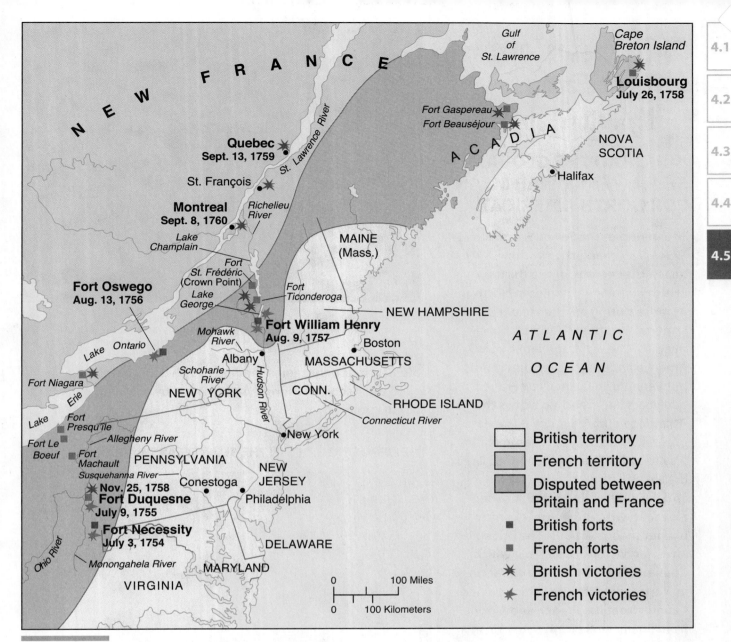

MAP 4.3 THE FRENCH AND INDIAN WAR, 1754–1763 Most of the battles of the French and Indian War occurred in the frontier regions of northern and western New York and the Ohio Valley. The influx of settlers into these areas created tensions that eventually developed into war.

for the promise not to fight again. Montcalm's Indian allies, 1,000 or more strong, were not to take prisoners, trophies, or plunder. The tragic result came to be known as the Massacre of Fort William Henry. Feeling betrayed by their French allies, the Indians took captives and trophies anyway. This action not only outraged the New England colonies (most of the victims were New Englanders) but also alienated the Indians on whom the defense of Canada depended.

For at the same time that the Europeanization of the war was weakening the French, the British moderated their policies and reached accommodation with the colonists. William Pitt, who as secretary of state directed the British war effort from late 1757 through 1761, realized that friction arose from the colonists' sense that they were bearing all the financial burdens of the war without having any say in how the war was fought. Pitt's ingenious solution was to promise reimbursements to the colonies in proportion to their contribution to the war effort, reduce the power of the commander in chief, and replace the arrogant Loudoun with a less objectionable officer.

✴ Explore the Seven Years' War on MyHistoryLab

This political allegory shows two opponents in Seven Years' War (1756–1763), Empress Maria Theresa of Austria and King Fredrick II of Prussia, playing chess with Mars, the Roman god of war.

WHAT DID THE GLOBAL SEVEN YEARS' WAR MEAN FOR NORTH AMERICA?

The period of the Seven Years' War, 1754–1763, marked a "world war" that tested the security of the thirteen British mainland colonies in North America during an intense period of imperial European—and global—rivalries. The war began in North America as conflict over land claims between Virginia and New France and two years later reached across the Atlantic to embroil many European powers, eventually spreading all the way to India. The conflict pitted Great Britain and its allies against France and its allies while both sides used alliances with Native Americans to bolster their positions. The British emerged victorious in 1763, which dramatically changed the situation in North America. The British gained Canada from the French and Florida from Spain, while Native American nations found that they could no longer play the French off the British and vice versa. In addition, colonists in the thirteen mainland British colonies found themselves no longer surrounded by competing colonial powers.

THE OPPOSING SIDES IN THE SEVEN YEARS' WAR

Great Britain, Prussia, Portugal, with allies

France, Spain, Austria, Russia, Sweden with allies

KEY QUESTIONS Use MyHistoryLab *Explorer* to answer these questions:

Response ▶▶▶ *How did other colonial claims in North America create instability for the thirteen British mainland colonies?*

Situate the location of these British colonies in relation to competing colonial claims.

Analysis ▶▶▶ *What made this eighteenth-century war a "world war"?*

Map the main battles in various parts of the world.

Consequences ▶▶▶ *In what ways did the territorial results of the war impact British mainland colonies?*

Conceptualize what these changes, especially the Proclamation Line of 1763, meant for the British colonists.

Pitt's money and measures restored colonial morale and launched the second phase of the war. He sent thousands of British soldiers to America to fight alongside colonial troops. As the Anglo-American forces grew stronger, they operated more successfully, seizing Louisbourg again in 1758. Once more, Canada experienced crippling shortages of supplies. But this time, the Anglo-Americans were united and able to take advantage of the situation. British emissaries persuaded the Delawares and Shawnees to abandon their French alliance, and late in 1758, an Anglo-American force again marched on Fort Duquesne. In command of its lead battalion was Colonel George Washington. The French defenders, abandoned by their native allies and confronted by overwhelming force, blew up the fort and retreated to the Great Lakes.

From this point on, the Anglo-Americans suffered no setbacks, and the French won no victories. The war became a contest in which the larger, better-supplied army would triumph. Montcalm, forced back to Quebec, decided to risk everything in a European-style, open-field battle against a British force led by General James Wolfe. At the Battle of Quebec (September 13, 1759), Montcalm lost the gamble—and his life (as did the victorious General Wolfe).

The French had not yet lost the war. If they could revive their Indian alliances, they still had a chance. What finally decided the outcome of the war in America was not the Battle of Quebec but two other developments: the Battle of Quiberon Bay in France (November 20, 1759) and the decision of the Iroquois to join the Anglo-American side in 1760. The sea battle cost the French navy its ability to operate in the Atlantic, preventing it from reinforcing Canada. Montcalm's successor could not rebuild the Indian alliances he so desperately needed. At the same time, the Iroquois decision to enter the war on the Anglo-American side tipped the balance irrevocably against the French. The last defenders of Canada surrendered on September 8, 1760.

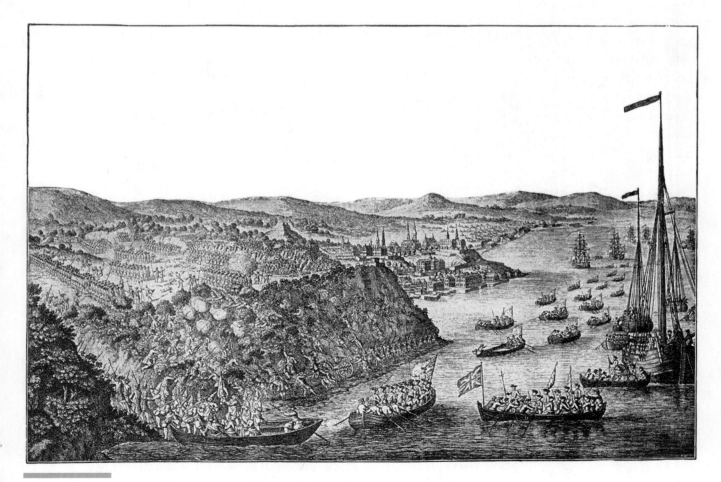

British soldiers faced a steep climb before they reached the battlefield where they ultimately defeated French forces at the Battle of Quebec in 1759.

The Triumph of the British Empire, 1763

The war pitting Britain against France and Spain (which had entered the fighting as a French ally in 1762) concluded with an uninterrupted series of British victories. In the Caribbean, where every valuable sugar island the French owned came under British control, the culminating event was the surrender of Havana on August 13, 1762. Even more spectacular was Britain's capture of the Philippine capital of Manila on October 5—a victory that literally carried British power around the world.

These conquests created the unshakable conviction that British arms were invincible. An immense surge of British patriotism spread throughout the American colonies. When news of the conquest of Havana reached Massachusetts, bells rang, cannons fired salutes, and bonfires blazed.

Treaty of Paris The formal end to British hostilities against France and Spain in February 1763.

Hostilities ended formally on February 10, 1763, with the conclusion of the **Treaty of Paris**. France regained its West Indian sugar islands—its most valuable colonial possessions—but lost the rest of its North American empire. France ceded to Britain all its claims to lands east of the Mississippi River (except the city of New Orleans) and compensated Spain for the losses it had sustained as an ally by handing over all claims to the Trans-Mississippi West and the port of New Orleans (see Map 4.4). Britain returned Cuba and the Philippines to Spain and in compensation received Florida. Now Great Britain owned everything east of the Mississippi, from the Gulf of Mexico to Hudson's Bay. With France and Spain both humbled and on the verge of financial collapse, Britain seemed preeminent in Europe and ready to dominate in the New World. Never before had Americans felt more pride in being British, members of the greatest empire on earth.

MAP 4.4 EUROPEAN EMPIRES IN NORTH AMERICA, 1750–1763 Great Britain's victory in the French and Indian War transformed the map of North America. France lost its mainland colonies, England claimed all lands east of the Mississippi, and Spain gained nominal control over the Trans-Mississippi West.

Conclusion

The George Washington who ordered a suit from England in 1763 longed to be part of the elite of the great British Empire. If he feared any threat to his position in that elite, it was not Parliament and the king but the uncomfortably large debts he owed to his London agents. But such worries, though real, were merely small, nagging doubts, shared by most of his fellow planters.

What was more real to Washington was the great victory that the British had just gained over France, a victory that he had helped to achieve. For Washington, as for virtually all other colonial leaders and many ordinary colonists, 1763 was a moment of great promise and patriotic devotion to the British Empire. They hoped that the colonies had embarked on a new stage in a political and cultural journey, moving them farther from their precarious origins as scattered English outposts and closer to an equal partnership with England itself in the world's most powerful empire. It was a time for colonists to rejoice in the fundamental British identity and liberty and rights that seemed to ensure that their lives would be better and more prosperous than ever.

For Suggested Readings go to MyHistoryLab.

Chapter Review

Economic Development and Imperial Trade in the British Colonies

4.1 How did trade policy shape the relationship between Britain and the colonies? p. 87

Parliament enacted a series of laws, known as the Navigation Acts, to knit Britain and the colonies into a prosperous commercial empire. Colonial raw materials flowed into Britain, while British manufactured goods were made available on favorable terms to colonial consumers.

The Transformation of Culture

4.2 In what ways did colonial culture change in the eighteenth century? p. 93

Colonial elites, worried about their provincial status, imported goods and cultivated genteel manners to become more like Britain. Some educated colonists took great interest in Enlightenment ideas about science and human progress. At the same time, evangelical religion flourished on both sides of the Atlantic, due to the revivals of the Great Awakening.

The Colonial Political World

4.3 How did the Glorious Revolution affect colonial politics? p. 99

The overthrow of James II in England and the end of the Dominion of New England symbolized the triumph of representative government over tyranny. Colonists came to see their legislatures as colonial equivalents of Parliament itself. They also understood their membership in the empire to be voluntary, not coerced.

Expanding Empires

4.4 In what ways did British, Spanish, and French expansion into new territories reflect patterns established earlier? p. 103

In the eighteenth as in the seventeenth century, British imperial expansion stemmed from a dramatic increase in its colonial population. The French continued to rely on trade and alliances with key Indian peoples, while the extension of Spanish colonization into Texas and California continued to involve Catholic missionaries.

A Century of Warfare

4.5 How significant were imperial wars in shaping colonial society? Which one had the most important impact on North America? p. 107

The imperial wars were significant in incorporating colonies into European diplomatic calculations. The most important conflict was the French and Indian War. The British victory in 1763 deprived France of its North American empire and inspired strong British patriotism in the colonies, whose soldiers had fought alongside British troops.

Timeline

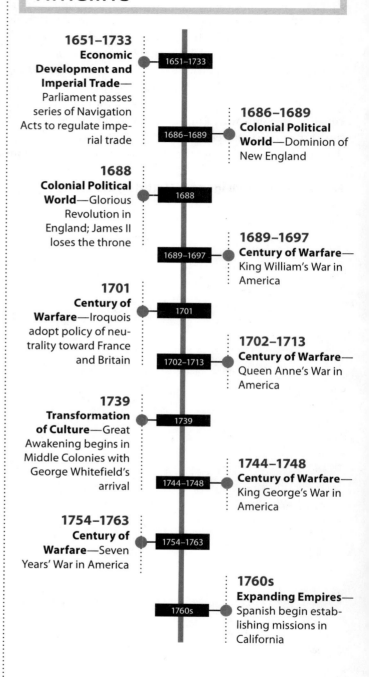

1651–1733
Economic Development and Imperial Trade—Parliament passes series of Navigation Acts to regulate imperial trade

`1651–1733`

1686–1689
Colonial Political World—Dominion of New England

`1686–1689`

1688
Colonial Political World—Glorious Revolution in England; James II loses the throne

`1688`

1689–1697
Century of Warfare—King William's War in America

`1689–1697`

1701
Century of Warfare—Iroquois adopt policy of neutrality toward France and Britain

`1701`

1702–1713
Century of Warfare—Queen Anne's War in America

`1702–1713`

1739
Transformation of Culture—Great Awakening begins in Middle Colonies with George Whitefield's arrival

`1739`

1744–1748
Century of Warfare—King George's War in America

`1744–1748`

1754–1763
Century of Warfare—Seven Years' War in America

`1754–1763`

1760s
Expanding Empires—Spanish begin establishing missions in California

`1760s`

5 Imperial Breakdown 1763–1774

One American Journey

Andrew Burnaby's Travel Journal

ndeed, it appears to me a very doubtful point, even supposing all the colonies of America to be united under one head, whether it would be possible to keep in due order and government so wide and extended an empire, the difficulties of communication, of intercourse, of correspondence, and all other circumstances considered.

A voluntary association or coalition, at least a permanent one, is almost as difficult to be supposed: for fire and water are not more heterogeneous than the different colonies in North America. Nothing can exceed the jealousy and emulation which they possess in regard to each other. . . . Even the limits and boundaries of each colony are a constant source of litigation. In short, such is the difference of character, of manners, of religion, of interest, of the different colonies, that I think, if I am not wholly ignorant of the human mind, were they left to themselves, there would

LEARNING OBJECTIVES

 Listen to Chapter 5 on MyHistoryLab

Having apparently originated in a May Day–like celebration of the repeal of the Stamp Act in the spring of 1766, liberty poles were particularly characteristic of New York City, where citizens of all social classes supported their erection (as in the picture). However, British soldiers repeatedly destroyed them, thereby prompting serious rioting. Elsewhere, liberty trees served similar symbolic functions. John C. McRae of New York published this print in 1875.

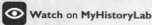 Watch the Video Series on MyHistoryLab

Learn about some key topics related to this chapter with the *MyHistoryLab Video Series: Key Topics in U.S. History.*

1 **The Burdens of an Empire: 1763–1775** Following the Seven Years' War, the American colonies chafed under an increased tax burden, military occupation, and a lack of influence in Great Britain's political system. This video surveys the economic and self-rule issues that led to a formal break with the mother country and revolution.

 Watch on MyHistoryLab

The Stamp Act The British government's efforts to pay off debts incurred during the Seven Years' War directly affected colonists in various ways. None was more despised than the Stamp Act. This video discusses the origins of the Stamp Act, the hostility to its imposition, and how the tax was rescinded, all of which strained the relationship between the British crown and its American colonies.

2

Watch on MyHistoryLab

3 **Boston Massacre** The Townshend Acts, coupled with Parliament's decision to enforce customs duties and station soldiers in Boston, came to a disastrous climax in Boston in 1770. This video provides the background as well as an explanation for this watershed event in the escalation of British control that further alienated the American colonists from Parliament and the British monarchy.

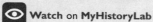 Watch on MyHistoryLab

The Boston Tea Party Parliament's passage of the Tea Act in 1773 provoked such resistance that a group of Bostonians, dressed as Native Americans, dumped a shipment of tea into Boston Harbor to avoid paying a tax on the product. As a result, Parliament passed the "Coercive Acts," which served as a galvanizing force to bring the American colonies together and inspire them to seek independence from Great Britain.

4

Watch on MyHistoryLab

soon be a civil war from one end of the continent to the other; while the Indians and negroes would, with better reason, impatiently watch the opportunity of exterminating them all together.

Andrew Burnaby, Travels Through the Middle Settlements in North America in the Years 1759 and 1760 [1775] (3rd ed., 1798; reprinted New York: Augustus M. Kelley, 1970), pp. 152–153.

Personal Journeys Online

- Mary Ambler, *Diary of M. Ambler*, 1770. This memoir records Ambler's trip to Baltimore to have her two young children inoculated for smallpox.

- Reverend John Ettwein, *Notes of Travel from the North Branch of the Susquehanna to the Beaver River, Pennsylvania*, 1772. This journal recorded the journey of about 122 Christianized Indians through western Pennsylvania to their new homes at the village of Friedenstadt.

- Nicholas Cresswell, *The Journal of Nicholas Cresswell, 1774–1777*. A prospective immigrant sails, having decided to go to America, but the Revolution changes his mind.

A ndrew Burnaby, an English clergyman, made these observations while on a tour of the colonies in 1759 and 1760. Few people on either side of the Atlantic would have disagreed with his assessment. The only union that he or anyone else at the time could imagine was the imperial connection that bound Great Britain to its American possessions. That connection seemed even stronger as Burnaby's journey came to a close in 1760, for by then Britain's victory in the French and Indian War was all but certain.

But the war had changed the British Empire in ways that few people immediately grasped. The first to understand the challenges of victory were British officials, who found themselves with a burdensome debt and vastly increased territory to administer—much of it occupied by erstwhile enemies. Their efforts to meet these challenges resulted in an unprecedented assertion of imperial control over the American colonies in order to secure the fruits of victory. From the vantage point of London, this new model of empire appeared both necessary and, to some officials, long overdue.

To many colonists, however, British reforms represented an unwarranted disruption of a well-functioning imperial relationship. Rather than seeing various reform measures as attempts to deal with practical problems, colonists regarded them as repeated assaults on their property and rights. For more than a decade, Great Britain and its American colonies engaged in an often acrimonious and occasionally violent debate over the proper structure of the postwar empire. Only at the end of that period did it become clear that the survival of the empire itself might be at stake.

The Crisis of Imperial Authority

5.1 What new challenges did the British government face in North America after 1763?

As the French and Indian War drew to a close, political shifts at the heart of London did not make the task of imperial administration any easier. In 1760, a rather naïve new monarch, George III, ascended the throne at the age of 22. Disputes among his advisers soon led to the resignation of William Pitt, the popular war minister who had helped England achieve its great victory. Political infighting at the highest reaches of government persisted until April 1763, when George Grenville became first lord of the treasury and the man responsible for ushering Britain and her colonies into the postwar era.

Challenges of Control and Finance

Britain's empire in 1763 was immense, and the problems its rulers faced were correspondingly large. Moreover, it still faced threats, if diminished ones, from its traditional European enemies. French territory on the North American mainland had been reduced to two tiny islands in the Gulf of St. Lawrence. Yet France's spectacular defeat would only whet its appetite for revenge.

Spain was a more significant presence on the North American mainland. At the end of the French and Indian War, it surrendered East and West Florida to Britain but got back its possessions in Cuba and the Philippines that the British had captured. Spain acquired Louisiana from its French ally as compensation for the loss of the Floridas.

Protecting Britain's enlarged empire from these familiar European rivals formed just part of the security problems facing British officials. With the Peace of Paris of 1763, Britain acquired not only new lands but also new subjects—few of whom had any reason to feel loyal toward George III or the British nation. Thousands of French inhabitants remaining in Canada and the Mississippi Valley would likely side with France in the event of another war with Britain. Even greater numbers of Native Americans, most of whom sided with France during the war, populated these regions.

Concerns about imperial authority extended to the inhabitants of the existing colonies themselves. Worries about the colonists' wartime smuggling and their assemblies' frequent obstruction of military orders fed an ongoing debate in London about the need for a more centralized form of imperial control. The assertiveness of colonial legislatures, many British officials thought, contributed to an unacceptable level of American insubordination.

But any plan for imperial restructuring, no matter how well designed, faced an enormous obstacle. Wartime expenses had caused England's national debt to balloon higher than ever before, from £72 million in 1755 to an astonishing £146 million in 1763. Half of the money collected from hard-pressed British taxpayers went just to pay the interest on this massive debt, and no more revenue could be squeezed from them without risking domestic unrest. Moreover, it seemed unfair to do so. Since the comparatively lightly taxed Americans benefited the most from the war, officials believed they should shoulder more of the financial burden of victory.

Native Americans and Frontier Conflict

As a first response to the new demands of empire, the British government decided to keep a substantial body of troops in America in peacetime—10,000 were initially planned. The soldiers would protect the new territories and existing colonies. More importantly, officials hoped that their presence would help to maintain peace with the Indians.

Even as the war with France had been drawing to a close, conflict with Cherokee Indians on the southern frontier had flared into violence. Longtime allies and trading partners of South Carolina, the Cherokees resented repeated incidents of theft, encroachment on Native lands, and violence perpetrated by frontier colonists. By early 1760, their frustration blossomed into the **Cherokee War** when they launched retaliatory attacks on western settlements in all the southern colonies. Three expeditions, manned by British as well as colonial troops, eventually forced the Cherokees to agree, in a 1761 treaty, to surrender land in the Carolinas and Virginia to the colonists.

The end of the Cherokee War did not necessarily ease frontier tensions. France's loss of its North American colonies deprived many Indians of a key ally, trading partner, and counterweight to British pressures for land. Britain's General Jeffrey Amherst confirmed their worst fears when he ordered a reduction in the gifts customarily supplied to the Iroquois and other Native allies. He saw no reason to continue offering what he regarded as bribes to maintain ties to Indians who could no longer threaten to desert Britain and ally with France. Amherst further infuriated western Indians by reneging on a promise to construct trading posts in the interior and withdraw troops. The persistence of military garrisons and the establishment of farming settlements near them suggested nothing less than a British intent to occupy Indian lands permanently.

The Indian response stunned the British with its fierceness and geographical range. It was also remarkable as an unprecedented example of Indian unity in the face of European expansion. The sources of that unity were as much spiritual as political. In 1761, Neolin, sometimes known as the Delaware Prophet, experienced a vision in which God commanded the Indians to reject their dependence on European goods and ways and embrace their own ancestral practices.

By May 1763, the Indians were ready to strike. Led by an Ottawa chief named Pontiac, a loose coalition of at least eight major Native American peoples launched attacks on more than a dozen British forts in the west, beginning at Detroit. Within months, **Pontiac's War** raged along the frontier from the Great Lakes to Virginia. Horrified by the prospect of an Indian victory, General Amherst urged his troops to adopt desperate measures. British tactics included killing Indian prisoners and, most notoriously, distributing smallpox-infected blankets as diplomatic gifts to local chiefs who had come to Fort Pitt during a temporary truce.

It was not smallpox but starvation that ultimately ended Pontiac's War. British forces attacked Indian food supplies as they waited for their adversaries to run out of ammunition. By late summer 1764, the Indian coalition had begun to disintegrate and fighting ceased. Pontiac finally accepted a treaty in 1766. Chastened by the conflict, British officials agreed to follow the practices the French had once used in the Great Lakes area by supplying western Indians with diplomatic gifts, encouraging trade, and mediating disputes.

Cherokee War Conflict (1759–1761) on the southern frontier between the Cherokee Indians and colonists from Virginia southward.

Pontiac's War Indian uprising (1763–1766) led by Pontiac of the Ottawas and Neolin of the Delawares.

This engraving depicts Native Americans delivering English captives to Colonel Henry Bouquet, a British officer, at the end of Pontiac's War.

Yet frontier animosities did not easily dissipate. Few colonists in vulnerable western settlements cared any longer to distinguish between friendly and hostile Indians; as far as they were concerned, all Indians were enemies. This kind of thinking provoked a group of Scots-Irish settlers in Paxton Township, Pennsylvania, upset at the colonial assembly's lack of aggressiveness in dealing with Indians, to take matters into their own hands. Unable to catch the Indians who were attacking their settlements, they slaughtered a defenseless group of Christian Conestogas living nearby. The so-called Paxton Boys went on to murder another group of Christian Indians two weeks later.

Dealing with the New Territories

Back in London, Pontiac's War gave British officials added incentive to assert imperial control over the vast territories acquired from France. Even as the war was going on, the king issued the **Proclamation of 1763**. The measure aimed to pacify Indians by prohibiting white settlement west of the ridgeline of the Appalachian Mountains.

Proclamation of 1763 Royal proclamation setting the boundary known as the Proclamation Line that limited British settlements to the eastern side of the Appalachian Mountains.

MAP 5.1 COLONIAL SETTLEMENT AND THE PROCLAMATION LINE OF 1763 This map depicts the regions claimed and settled by the major groups competing for territory in eastern North America. With the Proclamation Line of 1763, positioned along the crest of the Appalachian Mountains, the British government tried to stop the westward migration of settlers under its jurisdiction and thereby limit conflict with the Indians. The result, however, was frustration and anger on the part of land-hungry settlers.

Colonists who had already moved to the western side of this Proclamation Line were required "forthwith to remove themselves" back to the east (see Map 5.1). The royal proclamation contained two other key features. First, it obligated Britain to establish a regulated Indian trade in the interior in an effort to supply desired goods and curb traders' cheating of their Native American customers. Second, it established civilian governments in East and West Florida. For the time being, Canada—inhabited by more than 80,000 French Catholics—would remain under military rule.

The 10,000-man force that British officials planned to keep in America was not nearly large enough to ensure that the proclamation would be obeyed. Moreover, both the stationing of troops in peacetime and the establishment of the Proclamation Line aroused considerable resentment among colonists. Americans shared a traditional English distrust of standing armies, and worried that the soldiers could just as easily be used to coerce the colonists as to protect them. Their concerns were heightened when Parliament passed two **Quartering Acts** that required colonial assemblies to provide barracks and supplies for the soldiers.

News of the Proclamation Line was no more welcome. Colonial settlers and land speculators coveted the territories they had fought to win from France and resented the prohibition against their occupation. As it turned out, the prohibition against settlement was largely unenforceable. Within a few years, imperial authorities made several

Quartering Acts Acts of Parliament requiring colonial legislatures to provide supplies and quarters for the troops stationed in America.

adjustments to the settlement boundary line and returned supervision of the Indian trade to the individual colonies, concessions that revived many of the problems that the Proclamation of 1763 had meant to solve.

The Search for Revenue: The Sugar Act

In 1764, George Grenville and his fellow ministers turned from territorial control to matters of finance. Compounding the problem of the soaring national debt, a postwar recession had both Britain and the colonies in its grip. Parliament passed two laws that year to address imperial financial concerns. One statute responded to London merchants' protest against Virginia's use of colonial paper money as legal tender for payment of debts, because the money had lost nearly a sixth of its value during the recent war. The Currency Act of 1764 prohibited all colonial legislatures from making their paper money legal tender. It allowed creditors to demand repayment in specie (gold or silver), always in short supply in the colonies, and even more so during the postwar economic recession.

Parliament also passed the American Revenue Act, commonly known as the **Sugar Act**. This measure placed duties on a number of colonial imports, but its most important provision actually lowered the tax on imported molasses from six to three pence per gallon. The Molasses Act of 1733 had required the higher duty to discourage colonists from importing molasses (much of it used to make rum) from the French West Indies. But merchants evaded the high tax by bribing customs officials about a penny a gallon to certify French molasses as British. Grenville hoped that the three-pence-per-gallon Sugar Act tax was close enough to the going rate for bribes that colonial merchants would simply pay it.

The Sugar Act also took aim at smugglers by requiring that ships carry elaborate new documentation of their cargoes. Customs officials could seize ships for what their owners often regarded as minor technicalities. The act further ordered customs collectors to discharge their duties personally instead of relegating them to poorly paid deputies susceptible to bribes. Finally, Parliament gave responsibility for trying violations of the laws to vice-admiralty courts first in Halifax, Nova Scotia, and later in Boston, Philadelphia, and Charleston. Vice-admiralty courts, with jurisdiction over maritime affairs, normally operated without a jury and were therefore more likely to enforce trade restrictions.

New Englanders predominated among those colonists actively opposed to the Sugar Act. They feared that enforcement of the tax on foreign molasses would damage the northern rum industry. Earnings from rum were crucial to the New England–West Indies trade and also helped to pay for imported British goods. The postwar recession was hardly the time to stir up colonial fears about their economies. The assemblies of eight colonies collaborated on a set of petitions sent to royal authorities to protest the Sugar Act. Officials in London, however, simply ignored the petitions even as they labored to devise new colonial taxes.

Sugar Act Law passed in 1764 to raise revenue in the American colonies. It lowered the duty from six pence to three pence per gallon on foreign molasses imported into the colonies and increased the restrictions on colonial commerce.

Republican Ideology and Colonial Protest

5.2   How did republican ideology inform the colonists' view of their relationship to Britain?

Colonists stressed economic arguments in their petitions against the Sugar Act, but their unease about the measure also had political dimensions. Parliament had passed similar commercial regulations before, but its new assertiveness and its claim that additional taxes might be necessary stirred colonial fears that more than their pocketbooks were under threat. Colonists treasured their rights as Englishmen, but new imperial reforms threatened to encroach on their enjoyment of those rights as never before. Thus imperial reforms provoked colonists to reflect upon the character of the postwar empire and on the principles that governed their membership in it.

Power versus Liberty

Many colonists derived their understanding of politics from a set of ideas loosely grouped under the heading of **republicanism**. Influenced by writings from classical Rome, and linked to what was known in England as Country ("Real Whig") ideology (see Chapter 4), republican political thinkers acknowledged that governments must exercise power, but simultaneously cautioned that power could easily overwhelm liberty. Too much power in the hands of a ruler meant tyranny. Too much liberty in the hands of the people, however, was no better; it meant anarchy.

History offered many examples of tyrants gaining power through secrecy and corruption, buying off potential opponents with political offices or other favors. Tyrants then impoverished the people through heavy taxation and employed military force against any resistance. Once the people had lost their liberty, there was no turning back. They had, in effect, become slaves.

Republican ideology thus called upon the people to be ever vigilant against corruption and excessive power. Their main bulwark against tyranny was civil liberty, or maintaining the right of the people to participate in government. The people who did so, however, had to demonstrate virtue. To eighteenth-century republicans, virtuous citizens were those who focused not on their private interests but rather on what was good for the public as a whole. They were necessarily property holders, since only those individuals could exercise an independence of judgment impossible for those dependent on employers, landlords, masters, or (in the case of women and children) husbands and fathers.

The British Constitution

The key to good government was preserving a balance between the exercise of power and the protection of liberty. Colonists agreed that no government performed this crucial task better than Great Britain's, based as it was on the **British Constitution**. Then, as now, the British Constitution was not a written document. It consisted instead of the governing institutions, laws, and political customs of the realm as they had evolved over the centuries. It was understood, in short, as the way in which British government and society together *were constituted.*

The genius of Britain's government lay in the fact that its Constitution was "mixed and balanced." Society was comprised of three elements—the monarchy, aristocracy, and common people—and they had their governmental counterparts in the Crown, the House of Lords, and the House of Commons. Liberty would be preserved so long as none of the elements acquired the ability to dominate or corrupt the others.

The British Constitution protected that balance in a number of ways. Both Houses of Parliament, for instance, had to consent to laws in order for them to go into effect. Because taxation was such a sensitive subject, the House of Commons—the governmental unit closest to the people—retained the right to initiate tax laws and no tax could pass without the consent of the representatives of both houses. This parliamentary control of taxation operated as a crucial check on the monarch's power.

Taxation and Sovereignty

Colonists who had absorbed republican ideas were especially concerned about taxation because anyone who paid taxes in effect surrendered some of his property to do so. As long as the taxpayer consented to those taxes, however, it was unlikely that the taxes would become excessive enough to threaten his independence and liberty. Rumors from England that more taxes might follow the Sugar Act encouraged some colonists to consider whether they really consented to taxes passed by a Parliament to which they elected no representatives.

The fiscal measures required by imperial reform thus drew attention to differences between British and colonial understandings of representation. British authorities contended that colonists, like all inhabitants of Britain, were virtually represented in Parliament because that body's members served the interests of the British nation and empire as a whole. Colonists, however, thought they could only be represented by men for whom they had actually voted—such as the members of their colonial legislatures (see Chapter 4). And they insisted that the right to be taxed only by their own elected representatives was one of the most basic rights of Englishmen.

Few colonists realized yet that their concerns about taxation connected to the more fundamental issue of political **sovereignty**. Sovereignty was the supreme authority of the state, and it included both the right to take life (as in the case of executions for capital crimes) and to tax. If the state were deprived of its authority, it ceased to be sovereign. Were colonists to reach the point where they denied Parliament's right to tax them, they would in effect be denying that the British government had sovereign power over the colonies.

sovereignty The supreme authority of the state, including both the right to take life (as in the case of executions for capital crimes) and to tax.

The Stamp Act and Townshend Duty Act Crises

5.3 Why did the Stamp Act and Townshend Duty Act spark widespread unrest in the colonies?

Because revenue from the Sugar Act was not enough to solve Britain's debt problems, George Grenville proposed another measure, the **Stamp Act**. This legislation required all valid legal documents, as well as newspapers, playing cards, and various other papers, to bear a government-issued stamp, for which there was a charge. Colonists who opposed the Sugar Act had difficulty justifying their opposition to a measure that appeared to fall within Britain's accepted authority to regulate commerce. The Stamp Act was different. It was the first internal tax (as opposed to an external trade duty) that Parliament had imposed on the colonies.

Stamp Act Law passed by Parliament in 1765 to raise revenue in America by requiring taxed, stamped paper for legal documents, publications, and playing cards.

Colonial Assemblies React to the Stamp Tax

Colonial protests arose months before the Stamp Act was due to go into effect on November 1, 1765. Eight legislatures passed resolutions condemning the measure. In Virginia's House of Burgesses, 29-year-old Patrick Henry went so far as to propose a resolution asserting that Virginians could disobey any law to which their own legislature had not agreed. This resolution did not pass, but it testified to colonial outrage at what many regarded as an unconstitutional tax.

In October, nine colonies sent delegates to the **Stamp Act Congress** meeting in New York to coordinate the colonial response. The delegates affirmed their loyalty to the king and their "due subordination" to Parliament, but then adopted the **Declaration of Rights and Grievances**. This document denied Parliament's right to tax the colonies and petitioned the king and Parliament to repeal both the Sugar and Stamp acts. Parliament, shocked at this challenge to its authority, refused to receive this Declaration or any other colonial petitions.

While colonial assemblies and the Stamp Act Congress deliberated, a torrent of pamphlets and newspaper essays flowed from colonial presses. Some went beyond opposition to the Stamp Act itself to address broader issues, such as challenging the idea that colonists were virtually represented in Parliament. At the same time, merchants in several colonial cities resorted to economic pressure, pledging to cease importing British goods until the hated taxes were repealed. As important as these various measures were in solidifying colonial opposition, however, defeat of the Stamp Act came largely through actions, not words.

Stamp Act Congress October 1765 meeting of delegates sent by nine colonies, which adopted the Declaration of Rights and Grievances and petitioned against the Stamp Act.

Declaration of Rights and Grievances Asserted that the Stamp Act and other taxes imposed on the colonists without their consent were unconstitutional.

((• Read the Document Benjamin Franklin, Testimony Against the Stamp Act (1766)

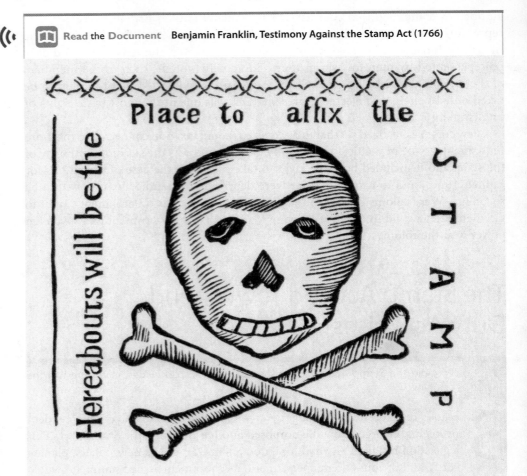

The Stamp Act required all colonial newspapers to bear a government-issued stamp. This newspaper protested the act by placing this death's-head image where the tax stamp would have gone.

Colonists Take to the Streets

In Boston, a group composed mainly of artisans and shopkeepers, with some prominent citizens playing behind-the-scenes roles, organized themselves as the **Sons of Liberty**. As part of their general protest against the Stamp Act, they planned to intimidate Andrew Oliver, who had been appointed to the office of stamp distributor, into resigning. In August 1765, they took to the streets, attacking Oliver's house. Two weeks later, a mob destroyed the home of Lieutenant Governor Thomas Hutchinson. Up and down the coast, rioters forced nearly every stamp distributor to resign his office before the law went into effect on November 1. After that date, the law was essentially nullified, because there was no one to distribute the hated stamps.

Colonial elites sympathetic to the cause of the rioters were nonetheless appalled at their violent tactics. The Stamp Act Congress convened, in large part, so that elites could try to regain control of the situation. When news of the protests reached London, imperial authorities were equally astonished. British merchants, feeling the sting of colonial boycotts of British goods, petitioned Parliament to repeal the Stamp Act and resolve the crisis before matters got further out of hand.

Repeal and the Declaratory Act

For reasons that had nothing to do with colonial unrest, George III decided to replace Grenville at the treasury with another man, the Marquis of Rockingham. Convinced that repealing the Stamp Act was the only way to calm colonial tempers, Rockingham

Sons of Liberty Secret organizations in the colonies formed to oppose the Stamp Act.

Samuel Adams, the leader of the Boston radicals, as he appeared to John Singleton Copley in the early 1770s. In this famous picture, thought to have been commissioned by another revolutionary leader, John Hancock, Adams points to legal documents guaranteeing American rights.

could count on the support of British merchants and manufacturers who wanted to see the trade boycotts ended. He faced a more delicate task, however, in getting Parliament and the king to agree to repeal. Both Crown and Parliament thought it preposterous for the world's mightiest empire simply to give way to unruly American mobs. They did not wish to give the slightest impression that they agreed with the colonists' assertion that the Stamp Act was unconstitutional, for to do so would be to call into question Parliament's right to legislate for the colonies at all.

In the end, Rockingham found a three-part solution that linked repeal to an unequivocal assertion of parliamentary sovereignty. First, the Stamp Act would be repealed only because it had damaged British commercial interests, and not because it allegedly violated the colonists' rights. Second, Parliament passed the **Declaratory Act**. This measure affirmed Parliament's sovereignty, declaring that it had "full power and authority to make laws and statutes of sufficient force and validity to bind the colonies and people of America . . . in all cases whatsoever." Third, Parliament passed the Revenue Act of 1766, which reduced the tax on molasses from three pence per gallon to one penny, but imposed it on all molasses—British and foreign—that came to the mainland colonies.

In London, Parliament had saved face and calmed the merchant community. In the colonies, people rejoiced. They regarded repeal as a vindication of their claim that the Stamp Act had been unconstitutional, and they saw little threat in the Declaratory Act because it did not explicitly assert Parliament's right to tax the colonies, but only "make laws" for them. The Revenue Act attracted little notice, even though it in fact generated considerable income for the empire. Tacit acceptance of this measure suggested that colonists remained willing to pay "external" taxes that regulated trade.

Declaratory Act Law passed in 1766 to accompany repeal of the Stamp Act that stated that Parliament had the authority to legislate for the colonies "in all cases whatsoever."

✳ Explore the Imperial Crisis on MyHistoryLab

WHY DID WIDESPREAD UNREST REACH THE THIRTEEN COLONIES BY THE 1760S?

At the end of the Seven Years' War in 1763, colonists in British North America were proud to be part of the world's largest empire. Soon, though, allegiance to the empire started to fade as Parliament in London began to find ways to pay for the costly war by imposing a variety of taxes on their American subjects across the Atlantic. Colonists began to protest that Parliament's actions violated their rights as British subjects, and the famous cry "No Taxation without Representation!" echoed up and down the Thirteen Colonies. Unfair taxation sparked riots in the American colonies, and some subjects even turned to violence.

The Boston Massacre occurred when British soldiers fired on a mob in Boston on March 5, 1770, and killed five civilians. This propaganda illustration depicts the event as an unprovoked atrocity.

RIOTS OF THE 1760s

Year	Colony	Location	Year	Colony	Location
1760	New York	New York City	1766	Connecticut	New Haven, New London
1763–1764	Pennsylvania	Lancaster, Millerstown, Philadelphia		Massachusetts (Maine)	Falmouth
1764	Massachusetts	Dighton		New York	Dutchess County
	New York	New York City		Virginia	Norfolk
	Rhode Island	Newport	1767	Virginia	Norfolk
1765	Massachusetts	Boston, Northampton	1767–1769	South Carolina	Western frontier
	New York	New York City	1768	Massachusetts	Boston
	North Carolina	Mecklenburg County		North Carolina	Hillsborough
	Pennsylvania	Cumberland County		Virginia	Norfolk
	Rhode Island	Newport	1769	Connecticut	New Haven, New London
1765 and 1769	Pennsylvania	Conococheague Valley		Pennsylvania	Philadelphia
1765–1771	North Carolina	Anson, Cumberland, Granville, Orange, and Rowan counties		Rhode Island	Newport
			Late 1760s	New York	New York City
				Rhode Island	Newport, Providence

SOURCE: "Violence and the American Revolution," in *Essays on the American Revolution,* eds. Stephen G. Kurtz and James H. Hutson (Chapel Hill: University of North Carolina Press, Published for the Institute of Early American History and Culture, 1973); Benjamin H. Irvin, "Tar, Feathers, and the Enemies of American Liberties, 1768–1776," *The New England QuarteRly* 76, no. 2 (Jun 2003), 197–238.

KEY QUESTIONS Use MyHistoryLab *Explorer* to answer these questions:

Consequence ▶▶▶ *How did different regional agricultural production influence colonists' reactions to the Revenue Acts?*

Map the various crops grown in the colonies to see this connection.

Cause ▶▶▶ *What sorts of mob actions were launched by the colonists?*

Chart the riotous manifestations to understand the range of grievances of colonists.

Analysis ▶▶▶ *Where did crowds of colonists take action against Parliament's new regulations?*

Consider the factors that may have affected the geographical distribution of these actions.

Townshend's Plan and Renewed Colonial Resistance

Peace between Britain and the colonies did not last long. In 1766 there was another shake-up in the British ministry. The king replaced Rockingham with William Pitt, who had accepted a peerage and was now known as Lord Chatham. As a noble, Pitt now sat in the House of Lords, leaving leadership in the House of Commons to Charles Townshend. Townshend, an unscrupulous politician whom few other British ministers fully trusted, was convinced that the colonists still needed to be taught a lesson in submission to parliamentary authority.

One focus of Charles Townshend's concern was New York, where the legislature refused to comply with the Quartering Act of 1765 that required colonial assemblies to raise money for housing and supplying British troops. New Yorkers had concluded that this measure amounted to taxation without representation. Townshend convinced Parliament to pass an act in 1767 that suspended the New York legislature. Although the New York assembly gave in before the act went into effect, the measure revived concerns about imperial power.

As chancellor of the exchequer, Townshend knew that much of Britain's postwar debt remained unpaid. It was all the more remarkable, then, that his fiscal plan was not really designed to reduce that debt. Townshend proposed new duties for the colonies but at the same time lowered certain taxes in Britain itself. He and other British officials were primarily interested in asserting parliamentary sovereignty over the colonies. The result was the **Townshend Duty Act of 1767**, which imposed new duties on imports that colonists got from Britain, including tea, paper, lead, glass, and paint. Revenue from the act would pay the salaries of governors and judges in the colonies, freeing them from dependence on the colonial assemblies that normally paid them. Charles Townshend died suddenly in September 1767 and thus did not live to see the consequences of his actions.

Townshend Duty Act of 1767
Imposed duties on colonial tea, lead, paint, paper, and glass.

Colonists who had absorbed republican ideology knew to be wary of corruption, and they suspected that Townshend's plan to pay governors and judges aimed to make these officials support their parliamentary paymasters rather than the colonial assemblies. Their fears grew when news arrived that there would be a new American Board of Customs Commissioners to see that the Townshend duties were paid. The board would be located in Boston, the presumed home port of many smugglers and the site of the fiercest protests against the Stamp Act.

Colonial protests were swift, if unorganized. Once again, colonial radicals called for a boycott of British goods, but trade embargoes hurt merchants and consumers alike, making it difficult to guarantee compliance in all port towns. For a boycott to be effective, unanimity was critical; a boycott in Boston was meaningless if British goods continued to flow into Philadelphia or New York. Support for nonimportation increased, however, after an incident in Boston in June 1768. When customs commissioners seized John Hancock's ship, *Liberty*, on charges of smuggling, their action sparked a riot. The terrified commissioners fled to Castle William, a fort on an island in Boston harbor, and petitioned London for help. In response, Britain sent two regiments of troops to Boston.

In the aftermath of the *Liberty* riot and with the impending arrival of British troops, merchants first in Boston and New York, and later Philadelphia, agreed to nonimportation. Enforcement of the trade boycotts energized the populace and drew more people, including artisans and laborers, into political action than ever before. Women, who normally had no formal political role because of their dependent status, found that their responsibilities for household production and purchasing gained political meaning. They, too, could announce their solidarity with fellow colonists by spurning British imports and instead making and wearing homespun clothing.

The **nonimportation movement** eventually produced a sharp drop in British imports. By early 1770, northern colonies had reduced imports by nearly two-thirds (see Figure 5.1). Once again, colonial economic pressure caught the attention of British merchants and members of Parliament. The troubles in America contributed to the king's decision to appoint a new prime minister, Frederick, Lord North, in January 1770. Lord

nonimportation movement
A tactical means of putting economic pressure on Britain by refusing to buy its exports in the colonies.

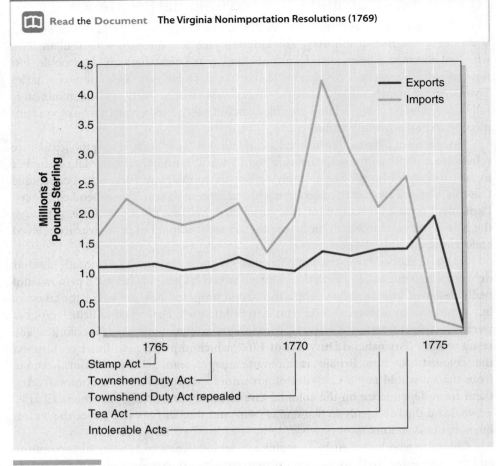

Read the Document   The Virginia Nonimportation Resolutions (1769)

FIGURE 5.1 VALUE OF AMERICAN EXPORTS TO AND IMPORTS FROM ENGLAND,
1763–1776 This figure depicts the value of American exports to and imports from England. The decrease of imports in 1765–1766 and the even sharper drop in 1769 illustrate the effect of American boycotts in response to the Stamp Act and Townshend duties.

SOURCE: U.S. Bureau of the Census, *Historical Statistics of the United States, Colonial Times to 1970*, Bicentennial Edition, Part 1 (1975).

North was prepared to concede that the Townshend duties had been counterproductive because they interfered with British trade. But even as he worked for their repeal, news arrived of another episode of violence in Boston—this time involving British troops.

The Boston Massacre

Ever since British troops had arrived in Boston in 1768, there had been friction between soldiers and civilians. By the summer of 1769, however, Boston seemed calm enough that British authorities thought it safe to remove half of the 1,000 troops stationed there. This action energized the Sons of Liberty, who saw an opportunity to confront the remaining soldiers more often. Crowds frequently gathered to taunt and throw stones at troops standing at guardposts. Townsmen also targeted off-duty soldiers who sought part-time employment at unskilled jobs. Many Bostonians, unemployed because of the weak economy, resented competition from soldiers who, because they derived some income from the army, could afford to accept lower wages from employers.

In early March 1770, these sporadic incidents culminated in a fatal confrontation. On March 5, a crowd gathered outside the customs house and began pelting the guardsmen with snowballs and rocks. The British officer, Captain Thomas Preston, ordered his men to fix bayonets and push the crowd back. But then one soldier evidently slipped, and his musket discharged as he fell. The remaining soldiers, perhaps believing that in the tumult Preston had ordered them to fire, shot into the crowd, killing five Bostonians and wounding six. Four of the dead men were white artisans or laborers; the fifth was Crispus Attucks, a free black sailor.

Captain Preston and six soldiers were tried for murder. They were defended in court by two prominent Boston lawyers, John Adams and Josiah Quincy, Jr., who—despite their radical political leanings—thought the soldiers deserved a proper legal defense. Preston and four soldiers were acquitted; two others were convicted of the lesser charge of manslaughter.

The **Boston Massacre** seemed to fulfill dire republican prophecies about a tyrannical Britain using military coercion to take away American liberties. Boston's radicals worked to ensure that the memory of the Massacre remained fresh in colonists' minds. Each year, Bostonians commemorated March 5 as "Massacre Day," with public speeches and other events. Orators warned colonists in other cities to be vigilant, since their turn might be next.

Partial Repeal and Its Consequences

Ironically, the Boston Massacre occurred on the same day that Lord North proposed that Parliament repeal all of the Townshend duties except the one on tea. As was the case after the Stamp Act, Parliament feared that complete repeal would make it seem that Britain had given in to the colonists. Retaining the tax on tea served as a statement of parliamentary authority; it also made fiscal sense in that most of the revenue raised by the Townshend duties came from the tax on tea.

The rejoicing that had followed the Stamp Act repeal was not repeated after partial repeal of the Townshend duties. For the colonists, this had been an incomplete victory, and recent events, especially the Boston Massacre, had seriously undermined their trust in British authority. On the surface, the years 1770–1773 looked like a time of relative calm. Underneath, however, colonial animosities against British policies continued to simmer.

Every now and then, some incident brought those animosities to a boil. Such was the case in 1772, when a British customs vessel, the *Gaspée*, ran aground near Providence, Rhode Island. Because its crew had allegedly harassed local residents, Rhode Islanders got even. Led by John Brown, a local merchant, they boarded and burned the ship. The British government appointed a commission of inquiry with instructions to arrest the culprits and send them to England for trial. Despite its offer of a reward for information, the commission learned nothing.

Such incidents, and in particular the British threat to send Americans to England for trial, led colonial leaders to resolve to keep one another informed about British actions. Twelve colonies established **committees of correspondence** for this purpose. In 1773, Boston radicals established similar committees in towns throughout Massachusetts. The committees aimed not only to keep abreast of events in Britain and in other colonies, but also to try and anticipate what Parliament's next move might be.

Boston Massacre After months of increasing friction between townspeople and the British troops stationed in the city, on March 5, 1770, British troops fired on American civilians in Boston.

committees of correspondence Committees formed in the colonies to keep Americans informed about British measures that would affect them.

Domestic Divisions

| 5.4 | What issues and interests divided the colonists? |

 ven as growing mistrust of Britain encouraged many colonists to see themselves as having common interests, local animosities could still divide them. The same issues that sparked opposition to Britain—property rights and political representation—often pitted colonists against one another.

Regulator Movements

The end of the Cherokee War of 1760–1761 had not brought peace to backcountry South Carolina. Gangs of outlaws displaced by that conflict roamed the countryside, plundering the estates of prosperous farmers and challenging anyone to stop them. When the colonial government, based more than a hundred miles away in Charleston, failed to respond, the aggrieved farmers took matters into their own hands. In 1767,

Regulators Vigilante groups active in the 1760s and 1770s in the western parts of North and South Carolina. The South Carolina Regulators attempted to rid the area of outlaws; the North Carolina Regulators were more concerned with high taxes and court costs.

they organized vigilante companies to fight against the marauders. Calling themselves "**Regulators**," they aimed to bring law and order to the backcountry. By March 1768, the Regulators had succeeded in killing or expelling most of the criminals.

The outlaws' threat to property and order was symptomatic of a larger problem of political representation. By the 1760s, most South Carolina settlers lived in the backcountry, but because the creation of legislative districts in the region had not kept pace with settlement, they elected only two of forty-eight assembly representatives. Moreover, there was no court system in the region for the resolution of disputes. Once the outlaws had been eliminated, the Regulators—many of whom were relatively prosperous farmers and shopkeepers—took it upon themselves to "regulate" the poor settlers in their neighborhoods. Their tactics included whipping and other forms of intimidation, which only created a new source of unrest. The crisis diminished only when the governor agreed to create circuit courts in the backcountry and the assembly established new districts that increased the region's political representation.

At about the same time, a Regulator movement emerged in North Carolina. Once again, political representation was a major grievance, for the western counties elected only seventeen of the assembly's seventy-eight members. And while North Carolina's backcountry did have county courts, they were plagued by corruption. Once again, aggrieved westerners resorted to extralegal protests. They refused to pay taxes, closed county courts, and attacked the most detested of tax officials.

Governor William Tryon matched force with force, sending 1,000 militiamen from eastern counties to subdue the protestors. In May 1771, the militiamen defeated more than 2,000 poorly armed Regulators in a battle at Alamance Creek that left 29 men dead and 150 wounded.

The battle at Alamance Creek was the most serious episode of unrest, but the tensions that produced it simmered throughout the backcountry. Western settlers—often recent immigrants from Scotland, Northern Ireland, and Germany—paid little attention to the threats to liberty and property posed by parliamentary measures. As far as they were concerned, the sources of corruption lay much closer to home, in eastern capitals where officials ignored western demands for good government. Until legislative districts were created in the region, backcountry farmers could legitimately complain about taxation without representation—imposed by their own colonial assemblies.

The Beginnings of Antislavery

In a similar vein, African slaves could have argued that their experience of actual enslavement was far more real than any potential threat to white colonists' liberty posed by imperial reforms. Black colonists, both slave and free, watched white colonists march in parades and riot in the streets, and heard their orators make fervent speeches on behalf of liberty. Although slavery would far outlast these decades, some colonists began to question the legitimacy of the oppressive institution.

Some slaves, particularly in New England, employed the language of liberty when they sued their owners for freedom. In Massachusetts, groups of slaves petitioned both the legislature and the governor for release from bondage. Although these legal maneuvers did bring freedom for some individual slaves, taking masters to court was expensive, and slavery as an institution was scarcely undermined.

The slave trade was temporarily interrupted in some colonies during the nonimportation movements. But the first significant attacks on the institution were generated by religious, not economic or political, concerns. In England, Methodists led the way; in the colonies, Quakers were the first to create an antislavery society and, in 1774, to abolish slaveholding among their membership.

The majority of colonists were nowhere near ready to endorse the end of slavery, and slave owners regarded calls for abolition as a threat to their property rights. Yet if the antislavery movement could claim few victories in these years, it in fact achieved a major accomplishment. For the first time, colonists who had grown accustomed to taking slavery for granted had to defend an institution that violated the very rights they claimed for themselves.

The Final Imperial Crisis

| 5.5 | What pushed the colonists from protest to rebellion? |

Themed the relative calm that marked the years 1770–1773 might have lasted far longer had Parliament not passed another law that reignited colonial protests. Ironically, the despised measure had nothing to do with imperial reform.

The Boston Tea Party

The measure that outraged colonists was actually designed to help a failing British corporation. The East India Company was tottering on the brink of bankruptcy. Millions of pounds of unsold tea sat in its warehouses, and the imminent failure of Britain's

📖 **Read the Document**   **John Andrews to William Barrell, Letter Regarding the Boston Tea Party (1773)**

Mr. and Mrs. Thomas Mifflin of Philadelphia. Mifflin was a prominent merchant and radical opponent of British policy toward the colonies. He and his wife were visiting Boston in 1773, when John Singleton Copley painted them. Working at a small loom, Sarah Morris Mifflin weaves a decorative fringe. She no doubt did the same during the nonimportation movement against the Townshend duties, thereby helping to make importation of such goods from England unnecessary.

From Then to Now
The Tea Party Movement

In 2009, a new political movement arose in the wake of Barack Obama's election as U.S. president and in opposition to his policies. Calling themselves the Tea Party movement, the members linked their concerns about the power of the federal government, the growing national debt, and the preservation of personal and economic freedom to one of the best-known incidents of the Revolutionary era. During the Boston Tea Party of December 1773, a group of colonists disguised themselves as Indians and dumped more than 300 chests of tea into Boston Harbor to protest a British tax to which they had not consented. Their action brought swift British retaliation, which in turn pushed Americans toward revolution.

Revolutionary-era Americans accorded less significance to the Tea Party than their descendants have. The Tea Party was not even known by that name until the 1830s, after the Revolutionary generation had largely passed away. Since then, numerous groups of Americans have appropriated the event to support their own agendas. In New York in the 1840s, for instance, farmers invoked the Tea Party in their protests against landlords and high rents. During the Vietnam era, some opponents of the war declared that their acts of civil disobedience were in the tradition of the Tea Party. Nearly thirty years later, in 1998, crusaders for tax reform boarded a replica of the original tea ship, placed a copy of the federal tax code in a chest marked "tea," and dumped it overboard. The recent emergence of the Tea Party movement, which helped to elect several conservative members to Congress in 2010 and participated in the 2012 elections, indicates that this Revolutionary event has lost none of its symbolic attraction to Americans who find themselves at odds with the political establishment.

Question for Discussion

- Why might the Tea Party have more symbolic significance to modern Americans than other episodes of protest during the 1760s and 1770s?

This engraving shows colonists dressed like Indians destroying British tea in December 1773 in protest against the Tea Act.

One participant in this 2011 Tea Party rally in Washington, DC, dressed up as George Washington to emphasize the movement's identification with the Revolutionary era.

largest corporation alarmed Lord North. If English and colonial consumers, who were purchasing cheaper, smuggled Dutch tea, could be induced to buy East India Company tea, the corporation might be saved without needing a major government subsidy.

North's proposed solution was the **Tea Act of 1773**. The measure made East India Company tea cheaper by exempting it from the duty normally collected as the tea was transshipped through Britain. For colonial consumers, the only tax that remained on the tea was the old Townshend duty. North assumed that the lure of cheaper tea would allow the colonists to accept the Townshend duty, and their increased purchases would save the beleaguered East India Company.

As it turned out, North spectacularly misjudged the colonial reaction. Merchants were outraged by a provision in the Tea Act that gave the company and its agents a monopoly on the sale of tea in the colonies. They were joined in protest by Americans in every colony, convinced that North meant to trick them into paying a tax to which they had not consented.

Tea Act of 1773 Permitted the East India Company to sell through agents in America without paying the duty customarily collected in Britain, thus reducing the retail price.

Colonial leaders realized that their most effective form of resistance was preventing the ships carrying tea from landing. In several ports, the Sons of Liberty threatened ship captains with violence, convincing them to return to England without unloading their cargo. But in Boston, some of the Company agents responsible for the tea happened to be the sons of Governor Thomas Hutchinson. The governor was determined to have the tea unloaded in Boston and the tax paid.

Boston's Sons of Liberty saw no alternative to taking decisive action. On December 16, 1773, a well-organized band of men disguised as Indians raced aboard the *Dartmouth* and two other tea ships, broke open 342 chests of tea, and heaved the contents into the harbor. In a similar action in 1774, residents of Annapolis, Maryland, forced some merchants to burn their own ship when it arrived with dutied tea. But it was the **Boston Tea Party** that captured the attention of Parliament and inspired its angry reaction.

The Intolerable Acts

The destruction of property in the Boston Tea Party shocked many people in Britain and America. Parliament understood that such an affront to its sovereignty demanded a vigorous response. Thus, in the spring of 1774, it passed a series of repressive measures known as the **Coercive Acts**.

The first of these, effective June 1, 1774, was the Boston Port Act, which closed the port of Boston until Bostonians paid for the tea and uncollected duties. The Administration of Justice Act allowed any British soldier or official who was charged with a crime while performing his duties to be tried in England (where he would almost certainly receive sympathetic treatment). A new Quartering Act permitted the army to lodge soldiers in any civilian building if necessary. The fourth and most detested measure, the Massachusetts Government Act, drastically modified that colony's charter of 1691. Henceforth, members of the governor's council and sheriffs would be appointed rather than elected. In addition, the act limited the number of town meetings that could be held without the governor's prior approval. As the Coercive Acts made their way through Parliament, the king chose General Thomas Gage, the commander of the British army in North America, as the new governor of Massachusetts.

On the same day that Parliament enacted these measures, it also passed an unrelated law, the **Quebec Act**. This statute extended Quebec's boundaries south to the Ohio River and stipulated that the colony was to be governed by an appointed governor and council but no elected assembly (see Map 5.2). Civil cases would be tried without a jury and the Catholic Church would enjoy the same privileges that it had under the French. The colonists linked the Quebec Act with the Coercive Acts and labeled them the **Intolerable Acts** (see Table 5.1 on page 137, New Restraints and Burdens on Americans, 1763–1774).

The Americans' Reaction

The Americans' response to all of these measures was swift, but also revealed divided opinions. The colonists came closest to unanimity in their opposition to the Quebec Act. As one colonist said, the establishment of the Catholic Church in Quebec "gave a General Alarm to all Protestants." Equally disturbing was the fact that the act gave Canada jurisdiction over lands north of the Ohio River claimed by Connecticut, Pennsylvania, and Virginia. Colonial settlers and land speculators in these colonies resented their exclusion from territory they had helped to win for Britain in the French and Indian War. Colonists also suspected that the autocratic government prescribed for Quebec—with appointed officials, no assemblies, and no civil juries—loomed as a model of British plans for their own colonies.

There was little the colonists could do to stop Gage from closing the port of Boston. Many merchants argued that the town should just pay for the tea and thus avoid an economic crisis. They were outnumbered, however, by many more Bostonians who called for another intercolonial boycott of British goods. Yet in New York and Philadelphia, merchants balked at a form of protest that hurt their businesses, and instead wanted an intercolonial congress called to coordinate an American response.

If Lord North thought that the Coercive Acts would drive a wedge between radical Boston and the rest of the colonies, he was utterly mistaken. Boston's committee of

Boston Tea Party Incident that occurred on December 16, 1773, in which Bostonians, disguised as Indians, destroyed £9,000 worth of tea belonging to the British East India Company in order to prevent payment of the duty on it.

Coercive Acts Legislation passed by Parliament in 1774; included the Boston Port Act, the Massachusetts Government Act, the Administration of Justice Act, and the Quartering Act of 1774.

Quebec Act Law passed by Parliament in 1774 that provided an appointed government for Canada, enlarged the boundaries of Quebec, and confirmed the privileges of the Catholic Church.

Intolerable Acts American term for the Coercive Acts and the Quebec Act.

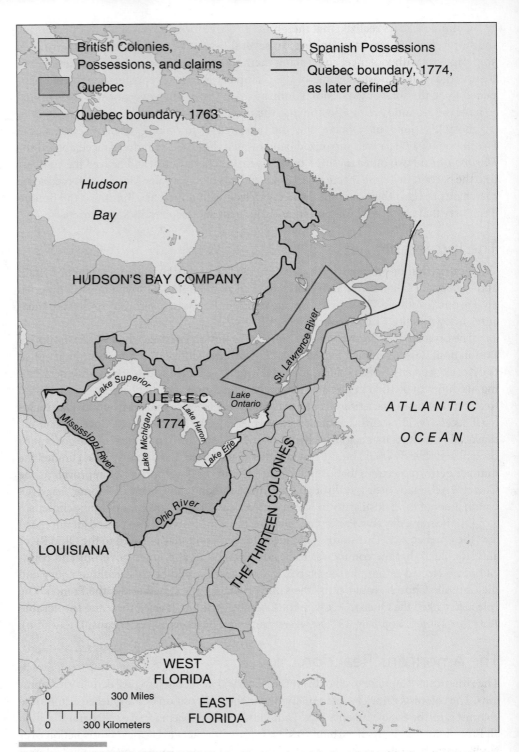

MAP 5.2 THE QUEBEC ACT OF 1774 The Quebec Act enlarged the boundaries of the Canadian province southward to the Ohio River and westward to the Mississippi, thereby depriving several colonies of claims to the area granted them by their original charters.

correspondence produced a steady stream of warnings about this latest and most serious threat to liberty that resonated throughout the colonies. As real economic hardship descended on the city, contributions of food and fuel flowed in from the countryside. The spirit of protest thus spread out from urban areas, where opposition to the Stamp Act and Townshend Duty Act had mainly occurred, into rural villages. More colonists were politicized than ever before.

When the assemblies in other colonies discussed joining the resistance movement, royal governors shut them down. This led colonists to organize "provincial congresses," or extralegal conventions that acted as proxies for the assemblies in mobilizing the public.

Read the Document John Dickinson, from *Letters from a Farmer in Pennsylvania* (1768)

5.1

5.2

5.3

5.4

5.5

TABLE 5.1 NEW RESTRAINTS AND BURDENS ON AMERICANS, 1763–1774

	Limits on Legislative Action	Curbs on Territorial Expansion	Burdens on Colonial Trade	Imposition of New Taxes
1763		Proclamation Line keeps white settlement east of the Appalachians	Peacetime use of navy and new customs officials to enforce Navigation Acts	
1764	Currency Act limits the colonial legislatures' ability to issue paper money		Vice-admiralty courts strengthened for Sugar Act	Sugar Act imposes taxes for revenue (modified 1766)
1765				Quartering Act requires assemblies to provide facilities for royal troops
				Stamp Act imposes internal taxes on various items (repealed 1766)
1766	Declaratory Act proclaims Parliament's right to legislate for colonies in all cases whatsoever			
1767	Royal instructions limit size of colonial assemblies		Vice-admiralty courts strengthened for Townshend duties; American Customs Service established in Boston	Townshend duties imposed on some imported goods in order to pay colonial officials; all but tax on tea repealed 1770
1773				Tea Act reduces duty and prompts Boston Tea Party
1774 (Intolerable Acts)	Massachusetts Government Act limits town meetings, changes legislature, and violates Massachusetts charter	Quebec Act enlarges Quebec at expense of colonies with claims in the Ohio River Valley	Boston Port Act closes harbor until East India Company's tea is paid for	Quartering Act of 1774 declares that troops can be lodged in virtually any uninhabited building in Boston

Massachusetts's Provincial Congress, meeting in the town of Concord, became the colony's de facto government. It voted to accept the **Suffolk Resolves**, which had been passed at a convention in Suffolk County (where Boston was located). These resolutions called for the payment of taxes to the Provincial Congress, not to Gage in Boston, and demanded creation of an armed force of "minutemen" ready to respond to any emergency. The Provincial Congress also authorized the stockpiling of arms and ammunition in Concord.

Suffolk Resolves Militant resolves adopted in 1774 in response to the Coercive Acts by representatives from the towns in Suffolk County, Massachusetts, including Boston.

The First Continental Congress

A consensus emerged in support of an intercolonial congress. In the end, twelve colonies (all except Georgia) sent representatives. The **First Continental Congress** met at Carpenter's Hall in Philadelphia from September 5 to October 26, 1774, with fifty-five delegates present at one time or another. The delegates quickly voted for nonimportation, remembering its utility in previous imperial confrontations. Virtually all of the delegates likewise agreed to a policy of nonexportation, to begin in August 1775 if Britain had not yet addressed colonial grievances. Despite concerns of more conservative members, radical delegates also succeeded in having the Congress endorse the Suffolk Resolves, declaring the Coercive Acts unconstitutional.

Delegates then engaged in an extended debate trying to define colonial rights, in effect specifying the terms by which the colonies would voluntarily retain their membership in the empire. The result was a declaration of rights and set of resolves that responded to a decade of imperial crises. The delegates went beyond declaring the Intolerable Acts unconstitutional to criticize all revenue measures passed since the end of the French and Indian War. They denounced the dissolution of colonial assemblies and the keeping of troops in the colonies during peacetime. Congress defined the colonists' rights to include "life, liberty, and property," and stated that colonial legislatures had exclusive powers to make laws and pass taxes, subject only to the royal veto. About the only concession it made was to pledge that Americans would "cheerfully" consent to trade regulations for the good of the empire.

First Continental Congress Meeting of delegates from most of the colonies held in 1774 in response to the Coercive Acts. The Congress endorsed the Suffolk Resolves, adopted the Declaration of Rights and Grievances, and agreed to establish the Continental Association.

Continental Association
Agreement adopted by the First Continental Congress in 1774 in response to the Coercive Acts to cut off trade with Britain until the objectionable measures were repealed.

The Continental Association

As Congress's proceedings came to an end, some delegates began to tinker with its recommendations to protect their own colonies' interests. Members from the Chesapeake colonies wanted to ensure that if the nonexportation policy had to go into effect in 1775, it would not begin until that year's tobacco crop had been shipped. Carolina delegates went so far as to threaten to walk out of the meeting if rice was not exempted from the nonexportation agreement.

Two final tasks remained. First, Congress needed an enforcement mechanism to ensure that its agreed-upon measures were followed. It created the **Continental Association**, a mutual pledge by the delegates to see that their colonies ceased importing any British goods after December 1, 1774, and, if the dispute with Britain was not resolved by September 1775, make sure that their provinces ceased exporting goods to Britain and the West Indies. Voters in every town, city, and county throughout the colonies were to choose committees to enforce the terms of the Association. The approximately 7,000 men who served on these committees during the winter of 1774–1775 in effect formed grassroots radical governments.

((• 📖 Read the Document   Patrick Henry, "Give Me Liberty or Give Me Death" (1775)

A New Method of MACARONY MAKING, as practised at BOSTON.

This image shows John Malcolm, an unpopular customs commissioner, being tarred and feathered in Boston. By 1774, radicals threatened others who defended British measures with similar punishment.

Second, Congress concluded its proceedings with an address not to Parliament, but to the king and the British and American people. This gesture confirmed the fact that delegates no longer considered Parliament to be a legitimate legislature over the colonies. Delegates instead asked George III to use his "royal authority and interposition" to protect his loyal subjects in America. So long as the king protected colonial rights, he could count on the Americans' allegiance.

Political Polarization

Scarcely anyone called for independence at this point. Even so, many Americans had moved far from the positions they had taken at the start of the imperial crisis. Instead of urging a return to the pre-1763 status quo, they agreed with the Congress's rejection of parliamentary sovereignty and its assumption that only allegiance to the king tied Americans to Britain.

Not all colonists accepted such a drastic reinterpretation of the imperial connection. Even if they regarded recent parliamentary measures as threats to American liberty, some colonists continued to recognize parliamentary authority over the colonies. Others had never quarreled with British policies at all. By late 1774, however, it became more dangerous to express such opinions. The local committees created under the Continental Association not only enforced the boycott against British goods but also intimidated their opponents into silence.

A new political order was emerging, requiring colonists to choose one side or the other. The advocates of colonial rights began to call themselves **Whigs** and condemned their opponents as **Tories**. These traditional English party labels dated from the late seventeenth century, when the Tories had supported the accession of the Catholic King James II, and the Whigs had opposed it. Colonial Whigs used this label to identify themselves as champions of liberty and called their opponents Tories to represent them as defenders of tyrannical royal government. As imperial ties proceeded to unravel, there appeared to be no third option.

Whigs The name used by advocates of colonial resistance to British measures during the 1760s and 1770s.

Tories A derisive term applied to loyalists in America who supported the king and Parliament just before and during the American Revolution.

Conclusion

Andrew Burnaby's confident assertion that colonial union was impossible rang hollow barely a decade after he made it. Yet imperial breakdown was as unexpected as it was rapid. British officials initiated their program of reform in 1763 in order to tighten the bonds of empire, not destroy them. But their plans went terribly awry. Colonists accustomed to local self-government and wedded to the belief that they were imperial partners, not subordinates, saw British reforms as infringements on their rights. For more than a decade, Britain and America engaged in a transatlantic debate—often punctuated with violence—about the terms under which the empire might endure.

Years of political turmoil inspired colonists to think more systematically about their rights than they had ever done before. As they did so, members of the elite and laborers, men and women, black colonists and white, were all drawn into the politics of resistance. They read (and sometimes wrote) letters and pamphlets, marched in the streets, boycotted tea, and wore homespun clothing. In so doing, they came to recognize their common interests as Americans and their differences from the British. They became aware, as Benjamin Franklin would later write, of the need to break "through the bounds, in which a dependent people had been accustomed to think, and act" so that they might "properly comprehend the character they had assumed."

In the winter of 1774–1775, however, the "character" of the Americans was not yet fully revealed. Although they had achieved an unprecedented level of unity in their opposition to Parliament, they did not all agree on where the path of resistance would lead. Americans had surely rebelled, but had not yet launched a revolution.

For Suggested Readings go to MyHistoryLab.

Chapter Review

The Crisis of Imperial Authority

5.1 What new challenges did the British government face in North America after 1763? p. 119

After 1763, Britain had to find ways to govern its enlarged territorial empire in North America and to pay off its enormous postwar debt. Indian conflict on the frontier and unregulated colonial settlement posed major challenges, and passage of the Sugar Act, intended to help address Britain's debt, sparked colonial protest.

Republican Ideology and Colonial Protest

5.2 How did republican ideology inform the colonists' view of their relationship to Britain? p. 123

Republican ideology encouraged colonists to be wary of excessive power and to protect their liberties. Many colonists regarded British imperial reforms, especially the passage of new taxes, as infringements on colonial liberty, since colonists did not elect representatives to the Parliament that imposed such taxes.

The Stamp Act and Townshend Duty Act Crises

5.3 Why did the Stamp Act and Townshend Duty Act spark widespread unrest in the colonies? p. 125

Colonists did not believe that Parliament had the constitutional right to tax them without their consent. They protested against the Stamp Act tax and the Townshend duties on imported goods in an attempt to preserve colonial liberties. Their protests included petitions for redress, trade boycotts, and violent mob actions.

Domestic Divisions

5.4 What issues and interests divided the colonists? p. 131

Some colonists, especially on the Carolina frontier, worried that local leaders were just as guilty as Parliament of encroaching on settlers' liberties. Groups like the Regulators fought back to protect their property rights and to call for political representation. Other colonists also began to question the legitimacy of the institution of slavery.

The Final Imperial Crisis

5.5 What pushed the colonists from protest to rebellion? p. 133

Parliament's passage of the Coercive Acts in response to the Boston Tea Party convinced many colonists that Britain aimed to rule the colonies by force. Thus colonists responded with another trade boycott and the calling of a Continental Congress to coordinate American resistance in an increasingly polarized political environment.

Timeline

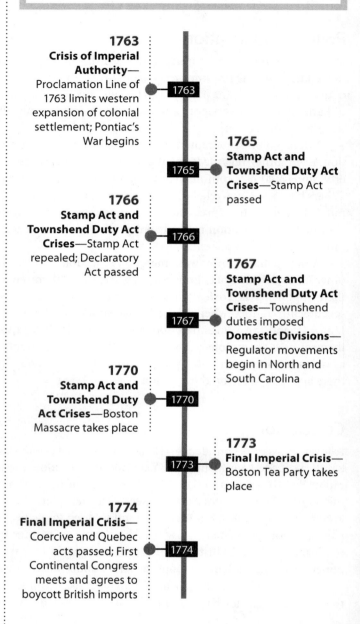

1763
Crisis of Imperial Authority—Proclamation Line of 1763 limits western expansion of colonial settlement; Pontiac's War begins

1765
Stamp Act and Townshend Duty Act Crises—Stamp Act passed

1766
Stamp Act and Townshend Duty Act Crises—Stamp Act repealed; Declaratory Act passed

1767
Stamp Act and Townshend Duty Act Crises—Townshend duties imposed
Domestic Divisions—Regulator movements begin in North and South Carolina

1770
Stamp Act and Townshend Duty Act Crises—Boston Massacre takes place

1773
Final Imperial Crisis—Boston Tea Party takes place

1774
Final Imperial Crisis—Coercive and Quebec acts passed; First Continental Congress meets and agrees to boycott British imports

6 The War for Independence 1774–1783

One American Journey

An American Soldier's Account of the Battle of Long Island, August 1776

t is impossible for me to describe the confusion and horror of the scene that ensued: the artillery flying with the chains over the horses' backs, our men running in almost every direction, and run which way they would, they were almost sure to meet the British or Hessians. And the enemy huzzahing when they took prisoners made it truly a day of distress to the Americans. I escaped by getting behind the British that had been engaged with Lord Stirling and entered a swamp or marsh through which a great many of our men were retreating. Some of them were mired and crying to their fellows for God's sake to help them out; but every man was intent on his own safety and no assistance was rendered. At the side of the marsh there was a pond which I took to be a millpond. Numbers, as soon as they came to this pond, jumped in, and some were drowned. Soon after I entered the marsh, a cannonading commenced from our batteries on the British, and they retreated, and I got safely into camp. Out of the eight men that were taken from the company to which I belonged the day before the battle on guard, I only escaped. The others were either killed or taken prisoner.

Michael Graham

John C. Dann, ed., *The Revolution Remembered: Eyewitness Accounts of the War for Independence* (Chicago: University of Chicago Press, 1980), p. 50.

John Trumbull's portrait of Washington shows the American general before the Battle of Trenton in December 1776. This battle turned out to be a key turning point in the war.

LEARNING OBJECTIVES

6.1 ((	6.2 ((	6.3 ((	6.4 ((	6.5 ((	6.6 ((
Why was reconciliation between the colonies and Britain virtually impossible by the beginning of 1775? p. 143	What functions did the Congress fulfill as it sought to manage the American rebellion? p. 144	What were the key differences between the British and American forces? p. 149	Why was the alliance with France a key turning point in the war? p. 152	How did the War for Independence affect women, African Americans, and Native Americans? p. 161	What were the key factors in the American victory in the Revolutionary War? p. 164

((Listen to **Chapter 6** on MyHistoryLab

6.1

6.2

6.3

6.4

6.5

6.6

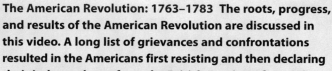 Watch the Video Series on MyHistoryLab

Learn about some key topics related to this chapter with the *MyHistoryLab Video Series: Key Topics in U.S. History.*

1 **The American Revolution: 1763–1783** The roots, progress, and results of the American Revolution are discussed in this video. A long list of grievances and confrontations resulted in the Americans first resisting and then declaring their independence from the British Empire. After eight years of warfare, the American colonies not only secured victory, but established a new unified nation.

 Watch on MyHistoryLab

The Second Continental Congress This video describes how the Second Continental Congress created an American army, named George Washington its commander, and debated the goals of the struggle. Its supreme achievement was the creation of the Declaration of Independence, the document that summed up the grievances and justifications of the American colonists, not just for themselves, but for the world. **2**

Watch on MyHistoryLab

3 **Declaring Independence** The background and outcome of declaring independence are examined in this video, which begins with an appreciation of Thomas Paine's "Common Sense." This discussion also includes the various declarations of independence authorized by the individual American colonies as well as the origin of the penultimate Declaration of Independence authored by Thomas Jefferson at the Second Continental Congress.

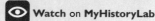 Watch on MyHistoryLab

Battle of Saratoga Using the 1777 Battle of Saratoga as a focal point, this video reveals the British plan to isolate New England from the other states and then conquer it. The plan not only failed, but the American victory at Saratoga resulted in a French alliance with the United States, broadening the scope of the war and ensuring Britain's defeat. **4**

Watch on MyHistoryLab

Personal Journeys Online

- George Washington, General Orders, 4 July 1775. Describes the creation of the Continental Army.
- Joseph Martin, *The Revolutionary Adventures of Joseph Plumb Martin,* 1776–1783. A Continental soldier remembers the Revolution.

Michael Graham, like other veterans of the Continental Army, had to offer a detailed account of his service when he applied for a military pension decades after the end of the War for Independence. Despite the passage of time, Graham's memory of the tumultuous Battle of Long Island remained extraordinarily vivid. A Pennsylvanian by birth, he was just 18 years old when he traveled with the army to New York and fought in this battle that British forces ultimately won. Graham's description of the event not only illuminates the confusion that characterized combat, but also serves as a reminder that, in the summer of 1776, many observers assumed that the powerful British army and navy would easily triumph over the ragtag American forces.

6.1

6.2

6.3

6.4

6.5

6.6

American colonists had long been suspicious of standing armies, fearing that they could be as easily used to oppress civilians as to defend them. But when the Revolutionary War began, it soon became clear that colonial militias alone would not be able to withstand attacks by a professional British army. Thus on July 4, 1775, the Continental Congress took control of the troops raised within the colonies and organized them into a Continental Army under the leadership of General George Washington.

The creation of the Continental Army marked a critical step in the Americans' journey from British colonists to an independent people. Yet the army's task was daunting and in the end required eight long years of fighting. The bloody conflict proved instrumental in convincing the Americans to abandon last-ditch efforts at compromise and declare independence. Victory, however, would require foreign help, particularly a crucial alliance in 1778 with France, eager for revenge against Britain after the French defeat in the Seven Years' War.

With the peace treaty signed in 1783, America's independent nationhood was secure. Americans celebrated their victory in a war hard-fought to preserve their liberty. Yet the conflict had also strained American society, and not all of the new nation's inhabitants would enjoy the liberty that soldiers such as Michael Graham had fought so hard to protect.

From Rebellion to War

6.1 Why was reconciliation between the colonies and Britain virtually impossible by the beginning of 1775?

When the First Continental Congress adjourned in October 1774, no one quite knew what the future would hold. Britain had adopted its harshest policies yet in response to the Boston Tea Party and appeared to be in no mood for reconciliation. At the same time, colonists in New England were stockpiling arms while committees of safety watched their neighbors in the cities and countryside, intimidating defenders of Britain into silence. Yet if tempers ran high, few people wished for bloodshed.

Contradictory British Policies

Britain held parliamentary elections in the fall of 1774, but if Americans hoped that the outcome would change the government's policy toward them, they were disappointed. Lord North's supporters won easily. A few members of Parliament urged their fellow legislators to adopt conciliatory measures before it was too late. However, such efforts failed to gain much support.

Lord North's next actions made matters worse. He ordered Thomas Gage, commander in chief of the British army in America and newly installed governor of Massachusetts, to destroy an arms stockpile in Concord and arrest the radical leaders John Hancock and Samuel Adams. North then introduced a measure that prohibited New Englanders from trading outside the British Empire or sending their ships to the North Atlantic fishing grounds. Both houses of Parliament followed a similar hard line by declaring the colony of Massachusetts to be in rebellion.

Yet at the same time Lord North introduced a **Conciliatory Proposition**, whereby Parliament pledged not to tax the colonies if their assemblies would voluntarily contribute to the defense of the empire and the costs of civil government and the judiciary in their own colonies. British officials, however, would decide what was a sufficient contribution—a provision that protected Parliament's claim to sovereignty—and could use force against colonies that did not pay their share. At one time, colonists might have found the Conciliatory Proposition acceptable. By the spring of 1775, it was too late.

Conciliatory Proposition Plan whereby Parliament would "forbear" taxation of Americans in colonies whose assemblies imposed taxes considered satisfactory by the British government.

6.1

6.2

6.3

6.4

6.5

6.6

Committee of Safety Any of the extralegal committees that directed the revolutionary movement and carried on the functions of government at the local level in the period between the breakdown of royal authority and the establishment of regular governments.

Minute Men Special companies of militia formed in Massachusetts and elsewhere beginning in late 1774.

Mounting Tensions in America

Colonists everywhere waited to hear what Britain's next move would be, but those in Massachusetts were most apprehensive. General Gage had begun fortifying Boston and had dissolved the Massachusetts legislature. The delegates assembled anyway, calling themselves the Provincial Congress. In October 1774, this body appointed an emergency executive body, the **Committee of Safety**, headed by John Hancock, to gather arms and ammunition and to organize militia volunteers. Some localities had already formed special companies of **Minute Men**, who were to be ready at "a minute's warning in Case of an alarm." Massachusetts had, in effect, created a revolutionary government.

As tensions grew, colonists everywhere found it increasingly dangerous to express opinions in favor of Britain, or even to try and remain neutral. Moderates who placed their hopes in George III were demoralized when the king declared the New England colonies to be in a state of rebellion. The king's threat that "blows must decide whether they are to be subject to this Country or independent" scarcely reassured those who hoped to avoid bloodshed. The initial clash between British and American forces was not long in coming.

The Battles of Lexington and Concord

Gage received his orders to seize the weapons at Concord and arrest Samuel Adams and John Hancock on April 14, 1775. On the night of April 18, hoping to surprise the colonists, he assembled 700 men on the Boston Common for a predawn march toward the towns of Lexington and Concord, some 20 miles away. But the army's maneuvers were hardly invisible to vigilant colonists. Adams and Hancock, who were staying in Lexington, escaped. Throughout the night, patriot riders—including the silversmith Paul Revere—spread the alarm through the countryside.

When the British soldiers reached Lexington at dawn, they found about seventy armed militiamen drawn up in formation on the village green. Outnumbered ten to one, the Americans probably did not plan to fight. More likely, they were there in a show of defiance, to demonstrate that Americans would not run at the sight of the king's troops. A British major ordered the militia to disperse. They were starting to obey when a shot from an unknown source shattered the stillness. The British responded with a volley that killed or wounded eighteen Americans.

The British troops pressed on to Concord and burned what few supplies the Americans had not hidden. But when their rear guard came under fire at Concord's North Bridge, the British panicked. As they retreated to Boston, patriot Minute Men and other militia harried them from both sides of the road. By the time the column reached safety, 273 British soldiers were dead, wounded, or missing. The Americans had suffered an additional 100 casualties.

Patriots made extraordinary efforts to spread the news of the **Battles of Lexington and Concord** as quickly as possible. The shots fired that April morning would, in the words of the nineteenth-century Concord philosopher and poet Ralph Waldo Emerson, be "heard round the world." They signaled the start of the American Revolution, which would help to inspire many revolutions elsewhere.

Battles of Lexington and Concord The first two battles of the American Revolution, which resulted in a total of 273 British soldiers dead, wounded, and missing and nearly 100 Americans dead, wounded, and missing.

The Continental Congress Becomes a National Government

6.2 What functions did the Congress fulfill as it sought to manage the American rebellion?

The First Continental Congress had adjourned in October 1774 with virtually everyone hoping that the imperial crisis could be resolved without war. When the delegates reconvened in Philadelphia on May 10, 1775, however, war had begun. Gage's troops had limped from Concord back into Boston, besieged there by a gathering force of patriot militia from all over New England. With no other intercolonial body available to do the job, the Second Congress by default assumed management of the rebellion as its members also debated what the colonies' ultimate goal should be. Even before America had declared itself a nation, it had acquired a national government.

6.1

6.2

6.3

6.4

6.5

6.6

The Second Continental Congress Convenes

It would be difficult to overstate the enormity of the task facing the **Second Continental Congress**. On the very day that the Congress convened—May 10, 1775—American forces from Vermont and Massachusetts captured the British garrison at Fort Ticonderoga at the southern end of Lake Champlain. Just over a month later, General Gage attempted to fortify territory south of Boston, where his cannons could command the harbor. But the Americans seized the high ground first, entrenching themselves on Breed's Hill north of town. On June 17, 1775, Gage sent 2,200 well-trained soldiers to drive the 1,700 patriot forces from their new position. The British succeeded, but at the cost of more than 1,000 casualties. One despondent British officer observed afterward that another such victory "would have ruined us." Misnamed for another hill nearby, this encounter has gone down in history as the Battle of Bunker Hill (see Map 6.1).

As the rebellion progressed, colonial assemblies remained in charge of making laws and imposing taxes. Congress, as the de facto national government, focused on the functions the Crown had formerly performed. It took command of the **Continental Army**, authorized the formation of a navy, established a post office, conducted diplomacy with Indian nations, and printed paper money to meet its expenses.

One of Congress's most momentous decisions was choosing a leader for the Continental Army. Although most of the patriot troops around Boston were New Englanders, delegates knew that they had to ensure military support from all colonies. Thus, at John Adams's suggestion, Congress asked a Virginian, George Washington, to take command.

Not yet ready to demand independence, Congress hoped that the fighting would compel Britain to accept a government that acknowledged the sovereignty of colonial assemblies and an imperial tie through allegiance to the Crown. Thus, even as delegates managed the war, they approved the **Olive Branch Petition** on July 5, 1775, in which they asked George III to protect his American subjects from the military actions ordered by Parliament. The following day, Congress approved the **Declaration of the Causes and Necessity of Taking Up Arms**, which listed colonial grievances and asserted the resolve of American patriots "to die freemen, rather than to live slaves." And at the end of the month, it formally rejected North's Conciliatory Proposition.

Early Fighting: Massachusetts, Virginia, the Carolinas, and Canada

Washington arrived in Boston in early July 1775 to take command of the American forces. Months of military standoff followed. During the winter of 1775–1776, however, the Americans dragged some sixty cannons 300 miles through snow and over mountains from Fort Ticonderoga to Boston. In March 1776, Washington mounted the newly arrived guns to overlook Boston harbor, putting the British in an indefensible position. The British then evacuated the city—which really had no strategic value for them—and moved their troops to Halifax, Nova Scotia. New England was for the moment secure for the patriots.

Second Continental Congress Convened in Philadelphia on May 10, 1775, the Second Continental Congress called for the patchwork of local forces to be organized into the Continental Army, authorized the formation of a navy, established a post office, and printed paper continental dollars to meet its expenses.

Continental Army The regular or professional army authorized by the Second Continental Congress and commanded by General George Washington during the Revolutionary War.

Olive Branch Petition A last effort for peace that avowed America's loyalty to George III and requested that he protect them from further aggressions.

Declaration of the Causes and Necessity of Taking Up Arms Declaration of the Second Continental Congress that Americans were ready to fight for freedom and liberty.

6.1

6.2

6.3

6.4

6.5

6.6

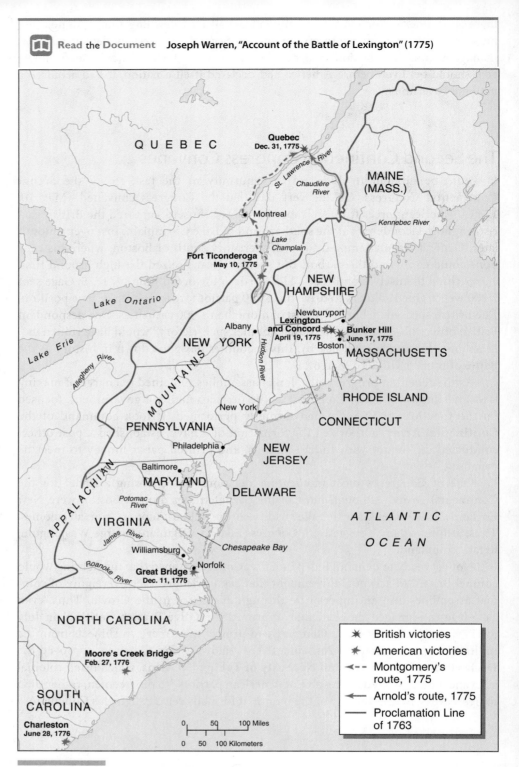

Read the **Document**   Joseph Warren, "Account of the Battle of Lexington" (1775)

British victories

American victories

◄-- Montgomery's route, 1775

◄— Arnold's route, 1775

—— Proclamation Line of 1763

MAP 6.1 EARLY FIGHTING, 1775–1776 As this map clearly reveals, even the earliest fighting occurred in widely scattered areas, thereby complicating Britain's efforts to subdue the Americans.

Fighting in the South also went well for the Americans. Virginia's last royal governor, Lord Dunmore, fled the capital, Williamsburg, and set up a base in nearby Norfolk. Promising freedom to slaves who joined him, he succeeded in raising a small force of black and white Loyalists and British marines. On December 9, 1775, most of these men died when they attacked a much larger force of 900 Virginia and North Carolina troops at Great Bridge, near Norfolk. On February 27, a force of Loyalist Scots suffered a similar defeat at Moore's Creek Bridge in North Carolina, and in June 1776, colonial forces successfully repulsed a large British expedition sent to attack Charleston, South Carolina.

6.1

6.2

6.3

6.4

6.5

6.6

Independence

The American forces' stunning early successes bolstered their confidence even as Britain continued to lose whatever colonial support remained. In October 1775, the British navy attacked and burned the town of Falmouth (now Portland) in Maine, an atrocity that outraged even those moderate colonists who held out hope for reconciliation. Slaveholders, particularly in Virginia, were equally appalled at Governor Dunmore's efforts to lure slaves away with a promise of freedom. When King George III rejected the Congress's Olive Branch Petition in August 1775 and proclaimed the colonies to be in rebellion, he unknowingly pushed more colonists toward independence.

It had taken more than a year of armed conflict to convince many Americans to accept the idea that independence from Britain, not reconciliation, should be the necessary outcome of their efforts. As it turned out, taking that final step required a push from an unexpected direction. It came from Thomas Paine, a ne'er-do-well Englishman, who had recently arrived on American soil. His pamphlet *Common Sense,* published in Philadelphia in January 1776, denounced King George and made a vigorously argued case for independence. Simple common sense, Paine concluded, dictated that "TIS TIME TO PART."

Common Sense, which sold more than 100,000 copies throughout the colonies, helped propel many Americans toward independence. Tactical considerations also influenced patriot leaders. Formal separation from Great Britain would make it easier for Americans to gain desperately needed aid from England's rival France and other foreign countries. France and Spain were already providing a small amount of secret aid, but would do much more for an independent nation. Declaring independence would also provide a better legal basis for American leaders' newly claimed authority. Accordingly, most of the states (as the rebellious colonies now called themselves) either instructed or permitted their delegates in the Congress to vote for independence.

On June 7, 1776, Virginian Richard Henry Lee introduced in the Congress a resolution stating that the united colonies "are, and of right ought to be, free and independent States." Postponing a vote on the issue, the Congress appointed a committee to draw up a declaration of independence. On June 28, after making revisions in a draft produced by Thomas Jefferson, the committee presented the document to Congress. In the debate that followed, a few delegates clung to the hope of remaining loyal to the Crown. But when the Congress voted on the resolution for independence on July 2, 1776, all voting delegations approved it. After further tinkering with the wording, the Congress officially adopted the **Declaration of Independence** on July 4, 1776.

Congress intended the declaration to be a justification for America's secession from the British Empire and an invitation to potential allies. But Jefferson's prose transformed a version of the **contract theory of government** into one of history's great statements of human rights. Developed by the late-seventeenth-century English philosopher John Locke and others, the contract theory maintains that legitimate government rests on an agreement between the people and their rulers. The people are bound to obey their rulers only so long as the rulers offer them protection.

The Declaration of Independence begins by announcing that all men are created equal, that they therefore have equal rights, and that they can neither give up these rights nor allow them to be taken away. Its first premise—that people establish governments to protect their fundamental rights to life, liberty, and property—is a restatement of contract theory. The second premise is a long list of charges meant to prove that George III had failed to defend his American subjects' rights. This indictment justified the Americans' rejection of their hitherto legitimate ruler. Then followed a dramatic conclusion: that Americans could rightfully overthrow King George's rule and replace it with something more satisfactory to them.

Declaration of Independence
The document by which the Second Continental Congress announced and justified its decision to renounce the colonies' allegiance to the British government.

contract theory of government
The belief that government is established by human beings to protect certain rights—such as life, liberty, and property—that are theirs by natural, divinely sanctioned law and that when government protects these rights, people are obligated to obey it.

6.1

6.2

6.3

6.4

6.5

6.6

📖 **Read the Document** Thomas Jefferson, "Original Rough Draught of the Declaration of Independence" (1776)

Thomas Jefferson, author of the Declaration of Independence and future president of the United States. Mather Brown, an American artist living in England, painted this picture of Jefferson for John Adams while the two men were in London on diplomatic missions in 1786. A companion portrait of Adams that Jefferson ordered for himself also survives. Brown's sensitive portrait of a thoughtful Jefferson is the earliest known likeness of him.

Although Jefferson proclaimed "all men" as being equal, many people were excluded from full participation in eighteenth-century American society. Women, Native Americans, slaves, and free black people fell outside the scope of that sweeping phrase. So, too, did men without property, who had restricted rights in colonial society. But if the words "all men are created equal" had limited practical meaning in 1776, they have ever since confronted Americans with a moral challenge to make good on them.

The Loyalists

The Declaration of Independence may have clarified matters for American Whigs, but it made the position of Loyalists, sometimes called Tories—those who professed loyalty to Britain—untenable. With the Declaration of Independence, these loyal subjects of Britain suddenly became enemies of the American people.

An estimated half a million colonists—20 percent of the free population—sided with Britain. Their numbers included rich merchants and farmers as well as poor settlers, and they could be found in every colony. Some were recent immigrants, especially Scots or Scots-Irish newcomers, who trusted the British government more than colonial elites to protect them. In New England, where they were a minority, Anglicans held fast to political as well as religious ties to Britain. Their experiences underscored the important point that the American Revolution was a civil conflict as well as a war for independence. It set neighbor against neighbor and created permanent rifts within families.

These divisions were intensified by the actions of the legislatures of newly independent states, which enacted new treason laws. Refusing to swear allegiance to the state and nation brought criminal penalties; taking up arms on behalf of Britain became a capital crime. Even so, about 19,000 colonists fought with the British, often in special units made up solely of Loyalists.

Up to 70,000 more Loyalists became refugees, fleeing mainly to Nova Scotia and Upper Canada (later the province of Ontario). In addition, some 20,000 escaped slaves who sought freedom with British forces likewise dispersed to other parts of the British Empire. By propelling thousands of people northward, the American Revolution can be said to have created two nations—the United States and, eventually, Canada.

The Combatants

6.1

6.2

6.3

6.4

6.5

6.6

6.3 What were the key differences between the British and American forces?

Republican theory mistrusted professional armies as the instruments of tyrants. A free people, republicans insisted, relied for defense on their own patriotism. But militiamen, as one American general observed, had trouble coping with "the shocking scenes of war" because they were not "steeled by habit or fortified by military pride." In real battles they often proved unreliable. Americans therefore faced a hard choice: develop a professional army or lose the war. In the end, they did what they had to do.

republican Used to describe a theory derived from the political ideas of classical antiquity, Renaissance Europe, and early modern England. Republicanism held that self-government by the citizens of a country, or their representatives, provided a more reliable foundation for the good society and individual freedom than rule by kings. The character of republican government depended on the virtue of the people, but the nature of republican virtue and the conditions favorable to it became sources of debate that influenced the writing of the state and federal constitutions as well as the development of political parties.

Professional Soldiers

Drawing on their colonial experience and on republican theory, the new state governments first tried to meet their military needs by relying on the militia and by creating new units based on short-term enlistments. Officers, particularly in the North, were often elected, and their positions depended on personal popularity. Discipline became a major problem in both the militia and the new state units, and often volunteers had barely received basic training before their term of duty ended and they returned home.

Washington sought to avoid these problems by professionalizing the new Continental Army. He eventually prevailed on Congress to adopt stricter regulations and to require enlistments for three years or the duration of the war. Although he used militia effectively, his consistent aim was to turn the Continental Army into a disciplined force that could defeat the British in the large engagements of massed troops characteristic of eighteenth-century European warfare, for only such victories could impress the other European powers and establish the legitimacy of the United States.

The enemy British soldiers—and the nearly 30,000 German mercenaries (Americans called them "Hessians") whom the British government employed—offered Americans the clearest model of a professional army. British regulars were not (as Americans assumed) the "dregs of society." Although most of the enlisted men came from the lower classes and from economically depressed areas, many also had skills. British officers usually came from wealthy families and had simply purchased their commissions. Only rarely could a man rise from the enlisted ranks to commissioned-officer status.

The lives of British soldiers were tough. They were frequently undernourished, and many more died of disease than of injury in battle. Medical care was, by modern standards, primitive. Severe discipline held soldiers in line. Striking an officer or deserting could bring death; lesser offenses usually incurred a beating.

6.1

6.2

6.3

6.4

6.5

6.6

After the winter of 1777–1778, conditions in the Continental Army more closely resembled those in the British army. Like British regulars, American recruits tended to be low on the social scale. They included young men without land, indentured servants, some criminals and vagrants—in short, men who lacked better prospects. The chances for talented enlisted men to win an officer's commission were greater than in the British army. But Continental soldiers frequently had little more than "their ragged shirt flaps to cover their nakedness," and their bare marching feet occasionally left bloody tracks in the snow.

The British and the Americans both had trouble supplying their troops. The British had plenty of sound money, which many American merchants and farmers were happy to take in payment for supplies. But they had to rely mostly on supplies shipped to them from the British Isles. The Continental Army, by contrast, had to pay for supplies in depreciating paper money. After 1780, the burden of provisioning the Continental Army fell on the states, which did little better than Congress had done. Unable to obtain sufficient supplies, the army sometimes threatened to seize them by force. Washington, however, did all he could to prevent his soldiers from foraging through the countryside, stealing much-needed provisions. He knew that such actions would erode public support for the army and the patriot cause.

The professional soldiers of the Continental Army developed a community of their own. The soldiers' spirit kept them together even in the face of misery. They groused, to be sure—sometimes alarmingly. In May 1780, Connecticut troops at Washington's camp in Morristown, New Jersey, staged a brief mutiny. On January 1, 1781, armed units from Pennsylvania that were stationed in New Jersey marched to Philadelphia, upset about the lack of supplies and back pay and also about the terms of their enlistments. To calm the situation down, the Pennsylvania Executive Council agreed to limit the men's service to a maximum of three years. Washington ordered subsequent mutinies by New Jersey and Pennsylvania troops to be suppressed by force.

Occasionally, American officers let their discontent get out of hand. The most notorious such case was that of Benedict Arnold, a general who compiled a distinguished record during the first three years of the war but then came to feel himself shabbily treated by Congress and his superiors. Seeking better rewards for his abilities, he offered to surrender the strategic fort at West Point (which he commanded) to the enemy. Before he could act, however, his plot was discovered, and he fled to the British, serving with them until the end of the war. Among Americans, his name became a synonym for traitor.

What was perhaps the most serious expression of army discontent—one that might have threatened the future of republican institutions and civilian government in the United States—occurred in March 1783, after the fighting was over. Washington's troops were then stationed near Newburgh, New York, waiting for their pay before disbanding. When the Congress failed to grant real assurances that any pay would be forthcoming, hotheaded young officers called a meeting that could have led to an armed coup. General Washington, who had scrupulously deferred to civilian authority throughout the war, asked permission to address the gathering and, in a dramatic speech, warned the men of all that they might lose by insubordination. A military coup would "open the flood Gates of Civil discord" and "deluge" the nation in blood; loyalty now, he said, would be "one more distinguished proof" of their patriotism. With the fate of the Revolution apparently hanging in the balance, the movement collapsed. Washington's quick response set a precedent for the subordination of the military to civilian government.

Women in the Contending Armies

Women accompanied many units on both sides, as was common in eighteenth-century warfare. A few were prostitutes. Some were officers' wives or mistresses, but most were the married or common-law consorts of ordinary soldiers. These "camp followers" fulfilled many of the support functions necessary to sustain the army. They cooked and washed for the troops, occasionally helped load artillery, and provided most of the nursing care. A certain number in a company were subject to military orders and were authorized to draw rations and pay.

Only a few women—disguised as men—managed to serve in the Continental Army's ranks. Perhaps the best-known example was Deborah Sampson of Massachusetts. She served for 17 months, seeing action in New York toward the end of the war.

African American Participation in the War

Early in the war, as we have seen, some royal officials like Lord Dunmore recruited slaves with promises of freedom. But these efforts often proved counterproductive, frightening potentially Loyalist slave owners and driving them to the Whig side. Thus it was not until June 30, 1779, that the British commander in chief, Sir Henry Clinton, promised to allow slaves who fled from rebel owners to join the royal troops to "follow . . . any Occupation" they wished. Hedged as this promise of freedom was, news of it spread quickly among the slave communities, and late in the war, African Americans flocked to the British army in South Carolina and Georgia.

Sharing prevailing racial prejudices, the British were often reluctant to arm blacks. Instead, they put most of the ex-slaves to work as agricultural or construction workers (many of the free and enslaved blacks accompanying American troops were similarly employed). However, a few relatively well-equipped black British dragoons (mounted troops) did see combat in South Carolina.

Approximately 5,000 African Americans fought for American independence, in militias and the Continental Army. Many were freemen from Massachusetts and Rhode Island. But farther south, John Laurens tried in vain to convince the South Carolina assembly to raise and arm black troops. Instead, the legislature eventually voted to give slaves confiscated from Loyalists to white volunteers as a reward for their service. It is therefore scarcely surprising that, as one Whig put it, many African Americans were "a little Toryfied," especially in the South.

Native Americans and the War

At first, most of the approximately 200,000 Native Americans east of the Mississippi River would probably have preferred to remain neutral. But Indians' skills and manpower were valuable, and by 1776 both the British and Americans sought their assistance. Forced to choose, many Native Americans favored the British, hoping thereby to safeguard their lands.

Prewar experience convinced Native Americans that British officials would be more apt to protect them against white settlers, and the British could provide more trade goods and arms. Many Indians, including the Cherokees, Creeks, Choctaws, and Chickasaws, therefore decided to back the British, and Cherokee warriors raided the southern frontier starting in 1776. Southern colonists countered with expeditions that repeatedly devastated Cherokee towns. When older chiefs sought peace, the more militant younger men established new communities in northern Georgia and continued to fight.

Caught between the British and the Americans, other Indian groups also split. Among these was the powerful Iroquois Confederation in upstate New York. Under the leadership of Thayendanegea—known to whites as Joseph Brant—the Mohawks and Senecas supported the British, while a minority of the Oneidas and Tuscaroras joined the Americans. The Revolution thus created an irreparable divide among the Iroquois, leading many to move to Canada during and after the war.

Frontier racism, which had scarcely dissipated since Pontiac's War (see Chapter 5), flared up again. Few Americans were willing to trust Indian claims of neutrality, and during the war conducted raids against native villages. In 1782, a group of Americans slaughtered 100 defenseless Moravian Christian Indians at Gnadenhutten in the Ohio country. Thus American behavior during the war did little to calm native fears for their lives and property in an independent United States.

6.1

6.2

6.3

6.4

6.5

6.6

6.1

6.2

6.3

6.4

6.5

6.6

From Then to Now
African American Soldiers

In late June 2012, a new chapter of the Daughters of the American Revolution was established in Queens, New York. What distinguished this group was the fact that five of its founding members were black Americans. The first black woman in modern times joined the DAR in 1977, but until recently, there were very few black members of this historically white organization. Because membership is limited to women who can prove that they are related to someone who fought on the American side during the Revolution, the creation of this new chapter helped to commemorate the participation of black soldiers in the fight for independence.

From the start of the war, New England militia units included black soldiers, many of whom gained their freedom through military service. The question of admitting black soldiers into the Continental Army, however, proved much more controversial. Southern slaveholders, with few exceptions, vehemently opposed black enlistment. Yet, as the war dragged on, manpower needs and a fear that the British would lure black colonists to their side led to a shift in practice. Several northern states recruited African American men to meet their quotas of soldiers, with both Massachusetts and Rhode Island creating all-black units. By war's end, an estimated 5,000 black troops served in the Continental Army or state militias.

Their actions marked the beginning of a long and distinguished tradition of black Americans' military service, which extends from the Revolution to the present day. Until 1948, African American soldiers served in segregated units, but that policy changed under President Harry Truman. Today, although African Americans constitute about 14 percent of the U.S. population, they make up nearly 20 percent of the active duty army and 13 percent of the National Guard.

Question for Discussion

- Why might African Americans have served so readily in the American military from the Revolution to the present?

This contemporary image depicts the Marquis de Lafayette at the battle of Yorktown; a black soldier holds his horse on the right. Although some African American soldiers served in similar noncombat positions, many others did see action.

This African American soldier prepares for the invasion of Iraq in 2003.

The War for Independence

6.4 Why was the alliance with France a key turning point in the war?

The Revolutionary War can be divided into three phases. In the first, from the outbreak of fighting in 1775 through 1777, most of the important battles took place in northern states, while the Americans faced the British alone. But in 1778, France entered the war on the American side, opening the second

6.1

6.2

6.3

6.4

6.5

6.6

phase of the war in which fighting would rage from 1778 to 1781, mainly in the South, at sea, and on the western frontier. The third phase of the war, from late 1781 to 1783, saw little actual fighting. With American victory assured, attention shifted to the diplomatic maneuvering leading up to the Peace of Paris (1783).

Britain Hesitates: Crucial Battles in New York and New Jersey

During the first phase of the war, the British concentrated on subduing New England. Replacing General Gage, the government appointed Sir William Howe as commander in chief of British forces and his brother, Richard Howe, as admiral of the naval forces in North American waters. The Howes made New York City their base of operations. To counter this move, Washington moved his forces to New York in the spring of 1776. In August 1776, the Howes landed troops on Long Island and, in the Battle of Brooklyn Heights, quickly drove the American forces deployed there back to Manhattan Island (see Map 6.2).

Following instructions to negotiate peace as well as wage war, Richard Howe then met on Staten Island with three envoys from Congress on September 11, 1776. The British commanders were prepared to offer fairly generous terms but could not grant independence. The Americans would accept nothing less. So the meeting produced no substantive negotiations.

In the ensuing weeks, British forces overwhelmed Washington's troops, driving them out of Manhattan and then, moving north, clearing them from the area around the city at the Battle of White Plains. But the Howes were hesitant to deal a crushing blow, and the Americans were able to retreat across New Jersey into Pennsylvania. The American cause seemed lost, however, and the Continental Army almost melted away. Realizing that without a success he would soon be without troops, Washington led his forces back across the icy Delaware and launched a successful surprise attack on a garrison of Hessian mercenaries at Trenton, New Jersey, on the morning of December 26. A week later, Washington overwhelmed a British force at Princeton, New Jersey. By raising morale, the victories at Trenton and Princeton probably saved the American cause.

The Year of the Hangman: Victory at Saratoga and Winter at Valley Forge

Contemporaries called 1777 the Year of the Hangman because the triple sevens suggested a row of gallows. It was in fact a critical year for the American cause. Mounting a major effort to end the rebellion, the British planned to send an army down the Hudson River from Canada. The goal was to have it link up with the Howes in New York City, isolate New England, and defeat the rebellion there. But there was little effort to coordinate strategy between the forces advancing from Canada and those in New York. The poorly planned and poorly executed campaign ended in disaster for the British.

Some 5,000 Redcoats and 3,000 German mercenaries assembled in Canada during the winter of 1776–1777. Under the command of the high-living and popular "Gentleman Johnny" Burgoyne, the army finally set off in June with 1,500 horses hauling its heavy artillery and ponderous supply train. A second, smaller column, supported by an Indian force under Thayendanegea (Joseph Brant), moved to the west to capture an American fort near Oriskany, New York, and then join up with Burgoyne's main force. On July 5, Burgoyne's army recaptured Fort Ticonderoga, but success eluded Burgoyne after that.

Trouble began as the troops started overland through the woods at the southern end of the lake. Huge trees felled by American axmen blocked their way, and the army crawled along at only two or three miles a day. Early in August, the column sent to capture the American fort near Oriskany turned back to Canada. Burgoyne's Indian allies under Joseph Brant likewise went home. Promised reinforcements never arrived. Ten days later, a Whig militia force wiped out a British force trying to gather supplies in Vermont.

6.1

6.2

6.3

6.4

6.5

6.6

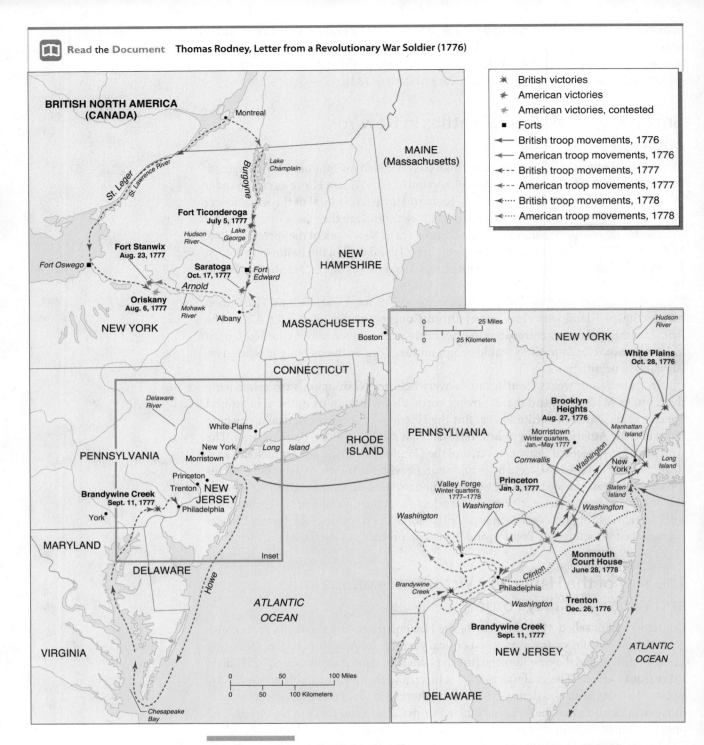

📖 **Read** the **Document**   Thomas Rodney, Letter from a Revolutionary War Soldier (1776)

MAP 6.2 THE WAR IN THE NORTH, 1776–1777 Most of the fighting between the British and Americans during the first part of the war occurred in the North, partly because the British commanders assumed that the New England colonies were the most rebellious.

By October 1777, Burgoyne's army was down to fewer than 6,000 men and faced disaster. Nearly 3,000 Continentals and 9,000 American militia, commanded by General Horatio Gates, exerted relentless pressure on the increasingly dispirited invaders. Unable to break through the American lines, Burgoyne surrendered his entire army to Gates following the Battle of Saratoga on October 17, 1777.

Meanwhile, General William Howe, rather than moving north to support Burgoyne, made plans to destroy Washington's army and capture Philadelphia. In July 1777, Howe's troops sailed from New York to Chesapeake Bay and from there marched on Philadelphia from the south. They met Washington's army on the banks of Brandywine Creek, near the Pennsylvania-Delaware border. The Americans put up a good fight before giving way with a loss of 1,200 killed or captured (twice as many as the British). Howe occupied Philadelphia, and his men settled down in comfortable winter quarters. The Congress fled to York, Pennsylvania, and the Continental Army established its winter camp outside Philadelphia at Valley Forge.

The Continental Army's miserable winter at **Valley Forge** has become famous for its hardships. Suffering from cold, disease, and starvation, as many as 2,500 soldiers died. Meanwhile, some congressmen and a few unhappy officers plotted unsuccessfully to replace Washington with Gates as commander in chief. Despite the difficulties, the Continental Army completed its transformation into a disciplined professional force. By spring, pleased observers felt that Washington at last had an army capable of meeting the British on equal terms.

Valley Forge Area of Pennsylvania approximately 20 miles northwest of Philadelphia where General George Washington's Continental troops were quartered from December 1777 to June 1778 while British forces occupied Philadelphia during the Revolutionary War.

The United States Gains an Ally

Since late 1776, Benjamin Franklin and a team of American diplomats had been in Paris negotiating French support for the patriot cause. In the winter of 1777–1778, aware that a Franco-American alliance was close, Parliament unsuccessfully tried to end the rebellion by giving the Americans everything they wanted except independence itself.

The American victory at Saratoga in October 1777 persuaded the French that the United States had a viable future. Eager for revenge against their old British enemy, French officials decided to act quickly lest any military reverses force the Americans to agree to reconciliation with Britain. In a move that astonished the British, France signed a commercial treaty and a military alliance with the United States on February 6, 1778. Both sides promised to fight together until Britain recognized the independence of the United States, and France pledged not to seek the return of lands in North America.

Foreign intervention transformed the American Revolution into a virtual world war, engaging British forces in heavy fighting not only in North America but also in the West Indies and India. French entry into the war was the first step in the consolidation of a formidable alliance of European powers eager to see Britain humbled and to gain trading rights in the former British colonies. France persuaded Spain to declare war on Britain in June 1779. New Orleans became a base for American privateers, and the Spanish fleet increased the naval power of the countries arrayed against Great Britain.

Catherine the Great of Russia suggested that the European powers form a League of Armed Neutrality to protect their trade with the United States and other warring countries against British interference. Denmark and Sweden soon joined; Austria, Portugal, Prussia, and Sicily eventually followed. Britain, which wanted to cut off Dutch trade with the United States, used a pretext to declare war on the Netherlands before it could join. Great Britain thus found itself isolated and even, briefly, threatened with invasion. These threats did not frighten the British leaders into suing for peace, but they forced them to make important changes in strategy.

In the spring of 1778, Britain replaced the Howes with a new commander, Sir Henry Clinton, and instructed him to send troops to attack the French West Indies. Knowing that he now faced a serious French threat, Clinton began consolidating his forces by evacuating Philadelphia and pulling his troops slowly back across New Jersey to New York.

On June 28, 1778, Washington caught up with the British at Monmouth Court House. This inconclusive battle proved to be the last major engagement in the North. Clinton withdrew to New York, and Continental troops occupied the hills along the Hudson Valley north of the city. The war shifted to other fronts.

Fighting on the Frontier and at Sea

Known as "a dark and bloody ground" to Native Americans, Kentucky became even bloodier after the British instructed their Indian allies to raid the area in 1777. Because the British post at Detroit coordinated these attacks, the Americans tried to take it in 1778. Three expeditions failed for various reasons, but during the last, under a Virginian,

6.1

6.2

6.3

6.4

6.5

6.6

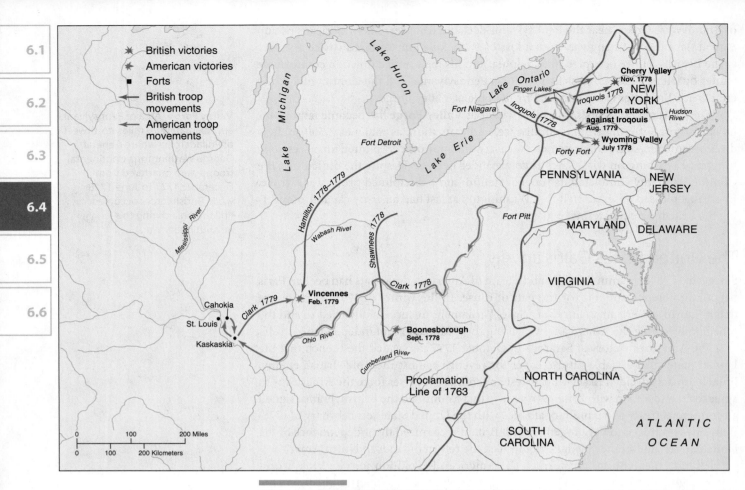

MAP 6.3 THE WAR ON THE FRONTIER, 1778–1779 Significant battles in the Mississippi Valley and the frontiers of the seaboard states added to the ferocity of the fighting and strengthened some American claims to western lands.

George Rogers Clark, the Americans did capture three key British settlements in the Mississippi Valley: Kaskaskia, Cahokia, and Vincennes (see Map 6.3). These successes may have strengthened American claims to the West at the end of the war.

In 1778 bloody fighting also occurred on the eastern frontiers. During the summer, a British force of 100 Loyalists and 500 Indians struck the Wyoming Valley of Pennsylvania. Four months later, a similar group of attackers burned farmsteads and slaughtered civilians at Cherry Valley, New York. Both raids stimulated equally savage reprisals against the Indians.

The Americans and British also clashed at sea throughout the war. Great Britain was the preeminent sea power of the age, and the United States never came close to matching it. But in 1775, Congress authorized the construction of thirteen frigates—medium-sized, relatively fast ships—as well as the purchase of several merchant vessels for conversion to warships. By contrast, the Royal Navy in 1779 had more than 100 large, heavily armed "ships of the line." The Americans therefore engaged in what was essentially a guerrilla war at sea.

The Congress and the individual states also supplemented America's naval forces by commissioning privateers. In effect legalized pirates, privateers preyed on British shipping. Captured goods were divided among the crew according to rank; captured sailors became prisoners of war. Some 2,000 American privateers took more than 600 British ships and forced the British navy to spread itself thin doing convoy duty.

The Land War Moves South

During the first three years of the war, the British made little effort to mobilize what they believed to be considerable Loyalist strength in the South. But in 1778, the enlarged threat from France prompted a change in strategy: Redcoats would sweep through a large area and then leave behind a Tory militia to reestablish loyalty to the Crown and suppress local Whigs. The British hoped thereby to recapture everything from Georgia to Virginia; they would deal with New England later.

The British southern strategy unfolded in November 1778, when General Clinton dispatched 3,500 troops to take control of Georgia (see Map 6.4). Meeting only light resistance, they quickly seized Savannah and Augusta and restored the old colonial government under civilian control. After their initial success, however, the British suffered

6.1
6.2
6.3
6.4
6.5
6.6

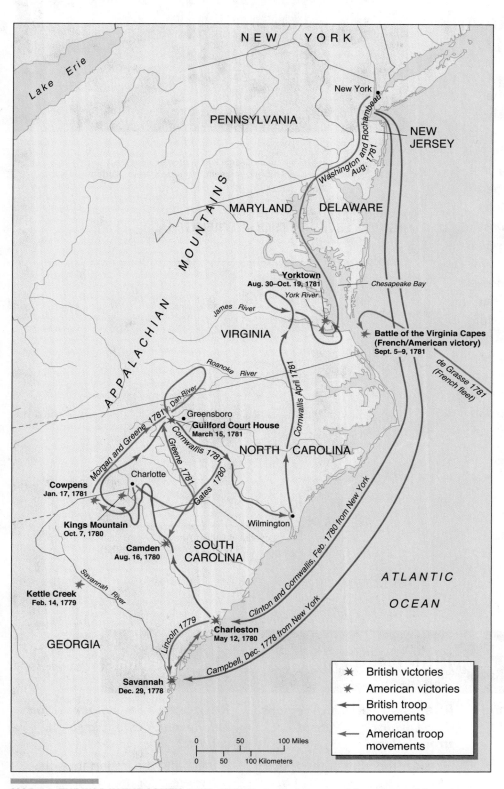

MAP 6.4 THE WAR IN THE SOUTH, 1778–1781 During the latter part of the war, most of the major engagements occurred in the South. British forces won most of the early ones but could not control the immense territory involved and eventually surrendered at Yorktown.

6.1

6.2

6.3

6.4

6.5

6.6

❄ Explore the American Revolution on MyHistoryLab

The idealized prominence of General George Washington as a war leader is shown as he meets with other generals and officers of the American colonies in a large state room.

HOW DID THE AMERICAN REVOLUTION UNFOLD?

Between 1775, when fighting broke out near Boston, and the 1783 Treaty of Paris, the British and rebellious American colonists fought the Revolutionary War. This war, however, was in reality a civil war, as some colonists remained loyal to the British Empire while their neighbors rebelled against imperial power. Even though George Washington's Continental Army was outmatched in military manpower and lost more major battles than it won, the superior decision making of its leaders combined with patriotic support throughout the colonies led to a victory for the Americans, and the Thirteen Colonies emerged as the independent United States of America.

HIGHEST LEVEL OF TROOP STRENGTH

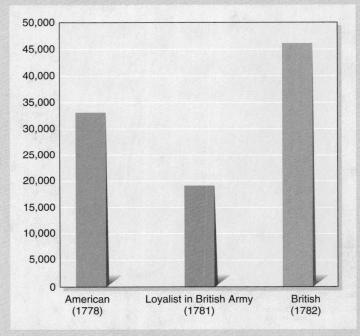

SOURCE: Longman American History Atlas, 1998

KEY QUESTIONS   Use **MyHistoryLab** *Explorer* to **answer** these **questions:**

Comparison ▶▶▶ *Where did the Americans have military successes?*

Map the losses and victories of the two sides in the Revolutionary War.

Analysis ▶▶▶ *Which regions were Loyalist and Patriot strongholds?*

Consider the roles of these two groups in the unfolding of the war.

Response ▶▶▶ *What position did the major cities play in the conflict?*

Understand the importance of urban areas for the two sides.

TABLE 6.1 IMPORTANT BATTLES OF THE REVOLUTIONARY WAR

6.1
6.2
6.3
6.4
6.5
6.6

	Battle	Date	Outcome
Early Fighting	Lexington and Concord, Massachusetts	April 19, 1775	Contested
	Fort Ticonderoga, New York	May 10, 1775	American victory
	Breed's Hill ("Bunker Hill"), Boston, Massachusetts	June 17, 1775	Contested
	Great Bridge, Virginia	December 9, 1775	American victory
	Quebec, Canada	December 31, 1775	British repulsed American assault
	Moore's Creek Bridge, North Carolina	February 27, 1776	American victory
The War in the North	Brooklyn Heights, New York	August 27, 1776	British victory
	White Plains, New York	October 28, 1776	British victory
	Trenton, New Jersey	December 26, 1776	American victory
	Princeton, New Jersey	January 3, 1777	American victory
	Brandywine Creek, Pennsylvania	September 11, 1777	British victory (opened way for British to take Philadelphia)
	Saratoga, New York	September 19 and October 17, 1777	American victory (helped persuade France to form an alliance with United States)
	Monmouth Court House, New Jersey	June 28, 1778	Contested
The War on the Frontier	Wyoming Valley, Pennsylvania	June and July 1778	British victory
	Kaskaskia and Cahokia, Illinois; Vincennes, Indiana	July 4, 1778– February 23, 1779	American victories strengthened claims to Mississippi Valley
	Cherry Valley, New York	November 11, 1778	British victory
The War in the South	Savannah, Georgia	December 29, 1778	British victory (took control of Georgia)
	Kettle Creek, Georgia	February 14, 1779	American victory
	Savannah, Georgia	September 3–October 28, 1779	British victory (opened way for British to take Charleston)
	Charleston, South Carolina	February 11–May 12, 1780	British victory
	Camden, South Carolina	August 16, 1780	British victory
	Kings Mountain, South Carolina	October 7, 1780	American victory
	Cowpens, South Carolina	January 17, 1781	American victory
	Guilford Court House, North Carolina	March 15, 1781	Contested
	Yorktown, Virginia	August 30–October 19, 1781	American victory (persuaded Britain to end war)

serious setbacks. Spain entered the war and seized British outposts on the Mississippi and Mobile rivers while Whig militia decimated a Loyalist militia at Kettle Creek, Georgia.

But the Americans could not beat the British army. In late September and early October 1779, a combined force of 5,500 American and French troops, supported by French warships, laid siege to Savannah. The assault failed, and the French sailed off.

The way was now open for the British to attack Charleston, the military key to the Lower South. In December 1779, Clinton sailed through stormy seas from New York to the Carolina coast with about 9,000 troops. In the Battle of Charleston, he encircled the city, trapping the patriot forces inside. On May 12, 1780, more than 5,000 Continentals and militia laid down their arms in the worst American defeat of the war.

The British were now poised to sweep the entire South. Most local Whigs, thinking the Revolution over, at first offered little resistance to the Redcoats striking into the Carolina backcountry. The British success seemed so complete that Clinton tried to force American prisoners to resume their duties as British subjects and join the Loyalist militia. Thinking that matters were now well in hand, Clinton sailed back to New York, leaving the southern troops under the command of Lord Cornwallis. Clinton's confidence that the South had returned to British allegiance, however, was premature.

American Counterattacks

In the summer of 1780, Congress dispatched a substantial Continental force to the South under General Horatio Gates, the hero of Saratoga. Local patriots flocked to join him. But instead of achieving another great victory, Gates and his men blundered into

The surrender of Lord Cornwallis at Yorktown on October 19, 1781, led to the British decision to withdraw from the war. Cornwallis, who claimed to be ill, absented himself from the ceremony and is not in the picture. Washington, who is astride the horse under the American flag, designated General Benjamin Lincoln (on the white horse in the center) as the one to accept the submission of a subordinate British officer. John Trumbull, who painted *The Battle of Bunker Hill* and some 300 other scenes from the Revolutionary War, finished this painting while he was in London about fifteen years after the events depicted. A large copy of the work now hangs in the rotunda of the U.S. Capitol in Washington, DC.

Cornwallis's British army near Camden, South Carolina, on August 16, and suffered a complete rout. More than 1,000 Americans were killed or wounded and many captured.

American morale revived on October 7, 1780, when "Overmountain Men" (militia) from Virginia, western North Carolina, and South Carolina defeated the British at Kings Mountain, South Carolina. And in December 1780, Nathanael Greene replaced the discredited Gates, bringing competent leadership to the Continentals in the South.

Ever resourceful, Greene divided his small forces, keeping roughly half with him in northeastern South Carolina and sending the other half westward under General Daniel Morgan. Cornwallis ordered Colonel Banastre Tarleton to pursue Morgan, who retreated northward until he reached Cowpens, South Carolina. There, on January 17, 1781, Morgan cleverly posted his least reliable troops, the militia, in the front line and ordered them to retreat after firing two volleys. When they did as told, the British thought the Americans were fleeing and charged after them—straight into devastating fire from Morgan's Continentals.

Cornwallis now badly needed a battlefield victory. Burning his army's excess baggage, he set off in hot pursuit of Greene and Morgan, whose rejoined forces retreated northward ahead of the British. On February 13, 1781, Greene's tired men crossed the Dan River into Virginia, and Cornwallis gave up the chase, marching his equally exhausted Redcoats southward. To his surprise, Cornwallis now found himself pursued—though cautiously—by Greene. On March 15, the opposing forces met at

Guilford Court House, North Carolina, in one of the war's bloodiest battles. Although the British held the field at the end of the day, an Englishman accurately observed, "another such victory would destroy the British Army." Cornwallis retreated to the coastal town of Wilmington, North Carolina, to rest and regroup.

By the late summer of 1781, British fortunes were waning in the Lower South. The Redcoats held only the larger towns and the immediately surrounding countryside. With their superior staying power, they won most major engagements, but these victories brought them no lasting gain. As General Greene observed, "We fight, get beat, and rise and fight again." When the enemy pressed him too hard, Greene retreated out of reach, advancing again as the British withdrew.

Disappointed and frustrated, Cornwallis decided to conquer Virginia to cut off Greene's supplies and destroy Whig resolve. British forces were already raiding the state. Cornwallis marched north to join them, reaching Yorktown, Virginia, during the summer of 1781.

The final military showdown of the war was at hand. By now, French soldiers were in America ready to fight alongside the Continentals, and a large French fleet in the West Indies had orders to support an attack on the British in North America. Faking preparations for an assault on British-occupied New York, the Continentals (commanded by Washington) and the French headed for the Chesapeake. Cornwallis and his 6,000 Redcoats soon found themselves besieged behind their fortifications at Yorktown by 8,800 Americans and 7,800 French. A French naval victory gave the allies temporary command of the waters around Yorktown. Cornwallis had nowhere to go, and Clinton—still in New York—could not reinforce him quickly enough. On October 19, 1781, the British army surrendered.

War and Society, 1775–1783

6.5 How did the War for Independence affect women, African Americans, and Native Americans?

Regular combatants were not the only ones to suffer during the struggle for independence. Eight years of warfare produced profound dislocations throughout American society. Military service wrenched families apart, sporadic raids brought the war home to vast numbers of people, and everyone endured economic disruptions. As a forge of nationhood, the Revolution tested all Americans, whatever their standing as citizens.

The Women's War

Women everywhere had to see their loved ones go off to fight and die. Such circumstances elevated women's domestic status. Wives frequently became more knowledgeable about the family's financial condition than their long-absent husbands. Women also assumed new public roles during the conflict. Some nursed the wounded. More wove cloth for uniforms. The Ladies' Association of Philadelphia was established in 1780 to demonstrate women's patriotism and raise money to buy shirts for the army. Similar associations formed in other states.

Despite their increasing private responsibilities and new public activities, it did not occur to most women to encroach on traditional male prerogatives. When John Adams's wife, Abigail, urged him and the Second Continental Congress to "Remember the Ladies," she was not expecting equal political rights. What she wanted were legal protections for women and recognition of their value and need for autonomy in the domestic sphere. "Remember," she cautioned, "all Men would be Tyrants if they could."

The Revolution in fact did little to change women's political status. Perhaps the most immediate outcome of the Revolution for American women was the politicization of their maternal responsibilities. As good "republican mothers," they could be trusted to instill patriotism in their sons, helping them to mature into virtuous citizens.

6.1

6.2

6.3

6.4

6.5

6.6

Although few women actually took up arms in the Revolutionary War, this 1779 image captures the patriotic spirit of women who helped the cause in other ways. Many women took on new public roles while their husbands were called away to battle.

Although this idea led to calls for enhancing women's educational opportunities, it was at best a limited improvement in their political role.

Effect of the War on African Americans

In the northern states, where slavery was already economically marginal and where black men could be volunteers in the Continental Army, the Revolutionary War helped to bring an end to slavery, although it remained legal there for some time (see Chapter 7). In the South, however, slavery was integral to the economy, and white planters viewed it as crucial to their postwar recovery. Thus, although British efforts to recruit black soldiers brought freedom to thousands and temporarily undermined slavery in the South, the war ultimately strengthened the institution, especially in the Carolinas and Georgia. Of the African Americans who left with the British at the end of the war, many, both slave and free, went to the West Indies. Others settled in Canada, and some eventually reached Africa, where Britain established the colony of Sierra Leone for them.

The War's Impact on Native Americans

Survivors among the approximately 13,000 Native Americans who fought for the British did not have the option of leaving with them at the end of the war. How many died during the conflict is not known, but certainly many did. Not only the Iroquois but other groups lost a great deal. The Americans repeatedly invaded the Cherokees' homeland in the southern Appalachian Mountains. Americans also attacked the Shawnees of Ohio.

In the peace treaty of 1783, Britain surrendered its territory east of the Mississippi, shocking and infuriating the Native Americans living there. They had not surrendered, and none of them had been at the negotiations in Paris. Because it enabled Americans to claim Indian territory by conquest, the Revolutionary War was a disaster for many Native Americans that opened the floodgates to a torrent of white settlers.

6.1
6.2
6.3
6.4
6.5
6.6

👁 **Watch** the **Video** **The American Revolution as Different Americans Saw It**

Ki-On-Twog-Ky, also known as Corn Planter (1732/40–1836), was a Seneca Indian chief who raided American settlements for the British, while he observed that "war is war, death is death, a fight is hard business." He later presided over the surrender of much land to the United States.

6.1

6.2

6.3

6.4

6.5

6.6

Economic Disruption

The British and American armies both needed enormous quantities of supplies. This heavy demand disrupted the normal distribution of goods and drove up real prices seven- or eightfold. In addition, widespread use of depreciating paper money by the American side triggered severe price inflation.

When the British did not simply seize what they needed, they paid for it in hard currency—gold and silver. American commanders, by contrast, had to rely on paper money because Congress and the states had almost no hard currency at their disposal. The Continental dollar, however, steadily declined in value, and by March 1780, the Congress was forced to admit officially that it was worthless.

Necessity, not folly, drove Congress and the states to rely on the printing press. Rather than alienate citizens by immediately raising taxes to pay for the war, the states printed paper money supposedly redeemable through future tax revenues. But because the quantity of this paper money rose faster than the supply of goods and services, prices skyrocketed, and the value of the money plunged. Those who had paper money tried to spend it before its value could drop further, whereas those who had salable commodities such as grain tended to hoard them in the hope that the price would go even higher. Prices also climbed faster than wages, leaving many working people impoverished.

The rampant inflation was demoralizing and divisive. Lucky speculators and unscrupulous profiteers could grow rich, while ordinary and patriotic people suffered. As usual, war and its deprivations brought out both the best and the worst in human nature.

Most Americans somehow managed to cope. But during the last years of the conflict, their economic and psychological reserves ran low. The total real wealth of private individuals declined by an average of 0.5 percent annually from 1774 to 1805, even with the returning prosperity of the 1790s. Such statistics suggest the true economic cost of the War for Independence. And the atrocities committed on both sides provide a comparable measure of the conflict's psychological cost.

The American Victory, 1782–1783

| 6.6 | What were the key factors in the American victory in the Revolutionary War? |

The British surrender at Yorktown marked the end of major fighting in North America, though skirmishes continued for another year. In April 1782, the Royal Navy defeated the French fleet in the Caribbean, strengthening the British bargaining position. Although George III insisted on continuing the war because he feared that defeat would threaten British rule in Canada and the West Indies, the majority in Parliament now felt that enough men and money had been wasted trying to keep the Americans within the empire. In March 1782, the king accepted Lord North's resignation and appointed a new prime minister, with a mandate to make peace.

The Peace of Paris

At the peace negotiations, which took place in Paris, the Americans demanded independence, significant territorial concessions, and access to the rich British-controlled fishing grounds in the North Atlantic. The new British prime minister, Lord Shelburne, was inclined to be conciliatory to help British merchants recover their lost colonial trade. The French had achieved their objective of weakening the British and now wanted out of an increasingly costly worldwide war. Spain had not won its most important goal, the recovery of British-held Gibraltar, and thus gave the Americans no support at all.

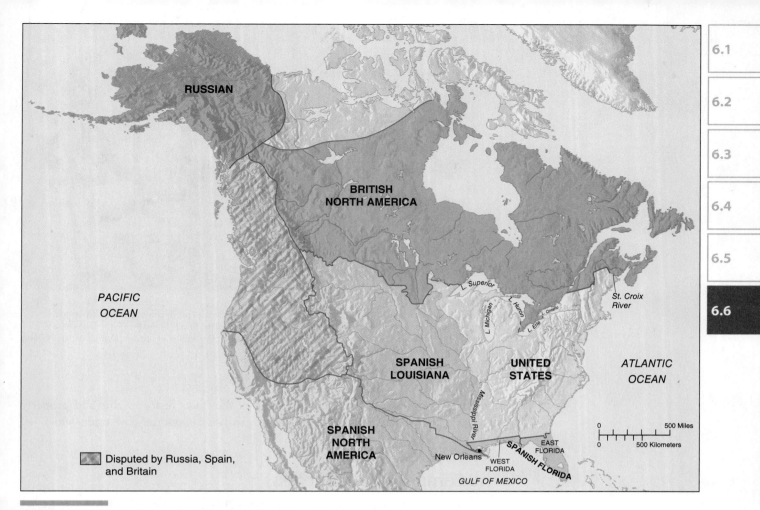

6.1

6.2

6.3

6.4

6.5

6.6

RUSSIAN

BRITISH
NORTH AMERICA

PACIFIC
OCEAN

Superior

L. Michigan

Huron

L. Erie L. Ontario

St. Croix
River

SPANISH
LOUISIANA

UNITED
STATES

ATLANTIC
OCEAN

Mississippi River

SPANISH
NORTH
AMERICA

New Orleans

WEST
FLORIDA

EAST
FLORIDA

SPANISH FLORIDA

0   500 Miles

0   500 Kilometers

Disputed by Russia, Spain,
and Britain

GULF OF MEXICO

MAP 6.5 NORTH AMERICA AFTER THE PEACE OF PARIS, 1783 The results of the American Revolution
redrew the map of North America, confining Britain to Canada and giving the United States most of the area east
of the Mississippi River, though Spain controlled its mouth for most of the next twenty years.

The American negotiators, Benjamin Franklin, John Adams, and John Jay, skillfully
threaded their way among these conflicting interests. With good reason, they feared
that the French and Spanish might strike a bargain with the British at the expense of the
United States. As a result, the Americans disregarded Congress's instructions to avoid
making peace unilaterally and secretly worked out their own arrangements with the
British. On November 30, 1782, the negotiators signed a preliminary Anglo-American
treaty of peace whose terms were embodied in the final **Peace of Paris**, signed by all the
belligerents on September 3, 1783.

The Peace of Paris gave the United States nearly everything it sought. Great Britain
acknowledged that the United States was "free, sovereign and independent." The
northern boundary of the new nation extended west from the St. Croix River (which
separated Maine from Nova Scotia) past the Great Lakes to what were thought to be
the headwaters of the Mississippi River (see Map 6.5). The Mississippi itself—down to
just north of New Orleans—formed the western border. Spain acquired the provinces
of East and West Florida from Britain. This territory included parts of present-day
Louisiana, Mississippi, Alabama, and Georgia.

Several provisions of the treaty addressed important economic issues. Adams,
on behalf of New Englanders, insisted on a provision granting American fishermen
access to the waters off eastern Canada. The treaty also required that British forces, on
quitting American soil, were to leave behind all American-owned property, including
slaves. Another provision declared existing debts between citizens of Britain and the
United States still valid, giving British merchants hope of collecting on their American

Peace of Paris Treaties signed
in 1783 by Great Britain, the
United States, France, Spain, and
the Netherlands that ended the
Revolutionary War.

6.1

6.2

6.3

6.4

6.5

6.6

American soldiers at Yorktown in 1781 as drawn by a young officer in the French army, Jean-Baptiste-Antoine de Verger. The African American on the left is an infantryman of the First Rhode Island Regiment; the next, a musketeer; the third, with the fringed jacket, a rifleman. The man on the right is a Continental artilleryman, holding a lighted match used to fire cannons.

accounts. Congress was to "recommend" that the states restore rights and property taken from Loyalists during the war. Nothing was said about the slave trade, which Jay had hoped to ban.

The Components of Success

The War for Independence was over. In December 1783, the last British troops left New York. The Continental Army had already disbanded during the summer of 1783. On December 4, Washington said farewell to his officers at New York City's Fraunces Tavern and later that month resigned his commission to the Congress and went home to Mount Vernon.

Washington's leadership was just one of the reasons why the Americans won the Revolutionary War. French assistance played a crucial role. Indeed, some historians contend that without the massive infusion of French men and money in 1781, the Revolution would have failed. The British also contributed heavily to their own downfall with mistakes that included bureaucratic inefficiency, hesitant command, and overconfidence. Finally, Great Britain had tried to solve a political problem by military means, but an occupying army is far more likely to alienate people than to secure their goodwill.

Yet it took 175,000 to 200,000 soldiers—Continentals and militia troops—to prevent Great Britain from recovering the colonies. Of these, some 7,000 died in battle. Perhaps 10,000 more succumbed to disease while on active duty, another 8,500 died while prisoners of war, and nearly 1,500 were reported missing in action. More than 8,000 were wounded and survived. Those who served in the Continental Army, probably more than half of all who fought, served the longest and saw the most action. Their casualty rate—30 to 40 percent—may have been the highest of any war in which the United States has been engaged.

Conclusion

Despite its devastation and divisiveness, many people in Europe and the United States were convinced that the War for Independence represented something momentous. The *Annual Register,* a popular and influential British magazine, commented in 1783 that the American Revolution "has already overturned those favourite systems of policy and commerce, both in the old and in the new world, which the wisdom of the ages, and the power of the greatest nations, had in vain endeavored to render permanent; and it seems to have laid the seeds of still greater revolutions in the history and mutual relations of mankind."

Americans, indeed, had fired a shot heard round the world. Thanks in part to its heavy investment in the American Revolution, France suffered a financial crisis in the late 1780s. This, in turn, ushered in the political crisis that culminated in the French Revolution of 1789. The American Revolution helped to inspire among French people (including soldiers returning from service in America) an intense yearning for an end to arbitrary government and undeserved social inequalities. Liberty also proved infectious to thousands of German troops who had come to America as mercenaries but stayed as free citizens after the war was over. The North American states had become an independent confederation, a grand experiment in republicanism whose fate mattered to enlightened men and women throughout the Western world.

In his written farewell to the rank and file of his troops at the end of October 1783, Washington maintained that "the enlarged prospects of happiness, opened by the confirmation of our independence and sovereignty, almost exceed the power of description." He urged those who had fought with him to maintain their "strong attachments to the union" and "prove themselves not less virtuous and useful as citizens, than they have been persevering and victorious as soldiers." The work of securing the promise of the American Revolution, Washington knew, would now shift from the battlefield to the political arena.

For Suggested Readings go to MyHistoryLab.

6.1

6.2

6.3

6.4

6.5

6.6

Chapter Review

From Rebellion to War

6.1 Why was reconciliation between the colonies and Britain virtually impossible by the beginning of 1775? p. 143

The combination of Parliament's refusal to consider conciliatory measures, Lord North's contradictory policies, and the Americans' decision to gather military supplies and form volunteer forces for self-defense left little room for reconciliation.

The Continental Congress Becomes a National Government

6.2 What functions did the Congress fulfill as it sought to manage the American rebellion? p. 144

The Continental Congress assumed executive functions the Crown had once performed. It took command of the army, authorized the creation of a navy, ran the post office, conducted Indian diplomacy, and printed paper money.

The Combatants

6.3 What were the key differences between the British and American forces? p. 149

The British had far greater experience with a well-disciplined professional army. The Americans, realizing that their militias would not suffice, had to create their own Continental Army and learn how to train its soldiers.

The War for Independence

6.4 Why was the alliance with France a key turning point in the war? p. 152

The French alliance provided Americans with key military and financial support. It also led other European nations to ally against Britain, forcing Britain to defend itself on multiple fronts in America, the Caribbean, and Europe.

War and Society, 1775–1783

6.5 How did the War for Independence affect women, African Americans, and Native Americans? p. 161

Although women supported the war effort on the home front, their political status scarcely changed. Some African Americans gained freedom through military service, but slavery persisted. Many Native Americans supported Britain, and suffered when America's victory let loose a flood of settlers on their lands.

The American Victory, 1782–1783

6.6 What were the key factors in the American victory in the Revolutionary War? p. 164

Despite their military prowess, the British suffered from overconfidence, inefficiency, and an inability to control the American countryside. Washington's leadership, the tenacity of the Continental Army, and the French alliance contributed to America's victory.

Timeline

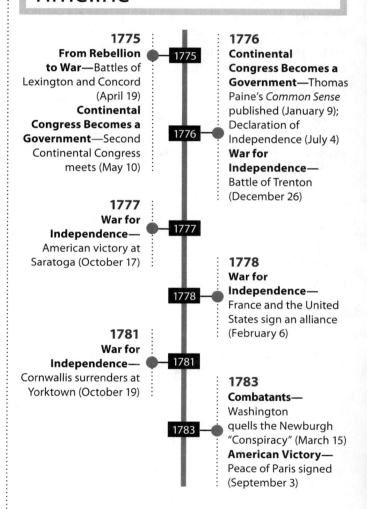

1775
From Rebellion to War—Battles of Lexington and Concord (April 19)
Continental Congress Becomes a Government—Second Continental Congress meets (May 10)

1776
Continental Congress Becomes a Government—Thomas Paine's *Common Sense* published (January 9); Declaration of Independence (July 4)
War for Independence—Battle of Trenton (December 26)

1777
War for Independence—American victory at Saratoga (October 17)

1778
War for Independence—France and the United States sign an alliance (February 6)

1781
War for Independence—Cornwallis surrenders at Yorktown (October 19)

1783
Combatants—Washington quells the Newburgh "Conspiracy" (March 15)
American Victory—Peace of Paris signed (September 3)

7 The First Republic
1776–1789

One American Journey

The Indictment of a Black Participant in Shays's Rebellion

The jurors of the Commonwealth of Massachusetts upon their oath present that Moses Sash of Worthington . . . a negro man & Labourer being a disorderly, riotous & seditious person & minding & contriving as much as in him lay unlawfully by force of arms to stir up promote incite & maintain riots mobs tumults insurrections in this Commonwealth & to disturb impede & prevent the Government of the same & the due administration of justice in the same, & to prevent the Courts of justice from sitting as by Law appointed for that purpose & to promote disquiets, uneasiness, jealousies, animosities & seditions in the minds of the Citizens of this Commonwealth on the twentieth day of January in the year of our Lord Seventeen hundred & eighty seven & on divers other days & times as well before as since that time at Worthington . . . unlawfully & seditiously with force & arms did advise persuade invite incourage & procure divers persons . . . of this Commonwealth by force of arms to oppose this Commonwealth & the Government thereof & riotously to join themselves to a great number of riotous seditious persons with force & arms thus opposing this Commonwealth & the Government thereof . . . and in pursuance of his wicked seditious purposes . . . did procure guns, bayonets, pistols, swords, gunpowder, bullets, blankets &

The illustration on this 1783 map of the United States pairs George Washington on the left with Liberty and Benjamin Franklin on the right with Justice in a symbolic identification of the new republic with the values of equality and individual dignity.

LEARNING OBJECTIVES

7.1 What people were deemed fit to have political rights in the new order of republicanism? p. 171

7.2 How did economic problems lead to political conflict in the 1780s? p. 178

7.3 What steps did Britain and Spain take to block American expansion? p. 185

7.4 What explains the call for a stronger centralized government and the divisions which emerged over the ratification of the new Constitution? p. 187

Listen to **Chapter 7** on **MyHistoryLab**

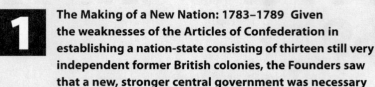

Watch the Video Series on MyHistoryLab

Learn about some key topics related to this chapter with the *MyHistoryLab Video Series: Key Topics in U.S. History.*

1 **The Making of a New Nation: 1783–1789** Given the weaknesses of the Articles of Confederation in establishing a nation-state consisting of thirteen still very independent former British colonies, the Founders saw that a new, stronger central government was necessary to safeguard the country. This video examines the Articles of Confederation and the Constitutional Convention that ultimately produced a new document and the federal union we have today.

👁 Watch on MyHistoryLab

Land Ordinances This video discusses the Land Ordinances (1785 and 1787) that created a rational and effective model for adding new states into the country. Along with guaranteeing the absence of slavery from the Northwest Territory, west of the Appalachians and north of the Ohio River, the Land Ordinances provided for an orderly method for as many as five new states to enter the union on an equal footing with the original states.

Watch on MyHistoryLab 👁 **2**

3 **Shays' Rebellion** Following the American Revolution, the primary problem for the federal, state, and local governments was a lack of hard currency. This money shortage, as well as economic depression, led to many rebellions over tax collection and debt payment. This video focuses on Shays' Rebellion (1786–1787) in Massachusetts. The ferocity of Shays and his followers as well as the military force needed to put it down would influence the need for a strong Constitution and central government.

👁 Watch on MyHistoryLab

The Constitutional Convention The Constitutional Convention in Philadelphia in 1787 has often been called the "Miracle in Philadelphia," as this video makes clear. The U.S. Constitution was truly the result of a series of compromises and deals on the part of the participants at the convention. However, to achieve a strong central government meant some lessening of the democratic power of the American people. **4**

Watch on MyHistoryLab 👁

provisions & other warlike instruments offensive & defensive . . . & did cause & procure them to be carried & conveyed to the riotous & seditious persons as aforesaid in evil example to others to offend in like manner against the peace of the Commonwealth aforesaid & dignity of the same.

Indictment of Moses Sash by the Supreme Judicial Court of Massachusetts for Suffolk County, April 9, 1787, cited in Sidney Kaplan and Emma Nogrady Kaplan, *The Black Presence in the Era of the American Revolution* (Amherst: University of Massachusetts Press, 1989), p. 259.

Personal Journeys Online

- William Shepard, *Letter to Governor Bowdoin, Jan. 26, 1787.* A militia captain describes the routing of the Shaysites at Springfield Arsenal.

- Henry Lee, *Letter to George Washington, Oct. 1, 1786.* One of Washington's former generals expresses his fears over the outbreak of agrarian insurgencies.

Thus, in the dry, legalistic language of the highest court in Massachusetts was Moses Sash, a 28-year-old African American veteran of the Revolutionary War, indicted by a grand jury for his role in Shays's Rebellion. Named after its leader,

Daniel Shays, another Revolutionary veteran, this armed insurgency pitted debt-ridden farmers in the western half of Massachusetts against conservative interests in the east. Farmers in western Massachusetts faced hard times in the 1780s brought on by falling farm prices, a shortage of money, heavy taxes, and mounting debts. Faced with an unresponsive state legislature controlled by eastern merchants and creditors, angry farmers reacted much as they had during the revolutionary agitation against the British a decade earlier: They organized, protested, and shut down the county courts.

Routed in a battle at Springfield Arsenal in January 1787 by an army raised by Governor Bowdoin, the Shaysites fled into the hills. Nearly all of them, including Sash, were pardoned by the new administration of Governor John Hancock. Sash moved to Connecticut and died in poverty.

More than any other domestic disturbance in the 1780s, Shays's Rebellion dramatized the fragile nature and conflicting values of America's first republic under the Articles of Confederation. White Americans debated the meaning of liberty and whether greater powers should be granted to the very weak national government established by the Articles in 1781. Moses Sash and countless other African Americans—slave or free—insisted that the Revolution bequeathed a promise of greater human rights that extended to all Americans regardless of race. Americans favoring a stronger, more centralized government repeatedly cited Shays's Rebellion as an example of the impending chaos that would destroy the republic unless fundamental changes were made. Those changes came with the writing of the U.S. Constitution in 1787 and its ratification in 1788.

The New Order of Republicanism

7.1   What people were deemed fit to have political rights in the new order of republicanism?

As royal authority collapsed during the Revolution, provincial congresses and committees assumed power in each of the former colonies. The Continental Congress, seeking to build support for the war effort, was concerned that these new institutions should have a firm legal and popular foundation. In May 1776, the Congress called on the colonies to form new state governments "under the authority of the people."

This call reflected the political philosophy of republicanism that animated the Revolution (see Chapter 6). To Americans, republicanism meant, first and foremost, that legitimate political authority derives from the people. Another key aspect of republicanism was the revolutionary idea that the people could define and limit governmental power through written constitutions. These core republican principles held that governmental authority should flow from the people, but it was not always clear just who was included in "the people."

Defining the People

Republicanism rested on the belief that the people were sovereign. But republicanism also taught that political rights should be limited to those who owned private property, because the independent will required for informed political judgment required economic self-sufficiency. This, in effect, restricted political participation to propertied white men. Virtually everyone else—propertyless white men, servants legally bound to others, women, slaves, and most free black people—were denied political rights. As for Native Americans, they were outside the U.S. body politic and exercised political rights within their own nations.

Because the ownership of property was relatively widespread among white men, some 60 to 85 percent of adult white men could participate in politics, a far higher proportion than elsewhere in the world of the eighteenth century. The greatest concentration of the remaining 25 percent or so who were shut out of the political process were unskilled laborers and mariners living in port cities.

suffrage The right to vote in a
political election.

Women and the Revolution

The Revolution did little to change the traditional patriarchal assumption that politics and public life should be the exclusive domain of men. Women, according to republican beliefs, were part of the dependent class and belonged under the control of propertied men, their husbands and fathers. Under common law (the customary, largely unwritten, law that Americans had inherited from Britain), women surrendered their property rights at marriage unless they made special arrangements to the contrary. Legally and economically, husbands had complete control over their wives. As a result, argued Theophilus Parsons of Massachusetts in 1778, women were, as a matter of course, "so situated as to have no wills of their own."

To be sure, some women saw in the political and social enthusiasm of the Revolution an opportunity to protest the most oppressive features of their subordination. "I won't have it thought that because we are the weaker sex as to bodily strength we are capable of nothing more than domestic concerns," wrote Eliza Wilkinson of South Carolina. Men, she lamented, "won't even allow us liberty of thought and that is all I want." Such protests, however, had little enduring effect. Most women were socialized to accept that their proper place was in the home with their families. In turn, the physical constraints on their lives—nearly endless chores as child providers and household managers and health issues related to frequent childbearing and deficient diets—left most women with neither the time nor the energy to push for a greater social role.

Gender-specific language, including such terms as "men," "Freemen," "white male inhabitants," and "free white men," explicitly barred women from voting in almost all state constitutions of the 1770s. Only the New Jersey constitution of 1776 defined **suffrage**, the right to vote, in gender-free terms—extending it to all adults "worth fifty pounds." As a result, until 1807, when the state legislature changed the constitution, propertied women, including widows and single women, enjoyed the right to vote in New Jersey.

The Revolution otherwise did bring women a few limited gains. They benefited from slightly less restrictive divorce laws and gained somewhat greater access to educational and business opportunities, changes that reflected the relative autonomy of many women during the war when their men were off fighting. The perception of women's moral status also rose. As the Philadelphia physician Benjamin Rush argued in his *Thoughts upon Female Education* (1787), educated and morally informed women were needed to instruct "their sons in the principles of liberty and government." Often called republican motherhood, this more positive view of women's influence entrusted

With the exception of New Jersey, where women meeting the property qualifications were eligible to vote, the state constitutions of the Revolutionary era prohibited women from voting.

mothers with the responsibility of passing on republican virtues from one generation to the next.

The Revolution and African Americans in the South. The Revolution had a more immediate impact on the lives of many African Americans, triggering the growth of free black communities and the development of an African American culture. Changes begun by the Revolution were the main factor in the tremendous increase of free blacks from a few thousand at mid-century to more than 100,000 by 1800 (see Figure 7.1). One key to this increase was a shift in the religious and intellectual climate. Revolutionary principles of liberty and equality and evangelical notions of human fellowship convinced many whites for the first time to challenge black slavery. As many whites grew more hostile to slavery, slaves in the North, drawing on republican political theory, submitted petitions for freedom to the new state legislatures, and blacks everywhere began to seize opportunities for freedom.

Upwards of 50,000 slaves, or one in ten of those in bondage, gained their freedom as a result of the war. One route was through military service, which generally carried a promise of freedom. When the British began raising black troops, the Americans followed suit. All the states except Georgia and South Carolina recruited black regiments. Some 5,000 blacks served in the Continental Army along with Moses Sash, and they, like their counterparts in British units, were mostly slaves. Most of the slaves who gained freedom during the war, however, had fled their owners and made their way to the port cities of the North.

By making slave property generally less secure, the Revolution encouraged many masters to free their slaves. A manumission act passed by the Virginia assembly in 1782 (but tightened a decade later) allowed individual owners to free their slaves. As the number of free blacks increased, those still enslaved grew bolder in their efforts to gain freedom. The fugitive slave Henny, warned a Maryland slaveowner in 1783, "will try to pass for a free woman as several have lately been set free in this neighborhood."

Northern Blacks and the Revolution. If the control mechanisms of slavery experienced some strain in the South during the Revolution, in the North, where slaves were only a small percentage of the population, they crumbled. Slaves pressured their owners for freedom by running away, damaging property, and committing arson. Most northern states ended slavery between 1777 and 1784. New York followed in 1799, and New Jersey in 1804. Nonetheless, although a majority of northern whites now agreed that slavery was incompatible with the Revolution's commitment to **natural rights** (the inherent human rights to life and liberty) and human freedom, they refused to sanction a sudden emancipation. The laws ending slavery in most of the northern states called for only the children of slaves to be freed, and only when they reached adulthood.

Northern blacks had to struggle to overcome white prejudice. Although black males were allowed to vote if they met the property qualifications, most were poor and held little property. Facing discrimination in jobs and housing, barred from juries, and

natural rights Political philosophy that maintains that individuals have an inherent right, found in nature and preceding any government or written law, to life and liberty.

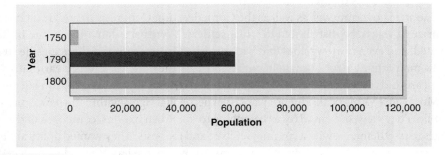

FIGURE 7.1 GROWTH OF THE FREE BLACK POPULATION BETWEEN 1750 AND 1800 Gradual emancipation in the North, the freeing of many slaves by their owners in the South, and the opportunities for freedom offered by the Revolution—all contributed to an explosive growth in the free population of African Americans in the second half of the eighteenth century.

SOURCE: *A Century of Population Growth in the United States, 1790–1900* (1909), p. 80. U.S. Bureau of the Census. Data for 1750 estimated.

((∙ 📖 **Read the Document** Prince Hall, A Free African American Petitions the Government for Emancipation of All Slaves (1777)

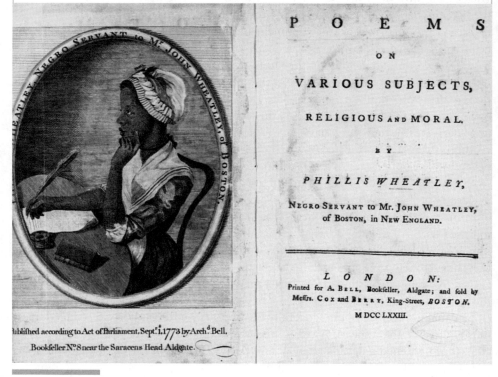

Phillis Wheatley was an acclaimed African American poet. Kidnapped into slavery as a child in Africa, she was a domestic slave to the Wheatley family of Boston when her first poems were published in 1773.

denied a fair share of funds for schools, urban blacks had to rely on their own resources. With the help of the small class of property holders among them, they began establishing their own churches and self-help associations such as the Free African Society in Philadelphia, founded in 1787.

The Revolution's Impact on Native Americans. Most Indian peoples had stayed neutral during the war or fought for the British (see Chapter 6). Just as the Americans sought to shake off British control, so the Indians, especially the western tribes and most of the Iroquois Confederation, sought to free themselves from American dominance. The British defeat was thus a double blow, depriving the Indians of a valuable ally and exposing them to the wrath of the victorious patriots. Late in the war a British officer observed of the pro-British southern Indians, "The minds of these people appear as much agitated as those of the unhappy Loyalists, they have very seriously proposed to abandon their country and accompany us [in an evacuation], having made all the world their enemies by their attachment to us."

The state governments, as well as the Confederation Congress, treated Indian lands as a prize of war to be distributed to white settlers. Territorial demands on the Indians escalated, and even the few tribes that had furnished troops for the American side struggled to maintain control over their homelands. As they did so, it was clear that white Americans did not consider Native Americans to be part of their republican society.

Most Native Americans did not want or expect equal rights within the new American republic. They viewed themselves as belonging to their own nations, composed of distinct villages and settlements, with a common culture and interests. They wanted political rights and control over the land within their nations. Above all, they wanted independence.

In seeking to defend their independence against the growing pressure of white Americans on their lands, Native Americans forged new confederacies in the 1780s that temporarily united them against a common enemy. They were encouraged in these efforts by the imperial powers of England and Spain, both of which sought to curb the

👁 Watch the Video   **Slavery and the Constitution**

Richard Allen, a former slave in Pennsylvania who purchased his freedom in the 1770s, was a cofounder in 1787 of the Free African Society in Philadelphia and later a bishop in the African Methodist Episcopal Church. This 1785 portrait conveys the firmness and calm dignity he brought to his leadership in the black community.

westward expansion of the United States. Thus, the immediate impact of the Revolution on Native Americans was a mixed one. On the one hand, the Revolution had created a new expansionist power in the United States that was intent on settling lands already occupied by Indians. On the other hand, American victory in the Revolution had broken the British monopoly of power in the region west of the Appalachian Mountains. Before the United States could consolidate its claim over the region, new imperial rivalries sprang up that allowed Native Americans to stake out a political middle ground between the competing powers. Throughout the 1780s, Native Americans continued to act as independent political agents in playing off outside powers against each other.

The State Constitutions

Ten new state constitutions were in place by the end of 1777. All these constitutions were written documents, a striking departure from the English practice of treating a constitution as a collection of customary rights and practices that had evolved over time. In the American view, a constitution was a formal expression of the people's sovereignty, a codification of the powers of government and the rights of citizenship that functioned as a fundamental law to which all public authority was held accountable.

Because Americans had come to associate tyranny with the privileges of royal governors, all the new state constitutions cut back sharply on executive power. Most important, for it struck at what patriots felt was the main source of executive domination and corruption, governors lost control over patronage, the power to appoint executive and judicial officials. As the new constitutions curbed the power of governors, they increased that of the legislatures, making them the focal point of government.

To make the legislatures more expressive of the popular will, the new constitutions included provisions that lowered property requirements for voting and officeholding, mandated annual elections, increased the number of seats in the legislatures, and made representation more proportional to the geographical distribution of population. Upper houses were made independent of the executive office and opened to popular election, as opposed to the colonial practice of having their members appointed by the governor.

Americans knew that legislatures, too, could act tyrannically, as they believed Britain's Parliament had done. So in a final check on arbitrary power, each state constitution eventually included some form of a **bill of rights** that set explicit limits on the power of government to interfere in the lives of citizens. The Virginia Declaration of Rights, written by the planter George Mason and adopted in June 1776, set the

bill of rights A written summary of inalienable rights and liberties.

precedent for this notable republican feature. By 1784, the constitutions of all thirteen states had provisions guaranteeing religious liberty, freedom of the press, and a citizen's right to such fair legal practices as trial by jury.

Toward Religious Pluralism. The new constitutions weakened but did not always sever the traditional tie between church and state. Many states, notably in New England, levied taxes for the support of religion. The states of New England also continued to maintain Congregationalism as the established, or state-supported, religion, while allowing dissenting Baptists and Methodists to use funds from the compulsory religious taxes to support their ministers. The "common people," explained the Baptist leader Isaac Backus, insisted that they had "as good a right to judge and act for themselves in matters of religion as civil rulers or the learned clergy."

The mid-Atlantic states lacked the religious uniformity of New England. This pluralism checked legislative efforts to impose religious taxes or designate any denomination as the established church. In the South, where many Anglican (or Episcopalian) clergymen had been Tories, the Anglican Church lost its former established status, a process speeded up by the refusal of religious dissenters in Virginia to serve in the Revolution unless granted exemption from taxes for the support of the Anglican establishment. These dissenters prized their religious freedom, but they hardly would have agreed with Thomas Jefferson's assertion regarding Virginia's religious freedom act of 1786 that "our civil rights have no dependence on our religious opinions any more than on opinions in physics or geometry."

Conflicting Visions of Republicanism. Although in general the executive lost power and the legislature gained power under the new state constitutions, the actual structure of each state government reflected the outcome of political struggles between radical and conservative visions of republicanism. The democratically inclined radicals wanted to open government to all male citizens and a political economy that favored a relative equality of wealth. The conservatives, fearing "mob rule," wanted to limit government to an educated elite of substantial property holders and to use the government to encourage large-scale capital accumulation. Although they agreed that government had to be derived from the people, most conservatives, like Jeremy Belknap of New Hampshire, thought that the people had to be "taught . . . that they are not able to govern themselves."

In South Carolina, where conservative planters gained the upper hand, the constitution mandated property qualifications that barred 90 percent of the state's white males from holding elective public office. By contrast, Pennsylvania had the most democratic and controversial constitution. Many of Pennsylvania's conservatives had discredited themselves during the Revolution by remaining neutral or loyal to the Crown. The Scots-Irish farmers and Philadelphia artisans who stepped into the resulting political vacuum held an egalitarian view of republicanism. The constitution they pushed through in 1776 gave the vote to all free males who paid taxes, regardless of wealth, and eliminated property qualifications for officeholding. In addition, the constitution concentrated power in a unicameral (single-house) legislature, eliminating both the office of governor and the more elite upper legislative house. To prevent the formation of an entrenched class of officeholders, the constitution's framers also required legislators to stand for election annually and barred them from serving more than four years out of seven.

Unlike the colonial assemblies, the new bicameral (two-house) state legislatures included substantially more artisans and small farmers and were not controlled by men of wealth. The proportion of legislators who came from a common background—those with property valued under £200—more than tripled to 62 percent in the North and more than doubled in the South from the 1770s to the 1780s.

Articles of Confederation Written document setting up the loose confederation of states that comprised the first national government of the United States from 1781 to 1788.

The Articles of Confederation

Once the Continental Congress decided on independence in 1776, it needed to create a legal basis for a permanent union of the states. According to the key provision of the **Articles of Confederation** that the Congress finally submitted to the states more than a year later, in November 1777, "Each State retains its sovereignty, freedom and independence, and every power, jurisdiction and right, which is not by this confederation expressly delegated to the United States, in Congress assembled." The effect was to create a loose confederation of autonomous states.

The powers the Articles of Confederation delegated to the central government were extremely limited, in effect little more than those already exercised by the Continental Congress. There were no provisions for a national judiciary or a separate executive branch of government. The Articles made Congress the sole instrument of national authority but restricted it with a series of constitutional safeguards that kept it from threatening the interests of the states. Each state had one vote in Congress. The delegates were chosen annually by their state legislatures and could serve only three years out of six. Important measures, such as finances or war and peace, required approval by nine states. Amendments to the Articles, including the levying of national taxes, required the unanimous consent of the states.

The Congress had authority primarily in the areas of foreign policy and national defense. It could declare war, make peace, conduct foreign affairs, negotiate with Native Americans, and settle disputes between the states. It had no authority, however, to raise troops or impose taxes; it could only ask the states to supply troops and money and hope that they would comply.

Most states quickly ratified the Articles of Confederation, but Maryland stubbornly held out until March 1781. Because they needed the approval of all thirteen states, only then did the Articles officially take effect.

The issue in Maryland concerned the unsettled lands in the West between the Appalachian Mountains and the Mississippi River (see Map 7.1). Some states claimed

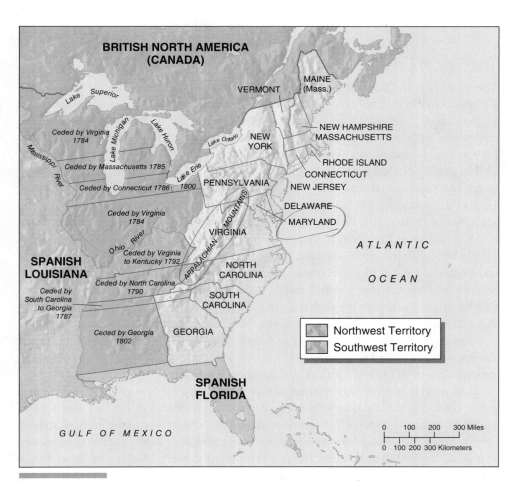

MAP 7.1 CESSION OF WESTERN LANDS BY THE STATES Eight states had claims to lands in the West after the Revolution, and their willingness to cede them to the national government was an essential step in the creation of a public domain administered by Congress.

these lands by virtue of their colonial charter rights and, led by Virginia and Massachusetts, they insisted on maintaining control over these territories. The so-called landless states—those with no claim to the West—insisted that the territories should be set aside as a national domain, a reserve of public land controlled by Congress for the benefit of all the states.

Threatened by the British presence in the Chesapeake area in early 1781, Virginia finally broke the impasse over the Articles. Though it retained control of Kentucky, Virginia gave up its claim in the West to a vast area extending north of the Ohio River. In turn, Maryland, the last holdout among the landless states and now desperate for military aid from the Congress, agreed to ratify the Articles.

Problems at Home

| 7.2 | How did economic problems lead to political conflict in the 1780s? |

Neither prosperity nor political stability accompanied the return of peace in 1783. The national government struggled to avoid bankruptcy, and in 1784 an economic depression struck. As fiscal problems deepened, creditor and debtor groups clashed angrily in state legislatures. When legislatures passed measures that provided relief to debtors at the expense of creditors, the creditors decried what they saw as the interference of ignorant majorities with the rights of private property. Raising the cry of "legislative despotism," the abuse of power by tyrannical lawmakers, the creditors joined their voices to those who early on had wanted the power of the states curbed by a stronger central government. The only solid accomplishment of the Confederation Congress during this troubled period was to formulate an orderly and democratic plan for the settlement of the West.

The Fiscal Crisis

The Continental Congress and the states had incurred heavy debts to finance the Revolutionary War. Unable to impose and collect sufficient taxes to cover the debts and without reserves of gold or silver, they had little choice but to borrow funds and issue certificates, or bonds, pledging repayment. The Congress had the largest responsibility for meeting the war's costs, and to do so, it printed close to $250 million in paper notes backed only by its good faith. By the end of the war in 1781, these Continental dollars were nearly worthless, and the national debt—primarily certificates issued by the Continental Loan Office—stood at $11 million. As Congress issued new securities to settle claims by soldiers and civilians, the debt rose to $28 million within just a few years.

The Congress never did put its tottering finances on a sound footing, and its fiscal problems ultimately discredited the Articles of Confederation in the eyes of the **nationalists**, a loose bloc of congressmen, army officers, and public creditors who wanted to strengthen the Confederation at the expense of the states. The nationalists first began to organize in the dark days of 1780 and 1781, when inflation was rampant, the army was going unpaid, the Congress had ceased paying interest on the public debt, and the war effort itself seemed in danger of collapsing. Galvanized by this crisis, the nationalists rallied behind Robert Morris, a Philadelphia merchant appointed as superintendent of finance for the Confederation government.

Morris sought to enhance national authority through a bold program of financial and political reform. He began by securing a charter from Congress in 1781 for the Bank of North America, the nation's first commercial bank. Morris wanted to use the bank to hold government funds, make loans to the government, and issue bank notes—paper money that could be used to settle debts and pay taxes owed to the United States. He met with some success, but his efforts ultimately depended on the Congress gaining taxing power.

In 1781, Morris proposed a national impost, or tariff, of 5 percent on imported goods. Because this was a national tax, it required an amendment to the Articles of

nationalists Group of leaders in the 1780s who spearheaded the drive to replace the Articles of Confederation with a stronger central government.

Confederation and the consent of all thirteen states. Twelve of the states quickly ratified the impost amendment, but Rhode Island—critically dependent on its own import duties to finance its war debt—rejected it, sending it down to defeat. When a revised impost plan was considered two years later, New York blocked its passage. These failures doomed Morris's financial reforms. He left office in 1784, and in the same year, the Bank of North America severed its ties to the national government and became a private corporation in Pennsylvania.

The failure of the impost tax was one of many setbacks that put the nationalists temporarily on the defensive. With the conclusion of peace in 1783, confidence in state government returned, taking the edge off calls to vest the central government with greater authority. The states continued to balk at supplying the money requisitioned by Congress and denied the Congress even limited authority to regulate foreign commerce. Most ominously for the nationalist cause, the states began to assume responsibility for part of the national debt. As Morris had warned in 1781, such a policy entailed "a principle of disunion . . . which must be ruinous." Without the power to tax, the Congress was a hostage to the sovereignty of the individual states with no real authority over the nation's economic affairs. When the economy plunged into a severe depression in 1784, Congress could only look on helplessly.

Economic Depression

During the Revolutionary War, Britain closed its markets to American goods. After the war, the British continued this policy, hoping to keep the United States weak and dependent. Meanwhile, British merchants were happy to satisfy America's pent-up demand for consumer goods after the war. Cheap British imports inundated the American market, and coastal merchants made them available to inland traders and shopkeepers by extending easy credit terms. In turn, these local businessmen sold the goods to farmers and artisans in the interior. Ultimately, however, the British merchants required payment in hard currency, gold and silver coins. Without access to its former export markets, America's only source of hard currency was foreign loans obtained by Congress and what money the French army had spent during the war. This was soon exhausted, and America's trade deficit with Britain—the excess of imports over exports—ballooned in the early 1780s (see Figure 7.2).

The result was an immense bubble of credit that finally burst in 1784, triggering a depression that would linger for most of the decade. As merchants began to press debtors for immediate payment, prices collapsed (they fell more than 25 percent between

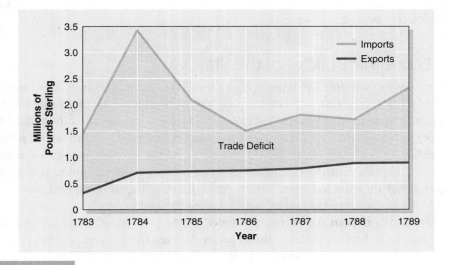

FIGURE 7.2 AMERICAN EXPORTS TO AND IMPORTS FROM BRITAIN BETWEEN 1783 AND 1789 During the 1780s, the United States imported far more from Britain than it exported there. The resulting huge trade deficit drained the country of gold and silver and was a major factor in the credit crisis that triggered an economic depression in the middle of the decade.

SOURCE: U.S. Bureau of the Census, *Historical Statistics of the United States: Colonial Times to 1970*, Pt. 2 (1975), p. 1176

1784 and 1786), and debtors were unable to pay. The best most could hope for was to avoid bankruptcy. Small farmers everywhere had trouble paying their debts.

In the cities, wages fell 25 percent between 1785 and 1789, and workers began to organize. They called for tariffs to protect them from cheap British imports and for legislative measures to promote American manufacturers. In the countryside, farmers faced lawsuits for the collection of debts and the dreaded possibility of losing their land.

With insufficient money in circulation to raise prices and reverse the downturn, the depression fed on itself. Congress was powerless to raise cash and was unable to pay off its old debts, including what it owed to the Revolutionary soldiers. Many state governments made things worse by imposing heavy taxes payable in the paper money they had issued during the Revolution. The result was to further reduce the amount of money in circulation, thus increasing deflationary pressures and forcing prices still lower.

Britain's trade policies caused particular suffering among New England merchants. No longer protected under the old Navigation Acts as British vessels, American ships were now barred from most ports in the British trading empire. Incoming cargoes from the West Indies to New England fell off sharply, and the market for whale oil and fish, two of New England's major exports, dried up. The economy of the mid-Atlantic region held up better, but even there the loss of the provisioning trade to the British West Indies cut into the income of merchants and farmers and forced layoffs among artisans who serviced the shipping trade.

In the southern states, British policies compounded the problem of recovering from the physical damage and labor disruptions inflicted by the war. Some 10 percent of the region's slaves had fled during the war, and production levels on plantations fell in the 1780s. Chesapeake planters needed a full decade to restore the prewar output of tobacco, and a collapse in tobacco prices in 1785 left most of them in the same chronic state of indebtedness that had plagued them on the eve of the Revolution.

Farther south, in the Carolina low country, the plantation economy was crippled. War damage had been extensive, and planters piled up debts to purchase additional slaves and repair their plantations and dikes. Burdened by new British duties on American rice, planters saw their rice exports fall by 50 percent.

By the late 1780s, the worst of the depression was over and an upturn was under way in the mid-Atlantic states. Food exports to continental Europe were on the rise, and American merchants were developing new trading ties with India and China. Commercial treaties with the Dutch, Swedes, and Prussians also opened up markets that had been closed to the colonists. Nonetheless, a full recovery had to await the 1790s.

As the economy stagnated in the 1780s, the population was growing rapidly. There were 50 percent more Americans in 1787 than there had been in 1775. As a result, living standards fell and economic conflict dominated the politics of the states during the Confederation period.

The Economic Policies of the States

The depression had political repercussions in all the states. Britain was an obvious target of popular anger, and merchants poorly positioned to adjust to the postwar dislocations of trade led a campaign to slap retaliatory duties on British ships and special taxes on British goods. Likewise artisans and workers, especially in the North, pushed for tariff barriers against cheap British goods as a way to encourage domestic manufacturing and protect their jobs and wages. Most northern states imposed anti-British measures, but these varied from state to state, limiting their impact and producing squabbles when goods imported in one state were shipped to another.

State legislatures in the North responded to the protests of artisans by passing tariffs, but the lack of a uniform national policy doomed their efforts. Shippers evaded high tariffs by bringing their cargoes in through states with no tariffs or less restrictive ones. States without ports, such as New Jersey and North Carolina, complained of economic discrimination. When they purchased foreign goods from a neighboring shipping state, they were forced to pay part of the tariff cost, but all the revenue from the tariff accrued to the importing state.

From Then to Now
Politics and Debt

A mericans demanded relief from high taxes and heavy debts in the 1780s much as they have in the early twenty-first century. Taxes levied to finance the Revolutionary War pushed up taxes in most states to three or four times the levels of the colonial period. Most of the tax revenue was funneled to the holders of state debts incurred to wage the war. Despite having purchased these debt securities at a sharp discount, the bondholders demanded payment at the face value of the debt. Furthermore, they blocked proposals to issue paper money so as to ensure they would not be paid back in depreciated currency. As land values and farm income fell during the depression of the 1780s, farmers found it increasingly difficult to come up with the hard money — gold and silver — to pay their taxes and private debts. Demands for debtor relief and paper money spread in all the states as farmers struggled to avoid foreclosures, scale back or suspend debt collections, and stay out of debtor prisons. Many of these debtors, most notoriously in Massachusetts, took up arms and closed courthouses. The conflict between debtors and creditors played itself out in newspapers and state legislatures and eventually shaped critical features of the new form of government hammered out in the Constitutional Convention.

By the 1830s the new federal government had paid off the Revolutionary War debt, including that of the states. With the exception of the huge outlays for World War II, which resulted in federal debt at almost 122 percent of GDP (gross domestic product) by 1946 before the debt was pared down, the federal debt never rose above the value of GDP until the cost of new wars in Iraq and Afghanistan, the bailout of the banks after the crash of 2008, and funds spent trying to revive the economy under President Obama sent it soaring once again. That debt, combined with near record levels of private indebtedness and calls for tax relief, returned American politics full circle to the raging debates of the 1780s.

Question for Discussion

• What are the differences and similarities in the ways in which Americans responded to issues of debt and taxation in the 1780s as compared to today?

The sluggish recovery from the financial crash of 2008 heightened concerns over wealth inequality and led to calls for greater economic fairness.

Armed with long muskets equipped with bayonets, Shays's supporters are depicted here gathering on the steps of a courthouse in western New England in 1786.

Tariff policies also fed sectional tensions between northern and southern states that undermined efforts to confer on the Congress the power to regulate commerce. The agrarian states of the South, which had little in the way of mercantile or artisan interests to protect, generally favored free trade policies that encouraged British imports. Southern planters were also happy to take advantage of the low rates charged by British ships for transporting their crops to Europe; by doing so, they put pressure on northern shippers to reduce their rates.

The most bitter divisions exposed by the depression of the 1780s, however, were not between states but between debtors and creditors within states. As the value of debt securities the states had issued to raise money dropped during the Revolutionary War, speculators bought them up for a fraction of their face value from farmers and soldiers

Shays's Rebellion An armed
movement of debt-ridden farmers
in western Massachusetts in the
winter of 1786–1787. The rebellion
shut down courts and created a
crisis atmosphere, strengthening
the case of nationalists that a
stronger central government was
needed to maintain civil order in
the states.

desperate for cash. The speculators then pressured the states to raise taxes and repay the debts in full in hard currency. Wealthy landowners and merchants likewise supported higher taxes and the rapid repayment of debts in hard currency.

Arrayed against these creditor groups by the mid-1780s was a broad coalition of debtors: middling farmers, small shopkeepers, artisans, laborers, and people who had overextended themselves speculating in western land. The debtors wanted the states to issue paper money that they could use instead of hard money—gold and silver—to pay their debts. The paper money would have an inflationary effect, raising wages and the prices of farm commodities and reducing the value of debts contracted in hard currency.

Shays's Rebellion. This was the economic context in which **Shays's Rebellion** exploded in the fall of 1786. Farm foreclosures and imprisonments for failure to pay debts had skyrocketed in western Massachusetts. When the creditor and seaboard

Read the **Document**   Daniel Gray and Thomas Grover, Reports on Shays's Rebellion (1786)

Benjamin Lincoln, the commander of the forces that suppressed Shays's rebellion, strikes a triumphant pose in this 1800 painting.

interests in the legislature refused to pass any relief measures, some 2,000 farmers took up arms against the state government in Shays's Rebellion.

Outside of western Massachusetts, discontented debtors generally stopped short of armed resistance because of their success in changing the monetary policy of their states. In 1785 and 1786, seven states enacted laws for new paper money issues. In most cases, the result was a qualified success. Controls on the supply of the new money kept it from depreciating rapidly, so that its inflationary effect was mild. Combined with laws that prevented or delayed creditors from seizing property from debtors to satisfy debts, the currency issues helped keep a lid on popular discontent.

The most notorious exception to this pattern of fiscal responsibility was in Rhode Island, already nicknamed "Rogue's Island" for the sharp trading practices of its merchants. A rural party that gained control of the Rhode Island legislature in 1786 pushed through a currency law that flooded the state with paper money that could be used to pay all debts. Creditors who balked at accepting the new money at face value were subject to heavy penalties. Shocked, they went into hiding or left the state entirely, and merchants denounced the law as outright fraud.

Debtors versus Conservatives.   The actions of the debtor party in Rhode Island alarmed conservatives everywhere, confirming their fears that legislative bodies dominated by common farmers and artisans rather than, as before the Revolution, by men of wealth and social distinction were dangerous. Conservatives, creditors, and nationalists alike now spoke of a democratic tyranny that would have to be checked if the republic were to survive and protect its property holders.

Congress and the West

The Peace of Paris and the surrender of charter claims by the states gave the Congress control of a magnificent expanse of land between the Appalachian Mountains and the Mississippi River. This was the first American West. In what would prove the most enduring accomplishment of the Confederation government, the Congress set forth a series of effective provisions for its settlement, governance, and eventual absorption into the Union.

Asserting for the national government the right to formulate Indian policy, the Congress negotiated a series of treaties with the Indians beginning in 1784 for the abandonment of their land claims in the West. By threatening to use military force, congressional commissioners in 1784 coerced the Iroquois Confederation of New York to cede half of its territory to the United States in the Treaty of Fort Stanwix. Similar tactics in 1785 resulted in the Treaty of Fort McIntosh, in which the Wyandots, Chippewas, Delawares, and Ottawas ceded much of their land in Ohio. Against the opposition of states intent on grabbing Indian lands for themselves, Congress resolved in 1787 that its treaties were binding on all the states. And anxious for revenue, Congress insisted on payment from squatters who had filtered into the West before provisions had been made for land sales.

The most pressing political challenge was to secure the loyalty of the West to the new and fragile Union. To satisfy the demands of settlers for self-government, the Congress resolved as early as 1779 that new states would be carved out of the western domain with all the rights of the original states. An early plan for organizing the territories, the Ordinance of 1784, was largely the work of Thomas Jefferson. In it, he proposed to create ten districts, or territories, each of which could apply for admission as a state when its population equaled that of the free inhabitants in the least populous of the existing states. Jefferson also proposed that settlers be permitted to choose their own officials, and he called for the prohibition of slavery in the West after 1800. Shorn of its no-slavery features, the ordinance passed Congress but was never put into practice.

As settlers and speculators began pouring into the West in 1784, however, the Congress was forced to move quickly to formulate a policy for conveying its public land into private hands. If it could not regulate land sales and pass on clear titles, Congress

Land Ordinance of 1785 Act passed by Congress under the Articles of Confederation that created the grid system of surveys by which all subsequent public land was made available for sale.

would, in effect, have surrendered its claim to govern. One way or another, settlers were going to get their land, but a pell-mell process of private acquisitions in widely scattered settlements threatened to touch off costly Indian wars, deprive the national government of vitally needed revenue, and encourage separatist movements.

The Congress responded with the **Land Ordinance of 1785**. The crucial feature of this seminal legislation was its stipulation that public lands be surveyed in a rectangular grid pattern before being offered for sale (see Figure 7.3). By requiring that land first be platted into townships of 36 uniform sections of 640 acres each, the ordinance adopted the New England system of land settlement, an approach that promoted compact settlements and produced undisputed land titles. In sharp contrast was the typical southern pattern, whereby settlers picked out a piece of land in a large tract ahead of a precise survey and then fought each other in the courts to secure legal title. In an effort to avoid endless litigation, Congress opted for a policy geared to order and regularity.

Congress also attempted to attract a certain type of settler to the West by offering the plots of 640 acres at the then hefty sum of no less than $640, or $1 per acre, payable in hard currency or its equivalent. The goal here was to keep out the shiftless poor and reserve the West for enterprising and presumably law-abiding farm families who could afford the entry cost. Concerned about westerners' reputation for lawlessness and afraid that the primitive living conditions might cause them to lapse into savagery,

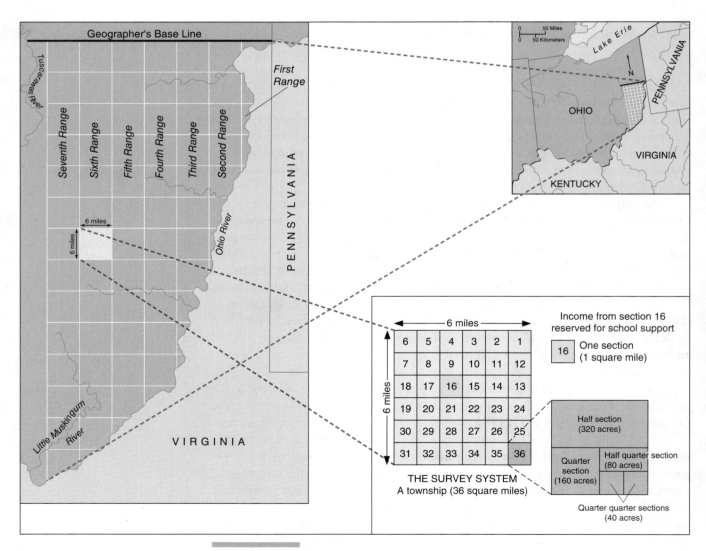

FIGURE 7.3 LAND ORDINANCE OF 1785 The precise uniformity of the surveying system initiated in the Land Ordinance of 1785 created a rectangular grid pattern that was the model for all future land surveyed in the public domain. The uniform grid system that was laid down ignored the natural contours of the land for the sake of speed and convenience in bringing the land to market.

Congress also set aside the income from the sale of the sixteenth section in each township for the support of public schools.

Before any land sales occurred under the Land Ordinance of 1785, impatient settlers continued to push north of the Ohio River and claim homesteads as squatters. They clashed both with local Indian tribes and with the troops sent by the Congress to evict them. Frustrated with the slow process of surveying, the Congress sold off 1.5 million acres to a group of New England speculators organized as the Ohio Company. The speculators bought the land with greatly depreciated loan-office certificates that had been issued to Revolutionary War veterans, and their cost per acre averaged less than 10 cents in hard money. They now pressed their allies in Congress to establish a governmental structure for the West that would protect their investment by bringing the unruly elements in the West under control.

Both the Congress and speculators wanted political stability and economic development in the West and a degree of supervision for settlers commonly viewed in the East as "but little less savage than the Indians." What was needed, wrote James Monroe of Virginia, were temporary controls—made acceptable by the promise of eventual statehood—that "in effect" would place the western territories under "a colonial government similar to that which prevail'd in these States previous to the revolution." The **Northwest Ordinance of 1787**, the most significant legislative act of the Confederation Congress, filled this need, creating a phased process for achieving statehood that neatly blended public and private interests.

According to the ordinance, controls on a new territory were to be strictest in the early stage of settlement, when Congress would appoint a territorial government consisting of a governor, a secretary, and three judges. When a territory reached a population of 5,000 adult males, those with 50 acres of land or more could elect a legislature. The actions of the legislature, however, were subject to an absolute veto by the governor. Once a territory had a population of 60,000, the settlers could draft a constitution and apply for statehood "on an equal footing with the original states in all respects whatsoever."

Most significant, it prohibited slavery. Southern congressmen agreed to the ban, in part because they saw little future for slavery in the region. More important, they expected slavery to be permitted in the region south of the Ohio River that was still under the administrative authority of Virginia, North Carolina, and Georgia in the 1780s. Indeed, slavery was allowed in this region when the **Southwest Ordinance of 1790** brought it under national control, a decision that would have grave consequences in the future sectionalization of the United States.

Although the Northwest Ordinance applied only to the national domain north of the Ohio River, it provided the organizational blueprint by which all future territory was brought into the Union. It went into effect immediately and set the original Union on a course of dynamic expansion through the addition of new states.

Northwest Ordinance of 1787 Legislation passed by Congress under the Articles of Confederation that prohibited slavery in the Northwest Territories and provided the model for the incorporation of future territories into the Union as coequal states.

Southwest Ordinance of 1790 Legislation passed by Congress that set up a government with no prohibition on slavery in U.S. territory south of the Ohio River.

Diplomatic Weaknesses

7.3 What steps did Britain and Spain take to block American expansion?

I n the international arena of the 1780s, the United States was a weak and often ridiculed nation. Under the Articles of Confederation, the Congress had the authority to negotiate foreign treaties but no economic or military power to enforce their terms.

Unable to regulate commerce or set tariffs, Congress had no leverage with which to pry open the restricted trading empires of France, Spain, and most important, Britain.

France and the United States, allies during the Revolutionary War, remained on friendly terms after it. Britain, however, treated its former colonies with contempt, and Spain was also openly antagonistic. Both of these powers sought to block American expansion into the trans-Appalachian West.

Impasse with Britain

The Confederation Congress was unable to resolve any of the major issues that poisoned Anglo-American relations in the 1780s. Key among those issues were provisions in the peace treaty of 1783 that concerned prewar American debts to the British and the treatment of Loyalists by the patriots. Britain used what it claimed to be America's failure to satisfy these provisions to justify its own violations of the treaty. The result was a diplomatic deadlock that hurt American interests in the West and in foreign trade.

Article 4 of the peace treaty called for the payment of all prewar debts at their "full value in sterling money"—that is, in gold or silver coin. Among the most numerous of those with outstanding debts to British creditors were tobacco planters in the Chesapeake region of Virginia and Maryland. During the Revolution, the British army had carried off and freed many of the region's slaves without compensating the planters. Still angry, the planters were in no mood to repay their debts. Working out a scheme with their respective legislatures, they agreed only to pay the face value of their debts to their state treasuries in state or Continental paper money. Since this money was practically worthless, the planters in effect repudiated their debts.

During the Revolution, all the states had passed anti-Loyalist legislation, and many state governments had seized Loyalists' lands and goods, selling them to raise revenue for the war effort. Upwards of 100,000 Loyalists fled to Canada and England, and their property losses ran into millions of dollars. Articles 5 and 6 of the peace treaty pledged the Congress to "recommend" to the states that they stop persecuting Loyalists and restore confiscated Loyalist property. But wartime animosities remained high, ebbing only gradually during the 1780s. Despite the pleadings of John Jay, the secretary for foreign affairs in the Confederation government, the states were slow to rescind their punitive legislation or allow the recovery of confiscated property.

Combined with the matter of the unpaid debts, the continued failure of the states to make restitution to the Loyalists gave the British a convenient pretext to hold on to the forts in the West that they had promised to relinquish in the Treaty of Paris. Their refusal to abandon the forts, which extended from Lake Champlain in upstate New York westward along the Great Lakes, was part of an overall strategy to keep the United States weak, divided, and small. The continued British presence in the region effectively shut Americans out of the fur trade with the Indians. It also insulted the sovereignty of the United States and threatened the security of its northern frontier.

For all of the British provocations in the West, American officials viewed Britain's retaliatory trade policies as the gravest threat to American security and prosperity. John Adams, the American minister to London, concluded that the British would never lift their trading and shipping restrictions until forced to do so by a uniform American system of discriminatory duties on British goods. Retaliatory navigation acts by individual states did little good because they left the British free to play one state off against another. Adams could denounce Parliament as a "parcel of sots" for restricting American trade, but only with a strong, centralized government could Americans fashion a navigation system that would command Britain's respect.

Spain and the Mississippi River

At the close of the Revolutionary War, Spain reimposed barriers on American commerce within its empire. Anxious to maintain as large a buffer zone as possible between its Louisiana and Florida possessions and the restless Americans, Spain also refused to recognize the southern and western boundaries of the United States as specified in the treaty with Britain in 1783, holding out instead for a more northerly border. And of greatest consequence, it denied the claim of the United States to free navigation of the entire length of the Mississippi River.

The Mississippi question was explosive because on its resolution hinged American settlement and control of the entire western region south of the Ohio River. Only with access to the Mississippi and the commercial right of deposit at New Orleans—that is, the right to transfer cargoes to oceangoing vessels—could the region's farmers, then mostly in what would become Tennessee and Kentucky, profitably reach national and international markets.

In the wake of the Revolution, the settlers of Kentucky, which was still part of Virginia, and Tennessee, which was still part of North Carolina, flirted with the idea of secession. Impatient to secure both political independence and the economic benefits that would come with access to the Mississippi, the separatists were not particular about whom they dealt with. They became entangled in a web of diplomatic intrigue that included the Spanish, the Indians, and American officials east of the mountains.

Spain sought to use the divided loyalties of American speculators and frontier settlers to its advantage, employing some of them as spies and informers. Spain likewise sought to exploit divisions among Indian groups. In a bewildering variety of treaties negotiated by the Congress, individual southern states, and land speculators, white Americans laid claim to much of the ancestral land of the major Indian nations in the Southeast—the Cherokee, Chickasaw, Choctaw, and Creek. Fraud was rampant, and many Native Americans believed, with good reason, that they had never been consulted in the dispossession of their land. The Spanish responded by recruiting disaffected Indians into an alliance system of their own. Their staunchest allies came from a faction of the Creeks led by Alexander McGillivray, the son of a trader father and a half-French, half-Creek mother. Supplied with arms by the Spanish, these Creeks succeeded in forcing white settlers off their tribal land in Georgia.

Spain stepped up pressure on the West in the summer of 1784, when it closed the Mississippi River within Spanish territory to American trade. Hoping now to benefit from American weakness, Spain also opened negotiations for a long-term settlement with the United States. The Spanish negotiator, Don Diego de Gardoqui, offered a deal that cleverly played the interests of the North against those of the South and West. In exchange for an American agreement to surrender claims to navigate the Mississippi for the next thirty years, Gardoqui proposed to grant the United States significant trading concessions in the Spanish empire that would open new markets and new sources of hard money to the financially pressed merchants of the northeastern states. John Jay, his American negotiating partner, reluctantly accepted the offer.

When Jay released the terms of the proposed treaty with Spain in 1786, Congress erupted in angry debate. Southerners, who had taken the lead in the settlement of the West, accused Jay of selling out their interests. The treaty threatened the agrarian alliance they hoped to forge with the West, increasing the odds that the West would break from the East and go its own way. Vowing that they would not surrender the West, southern congressmen united to defeat the treaty. Nine states' votes were required for ratification under the Articles, and Jay's treaty gained only seven—all in the North.

The regional antagonisms exposed by the Jay-Gardoqui talks heightened the alarm over the future of the republic provoked by Shays's Rebellion earlier in 1786. As the sense of crisis deepened in 1786, the nationalists grew in influence and numbers. Led by Alexander Hamilton of New York and James Madison of Virginia, they now argued that only a radical political change could preserve the republic and fulfill the promise of its greatness.

Toward a New Union

7.4 What explains the call for a stronger centralized government and the divisions which emerged over the ratification of the new Constitution?

I n September 1786, delegates from several states met at the **Annapolis Convention**, in Annapolis, Maryland, seeking to devise a uniform system of commercial regulation for the country. While there, a group of nationalist leaders issued a call for a convention at Philadelphia "to devise such further provisions as shall appear to them necessary to render the constitution of the Federal Government adequate to

Annapolis Convention
Conference of state delegates at Annapolis, Maryland, that issued a call in September 1786 for a convention to meet at Philadelphia in May 1787 to consider fundamental changes to the Articles of Confederation.

Constitutional Convention Convention that met in Philadelphia in 1787 and drafted the Constitution of the United States.

Constitution of the United States The written document providing for a new central government of the United States, drawn up at the Constitutional Convention in 1787 and ratified by the states in 1788.

the exigencies of the Union." The leaders who met at the **Constitutional Convention** in Philadelphia forged an entirely new framework of governance, the **Constitution of the United States**, which called for a federal republic with a powerful and effective national government. In 1788, after a close struggle in state ratifying conventions, the Constitution was adopted.

The Road to Philadelphia

Only nine states sent delegates to the Annapolis Convention, and only five from those states had actually arrived when the nationalists, at the prompting of Madison and Hamilton, abruptly adjourned the meeting. They then called on the states and the Congress to approve a full-scale constitutional convention for Philadelphia in May 1787.

The timing of the call for the Philadelphia Convention could not have been better. During the fall and winter of 1786, the agrarian protests unleashed by Shays's Rebellion in Massachusetts spilled over into other states. Coupled with talk of a dismemberment of the Union in the wake of the Jay-Gardoqui negotiations, the agrarian unrest strengthened the case of the nationalists for more centralized authority.

All the states except Rhode Island, which wanted to retain exclusive control over its own trade, sent delegates to Philadelphia. The fifty-five men who attended the convention represented an extraordinary array of talent and experience. Chiefly lawyers by training or profession, most had served in the Confederation Congress, and more than one-third had fought in the Revolution. Extremely well educated by the standards of the day, the delegates were members of the intellectual as well as the political and economic elite. As a group, they were far wealthier than the average American. Most had investments in land and the public securities of the United States. At least nineteen owned slaves. Their greatest asset as a working body was their common commitment to a nationalist solution to the crisis of confidence they saw gripping the republic. Most of the strong supporters of the Articles of Confederation refused to attend, perhaps because, as Patrick Henry of Virginia remarked, they "smelt a rat."

The Convention at Work

When it agreed to the Philadelphia Convention, the Congress authorized only a revision of the Articles of Confederation. Almost from the start, however, the delegates set about replacing the Articles altogether. Their first action was to elect George Washington unanimously as the convention's presiding officer, gaining credibility for their deliberations from his prestige. The most ardent nationalists then immediately seized the initiative by presenting the **Virginia Plan**. Drafted by James Madison, this plan replaced the Confederation Congress with a truly national government, organized like most of the state governments with a bicameral legislature, an executive, and a judiciary.

Two features of the Virginia Plan stood out. First, it granted the national Congress power to legislate "in all cases in which the separate states are incompetent" and to nullify any state laws that in its judgment were contrary to the "articles of Union." Second, it made representation in both houses of the Congress proportional to population. This meant that the most populous states would have more votes in Congress than the less populous states, giving them effective control of the government.

Delegates from the small states countered with the **New Jersey Plan**, introduced on June 15 by William Paterson. This plan kept intact the basic structure of the Confederation Congress—one state, one vote—but otherwise amended the Articles by giving the national government the explicit power to tax and to regulate domestic and foreign commerce. In addition, it gave acts of Congress precedence over state legislation, making them "the supreme law of the respective states."

Virginia Plan Proposal of the Virginia delegation at the 1787 Constitutional Convention calling for a national legislature in which the states would be represented according to population. The national legislature would have the explicit power to veto or overrule laws passed by state legislatures.

New Jersey Plan Proposal of the New Jersey delegation at the 1787 Constitutional Convention for a strengthened national government in which all states would have equal representation in a unicameral legislature.

The Great Compromise. The New Jersey Plan was quickly voted down, and the convention remained deadlocked for another month over how to apportion state representation in the national government. The issue was finally resolved on July 16 with the

Read the Document   James Madison, The Debates in the Federal Convention of 1787
(June 15, 1787)

7.1

7.2

7.3

7.4

This c. 1790 folk art depiction of Washington and his wife reveals how quickly Washington's fame became part of the public consciousness and made him the obvious choice to preside over the Constitutional Convention.

so-called **Great Compromise**. Small states were given equal footing with large states in the Senate, or upper house, where each would have two votes. In the lower house, the House of Representatives, the number of seats was made proportional to population, giving larger states the advantage. The Great Compromise also settled a sectional dispute over representation between the free (or about to be free) states and the slave states. The southern states wanted slaves counted for apportioning representation in the House but excluded from direct tax assessments. The northern states wanted slaves counted for tax assessments but excluded for apportioning representation. To settle the issue, the Great Compromise settled on an expedient, if morally troubling, formula: Free residents were to be counted precisely; to that count would be added, "excluding Indians not taxed, three-fifths of all other persons (meaning enslaved blacks)." Thus the slave states gained additional political representation, while the states in the North received assurance that the owners of nonvoting slaves would have to bear part of the cost of any direct taxes levied by the new government.

The Great Compromise ended the first phase of the convention, which had focused on the general framework of a stronger national government. In its next phase, the convention debated the specific powers to be delegated to the new government. It was at this point that the sectional cleavage between North and South over slavery and other issues came most prominently to the fore. As Madison had warned in late June, "the great division of interests" in the United States would arise from the effect of states "having or not having slaves."

Regulation of Commerce and the Issue of Slavery.   The sectional clash first erupted over the power of Congress to regulate commerce. At issue was whether Congress could regulate trade and set tariffs by a simple majority vote. Southerners worried that a northern majority would pass navigation acts favoring northern shippers and drive up the cost of sending southern commodities to Europe. To counter this threat, delegates from the Lower South demanded that a two-thirds majority be required to enact trade legislation. Suddenly, the central plank in the nationalists' program—the unified power to force trading concessions from Britain—was endangered.

In the end, Madison had his way; the delegates agreed that enacting trade legislation would require only a simple majority. In return, however, southerners exacted concessions on the slavery issue. When planters from South Carolina and Georgia

Great Compromise Plan proposed by Roger Sherman of Connecticut at the 1787 Constitutional Convention for creating a national bicameral legislature in which all states would be equally represented in the Senate and proportionally represented in the House.

made it clear that they would agree to join a new Union only if they could continue to import slaves, the convention abandoned a proposal to ban the foreign slave trade. Instead, Congress would be barred from acting against the slave trade for twenty years. In addition, bowing to the fears of planters that Congress could use its taxing power to undermine slavery, the convention denied Congress the right to tax exports from any state. And to alleviate southern concerns that slaves might escape to freedom in the North, the new Constitution included an explicit provision calling on the states to return "persons held to Service or Labour" in any other state.

After settling the slavery question in late August, the convention had one last significant hurdle to clear: the question of the national executive.

The Office of the Chief Executive.   In large part because of their confidence in George Washington, whom nearly everyone expected to be the first president, the delegates fashioned a chief executive office with broad discretionary powers. The prerogatives of the president included the rank of commander in chief of the armed forces, the authority to conduct foreign affairs and negotiate treaties, the right to appoint diplomatic and judicial officers, and the power to veto congressional legislation. The president's term of office was set at four years, with no limits on how often an individual could be reelected.

Determining how to elect the president proved a thorny problem. The delegates envisioned a forceful, energetic, and independent executive, insulated from the whims of an uninformed public and the intrigues of the legislature. As a result, they rejected both popular election and election by Congress. The solution they hit upon was the convoluted system of an "electoral college." Each state was left free to determine how it would choose presidential electors equal to the number of its representatives and senators. These electors would then vote by ballot for two persons. The person receiving a majority of all the electoral votes would become president and the second highest vote-getter the vice president. If no candidate received a majority of the electoral votes, the election would be turned over to the House of Representatives, where each state would have one vote.

After a style committee polished the wording in the final draft of the Constitution, thirty-nine of the forty-two delegates still in attendance signed the document on September 17. The Preamble, which originally began with a list of the states, was reworded at the last minute to begin simply: "We the people of the United States, in order to form a more perfect Union." This subtle change had significant implications. By identifying the people, and not a collection of states, as the source of authority, it emphasized the national vision of the framers and their desire to create a government quite different from a confederation of states.

Overview of the Constitution

Although not as strong as the most committed nationalists would have liked, the central government outlined in the Constitution was to have far more powers than were entrusted to Congress under the Articles of Confederation (see Table 7.1, The Articles of Confederation and the Constitution Compared). The Constitution's provision for a

TABLE 7.1 THE ARTICLES OF CONFEDERATION AND THE CONSTITUTION COMPARED

	Articles	Constitution
Sovereign power of central government	No power to tax or raise armies	Power granted on taxes and armed forces
Source of power	Individual states	Shared through federalism between states and national government
Representation in Congress	Equal representation of states in unicameral Congress	Bicameral legislature with equal representation of states in Senate and proportional representation in House
Amendment process	Unanimous consent of states	Consent of three-fourths of states
Executive	None provided for	Office of president
National judiciary	None provided for	Supreme Court

strong, single-person executive had no precedent in the Articles, nor did the provision for a Supreme Court. The Constitution vested this court, as well as the lower courts that Congress was empowered to establish, with the judicial power of the United States. In addition, the Constitution specifically delegated to Congress the powers to tax, borrow and coin money, regulate commerce, and raise armed forces, all of which the Confederation government had lacked.

Most of the economic powers of Congress came at the expense of the states. Further curbing the sovereignty of the states was a clause stipulating that the Constitution and all national legislation and treaties were to be "the supreme law of the land." This clause has subsequently been interpreted as giving the central government the power to declare state laws unconstitutional.

A no-nonsense realism, as well as a nationalist outlook, infused the Constitution. Its underlying political philosophy was that, in Madison's wonderful phrase, "ambition must be made to counter ambition." Madison and the other members of the national elite who met at Philadelphia were convinced that self-interest, not disinterested virtue, motivated political behavior. Accepting interest-group politics as inevitable and seeking to prevent a tyrannical majority from forming at the national level, the architects of the Constitution designed a central government in which competing blocs of power counterbalanced one another.

The Constitution placed both internal and external restraints on the powers granted to the central government. The functional division of the government into executive, legislative, and judicial branches, each with ways to keep the others from exercising excessive power, created an internal system of checks and balances.

Although the Constitution did not explicitly grant it, the Supreme Court soon claimed the right to invalidate acts of Congress and the president that it found to be unconstitutional. This power of **judicial review** provided another check against legislative and executive authority (see Chapter 9). To guard against an arbitrary federal judiciary, the Constitution empowered Congress to determine the size of the Supreme Court and to impeach and remove federal judges appointed by the president.

The external restraints on the central government were to be found in the nature of its relationship to the state governments. This relationship was based on **federalism**, the division of power between local and central authorities. By listing specific powers for Congress, the Constitution implied that all other powers were to be retained by the states. Thus, while strengthening the national government, the Constitution did not obliterate the sovereign rights of the states, leaving them free to curb the potential power of the national government in the ambiguous areas between national and state sovereignty.

This ambiguity in the federalism of the Constitution was both its greatest strength and its greatest weakness. It allowed both nationalists and advocates of states' rights to support the Constitution. But the issue of slavery, left unresolved in the gray area between state and national sovereignty, would continue to fester, sparking sectional conflict over the extent of national sovereignty that would plunge the republic into civil war three-quarters of a century later.

The Struggle over Ratification

The last article of the Constitution stipulated that it would go into effect when it had been ratified by at least nine of the states acting through specially elected popular conventions. The Congress, influenced by the nationalist sentiments of many of its members, one-third of whom had attended the Philadelphia Convention, and perhaps weary of its own impotence, accepted this drastic and not clearly legal procedure, submitting the Constitution to the states in late September 1787.

The delegates in Philadelphia had excluded the public from their proceedings. The publication of the Constitution lifted the veil of secrecy and touched off a great political debate. Although those who favored the Constitution could most accurately have been defined as nationalists, they referred to themselves as **Federalists**, a term that helped deflect charges that they favored an excessive centralization of political authority. By

judicial review A power implied in the Constitution that gives federal courts the right to review and determine the constitutionality of acts passed by Congress and state legislatures.

federalism The sharing of powers between the national government and the states.

Federalist A supporter of the Constitution who favored its ratification.

TABLE 7.2 FEDERALISTS VERSUS ANTIFEDERALISTS

	Federalists	Antifederalists
Position on Constitution	Favored Constitution	Opposed Constitution
Position on Articles of Confederation	Felt Articles had to be abandoned	Felt Articles needed only to be amended
Position on power of the states	Sought to curb power of states with new central government	Felt power of states should be paramount
Position on need for bill of rights	Initially saw no need for bill of rights in Constitution	Saw absence of bill of rights in proposed Constitution as threat to individual liberties
Position on optimum size of republic	Believed large republic could best safeguard personal freedoms	Believed only a small republic formed on common interests could protect individual rights
Source of support	Commercial farmers, merchants, shippers, artisans, holders of national debt	State-centered politicians, most backcountry farmers

Antifederalist An opponent of the Constitution in the debate over its ratification.

default, the opponents of the Constitution were known as **Antifederalists**, a negative-sounding label that obscured their support of the state-centered sovereignty that most Americans associated with federalism. Initially outmaneuvered in this way, the Antifederalists never did mount an effective campaign to counter the Federalists' pamphlets, speeches, and newspaper editorials (see Table 7.2, Federalists versus Antifederalists). The Antifederalists did attract some men of wealth and social standing. Most Antifederalists, however, were backcountry farmers, men with mud on their boots who lived far from centers of communication and market outlets for their produce. The Antifederalists clung to the belief that only a small republic, one composed of relatively homogeneous social interests, could secure the voluntary attachment of the people necessary for a free government. They argued that a large republic, such as the one framed by the Constitution, would inevitably become tyrannical because it was too distant and removed from the interests of common citizen-farmers.

However much the Antifederalists attacked the Constitution as a danger to the individual liberties and local independence that they believed the Revolution had been fought to safeguard, they were no political match for the Federalists. They lacked the wealth, social connections, access to newspapers, and self-confidence of the more cosmopolitan and better-educated Federalists. In addition, the Federalists could more easily mobilize their supporters, who were concentrated in the port cities and commercial farming areas along the coast.

Conservatives shaken by Shays's Rebellion lined up behind the Constitution. So, too, did groups—creditors, merchants, manufacturers, urban artisans, commercial farmers—whose interests would be promoted by economic development. The enhanced powers of the national government held out the promise of protecting the home market from British imports, enlarging foreign markets for American exports, promoting a stable and uniform currency, and raising revenues to pay off the Revolutionary War debt.

In the early stages, the Federalists scored a string of easy victories. Delaware ratified the Constitution on December 7, 1787, and within a month, so, too, had Pennsylvania, New Jersey, Georgia, and Connecticut. Except for Pennsylvania, these were small, sparsely populated states that stood to benefit economically or militarily from a stronger central government. The Constitution carried in the larger state of Pennsylvania because of the Federalists' strength in the commercial center of Philadelphia.

The Federalists faced their toughest challenge in the large states that had generally been more successful in going it alone during the 1780s. One of the most telling arguments of the Antifederalists in these and other states was the absence of a bill of rights in the Constitution. Realizing the importance of the issue, and citing Article 5 of the Constitution, which provided for an amendment process, the Federalists promised to recommend amending the Constitution with a bill of rights once it was ratified. By doing so, they split the ranks of the Antifederalists in Massachusetts.

This satire on Connecticut politics in 1787 shows two bitterly divided factions, the Federalists on the left and the Antifederalists on the right, pulling the debt-loaded wagon of state in opposite directions. The farmer in the middle with the plough and rake is complaining of heavy taxes.

After the Federalists gained the support of two venerable heroes of the Revolution, John Hancock and Sam Adams, the Massachusetts convention approved the Constitution by a close vote in February 1788.

The major hurdles remaining for the Federalists were Virginia, the most populous state, and strategically located New York. Technically, the Constitution could have gone into effect without them once Maryland, South Carolina, and New Hampshire had ratified it, bringing the total number of states to nine. But without Virginia, which ratified on June 25, and New York, which followed a month later, the new Union would have been weak and the Federalist victory far from assured.

To eke out victory in these crucial states, the Federalists drew on their pragmatism and persuasiveness. As in Massachusetts, they were helped by their promise of a bill of rights. And for the New York campaign, Madison, Jay, and Hamilton wrote an eloquent series of eighty-five essays known collectively as *The Federalist* to allay fears that the Constitution would so consolidate national power as to menace individual liberties. In the two most original and brilliant essays in *The Federalist,* essays 10 and 51, Madison turned traditional republican doctrine on its head. A large, diverse republic like the one envisaged by the Constitution, he reasoned, not a small and homogeneous one, offered the best hope for safeguarding the rights of all citizens. This was because a large republic would include a multitude of contending interest groups, making it difficult for any combination of them to coalesce into a tyrannical majority that could oppress minority rights. With this argument, Madison had developed a political rationale by which Americans could have both an empire and personal freedom.

North Carolina and Rhode Island did not ratify until after the new government was functioning. North Carolina joined the Union in 1789 once Congress submitted the amendments that constituted the Bill of Rights. The obstinate Rhode Islanders stayed out until 1790, when Congress forced them in with a threat of commercial reprisal.

⚜ Explore Ratification of the Constitution on MyHistoryLab

WHY DID RATIFICATION OF THE CONSTITUTION FACE OPPOSITION?

The early American republic found itself with a legal foundation based on the weak Articles of Confederation. Ratification of a new constitution, however, faced opposition up and down the new United States. For example, the inhabitants of cities, with economies linked tightly to commerce, were more likely to be divided on the issue, since the Constitution would provide the national government with more power over trade. Areas of the country with high populations of non-English Europeans, groups such as the Scots-Irish, often opposed ratification out of a concern that that the document would give those of English descent more power. Ratified—sometimes narrowly— by all the states via constitutional conventions between 1787 and 1790, the new document provided the young nation with a more powerful and centralized federal government.

The Constitution, the supreme law of the United States, was adopted on September 17, 1787, by the Constitutional Convention in Philadelphia. It replaced the Articles of Confederation and established a stronger central government.

RATIFICATION OF THE CONSTITUTION

State	Date of Ratification	Ratification Vote (yes–no)
Delaware	Dec. 8, 1787	30–0
Pennsylvania	Dec. 12, 1787	46–23
New Jersey	Dec. 18, 1787	38–0
Georgia	Jan. 2, 1788	26–0
Connecticut	Jan. 9, 1788	128–40
Massachusetts	Feb. 16, 1788	187–168
Maryland	April 28, 1788	63–11
South Carolina	May 23, 1788	149–73
New Hampshire	June 21, 1788	57–46
Virginia	June 25, 1788	89–79
New York	July 26, 1788	30–27
North Carolina	Nov. 21, 1789	184–77
Rhode Island	May 29, 1790	34–32

SOURCE: Orin Grant Libby, "The Geographical Distribution of the Vote of the Thirteen States on the Federal Constitution, 1787-8," *Bulletin of the University of Wisconsin, Economics, Political Science, and History Series 1*, no. 1 (June 1894), 1–116.

KEY QUESTIONS   Use **MyHistoryLab** *Explorer* to **answer** these **questions:**

Consequence ▶▶▶ *What was the relation between Loyalism in the Revolutionary War and subsequent views on ratification?*

Investigate area opinions on ratification in Loyalist strongholds.

Response ▶▶▶ *Did the level of slavery in an area affect opinion towards ratification?*

Map the level of opposition of ratification in slave-holding regions.

Analysis ▶▶▶ *What was the opinion in areas with a large German settler population?*

Conceptualize why members of this group and others saw the Constitution's adoption the way they did.

Conclusion

In freeing themselves from British rule, Americans embarked on an unprecedented wave of constitution-making that sought to put into practice abstract principles of republicanism that held that political power should derive from the people. Between 1776 and 1780, Americans developed a unique system of constitutionalism that went far beyond the British model of an unwritten constitution. They proclaimed the supremacy of constitutions over ordinary legislation, detailed the powers of government in a written document, provided protection for individual freedoms in bills of rights, and fashioned a process for framing governments through the election of delegates to a special constitutional convention and the popular ratification of the work of that convention. In all of these areas, Americans were pioneers in demonstrating to the rest of the world how common citizens could create their own governments.

In dealing with the legacy of slavery, however, white Americans were far more cautious, and most denied that their revolutionary experience included African Americans and should embrace black emancipation. Moses Sash and other African Americans, in keeping alive the dream of full black freedom, refused to passively accept the dictates of white authority. The revolution within a revolution they fought for was put off to the indefinite future by the delegates at the Constitutional Convention in 1787. Instead, they focused on achieving a peaceful, political revolution in securing the ratification of the Constitution. Their victory in creating a new central government with real national powers was built on the foundation of constitutional concepts and mechanisms that Americans had laid down in their state constitutions. The new Constitution rested on the consent of the governed, and it endured because it could be amended to reflect shifts in popular will and to widen the circle of Americans granted the rights of political citizenship and the enjoyment of liberty.

Accepting as a given that self-interest drove political action, the framers of the Constitution designed the new national government to turn ambition against itself. They created rival centers of power that forced selfish factions to compete in a constant struggle to form a workable majority. The struggle occurred both within the national government and between that government and the states in the American system of federalism. The Constitution thus set the stage for an entirely new kind of national politics.

For Suggested Readings go to MyHistoryLab.

Chapter Review

The New Order of Republicanism

7.1 What people were deemed fit to have political rights in the new order of republicanism? p. 171

Republican political thought in the 1780s was radical in its rejection of rule by divine right monarchs but conservative in its belief that only those who held a property stake in society should hold actual political power. In practice this limited political rights to white male property holders at the exclusion of the vast majority of women, working-class Americans, and free African Americans.

Problems at Home

7.2 How did economic problems lead to political conflict in the 1780s? p. 178

The Congress under the Articles of Confederation lacked the power to tax, and there was not nearly enough hard money, gold or silver, to pay off the debts incurred in waging the Revolutionary War and the large trade imbalance with Britain. Efforts led by debt-ridden farmers to inflate the currency with paper money were opposed by the holders of the national and state debts and led to bitter political conflicts in the states.

Diplomatic Weaknesses

7.3 What steps did Britain and Spain take to block American expansion? p. 185

By shutting off markets in its trading empire and flooding the new republic with cheap imports, Britain aimed to make the United States into an economic dependent with little real political independence. Spain stirred up separatist plots among American settlers south of the Ohio River and struck alliances with Native Americans in an attempt to check American expansion.

Toward a New Union

7.4 What explains the call for a stronger centralized government and the divisions which emerged over the ratification of the new Constitution? p. 187

To many in the nation's elite, as well as the military and political leaders of the Revolution, the Articles of Confederation left the republic helpless to deal with the threat of foreign encroachments and the problems of unpaid debts, a weak economy, and social unrest. They pushed through the drafting and ratification of the Constitution over the opposition of backcountry farmers and state-centered politicians who feared that a more centralized government would be a threat to their individual liberties.

Timeline

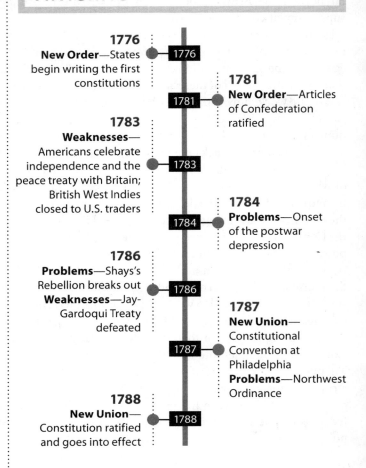

1776
New Order—States begin writing the first constitutions

1776

1781
New Order—Articles of Confederation ratified

1781

1783
Weaknesses—Americans celebrate independence and the peace treaty with Britain; British West Indies closed to U.S. traders

1783

1784
Problems—Onset of the postwar depression

1784

1786
Problems—Shays's Rebellion breaks out
Weaknesses—Jay-Gardoqui Treaty defeated

1786

1787
New Union—Constitutional Convention at Philadelphia
Problems—Northwest Ordinance

1787

1788
New Union—Constitution ratified and goes into effect

1788

8 A New Republic and the Rise of Parties 1789–1800

One American Journey

A Politician Comments in His Diary on Washington's First Inauguration

April 30, 1789
New York City

This is the great important day. Goddess of Etiquette assist me while I describe it. . . . The President was conducted out of the middle window into the Gallery [of Federal Hall] and the Oath administered by the Chancellor [Robert R. Livingston, Chancellor of New York]. Notice that the Business was done, was communicated to the Croud by Proclamation . . . who gave three Cheers. . . . As the Company returned into the Senate Chamber, the president took the Chair, and the Senate and representatives their Seats. He rose & all arose also and [he] addressed them [in his inaugural address]. This great Man was agitated and embarrassed more than ever he was by the levelled Cannon or pointed

This engraving shows respectful crowds greeting Washington as he passes through Trenton on the way to New York City for his inauguration as president.

LEARNING OBJECTIVES

8.1 ((	8.2 ((	8.3 ((	8.4 ((
What were the distinguishing features of the early republic's four major regions? p. 199	What challenges faced the Congress that assembled in New York between 1789 and 1791? p. 206	What forces shaped the development of party politics in America? p. 210	How did crises at home and abroad shape the administration of John Adams and help the Republicans win the election of 1800? p. 215

((**Listen to Chapter 8 on MyHistoryLab**

Watch the Video Series on MyHistoryLab

Learn about some key topics related to this chapter with the *MyHistoryLab Video Series: Key Topics in U.S. History.*

1 **The First Presidency** When George Washington took the oath of office on April 30, 1789, he became the first president of a large and diverse nation. The challenges facing the new American republic were legion, and the responses of Washington and his administration would vigorously test the core principles of the American Revolution and the newly ratified Constitution. This video introduces viewers to the issues that dominated Washington's time as chief executive and offers an assessment of his capabilities as a peacetime leader.

 Watch on MyHistoryLab

Regional Diversity in the New Republic The United States began its history as a new nation depleted by war and threatened by competing regional interests. This video examines the geographical and human differences that led four regions in the new United States—New England, the mid-Atlantic states, the slave-owning South, and the expanding West—to take on distinctive characteristics. It remained to be seen, however, if a single national government—could govern all Americans as a whole or if major faultlines would erupt along regional divides to dismantle the unity achieved by battling a common enemy. **2**

Watch on MyHistoryLab

3 **Government Based on a Constitution** In 1789, under Washington, the American experiment in self-government began in earnest. This video considers the actions taken by the newly elected president and by Congress to give form and substance to the framework for government outlined in the Constitution. A cabinet was formed, federal courts were organized, credit was established, and, when Congress prepared a list of amendments to the Constitution to reassure the public that the new national government would not become too powerful, Washington assisted in their adoption. The business of forging a new government was underway, all while the nation was growing in size and diversity.

 Watch on MyHistoryLab

The Development of Political Parties Much to the dismay of Washington, who advised his countrymen to resist excessive allegiance to both party and region, the rise of two political factions, or parties, was apparent by the end of his first term in office. Partisan differences between the Federalists and the Republicans, who had competing political visions for the new nation, resulted in the particularly bitter election of 1796, won narrowly by John Adams. Four years later, Thomas Jefferson, the leader of the Republicans, secured a razor-thin victory over the incumbent Federalist Adams. The transfer of power from a Federalist to a Republican administration, however, was admirably peaceful and orderly. Would discord and divergence in American party politics be entirely injurious to the new American republic or beneficial in some way not imagined by Washington? **4**

Watch on MyHistoryLab

Musket. He trembled and several times could scarce make out to read, tho it must be supposed he had often read it before. He put part of the fingers of his left hand, into the side, of what I think the Taylors call the fall, of his Breetches. Changing the paper into his left hand, after some time, he then did the same with some of the fingers of his right hand. When he came to the Words *all the World,* he made a flourish with his right hand, which left rather an ungainly impression. . . . He was dressed in deep brown, with Metal buttons, with an Eagle on them, White Stockings a Bag and Sword—from the Hall there was a grand Procession to St. Pauls Church where prayers were said by the Bishop. The Procession was well conducted and without accident, as far as I have heard. The Militias were all under Arms. [They] lined the Street near the Church, made a good figure and behaved well. The Senate returned to their Chamber after Service, formed & took up the Address. . . . In the Evening there were grand fire Works . . . and after this the People went to bed.

William Maclay

United States, First Congress, 1789–1781. Kenneth R. Bowling and Helen E. Veit, eds. *Documentary History of the First Federal Congress of the United States of Anerica, March 4, 1789–March 3, 1791,* Volume 9: *The Diary of William Maclay and Other Notes on Senate* Debates, pp. 3–11. © 1988 The Johns Hopkins University Press. Reprinted with permission of The Johns Hopkins University Press.

Personal Journeys Online

- New York *Daily Advertiser,* April 24, 1789. Newspaper description of Washington's arrival in New York.
- Tobias Lear, *Diary,* April 30, 1789. Account of presidential procession for Washington's inauguration.
- George Washington, *Excerpts from the First Inaugural Address,* April 30, 1789.

Senator **William Maclay** of Pennsylvania wrote, in his personal journal, this account of the inauguration of George Washington as the first president of the United States at Federal Hall in New York City on April 30, 1789. In the same caustic and witty style with which he had skewered Washington's performance at his inauguration, he continued his journal while in the Senate, and it remains one of our best documentary sources for the formative years of the Senate.

A Presbyterian with a strong sense of rectitude that often made him overly critical of others, he was one of the first of the original Federalists to break with the Washington administration over its fiscal and diplomatic policies.

Washington had every reason to dread taking on the burden of the presidency. As head of the new national government, he would put at risk the legendary status he had achieved during the Revolution. Most Americans intensely feared centralized authority, which is why the framers deliberately left the word *national* out of the Constitution. Washington somehow had to establish loyalty to a new government whose main virtue in the eyes of many was the very vagueness of its defined powers.

The Constitution had created the framework for a national government, but pressing problems demanded the fleshing out of that framework. The government urgently needed revenue to begin paying off the immense debt incurred during the Revolution. It also had to address the unstable conditions in the West, where the settlers wavered in their loyalties. Ultimately, the key to solving these and other problems was to inspire popular backing for the government's authority.

Washington's America

8.1   What were the distinguishing features of the early republic's four major regions?

The Americans whom Washington was called on to lead were hardly one unified people. They identified and grouped themselves according to many factors, including race, sex, class, ethnicity, religion, and degree of personal freedom. Geographical factors, including climate and access to markets, further divided them into regions and sections. The resulting hodgepodge sorely tested the assumption—and it was never more than an assumption in 1789—that a single national government could govern Americans as a whole (see Figure 8.1).

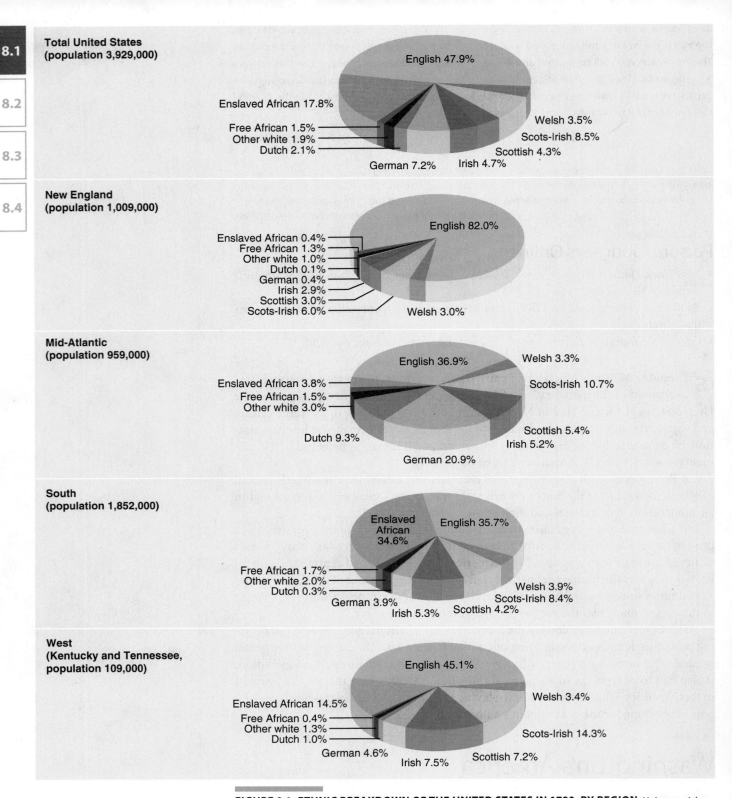

Total United States (population 3,929,000)

English 47.9%
Welsh 3.5%
Scots-Irish 8.5%
Scottish 4.3%
Irish 4.7%
German 7.2%
Dutch 2.1%
Other white 1.9%
Free African 1.5%
Enslaved African 17.8%

New England (population 1,009,000)

English 82.0%
Enslaved African 0.4%
Free African 1.3%
Other white 1.0%
Dutch 0.1%
German 0.4%
Irish 2.9%
Scottish 3.0%
Scots-Irish 6.0%
Welsh 3.0%

Mid-Atlantic (population 959,000)

English 36.9%
Welsh 3.3%
Scots-Irish 10.7%
Scottish 5.4%
Irish 5.2%
German 20.9%
Dutch 9.3%
Other white 3.0%
Free African 1.5%
Enslaved African 3.8%

South (population 1,852,000)

Enslaved African 34.6%
English 35.7%
Welsh 3.9%
Scots-Irish 8.4%
Scottish 4.2%
Irish 5.3%
German 3.9%
Dutch 0.3%
Other white 2.0%
Free African 1.7%

West (Kentucky and Tennessee, population 109,000)

English 45.1%
Welsh 3.4%
Scots-Irish 14.3%
Scottish 7.2%
Irish 7.5%
German 4.6%
Dutch 1.0%
Other white 1.3%
Free African 0.4%
Enslaved African 14.5%

FIGURE 8.1 ETHNIC BREAKDOWN OF THE UNITED STATES IN 1790, BY REGION Unique racial and ethnic patterns shaped each of the nation's four major regions in 1790. New England was most atypical in its lack of racial or ethnic diversity.

SOURCE: *The Statistics of the Population of the United States,* comp. by Francis A. Walker (1872), pp. 3–7; Thomas L. Purvis, "The European Ancestry of the United States Population, 1790," *William and Mary Quarterly,* 41(1984): p. 98.

The Uniformity of New England

The national census of 1790 counted nearly 4 million Americans, one in four of whom lived in New England. Although often viewed as the most typically "American" part of the young nation, New England in fact was rather atypical. It alone of the nation's formative regions had largely shut itself off from outsiders. The Puritan notions of religious liberty that prevailed in the region extended only to those who subscribed to the Calvinist orthodoxy of the dominant Congregationalist Church. Geography conspired with this religious exclusiveness to limit population diversity. New England's poor soils and long, cold winters made it an impractical place to cultivate cash crops like the tobacco and rice of the South. As a result, New England farmers had little need of imported white indentured servants or black slaves.

Puritan values and a harsh environment thus combined to make New England the most religiously and ethnically uniform region in the United States. Most of the people living there were descended from English immigrants who had arrived in the seventeenth century.

New Englanders found slavery incompatible with the natural-rights philosophy that had emerged during the Revolution and gradually began to abolish it in the 1780s (though they remained profitably tied to slavery through shipping plantation crops). Slavery had, in any case, always been marginal in New England's economy. Owning slaves as domestic servants or artisans had been a status symbol for wealthy urban whites in Boston, Portsmouth, and Newport. As a result, about 20 percent of New England's small African American population lived in cities, where jobs were relatively easy to find, in contrast to the white population, only 10 percent of which lived in cities.

Women outnumbered men in parts of New England in 1789. This pattern—not found in other parts of the country—was the result of the pressure of an expanding population and the practice of dividing family farms among male heirs. As farms in the older, more densely settled parts of New England were divided into ever-smaller lots, many young men migrated west in search of cheap, arable land.

Despite their superior numbers, women in New England, as elsewhere, remained subordinate to men. Even so, the general testing of traditional authority that accompanied the Revolution led some New England women to question male power. The Massachusetts poet Judith Sargeant Murray, for example, published essays asserting that women were the intellectual equals of men. Murray was the first woman to argue publicly in favor of equal educational opportunities for young women, and she boldly asserted that women should learn how to become economically independent. Republican ideology, emphasizing the need for women to be intellectually prepared to raise virtuous, public-spirited children, led reformers in New England to seek equal access to education for women. In 1789, Massachusetts became the first state to allocate funds specifically for girls' elementary education. And beginning in the 1780s, wealthy residents of eastern cities set up private academies for women that would later provide the foundation for women's higher education. Liberalized divorce laws in New England also allowed a woman to seek legal separation from an abusive or unfaithful spouse.

In other respects, political and social life in New England remained rooted in the Puritan past. Age, property, and reputation determined one's standing in a culture that valued a clearly defined social order. The moral code that governed town life promoted curbs on individual behavior for the benefit of the community as a whole. With their notions of collective liberty, New Englanders subscribed to a version of republicanism that favored strong government, setting themselves apart from most other Americans, who embraced a more individualistic idea of liberty and a suspicion of government power. New Englanders perceived government as a divine institution with a moral responsibility to intervene in people's lives. Acting through town meetings, they taxed themselves for public services at rates two to four times higher than in the rest of the country. Their courts were also far more likely than those elsewhere to punish individuals for crimes against public order (like failing to observe the Sabbath properly) and sexual misconduct.

The Pluralism of the Mid-Atlantic Region

The states of the mid-Atlantic region—New York, New Jersey, and Pennsylvania—were the most ethnically and religiously diverse in the nation. People of English descent constituted somewhat less than 40 percent of the population. Other major ethnic groups included the Dutch and Scots-Irish in New York and Germans and Scots-Irish in New Jersey and Pennsylvania. With ethnic diversity came religious diversity. Transplanted

Pietists Protestants who stress a religion of the heart and the spirit of Christian living.

New Englanders made up about 40 percent of New York's ethnic English population. Among others of English descent, Anglicans predominated in New York, and Quakers in New Jersey and Pennsylvania. The Dutch, concentrated in the lower Hudson Valley, had their own Dutch Reformed Church, and most Germans were either Lutherans or **Pietists**, such as the Mennonites and the Moravians, who stressed personal piety over theological doctrine. The Presbyterian Scots-Irish settled heavily in the backcountry.

This mosaic-like pattern of ethnic and religious groupings was no accident. In contrast to Puritan New England, the Middle Colonies had offered freedom of worship to attract settlers. In addition, economic opportunities for newcomers were much greater than in New England. The soil was better, the climate was milder, and market outlets for agricultural products were more abundant. These conditions made the mid-Atlantic region the nation's first breadbasket. Commercial agriculture fed urban growth and created a greater demand for labor in both rural and urban areas than in New England. The influx of Germans and Scots-Irish into the region in the eighteenth century occurred in response to this demand.

The demand for labor had also been met by importing African slaves. Blacks, both free and enslaved, made up 5 percent of the mid-Atlantic population in 1790, and, as in New England, they were more likely than whites to live in the maritime cities. New York had more slaveholders in 1790 than any other American city except Charleston, South Carolina. About 40 percent of the white families in the city's nearby rural outposts of Queens County, Brooklyn, and Staten Island owned slaves, a rate as high as in Maryland and South Carolina.

Despite its considerable strength in the port cities and adjacent rural areas, slavery was never an economically vital institution in most of the mid-Atlantic region. Commercial agriculture did not rest on a slave base, nor did it produce a politically powerful class of planters. As a result, slavery in the mid-Atlantic region gave way to demands for emancipation inspired by the natural-rights philosophy of the Revolution.

Pennsylvania in 1780, New York in 1799, and New Jersey in 1804 all passed laws of gradual emancipation. These laws did not free adult slaves but provided that children born of a slave mother were to be freed at ages ranging between 18 and 28. Soon after the laws were passed, however, adult slaves began hastening their own freedom. They ran away, set fires, and pressured their owners to accept cash payments in return for a short, fixed term of labor service. But even as they gained their freedom, African Americans had to confront enduring white racism. The comments of one white New Yorker suggest what they were up against. "We may sincerely advocate the freedom of black men," he wrote, "and yet assert their moral and physical inferiority."

The diversity of the mid-Atlantic region created a complex political environment. Competing cultural and economic interests prevented the kind of broad consensus on the meaning of republicanism that had emerged in New England.

Those who supported strong government included mercantile and financial leaders in the cities and commercial farmers in the countryside. These people tended to be Anglicans, Quakers, and Congregationalists of English descent. Those opposing them and favoring a more egalitarian republicanism tended to come from the middle and lower classes. They included subsistence farmers in the backcountry and artisans and day laborers in the cities. Most were Scots-Irish Presbyterians, but their number also included Dutch Calvinists and German Lutherans. Fiercely independent and proud of their liberties, they resented the claims of the wealthy to political authority. They resisted government aid to business as a form of political corruption that unfairly enriched those who were already economically powerful.

The Slave South and Its Backcountry

In the South—the region from Maryland and Delaware to Georgia—climate and soil conditions favored the production of cash staples for world markets. Cultivating these crops required backbreaking labor that white immigrants preferred to avoid. Southern planters relied on the coerced labor of African slaves, whose numbers made the South the most populous region in the country.

Idealized classical images of women—white, chaste, and pure—were popular emblems in the early republic to portray national ideals of liberty and republican motherhood.

Just under 40 percent of all southerners were slaves, but their concentration varied within the region. They were a majority in the Chesapeake Tidewater region, where slave ownership was widely distributed among white tobacco planters, including small and middling growers as well as the few great plantation owners. Farther south, in the tidal swamps of the South Carolina and Georgia low country, where draining and clearing the land required huge inputs of labor, blacks outnumbered whites five to one. In the low country, large planters, the richest men in the country, worked hundreds of slaves in the production of rice, indigo, and sea-island cotton.

Slaves were less numerous in the Piedmont, or foothills, region of the South that lies between the coastal plain and the Appalachian highlands. In the southern mountains, sloping to the southwest from the Blue Ridge in Virginia, the general absence of marketable crops diminished the demand for slave labor.

The free black population in the South had grown rapidly during the 1780s. Thousands of slaves fled behind British lines to win their freedom, and patriots freed others as a reward for enlisting in their forces. The Revolutionary values of liberty and equality also led many slave owners to question the morality of slavery. Legislatures in the Upper South passed laws making it financially easier than before for masters to manumit (free) their slaves. In Virginia alone, 10,000 slaves were manumitted in the 1780s. Slavery remained the foundation of the southern economy, however, and whites feared competition from freed blacks. As a result, no southern state embarked on a general program of emancipation, and slavery in the region survived the turbulence of the Revolutionary era.

Economic conditions in the South, where the raw poverty of the backcountry offset the great wealth of the low country, stamped the region's politics and culture. Tidewater planters were predominantly Anglican and of English descent. Piedmont farmers were more likely to be Scots-Irish Presbyterians and Baptists. More evangelical in their religion, and with simpler habits and tastes, the backcountry Baptists denounced the low-country planters for their luxury and arrogance. The planters retaliated by trying unsuccessfully to suppress the backcountry evangelicals.

The planters were indeed proud, domineering, and given to ostentatious displays of wealth. Planters understood liberty to mean the power of white males, unchecked by any outside authority, to rule over others. The only acknowledged check on this power was the planter's sense of duty, his obligation to adhere to an idealized code of conduct befitting a gentleman and a man of honor.

Backcountry farmers also jealously guarded their liberties. They shared with the planters a disdain for government and restraints on the individual. But they opposed the planters' belief in a social hierarchy based on wealth and birth that left both poor whites and black slaves in a subordinate position.

The Growing West

Between the Appalachian Mountains and the Mississippi River stretched the most rapidly growing region of the new nation, the West. Land-hungry settlers poured across the mountains once the British recognized the American claim to the region in the Treaty of Paris. During the 1780s, the white population of the West exploded from less than 10,000 to 200,000. The region's Native American population was about 150,000.

Indians strongly resisted white claims on their lands. A confederation of tribes in the Ohio Valley, led by the Miamis and supplied with firearms by the British in exchange for furs, kept whites out of the Old Northwest territory, the area north of the Ohio River. South of the Ohio, white settlements were largely limited to Kentucky and Tennessee. In what is today Alabama and Mississippi, the Creeks and their allies blocked American expansion.

Most white migrants in Kentucky and Tennessee were the young rural poor from the seaboard slave states. The West offered them the opportunity to claim their own farms and gain economic independence, free from the dominance of planters and the economic competition of slave labor. But planters also saw the West as a land of opportunity. The planters of Tidewater Virginia were especially likely to speculate in vast tracts of western land. And many planters' sons migrated to the West with a share of the family's slaves to become planters in their own right. This process laid the foundation for the extension of slavery into new regions. As early as 1790, slaves made up more than 10 percent of the population of Tennessee and Kentucky.

Isolation and uncertainty haunted frontier life. The Appalachians posed a formidable barrier to social and economic intercourse with the East. Few settlers had the labor resources, which chiefly meant slaves, to produce an agricultural surplus for shipment to market down the Ohio and Mississippi rivers. Most farmers lived at a semisubsistence level. Many of them, mostly Scots-Irish, did not own the land they cultivated. These squatters, as they were called, occupied the land hoping someday to obtain clear title to it.

In Kentucky, squatters, aligned with a small class of middling landowners, spearheaded the movement for political separation from Virginia that gained statehood for the territory in 1792. The settlers wanted to break the control that Tidewater planters had gained over most of the land and lucrative government offices in Kentucky. In their minds, planters, officeholders, land speculators, and gentlemen of leisure were all part of an aristocracy tied to the distant government in Richmond and intent on robbing them of their liberty.

Despite the movement in Kentucky for statehood, the ultimate political allegiance of the West was uncertain. Westerners wanted the freedom to control their own affairs and outlets for their crops. Apparently, they were willing to strike a deal with any outside power offering to meet these needs. Aware of the threat to the region posed by the British and Spanish, Washington had warned in 1784 that the political loyalties of the West wavered "on a pivot." The future of the region loomed as a major test for his administration.

Explore the Northwest Territory on MyHistoryLab

WHAT ROLE DID THE NORTHWEST TERRITORY PLAY IN AMERICAN HISTORY?

In 1787, the Northwest Ordinance transformed the course of the expansion of the young United States. A huge swath of territory north of the Ohio River had been claimed by eastern states, but these states relinquished their claims and the Northwest Ordinance organized the settlement of these lands. This territory eventually was divided among numerous modern American states and, importantly, slavery was not to be allowed in the region. However, the ordinance ignored that the area in 1787 belonged to and was populated by numerous Native American nations. During the next decade, conflict ensued when members of some nations formed the Western Indian Confederacy to fight against the United States in the Northwest Indian War as the region began to open to Euro-American settlement.

Established in 1783, the small southeast Indiana town of Clarksville holds the distinction of being the first American settlement in the Northwest Territory.

THE WESTERN INDIAN CONFEDERACY

Tribe
Anishinabes (Ojibwe)
Weas
Illinois
Ottawas
Menominees
Shawnees
Lenapes (Delawares)
Miamis
Kickapoos
Kinkashas

KEY QUESTIONS   Use **MyHistoryLab** *Explorer* to **answer** these **questions:**

Analysis ▶▶▶ *Why might potential settlers in this area resent being governed by an East Coast state?*

Map the claims of the eastern states prior to the Northwest Ordinance of 1787.

Consequence ▶▶▶ *How did the outcome of the Northwest Indian War affect subsequent Native American land cessations?*

Chart the extent of cessations in the Northwest Territory after 1795.

Comparison ▶▶▶ *How did the expansion of the U.S. population into the Northwest Territory compare to slavery's expansion in other areas?*

Map these two patterns to consider future possible conflict.

Forging a New Government

The Congress that assembled in New York (the temporary capital) from 1789 to 1791 faced a challenge scarcely less daunting than that of the Constitutional Convention of 1787. It had to give form and substance to the framework of the new national government outlined in the Constitution. Executive departments had to be established, a federal judiciary organized, sources of revenue found, terms of international trade and foreign policy worked out, and the commitment to add a bill of rights to the Constitution honored.

"Mr. President" and the Bill of Rights

The first problem for Washington and Congress was to decide just how the chief executive of the new republic should be addressed. In a debate that tied up Congress for a month, agreement was finally reached on "Mr. President." Whatever his title, Washington was intent on surrounding the presidency with an aura of respectability.

Meanwhile, Congress got down to business. James Madison, now a representative from Virginia, early emerged as the most forceful leader in the House. He pushed for speedy action on the bill of rights, which the Federalists had promised to add to the Constitution during the ratification debate. To allay the fears of Antifederalists that the Constitution granted too much power to the national government, the Federalists had promised to consider amendments that protected both individual rights and liberties and the rights of states. But Madison astutely kept the focus of the amendments on personal liberties. He submitted nineteen amendments, and Congress soon settled on twelve. Ten of these, known collectively as the **Bill of Rights**, were ratified by the states and became part of the Constitution as of December 15, 1791.

Bill of Rights A written summary of inalienable rights and liberties.

The Bill of Rights is one of the most enduring legacies of the first Congress. Most of the first eight amendments are concerned with individual rights. They guarantee religious freedom, freedom of expression, and the safeguarding of individuals and their property against arbitrary legal proceedings. Only three amendments speak of state interests. Citing the necessity of a "well regulated Militia" for "the security of a free State," the Second Amendment guarantees "the right of the people to keep and bear Arms." This assured the states that they could rely on their militias for protection against federal tyranny. The Ninth and Tenth Amendments stipulate that the powers not granted to the national government in the Constitution are retained by the people and the states.

The Bill of Rights broadened the government's base of popular support. Once Congress submitted the amendments to the states for ratification, North Carolina (1789) and Rhode Island (1790) overcame their lingering objections and joined the Union. The Bill of Rights also assured Americans that the central government would not try to impose a uniform national culture.

Departments and Courts

In the summer of 1789, Congress authorized the first executive departments: the State Department for foreign affairs, the Treasury for finances, and the War Department for the nation's defense. These departments already existed under the Articles of Confederation, and the only debate about them concerned the extent of presidential control over the officials who would head them. The Constitution was silent on whether the president could dismiss an official without the Senate's consent. Congress decided that the president could do so, setting an important precedent that bolstered presidential power. Department heads would now be closely bound to the president. As a group, they would evolve into the cabinet, the president's chief advisory body.

Greater controversy attended the creation of the federal judiciary. The Constitution called for "one Supreme Court" but left it up to Congress to authorize lower federal courts. The framers were deliberately vague about the federal judiciary, because Antifederalists and proponents of states' rights did not want national courts enforcing a uniform judicial system.

The **Judiciary Act of 1789** represented an artful compromise that balanced the concerns of the Antifederalists and states'-rights advocates with the concerns of nationalists who strongly opposed leaving matters of national law up to state courts. It created a hierarchical national judiciary based on thirteen federal district courts, one for each state. Appeals from these courts were to be heard in one of three circuit courts, and the Supreme Court was to have the final say in contested cases. In a major concession to the Antifederalists, however, the act limited jurisdiction in federal courts to legal issues stemming from the Constitution and the laws and treaties of the national government.

Judiciary Act of 1789 Act of Congress that implemented the judiciary clause of the Constitution by establishing the Supreme Court and a system of lower federal courts.

Revenue and Trade

The government's most pressing need was for revenue. Aware that Congress under the Articles of Confederation had been crippled by its inability to secure a reliable source of income, Madison acted to put the finances of the new federal government on a firm footing. Nearly everyone agreed that the government's chief source of income should be a tariff on imported goods and tonnage duties (fees based on cargo capacity) on ships entering American ports.

The **Tariff Act of 1789** was designed primarily to raise revenue, not to protect American manufacturers by keeping out foreign goods with high duties. It levied a duty of 5 percent on most imported goods but imposed tariffs as high as 50 percent on a limited number of items, such as steel, salt, cloth, and tobacco. The debate on the Tariff Act provoked some sectional sparring. Manufacturers, who were concentrated in the North, wanted high tariffs for protection against foreign competition. In contrast, farmers and southern planters wanted low tariffs to keep down the cost of the manufactured goods they purchased.

Tariff Act of 1789 The first national tariff was designed primarily to raise revenue and not to protect home industries.

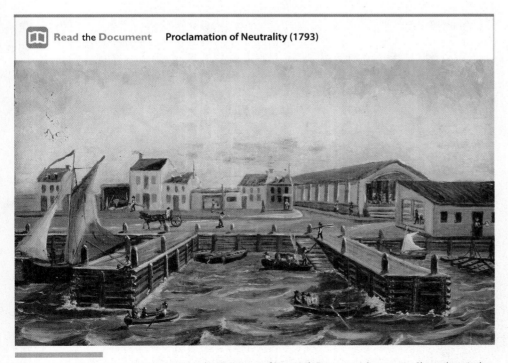

Read the Document   Proclamation of Neutrality (1793)

Waterborne commerce was the key in the early emergence of New York City as a trading center. Shown here is the Manhattan end of the Brooklyn Ferry in 1790.

Hamilton and the Public Credit

The Treasury was the largest and most important new department. To its head, Alexander Hamilton of New York, fell the task of bringing order to the nation's ramshackle finances. The basic problem was the huge debt left over from the Revolution. With interest going unpaid, the debt was growing, and by 1789 it had reached $52 million. Until the government set up and honored a regular schedule for paying interest, the nation's public credit would be worthless. Unable to borrow, the government would collapse.

At the request of Congress, Hamilton prepared a series of reports on the nation's finances and economic condition. In the first, issued in January 1790, Hamilton proposed a bold plan to address the Revolutionary War debt. The federal government, he maintained, should fund the national debt at full face value. To do this, he proposed exchanging the old debt, including accrued interest, for new government bonds bearing interest at about 4 percent. In addition, Hamilton maintained that the federal government should assume the remaining war debt of the state governments. The intent of this plan was to give the nation's creditors an economic stake in the stability of the new nation and to subordinate state financial interests to those of the central government.

In his second report, issued in December 1790, Hamilton called for an excise tax (a tax on the production, sale, or consumption of a commodity) on distilled whiskey produced within the United States. The purpose of the tax was to raise additional revenue for interest payments on the national debt and establish the government's authority to levy internal taxes on its citizens.

The third report recommended the chartering of a national bank, the Bank of the United States. Hamilton patterned his proposed bank after the Bank of England and intended it to meet a variety of needs. Jointly owned by the federal government and private investors, it would serve as the fiscal (financial) and depository agent of the government and make loans to businesses. Through a provision that permitted up to three-fourths of the value of bank stock to be purchased with government bonds, the bank would create a market for public securities and hence raise their value. Most important, the bank would provide the nation with a stable currency. At the time, the

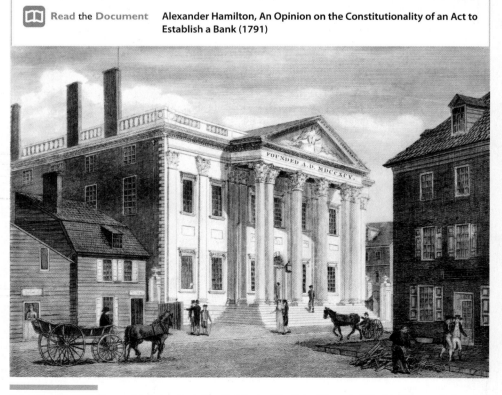

Read the Document **Alexander Hamilton, An Opinion on the Constitutionality of an Act to Establish a Bank (1791)**

Shown here in 1799, the neoclassical design of the First Bank of the United States in Philadelphia was a fitting expression of the grandeur of Hamilton's vision for a national bank.

country had only three private banks, and specie—hard currency in the form of gold and silver coins—was scarce. The government needed a reliable source of money, as did the economy as a whole. Hamilton proposed to allow the Bank of the United States to issue money in the form of paper banknotes that would be backed by a small reserve of specie and the security of government bonds. His goal was both to strengthen the economy and to consolidate the power of the national government.

Hamilton's final report, issued in December 1791, recommended government actions to promote industry. Looking, as always, to the British model of economic development, he argued that the United States would never become a great power until it diversified its largely agrarian economy. As long as the nation imported most of its manufactured goods, Hamilton warned, it would be no more than a second-rate power. Hamilton advocated aid in the form of protective tariffs (high tariffs meant to make imported goods more expensive than domestic goods) for such industries as iron, steel, and shoemaking—which had already begun to establish themselves—and direct subsidies to assist with start-up costs for other industries. Hamilton believed that such "patronage," as he called it, would ultimately foster interregional economic dependence. An industrializing Northeast, for example, would depend on the South and West for foodstuffs for its workers and raw materials for its factories. In turn, farmers and planters would buy manufactured goods from the Northeast. Thus, in Hamilton's vision, manufacturing, like a national currency, would be a great national unifier.

Reaction and Opposition

The breadth and boldness of Hamilton's program invited opposition. About half the members of Congress owned some of the nation's debt, and nearly all of them agreed with Hamilton that it should be paid off. Some opponents, however, were concerned that Hamilton's plan was unfair. Hard times had forced most of the original holders of the debt—by and large, ordinary citizens—to sell their certificates to speculators at a fraction of their face value. Should the government, asked Madison, reward speculators with a windfall profit when the debt was paid back in full and forget about the true patriots who had sustained the Revolution in its darkest hours?

Others objected, on republican grounds, that Hamilton had no intention of actually eliminating the government's debt. He envisioned instead a permanent debt, with the government making regular interest payments as they came due. The debt, in the form of government securities, would serve as a vital prop for the support of moneyed groups. One congressman saw this as a violation of "that great principle which alone was the cause of the war with Great Britain . . . that taxation and representation should go hand in hand." Future generations, he argued, would be unfairly taxed for a debt incurred by the present generation.

Opposition to Hamilton's proposal to have the federal government assume state debts reflected sectional differences. With the exception of South Carolina, the southern states had already paid back a good share of their war debts. Thus, Hamilton's plan stood to benefit the northern states disproportionately. Because Hamilton had linked the funding of the national debt with the assumption of state debts, southern opposition threatened funding as well. Tensions mounted as the deadlock continued into the summer of 1790. Frustrated over southern intransigence, New Englanders muttered about seceding. Southerners responded in kind.

Tempers cooled when a compromise was reached in July. Southerners agreed to accept funding in its original form because, as Hamilton correctly noted, it would be impractical, if not impossible, to distinguish between the original and current holders of the national debt. Assumption passed after Hamilton cut a deal with Virginians James Madison and Thomas Jefferson. In exchange for southern support of assumption, Hamilton agreed to a shift of the capital to Philadelphia for ten years and to line up northern votes for locating the nation's permanent capital on the banks of the Potomac

River, where it would be surrounded by the slave states of Maryland and Virginia. The package was sweetened by extra grants of federal money to states with small debts.

Hamilton's alliance with Madison and Jefferson proved short-lived, dissolving when Madison led the congressional opposition to Hamilton's proposed bank. Madison and most other southerners viewed the bank as evidence of a willingness to sacrifice the interests of the agrarian South in favor of the financial and manufacturing interests of the North. They feared that the bank, with its power to dispense economic favors, would re-create in the United States the kind of government corruption and privilege they associated with Great Britain. They argued that the Constitution did not explicitly authorize Congress to charter a bank or any other corporation.

The bank bill passed Congress on a vote that divided along sectional lines. And with Washington's signature on the bill, Hamilton's bank was chartered for twenty years. Congress also passed a hefty 25 percent excise tax on distilled liquor. Little, however, of Hamilton's plan to promote manufacturing survived the scrutiny of the agrarian opposition. Tariff duties were raised moderately in 1792, but no funds were forthcoming to accelerate industrial development.

The Emergence of Parties

8.3	What forces shaped the development of party politics in America?

Federalist A supporter of the Constitution who favored its ratification.

By the end of Washington's first term, Americans were dividing into two camps. On one side stood those who still called themselves **Federalists**. These were the supporters of Hamilton's program—speculators, creditors, merchants, manufacturers, and commercial farmers. They were the Americans most fully integrated into the market economy and in control of it. Concentrated in the North, they included New England Congregationalists and mid-Atlantic Episcopalians (former Anglicans), members of the more socially prestigious churches. In both economic and cultural terms, the Federalists were drawn from the more privileged segments of society. Jefferson and Madison shrewdly gave the name **Republican** to the party that formed in opposition to the Federalists, thus identifying it with individual liberties and the heritage of the Revolution (see Table 8.1). The Republicans accused Hamilton and the Federalists of attempting to impose a British system of economic privilege and social exploitation. The initial core of the party consisted of southern planters and backcountry Scots-Irish farmers, Americans outside the market economy or skeptical of its benefits. They feared that the commercial groups favored by Hamilton would corrupt politics in their pursuit of power and foster commerce and manufacturing at the expense of agriculture. The Republicans were committed to an agrarian America in which power remained in the hands of farmers and planters.

Republican Party headed by Thomas Jefferson that formed in opposition to the financial and diplomatic policies of the Federalist Party; favored limiting the powers of the national government and placing the interests of farmers and planters over those of financial and commercial groups.

TABLE 8.1 FEDERALIST PARTY VERSUS REPUBLICAN PARTY

Federalists	Republicans
Favored strong central government	Wanted to limit role of national government
Supported Hamilton's economic program	Opposed Hamilton's economic program
Opposed French Revolution	Generally supported French Revolution
Supported Jay's Treaty and closer ties to Britain	Opposed Jay's Treaty and favored closer ties to France
In response to threat of war with France, proposed and passed Direct Tax of 1798, Alien and Sedition Acts, and legislation to enlarge army	Opposed Alien and Sedition Acts and enlarged army as threats to individual liberties
Drew strongest support from New England; lost support in mid-Atlantic region after 1798	Drew strongest support from South and West

In 1792, parties were still in a formative stage. The political divisions that had appeared first in Congress and then spread to Washington's cabinet did not yet extend very deeply into the electorate. Washington remained aloof from the political infighting and was still seen as a great unifier. Unopposed, he was reelected in 1792. However, a series of crises in his second term deepened and broadened the incipient party divisions. One of the few lulls in the party battles came in August 1793, when all government business was suspended as a result of a yellow fever epidemic in Philadelphia. By 1796, rival parties were contesting the presidency and vying for the support of an increasingly politically organized electorate.

The French Revolution

The French Revolution began in 1789, and in its early phase, most Americans applauded it. France had been an ally of the United States during the Revolutionary War and now seemed to be following the example of its American friends in shaking off monarchical rule. By 1792, however, as threats against it mounted, the French Revolution turned violent and radical. Its supporters confiscated the property of aristocrats and the church, slaughtered suspected enemies, and executed the king, Louis XVI. The revolutionaries also passed an emancipation edict banning slavery in the French colonies, news of which produced rejoicing by African Americans on the streets of Philadelphia in 1794. Fearing that the old order was about to crumble, Britain and the European powers were at war against republican France by early 1793.

The excesses of the French Revolution and the European war that erupted in its wake touched off a bitter debate in America. Federalists drew back in horror from France's new regime. They insisted that the terror unleashed by the French was far removed from the reasoned republicanism of the American Revolution. For the Republicans, however, the French remained the standard-bearers of the cause of liberty for common people everywhere. Jefferson admitted that the French Revolution was tarnished by the loss of innocent lives, "but rather than it should have failed, I would have seen half the earth desolated." He was convinced that "the liberty of the whole earth was depending on the issue in the contest."

Franco-American Relations. When the new French ambassador, Edmond Genêt, arrived in the United States in April 1793—just as the debate in America over the French Revolution was heating up—Franco-American relations reached a turning point. The two countries were still bound to one another by the Franco-American Alliance of 1778. The alliance required the United States to assist France in the defense of its West Indian colonies and to open U.S. ports to French privateers if France were attacked. Genêt, it soon became clear, hoped to embroil the United States in the French war against the British. He commissioned U.S. privateers to attack British shipping and tried to enlist an army of frontiersmen to attack Spanish possessions in Louisiana and Florida.

Genêt's actions, as well as the enthusiastic reception that greeted him as he traveled from Charleston to Philadelphia, forced Washington to call a special cabinet meeting. The president feared that Genêt would stampede Americans into the European war, with disastrous results for the nation's finances. The bulk of U.S. foreign trade was with the British, and tariff duties on British imports were by far the main source of revenue to pay for Hamilton's assumption and funding programs. Hamilton urged Washington to declare U.S. neutrality in the European war, maintaining that the president could commit the nation to neutrality on his own authority when Congress, as was then the case, was not in session. Disputing Washington's power to act on his own, Jefferson maintained that the war-making powers of Congress reserved for it alone the right to issue a declaration of neutrality. Washington accepted Hamilton's argument on his authority to declare neutrality and issued a proclamation on April 22, 1793, stating that the United States would be "friendly and impartial toward the belligerent powers."

Despite this proclamation, Genêt continued to meddle. Washington was on the verge of forcing his recall to France when news arrived that a new and more radical

French government had decided to bring Genêt back as a political prisoner. The president graciously permitted Genêt to remain in the United States as a private citizen. Had he returned to France, he would have faced almost certain execution.

The Growth of Democratic-Republican Societies. Genêt quickly faded from public view, but U.S. politics became more open and aggressive in the wake of his visit. Pro-French enthusiasm lived on in a host of grassroots political organizations known as the Democratic-Republican societies. Nearly forty of these societies formed in 1793 and 1794. As their name suggests, these societies reflected a belief that democracy and republicanism were one and the same. This was a new concept in U.S. politics. Democracy had traditionally been equated with anarchy and mob rule. The members of the new societies argued, to the contrary, that only democracy—meaning popular participation in politics and direct appeals by politicians to the people—could maintain the revolutionary spirit of 1776, because the people were the only true guardians of that spirit.

The Democratic-Republican societies attacked the Washington administration for failing to assist France, and they expressed the popular feeling that Hamilton's program favored the rich over the poor. For the first time, Washington himself was personally assailed in the press.

The core members of the societies were urban artisans whose egalitarian views shocked the Federalists, who expected deference, not criticism and political activism, from the people. In their view, the Democratic-Republicans were rabble-rousers trying to dictate policy to the nation's natural leaders. The Federalists harshly condemned the emergence of organized political dissent from below, but in so doing they only enhanced the popular appeal of the growing Republican opposition.

Securing the Frontier

Control of the West remained an elusive goal throughout Washington's first term. Indian resistance in the Northwest Territory initially prevented whites from pushing north of the Ohio River. The powerful Miami Confederacy, led by Little Turtle, routed two ill-trained American armies in 1790 and 1791. The southern frontier was quieter, but the Spanish continued to use the Creeks and Cherokees as a buffer against American penetration south of the Tennessee River and to promote slavery as a means of securing the loyalty of the white settlers.

By 1793, many western settlers felt abandoned by the national government. They believed that the government had broken a promise to protect them against Indians and foreigners. Much of the popularity of the Democratic-Republican societies in the West fed off these frustrations. Westerners saw the French, who were at war with Britain and Spain, as allies against the foreign threat on the frontier, and they forwarded resolutions to Congress embracing the French cause. These resolutions also demanded free and open navigation on the Mississippi River. This, in the minds of westerners, was their natural right. Without it, they would be forever impoverished. "If the interest of Eastern America requires that we should be kept in poverty," argued the Mingo Creek society of western Pennsylvania, "it is unreasonable from such poverty to exact contributions. The first, if we cannot emerge from, we must learn to bear, but the latter, we never can be taught to submit to."

Submission to national authority, however, was precisely what the Federalists wanted from both the Indians and the western settlers. By the summer of 1794, Washington's administration felt prepared to move against the Indians. This time, it sent into the Ohio region not the usual ragtag crew of militia and unemployed city dwellers but a force built around veterans from the professional army. The commander, General Anthony Wayne, was a savvy, battle-hardened war hero.

Wayne's victory on August 4, 1794, at the Battle of Fallen Timbers, near present-day Toledo, broke the back of Indian military resistance in Ohio. In the resulting **Treaty of Greenville**, signed in August 1795, twelve tribes ceded most of the present state of Ohio to the U.S. government in return for an annual payment of $9,500. The Ohio country was now open to white settlement.

Treaty of Greenville Treaty of 1795 in which Native Americans in the Old Northwest were forced to cede most of the present state of Ohio to the United States.

The Whiskey Rebellion

Within a few months of Wayne's victory at Fallen Timbers, another American army was on the move. Its target was the so-called whiskey rebels of western Pennsylvania, who were openly resisting Hamilton's excise tax on whiskey. This tax had always been unpopular among western farmers. The high cost of transport across the mountains made it unprofitable for them to sell their grain in the East. But by distilling corn or rye into whiskey, they reduced it enough in bulk to lower transportation costs and earn a profit. Hamilton's excise tax wiped out this profit.

Hamilton was determined to enforce the tax and assert the supremacy of national laws. Although resistance to the tax was widespread, he singled out the Pennsylvania rebels. It was easier to send an army into the Pittsburgh area than into the Carolina mountains. Washington, moreover, was convinced that the Democratic-Republican societies of western Pennsylvania were behind the defiance of federal authority there. He welcomed the opportunity to chastise these organizations, which he identified with the dangerous doctrines of the French Revolution.

Washington called on the governors of the mid-Atlantic states to supply militia forces to crush the **Whiskey Rebellion**. The 13,000-man army that assembled at Harrisburg and marched into western Pennsylvania in October 1794 was larger than any Washington had commanded during the Revolution. The army met no resistance and expended considerable effort rounding up 20 prisoners. Two men were found guilty of treason, but Washington pardoned both. Still, at Hamilton's insistence, the Federalists had made their point: When its authority was openly challenged, the national government would use military force to compel obedience.

The Whiskey Rebellion starkly revealed the conflicting visions of local liberty and national order that divided Americans of the early republic. The non-English majority on the Pennsylvania frontier, Irish, Scots-Irish, German, and Welsh, justified resistance to the whiskey tax with the same republican ideology that had fueled the American Revolution. Mostly poor farmers, artisans, and laborers, they appealed to notions of liberty, equality, and freedom from oppressive taxation that were deeply rooted in backcountry settlements from Maine to Georgia. In putting down the Pennsylvania rebels, Washington and Hamilton acted on behalf of more English and cosmopolitan groups in the East who valued central power as a check on any local resistance movement that might begin unraveling the still fragile republic.

Whiskey Rebellion Armed uprising in 1794 by farmers in western Pennsylvania who attempted to prevent the collection of the excise tax on whiskey.

Treaties with Britain and Spain

Much of the unrest in the West stemmed from the menacing presence of the British and Spanish on the nation's borders. Washington's government had the resources to suppress Indians and frontier dissidents but lacked sufficient armed might to push Spain and especially Britain out of the West.

The British, embroiled in what they saw as a life-or-death struggle against revolutionary France, clamped a naval blockade on France and its Caribbean colonies in the fall of 1793. They also supported a slave uprising on the French island of Saint-Domingue (present-day Haiti), enraging southern planters who feared that slave rebellions might spread to the United States. The French countered by opening their colonial trade, which had been closed to outsiders during peacetime, to neutral shippers. American merchants stepped in and reaped profits by supplying France. The British retaliated by seizing American ships involved in the French trade. They further claimed the right to search American ships and impress, or forcibly remove, sailors they suspected of having deserted from the British navy. News of these provocations reached America in early 1794 and touched off a major war scare. Desperate to avert a war, Washington sent John Jay, the chief justice of the United States, to London to negotiate an accord.

From the American point of view, the resulting agreement, known as **Jay's Treaty**, was flawed but acceptable. Jay had to abandon the American insistence on the right of neutrals to ship goods to nations at war without interference (meaning in this case the right of the United States to continue trading with France without British harassment).

Jay's Treaty Treaty with Britain negotiated in 1794 in which the United States made major concessions to avert a war over the British seizure of American ships.

He also had to grant Britain "most favored nation" status, giving up the American right to discriminate against British shipping and merchandise. And he had to reconfirm the American commitment to repay in full pre-Revolutionary debts owed to the British. In return for these major concessions, Britain pledged to compensate American merchants for the ships and cargoes it had seized in 1793 and 1794, to abandon the six forts it still held in the American Northwest, and to grant the United States limited trading rights in India and the British West Indies.

Signed in November 1794, Jay's Treaty caused an uproar in the United States when its terms became known in March 1795. Southerners saw in it another sellout of their interests. It required them to pay their prewar debts to British merchants but was silent about the slaves Britain had carried off during the Revolution. And the concessions Britain did make seemed to favor the North, especially New England merchants and shippers. Republicans, joined now by urban artisans, were infuriated that Jay had stripped them of their chief weapon, economic retaliation, for breaking free of British commercial dominance. The Senate ratified the treaty in June 1795, but only because Washington backed it.

Jay's Treaty, combined with a string of French victories in Europe in 1795, convinced Spain to adopt a more conciliatory attitude toward the United States. In the **Treaty of San Lorenzo** in 1795 (also known as Pinckney's Treaty), Spain accepted the American position on the 31st parallel as the northern boundary of Spanish Florida and granted American farmers free transit through the port of New Orleans with the right of renewal after three years.

Treaty of San Lorenzo Treaty with Spain in 1795 in which Spain recognized the 31st parallel as the boundary between the United States and Spanish Florida.

The First Partisan Election

Partisanship, open identification with one of the two parties, steadily rose in the 1790s, fueled in large measure by a new print culture. The first opposition newspaper, the *National Gazette,* appeared in 1791, and the number of newspapers more than doubled within the decade. Circulated and discussed in taverns and coffeehouses, newspapers helped draw ordinary Americans into the political process. Ongoing involvement in the raucous, celebratory political culture that Americans fashioned also politicized them. Through festivals on July 4 honoring the nation's independence, street parades and demonstrations favoring or opposing such events as the French Revolution or Jay's Treaty, and an endless stream of toasts, speeches, banquets, and broadsides, various groups publicly proclaimed and acted out their version of what it meant to be an American. No single version held sway. National self-identity varied by class, race, sex, and region, but as newspaper reports of local activities were copied and disseminated across the country, Americans could feel that they were joined in a collective effort to define what the nation meant to them. As a national identity was being forged and contested, lines of partisanship were marked and deepened.

Women also participated in this public arena of political activism. Although denied formal political rights, they wrote and attended plays with explicit political messages, joined in patriotic rituals, and organized their own demonstrations. To show their support for the French Revolution, women in Menetomy, Massachusetts, wore liberty caps and cockades, the symbols of the French cause. Shocked by such pro-French sympathies and declarations of women's independence, the Federalists moved quickly to find a safe outlet for women's political activism. They invited women to join Federalist-sponsored events that denounced the French Revolution as a threat to all civilized order. By the late 1790s, both parties were seeking to broaden their popular appeal by including women in their partisan rallies.

As partisanship spread, no symbol of traditional authority, Washington included, was safe from challenge. He devoted most of his Farewell Address of September 1796 to a denunciation of partisanship. He also warned against any permanent foreign alliances and cautioned that the Union itself would be endangered if parties continued to be characterized "by geographical discriminations, *Northern* and *Southern, Atlantic* and *Western.*"

Read the Document   Matthew Carey, "A Short Account of the Malignant Fever ..." (1793)

This suburban estate outside Philadelphia was converted to a hospital for the victims of the city's yellow fever epidemic in 1793.

Confirming Washington's fears, the election of 1796 was the first openly partisan election in American history. John Adams was the Federalist candidate, and Thomas Jefferson, the Republican candidate. Each was selected by a party caucus, a meeting of party leaders. As a result of disunity in the Federalist ranks, the election produced the anomaly of a Federalist president (Adams) and a Republican vice president (Jefferson). Written with no thought of organized partisan competition for the presidency, the Constitution simply stated that the presidential candidate with the second-highest number of electoral votes would become vice president. In this case, that candidate was Jefferson.

Despite the election's confused outcome, the sectional pattern in the voting was unmistakable. Only the solid support of regional elites in New England and the mid-Atlantic states enabled the Federalists to retain the presidency. Adams received all the northern electoral votes, with the exception of Pennsylvania's. Jefferson was the overwhelming favorite in the South.

The Last Federalist Administration

8.4   How did crises at home and abroad shape the administration of John Adams and help the Republicans win the election of 1800?

The Adams administration got off to a rocky start from which it never recovered. The vice president was the leader of the opposition party; key members of the cabinet, which Adams had inherited from Washington, owed their primary loyalty to Hamilton; and the French, who saw Adams as a dupe of the British, instigated a major crisis that left the threat of war hanging over the entire Adams presidency.

The French Crisis and the XYZ Affair

An aggressive coalition known as the Directory gained control of revolutionary France in 1795 and denounced the Jay Treaty as evidence of an Anglo-American alliance against France. When Jefferson and the pro-French Republicans lost the election of 1796, the Directory turned openly hostile. In short order, the French annulled the commercial treaty of 1778 with the United States, ordered the seizure of American ships carrying goods to the British, and declared that any American sailors found on British ships, including those forcibly pressed into service, would be summarily executed. By the time Adams had been in office three months, the French had confiscated more than 300 American ships.

In the fall of 1797, Adams sent three commissioners to Paris in an effort to avoid war. The French treated the three with contempt. Through three intermediaries, identified by Adams only as X, Y, and Z when he informed Congress of the negotiations, the French foreign minister demanded a large bribe to initiate talks and an American loan of $12 million.

Read the Document **The Alien and Sedition Acts (1798)**

The slogan popularized in the XYZ Affair—Millions for our defence not a cent for tribute—streams across the top of this print of President John Adams framed by the arms of the then sixteen states.

In April 1798, the Senate published a full account of the insulting behavior of the French in what came to be called the **XYZ Affair**. The public was indignant, and war fever swept the country. The Federalists, who had always warned against the French, enjoyed greater popularity than they ever had or ever would again. Congress acted to upgrade the navy, and responsibility for naval affairs, formerly divided between the Treasury and War departments, was consolidated in a new Department of the Navy. By the fall of 1798, American ships were waging an undeclared war against the French in Caribbean waters, a conflict that came to be known as the **Quasi-War**.

The Federalists in Congress, dismissing Republican objections, also voted to create a vastly expanded army. They tripled the size of the regular army to 10,000 men and authorized a special provisional army of 50,000. Congress put the provisional army under Washington's command, but he declined to come out of retirement except for a national emergency. In the meantime, he insisted that Hamilton be appointed second in command and given charge of the provisional army's field operations. To pay for both the expanded army and the naval rearmament, the Federalists pushed through the Direct Tax of 1798, a levy on the value of land, slaves, and dwellings.

Crisis at Home

The thought of Hamilton in charge of a huge army convinced many Republicans that their worst nightmares were about to materialize. One congressman shuddered that "the monarchy-loving Hamilton is now so fixed, as to be able, with one-step, to fill the place of our present commander in chief." Adams shared such fears. He was furious that Hamilton had been forced on him as commander of the provisional army. As Adams came to realize, Hamilton's supporters, known as the High Federalists, saw the war scare with France as an opportunity to stamp out dissent, cement an alliance with the British, and strengthen and consolidate the powers of the national government.

The Federalists passed four laws in the summer of 1798, known collectively as the **Alien and Sedition Acts**, that confirmed the Republicans' fears. Three of these acts were aimed at immigrants, especially French and Irish refugees who voted for the Republicans. The president was empowered to deport foreigners who came from countries at war with the United States and to expel any alien resident he suspected of subversive activities. The Naturalization Act extended the residency requirement for U.S. citizenship (and hence the right to vote) from five to fourteen years. Worst of all in the minds of Republicans was the Sedition Act, a measure that made it a federal crime to engage in any conspiracy against the government or to utter or print anything "false, scandalous and malicious" against the government. Federalist judges were blatantly partisan in their enforcement of the Sedition Act. Twenty-five individuals, mostly Republican editors, were indicted under the act, and ten were convicted.

Outraged at this threat to the freedom of speech, Jefferson and Madison turned to the safely Republican legislatures of Kentucky and Virginia for a forum from which to attack the constitutionality of the Alien and Sedition Acts. Taking care to keep their authorship secret, they each drafted a set of resolutions—Jefferson for the Kentucky legislature, and Madison for the Virginia legislature—that challenged the entire centralizing program of the Federalists. In doing so, they produced the first significant articulation of the southern stand on **states' rights**.

The resolutions—adopted in the fall of 1798—proposed a compact theory of the Constitution. They asserted that the states had delegated specific powers to the national government for their common benefit. It followed that the states reserved the right to decide whether the national government had unconstitutionally assumed a power not granted to it. If a state decided that the national government had exceeded its powers, it could "interpose" its authority to shield its citizens from a tyrannical law. In a second set of resolutions, the Kentucky legislature introduced the doctrine of **nullification**, the right of a state to render null and void a national law it deemed unconstitutional.

Jefferson and Madison hoped that these resolutions would rally voters to the Republican Party as the defender of threatened U.S. liberties. Yet not a single additional

XYZ Affair Diplomatic incident in 1798 in which Americans were outraged by the demand of the French for a bribe as a condition for negotiating with American diplomats.

Quasi-War Undeclared naval war of 1797 to 1800 between the United States and France.

Alien and Sedition Acts Collective name given to four acts passed by Congress in 1798 that curtailed freedom of speech and the liberty of foreigners resident in the United States.

states' rights Favoring the rights of individual states over rights claimed by the national government.

nullification A constitutional doctrine holding that a state has a legal right to declare a national law null and void within its borders.

From Then to Now
A Presidential Address: ADVICE FOR AN EMPIRE

A lthough devoted primarily to domestic concerns, Washington's Farewell Address became a seminal document in the formulation of U.S. foreign policy. In his vision for American greatness he called not for a policy of isolation, for the United States has never been isolated from the rest of the world, especially in economic matters. Instead, he advised Americans "to steer clear of permanent alliances with any portion of the foreign world so far . . . as we now are at liberty to do it." Here was hardheaded advice grounded in the reality of America's still shaky independence and its threatened security in a world of hostile foreign powers. Rather than risk becoming the pawn of such powers or being dragged into a war in exchange for a temporary advantage, he counseled that the wisest course for the nation was to maintain its freedom of action, consolidate its strength, expand its commercial ties, and bide its time until American power could set its own terms.

The American empire that Washington saw in the future gradually took shape through territorial expansion in the nineteenth century and the emergence of the United States as first a world power in the twentieth century and then as the world power after the collapse of the Soviet Union in the late 1980s. The entry of the United States into World War I marked the first sharp departure from the tradition spawned by the Farewell Address of avoiding political and military involvement with the affairs of Europe, and the challenges of the Cold War replaced a policy of nonentangling alliances with unilateral military commitments across the globe. However, as Washington well understood, unilateral commitments undertaken without a judicious assessment of the nation's best interests and the limits of its power have a way of feeding upon themselves and becoming self-defeating.

Question for Discussion

- How would Washington have responded to those who wanted the United States to enter into a formal alliance with Britain, its major trading partner, against revolutionary France?

United States soldiers engaged in pacification efforts in the cities of Afghanistan.

General Anthony Wayne wins a decisive victory over the Miami Confederation at the battle of Fallen Timbers in 1794.

state seconded them. In the end, what aroused popular rage against the Federalists was not legislation directed against aliens and subversives but the high cost of Federalist taxes.

The Direct Tax of 1798 fell on all owners of land, dwellings, or slaves and provoked widespread resentment. Enforcing it required an army of bureaucrats—more than 500 for the state of Pennsylvania alone. In February 1799, in the heavily German southeastern counties of Pennsylvania, a group of men led by an auctioneer named John Fries released tax evaders from prison in Bethlehem. President Adams responded to Fries's Rebellion with a show of force, but the fiercest resistance the soldiers he sent to Pennsylvania encountered was from irate farm wives, who doused them with hot water and the contents of chamber pots. Fries and two other men were arrested, convicted of treason, and sentenced to be executed. (Adams later pardoned them.) But the Federalists had now lost much of their support in Pennsylvania.

The End of the Federalists

The events in Pennsylvania reflected the air of menace that gripped the country as the campaign of 1800 approached. The army was chasing private citizens whose only crime was resisting hateful taxes—in the eyes of many, a continuation of an honorable Revolutionary ideal. Federal soldiers also roughed up Republican voters at polling places. Southern Republicans talked in private of the possible need to resist Federalist tyranny by force and, failing in that, to secede from the Union. Hamilton and the High Federalists saw in the Kentucky and Virginia resolutions "a regular conspiracy to overturn the government." Reports that Virginia intended to strengthen its militia heightened their anxieties, and they proposed to meet force with force.

No one did more to defuse the charged atmosphere than President Adams. The Federalists depended for their popular support on the expectation of a war with France, which as late as 1798 had swept them to victory in the congressional elections. Still, Adams refrained from asking for a declaration of war. The United States had been successful in the Quasi-War against France. By early 1799, French ships had been forced out of the Caribbean and American coastal waters. And in Europe, the tide of war had turned against the French. As a result, Adams believed that the French would now be more open to conciliation. Of greater importance, Adams recognized that war with France could trigger a civil war at home. Hamilton and the High Federalists, he realized, would use war as an excuse to crush the Republican opposition in Virginia. Fearful of Hamilton's intentions and unwilling to run the risk of militarizing the government and saddling it with a huge war debt, Adams broke with his party and decided to reopen negotiations with France in February 1799.

The **Franco-American Accord of 1800** that resulted from Adams's initiative released the United States from its 1778 alliance with France. It also obligated the United States to surrender all claims against the French for damages done to U.S. shipping during the Quasi-War. Once peace with France seemed likely, the Hamiltonian Federalists lost their trump card in the election of 1800. The Republicans could no longer be branded as the traitorous friends of an enemy state. The enlarged army, with no foe to fight, became a political embarrassment, and the Federalists dismantled it. Although rumors of possible violence continued to circulate, the Republicans grew increasingly confident that they could peacefully gain control of the government.

The Federalists nonetheless ran a competitive race in 1800. Adams's peace policy bolstered his popularity. And because U.S. merchants had profited from supplying both sides in the European war, the country was enjoying a period of prosperity that benefited the president and his party. But the party wounds opened by Adams's decision to broker a peace with France continued to fester. Hamilton wrote a scathing attack on the president in a letter that fell into the hands of Aaron Burr, a crafty politician from New York whom the Republicans had teamed up with Jefferson for the presidential election. Burr published the letter, airing the Federalists' squabbling in public.

The Federalists, hampered by party disunity, could not counter the Republicans' aggressive organizational tactics. They found it distasteful to appeal to common people. One party member lamented that the Republicans sent spokesmen "to every class of men, and even to every individual man, that can be gained. Every threshing floor, every husting, every party at work on a house-frame or raising a building, the very funerals are infected with bawlers or whisperers against government."

Wherever they organized, the Republicans attacked the Federalists as monarchists plotting to undo the gains of the Revolution. The Federalists responded with emotional appeals that depicted Jefferson as a godless revolutionary whose election would usher in a reign of terror. "The effect," intoned the Reverend William Linn, "would be to destroy religion, introduce immorality, and loosen all bonds of society."

Attacks like Linn's reflected the fears of Calvinist preachers that a tide of disbelief was about to submerge Christianity in the United States. Church attendance had declined in the 1790s, particularly among men, and perhaps no more than one in twenty Americans was a member of any church. **Deism**, an Enlightenment religious philosophy

Franco-American Accord of 1800
Settlement reached with France that brought an end to the Quasi-War and released the United States from its 1778 alliance with France.

deism Religious orientation that rejects divine revelation and holds that the workings of nature alone reveal God's design for the universe.

219

popular among the leaders of the Revolutionary era, was now beginning to make inroads among ordinary citizens. Deists viewed God as a kind of master clockmaker who created the laws by which the universe runs but otherwise leaves it alone. They rejected revelation for reason, maintaining that the workings of nature alone reveal God's design.

These developments convinced Calvinist ministers, nearly all of them Federalists, that the atheism of the French Revolution was infecting U.S. republicanism. They lashed out at the Republicans, the friends of the French Revolution, as perverters of religious and social order. Jefferson, a deist known for his freethinking in religion, bore the brunt of their attack in 1800.

The Republicans won the election by mobilizing voters through strong party organizations. Voter turnout in 1800 was twice what it had been in the early 1790s, and most of the new voters were Republicans. The Direct Tax of 1798 cost the Federalists the support of commercial farmers in the mid-Atlantic states. Artisans in port cities had already switched to the Republicans in protest over Jay's Treaty, which they feared left them exposed to a flood of cheap British imports. Adams carried New England and had a smattering of support elsewhere. With New York added to their solid base in the South and the backcountry, the Jeffersonians gained an electoral majority (see Map 8.1).

Party unity among Republican electors was so strong that Jefferson and Burr each received seventy-three electoral votes. Consequently, the election was thrown into the House of Representatives, which, until the newly elected Congress was seated, was still dominated by Federalists. Hoping to deny Jefferson the presidency, the Federalists in the House backed Burr. The result was a deadlock that persisted into the early months of 1801. On February 16, 1801, the Federalists yielded. Informed through intermediaries that Jefferson would not dismantle Hamilton's fiscal system, enough Federalists cast blank ballots to give Jefferson the majority he needed for election. The

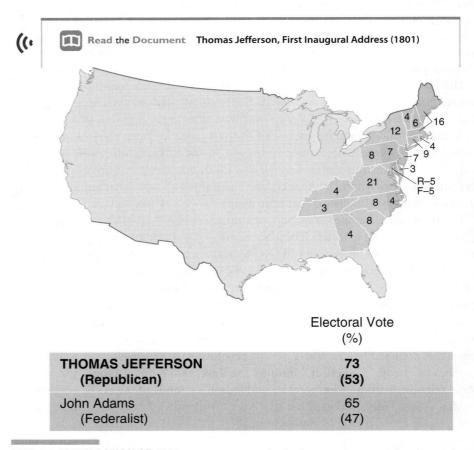

Read the **Document**   Thomas Jefferson, First Inaugural Address (1801)

	Electoral Vote (%)
THOMAS JEFFERSON **(Republican)**	**73** **(53)**
John Adams (Federalist)	65 (47)

MAP 8.1   THE ELECTION OF 1800 The sharp erosion of Federalist strength in New York and Pennsylvania after 1798 swung the election of 1800 to the Republicans.

Twelfth Amendment to the Constitution, ratified in 1804, prevented a similar impasse from arising again by requiring electors to cast separate ballots for president and vice president.

Conclusion

In 1789, the U.S. republic was little more than an experiment in self-government. The Federalists provided a firm foundation for that experiment. Hamilton's financial program, neutrality in the wars of the French Revolution, and the diplomatic settlement with Britain in Jay's Treaty bequeathed the young nation a decade of peace and prosperity.

Federalist policies, however, provoked strong opposition rooted in conflicting economic interests and contrasting regional views over the meaning of liberty and government in the new republic. As early as 1789, in the midst of debates in the Senate over a bill to establish a federal judiciary, Willaim Maclay saw the outlines of a plan to subvert republican liberties. As he put it, "The Constitution is meant to swallow up all the State Constitutions by degrees and this to swallow by degrees all the State Judiciaries. This at least is the design some Gentlemen seem driving at."

Federalist leadership initially depended on a coalition of regional elites in New England, the mid-Atlantic region, and the slave districts of the South. Fully sharing Maclay's fears over a consolidated government, southern planters were the first of the elites to bolt the Federalist coalition when they joined urban artisans and backcountry Scots-Irish farmers in opposing Jay's Treaty and the commercially oriented program of the Federalists. During John Adams's administration, Quaker and German farmers in the mid-Atlantic states defected from the Federalists over the tax legislation of 1798, and three of the four regions of the country lined up behind the Republicans. The new Republican majority was united by the belief that the actions of the New England Federalists—the expansion of the army, the imposition of new taxes, and the passage of the Alien and Sedition Acts—threatened individual liberty and regional autonomy. Non-English groups and farmers south of New England turned to the Republicans as the upholders of these threatened freedoms.

The openly partisan politics of the 1790s surprised the country's founders, who equated parties with the evils of factionalism. They had not foreseen that parties would forge a necessary link between the rulers and the ruled and create a mechanism by which group values and regional interests could be given a political voice. Party formation climaxed in the election of 1800, when the Republicans ended the Federalists' rule. The Republicans won by embracing the popular demand for a more egalitarian social and political order.

To the credit of the Federalists, they relinquished control of the national government peacefully. The importance of this precedent can scarcely be exaggerated. It marked the first time in modern political history that a party in power handed over the government to its opposition. It now remained to be seen what the Republicans would do with their newfound power.

For Suggested Readings go to MyHistoryLab.

Chapter Review

Washington's America

8.1 What were the distinguishing features of the early republic's four major regions? p. 199

Americans in the 1790s were a diverse people divided into four regional cultures and economies. Each of these regions—New England, the mid-Atlantic states, the South, and the West—had its own distinctive blend of ethnic and racial groups, labor systems, religious affiliations, and versions of republicanism.

Forging a New Government

8.2 What challenges faced the Congress that assembled in New York between 1789 and 1791? p. 206

The first Congress had to give substance to the governing guidelines in the Constitution by establishing executive departments, creating federal courts, and putting the nation's credit in good standing by agreeing on a plan to pay back the national debt. At the same time, it had to fashion a sense of national purpose without impinging on the needs and interests of the states.

The Emergence of Parties

8.3 What forces shaped the development of party politics in America? p. 210

The reaction to Hamilton's economic program sparked the first debates over interpreting the Constitution and produced early political divisions over the extent of federal powers. Conflicting views on the French Revolution and Jay's Treaty broadened and intensified these divisions into rival partisan parties, the Federalists and the Republicans.

The Last Federalist Administration

8.4 How did crises at home and abroad shape the administration of John Adams and help the Republicans win the election of 1800? p. 215

The Federalists divided into pro-Adams and pro-Hamilton factions in their response to the crisis in foreign policy produced by French raids on American shipping and the XYZ Affair. The unpopularity of the new Federalist legislation raising taxes and enlarging the military benefited the Republicans, who also proved far more adept in mobilizing voters on their behalf.

Timeline

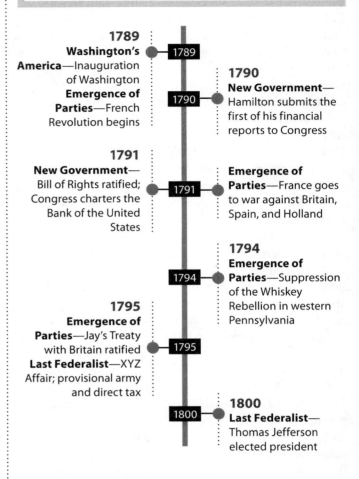

1789
Washington's America—Inauguration of Washington
Emergence of Parties—French Revolution begins

1790
New Government—Hamilton submits the first of his financial reports to Congress

1791
New Government—Bill of Rights ratified; Congress charters the Bank of the United States

Emergence of Parties—France goes to war against Britain, Spain, and Holland

1794
Emergence of Parties—Suppression of the Whiskey Rebellion in western Pennsylvania

1795
Emergence of Parties—Jay's Treaty with Britain ratified
Last Federalist—XYZ Affair; provisional army and direct tax

1800
Last Federalist—Thomas Jefferson elected president

9 The Triumph and Collapse of Jeffersonian Republicanism 1800–1824

One American Journey

A Letter from a Federalist Spreads the News of the British Attack on Washington, DC, in the War of 1812

Riversdale, 30 August 1814

My dear Sister,

Since I started this letter [on Aug. 9] we have been in a state of continual alarm, and now I have time to write only two or three lines to ask you to tell Papa that we are alive, in good health, and I hope safe from danger. I am sure that you have heard the news of the battle of Bladensburg where the English defeated the American troops with Madison "not at their head, but at their rear."

From there they went to Washington where they burned the Capitol, the President's House, all the public offices, etc. During the battle I saw several cannonballs with my own eyes, and I will write all the details to your husband. At the moment the English ships are at Alexandria which is also in their possession.

The British bombardment of Fort McHenry, Baltimore, on September 13–14, 1814, inspired the writing of "The Star Spangled Banner."

LEARNING OBJECTIVES

9.1	9.2	9.3	9.4	9.5
Why was the expansion of the United States so important to Jefferson? p. 226	What factors pushed Madison into a war with Britain? p. 232	What were the consequences of the War of 1812? p. 235	How did rising nationalism contribute to the spirit of the Era of Good Feelings? p. 240	Why did slavery become such a divisive issue in the years preceding the Missouri Compromise? p. 243

Listen to **Chapter 9** on MyHistoryLab

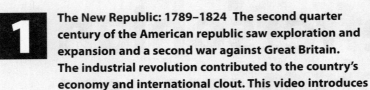

Watch the Video Series on MyHistoryLab

Learn about some key topics related to this chapter with the *MyHistoryLab Video Series: Key Topics in U.S. History.*

Captains Lewis & Clark holding a Council with the Indians Page 17

1 **The New Republic: 1789–1824** The second quarter century of the American republic saw exploration and expansion and a second war against Great Britain. The industrial revolution contributed to the country's economy and international clout. This video introduces this period in which the country prospered and, for a short time, Washington enjoyed politics virtually without factions as the rivalry between the Federalists and Democratic-Republicans ended with the so-called "Era of Good Feelings."

 Watch on MyHistoryLab

The Louisiana Purchase and Lewis and Clark One of the key events of the early national period is the purchase and exploration of the Louisiana Territory. This video examines why President Thomas Jefferson overcame personal and political considerations to buy the Louisiana Territory from France for $15 million. Then it profiles the expedition of Meriwether Lewis and William Clark that proved the wisdom of the "purchase." **2**

Watch on MyHistoryLab

3 **The War of 1812** With Great Britain seemingly overstretched in its wars against Napoleonic France and its allies, the United States invaded Canada, thus triggering the War of 1812. This video looks at the pretexts for war, namely, the British Navy's impressment of sailors serving aboard American merchant ships, Great Britain's failure to abandon frontier forts, and its support of Native Americans in their attempts to resist white expansion into their territories.

 Watch on MyHistoryLab

The "Era of Good Feelings" American success in the War of 1812, along with the election of James Monroe in 1816, combined to finally remove the last vestiges of the Federalist Party from American politics. This video explains why this period in American history was called the "Era of Good Feelings" despite the financial crises, sectional strife, and political manipulations that continued. **4**

Watch on MyHistoryLab

I don't know how all this will end, but I fear very badly for us. It is probable that it will also bring about a dissolution of the union of the states, and in that case, farewell to the public debt. You know I have predicted this outcome for a long time. Wouldn't it be wise to send your husband here without delay, in order to plan with me the best course to pursue for Papa's interests as well as yours?

This letter will go, I think, by a Dutch ship. If I have time with the confusion we are in, I will write again in a few days, perhaps by the same vessel. At present my house is full of people every day and at night my bedroom is full of rifles, pistols, sabers, etc. Many thanks to your husband for the information in his letter of 27 April, and tell him that I invested all his money in the May loan [of the U.S. Treasury]. Please give many greetings to my dear Father and to Charles [her brother]. Embrace your children for me and believe me.

Your affectionate sister,
Rosalie E. Calvert

Margaret Law Callcott, ed., *Mistress of Riversdale: The Plantation Letters of Rosalie Stier Calvert, 1795–1821*, pp. 271–272. © 1991 Johns Hopkins University Press. Reprinted with permission of The Johns Hopkins University Press.

9.1
9.2
9.3
9.4
9.5

Personal Journeys Online

- George Robert Gleig, *Burning of Washington*, August 23, 1814. A British soldier describes the destruction in Washington.

- Dolley Madison, *Letter to her sister*, August 23, 1814. Dolley Madison describes the abandonment of the White House.

- Lt. Col. R. E. Parker, *Letter to the governor*, June 11, 1814. A Virginia soldier relates how the slaves plotted to escape behind British lines.

9.1

9.2

9.3

9.4

9.5

Rosalie Calvert, from her plantation home in nearby Bladensburg, Maryland, wrote to her sister in Europe with news of the British attack on Washington, DC, in August 1814, the low point of the American cause in the War of 1812. The youngest of the three children of a wealthy Belgian family that had fled the advancing armies of revolutionary France, Rosalie was 16 when her family arrived in Philadelphia in the summer of 1794. Her father, Henri J. Stier, had planned in advance for his family's departure and brought with him a sizable fortune in gold, U.S. currency, and paintings. The family lived off the income from Henri's investments in U.S. securities and, unsurprisingly, was strongly Federalist in its political leanings. After resettling in Annapolis, most of the Stiers returned to Europe in 1803 when political conditions had stabilized. Left behind was Rosalie, entrusted with the management of the family's financial holdings. In 1799, Rosalie had married George Calvert, a descendant of the proprietors of the Maryland colony and a kinsman of the Washingtons.

The Calverts lived at Riversdale, a home built by her father, and shared in the responsibilities of managing three plantations worked by slave labor. Rosalie's wealth and elite social standing deepened her political conservatism. Moreover, the coming to power of the Jeffersonian Republicans in 1801 triggered bitter memories of the revolutionary turmoil she had experienced as a young woman in Belgium. In her eyes, Jefferson and his followers were demagogues who catered to the poor and threatened to infect the United States with the political radicalism of the French Revolution. She blamed the War of 1812 on ignorant, ill-conceived Republican policies and feared that the war would unleash massive unrest. Particularly alarming was the news that a mob in Baltimore had brutally beaten twelve prominent Federalists for their antiwar stand. Thus the sense of "continual alarm" that runs through her letter in August 1814, at a time when the war had spilled over into her home.

Her fears were overblown. The United States weathered the War of 1812, and the Calverts were spared property damage. Rosalie, however, survived the war by only six years. The strain of ten pregnancies in twenty-one years of marriage likely contributed to her death at the age of 43 from congestive heart failure. Despite her denunciations of the Republicans, Jefferson's party succeeded in promoting the growth and independence of the United States in the first quarter of the nineteenth century. Expansionist policies to the south and west more than doubled the size of the republic and fueled the westward spread of slavery. The war against Britain from 1812 to 1815, if less than a military triumph, nonetheless freed Americans to look inward for economic development.

At the height of Republican success just after the War of 1812, the Federalist Party collapsed, and with it the social and political elitism championed by Rosalie Calvert and her father. Without an organized opposition to enforce party discipline, the Republicans soon followed the Federalists into political oblivion. The nation's expansion produced two crises—a financial panic and a battle over slavery in Missouri—that shattered the facade of republican unity. By the mid-1820s, a new party system was emerging.

Jefferson's Presidency

9.1 Why was the expansion of the United States so important to Jefferson?

Thomas Jefferson believed that a true revolution had occurred in 1800, a peaceful overthrow of the Federalist Party and its hated principles of government consolidation and military force. In his eyes, the defeat of the monarchical Federalists reconfirmed the true political legacy of the Revolution by restoring the republican majority to its rightful control of the government.

Unlike the Hamiltonian Federalists, whose commercial vision of the United States accepted social and economic inequalities as inevitable, the Jeffersonians wanted a predominantly agrarian republic based on widespread economic equality for white yeomen families to counter any threat posed by the privileged few to the people's liberties. Thus, they favored territorial expansion as a means of adding enough land to maintain self-reliant farmers as the guardians of republican freedoms. They also favored the spread of slavery. As long as racial slavery promoted a sense of unity among free white men, they were confident that a populist democracy could coexist with elite rule.

Reform at Home

Believing that the Federalists had promoted aristocratic pretensions and courtly intrigue through such practices as weekly levees (formal receptions) for presidential

This 1808 print depicts the political aspirations of German Americans in Pennsylvania and their pride in their craft as butchers. It shows the butchers marching in a procession led by two African American fiddlers in honor of the Republican politician Simon Snyder, the first representative of German artisans and backcountry farmers to be elected governor of the state.

guests, Jefferson replaced the levees with small, men-only dinners, where he aired his political views. This effort to achieve republican purity in governance, one that denied women any political role, created a void in the capital's social life that was filled by the wives of cabinet members and women drawn from the social elite. It was their dinner parties and receptions that enabled politically minded women and men to come together, lobby on behalf of friends and relatives, and build the networks that influenced how political offices and favors were distributed. Influential Washington hostesses such as Dolley Madison soon wielded a good deal of informal political power as they helped make possible a national political culture.

The cornerstone of Republican domestic policy was retrenchment, a return to the frugal, simple federal establishment the Jeffersonians believed to be the original intent of the Constitution. Determined to root out what they viewed as Federalist corruption and patronage, the Republicans began by reforming fiscal policy. Jefferson's secretary of the treasury was Albert Gallatin, a native of Switzerland who emerged in the 1790s as the best financial mind in the Republican Party. He convinced Jefferson that the Bank of the United States was essential for financial stability and blocked efforts to dismantle it. Unlike Hamilton, however, Gallatin thought that a large public debt was a curse, a drag on productive capital, and an unfair burden on future generations. He succeeded in reducing the national debt from $83 million in 1800 to $57 million by 1809.

Gallatin's conservative fiscal policies shrank both the spending and taxes of the national government. The Republicans eliminated all internal taxes, including the despised tax on whiskey. Slashes in the military budget kept government expenditures below the level of 1800. The cuts in military spending, combined with soaring revenues from customs collections, left Gallatin with a surplus in the budget that he could devote to debt repayment.

Jeffersonian reform targeted the political character, as well as the size, of the national government. He moved to break the Federalist stranglehold on federal offices by appointing officials with sound Republican principles. Arch-Federalists, those Jefferson deemed guilty of misusing their offices for openly political reasons, were immediately replaced, and Republicans filled other posts opened up by attrition. By the time Jefferson left the presidency in 1809, Republicans held nearly all the appointive offices.

Jefferson moved most aggressively against the Federalists in the judiciary. Just days before they relinquished power, the Federalists passed the Judiciary Act of 1801, legislation that both enlarged the judiciary and packed it with more Federalists appointed by Adams, the outgoing president.

The Republicans fought back. Now dominant in Congress, they quickly repealed the Judiciary Act of 1801. Frustrated Federalists now turned to John Marshall, a staunch Federalist appointed chief justice of the United States by President Adams in 1801, hoping that he would rule that Congress had acted unconstitutionally in removing the recently appointed federal judges. Marshall moved carefully to avoid an open confrontation. He was aware that the Republicans contended that Congress and the president had at least a coequal right with the Supreme Court to decide constitutional questions.

The issue came to a head in the case of **_Marbury v. Madison_** (1803), which centered on Secretary of State James Madison's refusal to deliver a commission to William Marbury, one of Adams's "midnight appointments" (so-called because Adams made them on his next-to-last day in office) as a justice of the peace for the District of Columbia. Marshall held that although Marbury had a legal right to his commission, the Court had no jurisdiction in the case. The Court ruled that the section of the Judiciary Act of 1789 granting it the power to order the delivery of Marbury's commission was unconstitutional because it conferred on the Court a power not specified in the Constitution. Stating that it was "emphatically the province and duty of the judicial department to say what the law is," Marshall created the precedent of judicial review, the power of the Supreme Court to rule on the constitutionality of federal law. This doctrine rejected the Republican view expressed in the Virginia and Kentucky Resolutions that the states could decide on the constitutionality of federal laws and was of pivotal importance for the future of the Court.

Marbury v. Madison Supreme Court decision of 1803 that created the precedent of judicial review by ruling as unconstitutional part of the Judiciary Act of 1789.

The Louisiana Purchase

In foreign affairs, fortune smiled on Jefferson during his first term. The European war that had almost sucked in the United States in the 1790s subsided. Britain and France agreed on a truce in 1802.

The Anglo-French peace allowed Spain and France to reclaim their colonial trade in the Western Hemisphere. The new ruler of France, Napoleon Bonaparte, was also now free to develop his plans for reviving the French empire in America. In a secret treaty with Spain in 1800, Napoleon reacquired for France the Louisiana Territory, a vast, vaguely defined area stretching between the Mississippi River and the Rocky Mountains. Sketchy, unconfirmed reports of the treaty reached Jefferson in the spring of 1801, and he was immediately alarmed. French control of the Mississippi Valley, combined with the British presence in Canada, threatened to hem in the United States and deprive Jefferson's farmers of their empire of liberty.

Jefferson was prepared to reverse his party's traditional foreign policy to eliminate this threat. He opened exploratory talks with the British on an Anglo-American alliance to drive the French out of Louisiana. He also strengthened U.S. forces in the Mississippi Valley and secured congressional approval for the Lewis and Clark expedition through upper Louisiana. Although best known for its scientific discoveries, this expedition was designed initially as a military mission. Jefferson applied diplomatic and military pressure to induce Napoleon to sell New Orleans and a small slice of coastal territory to its east to the United States. This was his main objective: to possess New Orleans and control the mouth of the Mississippi River, outlet to world markets. To his surprise, Napoleon suddenly decided in early 1803 to sell all of the immense Louisiana Territory to the United States (see Map 9.1).

Watch the Video   Lewis and Clark: What Were They Trying to Accomplish?

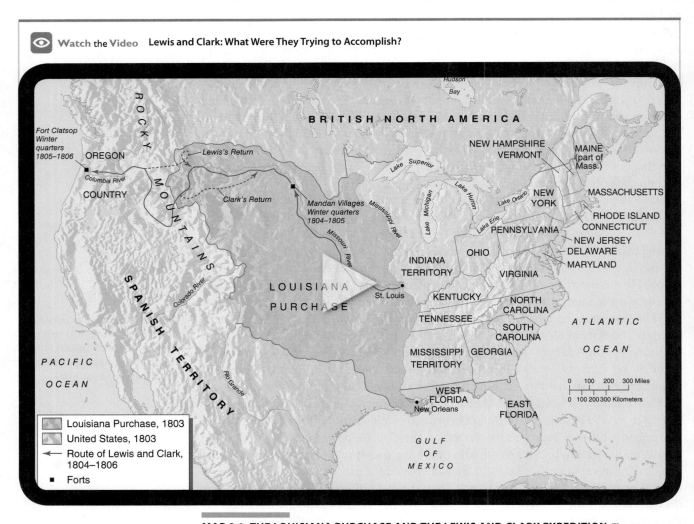

MAP 9.1 THE LOUISIANA PURCHASE AND THE LEWIS AND CLARK EXPEDITION The vast expanse of the Louisiana Purchase was virtually unknown territory to Americans before the Lewis and Clark expedition gathered a mass of scientific information about it.

Napoleon's failure to reconquer Saint-Domingue (modern-day Haiti) was instrumental in his about-face on plans for a revived French empire in America. He had envisioned this rich sugar island as the jewel of his new empire and intended to use the Louisiana Territory as a granary to supply the island. During the upheavals of the French Revolution, the slaves on the island, led by Touissant L'Ouverture, rebelled in a bloody and successful bid for independence that culminated in the second independent republic in the western Hemisphere. Napoleon sent a large army to reassert French control, but it succumbed to disease and the islanders' fierce resistance. Without firm French control of Saint-Domingue, Louisiana was of little use to Napoleon. For $15 million (including about $4 million in French debts owed to American citizens), he offered to part with the whole of Louisiana. The cost to the United States was about 3.5 cents per acre.

Jefferson, the strict constructionist, now turned pragmatist. Despite the lack of any specific authorization in the Constitution for the acquisition of foreign territory or the incorporation as U.S. citizens of the 50,000 French and Spanish descendants then living in Louisiana, he accepted Napoleon's deal. The Louisiana Purchase doubled the size of the United States and offered seemingly endless space to be settled by yeoman farmers. It also opened up another frontier for slaveholders in the lower Mississippi Valley.

Jefferson was willing, as the Federalists had been when they were in power, to stretch the Constitution to support his definition of the national good. Conversely, it was now the Federalists, fearful of a further decline in their political power, who relied on a narrow reading of the Constitution in a futile attempt to block the Louisiana acquisition.

Florida and Western Schemes

The magnificent prize of Louisiana did not satisfy Republican territorial ambitions. Still to be gained were river outlets on the Gulf Coast essential for the development of plantation agriculture in Alabama and Mississippi. The boundaries of the Louisiana Purchase were so vague that Jefferson felt justified in claiming Spanish-held Texas and the Gulf Coast eastward from New Orleans to Mobile Bay, including the Spanish province of West Florida. Against stiff Spanish opposition, he pushed ahead with his plans to acquire West Florida. This provoked the first challenge to his leadership of the party.

Once it was clear that Spain did not want to sell West Florida to the United States, Jefferson accepted Napoleon's offer to act as a middleman in the acquisition. Napoleon's price was $2 million. He soon lost interest in the project, however, and Jefferson lost prestige in 1806, when he pushed an appropriations bill through Congress to pay for Napoleon's services. Former Republican stalwarts in Congress denounced the bill as bribe money and staged a party revolt.

Jefferson's failed bid for West Florida emboldened westerners to demand that Americans seize the territory by force. In 1805 and 1806, Aaron Burr, Jefferson's first vice president, apparently became entangled in an attempt at just such a land grab.

Republicans had been suspicious of Burr since his dalliance with the Federalists in their bid to make him, rather than Jefferson, president in 1800. He further alienated the party when he involved himself with the efforts of a minority of die-hard Federalists known as the Essex Junto. The members of this group feared that incorporation of the vast Louisiana Purchase into the United States would leave New England powerless in national affairs. They concocted a plan for a northern confederacy in which New York would play a key role. Rebuffed by Hamilton, they turned to Burr and backed him in the New York gubernatorial race of 1804. Burr lost, largely because Hamilton denounced him. The enmity between the two men reached a tragic climax in July 1804, when Burr killed Hamilton in a duel at Weehawken, New Jersey. Although outlawed in the northern states, this centuries-old ritual of settling affairs of honor still appealed to men who felt their integrity had been impugned. Burr, indicted for murder in the state of New Jersey, was nonetheless able to return to Washington where he both resumed his duties as vice president and hatched a separatist plot for the West.

From Then to Now
Lewis and Clark Expedition: IN THEIR WORLD AND OURS

In its day the Lewis and Clark expedition was as daring a venture as space exploration is today. The expedition, which began in 1803 and ended in 1806, brought Americans their first knowledge of the vast territory they had secured in the Louisiana Purchase. The West described by Lewis and Clark was a land of change, diversity, and abundance. They catalogued 122 animals and 178 plants that were new to American science. Traveling through present-day South Dakota in September 1804, Lewis observed "Vast herds of Buffaloe deer elk and Antilopes . . . feeding in every direction as far as the eye of the observer could reach." Clark wrote that the numbers of salmon in the Columbia River were "almost inconceivable." Before the end of the nineteenth century, the great herds of grazing animals in the West and the carnivores that stalked them had nearly been wiped out by government-sponsored extermination programs. Most of the vast prairie landscape that Lewis and Clark crossed has disappeared, replaced by uniform fields of row-to-row crops. The prairie grasslands were once the largest ecosystem in North America, a patchwork of native grasses and herbs that supported a wide diversity of habitats.

The journals of Lewis and Clark provide a baseline from which to gauge how much the West has changed, putting Americans in a better position to preserve what is left and even restore some of what has been lost.

Question for Discussion

- What successful restoration programs have been undertaken in the modern trans-Mississippi West?

Corn fields now stretch across the plains crossed by Lewis and Clark.

The Amerindian Sacajawea was an indispensable guide for Lewis and Clark on their famed expedition.

The Burr conspiracy remains mysterious. Burr was undoubtedly eager to pry land loose from the Spanish and Indians, and he may have been thinking of carving out a separate western confederacy in the lower Mississippi Valley. Whatever he had in mind, he blundered in relying on General James Wilkinson as a co-conspirator. Wilkinson, the military governor of the Louisiana Territory and also a double agent for Spain, betrayed Burr. Burr was tried for treason in 1807, and Jefferson made extraordinary efforts to secure his conviction. He was saved by the insistence of Chief Justice Marshall that the Constitution defined treason only as the waging of war against the United States or the rendering of aid to its enemies. The law also required the direct testimony of two witnesses to an "overt act" of treason for conviction. Lacking such witnesses, the government failed to prove its case, and Burr was acquitted.

Embargo and a Crippled Presidency

Concern about a possible war against Britain in 1807 soon quieted the uproar over Burr's trial. After Britain and France had resumed their war in 1803, the United States became enmeshed in the same quarrels over neutral rights, blockades, ship seizures, and **impressment** of U.S. sailors that had almost dragged the country into war in

impressment The coercion of American sailors into the British navy.

the 1790s. Britain proclaimed a blockade of the European continent, which was controlled by Napoleon, and confiscated the cargoes of ships attempting to run the blockade. Napoleon retaliated with seizures of ships that submitted to British searches and accepted the British-imposed licensing system for trading with Europe. Caught in the middle, but eager to supply both sides, was the U.S. merchant marine, the world's largest carrier of neutral goods.

United States merchants and shippers had taken full advantage of the opportunities opened by the European war. Despite French and British restrictions, American merchants traded with anyone they pleased. They dominated commerce, not only between Britain and the United States, but also between the European continent and the French and Spanish colonies in the West Indies. Profits were so great that merchants made money even when only one-third of their ships evaded the blockades.

In June 1807, however, a confrontation known as the ***Chesapeake* Incident** nearly triggered an Anglo-American war. A British ship, the *Leopard,* ordered a U.S. frigate, the *Chesapeake,* to submit to a search in coastal waters off Norfolk, Virginia. When the commander of the *Chesapeake* refused, the *Leopard* opened fire and three Americans were killed. Jefferson resisted the popular outcry for revenge. Instead, he barred U.S. ports to British warships and called for both monetary compensation and an end to impressments, not only because the country was woefully unprepared for war but also because he passionately believed that international law should settle disputes between nations.

In a last burst of the idealism that had animated the republicanism of the Revolution, Jefferson resorted to a trade embargo as a substitute for war. The **Embargo Act of 1807**, an expression of Jefferson's policy of "peaceable coercion," prohibited U.S. ships from leaving port to any nation until Britain and France repealed their trading restrictions on neutral shippers.

The premise of the embargo was that Europe was so dependent on American foods and raw materials that it would do America's bidding if faced with a cutoff. This premise was not so much wrong as unrealistic. The embargo did hurt Europe, but the people who first felt the pain were British textile workers and slaves in the colonies, hardly those who wielded the levers of power. Meanwhile, politically influential landlords and manufacturers benefited from short-term shortages by jacking up prices.

The U.S. export trade and its profits dried up with Jefferson's self-imposed blockade. Except for manufacturers, who now had the U.S. market to themselves, nearly all economic groups suffered under the embargo. Especially hard hit were New England shippers and merchants, and they accused the Republicans of near-criminal irresponsibility

***Chesapeake* Incident** Attack in 1807 by the British ship *Leopard* on the American ship *Chesapeake* in American territorial waters.

Embargo Act of 1807 Act passed by Congress in 1807 prohibiting American ships from leaving for any foreign port.

This Federalist cartoon satirizes Jefferson, in the form of a prairie dog, coughing up the $2 million bribe to Napoleon for the acquisition of West Florida, while a French diplomat stands by dancing and taunting Jefferson.

for forcing a depression on the country. Jefferson responded to these criticisms and to widespread violations of the embargo with a series of enforcement acts that consolidated executive powers far beyond what the Federalists themselves had been able to achieve while in power.

As the embargo tightened and the 1808 presidential election approached, the Federalist Party revived. The Federalist presidential candidate, Charles C. Pinckney, running against Secretary of State James Madison, Jefferson's handpicked successor, polled three times as many votes as he had in 1804. Madison won only because he carried the South and the West, the Republican heartland.

Before Madison took office, the Republicans abandoned Jefferson's embargo, replacing it with the Nonintercourse Act, a measure that prohibited U.S. trade only with Britain and France. At the president's discretion, trade could be reopened with either nation once it lifted its restrictions on U.S. shipping.

Madison and the Coming of War

9.2   What factors pushed Madison into a war with Britain?

F rail-looking and short, Madison struck most contemporaries as an indecisive and weaker version of Jefferson. Yet in intellectual toughness and resourcefulness he was at least Jefferson's equal. He failed because of an inherited foreign policy that was partly of his own making as Jefferson's secretary of state. The Republicans' idealistic stand on neutral rights was ultimately untenable unless backed up by military and political force. Madison concluded as much when he decided on war against Britain in the spring of 1812.

A war against America's old enemy also promised to restore unity to a Republican Party increasingly divided over Madison's peaceful diplomacy. Thus did Madison and his fellow Republicans push for a war they were eager but unprepared to fight.

The Failure of Economic Sanctions

As pressure mounted to reopen all trade routes, Congress responded in 1810 by replacing the Nonintercourse Act with Macon's Bill No. 2, named after Congressman Nathaniel Macon. This measure threw open American trade to everyone but stipulated that if either France or England lifted its restrictions, the president would resume trading sanctions against the other. Napoleon now duplicitously promised to withdraw his decrees against U.S. shipping on the condition that if Britain did not follow suit, Madison would force the British to respect U.S. rights. To Madison's chagrin, French seizures of U.S. ships continued. By the time Napoleon's duplicity became clear, he had already succeeded in worsening Anglo-American tensions. In November 1810, Madison reimposed nonintercourse against Britain, putting the two nations on a collision course.

The Frontier and Indian Resistance

Mounting frustrations in the South and West also pushed Madison toward a war against Britain. Nearly a million Americans lived west of the Appalachian Mountains in 1810, a tripling of the western population in just a decade. Farm prices, including those for the southern staples of cotton and tobacco, plunged when Jefferson's embargo shut off exports, and they stayed low after the embargo was lifted. Blame for the persistent agricultural depression focused on the British and their stranglehold on overseas trade after 1808. Western settlers also accused the British of inciting Indian resistance. However, it was the unceasing demand of Americans for ever more Indian land, not any British incitement, that triggered the **pan-Indian resistance movement** that so frightened western settlers on the eve of the War of 1812.

In the Treaty of Greenville (1795) (see Chapter 8), the U.S. government had promised that any future acquisitions of Indian land would be approved by all native peoples in the region. Nonetheless, government agents continued to play one group against another and divide groups from within by lavishing money and goods on the more accommodationist Christianized Indians. By such means, William Henry Harrison, the governor of the Indiana Territory, procured most of southern Indiana in the Treaty of Vincennes of 1804. Two extraordinary leaders, the Shawnee chief Tecumseh and his brother, the Prophet Tenkswatawa, channeled Indian outrage over this treaty into a movement to unify tribes throughout the West for a stand against the white invaders.

The message of pan-Indianism was unwavering: White encroachments had to be stopped and tribal and clan divisions submerged in a return to native rituals and belief systems. With the assistance of Tecumseh, Tenkswatawa established the Prophet's Town in 1808. At the confluence of the Wabash and Tippecanoe rivers in north-central Indiana, this encampment became headquarters of an intertribal confederation. As he tried to explain to the worried Governor Harrison, his goals were peaceful. He admonished his followers, "[Do] not take up the tomahawk, should it be offered by the British, or by the long knives: do not meddle with any thing that does not belong to you, but mind your own business, and cultivate the ground, that your women and your children have enough to live on."

That ground, of course, was the very reason the Indians could not live in peace and dignity. White settlers wanted it and would do anything to get it. In November 1811, Harrison marched an army to Prophet's Town and provoked the Battle of Tippecanoe. Losses were heavy on both sides, but Harrison regrouped his forces, drove the surviving Indians away, and burned the abandoned town. Harrison's victory came at a high cost: Tecumseh now joined forces with the British, leaving the frontier more unsettled than ever.

While Harrison's aggressiveness was converting fears of a British-Indian alliance into a self-fulfilling prophecy, expansionist-minded southerners struck at Britain through Spain, now its ally against Napoleon. With the covert support of President Madison, U.S. adventurers staged a bloodless revolt in Spanish West Florida between Louisiana and the Pearl River. This "republic" was quickly recognized by the U.S. government and annexed as part of Louisiana in 1811. Hatred of Native Americans, expansionist pressures, the lingering agricultural depression, and impatience with the administration's policy of economic coercion all pointed in the same direction, a war against Britain coupled with a U.S. takeover of British Canada and Spanish Florida. This was the rallying cry of the **War Hawks**, the forty or so pro-war congressmen swept into office in 1810. Generally younger men from the South and West, the War Hawks were led by Henry Clay of Kentucky. Along with other outspoken nationalists, such as John C. Calhoun of South Carolina, Clay played a key role in building congressional support for Madison's growing aggressiveness on the British issue.

Decision for War

In July 1811, Madison issued a Proclamation calling Congress into an early session on November 4. When Congress met, Madison tried to lay the groundwork for war. But the Republican-controlled Congress balked at strengthening the military or raising taxes to pay for war. Madison secretly asked Congress on April 1, 1812, for a sixty-day embargo, a move designed to give U.S. merchant ships time to return safely to their home ports. On June 1, he sent a war message to Congress in which he laid out the stark alternative of submission or resistance to British control of U.S. commerce. Madison was now convinced that British commercial restrictions were not just a defensive measure aimed at France but an aggressive attempt to reduce the United States to the permanent status of colonial dependent.

pan-Indian resistance movement Movement calling for the political and cultural unification of Indian tribes in the late eighteenth and early nineteenth centuries.

War Hawks Members of Congress, predominantly from the South and West, who aggressively pushed for a war against Britain after their election in 1810.

Read the Document *Pennsylvania Gazette*, "Indian Hostilities" (1812)

The Prophet Tenkswatawa was the spiritual leader of the pan-Indian movement that sought to revitalize native culture and block the spread of white settlement in the Old Northwest.

For Madison and most other Republicans, the impending conflict was a second war for independence. Free and open access to world markets was certainly at stake, but so was national pride. The arrogant British policy of impressment was a humiliating affront to U.S. honor and headed the list of grievances in Madison's war message. The British had seized some 6,000 U.S. sailors in the three years leading up to the war.

A divided Congress declared war on Britain. The vote in the House on June 4 was 79 in favor and 49 opposed; on June 17, the Senate concurred, 19 to 13. Support for the war was strongest in regions whose economies had been damaged the most by the British blockade and control of Atlantic commerce. Thus, the South and the West, trapped in an agricultural depression and anxious to eliminate foreign threats at their frontiers, favored war. Conversely, mercantile New England, a region that had, ironically, prospered as a result of British interference with ocean commerce, opposed the war.

The votes that carried the war declaration came from northern Republicans, who saw the impending struggle as a defense of America's experiment in self-government. Nine-tenths of the congressional Republicans voted for war, but not a single Federalist did so. For the Federalists, the real enemy was France, which had actually seized more U.S. ships than had the British. From their strongholds in coastal New England, the Federalists condemned the war as a French-inspired plot and predicted that it would end in financial ruin.

The Federalists' anger increased when they learned that the British had been prepared to yield on one of the most prominent issues. On June 23, the British government revoked for one year its Orders in Council against the United States. A poor harvest and the ongoing economic pressure exerted by Madison had finally caused hard times in England and produced a policy reversal intended to placate the Americans. This concession, however, did not address impressment or monetary compensation, and news of it reached America too late to avert a war.

The War of 1812

| 9.3 | What were the consequences of the War of 1812? |

The Republicans led the nation into a war that it was unprepared to fight. Still, the apparent vulnerability of Canada to invasion and the British preoccupation with Napoleon in Europe made it possible to envision a U.S. victory.

Setbacks in Canada

The **War of 1812** unleashed deep emotions that often divided along religious lines. From their strongholds in the Congregationalist churches in New England, the Federalists preached that all true Christians opposed a war "against the nation from which we are descended, and which for many generations has been the bulwark of the religion we profess." Such antiwar sentiments, however, outraged the Baptists and Methodists, the largest and most popularly rooted denominations. They believed, as resolved by the Georgia Baptist Association in 1813, that the British government was "corrupt, arbitrary, and despotic" and that the war was "just, necessary, and indispensable."

Fiercely loyal to Madison, who had championed religious freedom in Virginia, these Methodists and Baptists harbored old grudges against the established churches of both Britain and New England for suppressing their religious rights. Especially for the Baptists, the war became something of a crusade to secure civil and religious liberties against their traditional enemies. Madison hoped to channel this Christian anti-British patriotism into the conquest of Canada. Instead, he unleashed what in part was a civil war in which American-born residents on both sides of the border sorted themselves out into Americans and Canadians. Two out of three Canadians were native-born Americans, the result of the exodus of Loyalists during and after the Revolution and more recent migrants attracted by offers of free land. These Canadians, it was assumed, would welcome the U.S. Army with open arms. Only 5,000 British troops were initially stationed in Canada, and Canadian militia were outnumbered nine to one by their U.S. counterparts.

Canada was also the only area where the United States could strike directly against British forces. Although officially a war to defend America's neutrality on the high seas, the War of 1812 was largely a land war. The United States simply did not have enough ships to do more than harass the powerful British navy.

By seizing Canada, Madison also hoped to weaken Britain's navy and undercut its maritime system. Madison had been convinced that withholding U.S. foodstuffs and provisions from the British West Indies would quickly force the British to yield to

War of 1812 War fought between the United States and Britain from June 1812 to January 1815 largely over British restrictions on American shipping.

U.S. economic pressure. But the British had turned to Canada as an alternative source of supplies. Madison hoped to close off that source. And if, as Madison expected, Napoleon denied the British access to the naval stores of the Baltic region in Europe, a U.S. monopoly on Canadian lumber would cripple British naval power. Facing such a threat, the British would have to end the war on U.S. terms.

Madison's strategic vision was clear, but its execution was pathetic. Three offensives against Canada in 1812 were embarrassing failures. Most Canadians, nearly all of whom resented the plundering of U.S. troops, fought against, not with, the Americans. Reliance on state militias proved disastrous. Poorly trained and equipped, the militias, when they did show up for battle, could not match the discipline of British soldiers or the fighting skills of their Native American allies. Nor was U.S. generalship on a par with that of the British. Primitive land communications made the movement and coordination of troops a nightmare. New England, the obvious base for operations against the strategically critical St. Lawrence River Valley—the entry point for all British supplies and reinforcements—withheld many of its state forces from national service. Consequently, the invasions were piecemeal ineffective forays launched from western areas where anti-British and anti-Indian sentiment ran high.

Republican expectations of victory in Canada had been wishful thinking. All the Republicans had to show for the first year of the war were morale-boosting but otherwise insignificant naval victories. In individual combat between ships, the small U.S. Navy acquitted itself superbly. Early in the war, U.S. privateers harassed British merchant vessels, but the easy pickings were soon gone. British naval squadrons were redeployed to protect shipping, and other warships kept up a blockade that stifled U.S. commerce.

Military setbacks and antiwar feeling in much of the Northeast hurt the Republicans in the election of 1812. Madison won only narrowly. Federalists and other disaffected northerners rallied behind DeWitt Clinton, an anti-administration Republican from New York. The now familiar regional pattern in voting repeated itself. Madison swept the electoral vote of the South and West. He ran poorly in the Northeast and won only because his party held on to Pennsylvania.

Western Victories and British Offensives

United States forces fared better in 1813. In September, the navy won a major engagement on Lake Erie that opened up a supply line in the western theater. Commodore Oliver Hazard Perry attacked the British fleet in the **Battle of Put-in-Bay**, on the southwestern shore of the lake, and forced the surrender of all six British ships. The victory signaled General William Henry Harrison to launch an offensive in the West.

Battle of Put-in-Bay American naval victory on Lake Erie in September 1813 in the War of 1812 that denied the British strategic control over the Great Lakes.

With the loss of Lake Erie, the British were forced to abandon Detroit. Harrison caught up with the British garrison and their Indian allies on the banks of the Thames River in southern Ontario. Demonstrating bold leadership and relying on battle-tested western militias, Harrison won a decisive victory. Tecumseh, the most visionary of the Indian warriors, was killed, and the backbone of the Indian resistance was broken. The Old Northwest was again safe for U.S. settlement.

The Battle of the Thames ended British plans for an Indian buffer state. But by 1814, Britain had bigger goals in mind. A coalition of European powers forced Napoleon to abdicate in April 1814, thus freeing Britain to focus on the U.S. war. It now seemed poised to win the war with a clear-cut victory. British strategy in 1814 called for two major offensives—an invasion south from Montreal down Lake Champlain in upstate New York, and an attack on Louisiana aimed at seizing New Orleans with a task force out of Jamaica. Meanwhile, diversionary raids along the mid-Atlantic coast were to pin down U.S. forces and undermine morale. The overall objective was nothing less than a reversal of America's post-1783 expansion.

The British attacks could hardly have come at a worse time for the Madison administration. The Treasury was nearly bankrupt. Against the wishes of Treasury Secretary Gallatin, Congress had refused to preserve the Bank of the United States when its charter expired in 1811. Lacking both a centralized means of directing wartime finances and any significant increase in taxes, the Treasury was forced to rely on makeshift loans. These loans were poorly subscribed, largely because the cash-rich New England banks refused to buy them. Inflation also became a problem when state banks, no longer restrained by the control of a national bank, overissued paper money in the form of bank notes.

As the country's finances tottered toward collapse, political dissent in New England was reaching a climax. In 1814, the British extended their blockade of U.S. commerce northward to include New England. Federalist merchants and shippers, who had earlier profited from their illegal trade with the British, now felt the economic pinch of the war. Cries for resistance against "Mr. Madison's war" culminated in a call issued by the Massachusetts legislature for a convention to consider "a radical reform of the national compact." The convention was scheduled for December in Hartford, Connecticut.

The darkest hour came in August 1814. A British amphibious force occupied and torched Washington, DC, in retaliation for a U.S. raid on York (now Toronto), the capital of Upper Canada. Still, the British actions stiffened U.S. resistance, and the failure of a follow-up attack on Baltimore deprived the British of any strategic gain. Baltimore's defenses held, stirring Francis Scott Key, a young lawyer who viewed the bombardment from a British prisoner-of-war ship, to write "The Star-Spangled Banner." Fittingly in this strange war, the future national anthem was set to the tune of a British drinking song.

The Chesapeake raids were designed to divert U.S. attention from the major offensive General George Prevost was leading down the shores of Lake Champlain. Prevost commanded the largest and best-equipped army the British had yet assembled, but he was forced to turn back when Commodore Thomas McDonough defeated a British fleet on September 11 at the **Battle of Plattsburgh**.

The tide had turned. When news of the setbacks at Baltimore and Plattsburgh reached England, the Foreign Office scaled back the demands it had been making on U.S. negotiators at peace talks in the city of Ghent, in present-day Belgium. The British were ready for peace, but one of their trump cards had yet to be played—the southern offensive against New Orleans. The outcome of that campaign could still upset whatever was decided at Ghent.

Battle of Plattsburgh Victory of Commodore Thomas McDonough over a British fleet in Lake Champlain, September 11, 1814.

The Treaty of Ghent and the Battle of New Orleans

By the fall of 1814, the British were eager to redraw the map of post-Napoleonic Europe, restore profitable relations with America, and reduce their huge war debt. The British negotiators at Ghent agreed to a peace treaty on terms the Americans were delighted to accept. The **Treaty of Ghent**, signed on Christmas Eve, 1814, simply restored relations to their status at the start of the war. No territory changed hands, and nothing was said about impressment or the rights of neutrals. The ink had barely dried on the Treaty of Ghent when the British government sent reinforcements to General Edward Pakenham, the commander of the Louisiana invasion force. By this action, the British indicated that they were not irrevocably committed to the peace settlement, which, though signed, could not be formally ratified until weeks later, when it was sent across the Atlantic. Far from being an anticlimax to a war that was already over, the showdown between British and U.S. forces at the **Battle of New Orleans** in January 1815 had immense strategic significance for the United States.

The hero of New Orleans, in song and legend, was Andrew Jackson. A planter-politician from Tennessee, Jackson rose to prominence during the war as a ferocious

Treaty of Ghent Treaty signed in December 1814 between the United States and Britain that ended the War of 1812.

Battle of New Orleans Decisive American War of 1812 victory over British troops in January 1815 that ended any British hopes of gaining control of the lower Mississippi River Valley.

Indian fighter. As a general in the Tennessee militia, Jackson crushed Indian resistance in the Old Southwest at the Battle of Horseshoe Bend in March 1814. The number of Indians who fought and died in this battle was the largest in the history of American-Indian warfare. Jackson then forced the vanquished Creeks to cede two-thirds of their territory to the United States. On the southern frontier as well as the northern, Native Americans emerged as the major losers of the war.

After his Indian conquests, Jackson was promoted to general in the regular army and given command of the defense of the Gulf Coast. In November 1814, he seized Pensacola in Spanish Florida to deny the British its use as a supply depot and then hurried to defend New Orleans. The overconfident British frontally attacked Jackson's lines on January 8, 1815. The result was a massacre. Artillery fire laid down by French-speaking cannoneers from New Orleans accounted for most of the carnage. More than 2,000 British soldiers were killed or wounded, while U.S. casualties totaled 21.

Strategically, Jackson's smashing victory at New Orleans ended any possibility of a British sphere of influence in Louisiana. Politically, it was a deathblow to Federalism. At the Hartford Convention in December 1814, party moderates had forestalled talk of secession with a series of proposed constitutional amendments designed to limit southern power in national affairs. At the top of their list was a demand for eliminating the three-fifths clause by which slaves were counted for purposes of congressional representation. They also wanted to require a two-thirds majority in Congress for the admission of new states, declarations of war, and the imposition of embargoes. These demands became public as Americans were rejoicing over the Treaty of Ghent and Jackson's rout of the British. Set against the revived nationalism that marked the end of the war, the Federalists now seemed to be parochial sulkers who put regional interests above the national good. Worse yet, they struck many Americans as quasi-traitors who had been prepared to desert the country in the face of the enemy. As a significant political force, Federalism was dead.

Read the Document   Letter from Dolley Payne Madison to Lucy Payne Todd (1814)

Among the troops that Jackson led to victory at the Battle of New Orleans were a contingent of African Americans, the Free Men of Color from New Orleans.

✷ Explore the War of 1812 on MyHistoryLab

WHAT BROUGHT ABOUT THE WAR OF 1812?

By the beginning of the 1800s, the young United States found itself under various pressures. The British had never completely withdrawn its forces from the Northwest Territory. During its ongoing war with Napoleonic France, tensions with Great Britain, the former mother country, grew when the British navy refused to respect the rights of neutral American ships and impressed American sailors at sea deemed to be British citizens into forced military service. Moreover, war with Native Americans seemed imminent after many years of encroachment by the U.S. military and American settlers on Indian lands. By 1812, the United States was at war with the British and Native American groups living in the Southeast and Northwest.

The Native American allies of the British during the War of 1812 received bounties for the scalps of dead American combatants. Cartoons such as these inspired genocidal U.S. government policies in later years.

NATIVE AMERICAN ALLIANCES DURING THE WAR OF 1812

Supplying Warriors against the United States	U.S. Allies
Upper Creeks, Shawnees, Lenapes (Delawares), Miamis, Potawatomis, Ojibwes	Cherokees, Choctaws, Lower Creeks

KEY QUESTIONS   Use **MyHistoryLab** *Explorer* to **answer** these **questions:**

Consequence ▶▶▶ *Where had Native Americans been forced to cede lands?*

Consider how this might affect relations between Native Americans and settlers.

Cause ▶▶▶ *In what areas was support for war with Britain strongest?*

Theorize the reasons for regional differences in the desire for conflict.

Analysis ▶▶▶ *Where were major battles fought, by whom, and with what outcomes?*

Understand the strategies of the various parties in the War of 1812.

Era of Good Feelings The period from 1817 to 1823 in which the disappearance of the Federalists enabled the Republicans to govern in a spirit of seemingly nonpartisan harmony.

Second Bank of the United States A national bank chartered by Congress in 1816 with extensive regulatory powers over currency and credit.

The Era of Good Feelings

9.4 How did rising nationalism contribute to the spirit of the Era of Good Feelings?

I n 1817, on the occasion of a presidential visit by James Monroe, a Boston newspaper proclaimed the **Era of Good Feelings**, an expression that nicely captured the spirit of political harmony and sectional unity that washed over the republic in the immediate postwar years. National pride surged with the humbling of the British at New Orleans, the demise of the Federalists lessened political tensions, and the economy was booming. The Republicans had been vindicated, and for a short time they enjoyed de facto status as the only governing party.

Economic Nationalism

The War of 1812 had taught the Republicans to appreciate the old Federalist doctrines on centralized national power. In his annual message of December 1815, Madison outlined a program of economic nationalism that was pushed through Congress by Henry Clay and John C. Calhoun, the most prominent of the new generation of young, nationalist-minded Republicans.

The first order of business was to create a new national bank. Reliance on state banks for wartime financing had proved a major mistake. The demand for credit was met by a flood of state bank notes that fell in value because there was insufficient gold and silver to back them. Many banks suspended specie payments for their notes, and inflation was a persistent problem. Throughout the war the Treasury could borrow only at high interest rates. Fiscal stability required the monetary coordination and restraint that only a new Bank of the United States could provide. Introduced by Calhoun, the bank bill passed Congress in 1816. Modeled after Hamilton's original bank and also headquartered in Philadelphia, the **Second Bank of the United States** was capitalized at $35 million, making it by far the nation's largest bank. Its size and official status as the depository and dispenser of the government's funds gave the bank tremendous economic power. It also enjoyed the exclusive privilege of being able to establish branches in any state.

After moving to repair the fiscal damage of the war, the Republicans then acted to protect what the war had fostered. Embargoes followed by three years of war had forced U.S. businessmen to manufacture goods they previously had imported. This was especially the case with iron and textile goods long supplied by the British. In 1815 and again in 1816, the British inundated the U.S. market with cheap imports to strangle U.S. industry in its infancy. Responding to this challenge to the nation's economic independence, the Republicans passed the Tariff of 1816, the first protective tariff in U.S. history. The act levied duties of 20 to 25 percent on imported goods that could be produced in the United States.

Congress earmarked revenue from the tariff and $1.5 million from the Bank of the United States (a cash payment in return for its charter) for transportation projects. The lack of a road system in the trans-Appalachian region had severely hampered troop movements during the war. Also, as settlers after the war moved onto lands seized from the pro-British Indians, western congressmen demanded improved outlets to eastern markets.

In early 1817, an internal-improvements bill sponsored by Calhoun passed Congress. Though in agreement with the bill's objectives, President Madison was convinced that the Constitution did not permit federal financing of primarily local projects. He vetoed the bill just before he left office.

Congressional passage of Calhoun's internal-improvements bill marked the pinnacle of the Republicans' economic nationalism. Frightened by the sectional disunity of the war years, a new generation of Republicans jettisoned many of the ideological trappings of Jefferson's original agrarian party. Their program was a call for economic, and therefore political, unity. Support for this program was strongest in the mid-Atlantic and western states, the regions that stood to gain the most economically. Opposition centered in the Southeast, notably among die-hard proponents of states' rights in the old tobacco belt of Virginia and North Carolina and in New England, a region not only well served already by banks and a road network but also anxious not to be politically overshadowed by the rising West. This opposition took on an increasingly hard edge in the South as the Supreme Court outlined an ever more nationalist interpretation of the Constitution.

Judicial Nationalism

Under Chief Justice John Marshall, the Supreme Court had long supported the nationalist perspective Republicans began to champion after the war. Two principles defined Marshall's jurisprudence: the primacy of the Supreme Court in all matters of constitutional interpretation and the sanctity of contractual property rights. In *Fletcher v. Peck* (1810), for example, the Court ruled that a Georgia law voiding a land grant made by an earlier legislature—on the grounds that it had involved massive fraud—violated the constitutional provision barring any state from "impairing the obligation of contracts." Marshall held that despite the fraud, the original land grant constituted an unbreakable legal contract.

Fletcher v. Peck Supreme Court decision of 1810 that overturned a state law by ruling that it violated a legal contract.

Out of the political limelight since the Burr trial in 1807, the Court was thrust back into it by two controversial decisions in 1819. The first involved Dartmouth College and the attempt by the New Hampshire legislature to amend its charter in the direction of greater public control over this private institution. In *Dartmouth College v. Woodward*, the Court ruled that Dartmouth's original royal charter of 1769 was a contract protected by the Constitution. Therefore, the state of New Hampshire could not alter the charter without the prior consent of the college. By sanctifying charters, or acts of incorporation, as contracts, the Court prohibited states from interfering with the rights and privileges they had bestowed on private corporations.

Dartmouth College v. Woodward Supreme Court decision of 1819 that prohibited states from interfering with the privileges granted to a private corporation.

The second important decision in 1819, *McCulloch v. Maryland*, rested on a positive assertion of national power over the states. The case involved the Bank of the United States. In 1818, the Maryland legislature placed a heavy tax on the branch of the Bank of the United States established in Baltimore (and on all other banks in the state established without legislative authority). James McCulloch, the cashier of the Baltimore branch, refused to pay the tax. This set up a test case that involved two fundamental legal issues: Was the bank itself constitutional? And could a state tax federal property within its borders?

McCulloch v. Maryland Supreme Court decision of 1819 that upheld the constitutional authority of Congress to charter a national bank, and thereby to regulate the nation's currency and finances.

A unanimous Court, in language similar to but even more sweeping than that used by Alexander Hamilton in the 1790s, upheld the constitutional authority of Congress to charter a national bank and thereby regulate the nation's currency and finances. As long as the end was legitimate "within the scope of the Constitution," Congress had full power to use any means not expressly forbidden by the Constitution to achieve that end. As for Maryland's claim of a constitutional right to tax a federal agency, Marshall stressed that "the power to tax involves the power to destroy." Surely, he reasoned, when the people of the United States ratified the Constitution, they did not intend the federal government to be controlled by the states or rendered powerless by state action. Here was the boldest statement to date of the loose, or "implied powers," interpretation of the Constitution.

Toward a Continental Empire

Marshall's legal nationalism paralleled the diplomatic nationalism of John Quincy Adams, secretary of state from 1817 to 1825. A former Federalist and the son of the second president, Adams broke with the party over its refusal to support an expansionist policy and held several diplomatic posts under the Madison administration.

Rush-Bagot Agreement Treaty of 1817 between the United States and Britain that effectively demilitarized the Great Lakes by sharply limiting the number of ships each power could station on them.

Anglo-American Accords Series of agreements reached in the British-American Conventions of 1818 that fixed the western boundary between the United States and Canada, allowed for joint occupation of Oregon, and restored American fishing rights.

Trans-Continental Treaty of 1819 Treaty between the United States and Spain in which Spain ceded Florida to the United States, surrendered all claims to the Pacific Northwest, and agreed to a boundary between the Louisiana Purchase territory and the Spanish Southwest.

Monroe Doctrine In December 1823, Monroe declared to Congress that the Americas "are henceforth not to be considered as subjects for future colonization by any European power."

Adams shrewdly exploited Britain's desire for friendly and profitable relations after the War of 1812. The British wanted access to U.S. cotton and foodstuffs in exchange for manufactured goods and investment capital. The United States wanted more trading opportunities in the British Empire and a free hand to deal with Spain's disintegrating empire in the Americas.

The **Rush-Bagot Agreement** of 1817 signaled the new pattern of Anglo-American cooperation. The agreement strictly limited naval armaments on the Great Lakes, thus effectively demilitarizing the border with Canada. The **Anglo-American Accords** of the following year resolved several issues left hanging after the war. The British once again recognized U.S. fishing rights off Labrador and Newfoundland, a concession that was of great importance to New England. The boundary of the Louisiana Territory abutting Canada was set at the 49th parallel, and both nations agreed to the joint occupation of Oregon, the territory in the Pacific Northwest that lay west of the Rocky Mountains.

Having secured the northern flank of the United States, Adams was now free to deal with the South and West. Adams wanted all of Florida and an undisputed American window on the Pacific. The adversary here was Spain. In trying to hold off the tenacious Adams, Spain resorted to delaying tactics. Negotiations remained deadlocked until Andrew Jackson gave Adams the leverage he needed.

In March 1818, Jackson led his troops across the border into Spanish Florida. He destroyed encampments of the Seminole Indians, seized two Spanish forts, and executed two British subjects on the grounds that they were selling arms to the Seminoles for raids on the Alabama-Georgia frontier. Despite later protestations to the contrary, Jackson had probably exceeded his orders. He might well have been censured by the Monroe administration had not Adams supported him, telling Spain that Jackson was defending U.S. interests and warning that he might be unleashed again.

Spain yielded to the U.S. threat in the **Trans-Continental Treaty of 1819**. The United States annexed East Florida, and Spain recognized the prior U.S. seizures of West Florida in 1810 and 1813. Adams secured a U.S. hold on the Pacific Coast by drawing a boundary between the Louisiana Purchase and the Spanish Southwest that ran stepwise up the Sabine, Red, and Arkansas rivers to the Continental Divide and then due west along the 42nd parallel to the Pacific (see Map 9.2). Spain renounced any claim to the Pacific Northwest; the United States in turn renounced its shaky claim to Texas under the Louisiana Purchase and assumed $5 million in Spanish debts to American citizens.

Adams's success in the Spanish negotiations turned on the British refusal to threaten war or assist Spain in the wake of Jackson's high-handed actions in Florida. Spanish possessions and the lives of two British subjects were worth little when weighed against the economic advantages of retaining close trading ties with the United States. Moreover, Britain, like the United States, had a vested interest in developing trade with the newly independent Latin American countries. Recognizing this common interest, George Canning, the British foreign minister, proposed in August 1823 that the United States and Britain issue a joint declaration opposing any European attempt to recolonize South America or to assist Spain in regaining its colonies.

President Monroe rejected the British overture, but only at the insistence of Adams. Canning's offer had a string attached to it: a mutual pledge by the British and Americans not to annex former Spanish territory. But Adams was confident that within a generation, the United States would acquire California, Texas, and perhaps Cuba as well. He wanted to maintain the maximum freedom of action for future U.S. policy and avoid any impression that America was beholden to Britain. He also wanted to cement relations with the new nations of Latin America that he had refused to recognize formally until 1822. Thus originated the most famous diplomatic statement in early American history, the **Monroe Doctrine**.

In his annual message to Congress in December 1823, Monroe declared that the Americas "are henceforth not to be considered as subjects for future colonization

Read the Document   Thomas Jefferson, Response to John Holmes on the Missouri Compromise (1820)

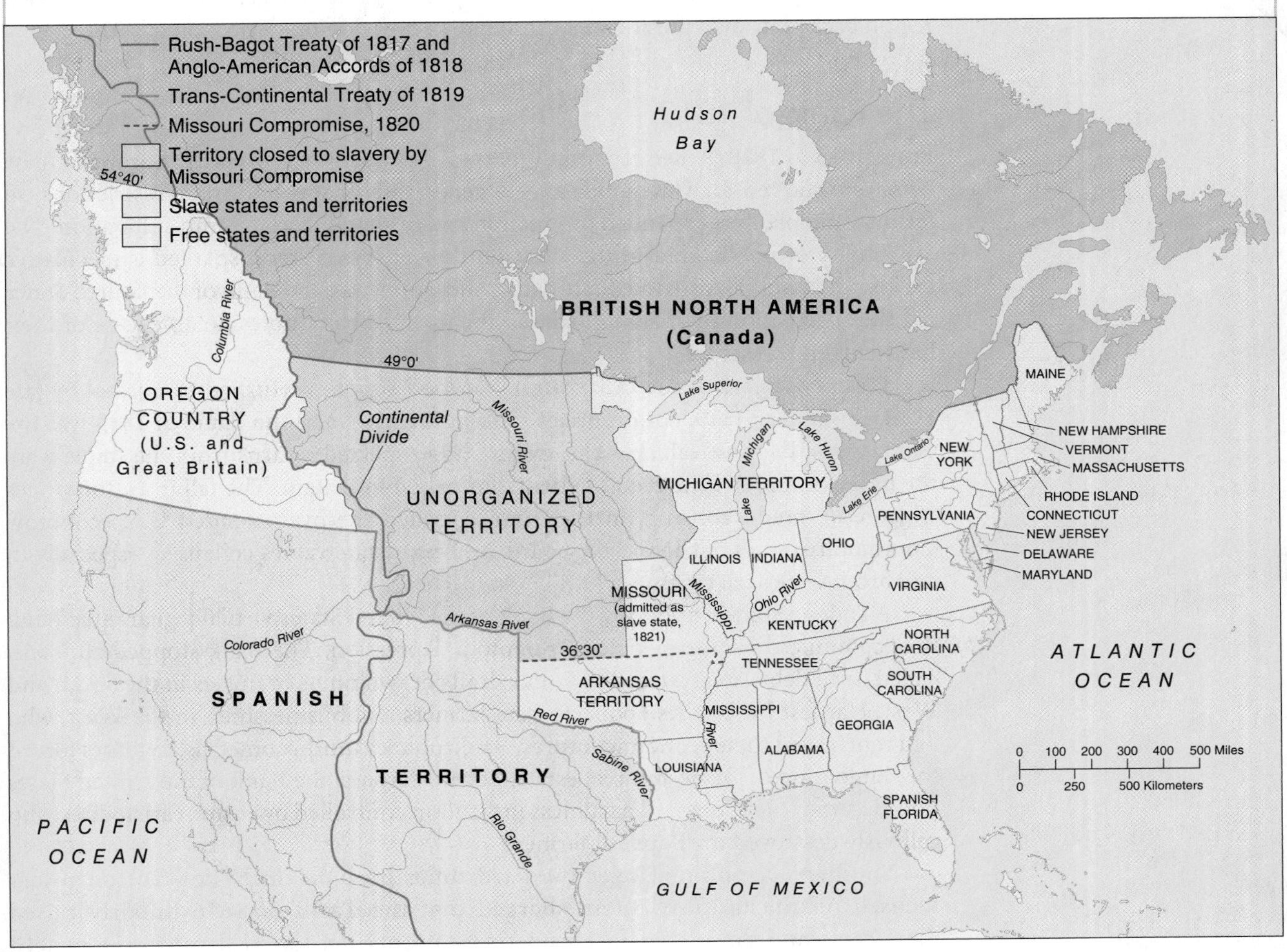

9.1

9.2

9.3

9.4

9.5

MAP 9.2 THE MISSOURI COMPROMISE OF 1820 AND TERRITORIAL TREATIES WITH BRITAIN AND SPAIN, 1818–1819 Treaties with Britain and Spain in 1818 and 1819 clarified and expanded the nation's boundaries. Britain accepted the 49th parallel as the boundary between Canada and the United States in the Trans-Mississippi West and agreed to the joint occupation of the Oregon Country. Spain ceded Florida to the United States and agreed to a boundary stretching to the Pacific between the Louisiana Purchase territory and Spanish possessions in the Southwest. Sectional disputes over slavery led to the drawing of the Missouri Compromise line of 1820 that prohibited slavery in the Louisiana Territory north of 36°30'.

by any European power." In turn, Monroe pledged that the United States would not interfere in the internal affairs of European states. With its continental empire rapidly taking shape and new Latin American republics to be courted, the United States was more than willing to proclaim a special position for itself as the guardian of New World liberties.

The Breakdown of Unity

9.5 Why did slavery become such a divisive issue in the years preceding the Missouri Compromise?

For all the intensity with which he pursued his continental vision, John Quincy Adams worried in early 1819 that "the greatest danger of this union was in the overgrown extent of its territory, combining with the slavery question." His words were prophetic. A sectional crisis flared in 1819 over slavery and its expansion when the territory of Missouri sought admission to the Union as a slave state. Simultaneously, a financial panic ended postwar prosperity and crystallized regional discontent over banking and tariff policies. Party unity cracked under these pressures, and each region backed its own presidential candidate in the wide-open election of 1824.

The Panic of 1819

From 1815 to 1818, Americans enjoyed a wave of postwar prosperity. European markets were starved for U.S. goods after a generation of war and trade restrictions, so farmers and planters expanded production and brought new land into cultivation. The availability of public land in the West on easy terms of credit sparked a speculative frenzy, and land sales soared. State banks and, worse yet, the Bank of the United States fed the speculation by making loans in the form of bank notes far in excess of their hard-currency reserves.

European markets for U.S. cotton and food supplies returned to normal by late 1818. In January 1819, cotton prices sank in England, and the Panic of 1819 was on. Cotton was the most valuable U.S. export, and expected returns from the staple were the basis for an intricate credit network anchored in Britain. The fall in cotton prices triggered a credit contraction that soon engulfed the overextended U.S. economy. Commodity prices fell across the board, and real estate values collapsed, especially in and around western cities.

A sudden shift in policy by the Bank of the United States virtually guaranteed that the economic downturn would settle into a depression. The Bank stopped all loans, called in all debts, and refused to honor drafts drawn on its branches in the South and West. Hardest hit by these policies were farmers and businessmen in the West, who had mortgaged their economic futures. Bankruptcies mushroomed as creditors forced the liquidation of farms and real estate. For westerners, the Bank of the United States now became "the Monster," a ruthless institution controlled by eastern aristocrats who callously destroyed the hopes of farmers.

Southern resentment over the hard times brought on by low cotton prices focused on the tariff. Planters charged that the Tariff of 1816 unfairly raised their costs and amounted to an unconstitutional tax levied for the sole benefit of northern manufacturers. Unreconstructed Jeffersonians, now known as the Old Republicans, spearheaded a sharp reaction against the South's flirtation with nationalist policies in the postwar period by demanding a return to strict states'-rights doctrines.

The Missouri Compromise

Until 1819, slavery was not a major divisive issue in U.S. politics. The Northwest Ordinance of 1787, which banned slavery in federal territories north of the Ohio River, and the Southwest Ordinance of 1790, which permitted slavery south of the Ohio, represented a compromise that had allowed slavery in areas where climate and soil conditions favored slave-based agriculture. What was unforeseen in the 1780s, however, was the explosive demand for slave-produced cotton generated by the English textile industry in the early nineteenth century (see Chapter 11). A thriving cotton market was underwriting slavery's expansion across the South, and even Missouri, a portion of the Louisiana Purchase that northerners initially assumed would be inhospitable to slavery, fell under the political control of slaveholders.

The Missouri issue increased long-simmering northern resentment over the spread of slavery and the southern dominance of national affairs under the Virginia presidents. In February 1819, James Tallmadge, a Republican congressman from New York, introduced an amendment in the House mandating a ban on future slave imports and a program of gradual emancipation as preconditions for the admission of Missouri as a state. Without a two-party system in which each party had to compromise to protect its interests, voting followed sectional lines. The amendment passed in the northern-controlled House, but it was repeatedly blocked in the Senate, which was evenly divided between free and slave states. The debates were heated, and southerners spoke openly of secession if Missouri were denied admission as a slave state.

The stalemate over Missouri persisted into the next session of Congress. Finally, Speaker of the House Henry Clay engineered a compromise in March 1820. Congress put no restrictions on slavery in Missouri, and the admission of Missouri as a slave state was balanced by the admission of Maine (formerly part of Massachusetts) as a free state. In return for their concession on Missouri, northern congressmen demanded a prohibition on slavery in the remainder of the Louisiana Purchase north of the 36° 30' parallel, the southern boundary of Missouri (see Map 9.2). With the **Missouri Compromise**, the Louisiana Purchase was closed to slavery in the future, except for the Arkansas Territory and what would become the Indian Territory of Oklahoma.

The compromise almost unraveled the following November when Missouri submitted a constitution that required the state legislature to bar the entry of free black people. Missouri's restrictionist policy obviously denied African American citizens the constitutional right to move from one state to any other state. The nearly universal acceptance by white Americans of second-class citizenship for free black Americans permitted Clay to dodge the issue. Missouri's constitution was accepted with the proviso that it "shall never be construed" to discriminate against citizens in other states. With these meaningless words, the Missouri Compromise was salvaged. By sacrificing the claims of free black citizens for equal treatment, the Union survived its first great sectional crisis over slavery.

The Missouri crisis made white southerners aware that they were now a political minority within the Union. More rapid population growth in the North had reduced southern representation in the House to just over 40 percent. Of greater concern was the crystallization in Congress of a northern majority array against the expansion of slavery. Southern threats of secession died out in the aftermath of the Missouri Compromise, but it was an open question whether the sectional settlement really solved the intertwined issues of slavery and expansion or merely sidestepped them for a day of final reckoning.

Missouri Compromise Sectional compromise in Congress in 1820 that admitted Missouri to the Union as a slave state and Maine as a free state and prohibited slavery in the northern Louisiana Purchase territory.

The Election of 1824

The election of 1820 made Monroe, like both his Republican predecessors, a two-term president. The Federalists were too weak to run a candidate, and although Monroe won all but one of the electoral votes, Republican unity was more apparent than real. Voters had no choice in 1820, and without two-party competition, no outlets existed for expressing popular dissatisfaction with the Republicans. Instead, the Republicans split into factions as they began jockeying almost immediately for the election of 1824 (see Map 9.3).

Monroe had no obvious successor, and five candidates competed to replace him. All of them were nominal Republicans, and three were members of his cabinet. Secretary of War John C. Calhoun soon dropped out. He preferred to accept a nomination as vice president, confident that his turn would come in 1828. The other candidates, Secretary of the Treasury William Crawford from Georgia, Secretary of State John Quincy Adams from Massachusetts, Henry Clay from Kentucky, and Andrew Jackson from Tennessee, each had a strong regional following. As the Republican Party fragmented, sectional loyalties were replacing partisan allegiances.

None of the candidates ran on a platform, but Crawford was identified with states' rights, and Clay and Adams with centralized government. Clay in particular was associated with the national bank, protective tariffs, and federally funded internal improvements, a package of federal subsidies he called the **American System**. Jackson took no stand on any of the issues.

American System The program of government subsidies favored by Henry Clay and his followers to promote American economic growth and protect domestic manufacturers from foreign competition.

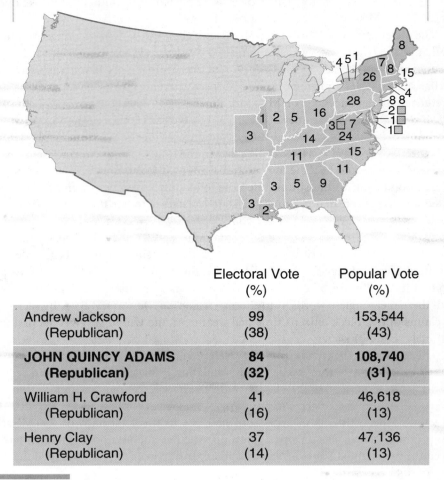

Read the Document John Quincy Adams, A Corrupt Bargain? from the *Memoirs of John Quincy Adams* (1824)

	Electoral Vote (%)	Popular Vote (%)
Andrew Jackson (Republican)	99 (38)	153,544 (43)
JOHN QUINCY ADAMS (Republican)	**84 (32)**	**108,740 (31)**
William H. Crawford (Republican)	41 (16)	46,618 (13)
Henry Clay (Republican)	37 (14)	47,136 (13)

MAP 9.3 THE ELECTION OF 1824 The regional appeal of each of the four presidential candidates in the election of 1824 prevented any candidate from receiving a majority of the electoral votes. Consequently, and as set forth in the Constitution, the House of Representatives now had to choose the president from the three leading candidates. Its choice was John Quincy Adams.

Jackson's noncommittal stance turned out to be a great asset. It helped him to project the image of a military hero, fresh from the people, who was unsullied by any connection with Washington politicians, whom the public associated with hard times and sectional controversies. He was the highest vote-getter (43 percent of the popular vote), but none of the four candidates had a majority in the electoral college.

As in 1800, the election was thrown into the House of Representatives. Each state had one vote. Clay, who had received the fewest electoral votes, was eliminated. Crawford had suffered a debilitating stroke and was no longer a viable candidate. Thus it came down to Adams or Jackson. Anxious to undercut Jackson, his chief rival in the West, Clay used his influence as speaker of the House to line up support for Adams, a fellow advocate of a strong centralized government. Adams won the election, and he immediately named Clay as his secretary of state, the office traditionally viewed as a stepping-stone to the presidency. Jackson and his followers were outraged. They smelled a "corrupt bargain" in which Clay had bargained away the presidency to the highest bidder. Vowing revenge, they began building a new party that would usher in a more democratic era of mass-based politics.

Conclusion

In 1800, the Republicans were an untested party whose rise to power frightened many Federalists into predicting the end of the Union and constitutional government. The Federalists were correct in sensing that their days of power had passed, but they underestimated the ideological flexibility the Republicans would reveal once in office and the imaginative ways in which Jefferson and his successors would wield executive power to expand the size of the original Union. Far from being anarchists and demagogues, the Republicans were shrewd empire builders astute enough to add to their base of political support in the South and West. They also paved the way for the nation to evolve as a democratic republic rather than the more aristocratic republic preferred by the Federalists and Rosalie Calvert and her family.

Although foreign-policy issues leading up to the War of 1812 kept the Federalists alive and even briefly revived the party, Jackson's victory at the Battle of New Orleans ended the war in a burst of U.S. glory, and the Federalists were swept aside by the postwar surge of nationalism. With no Federalist threat to enforce party discipline, the Republicans lost their organizational strength. Embracing economic nationalism after the war made the party's original focus on states' rights all but meaningless. Ideologically and organizationally adrift, the party split into regional coalitions in the wake of the Missouri controversy and the panic of 1819. But before it dissolved, the party left as its most enduring legacy the foundations of a continental empire.

For Suggested Readings go to MyHistoryLab.

Chapter Review

Jefferson's Presidency

9.1 Why was the expansion of the United States so important to Jefferson? p. 226

Jefferson believed that political independence in a republican form of government depended on a property-holding citizenry, especially farmers who owned their own land. Without an increasing supply of land acquired through expansion, he feared that Americans would become wage laborers dependent on others for their livelihood and incapable of independent political decisions.

Madison and the Coming of War

9.2 What factors pushed Madison into a war with Britain? p. 232

Madison was faced with a Britain that refused to respect the independence and sovereignty of the United States. British policies of restricting U.S. global trade, impressing American sailors, and relying on Native Americans as allies to check American expansion stirred up popular resentments against the British and led to calls for a second war of independence.

The War of 1812

9.3 What were the consequences of the War of 1812? p. 235

The War of 1812 smashed the power of Native Americans in the Old Northwest and strengthened nationalist feelings on both sides of the newly solidified boundary across the Great Lakes between British Canada and the United States. The war also convinced both the British and the Americans of the need each had of the other as a vital trading partner.

The Era of Good Feelings

9.4 How did rising nationalism contribute to the spirit of the Era of Good Feelings? p. 240

Jackson's victory at the Battle of New Orleans eliminated the pro-British Federalists as a major political power. As the economy boomed until 1819 in a period of political and sectional harmony, improved relations with the British made possible a more aggressive foreign policy that soon made the United States a transcontinental power.

The Breakdown of Unity

9.5 Why did slavery become such a divisive issue in the years preceding the Missouri Compromise? p. 243

The steady expansion of slavery in the early nineteenth century put an end to earlier hopes in the North that slavery would gradually wither and die. Northerners also grew increasingly frustrated over southern dominance of the federal government through the administrations of slaveholding presidents. Once Missouri, part of the Louisiana Purchase, seemed poised to enter the Union as another slaveholding state, northern congressmen decided to take a stand against the extension of slavery.

Timeline

1801
Jefferson's Presidency—Thomas Jefferson is inaugurated, the first Republican president
`1801`

`1803`
1803
Jefferson's Presidency—Louisiana Purchase

1807
Jefferson's Presidency—Congress passes the Embargo Act
`1807`

`1810`
1810
Madison and the Coming of War—Macon's Bill No. 2 reopens trade with Britain and France

1812
The War of 1812—Congress declares war on Britain
`1812`

`1815`
1815
The War of 1812—Jackson routs British at the Battle of New Orleans

1818
The Era of Good Feelings—Anglo-American Accords on trade and boundaries
`1818`

`1819`
1819
The Era of Good Feelings—Trans-Continental Treaty between United States and Spain

1819
The Breakdown of Unity—Financial panic sends economy into a depression
`1819`

`1820`
1820
The Breakdown of Unity—Missouri Compromise on slavery in the Louisiana Purchase

1823
The Breakdown of Unity—Monroe Doctrine proclaims Western Hemisphere closed to further European colonization
`1823`

10 The Jacksonian Era 1824–1845

One American Journey

Journal Entry on the Political Excitement in 1828

September, 1828
Newport, New Hampshire

Wherever a person may chance to be in company, he will hear nothing but politicks discussed. In the ballroom, or at the dinner table, in the Stagecoach & in the tavern; even the social chitchat of the tea table must yield up to the everlasting subject.

How many friendships are broken up! With what rancor the political war is carried on between the editorial corps! To what meanness[,] vulgarity & abuse is that champion of liberty, in proper hands, the press prostituted! With what lies and scandal does the columns of almost every political paper abound! I blush for my country when I see such things, & I often tremble with apprehension that our Constitution will not long withstand the current which threatens to overwhelm it. Our government is so based that an honest difference between American citizens must always exist. But the rancorous excitement which now threatens our civil liberties and a dissolution of this Union does not emanate from an honest difference of opinion, but from a determination of an unholy

LEARNING OBJECTIVES

10.1	10.2	10.3	10.4	10.5
What factors contributed to the democratization of American politics and religion in the early nineteenth century? p. 251	How did the Jacksonian Democrats capitalize on the new mass politics? p. 257	What challenges did Van Buren face during his presidency? p. 265	What was the basis of Whig popularity and what did they claim to stand for? p. 270	Why was William Henry Harrison's death such a blow to the Whig agenda? p. 274

This painting of an election scene in a small Midwestern town in the mid-nineteenth century depicts the rituals of voting as a collective community, bringing together white males across class lines.

((· Listen to Chapter 10 on MyHistoryLab

Watch the Video Series on MyHistoryLab

Learn about some key topics related to this chapter with the *MyHistoryLab Video Series: Key Topics in U.S. History.*

1 **A Democracy Grows: 1819–1832** The Age of Andrew Jackson was an era of expanding American democracy. This video profiles Jackson and assesses the accomplishments of his presidency, as well as the controversies that still cause debate, including his policy of removing Native Americans from their lands without just compensation and his attempts to break the power of the National Bank.

 Watch on **MyHistoryLab**

The Frontier President: Andrew Jackson This video discusses the path taken by Andrew Jackson from his early childhood to winning the presidency of the United States. Jackson represented the popular image of "everyman" to his contemporaries. However, the real Jackson did not fit the benign, backwoods "Old Hickory" image that Americans still have of him. **2**

Watch on **MyHistoryLab**

3 **The Indian Removal Act** Andrew Jackson's controversial order to remove Native American tribes from east of the Mississippi River to the Oklahoma Territory is still seen as one of the cruelest events in American history and a forerunner of such practices as ethnic cleansing. This video assesses Jackson's Indian Removal Act in the light of his times and its legacy today, especially for its primary victims, the Native American nations that comprised the "Five Civilized Tribes."

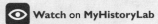 **Watch** on **MyHistoryLab**

"Monster Bank!" This video looks at Andrew Jackson's attempt to prevent the rechartering of the Second Bank of the United States and to dismantle an institution which he believed served the interests of an economic elite. The Bank War remains one of the defining moments of Jackson's tenure in office and contributed to his reputation as a representative of the common man. **4**

Watch on **MyHistoryLab**

league to trample down an Administration, be it ever so pure, & be its acts ever so just. It must not be. There is a kind Providence that overlooks the destinies of this Nation and will not suffer it to be overthrown by a party of aspiring office seekers & political demagogues.

Benjamin B. French

Donald B. Cole and John J. McDonough, eds., *Witness to the Young Republic: A Yankee's Journal, 1828–1870.* © 1988 University Press of New England, Lebanon, NH. Reprinted with permission, pages 15–16.

Personal Journeys Online

- Alexis de Tocqueville, *Travel account,* 1835. A Frenchman gives his impressions of American democracy.

- Michael Chevalier, *Travel account,* 1831. A Frenchman describes the spectacle of electoral politics.

Benjamin Brown French, a young editor and county clerk in Newport, New Hampshire, penned these words in his journal in September 1828. Like most other Americans, he was amazed, indeed shocked, by the intense, seemingly all-pervasive partisanship stirred up in the presidential election of 1828 between Andrew Jackson and John Quincy Adams. Whether measured by the vulgar personal attacks launched by a partisan press, the amount of whiskey and beef consumed at political barbecues, or the huge increase in voter turnout, this election marked the entrance of ordinary Americans onto the political stage.

The sense of shock soon wore off for French. The son of a wealthy Federalist lawyer with whom he was always at odds, French broke with his father at the age of 25, when he married without his permission. With no income, job, or family support, he now began to make a business out of law, politics, and journalism. In so doing he was part of the first generation of professional politicians, young men who compensated for their lack of social connections and family wealth by turning to politics. The partisanship that French found so disturbing in 1828 quickly became the basis of his livelihood. After rejecting his father's politics by joining the Democrats in 1831, he spent most of his subsequent years as a political officeholder in Washington, holding a variety of appointive jobs until his death in 1870.

What made French's career possible was the ongoing democratization of U.S. politics in the early decades of the nineteenth century. The number and potential power of the voters expanded, and professional politicians realized that party success now depended on reaching and organizing this enlarged electorate. Men like French, working for the party, could help them do this. The Jacksonian Democrats, named for their leader, Andrew Jackson, were the first party to learn this fundamental lesson. Trumpeting Andrew Jackson as the friend of the common man and the foe of aristocratic privilege, they won a landslide victory in 1828 and held national power through the 1830s. The Jacksonians promised to protect farmers and workers from the monied elite, whom they portrayed as the enemies of equality and the corruptors of public morality.

The Egalitarian Impulse

10.1 What factors contributed to the democratization of American politics and religion in the early nineteenth century?

Demands for democratic reform were heard on both sides of the Atlantic after 1815. Sparked by the egalitarian promise of the French Revolution and the social changes unleashed by a spreading industrial revolution, these demands in Europe were held at bay by entrenched monarchical orders that were buttressed by the legal privileges of the landed aristocracies. Only in the United States did the egalitarian impulse make significant gains.

Political democracy, defined as the majority rule of white males, was far from complete in early nineteenth-century America. Acting on the belief that only property owners with a stake in society should have a voice in governing it, the landed and commercial elites of the Revolutionary era erected legal barriers against the full expression of majority sentiments. These barriers, property requirements for voting and office-holding, the prevalence of appointed over elected offices, and the overrepresentation of older and wealthier regions in state legislatures, came under increasing attack after 1800 and were all but eliminated by the 1820s.

As politics opened to mass participation, popular styles of religious leadership and worship emerged in a broad reaction to the formalism and elitism of the dominant Protestant churches. The same egalitarian impulse drove these twin democratic revolutions, and both represented an empowerment of the common man. Popular movements now spoke his language and appealed to his quest for republican equality. (Women would have to wait longer.)

The Extension of White Male Democracy

In 1789, Congress set the pay of representatives and senators at $6 a day plus travel expenses. By 1816, inflation had so eroded this salary that many government clerks

((◄ 📖 **Read** the Document   Alexis de Tocqueville, *Democracy in America* (1835–1840)

Alexis de Tocqueville, a French aristocrat with republican sensibilities, wrote a penetrating account of Jacksonian society and its democratic institutions after visiting the United States in the early 1830s.

earned more than members of Congress. Thus Congress thought itself prudent and justified when it voted itself a hefty raise to $1,500 a year. The public thought otherwise.

So sharp was the reaction against the Salary Act of 1816 that 70 percent of the members of Congress were turned out of office at the next election. Chastised congressmen quickly repealed the salary increase. As Richard M. Johnson of Kentucky noted, "The presumption is, that the people are always right."

The uproar over the Salary Act marked a turning point in the transition from the deferential politics of the Federalist-Republican period to the egalitarianism of the coming Jacksonian era. The public would no longer passively accept decisions handed down by local elites or established national figures. Individual states, not the federal government, defined who could vote. Six states, Indiana, Mississippi, Illinois, Alabama, Missouri, and Maine, entered the Union between 1816 and 1821, and none of them required voters to own property. Meanwhile, proponents of suffrage liberalization won major victories in the older states. Constitutional conventions in Connecticut in 1818 and Massachusetts and New York in 1821 eliminated property requirements for voting. By the end of the 1820s, near universal white male suffrage was the norm everywhere except Rhode Island, Virginia, and Louisiana.

Extending the Suffrage and Democratic Reform. Broadening the suffrage was part of a general democratization of political structures and procedures in the state governments. Most significant for national politics, voters acquired the power to choose presidential electors. In 1800, only two states had provided for a statewide popular vote in presidential elections. By 1824, most did so, and by 1832 only South Carolina still clung to the practice of having the state legislature choose the electors.

Several currents swelled the movement for democratic reform. Limiting voting rights to those who owned landed property seemed increasingly elitist when economic changes were producing new classes—workers, clerks, and small tradesmen—whose livelihoods were not tied directly to the land. Renters, more than 77 percent of the voters in New York City by 1814, joined homeowners in an expanded electorate. The middling and lower ranks of society demanded the ballot and access to offices to protect themselves from the commercial and manufacturing interests that benefited most from economic change.

Of greatest importance, however, was the incessant demand that all white men be treated equally. The logical extension of the ideology of the American Revolution, with its leveling attacks against kings and aristocrats, this demand for equality made republicanism by the 1820s synonymous with simple majority rule. If any white male was the equal of any other, regardless of wealth or property holdings, then only the will of the majority could be the measure of a republican government.

The Disfranchisement of Free Blacks and Women. As political opportunities expanded for white males, they shrank for women and free black people. In the state constitutions of the Revolutionary era, free black males who met the minimum property requirements usually had the same voting rights as white males. New Jersey's constitution of 1776 was exceptional in also granting the suffrage to single women and widows who owned property. By the early 1800s, race and gender began to replace wealth and status as the basis for defining the limits of political participation. Thus, in 1807, New Jersey's new constitution broadened suffrage by requiring only a simple taxpaying qualification to vote, but it also denied the ballot to women and free black men. In state after state, the same constitutional conventions that embraced universal suffrage for white men deprived black men of the vote or burdened them with special property qualifications. Moreover, none of the ten states that entered the Union from 1821 to 1861 allowed black suffrage. African Americans protested in vain. "Foreigners and aliens to the government and laws," complained black New Yorkers in 1837, "strangers to our institutions, are permitted to flock to this land and in a few years are endowed with all the privileges of citizens; but we native born Americans . . . are most of us shut out." By the 1850s, black males could vote only in certain New England states.

Advocates of greater democratization explicitly argued that only white males had the intelligence and love of liberty to be entrusted with political rights. Women, they said, were too weak and emotional, black people too lazy and lascivious. In denouncing distinctions drawn on property as artificial and demeaning, the white egalitarians simultaneously erected new distinctions based on race and sex that were supposedly natural and hence immutable. Thus personal liberties were now to be guarded not by propertied gentlemen but by all white men, whose equality ultimately rested on assumptions of their shared natural superiority over women and nonwhite people.

Second Great Awakening Series of religious revivals in the first half of the nineteenth century characterized by great emotionalism in large public meetings.

The Popular Religious Revolt

In religion as well as politics, ordinary Americans demanded a greater voice in the early nineteenth century. Insurgent religious movements rejected the formalism and traditional Calvinism of the Congregational and Presbyterian churches, the dominant Protestant denominations in Washington's America. In a blaze of fervor known as the **Second Great Awakening** (recalling the Great Awakening of colonial America), evangelical sects led by the Methodists and Baptists radically transformed the religious landscape between 1800 and 1840. A more popularly rooted Christianity moved outward and downward as it spread across frontier areas and converted marginalized and common folk. By 1850, one in three Americans was a regular churchgoer, a dramatic increase since 1800.

The Baptists and Methodists, both spinning off numerous splinter groups, grew spectacularly and were the largest religious denominations by the 1820s. The key to their success was their ability to give religious expression to the popular impulse behind democratic reform. Especially in the backcountry of the South and West, where the first revivals occurred, itinerant preachers reshaped religion to fit the needs and values of ordinary Americans.

The evangelical religion of the traveling preachers was democratic in its populist rejection of traditional religious canons and its encouragement of organizational forms that gave a voice to popular culture. Salvation was no longer simply bestowed by an implacable God, as taught by the Calvinist doctrine of individual predestination (see Chapter 1). Ordinary people could now actively choose salvation, and this possibility was exhilarating.

📖 Read the Document   Charles Finney, "What a Revival of Religion Is" (1835)

The Second Great Awakening originated on the frontier. Preachers were adept at arousing emotional fervor, and women in particular responded to the evangelical message of spiritual equality open to all who would accept Christ into their lives.

Evangelicalism and Minority Rights.   Evangelicalism was a religion of the common people, and it appealed especially to women and African Americans. The revivals converted about twice as many women as men. Excluded from most areas of public life, women found strength and comfort in the evangelical message of Christian love and equality. As the wife of a Connecticut minister explained, church membership offered women a welcome release from "being treated like beasts of burden [and] drudges of domineering masters." In the first flush of evangelical excitement, female itinerant preachers spread the gospel up and down the East Coast. By thus defying social convention, these women offered a model of independent action. Other women organized their own institutions within denominations still formally controlled by men. Women activists founded and largely directed hundreds of church-affiliated charitable societies and missionary associations.

Evangelicalism also empowered black Americans. African American Christianity experienced its first sustained growth in the generation after the Revolutionary War. As a result of their uncompromising commitment to convert slaves, the Baptists and Methodists led the way. They welcomed slaves at their revivals, encouraged black preachers, and above all else, advocated secular and spiritual equality. Many of the early Baptist and Methodist preachers directly challenged slavery. In converting to Methodism, one slave stated that "from the sermon I heard, I felt that God had made all men free and equal, and that I ought not be a slave." Perceiving in it the promise of liberty and deliverance, the slaves received the evangelical gospel in loud, joyous, and highly emotional revivals. They made it part of their own culture, fusing Christianity with folk beliefs from their African heritage.

The Limits of Equality. But for all its liberating appeal to women and African Americans, evangelicalism was eventually limited by race and gender in much the same way as the democratic reform movement. Denied positions of authority in white-dominated churches and resentful of white opposition to integrated worship, free black northerners founded their own independent churches.

As increasing numbers of planters embraced evangelicalism after the 1820s, southern evangelicals first muted their attacks on slavery and then developed a full-blown religious defense of it based on the biblical sanctioning of human bondage. They similarly cited the Old Testament patriarchs to defend the unquestioned authority of fathers over their households, the masters of slaves, women, and children. Whether in religion or politics, white men retained the power in Jacksonian America. Still, the Second Great Awakening removed a major intellectual barrier to political democracy. Traditional Protestant theology, whether Calvinist, Anglican, or Lutheran, viewed the mass of humanity as sinners predestined to damnation and hence was loath to accept the idea that those same sinners, by majority vote, should make crucial political decisions. In rejecting this theology, ordinary Americans made a fundamental intellectual breakthrough. "Salvation open to all" powerfully reinforced the legitimacy of "one man, one vote."

The Rise of the Jacksonians

The Jacksonian Democrats were the first party to mold and organize the democratizing impulse in popular culture. At the core of the Jacksonian appeal was the same rejection of established authority that marked the secular and religious populists. Much like the revivalists and the democratic reformers, the Jacksonians fashioned communications techniques that tapped into the hopes and fears of ordinary Americans. In so doing, they built the first mass-based party in U.S. history.

In Andrew Jackson the new **Democratic Party** that formed between 1824 and 1828 had the perfect candidate for the increasingly democratic temperament of the 1820s. Born of Scots-Irish ancestry on the Carolina frontier in 1767, Jackson was a self-made product of the southern backcountry. Lacking any formal education, family connections, or inherited wealth to ease his way, he relied on his own wits and raw courage to

Democratic Party Political party formed in the 1820s under the leadership of Andrew Jackson; favored states' rights and a limited role for the federal government, especially in economic affairs.

carve out a career as a frontier lawyer and planter in Tennessee. He won fame as the military savior of the republic with his victory at the Battle of New Orleans. Conqueror of the British, the Spanish, and the Indians, all of whom had blocked frontier expansion, he achieved incredible popularity in his native South. His strengths and prejudices were those most valued by the restless, mobile Americans to whom he became a folk hero.

As a presidential candidate, Jackson's image was that of the anti-elitist champion of the people. Jackson lost the election of 1824, but his defeat turned out to be a blessing in disguise. The wheeling and dealing in Congress that gave the presidency to John Quincy Adams enveloped his administration in a cloud of suspicion from the start. It also enhanced Jackson's appeal as the honest tribune of the people whose rightful claim to the presidency had been spurned by intriguing politicians in Washington by the "corrupt bargain" between Adams and Clay (see page 246). Moreover, the ill-fated Adams presidency virtually destroyed itself. Adams seemed frozen in an eighteenth-century past. Uncomfortable with the give and take of politics or the idea of building a coalition to support himself, Adams was out of touch with the political realities of the 1820s.

Just how out of touch was revealed when Adams delivered his first annual message to Congress in 1825. He presented a bold vision of an activist federal government promoting economic growth, social advancement, and scientific progress. Such a vision might have received a fair hearing in 1815, when postwar nationalism was in

📖 **Read the Document**   Andrew Jackson, The "Commoner" Takes Office (1829)

To the opponents of the Jacksonians, elections had become a degrading spectacle in which conniving Democratic politicians, such as the one shown above handing a voting ticket to the stereotypical Irishman in the light coat, were corrupting the republic's political culture.

full stride. By 1825, postwar nationalism had dissolved into sectional bickering and burning resentments against banks, tariffs, and the political establishment, which were blamed for the hard times after the Panic of 1819.

Little of Adams's program passed Congress, and his nationalist vision drove his opponents into the Jackson camp. Southern planters jumped onto the Jackson bandwagon out of fear that Adams might use federal power against slavery; westerners joined because Adams revived their suspicions of the East. The most important addition came from New York, where Martin Van Buren had built the **Albany Regency**, a tightly disciplined state political machine.

Albany Regency Popular name after 1820 for the state political machine in New York headed by Martin Van Buren.

Van Buren belonged to a new breed of professional politicians. The son of a tavern keeper, he quickly grasped, as a young lawyer, how politics could open up career opportunities. The discipline and regularity of strict party organization gave him and others from the middling ranks a winning edge in competition against their social betters. In battling against the system of family-centered wealth and prestige on which politics had previously been based, Van Buren redefined parties as something good in and of themselves. Indeed, he and his followers argued that parties were indispensable instruments for the successful expression of the popular will against the dominance of elites.

State leaders such as Van Buren organized the first national campaign that relied extensively on new techniques of mass mobilization. In rallying support for Jackson against Adams in 1828, these state leaders put together chains of party-subsidized newspapers and coordinated a frantic schedule of meetings and rallies. Grassroots Jackson committees reached out to voters by knocking on their doors, pressing party literature into their hands, dispensing mass-produced medals and buttons with a likeness of Jackson, and lavishly entertaining all who would give them a hearing. Politics became a folk spectacle as torchlight parades awakened sleepy towns and political barbecues doled out whiskey and food to farmers from the surrounding countryside.

The election of 1828 centered on personalities, not issues. This in itself was a victory for Jackson's campaign managers, who proved far more skillful in the new presidential game of image making than did their Adams counterparts, now known as the National Republicans.

Jackson carried every state south and west of Pennsylvania in 1828 and polled 56 percent of the popular vote. Voter turnout shot up to 55 percent from the apathetic 25 percent of 1824. Adams ran well only in New England and in commercialized areas producing goods for outside markets. Aside from the South, where he was virtually untouchable, Jackson's appeal was strongest among ordinary Americans who valued their local independence and felt threatened by outside centers of power beyond their control. He rolled up heavy majorities from Scots-Irish farmers in the Baptist-Methodist evangelical belt of the backcountry and from unskilled workers with an Irish Catholic background. To these voters, Jackson was a double hero, for he had defeated their hated British enemy and promised to do the same to the Yankee capitalists of the Northeast and all the elitist politicians. Democracy, they were convinced, had at last come to presidential politics.

Jackson's Presidency

10.2 How did the Jacksonian Democrats capitalize on the new mass politics?

Once in office, Jackson proved to be the most forceful and energetic president since Jefferson. Like a military chieftain tolerating no interference from his subordinates, Jackson dominated his presidency with the sheer force of his personality.

The Jacksonians had no particular program in 1828. Apart from removing Indians to areas west of the Mississippi River, Jackson's first term was notable primarily for its political infighting. Two political struggles that came to a head in 1832–1833, the Bank War and the nullification crisis, stamped the Jacksonians with a lasting party identity.

Jackson's Appeal

Although they were led by wealthy planters and entrepreneurs—hardly average Americans—the Jacksonians skillfully depicted themselves as the champions of the common man against aristocratic interests that had enriched themselves through special privileges granted by the government. Jackson proclaimed his task as one of restoring the federal government to the ideal of Jeffersonian republicanism, in which farmers and artisans could pursue their individual liberty free of any government intervention that favored the rich and powerful.

Jackson began his assault on special privilege by proclaiming a reform of the appointment process for federal officeholders. Accusing his predecessors, especially

((• 📖 **Read** the Document   **Andrew Jackson, First Annual Message to Congress (1829)**

This bust portrait of Jackson in uniform, issued as print during the 1832 presidential race, invokes his military image and especially his victory at New Orleans in 1815.

Adams, of having created a social elite of self-serving bureaucrats, he vowed to make government service more responsive to the popular will. He insisted that federal jobs required no special expertise or training and proposed to rotate honest, hard-working citizens in and out of the civil service.

Jackson's reform of the federal bureaucracy had more style than substance. He removed only about one-fifth of the officeholders he inherited, and most of his appointees came from the same relatively high-status groups as the Adams people. But by providing a democratic rationale for government service, he opened the way for future presidents to move more aggressively against incumbents. Thus emerged the **spoils system**, in which the victorious party gave government jobs to its supporters and removed the appointees of the defeated party. This parceling out of jobs was a powerful technique for building party strength, because it tied party loyalty to the reward of a federal appointment.

10.1

10.2

10.3

10.4

10.5

spoils system The awarding of government jobs to party loyalists.

When Jackson railed against economic privilege, he most often had in mind Henry Clay's American System (see Chapter 9). Clay's program called for a protective tariff, a national bank, and federal subsidies for internal improvements; his goal was to bind Americans together in an integrated national market. To the Democrats, Clay's system represented government favoritism at its worst, a set of costly benefits at the public's expense for special-interest groups that corrupted politicians in their quest for economic power. In 1830, Jackson struck a blow for the Democratic conception of the limited federal role in economic development. He vetoed the Maysville Road Bill, which would have provided federal money for a road to be built entirely within Kentucky, Clay's home state. The bill was unconstitutional, he claimed, because it benefited only the citizens of Kentucky and not the U.S. people as a whole.

On the issue of internal improvements, as with bureaucratic reform, the Democrats placed party needs ahead of ideology. Jackson's Maysville veto did not rule out congressional appropriations for projects deemed beneficial to the general public. This pragmatic loophole gave Democrats all the room they needed to pass more internal-improvement projects during Jackson's presidency than during all of the previous administrations together. Having built a mass party, the Democrats soon discovered that they had to funnel federal funds to their constituents back home.

The Democrats also responded to the demand for Indian removal that came out of their strongholds in the South and West. By driving Native Americans from these regions, Jackson more than lived up to his billing as the friend of the common (white) man.

Indian Removal

Some 125,000 Indians lived east of the Mississippi when Jackson became president. The largest concentration was in the South, where five Indian nations, the Cherokees, Creeks, Choctaws, Chickasaws, and Seminoles, controlled millions of acres of land in what soon would become the great cotton frontiers of southwestern Georgia and central Alabama and Mississippi. That, of course, was the problem: Native Americans held land that white farmers coveted for their own economic gain.

Pressure from the states to remove the Indians had been building since the end of the War of 1812. It was most intense in Georgia. In early 1825, Georgia authorities finalized a fraudulent treaty that ceded most of the Creek Indians' land to the state. When Adams tried to obtain fairer terms for the Creeks in a new treaty, he was brazenly denounced in Georgia, which based its case for grabbing Indian territory on the inviolability of states' rights.

In 1828, Georgia moved against the Cherokees, the best-organized and most advanced (by white standards) of the Indian nations. By now a prosperous society of small farmers with their own newspaper and schools for their children, the Cherokees wanted to avoid the fate of their Creek neighbors. In 1827, they adopted a constitution declaring themselves an independent nation with complete sovereignty over their land. The Georgia legislature reacted by placing the Cherokees directly under state law, annulling Cherokee laws and even the right of the Cherokees to make laws, and

✳ Explore Indian Removal on MyHistoryLab

HOW DID U.S. INDIAN POLICY IMPACT THE "FIVE CIVILIZED TRIBES"?

The Cherokees, the Creeks, the Choctaws, the Chickasaws, and the Seminoles represented the so-called "Five Civilized Tribes" of the American Southeast. In the 1790s, the U.S. federal government had signed treaties that promised to recognize the rights of these tribes as autonomous nations. In the 1820s and 1830s, American citizens, the state of Georgia, and, finally, the U.S. government began a concerted effort of denying the rights established by those treaties. During this era, the "Five Civilized Tribes" faced legal harassment alongside the intrusive settlement of Euro-Americans upon their lands. The culmination of U.S. policy toward American Indians in the 1830s was the forcible removal of these five southeastern Native American nations from their traditional lands. The accompanying table details the cost of this removal in terms of human lives.

For the Cherokees, the Trail of Tears stretched 1,200 miles from the homeland in the East to what became the Indian Territory in Oklahoma.

INDIAN REMOVAL AND MORTALITY FIGURES FOR THE "FIVE CIVILIZED TRIBES"

Tribe	Period	Removed	Deaths
Cherokees	1836–1838	20,000	4,000–8,000
Choctaws	1831–1836	12,500	2,000–4,000
Chickasaws	1837–1847	4,000	500–800
Creeks	1834–1837	19,600	3,500
Seminoles	1832–1842	2,833	700*

*Including Second Seminole War casualties.

SOURCE: Prucha, Francis Paul. *American Indian Treaties: The History of a Political Anomaly. University of California Press*, 1994; Foreman, Grant. *Indian Removal: The Emigration of the Five Civilized Tribes of Indians*. Norman, Oklahoma: University of Oklahoma Press, 1932, 11th printing 1989; Thornton, Russell. *American Indian Holocaust and Survival: A Population History Since 1492*. Norman, Oklahoma: University of Oklahoma Press, 1987; Wallace, Anthony F.C. *The Long, Bitter Trail: Andrew Jackson and the Indians*. New York: Hill and Wang, 1993; Goins, Charles Robert et al. *The Historical Atlas of Oklahoma*. Norman: University of Oklahoma Press, 2006; Wishart, David M. "Evidence of Surplus Production in the Cherokee Nation Prior to Removal," *The Journal of Economic History*. 55.1, 120–138.

KEY QUESTIONS Use **MyHistoryLab** *Explorer* to **answer** these **questions:**

Cause ▶▶▶ *Why were the "Five Civilized Tribes" driven from their lands?*

Map the expansion of white settlement in the United States up to 1830.

Consequence ▶▶▶ *What was the fate of the "Five Civilized Tribes" and other Indian nations after removal?*

Map the removal of the Five Civilized Tribes and other nations in the 1830s–1850s.

Choices ▶▶▶ *What were the alternatives to the forcible removal of the "Five Civilized Tribes"?*

Map the spread of Indian land cessions up to 1830.

📖 **Read** the **Document** *Nile's Weekly Register,* "Memorial of the Cherokee Nation" (1830)

Sequoyah, a Cherokee scholar, developed a written table of syllables for the Cherokee language that enabled his people to publish a tribal newspaper in both Cherokee and English.

legally defining the Cherokees as tenants on land belonging to the state of Georgia. By also prohibiting Indian testimony in cases against white people, the legislature stripped the Cherokees of any legal rights. Alabama and Mississippi followed Georgia's lead in denying Indians legal rights.

Thus the stage was set for what Jackson always considered the most important measure of the early days of his administration, the **Indian Removal Act**. Jackson had long considered the federal policy of negotiating with the Indians as sovereign entities a farce. But it was awkward politically for the president to declare that he had no intention of enforcing treaty obligations of the U.S. government. The way out of this dilemma was to remove Native Americans from the center of the dispute. In his first annual message, Jackson sided with state officials in the South and advised the Indians "to emigrate beyond the Mississippi or submit to the laws of those States." This advice enabled Jackson to pose as the friend of the Indians, the wise father who would lead them out of harm's way and save them from rapacious white people.

Indian Removal Act Legislation passed by Congress in 1830 that provided funds for removing and resettling eastern Indians in the West. It granted the president the authority to use force if necessary.

Congress acted on Jackson's recommendation in the Indian Removal Act of 1830. The act appropriated $500,000 for the negotiation of new treaties under which Indians would surrender their territory and be removed to land in the trans-Mississippi area (primarily present-day Oklahoma). Although force was not authorized and Jackson stressed that removal should be voluntary, no federal protection was provided for Indians harassed into leaving by land-hungry settlers. Ultimately, Jackson did deploy the U.S. Army, but only to round up and push out Indians who refused to comply with the new removal treaties.

And so most of the Indians left the eastern United States, the Choctaws in 1830, the Creeks and Chickasaws in 1832, and the Cherokees in 1838 (see Map 10.1). The government was ill prepared to supervise the removal. The private groups that won the federal contracts for transporting and provisioning the Indians were the ones that had entered the lowest bids; they were a shady lot, interested only in a quick profit. Thousands of Indians, perhaps as many as one-fourth of those who started the trek, died on the way to Oklahoma, the victims of cold, hunger, disease, and the general callousness of the white people they met along the way. It was indeed, as recalled in the collective memory of the Cherokees, a **Trail of Tears**.

Tribes that resisted removal were attacked by white armies. Federal troops joined local militias in 1832 in suppressing the Sauk and Fox Indians of Illinois and Wisconsin in what was called **Black Hawk's War**. More a frantic attempt by the Indians to reach safety on the west bank of the Mississippi than an actual war, this affair ended in the slaughter of 500 Indian men, women, and children by white troops and their Sioux

Trail of Tears The forced march in 1838 of the Cherokee Indians from their homelands in Georgia to the Indian Territory in the West; thousands of Cherokees died along the way.

Black Hawk's War Short 1832 war in which federal troops and Illinois militia units defeated the Sauk and Fox Indians led by Black Hawk.

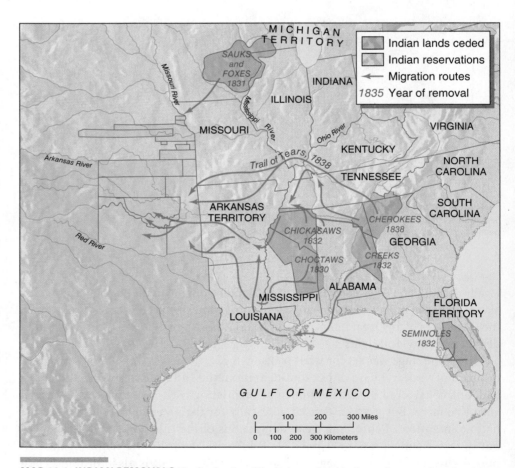

MAP 10.1 INDIAN REMOVALS The fixed policy of the Jackson administration and pressure from the states forced Native Americans in the 1830s to migrate from their eastern homelands to a special Indian reserve west of the Mississippi River.

allies. The Seminoles, many of whose leaders were runaway slaves adopted into the tribe, fought the army to a standstill in the swamps of Florida in what became the longest Indian war in U.S. history.

Jackson forged ahead with his removal policy despite the opposition of eastern reformers and Protestant missionaries. Aligned with conservatives concerned by Jackson's cavalier disregard of federal treaty obligations, they came within three votes of defeating the removal bill in the House of Representatives. Jackson ignored their protests as well as the legal rulings of the Supreme Court. In *Cherokee Nation v. Georgia* (1831) and *Worcester v. Georgia* (1832), the Court ruled that Georgia had violated the U.S. Constitution in extending its jurisdiction over the Cherokees. Chief Justice John Marshall defined Indian tribes as "dependent domestic nations" subject only to the authority of the federal government. Marshall may have won the legal argument, but he was powerless to enforce his decisions without Jackson's cooperation. Aware that southerners and westerners were on his side, Jackson ignored the Supreme Court rulings and pushed Indian removal to its tragic conclusion.

The Nullification Crisis

Jackson's stand on Indian removal confirmed the impression of many of his followers that when state and national power conflicted, he could be trusted to side with the states. But when states'-rights forces in South Carolina precipitated the **nullification crisis** by directly challenging Jackson in the early 1830s over tariff policy, Jackson revealed himself to be an ardent nationalist on the issue of majority rule in the Union.

After the first protective tariff in 1816, rates increased further in 1824 and then jumped to 50 percent in 1828 in what was denounced as the "Tariff of Abominations," a measure contrived by northern Democrats to win additional northern support for Jackson in the upcoming presidential campaign. The outcry was loudest in South Carolina, an old cotton state losing population to the West in the 1820s as cotton prices remained low after the Panic of 1819. For all of the economic protests that high tariffs worsened the agricultural depression by raising the cost of manufactured goods purchased by farmers and planters and lowering the foreign demand for agricultural exports, the tariff issue was a stalking-horse for the more fundamental issue of setting limits on national power so that the federal government could never move against slavery.

South Carolina was the only state where African Americans made up the majority of the population. Slaves were heavily concentrated in the marshes and tidal flats south of Charleston, the lowcountry district of huge rice plantations. Ever fearful that growing antislavery agitation in the North and in England was feeding slave unrest, state leaders such as James Hamilton Jr. warned that the time had come to "stand manfully at the Safety Valve of Nullification."

With the lowcountry planters in charge, the anti-tariff forces in South Carolina controlled state politics by 1832. They called themselves the nullifiers, a name derived from the constitutional theory developed by John C. Calhoun in an anonymous tract of 1828 titled *The South Carolina Exposition and Protest*. Pushing to its logical extreme the states'-rights doctrine first outlined in the Kentucky and Virginia Resolutions of 1798, Calhoun argued that a state, acting through a popularly elected convention, had the sovereign power to declare an act of the national government null and inoperative.

Calhoun, who had been elected vice president in 1828, openly embraced nullification after he broke with Jackson in 1830. With Calhoun's approval, a South Carolina convention in November 1832 nullified the tariffs of 1828 and 1832 (a compromise tariff that did not reduce rates to a low enough level to satisfy the nullifiers). The

nullification crisis Sectional crisis in the early 1830s in which a states' rights party in South Carolina attempted to nullify federal law.

convention decreed that customs duties were not to be collected in South Carolina after February 1, 1833.

In January 1833, Jackson, in the Force Bill, asked for and received from Congress full authorization to put down nullification by military force. Meanwhile, a compromise tariff in 1833 provided for the lowering of tariff duties to 20 percent over a ten-year period. Up against this combination of the carrot and the stick, the nullifiers backed down, but not before they scornfully nullified the Force Bill.

Jackson's stand established the principle of national supremacy grounded in the will of the majority. Despite his victory, however, states'-rights doctrines remained popular both in the South and among many northern Democrats. South Carolina had been isolated in its stand on nullification, but many southerners, and especially slaveholders, agreed that the powers of the national government had to be strictly limited. By dramatically affirming his right to use force against a state in defense of the Union, Jackson drove many planters out of the Democratic Party. In the shock waves set off by the nullification crisis, a new anti-Jackson coalition began to form in the South.

The Bank War

Bank War The political struggle between President Andrew Jackson and the supporters of the Second Bank of the United States.

What amounted to a war against the Bank of the United States became the centerpiece of Jackson's presidency and a defining event for the Democratic Party. The **Bank War** erupted in 1832, when Jackson vetoed draft legislation for the early rechartering of the national bank.

Like most westerners, Jackson distrusted banks. Because gold and silver coins were scarce and the national government did not issue or regulate paper currency, money consisted primarily of notes issued as loans by private and state banks. These bank notes fluctuated in value according to the reputation and creditworthiness of the issuing banks. In the credit-starved West, banks were particularly unreliable. All of this struck many Americans, and especially farmers and workers, as inherently dishonest. They wanted to be paid in "real" money, gold or silver coin, and they viewed bankers as parasites who did nothing but fatten their own pockets by manipulating paper money. The largest and most powerful bank was the Bank of the United States, and citizens who were wiped out or forced to retrench drastically by the Panic of 1819 never forgave the Bank for saving itself at the expense of its debtors. Still, under the astute leadership of a new president, Nicholas Biddle of Philadelphia, the Bank performed well in the 1820s. Prosperous times had returned, and the Bank underwrote the economic expansion with its healthy credit reserves, stable bank notes, and policing of the state banks through its policy of returning their notes for redemption in specie. By 1832, the Bank was as popular as it ever would be.

Searching for an issue to use against Jackson in the presidential campaign of 1832, Clay forced Jackson's hand on the Bank. Clay convinced Biddle to apply to Congress for a new charter, even though the current charter would not expire until 1836. Confident of congressional approval, Clay reasoned that he had Jackson trapped. If Jackson went along with the new charter, Clay could take credit for the measure. If he vetoed it, Clay could attack Jackson as the enemy of a sound banking system.

Clay's clever strategy backfired. Jackson turned on him and the Bank with a vengeance. As he told his heir apparent, "The bank, Mr. Van Buren, is trying to kill me, but *I will kill it!*" Jackson and his advisers realized that the Bank was vulnerable as a symbol of privileged monopoly, a monstrous institution that deprived common Americans of their right to compete equally for economic advantage. Moreover, many of these advisers were also state bankers and local developers, who backed Jackson precisely because they wanted to be free of federal restraints on their business activities. On July 10, 1832, Jackson vetoed the rechartering bill for the Bank in a message that appealed both to state bankers and to foes of all banks. He took a ringing "stand against all new grants of monopolies and exclusive privileges, against any prostitution of our Government to the advancement of the few at the expense of the many."

The business community and eastern elites lashed out at Jackson's veto as the demagogic ravings of an economic fool. For Biddle, the veto message had "all the fury of a chained panther, biting the bars of his cage." In rejecting Jackson's claims that the Bank had fostered speculative and corrupt financial practices, the pro-Bank forces had the better of the economic argument. But Jackson won the political battle, and he went to the people in the election of 1832 as their champion against the banking aristocracy. Although his support was no stronger than it had been in 1828, he easily defeated Clay, the candidate of the short-lived National Republican Party, which had also backed Adams in 1828.

After Congress failed to override his veto, Jackson then set out to destroy the Bank. He claimed that the people had given him a mandate to do so by reelecting him in 1832. In Roger B. Taney he finally found a secretary of the treasury (his first two choices refused) who agreed to sign the order removing federal deposits from the Bank in 1833. Drained of its lifeblood, the deposits, the Bank was reduced by 1836 to seeking a charter as a private corporation in the state of Pennsylvania. In the meantime, the government's moneys were deposited in "pet banks," state banks controlled by loyal Democrats.

Jackson won the Bank War, but he left the impression that the Democrats had played fast and loose with the nation's credit system. The economy overheated in his second term. High commodity prices and abundant credit, both at home and abroad, propelled a buying frenzy of western lands. Prices soared, and inevitably the speculative bubble had to burst. When it did, the Democrats would be open to the charge of squandering the people's money by shifting deposits to reckless state bankers who were part of a corrupt new alliance between the government and private economic interests. Jackson was out of office when the Panic of 1837 hit; Van Buren, his successor, paid the political price for Jackson's economic policies.

Van Buren and Hard Times

10.3 What challenges did Van Buren face during his presidency?

Like John Adams and James Madison, Martin Van Buren followed a forceful president who commanded a strong popular following. Fairly or not, he would come out, as they did, second-best compared to his predecessor.

Facing a sharp economic downturn, Van Buren appeared indecisive and unwilling to advance a bold program. When the rise of a radical **abolitionist movement** in the North revived sectional tensions over slavery, he awkwardly straddled the divisive issue. In the end, he undermined himself by failing to offer a compelling vision of his presidency.

abolitionist movement A radical antislavery crusade committed to the immediate end of slavery that emerged in the three decades before the Civil War.

The Panic of 1837

Van Buren was barely settled into the White House when the nation was rocked by a financial panic. For over a decade, the economy had benefited from a favorable business cycle. A banking crisis in 1837 produced a painful economic reckoning.

Even as it expanded, the U.S. economy had remained vulnerable to disruptions in the supply of foreign capital and the sale of agricultural exports that underpinned

From Then to Now
Speculative Bubbles and Economic Busts

The hard times that marked the Van Buren presidency and persisted into the 1840s marked the nation's first great depression. But it would hardly be the last time that speculative binges in the economy ended up in crippling depressions. Similar boom-bust cycles shook America in the 1870s, the 1890s, the Great Depression of the 1930s, and, more recently, what has been termed the Great Recession, which resulted from the collapse of the housing market in 2008 and the hopelessly complex structure of arcane financial instruments created to sustain the surge of borrowing.

In the 1830s, as well as in the early twenty-first century, governments and private banks played major roles in promoting near reckless economic expansion. Easy credit was lavished on the construction of roads, canals, and railroads, economic infrastructure that the states competed against each other to provide for their citizens and went into debt to finance. Meanwhile, both the Second Bank of the United States before Jackson destroyed it and the state banks issued bank notes that helped fuel an unsustainable rise in the price of land and commodities such as cotton. Heavily dependent on British commodity markets and credit arrangements, the economy lurched into reverse when the Bank of England raised interest rates and cotton prices fell. Banks suspended specie payments, called in loans and stopped issuing new ones, and wrote off bad debts. The states that had borrowed to the hilt to finance

This 1838 lithograph portrays the plight of a tradesman and his family caught up in the Panic of 1837.

The post-2008 housing crisis left many home owners underwater on their mortgages, that is, they owed more on their mortgages than the resale value of their homes.

internal improvements, as well as the territorial government of Florida, defaulted on their bonds. Politically, defaulting was easier than facing the wrath of voters if taxes were raised enough to pay off the bonds. Unlike today, there was no possibility then of a federal bailout. President John Tyler made that clear to British investors, the holders of many of the defaulted bonds, when he lectured them on the constitutional difference between state and federal governments.

The names are different in the post-2008 global squeeze on debtors, both public and private, and the sums of money involved are far greater; but the underlying mechanism at play remains the same. Economic growth requires capital and risk takers, and when growth seems endless in heady times all caution is thrown to the wind. And then as now, the question of who should pick up the tab for the recklessness—taxpayers on behalf of their governments or the private investors who risked too much—shaped the political debates on how to cope with the economic wreckage.

Question for Discussion

- How would you stake out a position on whether governments or private investors should bear the major costs of dealing with a severe economic downturn?

prosperity. The key foreign nation was Britain, a major source of credit and demand for exports. In late 1836, the Bank of England tightened its credit policies. Concerned about the large outflow of specie to the United States, it raised interest rates and reduced the credit lines of British merchants heavily involved in U.S. trade. Consequently, the British demand for cotton fell and with it the price of cotton (see Figure 10.1 on page 268). Because cotton, as the leading export, was the main security for most loans issued by U.S. banks and mercantile firms, its drop in value set off a chain reaction of contracting credit and falling prices. When panic-stricken investors rushed to the banks to redeem their notes in specie, the hard-pressed banks suspended specie payments.

The shock waves hit New Orleans in March 1837 and spread to the major New York banks by May. What began as a bank panic soon dragged down the entire economy. State governments, which had borrowed lavishly during the boom

THE MODERN BALAAM AND HIS ASS.

This Whig cartoon blaming Jackson for the Panic of 1837 introduced the donkey as the symbol of the Democratic Party.

years to finance canals and other internal improvements, slashed their budgets and halted all construction projects. As unemployment mounted and workers mobilized mass protest meetings in eastern cities, conservatives feared the worst. "Workmen thrown out of employ by the hundred daily," nervously noted a wealthy merchant in New York City in May 1837. He half expected that "we shall have a revolution here."

After a brief recovery in 1838, another round of credit contraction drove the economy into a depression that did not bottom out until 1843. In the manufacturing and commercial centers of the Northeast, unemployment reached an unheard-of 20 percent. The persistence of depressed agricultural prices meant that farmers and planters who had incurred debts in the 1830s faced the constant threat of losing their land or their slaves. Many fled west to avoid their creditors.

The Independent Treasury

Although the Democrats bore no direct responsibility for the economic downturn, they could not avoid being blamed for it. Their political opponents, now coalescing as the **Whig Party**, claimed that Jackson's destruction of the Bank of the United States had undermined business confidence. In their view, Jackson had then compounded his error by trying to force a hard-money policy on the state banks that had received federal deposits. The "pet banks" were required to replace small-denomination bank notes with coins or hard money. This measure, it was hoped, would protect the farmers and workers from being paid in depreciated bank notes.

Whig Party Political party, formed in the mid-1830s in opposition to the Jacksonian Democrats, that favored a strong role for the national government in promoting economic growth.

267

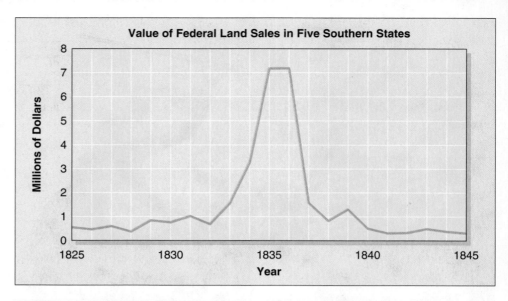

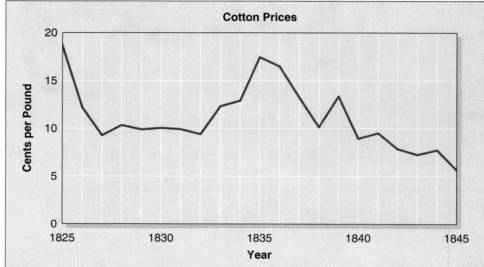

FIGURE 10.1 COTTON PRICES AND THE VALUE OF FEDERAL LAND SALES IN FIVE SOUTHERN STATES, 1825–1845
Because the U.S. economy was heavily dependent on cotton exports as a source of credit, the collapse of cotton prices, and a corresponding plunge in the sales of federal land after a speculative run-up in the newer cotton regions of the South, triggered a financial panic in the late 1830s.

SOURCE: Douglas C. North, *The Economic Growth of the United States, 1790–1860* (1966 W.W. Norton), tab. A-X, p. 257.

Specie Circular Proclamation issued by President Andrew Jackson in 1836 stipulating that only gold or silver could be used as payment for public land.

Jackson had taken his boldest step against paper money when he issued the **Specie Circular** of 1836, which stipulated that large tracts of public land could be bought only with specie. Aimed at breaking the speculative spiral in land purchases, the Specie Circular contributed to the Panic of 1837 by requiring the transfer of specie to the West for land transactions just when eastern banks were strapped for specie reserves. Bankers and speculators denounced Jackson for interfering with the natural workings of the economy and blundering into a monetary disaster.

Conservative charges of Democratic irresponsibility were overblown, but the Democrats were caught in a dilemma. By dramatically politicizing the banking issue and removing federal moneys from the national bank, the Democrats had in effect assumed the burden of protecting the people from the banking and business community. Once they shifted treasury receipts to selected state banks, they had to try to regulate these banks. Otherwise they would be accused of creating a series of little "monsters" and feeding the paper speculation they so decried. But any regulatory policy contradicted the Democratic commitment to limit governmental power.

The only way out of the dilemma was to make a clean break between the government and banking. Van Buren reestablished the Democrats' tarnished image as the party of limited government when he came out for the **Independent Treasury System**. Under this plan, the government would dispense with banks entirely. The Treasury would conduct its business only in gold and silver coin and would store its specie in regional vaults or subtreasuries. First proposed in 1837, the Independent Treasury System finally passed Congress in 1840 on the heels of a second wave of bank failures.

The Independent Treasury System made more political than economic sense. It restored the ideological purity of the Democrats as the friends of honest money, but it prolonged the depression. Specie locked up in government vaults was unavailable for loans in the private banking system that could have expanded the credit needed to revive the economy. The end result was to reduce the money supply and further depress prices.

Uproar over Slavery

In 1831, William Lloyd Garrison of Boston inaugurated a radical new phase in northern attacks on slavery with the publication of his abolitionist paper the *Liberator*. The abolitionists embraced the doctrine of immediatism, an immediate moral commitment to begin the work of emancipation. Inspired by the wave of religious revivals sweeping the North in the late 1820s, they seized on slavery as the greatest sin of all. (For more on the abolitionists, see Chapter 12.)

The abolitionists touched off a political uproar when they launched a propaganda offensive in 1835. Taking advantage of technological improvements in the printing industry, they produced more than a million pieces of antislavery literature, much of which was sent to the South through the U.S. mail. Alarmed white southerners vilified the abolitionists as fanatics intent on enticing the slaves to revolt. Abolitionist tracts were burned, and, with the open approval of Jackson, southern postmasters violated federal law by censoring the mail to keep out antislavery materials.

Unable to receive an open hearing in the South, the abolitionists now focused on Congress. Beginning in 1836 and continuing through Van Buren's presidency, hundreds of thousands of antislavery petitions, some with thousands of signatures, flooded into Congress. Most called for the abolition of slavery in the District of Columbia. Southern congressmen responded by demanding that free speech be repressed in the name of southern white security. The enemy, they were convinced, was fanaticism, and nearly all agreed with Francis Pickens of South Carolina that they must "meet it and strangle it in its infancy." The strangling took the form of the **gag rule**, a procedural device whereby antislavery petitions were automatically tabled with no discussion.

The gag rule was first passed in 1836 and was renewed in a series of raucous debates through 1844. Only the votes of some three-fourths of the northern Democrats enabled the southern minority to have its way. With Van Buren's reluctant support, the gag rule became a Democratic Party measure, and it identified the Democrats as a pro-southern party in the minds of many northerners. Ironically, while Van Buren was attacked in the North as a lackey of the slave interests, he was damned in the South, if only because he was a nonslaveholder from the North, as being unsafe on the slavery issue. In short, tensions over slavery and the economy doomed Van Buren to be cast as a vacillating president fully trusted by neither section.

Independent Treasury System Fiscal arrangement first instituted by President Martin Van Buren in which the federal government kept its money in regional vaults and transacted its business entirely in hard money.

gag rule Procedural rule passed in the House of Representatives that prevented discussion of antislavery petitions from 1836 to 1844.

The Rise of the Whig Party

| **10.4** | What was the basis of Whig popularity and what did they claim to stand for? |

The early opponents of the Democrats were known as the National Republicans, a label that captured the nationalist vision of former Jeffersonian Republicans who adhered to the economic program of Henry Clay and John Quincy Adams. The Bank War and Jackson's reaction to nullification shook loose pro-Bank Democrats and many southern states'-righters from the original Jacksonian coalition, and these groups joined the opposition to Jackson. By 1834, the anti-Jacksonians started to call themselves Whigs, a name associated with eighteenth-century American and British opponents of monarchical tyranny. The name stuck because of the party's constant depiction of Jackson as King Andrew, a tyrant who ran roughshod over congressional prerogatives and constitutional liberties.

By 1840, the Whigs had mastered the techniques of political organization and mobilization pioneered by the Democrats in the late 1820s. They ran William Henry Harrison, their own version of a military hero, and swept to victory. The **second party system** of intense national competition between Whigs and Democrats was now in place (see Table 10.1). It would dominate politics until the rise of the antislavery Republican Party in the 1850s.

second party system The national two-party competition between Democrats and Whigs from the 1830s through the early 1850s.

The Party Taking Shape

The Whig party was born in the congressional reaction to Jackson's Bank veto and his subsequent attacks on the national bank. What upset the congressional opposition, apart from the specific content of Jackson's policies, was how he enforced his will. Jackson wielded his executive power like a bludgeon. Whereas all earlier presidents together had used the veto only ten times, Jackson did so a dozen times. He openly defied the Supreme Court and Congress, and unlike his predecessors, he took each case directly to the people.

Local and state Whig coalitions sent an anti-Jackson majority to the House of Representatives in 1835. The most powerful of these coalitions was in New York, where a third party, the **Anti-Masons**, joined the Whigs. The party had originated in western New York in the late 1820s as a grassroots response to the sudden disappearance and presumed murder of William Morgan, an itinerant artisan who threatened to expose the secrets of the Order of Freemasons. An all-male order steeped in ritual and ceremony, the Masons united urban and small-town elites into a tightly knit brotherhood through personal contacts and mutual aid. When efforts to investigate Morgan's disappearance ran into a legal dead end, rumors spread that the exclusivist Masons

Anti-Masons Third party formed in 1827 in opposition to the presumed power and influence of the Masonic order.

TABLE 10.1 THE SECOND PARTY SYSTEM

	Democrats	Whigs
Ideology	Favor limited role of federal government in economic affairs and matters of individual conscience; support territorial expansion	Favor government support for economic development and controls over individual morality; opposed to expansion
Voter support	Mainly subsistence farmers, unskilled workers, and Catholic immigrants	Mainly manufacturers, commercial farmers, skilled workers, and northern evangelicals
Regional strength	South and West	New England and Upper Midwest

constituted a vast conspiracy that conferred special privileges and legal protection on its members.

Western New York, an area of religious fervor and rapid economic change after the opening of the Erie Canal in 1825, provided fertile ground for the growth of the new party. With close ties to rural landlords and town creditors, the Masons were vulnerable to the charge of economic favoritism. In addition, evangelicals accused the Masons of desecrating the Christian faith with their secret rituals. The Anti-Masons were thus the first party to combine demands for equal opportunity with calls for the moral reform of a sinful society. They were also the first party to select their presidential ticket in a national nominating convention, a precedent immediately followed by the Whigs and Democrats.

Although it spread into New England and the neighboring mid-Atlantic states, the Anti-Mason party was unable to sustain itself. Its presidential candidate in 1832, William Wirt of Maryland, won only Vermont. Recognizing that the opponents of the Anti-Masons were usually the entrenched local interests of the Democratic Party, shrewd politicians, led by Thurlow Weed and William Seward of New York, took up the movement and absorbed most of it into the anti-Jackson coalition. They did so by calling for equal opportunity and for such evangelical reforms as a ban on the sale of alcohol. The Whigs thus broadened their popular base and added an egalitarian message to their appeal.

By 1836, the Whigs were strong enough to mount a serious challenge for the presidency. However, they still lacked an effective national organization that could unite their regional coalitions behind one candidate. They ran four sectional candidates, and some Whigs hoped that the regional popularity of these candidates would siphon off enough votes from Van Buren to throw the election into the House of Representatives. The strategy, if such it can be called, failed. Van Buren won an electoral majority by holding on to the populous mid-Atlantic states and improving on Jackson's showing in New England. Still, the Whigs were encouraged by the results. Compared to Jackson, Van Buren did poorly in what had been the overwhelmingly Democratic South, which was now open to further Whig inroads.

Whig Persuasion

The Whigs, like the Democrats, based their mass appeal on the claim that they could best defend the republican liberties of the people. Whereas the Democrats attributed the threat to those liberties to privileged monopolies of government-granted power, the Whigs found it in the expansive powers of the presidency as wielded by Jackson and in the party organization that put Jackson and Van Buren into office. In 1836, the Whigs called for the election of "a president of the nation, not a president of party." Underlying this call was the persistent Whig belief that parties undermined individual liberties and the public good by fostering and rewarding the selfish interests of the party faithful. Although the Whigs dropped much of this ideology when they matured as a party, they never lost their fear of the presidency as an office of unchecked, demagogic power. They always insisted that Congress should be the locus of power in the federal system.

Most Whigs viewed governmental power as a positive force to promote economic development. They favored the spread of banking and paper money, chartering corporations, passing protective tariffs to support U.S. manufacturers, and opening up new markets for farmers through government-subsidized transportation projects. Such policies, they held, would widen economic opportunities for Americans and provide incentives for material self-improvement.

In addition to drawing heavily from commercial and planting interests in the South, the Whigs appealed to bankers, manufacturers, small-town entrepreneurs, farmers prospering from the market outlets of canals and railroads, and skilled workers who valued a high tariff as protection from the competition of foreign goods. These Whig supporters also tended to be native-born Protestants of New England or Yankee ancestry, particularly those caught up in the religious revivals of the 1820s and 1830s. The strongest Whig constituencies comprised an arc of Yankee settlements stretching from rural New England through central New York and around the southern shores of the Great Lakes.

Whether as economic promoters or evangelical reformers, Whigs believed in promoting social progress and harmony through an interventionist government. The Whigs favored such social reforms as prohibiting the consumption of alcohol, preserving the sanctity of the Protestant Sabbath through bans on business activities on Sundays, caring for orphans, the physically handicapped, and the mentally ill in state-run asylums and hospitals, and teaching virtuous behavior and basic knowledge through a centralized system of public education. Whig ideology blended economic, social, and spiritual reform into a unified message of uplift. An activist government would provide economic opportunities and moral guidance for a harmonious, progressive society of freely competing individuals whose behavior would be shaped by the evangelical norms of thrift, sobriety, and self-discipline. Much of the Whigs' reform impulse was directed against non-English and Catholic immigrants, those Americans who the Whigs believed most needed to be taught the virtues of self-control and disciplined work habits. Not coincidentally, these groups, the Scots-Irish in the backcountry, the Reformed Dutch, and Irish and German Catholics, were the most loyal Democrats. They resented the Whigs' aggressive moralism and legislative attempts to interfere with their drinking habits and Sunday amusements. These Democrats were typically subsistence farmers on the periphery of market change and unskilled workers forced by industrial change to abandon their hopes of ever opening their own shops. They equated an activist government with special privileges for the economically and culturally powerful and identified with the Democrats' desire to keep the government out of the economy and individual religious practices.

The Election of 1840

One of the signs of the Whigs' maturing as a party was their decision in 1840 to place victory above principle. Because of the lingering economic depression, Democratic rule had been discredited for many voters. Henry Clay, who promised that his American System would revive the economy with government aid, appeared the most likely Whig candidate for president against Van Buren in 1840. Yet Whig power brokers dumped Clay, who represented the party's ideological heart, for a popular military hero, William Henry Harrison of Ohio.

Harrison had run surprisingly well as one of the Whigs' regional candidates in 1836 and had revealed a common touch with the voters. Unlike Clay, he was untainted by any association with the Bank of the United States, the Masonic Order, or slaveholding. As the victor at the Battle of Tippecanoe and a military hero in the War of 1812, he enabled Whig image-makers to cast him, like Jackson, as the honest, patriotic soldier worthy of the people's trust. In a decision that came back to haunt them, the Whigs geographically balanced their ticket by selecting John Tyler, a planter from Virginia, as Harrison's running mate. Tyler was an advocate of states' rights and a former Democrat who had broken with Jackson over the Force Bill.

The Democrats inadvertently gave the Whig campaign a tremendous boost. A Democratic editor wisecracked that "Old Granny" Harrison (he was 67) was such a simpleton that he would like nothing better than to retire to a log cabin with a government pension and a barrel of hard cider. Pouncing on this sneer, the Whigs created a Harrison who never was, a yeoman farmer of humble origins and

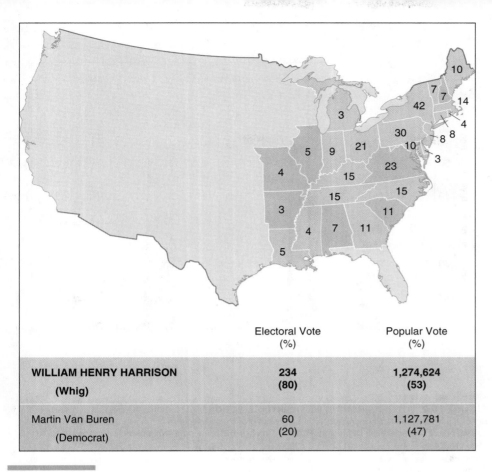

	Electoral Vote (%)	Popular Vote (%)
WILLIAM HENRY HARRISON (Whig)	**234** **(80)**	**1,274,624** **(53)**
Martin Van Buren (Democrat)	60 (20)	1,127,781 (47)

MAP 10.2 THE ELECTION OF 1840 Building upon their strength in the commercializing North, the Whigs attracted enough rural voters in the South and West to win the election of 1840.

homespun tastes, whose rise to prominence was a democratic model of success for other Americans to follow. Thus Harrison, who was descended from the Virginia slaveholding aristocracy, became a symbol of the common man, and the Whigs were finally able to shed their aristocratic image. Indeed, they pinned the label of the dandified and elitist aristocrat on Van Buren. "Martin Van Ruin," as effectively portrayed by the Whigs, squandered public revenue on effete luxuries and was concerned only with the spoils of office.

The Whigs beat the Democrats at their own game of mass politics in 1840. They reversed the roles and symbolism of the Jackson-Adams election of 1828 and seized the high ground as the party of the people. In a further adaptation of earlier Democratic initiatives, the Whigs put together a frolicking campaign of slogans, parades, and pageantry.

Much to the disgust of Benjamin French, who accused the Whigs of running a campaign based on "fraud & humbug," the Whigs gained control of both Congress and the presidency in 1840. Harrison won 53 percent of the popular vote, and for the first time the Whigs carried the South (see Map 10.2). With the arrival of politics as mass spectacle, the turnout surged to an unprecedented 78 percent of eligible voters, a whopping increase over the average of 55 percent in the three preceding presidential elections (see Figure 10.2). The Whigs claimed most of the new voters and were now fully competitive with the Democrats in all parts of the nation. As the new majority party, they finally had the opportunity, or so they thought, to implement their economic program.

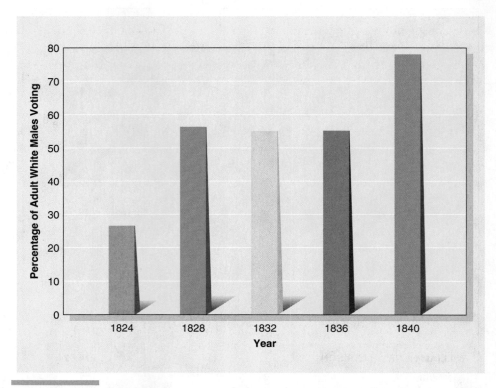

FIGURE 10.2 VOTER TURNOUT IN PRESIDENTIAL ELECTIONS, 1824–1840 The creation of mass-based political parties dramatically increased voter turnout in presidential elections. Voting surged in 1828 with the emergence of the Jacksonian Democratic Party and again in 1840 when the Whig party learned to appeal to the mass electorate.

SOURCE: Richard P. McCormick, "New Perspectives on Jacksonian Politics," in *The Nature of Jacksonian America*, edited by Douglas T. Miller, p. 103. Copyright © 1972. Reproduced with permission of John Wiley & Sons, Inc.

The Whigs in Power

10.5 Why was William Henry Harrison's death such a blow to the Whig agenda?

Although the Whigs had been noncommittal on their plans during the campaign of 1840, it was common knowledge that Clay would move quickly on Whig economic policies by marshaling his forces in Congress and trying to dominate a pliant Harrison. But Harrison died from pneumonia in April 1841, barely a month after his inauguration, ruining Clay's plans.

Harrison and Tyler

Harrison had pledged to follow the dictates of party leaders in Congress and defer to the judgment of his cabinet. Bowing to Clay's demands, he agreed to call Congress into special session to act on Whig party measures. Precisely because he was the type of president the Whigs needed and wanted, his death was a real blow to Whig hopes of establishing the credibility of their party as an effective agent for positive change.

Just how serious that blow was soon became apparent when Tyler became president, the first vice president to succeed on the death of a president. Tyler was cut from quite different cloth from Harrison. This stiff, unbending planter subscribed to a states'-rights agrarian philosophy that put him at odds with the urban and commercial elements of the Whig party even in his home state of Virginia. Clay's economic nationalism struck him as a program of rank corruption that surrendered the constitutional rights of the South to power-hungry politicians and manufacturers in the

North. Clay refused to cultivate Tyler's prickly pride with soothing gestures, and he forged ahead with the party agenda, the repeal of the Independent Treasury System and its replacement by a new national bank, a protective tariff, and the distribution of the proceeds of the government's public land sales to the states as funds for internal improvements.

Tyler used the negative power of presidential vetoes to stymie the Whig program. He twice vetoed bills to reestablish a national bank. The second veto led to the resignation of the cabinet he had inherited from Harrison, save for Secretary of State Daniel Webster, who was in the midst of negotiations with the British. Enraged congressional Whigs then expelled Tyler from the party.

Clay's legislative efforts got him nowhere. When the Whigs passed a higher tariff in 1842 with a provision for distribution, Tyler vetoed it and forced them to settle for a protective tariff with no distribution. In the end, Clay had no national bank, no funds for internal improvements, and only a slightly higher tariff. Although Clay's leadership of the Whigs was strengthened, Tyler had deprived that leadership of meaning by denying the Whigs the legislative fruits of their victory in 1840.

The Texas Issue

Constrained by his states'-rights view to a largely negative role in domestic policy, Tyler was a much more forceful president in foreign policy, an area in which the Constitution gives the chief executive considerable latitude. In 1842, Tyler's secretary of state, Daniel Webster, wrapped up his negotiations with the British over a long-standing boundary dispute. The **Webster-Ashburton Treaty** of that year established the boundary between British Canada and Maine and parts of the Upper Midwest. An agreement was also reached to cooperate in suppressing the African slave trade. Webster now resigned from the cabinet to join his fellow Whigs, allowing Tyler to follow a pro-southern policy of expansion that he hoped would gain him the Democratic nomination for the presidency in 1844. His goal was the annexation of Texas.

Texas had been a slaveholding republic since 1836, when rebellious Americans, joined by some *tejanos* (Texans of Mexican descent), declared their independence from Mexico. Jackson extended diplomatic recognition before leaving office, but he refused the new nation's request to be annexed to the United States out of fear of provoking a war with Mexico, which did not recognize Texan independence.

For the sake of sectional harmony, party leaders sidestepped the Texas issue after 1836. Tyler renewed the issue in 1843 to curry favor among southern and western Democrats. He replaced Webster as secretary of state with a pro-annexationist Virginian, Abel P. Upshur, and secretly opened negotiations with the Texans. After Upshur's death in an accidental explosion on the battleship *Princeton,* John C. Calhoun, his successor, completed the negotiations and dramatically politicized the slavery issue. In the spring of 1844, Calhoun and Tyler submitted to the Senate a secretly drawn up treaty annexing Texas to the United States. Calhoun also made public his correspondence with Richard Pakenham, the British minister in Washington. In his letter, Calhoun accused the British of seeking to force emancipation on Texas in return for economic aid and a British-brokered Mexican recognition of Texan independence. These British efforts, warned Calhoun, were just the opening wedge in a master plan to block U.S. expansion and destroy slavery in the South. After pointedly defending slavery as a benign institution, Calhoun concluded that the security and preservation of the Union demanded the annexation of Texas. The Pakenham letter hit the Senate like a bombshell, convincing antislavery Northerners that the annexation of Texas was a slaveholders' conspiracy to extend slavery and swell the political power of the South. In June 1844, the Senate rejected Calhoun's treaty of annexation by a two-to-one margin. All but one Whig senator voted against it. Still, the issue was hardly dead. Thanks to Tyler and Calhoun, Texas dominated the election of 1844.

Webster–Ashburton Treaty
Treaty signed by the United States and Britain in 1842 that settled a boundary dispute between Maine and Canada and provided for closer cooperation in suppressing the African slave trade.

The Election of 1844

The Whig and Democratic National Conventions met in the spring of 1844 in the midst of the uproar over Texas. Both Clay, who had the Whig nomination locked up, and Van Buren, who was the strong favorite for the Democratic one, came out against immediate annexation. But Van Buren's anti-Texas stand cost him his party's nomination. In a carefully devised strategy, western and southern Democrats united to deny him the necessary two-thirds vote of convention delegates. A deadlocked convention turned to James K. Polk of Tennessee, a confirmed expansionist who had the blessing of Jackson, the party's patriarch.

To counter the charge that they were a pro-southern party, the Democrats ran in 1844 on a platform that linked Oregon to Texas as a territorial objective. Oregon had first attracted public attention during the Tyler presidency. Glowing reports from Protestant missionaries of the boundless fertility of Oregon's Willamette Valley triggered a migration to the new promised land on the shores of the Pacific by midwestern farm families still reeling from the Panic of 1837. At the same time, the report of a naval expedition sent to explore the Pacific aroused the interest of New England merchants in using Oregon as a jumping-off point for expanded trade with China.

Some 6,000 Americans were in Oregon by the mid-1840s, and demands mounted, especially from northern Democrats, that the United States abandon its 1818 agreement of joint occupation with the British and lay exclusive claim to Oregon as far north as the 54°40' parallel, the border with Russian-owned Alaska. These were bold, even reckless, demands, because the actual area of U.S. settlement in Oregon was south of the Columbia River, itself well south of even the 49th parallel. Nonetheless, the Polk Democrats seemed to endorse them when they asserted a U.S. claim "to the whole of the Territory of Oregon."

Polk's expansionist program united the Democrats and enabled them to campaign with much more enthusiasm than in 1840. Acquiring Texas and Oregon not only held out the hope of cheap, abundant land to debt-burdened farmers in the North and planters in the South but also played on the anti-British sentiments of many voters. In contrast, the Whig campaign was out of focus. Clay sensed that his opposition to the immediate annexation of Texas was hurting him in the South, and he started to hedge by saying that he would accept Texas if the conditions were right. This wavering, however, failed to stem the defection of pro-slavery southern Whigs to the Democrats and cut into his support among antislavery Whigs in the North. Clay lost to Polk by less than 2 percent of the popular vote.

Tyler claimed Polk's victory as a mandate for the immediate annexation of Texas. He knew that it would still be impossible to gain the two-thirds majority in the Senate necessary for the approval of a treaty. Thus, he resorted to the constitutionally unprecedented expedient of a joint resolution in Congress inviting Texas to join the Union. By the narrow margin of 27 to 25, the Senate concurred with the House in favor of annexation. Tyler signed the joint resolution on March 1, 1845.

Although Tyler had failed to secure the Democratic nomination in 1844, he had gained Texas. He also had the satisfaction of getting revenge against the Whigs, the party that had disowned him. Texas, more than any other issue, defeated Clay and the Whigs in 1844.

Conclusion

The Jacksonian era ushered in a revolution in U.S. political life. Responding to a surge of democratization that was in full swing by the 1820s, politicians learned how to appeal to a mass electorate and to build disciplined parties that channeled popular desires into distinctive party positions. In the two decades after 1824, voter participation in national elections tripled, and Democrats and Whigs competed on nearly equal terms in every region.

Although the origins of a national political culture can be traced back to the Federalists and the Jeffersonian Republicans, politics did not fully enter the mainstream of U.S. life until the rise of the second party system of Democrats and Whigs. The election of 1824 revived interest in presidential politics, and Jackson's forceful style of leadership highlighted the presidency as the focal point of U.S. politics. Professional politicians soon mastered the art of tailoring issues and images to reach the widest popular audience. Voters in favor of government aid for economic development and a social order based on Protestant moral controls turned to the Whigs. Conversely, those who saw an activist government as a threat to their economic and cultural equality turned to the Democrats.

The national issues around which the Democrats and Whigs organized and battled down to 1844 were primarily economic. As long as this was the case, party competition tended to diffuse sectional tensions and strengthen a national political culture. Slavery, in the form of the Texas question, replaced the economy as the decisive issue in the election of 1844. With this shift, party appeals began to focus on the place of slavery in U.S. society, creating an escalating politics of sectionalism that saw such loyal party workers as Benjamin French switch their allegiances to a new sectional party. Within a decade, the slavery issue would rip apart the second party system.

For Suggested Readings go to MyHistoryLab.

Chapter Review

The Egalitarian Impulse

10.1 What factors contributed to the democratization of American politics and religion in the early nineteenth century? p. 251

After the War of 1812 Americans increasingly demanded an end to elitist dominance in their political and religious affairs. The greatest expression of this in politics was the expansion of suffrage to include virtually all adult white males as traditional property qualifications for voting were dropped. A quest for equality transformed American Christianity as a series of revivals spiritually empowered common Americans, especially women and African Americans.

Jackson's Presidency

10.2 How did the Jacksonian Democrats capitalize on the new mass politics? p. 257

A rising generation of career politicians led by Martin Van Buren linked their fortunes to the popularity of Andrew Jackson and developed new techniques of party organization and voter mobilization that enabled them to appeal to the mass electorate that had formed by the 1820s.

Van Buren and Hard Times

10.3 What challenges did Van Buren face during his presidency? p. 265

Enflamed sectional tensions over the rise of the abolitionist movement and the worst economic depression to date hampered all of Van Buren's efforts to exercise effective leadership. He never succeeded in convincing many Americans that his party was not to blame for their economic troubles.

The Rise of the Whig Party

10.4 What was the basis of Whig popularity and what did they claim to stand for? p. 270

The Whigs offered a vision of social progress and moral control. Their program of economic development was promoted by the government and appealed to Americans who embraced economic change and expected to benefit from it. The Whigs' support of moral reform won them the backing of Protestants who were anxious to establish a Christian republic.

The Whigs in Power

10.5 Why was William Henry Harrison's death such a blow to the Whig agenda? p. 274

Most Whigs expected the politically inexperienced Harrison to go along with Henry Clay's package of congressional measures that were intended to revive the economy and associate the Whigs with renewed prosperity. Harrison's death upended all of Clay's plans. Harrison's successor, John Tyler, used his veto powers to crush Clay's program.

Timeline

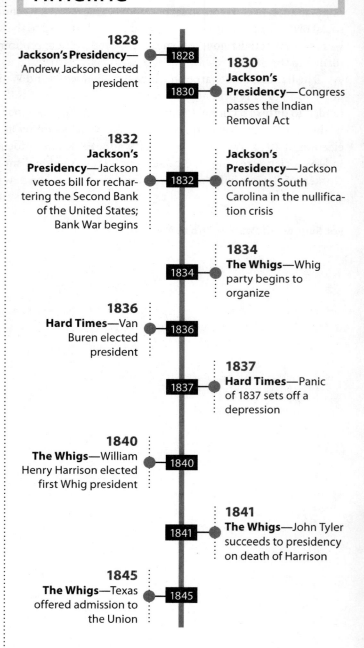

1828
Jackson's Presidency— Andrew Jackson elected president

1830
Jackson's Presidency—Congress passes the Indian Removal Act

1832
Jackson's Presidency—Jackson vetoes bill for rechartering the Second Bank of the United States; Bank War begins

Jackson's Presidency—Jackson confronts South Carolina in the nullification crisis

1834
The Whigs—Whig party begins to organize

1836
Hard Times—Van Buren elected president

1837
Hard Times—Panic of 1837 sets off a depression

1840
The Whigs—William Henry Harrison elected first Whig president

1841
The Whigs—John Tyler succeeds to presidency on death of Harrison

1845
The Whigs—Texas offered admission to the Union

11 Slavery and the Old South 1800–1860

One American Journey

Excerpt from a Novel Written by a Female Black Slave

Had Mrs Wheeler condemned me to the severest corporal punish, or exposed me to be sold in the public slave market in Wilmington [New Carolina] I should probably have resigned myself with apparent composure to her cruel behests. But when she sought to force me into a compulsory union with a man whom I could only hate and despise it seemed that rebellion would be a virtue, that duty to myself and my God actually required it, and that whatever accidents or misfortunes might attend my flight nothing could be worse than what threatened my stay.

Marriage like many other blessings I considered to be especially designed for the free, and something that all the victims of slavery should avoid as tending essentially to perpetuate that system. Hence to all overtures of that kind from whatever quarter they might come I had invariably turned a deaf ear. I had spurned domestic ties not because my heart was hard, but because it was my unalterable resolution never to entail slavery on any human being. And now when I had voluntarily renounced the society of those I might

The spectacle of the slave market was commonplace in the cities of the antebellum South. The above scene is of a slave auction in Richmond, Virginia.

LEARNING OBJECTIVES

11.1 How did the increasing demand for cotton shape the development of slavery in the Lower South? p. 281

11.2 What caused the decline of slavery after 1800 in the Upper South? p. 285

11.3 What was life like for African American slaves in the first half of the nineteenth century? p. 290

11.4 How was free society in the South structured? p. 296

11.5 How did the southern defense of slavery change between the early nineteenth century and the 1850s? p. 301

((• Listen to Chapter 11 on MyHistoryLab

Watch the Video Series on MyHistoryLab

Learn about some key topics related to this chapter with the *MyHistoryLab Video Series: Key Topics in U.S. History.*

1 **The Upper and Lower South: 1800–1860** Differences in climate, geography, economic incentives, and the degree of agricultural diversification all contributed to the distinctive character of various regions in the South in the first half of the nineteenth century. As this video shows, the regional diversity of the Upper and Lower South are particularly revealing of southern life, southern customs, southern wealth, and the deep-rootedness of the slave system on which everything rested.

 Watch on **MyHistoryLab**

Cotton and Slavery The South became the world's leading supplier of cotton after 1800, producing more than 4 million bales in the years just before the start of the Civil War. Growing conditions in the Lower South were particularly well suited to cotton production, and white southerners were quick to exploit this advantage by employing larger and larger numbers of slaves to support expansive cotton plantations. **2**

Watch on **MyHistoryLab**

3 **Slave Life and Culture** Slave life and culture were shaped by many forces, not least of which was the unrelenting labor extracted from slaves by their masters. Their status as property, reinforced by repressive slave codes, disrupted the social relations of slaves, whose families could be broken up by the sale or forced removal of parents, spouses, and children. Poor diet and inadequate housing were constant torments even though slave owners had strong and obvious economic incentives to provide better living conditions. Despite these and other obstacles arrayed against them, slaves often produced extensive and supportive ties to kin and community and challenged their enslavement with both everyday acts and with forms of resistance that were sometimes direct and violent.

 Watch on **MyHistoryLab**

Pro-Slavery Argument In response to increasing numbers of stinging attacks on slavery from quarters within and without the American South, some white southerners took steps to reinforce the institution, defending slavery, not as a necessary evil, but as a benevolent form of social organization that protected and nurtured an inferior race. The suppression of antislavery sentiment, by the 1850s, was a common cause among southern politicians, intellectuals, and evangelical ministers who vehemently argued, from the statehouse, the public square, and the pulpit, that slavery was a positive good. **4**

Watch on **MyHistoryLab**

have learned to love should I be compelled to accept one, whose person, and speech, and manner could not fail to be ever regarded by me with loathing and disgust. Then to be driven in to the fields beneath the eye and lash of the brutal overseer, and those miserable huts, with their promiscuous crowds of dirty, obscene and degraded objects, for my home I could not, I would not bear it.

Hannah Crafts

Personal Journeys Online

- Marie Perkins, *Letter*, 1852. A slave writes her husband informing him of the sale of their son.
- Lucy Skipwith, *Letter*, 1855. A slave writes her master in Virginia from his plantation in Alabama.
- Stephen Pembroke, *Speech by a slave*, 1854. A former slave describes his life under slavery.

H **annah Crafts** was the name an African American woman adopted after she escaped from slavery in the late 1850s. This passage is from *The Bondwoman's Narrative*, a recently discovered manuscript that stands as the only known novel written by a female black slave. Although the precise identity of Crafts remains uncertain, the evidence strongly suggests that she was a house slave of John Hill Wheeler of North Carolina who fled north in the spring of 1857, married a Methodist clergyman, and merged into the black middle class of southern New Jersey.

Only the system of slavery that Crafts described with revulsion makes it possible to speak of the antebellum South as a single region despite its geographical and cultural diversity. It was black slavery that created a bond among white southerners and cast them in a common mold.

Not only did slavery make the South distinctive, but it was also the source of the region's immense agricultural wealth, the foundation on which planters built their fortunes, the basis for white upward mobility, and the means by which white people controlled a large black minority. Precisely because slavery was so deeply embedded in southern life and customs, white leadership reacted to the mounting attacks on slavery after 1830 with an ever more defiant defense of the institution. That defense, in turn, reinforced a growing sense of sectionalism among white southerners, the belief that their values divided them from their fellow citizens in the Union.

Economically and intellectually, the Old South developed in stages. The South of 1860 was geographically much larger and more diverse than it had been in 1800. It was also more uniformly committed to a single cash crop, cotton. Cotton became king, as contemporaries put it, and it provided the economic basis for southern sectionalism. During the reign of King Cotton, however, regional differences emerged between the Lower South, where the linkage between cotton and slavery was strong, and the Upper South, where slavery was relatively less important and the economy was more diversified. In both regions the control mechanisms of slavery were very tight, and Hannah Crafts was exceptional in her successful flight to freedom.

The Lower South

11.1 How did the increasing demand for cotton shape the development of slavery in the Lower South?

S outh and west of South Carolina stretched some of the best cotton land in the world. A long growing season, adequate rainfall, navigable rivers, and untapped fertility gave the Lower South—consisting, in 1850, of South Carolina, Georgia, Florida, Alabama, Mississippi, Louisiana, and Texas—incomparable natural advantages for growing cotton. Ambitious white southerners exploited these advantages by extending slavery to the newer cotton lands that opened up in the Lower South after 1800 (see Map 11.1). Cotton production and slavery thus went hand in hand.

Cotton and Slaves

Before 1800, slavery was associated with the cash crops of tobacco, rice, and sea island (or long-staple) cotton. Tobacco, the mainstay of the colonial Chesapeake economy, severely depleted the soil. Its production stagnated after the Revolutionary War, when

Watch the Video **The Slave Trade**

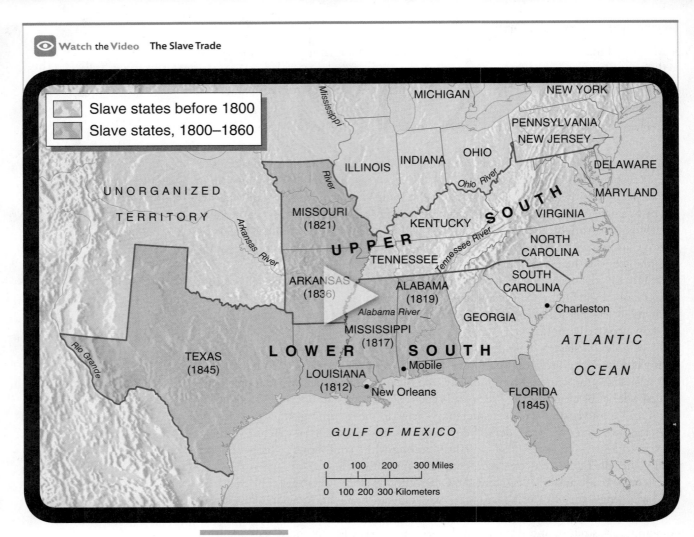

Slave states before 1800
Slave states, 1800–1860

MAP 11.1 THE SPREAD OF SLAVERY: NEW SLAVE STATES ENTERING THE UNION, 1800–1850
Seven slave states entered the Union after 1800 as cotton production shifted westward.

it lost its formerly protected markets in Britain. Rice and long-staple cotton, named for its long, silky fibers, were profitable but geographically limited to the humid sea islands and tidal flats off the coast of South Carolina and Georgia. Like sugar cane, introduced into Louisiana in the 1790s, they required a huge capital investment in special machinery, dikes, and labor. Upland, or short-staple, cotton faced none of these constraints, once the cotton gin removed the technical barrier to its commercial production (see Chapter 13). It could be planted far inland, and small farmers could grow it profitably because it required no additional costs for machinery or drainage systems.

As a result, after the 1790s, the production of short-staple cotton boomed. Moreover, like the South's other cash crops, upland cotton was well suited for slave labor because it required fairly continuous tending throughout the year. The long work year maximized the return on capital invested in slave labor.

The linkage of cotton and slaves was at the heart of the plantation system that spread westward after the War of 1812. From its original base in South Carolina and Georgia, the cotton kingdom moved into the Old Southwest and then into Texas and Arkansas. As wasteful agricultural practices exhausted new lands, planters moved to the next cotton frontier farther west. Cotton output exploded from 73,000 bales (a bale weighed close to 500 pounds) in 1800 to more than 2 million bales by mid-century, thanks to the fertility of virgin land and to technological changes, such as improved seed varieties and steam-powered cotton gins (see Figure 11.1). Slave labor accounted for more than 90 percent of cotton production.

Plantations, large productive units specializing in a cash crop and employing at least twenty slaves, were the leading economic institution in the Lower South. Planters

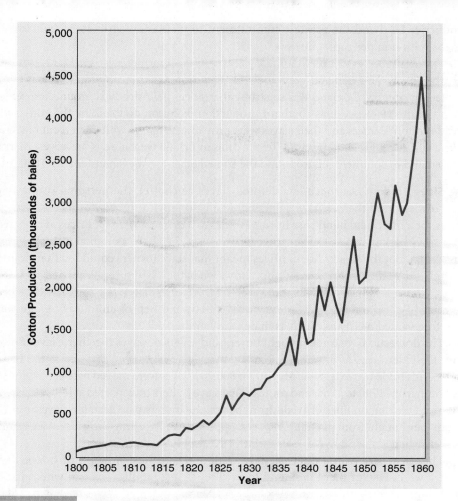

FIGURE 11.1 U.S. COTTON PRODUCTION, 1800–1860 Cotton production spiraled upward after 1800, and the South became the world's leading supplier.

SOURCE: U.S. Bureau of the Census, *Historical Statistical Abstract of the United States* (1960).

were the most prestigious social group, and, although fewer than 5 percent of white families were in the planter class, they controlled more than 40 percent of the slaves, cotton output, and total agricultural wealth. Most had inherited or married into their wealth, but they could stay at the top of the South's class structure only by continuing to profit from slave labor.

Plantations were generally more efficient producers of cotton than small farms. A variety of factors contributed to this efficiency. Most important, the ownership of twenty or more slaves enabled planters to use gangs to do both routine and specialized agricultural work. This **gang system**, a crude version of the division of labor that was being introduced in northern factories, permitted a regimented work pace. Teams of field hands, made up of women as well as men, had to work at a steady pace or else feel the lash.

The plantation districts of the Lower South stifled the growth of towns and economic enterprise. Planters, as well as ordinary farmers, strove to be self-sufficient. The most significant economic exchange, exporting cotton, took place in international markets and was handled by specialized commission merchants in Charleston, Mobile, and New Orleans. The Lower South had amassed great wealth, but most outsiders saw no signs of progress there.

gang system The organization and supervision of slave field hands into working teams on southern plantations.

The Profits of Slavery

Slavery was profitable on an individual basis. Most modern studies indicate that the average rate of return on capital invested in a slave was about 10 percent a year, a rate that at least equaled that of alternative investments in the South or the North. Not surprisingly, the newer regions of the cotton kingdom in the Lower South, with the most

283

productive land and the greatest commitment to plantation agriculture, consistently led the nation in per capita income.

The profitability of slavery ultimately rested on the enormous demand for cotton outside the South. This demand grew at about 5 percent a year during the first half of the nineteenth century. Demand was so strong that prices held steady at around ten cents a pound in the 1850s, even as southern production of cotton doubled. By the end of that decade cotton planters and their slaves were providing England with 77 percent of its raw cotton and France with 90 percent. Textile mills in Britain were always the largest market, but demand in continental Europe and the United States grew even faster after 1840.

The Slave Trade.   Southern law defined slaves as chattel, the personal property of their owners, and their market value increased along with the profitability of slavery. Prices for a male field hand rose from $250 in 1815 to $900 by 1860. Prices at any given time varied according to the age, sex, and skills of the slave, as well as overall market conditions, but the steady rise in prices meant that slave owners could sell their human chattel and realize a profit over and above what they had already earned from the slaves' labor. This was especially the case with slave mothers; the children they bore increased the capital assets of their owners. Slave women of childbearing age were therefore valued nearly as much as male field hands.

The domestic slave trade brought buyers and sellers of slaves together. Slaves flowed from the older areas of the Upper South to the newer plantation districts in the Lower South. This trade was extensive: More than 800,000 slaves were moved between regions in the South from 1790 to 1860, and professional slave traders transported at least 60 percent of them. Drawing on lines of credit from banks, the traders paid cash for slaves, most of whom they bought from plantations in the Upper South. By selling these slaves in regional markets where demand had driven up the price, they turned a tidy profit.

The sheer size of the internal slave trade indicates just how profit-driven slave owners were. Few of them hesitated to break up slave families for sale when market conditions were right. About half of all slave sales separated family members. Slave children born in the Upper South after 1820 stood a one-in-three chance of being sold during their lifetime. Most of the profits from slave labor and sales went into buying more land and slaves. As long as slaves employed in growing cash staples returned 10 percent a year, slave owners had little economic incentive to shift their capital resources into manufacturing or urban development. The predictable result was that industrialization and urbanization fell far behind the levels in the free states.

(((• 📖 **Read the Document**   Henry Watson, A Slave Tells of His Sale at Auction (1848)

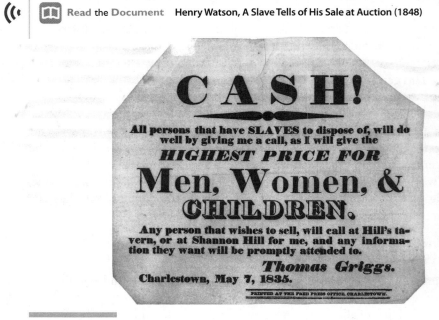

Like most slave traders, Thomas Griggs of Charleston offered cash for all slaves he purchased.

Nowhere was the indifference of planters to economic diversification more evident than in the Lower South, which had the smallest urban population and the fewest factories. Planters here were not opposed to economic innovations that promised greater profits, but they feared social changes that might undermine the stability of slavery. Urbanization and industrialization both entailed such risks. Most planters suspected that the urban environment weakened slavery.

Urban Slavery. Urban slaves were artisans, semiskilled laborers, and domestics, and, unlike their rural counterparts, they usually lived apart from their owners. They had much more freedom than field hands to move around, interact with white people and other black people, and experiment with various social roles. Many of them, especially if they had a marketable skill, such as carpentry or tailoring, could hire out their labor and retain some of their wages for themselves after reimbursing their owners. In short, the direct authority of the slave owner was less clear-cut in the town than in the country.

Urban slavery declined from 1820 to 1860 as slaves decreased from 22 percent to 10 percent of the urban population. This decline reflected both doubts about the stability of slavery in an urban setting and the large profits that slave labor earned for slave owners in the rural cotton economy.

Industrial Slavery. The ambivalence of planters toward urban slavery also characterized their attitudes toward industrial slavery and, indeed, to industrialization itself. If based on free labor, industrialization risked promoting an antislavery class consciousness among manufacturing laborers that would challenge the property rights of slave owners. But the use of slaves as factory operatives threatened slave discipline because an efficient level of production required special incentives. A Virginian noted of slaves that he had hired out for industrial work, "They were worked hard, and had too much liberty, and were acquiring bad habits. They earned money by overwork, and spent it for whisky, and got a habit of roaming about and *taking care of themselves;* because, when they were not at work in the furnace, nobody looked out for them."

No more than 5 percent of the slaves in the Lower South ever worked in manufacturing, and most of these were in rural enterprises serving local markets too small to interest northern manufacturers. Ever concerned to preserve slavery, planters would not risk slave discipline or the profits of cotton agriculture by embracing the unpredictable changes that industrialization was sure to bring.

The Upper South

11.2 What caused the decline of slavery after 1800 in the Upper South?

Climate and geography distinguished the Upper South from the Lower South. The eight slave states of the Upper South lay north of the best growing zones for cotton. The northernmost of these states—Delaware, Maryland, Kentucky, and Missouri—bordered on free states and were known as the Border South. The four states south of them—Virginia, North Carolina, Tennessee, and Arkansas—constituted a middle zone. Slavery was entrenched in all these states, but it was less dominant than in the cotton South.

The key difference between the Upper and Lower South was the suitability of the Lower South for growing cotton with gangs of slave laborers. Except for prime cotton districts in middle Tennessee, eastern Arkansas, and parts of North Carolina, the Upper South lacked the fertile soil and long growing season necessary for the commercial production of cotton, rice, or sugar (see Map 11.2). Consequently, the demand for slaves was weaker than in the Lower South. Two-thirds of white southerners lived in the Upper South in 1860, but they held only 45 percent of all slaves. Percentages of slave ownership and of slaves in the overall population were roughly half those in the cotton

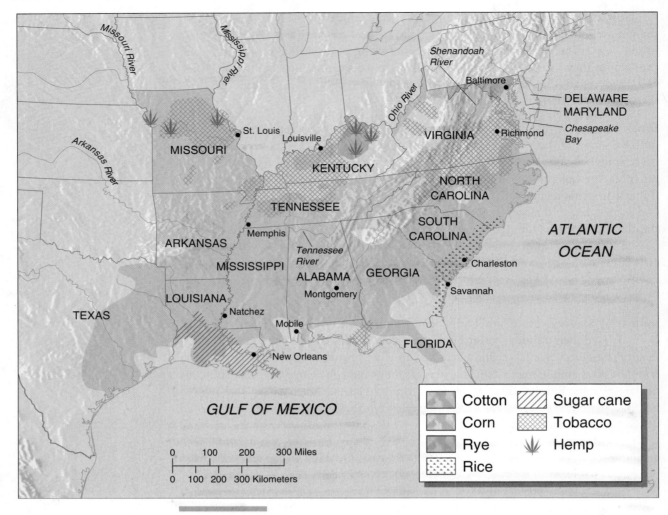

MAP 11.2 COTTON AND OTHER CROPS IN THE SOUTH, 1860 Most of the Upper South was outside the cotton belt, where the demand for slave labor was greatest.

South. While the Lower South was undergoing a cotton boom after the War of 1812, the Upper South was mired in a long economic slump, from which it did not emerge until the 1850s. The improved economy of the Upper South in the late antebellum period increasingly relied on free labor, a development that many cotton planters feared would diminish southern unity in defense of slavery.

A Period of Economic Adjustment

To inhabitants and visitors alike, vast stretches of the Upper South presented a dreary spectacle of exhausted fields and depopulation in the 1820s and 1830s. The soil was most depleted where tobacco had been cultivated extensively. Even where the land was still fertile, farmers could not compete against the fresher lands of the Old Southwest. Land values fell as farmers dumped their property and headed west.

Agricultural reform emerged in the 1830s as one proposed solution to this economic crisis. Its leading advocate was Edmund Ruffin, a Virginia planter who tirelessly promoted the use of marl (calcium-rich seashell deposits) to neutralize the overly acidic and worn-out soils of the Upper South. He also called for deeper plowing, systematic rotation of crops, and upgrading the breeding stock for animal husbandry.

Ruffin's efforts, and those of the agricultural societies and fairs spawned by the reform movement, met with some success, especially in the 1840s, when the prices of all cash staples fell. Still, only a minority of farmers ever embraced reform. These were generally the well-educated planters who read the agricultural press and could afford to change their farming practices.

From Then to Now
Overcoming the Economic Legacy of Slavery

S lavery generated immense wealth for the planter elite and consistent profits from the production and export sale of cash staples such as cotton. As long as plantation agriculture remained profitable, planters had little incentive to diversify the southern economy along the path of manufacturing and transportation improvements followed by the antebellum North. At the same time, the vast bulk of southerners—black slaves to be sure as well as most nonslaveholding whites—lacked the cash income and educational skills needed to create a sectional demand for consumer goods or improvements in their standard of living. Defeat in the Civil War and the revolutionary changes that emancipation brought to southern agriculture wiped out capital reserves and left in its wake persistent poverty and underdevelopment. From near parity in 1860, the region's per capita income fell to but half that of the nation as a whole by 1880 and remained at that trough until well into the twentieth century. It is no wonder that by the 1930s the South was labeled as the nation's number-one economic problem.

Massive federal spending programs associated with the New Deal initiated a tentative upswing in the southern economy.

Then, during World War II, abundant, well-paying jobs accelerated the outflow of the South's low-skilled workers, and federal money poured into the South for new defense plants and war-related projects. By the 1950s, the southern economy had turned the corner. Southern politicians became adept at attracting new sources of capital and large federal subsidies, and the white business elite, at first reluctantly and then with increasing speed, backed the formal end of segregation in order to improve the South's image. Today, well over a century after slavery placed it on a separate path of economic development, the southern economy has entered the national mainstream and enjoys one of the highest rates of economic growth in the nation.

Question for Discussion

- How would you explain the role that the sudden end of slavery played in the chronic poverty that plagued the South for so long?

A common scene at harvest time in the Lower South: slaves working in a cotton field under the supervision of a white overseer, shown here mounted on his horse.

BMW workers on an assembly line in a new production plant in the South.

Although soil exhaustion and wasteful farming persisted, agriculture in the Upper South had revived by the 1850s. A rebound in the tobacco market accounted for part of this revival, but the growing profitability of general farming was responsible for most of it.

Particularly in the Border South, the trend was toward agricultural diversification. Farmers and planters lessened their dependence on slave labor or on a single cash crop and practiced a thrifty, efficient agriculture geared to producing grain and livestock for urban markets. Western Maryland and the Shenandoah Valley and northern sections of Virginia grew wheat, and in the former tobacco districts of the Virginia and North Carolina Tidewater, wheat, corn, and garden vegetables became major cash crops.

Expanding urban markets and a network of internal improvements facilitated the transition to general farming. Both these developments were outgrowths of the movement for industrial diversification launched in the 1820s in response to the heavy outflow of population from the Upper South.

Growing Urbanization. Although not far advanced by northern standards, urbanization and industrialization in the Upper South were considerably greater than in the Lower South. The region had twice the percentage of urban residents of the cotton South, and it contained the leading manufacturing cities in the slave states, St. Louis, Baltimore, and Louisville. Canals and railroads linked cities and countryside in a denser transportation grid than in the Lower South.

With an economy more balanced among agriculture, manufacturing, and trade than a generation earlier, the Upper South at mid-century was gradually becoming less tied to plantation agriculture and slave labor. The rural majority increasingly prospered by growing foodstuffs for city dwellers and factory workers. The labor market for railroad construction and manufacturing work attracted northern immigrants, helping to compensate for the loss of the native-born population through migration to other states.

The economic adjustment in the Upper South converted the labor surplus of the 1820s into a labor scarcity by the 1850s. "It is a fact," noted Edmund Ruffin in 1859, "that labor is greatly deficient in all Virginia, and especially in the rich western counties, which, for want of labor, scarcely yet yield in the proportion of one tenth of their capacity." Ruffin's commitment to agricultural reform was exceeded only by his devotion to slavery. He now feared that free labor was about to replace scarce and expensive slave labor in Virginia and much of the Upper South.

The Decline of Slavery

Slave owners tended to exaggerate all threats to slavery, and Ruffin was no exception. But slavery was clearly growing weaker in the Upper South by the 1850s (see Figure 11.2). The decline was most evident along the northern tier of the Upper South, where the proportion of slaves to the overall population fell steadily after 1830.

Elsewhere in the Upper South, slavery was holding its own by the 1850s. Tobacco and cotton planters in North Carolina and Tennessee continued to rely heavily on slave labor, but most small farmers were indifferent, if not opposed, to the institution. Only

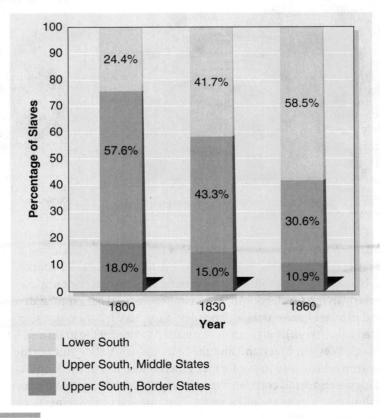

FIGURE 11.2 THE CHANGING REGIONAL PATTERN OF SLAVERY IN THE SOUTH, 1800–1860 As the nineteenth century progressed, slavery increasingly became identified with the cotton-growing Lower South.
SOURCE: U.S. Census Bureau

in Arkansas, whose alluvial lands along the Mississippi River offered a new frontier for plantation agriculture, was slavery growing rapidly. Slaves, however, still made up only 25 percent of the population of Arkansas in 1860 and were confined mainly to the southeastern corner of the state. Geographically dominated by the Ozark Highlands, Arkansas was best suited to general farming.

The region's role as a slave exporter to the Lower South hastened the decline of slavery in the Upper South. In every decade after 1820, the internal slave trade drained off about 10 percent of the slaves in the Upper South, virtually the entire natural increase. Slave traders initially made most of their purchases in Virginia and Maryland, but by the 1850s, they were also active in the Carolinas, Kentucky, and Missouri.

Selling slaves to the Lower South reinforced the Upper South's economic stake in slavery at a time when the institution was otherwise barely profitable there. The sale of surplus slaves was a windfall for planters whose slaves had become an economic burden. This same windfall gave planters the capital to embark on agricultural reform and shift out of tobacco production. Investment capital in the Upper South was not flowing into slave property but into economic diversification that expanded urban manufacturing. Both of these structural changes increasingly put slavery at a competitive disadvantage against free labor.

The wheat, corn, oats, and fodder crops that replaced tobacco in much of the Upper South did not require continuous attention. Unlike tobacco, wheat needed intensive labor only at planting and harvest. Thus, as planters abandoned tobacco, they kept fewer slaves and relied on cheap seasonal workers to meet peak labor demand.

The cheapness and flexibility of free labor made it better suited than slave labor for general farming. Urban manufacturers likewise wanted workers who could be hired and fired at a moment's notice. Despite the successful use of slaves in tobacco manufacturing and at the large Tredegar Iron Works in Richmond, immigrant workers displaced slaves in most of the factories in the Border South. By 1860, slaves made up just 1 percent of the population in St. Louis and Baltimore, the South's major industrial cities.

The internal slave trade was the primary means by which the slaves of the Upper South were brought into the plantation markets of the Old Southwest. Shown here are slaves being driven south.

Slavery was in economic retreat across the Upper South after 1830. There were still plantation districts with large concentrations of slaves, and slave owners retained enough political power to defeat all challenges to their property interests. Nevertheless, the gradual turn to free labor was unmistakable. As Alfred Iveson, a Georgia planter, noted with alarm in 1860, "Those border States can get along without slavery. Their soil and climate are appropriate to white labor; they can live and flourish without African slavery; but the cotton States cannot."

Slave Life and Culture

11.3 What was life like for African American slaves in the first half of the nineteenth century?

Nearly 4 million slaves lived in the South by 1860, a more than fivefold increase since the ratification of the Constitution. This population gain was overwhelmingly due to an excess of births over deaths. The British-led effort to suppress the foreign slave trade was successful in closing off fresh supplies from Africa after 1807.

Almost all southern slaves were thus native-born by the mid-nineteenth century. They were not Africans but African Americans, and they shared the common fate of bondage. By resisting an enslavement they could not prevent, they shaped a culture of their own that eased their pain and raised their hopes of someday being free. They retained their dignity in the face of continual humiliation and relied on their family life and religious beliefs as sources of strength under nearly intolerable circumstances.

Work Routines and Living Conditions

Being treated as a piece of property to be worked for profit and bought and sold when financially advantageous to one's owners—this was the legal and economic reality that all slaves confronted. Each southern state had its own **slave code,** laws defining the status of slaves and the rights of masters; the codes gave slave owners near-absolute power over their human property.

Slaves could not own property, make contracts, possess guns or alcohol, legally marry (except in Louisiana), leave plantations without the owner's written permission, or testify against their masters or any other white person in a court of law. Many states also prohibited teaching a slave to read or write. The law assumed that the economic self-interest of masters in their slave property gave slaves adequate legal protection against injury. The murder of a slave by a master was illegal, but in practice, the law and community standards looked the other way if a disobedient slave was killed while being disciplined.

The slave codes penalized any challenge to a master's authority or any infraction of plantation rules. Whippings were the most commonly authorized punishment: 20 lashes on the bare back for leaving a plantation without a pass, 100 lashes for writing a pass for another slave, and so on. Striking a master, committing arson, or conspiring to rebel were punishable by death. Most masters recognized that it made good business sense to feed, clothe, and house their slaves well enough to ensure productive labor and to encourage a family life that would enable the slave population to reproduce itself. Thus planters' self-interest probably improved the living standards for slaves in the first half of the nineteenth century, and the slave population grew at a rate only slightly below that of white southerners.

Diet and Housing. Planters rarely provided their slaves with more than the bare necessities. The slaves lived mainly on rations of cornmeal and salt pork, supplemented with vegetables they grew on the small garden plots that many planters permitted and with occasional catches of game and fish. This diet provided ample calories but often insufficient vitamins and nutrients to protect slaves (as well as the many poor

slave code A series of laws passed mainly in the southern colonies in the late seventeenth and early eighteenth centuries to defend the status of slaves and codify the denial of basic civil rights to them.

whites who ate the same diet) against such diseases as beriberi and pellagra. Intestinal disorders were chronic, and dysentery and cholera were common. About 20 percent of the slaves on a typical plantation were sick at any given time. Infant mortality was twice as high among slaves as among white southerners in 1850; so was mortality among slave children up to age 14. According to one study, the life expectancy for slaves at birth was 21 to 22 years, roughly half the white life expectancy.

Planters furnished slaves with two sets of coarse clothing, one for summer and one for winter. Their housing, typically a 15-by-15-foot, one-room cabin for five or six occupants, provided little more than basic shelter against the elements. Small and unadorned, slave cabins showed the planters' desire to minimize housing costs and their determination to treat slaves as a regimented collective population. Large planters placed these cabins in a row, an arrangement that projected precision and undifferentiated order. Slaves expressed their individuality by furnishing their cabins with handmade beds and benches and by pushing for the right to put in gardens.

Working Conditions. The diet and housing of most slaves may have been no worse than that of the poorest whites in both the North and the South, but their workload was undoubtedly heavier. Just over half of the slave population at mid-century was concentrated on plantation units with twenty or more slaves, and most of these slaves worked as field hands in gang labor. Overseers freely admitted that they relied on whippings to make slaves in the gangs keep at their work.

Most plantation slaves toiled at hard physical labor from sunup to sundown. The work was more intense and sustained than that of white farmers or white factory hands. The fear of the whip on a bare back set the pace.

Some 15 to 20 percent of plantation slaves were house servants or skilled artisans who had lighter and less regimented workloads than field hands. Some planters used the prospect of transfer to these relatively privileged positions as an incentive to field hands to work harder. Extra rations, time off on weekends, passes to visit a spouse on a nearby plantation, and the right to have a garden plot were among the other incentives planters used to keep labor productivity high. However, what a planter viewed as privileges, benevolently bestowed, slaves quickly came to see as customary rights. Despite the power of the whip, if planters failed to respect these "rights," slave morale would decline, and the work routine would be interrupted.

Nearly three-fourths of the slaves worked on plantations and medium-sized farms. Most of the remainder, those in units with fewer than ten slaves, worked on small farms in close contact with the master's family. Their workloads were more varied and sometimes less taxing than those of plantation hands, but these slaves were also more directly exposed to the whims of their owners and less likely to live in complete family units. Slave couples on small holdings were more likely to live on separate farms. Owners with only a few slaves were also more vulnerable than planters to market downturns that could force them to sell slaves and further divide families.

Of all slaves, 10 percent were not attached to the land, laboring instead at jobs that most white workers shunned. Every southern industry, but most particularly extractive industries such as mining and lumbering, relied heavily on slaves. The Tredegar Iron Company in Richmond, the largest iron foundry in the South, used slaves as its main workforce after 1847, partly to curb strikes by its white workers. Racial tensions often flared in southern industry, and when the races worked together, skilled white laborers typically insisted on being placed in supervisory positions.

Digging coal as miners or shoveling it as stokers for boilers on steamboats, laying down iron for the railroads or shaping hot slabs of it in a foundry, industrial slaves worked at least as hard as field hands. Compared to plantation slaves, however, they had more independence off the job and greater opportunities to earn money of their own. Because many of them had to house and feed themselves, they could also enjoy more time free from direct white scrutiny. By undertaking extra factory work, known as "overwork," industrial slaves could earn $50 or more a month, money they could use to buy goods for their families or, in rare cases, to purchase their freedom.

Families and Religion

The core institution of slave life was the family. Except in Louisiana, southern law did not recognize slave marriages, but masters permitted, even encouraged, marital unions in order to raise the morale of their labor force and increase its value by having it produce marketable children. Slaves embraced their families as a source of loving warmth and strength in a system that treated them as commodities.

Despite all the obstacles arrayed against them, many slave marriages produced enduring commitments and a supportive moral code for family members. Most slave unions remained intact until the death or, frequently, the sale of one spouse. Close to one-third of slave marriages were broken up by sales or forced removals.

Both parents were present in about two-thirds of slave families, the same ratio as in contemporary peasant families in Western Europe. Although the father's role as protector of and provider for his wife and children had no standing under slavery, most slave fathers struggled to help feed their families by hunting and fishing, and they risked beating and death to defend their wives against sexual abuse by the overseer or master. Besides their field labors, slave mothers had all the burdens of pregnancy, childcare, laundry, and cooking.

No anguish under slavery was more heartrending than that of a mother whose child was sold away from her. "Oh, my heart was too full!" recalled Charity Bowery on being told that her boy Richard had been sold. "[My mistress] had sent me away on an errand, because she didn't want to be troubled with our cries. I hadn't any chance to see my poor boy. I shall never see my poor boy. I shall never see him again in this world. My heart felt as if it was under a great load."

Charity Bowery's experience was hardly unique. Slave parents had to suppress the rage they felt at their powerlessness to protect their children from the cruelties of slavery. Most parents could only teach their children the skills of survival in a world in which white people had a legal monopoly on violence. The most valuable of these skills was the art of hiding one's true feelings from white people and telling them what they wanted to hear.

Extensive kinship ties provided a support network for the vulnerable slave family. Thickest on the older and larger plantations, these networks included both blood relatives and other significant people. Children were taught to address elders as "Aunt" and "Uncle" and fellow slaves as "Sister" and "Brother." If separated from a parent, a child could turn to relatives or the larger slave community for care and assistance.

Slaves followed West African customs by prohibiting marriage between cousins and by often naming their children after departed grandparents. They also drew on an African heritage kept alive through folklore and oral histories to create a religion that fit their needs. The ancestors of nineteenth-century slaves brought no common religion with them when they were taken to the New World. However, beliefs common to a variety of African religions survived. Once slaves began to embrace Christianity in the late eighteenth century, they blended these beliefs into an African Christianity. In keeping with African traditions, the religion of the slaves fused the natural and spiritual worlds, accepted the power of ghosts over the living, and relied on an expressive form of worship in which the participants shouted and swayed in rhythm with the beat of drums and other instruments.

By most estimates, no more than 30 percent of slaves ever converted to Christianity. Those who did found in Christianity a message of deliverance rooted in the liberation of Moses's people from bondage in Egypt. The Jesus of the New Testament spoke to them as a compassionate God who had shared their burden of suffering, so that all peoples could hope to find the Promised Land of love and justice. By blending biblical imagery into their spirituals, the slaves expressed their yearning for freedom: "Didn't my Lord deliver Daniel/Then why not every man?"

The initial exposure of slaves to Christianity usually came from evangelical revivalists, and slaves always favored the Baptists and Methodists over other denominations. The evangelical message of universal spiritual equality confirmed the slaves' sense of personal worth. Less formal in both their doctrines and organization than the Presbyterians and Episcopalians, the evangelical sects allowed the slaves more leeway to choose their own preachers and engage in their physical call-and-response pattern of worship. Perhaps because they baptized by total immersion, which evoked the purifying power of water so common in African religions, the Baptists gained the most slave converts.

Most planters were pragmatic about encouraging Christianity among their slaves. They wished to control religion, as they did other aspects of slaves' lives. Thus, while many planters allowed black preachers at religious services on their plantations, they usually insisted that white observers be present. Worried that abolitionist propaganda might attract the slaves to Christianity as a religion of secular liberation, some planters in the late antebellum period tried to convert their slaves to their own version of Christianity. They invited white ministers to their plantations to preach a gospel of passivity and obedience, centered on Paul's call for servants to "obey in all things your Masters."

Although most slaves viewed the religion of their owners as hypocritical and the sermons of white ministers as propaganda, they feigned acceptance of the religious wishes of their masters. As much as they could, the slaves hid their genuine religious life from white people. Many slaves experienced religion as a spiritual rebirth that gave them the inner strength to endure their bondage. As one recalled, "I was born a slave and lived through some hard times. If it had not been for my God, I don't know what I would have done."

Resistance

Open resistance to slavery was futile. The persistently disobedient slave would be sold "down river" to a harsher master or, in extreme cases, killed. Nevertheless, although the odds of succeeding were infinitesimal, slaves did plot rebellion in the nineteenth century.

The first major uprising, **Gabriel Prosser's Rebellion** in 1800, involved about fifty armed slaves around Richmond, though perhaps as many as 1,000 slaves knew about Prosser's plans. The rebels' failure to seize a key road to Richmond and a slave informer's warning to white authorities doomed the rebellion before it got under way. State authorities executed Prosser and twenty-five of his followers.

In January 1811, in what seems to have been a spontaneous bid for freedom, several hundred slaves in the river parishes (counties) above New Orleans marched on the city. Poorly armed, they were no match for the U.S. Army troops and militiamen who stopped them. Led by the slave driver Charles Deslondes, the rebels killed two white men. Nearly 100 slaves died. Some, like Deslondes, were mutilated before their bodies were burned; others were "tried" and then executed by hanging or decapitation. The heads of the leading rebels were posted on poles along the Mississippi River to warn others of the fate that awaited rebellious slaves. It was macabre scene. "I am told," one observer wrote, "[the heads] look like crows sitting on long poles."

The most carefully planned slave revolt (at least in the minds of whites who resorted to torture to gain "confessions"), **Denmark Vesey's Conspiracy**, like Prosser's, failed before it got started. Vesey, a literate carpenter and lay preacher in Charleston who had purchased his freedom, allegedly planned the revolt in the summer of 1822. The plot collapsed when two domestic servants betrayed it. White authorities responded swiftly and savagely. They hanged thirty-five conspirators, including Vesey, and banished thirty-seven others from the state. After destroying the African Methodist Episcopal church where Vesey had preached and the purported conspirators had met, they tried to seal off the city from subversive outsiders by passing the Negro Seamen's Act, which mandated the imprisonment of black sailors while their ships were berthed in Charleston.

Nat Turner's Rebellion, in Southampton County, Virginia, erupted before it could be suppressed. Turner was a literate field hand driven by prophetic visions of black vengeance against white oppressors. Convinced by what he called "signs in heaven" that he should "arise and prepare myself and slay my enemies with their own weapons," he led a small band of followers on a murderous rampage in late August 1831. The first white man to be killed was Joseph Travis, Turner's owner. In the next two days, the rebels killed sixty other white people. An enraged posse, aided by slaves, captured or killed most of Turner's party. Turner hid for two months before being apprehended. He and more than thirty other slaves were executed, and panicky white people killed more than a hundred others.

Gabriel Prosser's Rebellion Slave revolt that failed when Gabriel Prosser, a slave preacher and blacksmith, organized a thousand slaves for an attack on Richmond, Virginia, in 1800.

Denmark Vesey's Conspiracy The most carefully devised slave revolt in which rebels planned to seize control of Charleston in 1822 and escape to freedom in Haiti, a free black republic, but they were betrayed by other slaves, and thirty-five conspirators were executed.

Nat Turner's Rebellion Uprising of slaves led by Nat Turner in Southampton County, Virginia, in the summer of 1831 that resulted in the death of up to sixty white people.

Read the Document   Thomas R. Gray, *The Confessions of Nat Turner* (1831)

This contemporary woodcut of Nat Turner's Rebellion depicts the fervency of both the actions of the slaves and the response of the whites.

Slaves well understood that the odds against a successful rebellion were insurmountable. They could see who had all the guns. White people were also more numerous. In contrast to the large black majorities in the slave societies of the West Indies and Brazil, majorities made possible only by the continuous heavy importation of Africans, slaves made up only one-third of the population of the antebellum U.S. South. They lacked the numbers to overwhelm the white population and could not escape to mountain hideaways or large tracts of jungle. Surveillance by mounted white patrols, part of the police apparatus of slavery, limited organized rebellion by slaves to small, local affairs that were quickly suppressed.

Nor could many slaves escape to freedom. Few runaways made it to Canada or to a free state. White people could stop black people and demand to see papers documenting their freedom or right to travel without a master. The **Underground Railroad,** a secret network of stations and safe houses organized by Quakers and other black and white antislavery activists, provided some assistance. However, fellow slaves or free black people, especially in the cities of the Border South, provided the only help most runaways could count on. Out of more than 3 million slaves in the 1850s, only about 1,000 a year permanently escaped.

Running away was common, but most runaways fled no farther than to nearby swamps and woods. Most voluntarily returned or were tracked down by bloodhounds within a week. Aside from those who were protesting a special grievance or trying to avoid punishment, slaves who ran away usually did so to visit a spouse or loved one. Occasionally, runaways could bargain for lenient treatment in return for faithful service in the future. Most were severely punished. Such temporary flights from the master's control siphoned off some of the anger that might otherwise have erupted in violent, self-destructive attacks on slave owners. All planters had heard about the field hand who took an ax to an overseer, the cook who poisoned her master's family, or the house servant who killed a sleeping master or mistress.

Slaves resisted complete domination by their masters in less overt ways. They mocked white people in folktales like those about B'rer Rabbit, for example, in which weak but wily animals cunningly outsmart their stronger enemies. Slave owners routinely complained

Underground Railroad Support system set up by antislavery groups in the Upper South and the North to assist fugitive slaves in escaping the South.

Explore the Underground Railroad on MyHistoryLab

The Resurrection of Henry Box Brown at Philadelphia is a lithograph that depicts Henry Brown emerging from the shipping crate he and abolitionists used to ship him from Richmond, Virginia, to freedom in Philadelphia in 1849.

WHAT WAS THE PURPOSE OF THE UNDERGROUND RAILROAD?

In the early 1800s, a secret network emerged in the United States as the nation became increasingly divided over the issue of slavery. Opponents of slavery helped organize various secret routes and safe houses to covertly smuggle slaves from the slave states of the South to the free states of the North. "Railroad" came to be the code word for the system. "Conductors" guided and assisted the escaped slaves, who were called the "freight." Canada was often the final destination, especially after the Fugitive Slave Law of 1850. Slaves and those helping them to escape faced significant legal and geographical obstacles; nevertheless, the network of departure points in Border States and southern ports, as well as safe houses ("stations") and routes, increased over the decades prior to the Civil War.

SELECTED UNDERGROUND RAILROAD POINTS OF DEPARTURE

SOURCE: Prentice Hall Historical Atlas, 1999 page 28.

KEY QUESTIONS   Use **MyHistoryLab** *Explorer* to answer these **questions:**

Cause ▶▶▶ *What geographic features made passage on the Underground Railroad more difficult?*

Map major "routes" and obstacles along the way.

Analysis ▶▶▶ *Which regions of the South provided the most slaves on the railroad?*

Consider the reasons for such patterns.

Consequence ▶▶▶ *How did Congress's Fugitive Slave Law of 1850 affect the railroad?*

Explore the impact of this on "stations," "routes," and "freight."

Watch the Video   Underground Railroad

The $100 reward offered in this newspaper ad for helping capture a slave runaway in Missouri in 1860 would be worth well over $2,000 in today's currency.

of slaves malingering at work, abusing farm animals, losing tools, stealing food, and committing arson. These subversive acts of protest never challenged the system of slavery itself, but they did help slaves to maintain a sense of dignity and self-respect.

Free Society

11.4   How was free society in the South structured?

The abolitionists and the antislavery Republican Party of the 1850s portrayed the social order of the slave South as little more than haughty planters lording it over shiftless poor white people. The reality was considerably more complex (see Table 11.1). Planters, who set the social tone for the South as a whole, did act superior, but they were a tiny minority and had to contend with an ambitious middle class of small slaveholders and a majority of nonslaveholding farmers. Some landless white people on the margins of rural society fit the stereotype of "poor whites," but they were easily outnumbered by self-reliant farmers who worked their own land. Southern cities, though small by northern standards, provided jobs for a growing class of free workers who increasingly clashed with planters over the use of slave labor. These same cities, notably in the Upper South, were also home to the nation's largest concentration of free black people.

The Slaveholding Minority

The white-columned plantation estate approached from a stately avenue of shade trees and framed by luxuriant gardens remains the most popular image of the slave South. In fact, such manorial estates were utterly unrepresentative of the lifestyle of the typical

TABLE 11.1 STRUCTURE OF FREE SOCIETY IN THE SOUTH, c. 1860

Group	Size	Characteristics
Large planters	Less than 1 percent of white families	Owned 50 or more slaves and plantations in excess of 1,000 acres; the wealthiest class in the United States
Planters	About 3 percent of white families	Owned 20 to 49 slaves and plantations in excess of 100 acres; controlled bulk of southern wealth and provided most of the political leaders
Small slaveholders	About 20 percent of white families	Owned fewer than 20 slaves and most often fewer than 5; primarily farmers, though some were part of a small middle class in towns and cities
Nonslaveholding whites	About 75 percent of white families	Mostly yeomen farmers who owned their own land and stressed production for family use; one in five owned neither slaves nor land and squatted on the least desirable land where they planted some corn and grazed some livestock; in cities they worked as artisans or, more typically, day laborers
Free blacks	About 3 percent of all free families	Concentrated in the Upper South; hemmed in by legal and social restrictions; mostly tenants or farm laborers; about one-third lived in cities and generally were limited to lowest-paying jobs

slaveholder. Only the wealthiest planters could live in such splendor, and they constituted less than 1 percent of southern white families in 1860. Yet their wealth and status were so imposing that they created an idealized image of grace and grandeur that has obscured the cruder realities of the slave regime.

Large Planters.   Only in the rice districts of the South Carolina low country and in the rich sugar- and cotton-growing areas of the Mississippi Delta were large planters more than a small minority of the slaveholding class, let alone the general white population. Families of the planter class, those who held a minimum of twenty slaves, constituted only around 3 percent of all southern families in 1860. Fewer than one out of five planter families, less than 1 percent of all families, owned more than fifty slaves. Far from conspicuously exhibiting their wealth, most planters lived in drab log cabins, not grand, white-columned houses. Most planters wanted to acquire wealth, not display it. They were restlessly eager to move on and abandon their homes when the allure of profits from a new cotton frontier promised to relieve them of the debts they had incurred to purchase their slaves.

Planters' Wives.   Most planters expected their wives to help supervise the slaves and run the plantation. Besides raising her children, the plantation mistress managed the household staff, oversaw the cooking and cleaning, gardened, dispensed medicine and clothing to the slaves, and often assisted in their religious instruction. When guests or relatives came for an extended visit, the wife had to make all the special arrangements that such occasions entailed. When the master was called off on a business or political trip, she kept the plantation accounts. In many respects, she worked harder than her husband.

Planters' wives often complained in their journals and letters of their isolation from other white women and the physical and mental toil of managing slaves. The women with whom they had the closest daily contact were often their female domestic slaves and, as Hannah Crafts noted, they treated some of these slaves with an intimacy that abolitionist propaganda refused to acknowledge. Whatever their misgivings about slavery, plantation mistresses enjoyed a wealth and status unknown to most southern women and only rarely questioned the institution of slavery. Their deepest anger stemmed from their humiliation by husbands who kept slave mistresses or sexually abused slave women. Bound by their duties as wives not to express this anger publicly, and unwilling to renounce the institution that both victimized and benefited them, white women tended to vent their frustrations on black women whose alleged promiscuity they blamed for the sexual transgressions of white males.

Small Slaveholders.   Despite the tensions and sexual jealousies it aroused, owning slaves was the surest means of social and economic advancement for most white families. Most slave owners, however, never attained planter status. Nine out of ten slave owners in 1860 owned fewer than twenty slaves, and fully half of them had fewer than five. Many white people also rented a few slaves on a seasonal basis.

Generally younger than the planters, small slaveholders were a diverse lot. About 10 percent were women, and another 20 percent or so were merchants, businessmen, artisans, and urban professionals. Most were farmers trying to acquire enough land and slaves to become planters. To keep costs down, they often began by purchasing children, the cheapest slaves available, or a young slave family, so that they could add to their slaveholdings as the slave mother bore more children.

Small slaveholders had scant economic security. A deadly outbreak of disease among their slaves or a single bad crop could destroy their credit and force them to sell their slaves to clear their debts. Owners of fewer than ten slaves stood a fifty-fifty chance within a decade of dropping out of the slaveholding class. Nor could small holders hope to compete directly with the planters. In any given area suitable for plantations, they were gradually pushed out as planters bought up land to raise livestock or more crops. In general, only slave owners who had established themselves in business or the professions had the capital reserves to rise into the planter elite.

The White Majority

Three-fourths of southern white families owned no slaves in 1860. Although most numerous in the Upper South, nonslaveholders predominated wherever the soil and climate were not suitable for plantation agriculture. Most were yeoman farmers who worked their own land with family labor.

These farmers were quick to move when times were bad and their land was used up, but once settled in an area, they formed intensely localized societies in which fathers and husbands held sway over their families. The community extended 5 to 10 miles around the nearest country store or county courthouse. Networks of kin and friends provided labor services when needed, fellowship in evangelical churches, and staple goods that an individual farm could not produce. Social travel and international markets, so central to the lives of planters, had little relevance in the farmers' community-centered existence. The yeomanry aimed to be self-sufficient and limited their market involvement to the sale of livestock and an occasional cotton crop that could bring in needed cash.

Yeoman farmers jealously guarded their independence, and in their tight little worlds of face-to-face relationships, they demanded that planters treat them as social equals. Ever fearful of being reduced to dependence, they avoided debt and sought to limit government authority. Rather than risk financial ruin by buying slaves on credit to grow cotton, they grew food crops and depended on their sons and, when needed, their wives and daughters to work the fields.

Nonslaveholding farmers from the mountains and planters on the bottomlands rarely mixed, and their societies developed in isolation from each other. In areas where there were both small farms and scattered plantations, the interests of the yeomen and the planters were often complementary. Planters provided local markets for the surplus grain and livestock of nonslaveholders and, for a small fee, access to gristmills and gins for grinding corn and cleaning cotton. They lent small sums to poorer neighbors in emergencies or to pay taxes. The yeomen staffed the slave patrols and became overseers on the plantations. Both groups sought to protect property rights from outside interference and to maintain a system of racial control in which white liberties rested on black degradation.

When yeomen and planters clashed, it was usually over economic issues. Large slaveholders needing better credit and marketing facilities gravitated toward the Whig Party, which called for banks and internal improvements. Nonslaveholding farmers, especially in the Lower South, tended to be Democrats who opposed banks and state-funded economic projects. They viewed bankers as grasping outsiders who wanted to rob them of their economic independence, and they suspected that state involvement in the economy led only to higher taxes and increased public debt. These partisan battles, however, rarely involved a debate about the merits of slavery. As long as planters deferred to the egalitarian sensibilities of the yeomen by courting them at election time and promising to safeguard their liberties, the planters were able to maintain broad support for slavery across class lines.

Around 15 percent of rural white families owned neither land nor slaves. These were the so-called poor whites, stigmatized by both abolitionists and planters as lazy and shiftless. The abolitionists considered them a kind of underclass who proved that slavery so degraded the dignity of labor that it led people to shun work and lapse into wretched poverty. To the planters, they were a constant nuisance and a threat to slave discipline. Planters habitually complained that poor whites demoralized their slaves by showing that a person could survive without steady labor. Planters also accused them of trading guns and alcohol with slaves for stolen plantation property. Despite the efforts of slave owners to crack down on this illicit trade, poor whites and slaves continued to swap goods and socially intermingle on the fringes of the plantations.

Some landless white people did live down to their negative stereotype. Still, the "poor white trash" label with which they were stigmatized is misleading. Some moved around, taking whatever work they could find on a daily or seasonal basis. Others were resourceful and enterprising enough to supply themselves with all the material comforts they wanted. Not having to do steady work for survival, they hunted, fished, and took orders from no one. Although poor by most standards, they were also defiantly self-reliant.

Nonslaveholders were a growing majority in southern cities, especially among the working classes. These urban workers shared no agricultural interests or ties with the planters. Nor were most of them, especially in the unskilled ranks, southern-born. Northerners and immigrants dominated the urban workforce. Free workers, especially Irish and German immigrants, increasingly replaced slaves in urban labor markets. These white workers bitterly resented competition from black slaves, and their demands to exclude slaves from the urban workplace reinforced planters' belief that cities bred abolitionism. When urban laborers protested against slave competition in the 1850s, planters singled them out as the nonslaveholders most likely to attack slavery.

Free Black People

A small minority of southern black people, 6 percent of the total in 1860, were "free persons of color." They constituted 3 percent of the free population in the South (see Figure 11.3). These free black people occupied a precarious and vulnerable position between degraded enslavement and meaningful freedom. White intimidation and special legal provisions known as **black codes** (found throughout the North as well) denied them nearly all the rights of citizenship. Because of the legal presumption in the South that all black people were slaves, they had to carry freedom papers, official certificates of their freedom. They were shut out of the political process and could not testify against white people in court. Many occupations, especially those involved in the communication of ideas, such as the printing trades, were closed to them.

Every slave state forbade the entry of free black people, and every municipality had rules and regulations that forced them to live as an inferior caste. Any sign of upward mobility or intimation of equal standing was ruthlessly suppressed. More than four-fifths of the southern free black population lived in the Upper South. Most were the offspring of slaves freed by private manumissions between 1780 and 1800, when slavery temporarily loosened in the Chesapeake region in the wake of the Revolutionary War. Manumissions dropped sharply after 1810, the result of heightened white anxieties after Prosser's Rebellion and the rising demand for slaves in the Lower South.

As in the North, legal barriers and white prejudice generally confined free black people to the poorest-paying and most menial work. In rural areas, a handful became independent farmers, but most worked as farm laborers or tenants. The best economic opportunities were in the cities, where some found factory jobs and positions in the skilled trades. Because the South had a general shortage of skilled labor, free black artisans—carpenters, barbers, shoemakers, tailors, and plasterers—could earn a respectable income. Indeed, the percentage of black people in the skilled trades was generally higher in the South than in the North.

One-third of the free black people in the Upper South lived in cities, a much higher proportion than among white people. Cities offered black people not only jobs but also enough social space to found their own churches and mutual-aid associations. Especially after 1840, urban African American churches became the center of black community

black codes Laws passed by states and municipalities denying many rights of citizenship to free black people before the Civil War.

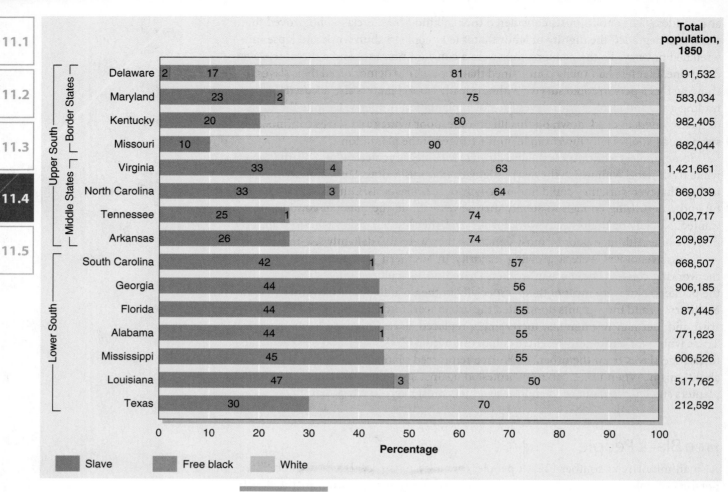

FIGURE 11.3 SLAVE, FREE BLACK, AND WHITE POPULATION IN SOUTHERN STATES, 1850
Except for Texas, slaves by 1850 comprised over 40 percent of the population in every state of the Lower South. The small population of free black people was concentrated in the Upper South.
SOURCE: U.S. Census Bureau

life. Church Sunday schools and day schools provided black people practically their only access to education, which they persisted in pursuing despite white opposition.

Less than 2 percent of the black people in the Lower South were free in 1860. Given the greater profitability of slavery there, manumissions were rare. Most of the Lower South's free black population descended from black emigrants who fled the revolutionary unrest in Haiti in the 1790s. These refugees were artisans, shopkeepers, and farmers who settled primarily in Charleston and New Orleans. Able to secure a solid economic footing, they left their descendants wealthier than any other free black people in the United States. Free black people in the Lower South were more likely than those in the Upper South to have a marketable skill, and two-thirds of them lived in cities.

A light skin enhanced the social standing of free black people among color-conscious whites in the Lower South. Nearly 70 percent of free black people in 1860 were mulattoes, and from their ranks came nearly all of the very small number of black planters. A mulatto elite emerged in Charleston, Mobile, and New Orleans that carefully distanced itself from most black people, slave or free. Even in these cities, however, the mulatto elite remained suspended between black and white worlds, never fully accepted by either.

Despite the emergence of a three-tiered racial hierarchy in the port cities of the Lower South, white officialdom insisted on maintaining a white and black racial dichotomy. As the racial defense of slavery intensified in the 1850s, more calls were made for laws to banish or enslave free black people. Arkansas passed such a law in 1859, and similar bills were proposed in Florida, Tennessee, Mississippi, and Missouri. Even Maryland held a referendum in 1859 on whether to reenslave its free black population, among the largest in the South. Only the opposition of nonslaveholders heavily dependent on cheap free black labor defeated the referendum.

The Pro-Slavery Argument

11.5 How did the southern defense of slavery change between the early nineteenth century and the 1850s?

n the early nineteenth century, white southerners made no particular effort to defend slavery, because the institution was not under heavy outside attack. If pressed, most white people would have called slavery a necessary evil, an unfortunate legacy from earlier generations that was needed to maintain racial peace.

The 1830s marked a turning point. After the twin shocks of Nat Turner's Rebellion and the onset of the abolitionist crusade (for more on this crusade, see Chapter 12), white mobs emerged to stifle any open criticism of slavery in the Lower South. White southerners also began to develop a defense of slavery. By the 1850s, politicians, intellectuals, and evangelical ministers were arguing that slavery was a positive good.

Religious Arguments

Evangelical Protestantism dominated southern religious expression by the 1830s, and its ministers took the lead in combating abolitionist charges that slavery was a moral and religious abomination. Except for a radical minority of antislavery evangelicals in the Upper South, a group largely silenced or driven out by the conservative reaction following Nat Turner's uprising, southern churches had always supported slavery. This support grew more pronounced and articulate once the abolitionists stepped up their attacks on slavery in the mid-1830s.

Southern evangelicals accepted the Bible as God's literal word, and through selective reading they found abundant evidence to proclaim slavery fully in accord with His moral dictates. They pointed out, for example, that the patriarchs of Israel had owned slaves. Slavery had been practiced throughout the Roman world at the time of Christ, they noted, and the apostles had urged obedience to all secular laws, including those governing slavery.

Southern evangelicals also turned to the Bible to support their argument that patriarchal authority, the unquestioned power of the father, was the basis of all Christian communities. Part of that authority extended over slaves, and slavery thus became a matter of family governance, a domestic institution in which Christian masters of slaves, unlike capitalist masters of free "wage slaves" in the North, accepted responsibility for caring for their workers in sickness and old age. Far from being a moral curse, therefore, slavery was part of God's plan to Christianize an inferior race and teach its people how to produce raw materials that benefited the world's masses.

The growing commitment of southern evangelicals to slavery as a positive good clashed with the antislavery position and the generally more liberal theology of northern evangelicals. In 1837, the Presbyterians split along sectional lines in part because of differences over slavery. In 1844, as a direct result of the slavery issue, the Methodist Episcopal Church, the nation's largest, divided into northern and southern churches. The Baptists did the same a year later. These religious schisms foreshadowed the sectionalized political divisions of the 1850s; they also severed one of the main emotional bonds between whites in the North and the South. The religious defense of slavery was central to the slaveholding ethic of paternalism that developed after 1830. By the 1850s, planters commonly described slaves as members of an extended family who were treated better than free workers in the North.

The crusade to sanctify slavery won few converts outside the South. Most northern churches did not endorse abolitionism but did have moral qualms about slavery. In a particularly stinging rebuke to southern church leaders in the 1850s, black abolitionists succeeded in having slaveholders barred from international religious conventions.

Racial Arguments

More common than the biblical defense of slavery was the racial argument that black people were unfit for freedom. Drawing in part on the scientific wisdom of the day, the racial defense alleged that black people were naturally lazy and inherently inferior to white people. If freed, so went the argument, they would turn to crime and sexually assault white women. Only the controls of slavery enabled the races to coexist in the South.

The racial argument resonated powerfully among white people because nearly all of them, including those otherwise opposed to slavery, dreaded emancipation. The attitude of a Tennessee farmer, as recorded by a northern traveler in the 1850s, was typical: "He said he'd always wished there hadn't been any niggers here . . . , but he wouldn't like to have them free." Unable to conceive of living in a society with many free black people, most white people could see no middle ground between slavery and the presumed social chaos of emancipation.

The existence of *black* slavery also had egalitarian implications for the nonslave-holding majority of whites. Slavery supposedly spared white southerners from the menial, degrading labor that white northerners had to perform. Moreover, because

📖 **Read the Document**   Thomas R. Dew, Defense of Slavery (1832)

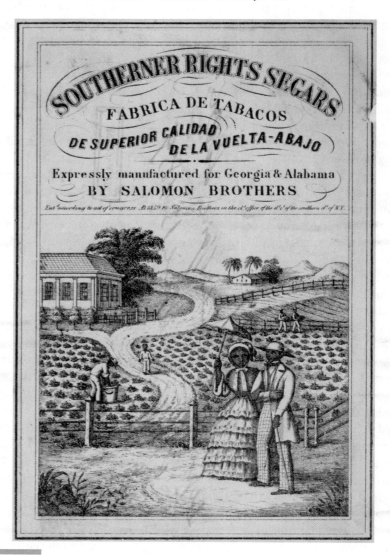

As this printed label from the 1850s for a box of cigars reveals, antebellum manufacturers of consumer goods produced by slave labor had every incentive to present an idealized picture of slave life in the South.

slaves lacked political rights, champions of slavery argued that black bondage buttressed the political liberties of all white males by removing from politics the leveling demands of the poor and propertyless for a redistribution of wealth.

Despite its apparent success in forging white solidarity, the racial argument could be turned on its head and used to weaken slavery. Most white northerners were about as racist as their southern counterparts, but they were increasingly willing to end slavery on the grounds that the stronger white race should help black people improve themselves as free persons. In short, nothing in the internal logic of racist doctrines required enslaving black people. The same logic also encouraged some white southerners to challenge the economic prerogatives of slaveholders. Why, for example, should any white people, as members of the master race, be forced into economic competition against skilled slave artisans? Why should not all nonagricultural jobs be legally reserved for white people? Doctrines of black inferiority could not prevent white unity from cracking when the economic interests of nonslaveholders clashed with those of planters.

Conclusion

Slavery and a biracial social order defined the South as a distinctive region. The spread of plantation agriculture across the Lower South after 1830 deepened the involvement of white southerners in cotton and slavery. As southern interests became more enmeshed in an institution that outsiders condemned, religious and intellectual leaders portrayed slavery as a Christian institution and a positive good necessary for white democracy and harmonious race relations. Pro-slavery ideologues stridently insisted that the South was separate from and superior to the rest of the nation.

The pro-slavery argument depicted a nearly ideal society blessed by class and racial harmony. In reality, social conditions in the slave South were contradictory and conflict-ridden. Slaves were not content in their bondage. Hannah Crafts spoke for nearly all of them when she described slavery as a coarse, brutalizing institution that demeaned all it touched. They dreamed of freedom and sustained that dream through their own forms of Christianity and the support of family and kin. Relations between masters and their slaves were antagonistic, not affectionate, and wherever the system of control slackened, slaves resisted their owners.

Nor did all white southerners, who confronted increasing economic inequality after 1830, accept racial slavery as in their best interests. It divided as well as united them. The publication of Hinton Rowan Helper's *The Impending Crisis of the South* in 1857, a scathing indictment by a white North Carolinian of slavery's harmful effect on economic opportunities for average white people, vividly showed that not all were convinced by the pro-slavery argument.

During the 1850s, the size of the slaveholding class fell from 31 percent of southern white families to 25 percent. Slave owners were a shrinking minority, and slavery was in decline throughout the Upper South. In the Border South, free labor was replacing slavery as the dominant means of organizing economic production. In these states, slavery was a vulnerable institution. Planters were not fooled by the public rhetoric of white unity. They knew that slavery was increasingly confined to the Lower South, and that elsewhere in the South white support for it was gradually eroding. Planters feared the double-edged challenge to their privileged position posed by outside interference with slavery and internal white disloyalty. By the 1850s, many of them were concluding that the only way to resolve their dilemma was to make the South a separate nation.

For Suggested Readings go to MyHistoryLab.

Chapter Review

The Lower South

11.1 How did the increasing demand for cotton shape the development of slavery in the Lower South? p. 281

The increasing demand and rising price for cotton acted as an incentive for southern whites to shift slaves out of the Upper South and use them as plantation laborers on the cheap and fertile lands that opened up as the United States expanded to the south and west. Cotton and slavery became linked as a new cotton kingdom spread across much of the Lower South.

The Upper South

11.2 What caused the decline of slavery after 1800 in the Upper South? p. 285

Declining soil fertility on overworked tobacco fields and falling land prices led to an exodus of whites and their slaves as new plantation regions were established in the Old Southwest. The economic recovery that set in by the mid-nineteenth century was based on a pattern of agricultural diversification that increasingly relied on free labor.

Slave Life and Culture

11.3 What was life like for African American slaves in the first half of the nineteenth century? p. 290

Material conditions in diet and housing improved as slave owners had a strong incentive to promote better living conditions once the congressional ban on the foreign slave trade closed off the market in cheap slaves from Africa. However, hard physical labor enforced by frequent whippings remained the lot of most slaves, and all slave families lived in dread of the possibility that family members would be separated through sales in the domestic slave trade.

Free Society

11.4 How was free society in the South structured? p. 296

Only a tiny minority of whites ever reached the status of a large planter, and in the slave states as a whole, only one in four white families owned slaves, generally fewer than ten. Most southern whites were part of a class of landowning farmers who rarely owned any slaves. Towns and cities contained a small middle class of professionals and businessmen along with white artisans who increasingly opposed competition from slave labor.

The Pro-Slavery Argument

11.5 How did the southern defense of slavery change between the early nineteenth century and the 1850s? p. 301

Primarily in response to the moral indictment of slavery by the abolitionists, southern whites shifted the defense of slavery from that of a necessary evil to a positive good. Evangelical ministers took the lead in depicting slavery as a benevolent institution ordained by God for the material improvement and moral uplift of an inferior race.

Timeline

1793
The Lower South—Eli Whitney patents the cotton gin

1793

1800
The Upper South—Gabriel Prosser leads a rebellion in Richmond, Virginia

1800

1808
Slave Life and Culture—Congress prohibits the African slave trade

1808

1811
The Lower South—Slaves rebel in Louisiana

1811

1822
The Lower South—Denmark Vesey's Conspiracy fails in Charleston, South Carolina

1822

1831
The Upper South—Nat Turner leads a rebellion in Southampton County, Virginia

1831

1832
The Pro-Slavery Argument—Thomas R. Dew publishes the first full-scale defense of slavery

1832

1837–1845
The Pro-Slavery Argument—Slavery issue divides Presbyterians, Methodists, and Baptists into separate sectional churches

1837–1845

1857
Free Society—Hinton R. Helper publishes *The Impending Crisis of the South*

1857

12 The Market Revolution and Social Reform 1815–1850

One American Journey

Letter from an Advocate for Women's Rights

East Boylston, Mass.
10th mo. 2d, 1837

Dear Friend: . . .

The investigation of the rights of the slave has led me to a better understanding of my own. I have found the Anti-Slavery cause to be the high school of morals in our land—the school in which *human rights* are more fully investigated, and better understood and taught, than in any other. Here a great fundamental principle is uplifted and illuminated, and from this central light, rays innumerable stream all around. Human beings have *rights,* because they are *moral* beings: the rights of *all* men grow out of their moral nature; and as all men have the same moral nature, they have essentially the same rights. These rights may be wrested from the slave, but they cannot be alienated: his title to himself is as perfect now, as is that of Lyman Beecher [a prominent minister]: it is stamped on his moral being, and is, like it, imperishable. Now if rights are founded on the nature of our moral being, then the

Whether at home or on the road, the contributions of women were indispensable to the success of antebellum reform movements.

LEARNING OBJECTIVES

12.1
How did industrialization contribute to growing inequality and the creation of new social classes? p. 307

12.2
What role did religion play in the reform movements that followed the War of 1812? p. 321

12.3
How did Enlightenment ideas shape the reform of institutions for the poor, criminals, and the mentally ill? p. 326

12.4
What was the relationship between abolitionism and the women's rights movement? p. 330

((• Listen to Chapter 12 on **MyHistoryLab**

Watch the Video Series on MyHistoryLab

Learn about some key topics related to this chapter with the *MyHistoryLab Video Series: Key Topics in U.S. History.*

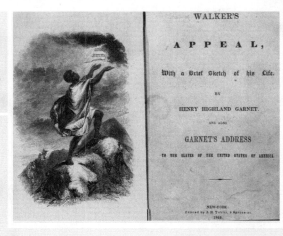

1 **The Republic of Reform: 1820–1850** During the second quarter of the nineteenth century, in the wake of the Second Great Awakening, the United States saw the growth and spread of reform movements. The most important of these are discussed in this video, including the temperance, abolitionist, women's rights, as well as the prison and asylum reform movements that sought to alleviate numerous social problems and inequalities. Since these movements were inspired by faith, as well as the founding principles of the country, they not only added a religious dimension to their reforms, but also resulted in the development of new spiritual movements and sects.

 Watch on **MyHistoryLab**

The Second Great Awakening This video focuses on the ongoing development of religious faith and spiritualism in American society known as the Second Great Awakening. The frontier experience played an important part in the religious convictions and identity of U.S. citizens during this period and resulted in the development of entirely new and uniquely American religious groups, such as the Mormons and the Unitarian church. **2**

Watch on **MyHistoryLab**

3 **David Walker's "Appeal"** The "Appeal," penned by a former slave, David Walker, is one of the earliest documents calling for emancipation and the abolition of slavery. This video examines the historical context in which it was written during the 1820s as well as Walker's demands and his belief in the armed resistance of slaves.

 Watch on **MyHistoryLab**

Seneca Falls Convention The reform movements of the nineteenth century involved many outspoken women. In 1848, a number of them in gathered at Seneca Falls, New York, in order to demand reforms for themselves as well. This video discusses what brought those women together and their demands for nothing less than full equality with men. The leaders at Seneca Falls, chief among them Lucretia Mott and Elizabeth Cady Stanton, borrowed the language of the Declaration of Independence to write their own Declaration of Sentiments and Resolutions for women. **4**

Watch on **MyHistoryLab**

mere circumstance of sex does not give to man higher rights and responsibilities, than to woman. My doctrine then is, that whatever it is morally right for man to do, it is morally right for woman to do. Our duties originate, not from difference of sex, but from the diversity of our relations in life, the various gifts and talents committed to our care, and the different eras in which we live.

Angelina Emily Grimké

Angelina E. Grimké, *Letters to Catherine Beecher, in reply to an Essay of Slavery and Abolition, Addressed to A. E. Grimké*, rev. ed., Boston: Isaac Knapp, 1838, pp. 114–121.

Personal Journeys Online

- Margaret Fuller, *Excerpt from book*, 1845. Arguments for women's rights.
- Lydia Maria Child, *Letter*, 1839. Issue of women's rights in the antislavery movement.

B orn in 1805 to a wealthy slaveholding family in Charleston, Angelina Grimké was the daughter of a prominent jurist. Despite all the social and economic benefits that membership in the planter class conferred upon her, she passionately rejected slavery when she became a young adult. As was also true for her sister Sarah, this rejection was part of a religious conversion to Quakerism. Angelina left her home in Charleston in 1829 and joined her sister in Philadelphia. The sisters joined the abolitionist movement in 1835, and within two years had become the crusade's most celebrated (and notorious) platform lecturers.

Although Angelina, in her commitment to radical reform, was hardly typical of antebellum U.S. women, let alone women of the planter class, her journey from a privileged life in Charleston to one of social activism in the North speaks to the radicalizing potential of the reform impulse that swept over the nation after the War of 1812.

This reform impulse was strongest in the North, where traditional social and economic relations were undergoing wrenching changes as a market revolution accelerated the spread of cities, factories, and commercialized farms. New middle and working classes evolved in response to such changes, which were the most pronounced in the Northeast. The North was also the area where the emotional fires of evangelical revivals burned the hottest.

The religious message of the Second Great Awakening, which began in the early 1800s, provided a framework for responding to the changes that accompanied the market revolution. Evangelicalism taught that in both the spiritual and secular realms, individuals were accountable for their own actions. Through Christian activism, individuals could strive toward moral perfectibility and cleanse society of its evils.

The first wave of reform after the War of 1812 focused on individual behavior, targeting drinking, gambling, sexual misconduct, and Sabbath-breaking. By the 1830s, a second phase of reform turned to institutional solutions for crime, poverty, and social delinquency, largely untouched by voluntary moral suasion. The third phase of the reform cycle rejected the social beliefs and practices that prescribed fixed and subordinate positions to certain Americans based on race and also on sex. This radical phase culminated in abolitionism and the campaign for women's rights, movements that came together in Angelina Grimké's journey out of her native South.

Industrial Change and Urbanization

12.1 How did industrialization contribute to growing inequality and the creation of new social classes?

I n 1820, 80 percent of the free labor force worked in agriculture, and manufacturing played a minor role in overall economic activity. Over the next three decades, however, the United States joined England as a world leader in industrialization.

The most direct cause of this rapid and sustained surge in manufacturing was increased consumption within the United States of the goods the country was producing. The **transportation revolution** dramatically reduced transportation costs and shipping times, opened up new markets for farmers and manufacturers alike, and provided an incentive for expanding production (see Table 12.1). As agricultural and manufactured goods were exchanged more efficiently, a growing home market continually stimulated the development of U.S. manufacturing.

transportation revolution
Dramatic improvements in transportation that stimulated economic growth after 1815 by expanding the range of travel and reducing the time and cost of moving goods and people.

TABLE 12.1 IMPACT OF THE TRANSPORTATION REVOLUTION ON TRAVEL TIME

Route	1800	1830	1860
New York to Philadelphia	2 days	1 day	Less than 1 day
New York to Charleston	More than 1 week	5 days	2 days
New York to Chicago	6 weeks	3 weeks	2 days
New York to New Orleans	4 weeks	2 weeks	6 days

The Transportation Revolution

Aside from some 4,000 miles of toll roads in the Northeast, the nation had nothing approaching a system of transportation in 1815. The cost of moving goods by land transportation was prohibitively high. It cost just as much to haul heavy goods by horse-drawn wagons 30 miles into the interior as to ship them 3,000 miles across the Atlantic Ocean. Water transportation was much cheaper, but it was limited to the coast or navigable rivers. Thus, only farmers located near a city or a river could grow surplus crops for sale in an outside market. Western farm surpluses followed the southerly flow of the Ohio and Mississippi river systems to market outlets in New Orleans.

Steamboats and Canals. Steamboats provided the first transportation breakthrough. In 1807, Robert Fulton demonstrated their commercial practicality when he sent the *Clermont* 150 miles up the Hudson River from New York City to Albany. By the 1820s, steamboats had reduced the cost and the time of upriver shipments by 90 percent. As steamboats spread to western waters, more and more farmers could reap the economic benefits of exporting corn, pork, and other foodstuffs.

Western trade did not start to flow eastward until the completion of the Erie Canal in 1825, the first and most successful of the artificial waterways designed to link eastern seaboard cities with western markets (see Map 12.1). Funded by the New York legislature, the Erie Canal stretched 364 miles from Albany to Buffalo, a small port on Lake Erie. An immediate success, the Erie Canal reduced the cost of sending freight from Buffalo to New York City by more than 90 percent, and by the 1840s, it was pulling in more western trade than was being sent to New Orleans on the Mississippi River.

Anxious to match the Erie's success, other states launched plans for competing canals to the West. More than 3,000 miles of canal were in place by 1840, but no other canal could overcome the tremendous advantage of the Erie's head start in fixing trading patterns along its route. Before the Panic of 1837 abruptly ended the canal boom by drying up financing, three broad networks of canals had been built. One set linked seaboard cities on the Atlantic with their agricultural hinterlands, another connected the mid-Atlantic states with the Ohio River Valley, and a third funneled western grain to ports on the Great Lakes.

Railroads. Railroads were the last and ultimately the most important of the transportation improvements that spurred economic development in Jacksonian America. Moving at 15 to 20 miles per hour, four times as fast as a canal boat and twice the speed of a stagecoach, the railroads of the 1830s were a radically new technology that overturned traditional notions of time and space.

In 1825, the same year the Erie Canal was completed, the world's first general-purpose railroad opened in England. The construction of the first American railroads began in the late 1820s, and they all pushed outward from seaboard cities eager to connect to the western market. By 1840, the railroads had become the most dynamic booster of interregional trade. Whereas the canal network stopped expanding after 1840, the railroads tripled their mileage in the 1840s. By 1849, trunk lines built westward from Atlantic Coast cities had reached the Great Lakes and the Ohio Valley and were about to enter the Mississippi Valley.

The rail network in place by mid-century was already altering the North-South sectional balance. The bulk of western trade no longer went downriver to New Orleans but was shipped east by rail. Moving in the opposite direction, to the West, were northern-born settlers, manufactured goods, and cultural values that increasingly unified the free states east of the Mississippi into a common economic and cultural unit. As the distinctions between them blurred, the Northeast and the Old Northwest were becoming just the North. Significantly, no direct rail connection linked the North and the South.

Government and the Transportation Revolution. Both national and state government promoted the transportation revolution. Given the high construction costs and uncertain profits, private investors were leery of risking their scarce capital in long-term

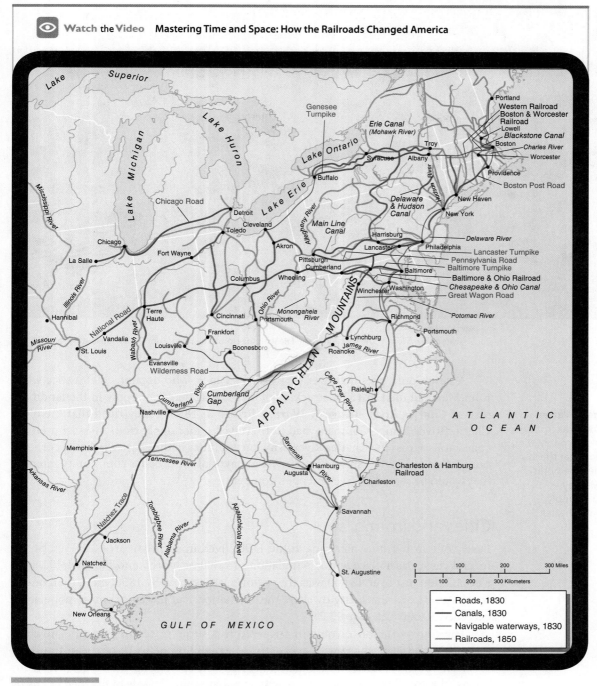

MAP 12.1 THE TRANSPORTATION REVOLUTION By 1830, a network of roads, canals, and navigable rivers was spurring economic growth in the first phase of the transportation revolution. By 1850, railroads, the key development in the second phase of the transportation revolution, were opening up additional areas to commercial activity.

transportation projects. State legislatures stepped in and furnished some 70 percent of the funding for canals and about half of all railroad capital. The federal government provided engineers for railroad surveys, lowered tariffs on iron used in rail construction, and granted subsidies to the railroads in the form of public land.

Most important, however, were two Supreme Court decisions that helped open up the economy to competition. In *Gibbons v. Ogden* (1824), the Court overturned a New York law that had given Aaron Ogden a monopoly on steamboat service between New York and New Jersey. Thomas Gibbons, Ogden's competitor, had a federal license for the coastal trade. The right to compete under the national license, the Court ruled, took legal precedence over Ogden's monopoly. The decision affirmed the supremacy of the national government to regulate interstate commerce.

Gibbons v. Ogden Supreme Court decision of 1824 involving coastal commerce that overturned a steamboat monopoly granted by the state of New York on the grounds that only Congress had the authority to regulate interstate commerce.

Canal boats below a lock at the junction of the Erie with the Northern (Champlain) Canal. Aquatint by John Hill.

Charles River Bridge v. Warren Bridge Supreme Court decision of 1837 that promised economic competition by ruling that the broader rights of the community took precedence over any presumed right of monopoly granted in a corporate charter.

A new Court, presided over by Roger B. Taney, who became chief justice when John Marshall died in 1835, struck a bolder blow against monopoly in the landmark case of **Charles River Bridge v. Warren Bridge** in 1837. Taney ruled that the older Charles River Bridge Company had not received a monopoly from Massachusetts to collect tolls across the Charles River. Any uncertainties in the charter rights of corporations, reasoned Taney, should be resolved in favor of the broader community interests that would be served by free and open competition.

Cities and Immigrants

Barely one in twenty Americans in the 1790s lived in an urban area (defined by the federal census as a place with a population of 2,500 or more), and Philadelphia, with a population just over 40,000, was the nation's largest city. By 1850, more than one in seven Americans was a city dweller, and the nation had ten cities whose population exceeded 50,000 (see Map 12.2).

The transportation revolution triggered this surge in urban growth. The cities that prospered were those with access to the expanding network of cheap transport on steamboats, canals, and railroads. This network opened up the rural interior for the purchase of farm commodities by city merchants and the sale of finished goods by urban importers and manufacturers. A huge influx of immigrants after the mid-1840s and simultaneous advances in steam engines provided the cheap labor and sources of power that increasingly made cities focal points of manufacturing production.

The Port Cities. America's largest cities in the early nineteenth century were its Atlantic ports: New York, Philadelphia, Baltimore, and Boston. All these cities grew as a result of transportation improvements, but only New York experienced phenomenal growth. By 1810, New York had become the largest U.S. city, and by the 1850s its population exceeded 800,000.

New York's harbor gave oceangoing ships direct, protected access to Manhattan Island, and from there, the Hudson River provided a navigable highway flowing 150 miles north to Albany, deep in the state's agricultural interior. No other port was so ideally situated for trade. And no other had the advantage of access to the Erie Canal. New Yorkers plowed the profits of this trade into local real estate, which soared in value fiftyfold between 1823 and 1836, and into financial institutions such as the New York

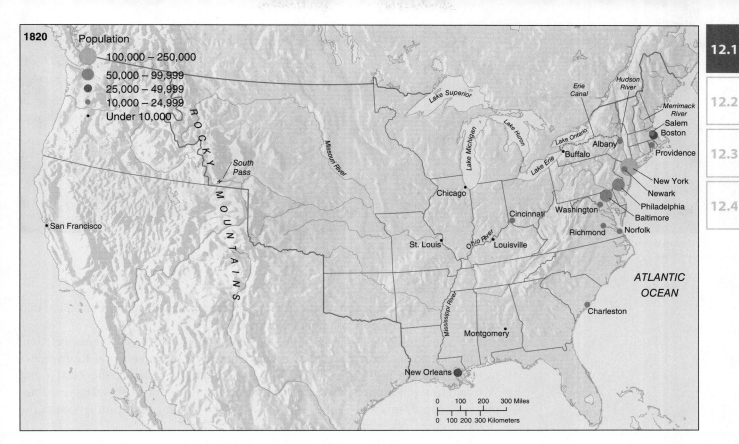

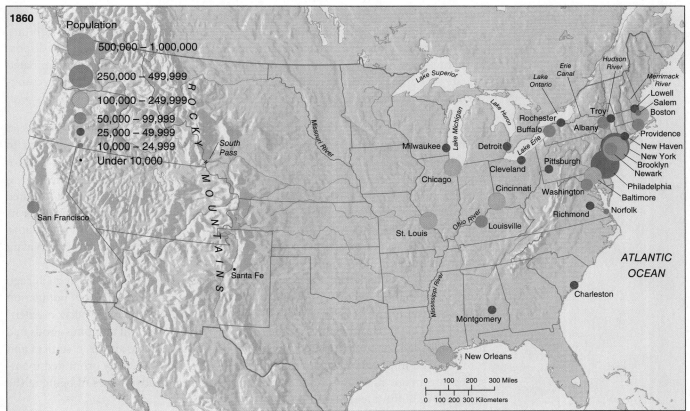

MAP 12.2 THE GROWTH OF CITIES, 1820–1860 In 1820, most cities were clustered along the Atlantic seaboard. By 1860, new transportation outlets—canals and railroads—had fostered the rapid growth of cities in the interior, especially at trading locations with access to navigable rivers or to the Great Lakes. Much of this growth occurred in the 1850s.

SOURCE: *Statistical Abstract of the United States.*

New York City's busy harbor was the entry to the largest metropolitan center that emerged in the nineteenth-century United States.

Stock Exchange, founded in 1817. The city's banks brought together the capital that made New York the country's chief financial center.

As they grew, the Atlantic ports pioneered new forms of city transportation. Omnibuses, horse-drawn coaches carrying up to twenty passengers, and steam ferries were in common use by the 1820s. The first commuter railroad, the Boston and Worcester, began service in 1838. At mid-century, horse-drawn street railway lines moved at speeds of about 6 miles an hour, overcoming some of the limitations of the "walking cities" of the early nineteenth century.

Accompanying this growth were the first slums, the most notorious of which was the Five Points district of New York City. Small, flimsy wooden structures, often crammed into back alleys, housed the working poor in cramped, fetid conditions. Backyard privies, supplemented by chamber pots, were the standard means of disposing of human waste. These outhouses overflowed in heavy rain and often contaminated private wells, the source of drinking water. Garbage and animal wastes simply accumulated on streets, scavenged by roving packs of hogs.

Inland Cities.   The fastest-growing cities were in the interior. Pittsburgh, at the head of the Ohio River, was the first western city to develop a manufacturing sector to complement its exchange function. With access to the extensive coalfields of western Pennsylvania, Pittsburgh had a cheap fuel that provided the high heat needed to manufacture iron and glass. It emerged as America's best-known and most polluted manufacturing city. Cincinnati, downstream on the Ohio, soon became famous for its hogs. "Porkopolis," as it was called, was the West's first meatpacking center. St. Louis, just below the merger of the Missouri and Mississippi rivers, prospered by servicing American trade with the Trans-Mississippi West.

By the 1840s, the Great Lake ports of Cleveland, Detroit, Milwaukee, and Chicago were the dynamic centers of western urbanization. Their combined population increased twenty-five-fold between 1830 and 1850. The Great Lakes served as an extension of the Erie Canal, and cities on the lakes where incoming and outgoing goods had to be unloaded for transshipment benefited enormously. They attracted settlers and soon evolved into regional economic centers. They also aggressively promoted themselves into major rail hubs and thus reaped the economic advantages of being at the junctions of both water and rail transport.

New Industrial Cities.   The only other cities growing as fast as the Great Lakes ports were the new industrial towns. The densest cluster of these was in rural New England along the fall line of rivers, where the rapidly falling water provided cheap power to drive the industrial machinery of factories and machine shops. Each town was tied to a transportation network that brought in raw cotton for the textile mills from the mercantile centers of Boston and Providence and shipped out the finished goods.

Read the Document   A New England Factory Issues Regulations for Workers (1825)

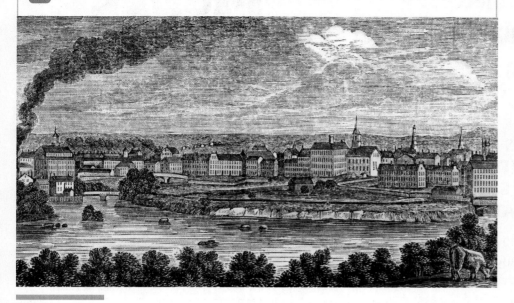

Built along the Merrimack River, Lowell was the nation's leading textile center and the second-largest city in Massachusetts by 1850.

Lowell, Massachusetts, was America's first large-scale planned manufacturing city. Founded in 1822 by Boston businessmen, Lowell was built around the falls of the Merrimack River. Within a decade, rural fields had been transformed into a city of 18,000 people. Lowell's success became a model for others to follow, and by 1840, New England led the North in both urbanization and industrialization.

Immigration.   Swelling the size of nearly all the cities was a surge of immigrants after the 1830s. The number of immigrants from 1840 to 1860, 4.2 million, represented a tenfold increase over the number that had come in the two preceding decades. At mid-century, most of the population of New York was foreign-born, and in all the port cities of the Northeast, immigrants dominated the manufacturing workforce. Most of these immigrants were Irish and German (see Figure 12.1, page 315).

In the 1840s, economic and political upheavals in Europe spurred mass migration, mostly to the United States. Catholic peasants in Ireland, dominated by their Protestant English landlords, eked out a subsistence as tenants on tiny plots of land. A potato blight wiped out the crop in 1845 and 1846, and in the next five years about 1 million Irish died of malnutrition and disease. Another 1.5 million fled, many to the United States.

The Irish had no money to buy land or move west unless they joined construction gangs for canals and railroads. Without marketable skills, they had to take the worst and lowest-paying jobs. Wives and daughters became laundresses and maids for the urban middle class. Packed into dark cellars, unventilated attics, and rank tenements, the Irish suffered from very high mortality rates. Still, cash wages and access to food made the U.S. city preferable to the prospect of starvation in Ireland.

German immigrants were second in number only to the Irish by the 1850s. They came to America to escape poor harvests and political turmoil. Far more Germans than Irish had owned property as farmers, artisans, and shopkeepers and had the capital to purchase land in the West and the skills to join the ranks of small businessmen in the cities. They were also more likely than the Irish to have entered the country through Baltimore or New Orleans, southern ports engaged in the tobacco and cotton trade with continental Europe. From there they fanned out into the Mississippi and Ohio valleys. With their diversified skills, they found ample economic opportunities in the fast-growing cities of the West and a setting in which to build tightly knit communities with German-speaking shops, churches, schools, and benevolent societies. About four in five

✳ Explore Early Nineteenth-Century Urbanization and the Transportation Revolution on MyHistoryLab

HOW DID CHANGES IN URBANIZATION AND TRANSPORTATION SHAPE THE YOUNG UNITED STATES?

Between approximately 1800 and 1850, the United States underwent major changes in where people lived and their means of travel and transportation. As the industrial revolution reached the country, the older cities of the East Coast continued to grow while new urban centers developed rapidly in the Midwest. Cities offered not only jobs in factories but also markets and services for those living in the countryside. Moreover, a transportation revolution brought new canals, wagon roads, and, particularly, railroads— the wonder of the age— tying together certain regions and dramatically reducing travel times. These developments in transportation helped to knit together a national economic system.

This 1837 handbill reveals the mixed transportation infrastructure of the early 1800s, which connected cities via a system of railroads, canals, and river steamboats for travel and commerce.

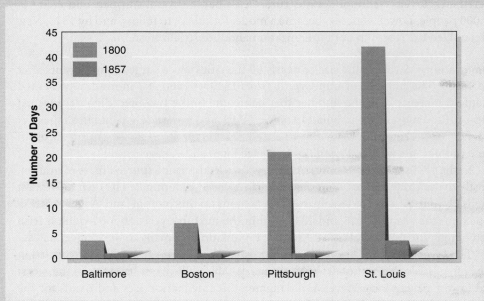

CHANGES IN TRAVEL TIMES FROM NEW YORK CITY BETWEEN 1800 AND 1857

(Bar chart showing Number of Days on the y-axis from 0 to 45, with two bars — 1800 and 1857 — for each city: Baltimore, Boston, Pittsburgh, St. Louis)

KEY QUESTIONS   Use **MyHistoryLab** *Explorer* to **answer** these **questions:**

Response ▶▶▶ *To what degree did urbanization affect various parts of the country?*

Chart population changes of urban centers.

Analysis ▶▶▶ *Where were the new canals, wagon roads, and railroads built?*

Map these important developments.

Consequence ▶▶▶ *Which regions were linked closely together by the transportation revolution?*

Consider the effects of these connections for later growth.

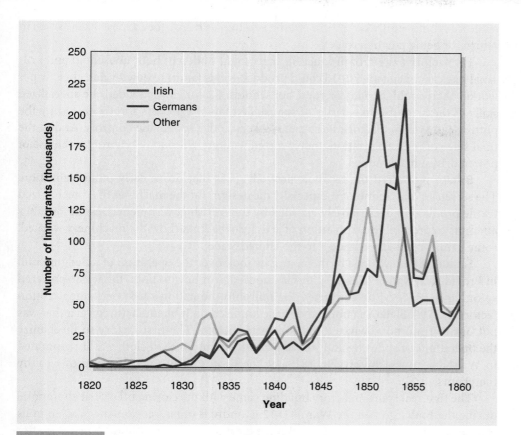

FIGURE 12.1 IMMIGRATION TO THE UNITED STATES, 1820–1860 The potato famine in Ireland and economic and political unrest on the continent led to a surge in immigration in the 1840s. The pace slackened in the mid-1850s, when economic conditions in Europe improved.

SOURCE: U.S. Bureau of the Census, *Historical Statistics of the United States, Colonial Times to 1957* (1960), p. 57.

of all the immigrants arriving after 1840 settled in the New England and mid-Atlantic states. Their sheer numbers transformed the size and ethnic composition of the working class, especially in the cities of the Northeast. And their cheap labor provided the final ingredient in the expansion of industrialization that began after the War of 1812.

The Industrial Revolution

The Northeast led America's industrial revolution. In 1815, this region had the largest cities, the most developed capital markets, the readiest access to the technological skills of artisans, and the greatest supply of available labor. The first large-scale factories, the textile mills, were erected in New England in the 1820s. For the next thirty years, the United States had the most rapidly developing industrial economy in the world.

The household and the small workshop were the sites of manufacturing in Jefferson's America. Wider markets for household manufactures began to develop in the late eighteenth century with the coming of the **putting-out system**. Local merchants furnished ("put out") raw materials to rural households and paid at a piece rate for the labor that converted the raw materials into manufactured products. The supplying merchant then marketed and sold these goods.

In the cities and larger towns, most manufacturing was done by artisans, skilled craftsmen known as mechanics. Working in their own shops and with their own tools, they produced small batches of finished goods. Each artisan had a specific skill that set him above common laborers—shoemaking, furniture making, silver smithing. These skills came from hands-on experience and craft traditions that were handed down from one generation to the next.

Master craftsmen taught the "mysteries of the craft" to the journeymen and apprentices who lived with them and worked in their shops. Journeymen had learned the skills of their craft but lacked the capital to open their own shops. Apprentices were

putting-out system System of manufacturing in which merchants furnished households with raw materials for processing by family members.

315

adolescent boys legally sent by their fathers to live with and obey a master craftsman in return for being taught a trade.

The factory system of production that would undercut both household and artisanal manufacturing after 1815 could produce goods far more quickly and cheaply per worker than could artisans or rural households. Factories subdivided the specialized skills of the artisan into a series of semiskilled tasks, a process foreshadowed by the putting-out system. Factories also put workers under systematic controls. And in the final stage of industrialization, they boosted workers' productivity through the use of power-driven machinery.

Britain pioneered the technological advances that drove early industrialization. The secrets of this technology, especially the designs for the machines that mechanized textile production, were closely guarded by the British government. Despite Britain's attempts to prohibit the emigration of artisans who knew how the machinery worked, some British mechanics made it to the United States.

Samuel Slater was one of them, and he took over the operation of a fledgling mill in Providence, Rhode Island. With his knowledge of how to build the water-powered spinning machinery, he converted the mill into the nation's first permanent cotton factory in 1790. Slater's factory, and those modeled on it, manufactured yarn that was put out to rural housewives to be woven into cloth. The first factory to mechanize the operations of spinning and weaving and turn out finished cloth was incorporated in Waltham, Massachusetts, in 1813, by the Boston Associates, a group of wealthy merchants.

The first real spurt of factory building came with the closing off of British imports during the Embargo and the War of 1812. Hundreds of new cotton and woolen mills were established from 1808 to 1815. But the great test of U.S. manufacturing came after 1815, when peace with Britain brought a flood of cheap British manufactured goods. If factories were to continue to grow, U.S. manufacturers had to reach more consumers in their home market and overcome the British advantage of lower labor costs.

Sources of Labor.   Industrial labor was more expensive in America than in England, where the high cost of land forced the rural poor into the cities to find work. In contrast, land was cheap and plentiful in the United States, and Americans preferred the independence of farm work to the dependence of factory labor. Consequently, the first mill workers were predominantly children. The owners set up the father on a plot of company-owned land, provided piecework for the mother, and put the children to work in the mills.

Although this so-called **Rhode Island system** of family employment sufficed for small mills, it was inadequate for the larger, more mechanized factories that were built in New England after the War of 1812. The owners of these mills recruited unmarried adolescent daughters of farmers from across New England as their laborers in the **Waltham system**. Although factory wages were low, they were more than these young women could earn doing piecework in the home or as domestics. The wages also brought a liberating degree of financial independence. "When they felt the jingle of silver in their pockets," recalled Harriet Hanson Robinson of her fellow workers at Lowell in the 1830s, "there for the first time, their heads became erect and they walked as if on air."

To overcome parental fears that their daughters might be exposed to morally corrupting conditions in the mills and mill towns, New England manufacturers set up paternalistic moral controls. Single female workers had to live in company-owned boardinghouses that imposed curfews, screened visitors, and mandated church attendance. The mill women worked six days a week from dawn to dusk for low wages. There were limits to what the women would endure, and in 1834 and 1836 the female hands at Lowell "turned out" to protest wage reductions in demonstrations that were the largest strikes in American history up to that time.

After the economic downturn of the late 1830s, conditions in the mills grew worse. By the mid-1840s, however, the Irish, desperate for work, sent their children into the

Rhode Island system During the industrialization of the early nineteenth century, the recruitment of entire families for employment in a factory.

Waltham system During the industrialization of the early nineteenth century, the recruitment of unmarried young women for employment in factories.

mills at an earlier age than Yankee families. These workers did not leave after two or three years of building up a small dowry for marriage, as many New Englanders did. By the early 1850s, more than half the textile operatives were Irish women.

In the mid-Atlantic region, where the farm population was more prosperous than in New England and fewer young women were available for factory work, immigrants were an important source of manufacturing workers as early as the 1820s. They played an especially crucial role in urban manufacturing. The port cities lacked usable water-power, but by drawing on a growing pool of cheap, immigrant labor, manufacturers could expand production while driving down the cost.

Except in New England textile factories and the smaller factories and shops in the seaboard cities, native-born males were the largest group of early manufacturing work-ers. They came from poor rural families that lacked enough land to pass on to male heirs. As late as 1840, women, including those working at home, made up about half of the manufacturing workforce and one-quarter of the factory hands. Regardless of their sex, few of these workers brought any specific skills to their jobs, and thus they had little bargaining power. Economic necessity forced them to accept low wages and harsh working conditions. The sheer increase in their numbers, as opposed to any productivity gains from technological innovations, accounted by 1850 for two-thirds of the gains in manufacturing output.

Technological Gains. After 1815, U.S. manufacturers began to close the technological gap with Britain by drawing on the versatile skills of U.S. mechanics. Mechanics experimented with new designs, improved old ones, and patented inventions that found industrial applications outside their own crafts.

The most famous early American invention was the cotton gin. Eli Whitney, a Massachusetts Yankee, built the prototype of the gin in 1793 while working as a tutor on a Georgia plantation. By cheaply and quickly removing the seeds from cotton fibers, the cotton gin spurred the cultivation of cotton across the South.

Whitney also pushed the idea of basing production on interchangeable parts. After receiving a federal contract to manufacture muskets, he designed new milling machines and turret lathes that transformed the technology of machine tool production. The new techniques were first applied in 1815 to the manufacture of wooden clocks and by the 1840s to sewing machines, farm machinery, and watch parts. The **American system of manufacturing**—low-cost, standardized mass production, built around interchange-able parts stamped out by machines—was America's unique contribution to the indus-trial revolution.

As the pace of technological innovation accelerated after 1840, so did the growth of manufacturing. Indeed, the 1840s registered the highest rate of expansion in the manufacturing sector of the economy in the nineteenth century. The adoption of the stationary steam engine in urban manufacturing fueled much of this expansion. High-pressure steam engines enabled power-driven industry to locate in the port cit-ies of the Northeast and the booming cities on the Great Lakes. With limited access to waterpower, early manufacturing in the West was confined to the processing of farm goods. By turning to steam power and new machine tools, western manufactur-ers after 1840 enlarged their region's industrial base and created a new industry, the mass production of agricultural implements. The West was the center of the farm-machinery industry, and the region produced 20 percent of the nation's manufactur-ing output by the 1850s.

A greater control over natural resources, as well as new technologies, drove indus-trial growth. To provide their mills with a steady, reliable source of water, one that would not be affected by the whims of nature, the Boston Associates constructed a series of dams and canals that extended to the headwaters of the Merrimack River in northern New Hampshire. Inevitably, the ecology of the region changed. The level of the lakes was altered, the flow of rivers interrupted, the upward migration of spawn-ing fish blocked, and the foraging terrain of wild game flooded. Farmers protested when their fields and pastures were submerged, but lawyers for the Boston Associates

American system of manufacturing A technique of production pioneered in the United States in the first half of the nineteenth century that relied on precision manufacturing with the use of interchangeable parts.

successfully argued that water, like other natural resources, should be treated as a commodity that could contribute to economic progress. Increasingly, the law treated nature as an economic resource to be engineered and bought and sold.

Growing Inequality and New Classes

In the first half of the nineteenth century, the economy grew three times faster than in the eighteenth century, and per capita income doubled. Living standards for most Americans improved. There was a price to be paid, however, for the benefits of economic growth. Half of the adult white males were propertyless at mid-century. Wealth had become more concentrated, and extremes of wealth and poverty eroded the Jeffersonian ideal of a republic of independent proprietors who valued liberty because they were economically free.

The gap between the rich and the poor widened considerably in the early phases of industrialization (see Figure 12.2). In 1800, the richest 10 percent of Americans owned 40 to 50 percent of the national wealth. By the 1850s, their share was about 70 percent. The most glaring discrepancies in wealth appeared in the large cities. In all cities by the 1840s, the top 10 percent of the population owned 80 percent of urban wealth.

The New Middle Class. The faster pace of economic growth that enabled the urban rich to increase their wealth also created opportunities for a rapidly expanding new middle class. This class grew as the number of nonmanual jobs increased. Most of these jobs were in northern cities and bustling market towns, where the need was greatest for office and store clerks, managerial personnel, sales agents, and independent retailers.

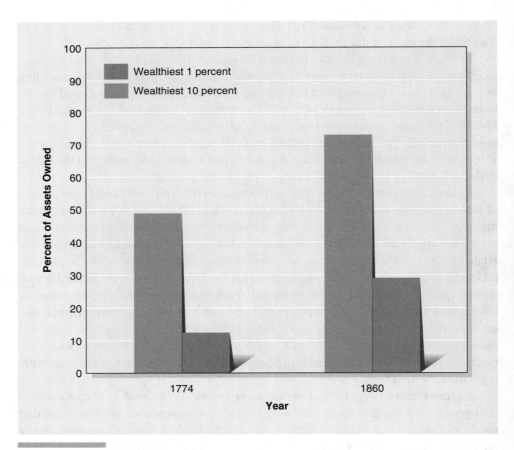

FIGURE 12.2 GROWTH IN WEALTH INEQUALITY, 1774–1860 The two benchmark years for the gathering of data on the nationwide distribution of wealth are 1774 and 1860. Specialized studies on regions and subregions indicate that wealth inequality increased most sharply from the 1820s to 1850, the period that coincides with early industrialization.

SOURCE: Data from Jeffrey G. Williamson and Peter H. Lindert, *American Inequality: A Macroeconomic History*, p. 38. Copyright © 1980. Reprinted by permission of the authors.

The result by mid-century was a new middle class superimposed on the older one of independent farmers, artisans, shopkeepers, and professionals.

The separation of work and home constituted the first step in an evolving sense of class consciousness. As the market revolution advanced, the workplace increasingly became a specialized location of production or selling. Middle-class fathers now left for work in the morning, while mothers governed households that were primarily residential units and places of material comfort, where growing quantities of consumer goods were on display. Having servants became a status symbol. Shunned as degrading by most native-born white women, these low-paying jobs were filled by African American and young immigrant (especially Irish) women. Work had not left the middle-class home; instead, it was disguised as the "domestic duties" of middle-class wives who supervised the servants.

Besides turning to etiquette books for advice on proper manners in public and in the home, the middle class also tried to shape its behavior by the tenets of evangelical religion. Revivals swept northern cities in the late 1820s. Charles G. Finney led the most dramatic and successful ones in the cities along the Erie Canal in upstate New York. Finney preached that salvation was available to those who willed it. He also stressed that both economic and moral success depended on the virtues of sobriety, self-restraint, and hard work. Aggressiveness and ambition at work were not necessarily sinful so long as businessmen reformed their own moral lives and helped others do the same. This message was immensely reassuring to employers and entrepreneurs, for it confirmed and sanctified their own pursuit of economic self-interest. It also provided them with a religious inspiration for attempting to exert moral control over their communities and employees. **Temperance**, the prohibition of alcoholic beverages, was the greatest of the evangelically inspired reforms, and abstinence from alcohol became the most telling evidence of middle-class respectability.

temperance Reform movement originating in the 1820s that sought to eliminate the consumption of alcohol.

Women and the Cult of Domesticity.   In a reversal of traditional Calvinist doctrine, the evangelical ministers of the northern middle class enshrined women as the moral superiors of men. Though considered weak and passive, women were also held to be uniquely pure and pious. Women, who easily outnumbered men at Sunday services and weeknight prayer meetings, were now responsible for converting their homes into loving, prayerful centers of domesticity, and the primary task of motherhood became the Christian nurturing of souls entrusted to a mother's care.

This sanctified notion of motherhood reflected and reinforced shifting patterns of family life. Families became smaller as the birthrate fell by 25 percent in the first half of the nineteenth century. The decline was greatest in the urban middle class after 1820. Children were no longer an economic asset as they had been on a family farm. Middle-class couples consciously limited the size of their families, and women stopped having children at an earlier age. As a result, parents devoted more care and financial resources to child rearing. Middle-class children lived at home longer than children had in the past and received more schooling than working-class children.

Beginning in the 1820s, ministers and female writers elevated the family role of middle-class women into a **cult of domesticity**. This idealized conception of womanhood insisted that the biological differences of God's natural order determined separate social roles for men and women. Characterized as strong, aggressive, and ambitious, men naturally belonged in the competitive world of business and politics. Women's providential task was to preserve religion and morality in the home and family.

cult of domesticity The belief that women, by virtue of their sex, should stay home as the moral guardians of family life.

The Working Classes.   The economic changes that produced a new middle class also fundamentally transformed the working class. In the preindustrial United States, the working class was predominantly native-born and of artisan origins. By mid-century, most urban workers were immigrants or the children of immigrants and had never been artisans in a skilled craft.

Job skills, sex, race, and ethnicity all divided workers after 1840. Master craftsmen were the most highly skilled and best-paid workers. As industrialization proceeded, the unity of the old artisan class splintered. Ambitious master craftsmen with access to

This pen-and-watercolor drawing of a middle-class family illustrates how the home, as it lost its productive functions, became idealized as a center of domestic refinement and material comfort.

capital rose into the ranks of small businessmen and manufacturers. They expanded output and drove down the cost of production by contracting out work at piece wages and hiring the cheapest workers they could find. The result was to transform the apprentice system into a system of exploited child labor.

By the 1830s, journeymen were becoming permanent wage earners with little prospect of opening their own shops. To protect their liberties from what they considered a new aristocracy of manufacturers, they organized workingmen's parties in the 1830s, centered in the eastern cities. At the top of these parties' lists of reforms were free public education, the abolition of imprisonment for debt, and a 10-hour workday.

Early Trade Unions. Journeymen also turned to trade union activity in the 1820s and 1830s to gain better wages, shorter hours, and enhanced job security. Benefiting from a strong demand for their skills, workers in the building trades organized the first unions. They were soon followed by shoemakers, printers, and weavers, workers in trades where pressure on urban journeymen was the most intense. Locals from various trades formed the National Trades Union, the first national union, in 1834. The new labor movement launched more than 150 strikes in the mid-1830s.

Although the Panic of 1837 decimated union membership, the early labor movement did achieve two notable victories. First, by the late 1830s, it had forced employers to accept the 10-hour day as the standard for most skilled workers. Second, in a landmark decision handed down in 1842, the Massachusetts Supreme Court ruled in *Commonwealth v. Hunt* that a trade union was not necessarily subject to laws against criminal conspiracies and that a strike could be used to force employers to hire only union members.

The unions defended artisanal rights and virtues, and they ignored workers whose jobs had never had craft status. As massive immigration merged with industrialization after 1840, this basic division between workers widened. On one side was the male,

Protestant, and native-born class of skilled artisans. On the other side was the working-class majority of factory laborers and unskilled workers, predominantly immigrants and women who worked for a wage as domestics or factory hands. On average, they earned less than $500 a year, about half what skilled workers earned. Their financial survival rested on a family economy in which all members contributed whatever they could earn.

Increasingly fearing these workers as a threat to their job security and Protestant values, in the 1840s U.S.-born artisans joined **nativist** organizations that sought to curb mass immigration from Europe and limit the political rights of Catholic immigrants. Whereas immigrants viewed temperance as business-class meddling in their lives, nativist workers tended to embrace the evangelical, middle-class ideology of temperance and self-help. One of the few issues that brought immigrants and nativists together was the nearly universal demand of white workers that black workers be confined to the most menial jobs.

Gender also divided workers. Working-class men shared the dominant ideology of female dependence. They measured their own status as husbands by their ability to support their wives and daughters. Beginning in the 1830s, male workers argued that their wages would be higher if women were barred from the labor force.

With these views, male workers helped lock wage-earning women into the lowest-paying and most exploited jobs. "If we do not come forth in our defence, what will become of us?" asked Sarah Monroe of New York City in the midst of a strike by seamstresses in 1831. Women workers tried to organize, but the male labor movement refused to lend much support. The men tried to channel the discontent of women workers into "proper female behavior" and generally restricted their assistance to pushing for legislation that would limit the hours worked by women and children, a stand that enhanced their male image as protectors of the family.

nativist Favoring the interests and culture of native-born inhabitants over those of immigrants.

Reform and Moral Order

12.2 What role did religion play in the reform movements that followed the War of 1812?

The rapidity and extent of the social and economic changes that accompanied the market revolution were disorienting, even frightening, to many Americans, particularly religious leaders and wealthy businessmen in the East (see Table 12.2 for these changes). They saw signs of moral wickedness and disorder all around them in the more fluid, materialistic society that was emerging. In their eyes, licentiousness was rampant in the cities, and the evils of drink were causing

TABLE 12.2 CHANGES PROMOTING GROWTH IN THE TRANSFORMED ECONOMY

Sector	1815	1850
Travel and transportation	By foot and horse-drawn wagon	Cheaper and faster with canals, steamboats, and railroads opening up new markets
Population	Overwhelmingly native-born, rural, and concentrated east of Appalachian Mountains	Four times larger as a result of natural increase and surge of immigration after 1840; settlement of West and growth of cities
Wage labor	Native-born, primarily women and children in manufacturing	Expanding as rural poor and immigrants enter manufacturing workforce
Power	Water-driven mills	Steam-driven engines
Farming	Subsistence-oriented; surplus sold in localized markets	Commercialized agriculture spreading in response to improvements in transportation
Manufacturing	Small-scale production in household units and artisan shops	Large-scale production in eastern cities and factories

From Then to Now
Immigration: AN AMBIVALENT WELCOME

Americans have long extended an ambivalent welcome to newcomers. Yet the United States, whose founding ideals promise equality and opportunity to all, is a nation settled and built by immigrants. And for much of its history it has offered asylum for the world's oppressed.

The first sustained attack against newcomers emerged as a result of the surge in immigration during the 1840s and 1850s. It was directed by established immigrant groups, the descendants of settlers from Britain and northwestern Europe, at unfamiliar newcomers, particularly the Irish. These nativists especially feared religious contamination, claiming that the Catholicism of the Irish was alien to the Protestant values held to be indispensable to the preservation of American liberties.

In the late nineteenth century, a massive new immigrant surge dominated by people from southern and eastern Europe seeking economic opportunity and fleeing religious oppression transformed U.S. society and renewed nativist fears. This time, race replaced religion as the basis for drawing invidious comparisons between established residents and the newcomers. Pseudoscientific theories relegated Jews, Slavs, and Mediterranean peoples,

together with Africans, to an inferior status below people of northern Europe. The newcomers, it was claimed, were unfit for democratic government and would endanger American civilization. Strict anti-immigrant legislation in the 1920s sharply curtailed immigration from outside the Western Hemisphere, banning Asians entirely and setting quotas based on national origin for others.

Recent concerns about immigration result from the unforeseen consequences of a 1965 reform of the immigration law that abolished quotas. Since then, immigration has risen sharply, and the vast majority of the immigrants come from areas outside of Europe. As cries are again raised that alien newcomers are threatening the cohesiveness of the nation's institutions and values, Americans would do well to recall the words of Abraham Lincoln: "What held the nation together was an idea of equality that every newcomer could claim and defend by free choice."

Question for Discussion

- What recurring patterns occur in the ambivalence with which resident Americans have viewed the acceptance of newcomers?

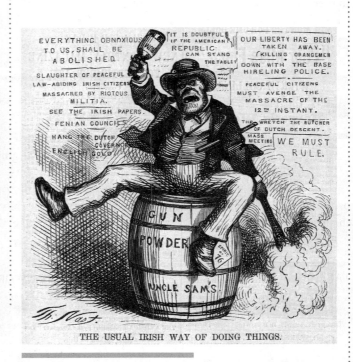

These Italian children on board an immigrant ship were part of the huge influx of southern and eastern Europeans after 1880.

Their nativist critics depicted the Irish as drunken brawlers with the derogatory racial characteristics that native-born whites assigned to African Americans.

benevolent empire Network of reform associations affiliated with Protestant churches in the early nineteenth century dedicated to the restoration of moral order.

workers to forsake God and their families. Alarmed by what they perceived as a breakdown in moral authority, they sought to impose moral discipline on Americans.

These eastern elites, with the indispensable support of their wives and daughters, created a network of voluntary church-affiliated reform organizations known collectively as the **benevolent empire**. Revivals in the 1820s and 1830s broadened the base of reform to include the newly evangelicalized middle class in northern cities and towns.

The Benevolent Empire

Evangelical businessmen in the seaboard cities backed the call to restore moral order. Worried by the increasing number of urban poor, wealthy merchants contributed vital financial support for a network of reform associations. The reform societies built on the Second Great Awakening's techniques of organization and communication. The Protestant reformers sent out speakers on regular schedules along prescribed routes. They developed organizations that maintained a constant pressure for reform. National and local boards of directors supervised the work of salaried managers, who inspired volunteers to combat sin among the unconverted.

When steam presses and stereotype plates halved the cost of printing and dramatically increased its speed, the American Bible Society was the first organization to exploit this revolution in the print media. Between 1790 and 1830, the number of religious newspapers grew from 14 to more than 600. By then, religious presses were churning out more than 1 million Bibles and 6 million tracts a year.

A host of local societies targeted individual vices. Their purpose, as summed up by a Massachusetts group, the Andover South Parish Society for the Reformation of Morals, was "to discountenance [discourage] immorality, particularly Sabbath-breaking, intemperance, and profanity, and to promote industry, order, piety, and good morals." These goals linked social and moral discipline, appealing both to churchgoers concerned about godlessness and profit-oriented businessmen eager to curb their workers' unruly behavior.

The boldest expression of the drive to enhance Protestant Christian power was the **Sabbatarian movement**. In 1828, evangelicals led by Reverend Lyman Beecher formed the General Union for Promoting the Observance of the Christian Sabbath. Their immediate goal was the repeal of a law passed by Congress in 1810 directing post offices to deliver mail on Sunday. Their broader mission was to enforce local statutes that shut down business and leisure activities on Sundays. The Sabbatarians considered such statutes no less "necessary to the welfare of the state" than "laws against murder and polygamy."

In 1829, insisting on the separation of church and state, the Democratic Congress upheld the postal law of 1810. The Sabbatarians had outraged canal operators, hotelkeepers, tavern owners, and other businesses threatened with the loss of their Sunday trade. Businessmen, workingmen, southern evangelicals, and religious conservatives all felt that the Sabbath purists had gone too far in a movement now seen as a threat to civil liberties and the rights of private property.

The General Union disbanded in 1832, but it left an important legacy for future reform movements. On the one hand, it developed techniques that converted the reform impulse into direct political action. In raising funds, training speakers, holding rallies, disseminating literature, lobbying for local Sunday regulations, and coordinating a petition to Congress, the Sabbatarians created an organizational model for other reformers to follow in mobilizing public opinion and influencing politicians. On the other hand, the failure of the Sabbatarians revealed that a new approach was needed that encouraged individuals to reform themselves without coercive controls. It soon emerged in the temperance movement.

The Temperance Movement

Temperance, the drive against the consumption of alcohol, had the greatest impact on the most people of any reform movement. Its success rested on what Lyman Beecher called "a new moral power." Dismayed by popular resistance to the coercive moralism of the first wave of Protestant reform, evangelicals concluded that reform had to rest on persuasion, and it had to begin with the voluntary decision of individuals to free themselves from sin.

In 1826, evangelicals founded the **American Temperance Society**. Their goal was to bring about a radical change in U.S. attitudes toward alcohol and its role in social

Sabbatarian movement Reform organization founded in 1828 by Congregationalist and Presbyterian ministers that lobbied for an end to the delivery of mail on Sundays and other Sabbath violations.

American Temperance Society National organization established in 1826 by evangelical Protestants that campaigned for total abstinence from alcohol and was successful in sharply lowering per capita consumption of alcohol.

Watch the Video   **Drinking and the Temperance Movement in Nineteenth-Century America**

Temperance cartoon

life. Taverns easily outnumbered churches as gathering places. Alcohol was used to pay common laborers and itinerant preachers on the early Methodist circuit. Masters and journeymen shared a drink as a customary way of taking a break from work, and no wedding, funeral, or meeting of friends was complete without alcohol.

For the temperance crusade to succeed, the reformers had to finance a massive propaganda campaign and link it to an organization that could mobilize and energize thousands of people. They built such a mass movement by merging temperance into the network of churches and lay volunteers that the benevolent empire had developed and by adopting the techniques of revivals to win converts.

Evangelical reformers denounced intemperance as the greatest sin of the land. Alcohol represented all that was wrong in America: crime, poverty, insanity, broken families, boisterous politicking, Sabbath-breaking. This message thundered from the pulpit and the public lectern. Thanks to the generous financial subsidies of wealthy benefactors, it was also broadcast in millions of tracts printed on the latest high-speed presses. Like revivals, temperance rallies combined emotionally charged sermons with large, tearful prayer meetings to evoke guilt among sinners, who would then seek release by taking the pledge of abstinence.

Within a decade, the American Temperance Society had more than 5,000 local chapters and statewide affiliates, most in the Northeast. A million members had pledged abstinence by 1833. Women constituted one-third to more than one-half of the members in local temperance societies. Lacking legal protections against abusive husbands who drank away the family resources, women had a compelling reason to join the crusade. As the moral protectors of the family, they pressured their husbands to take the teetotaler's pledge and stick by it, raised sons to shun alcohol, and banished liquor from their homes. By the 1840s, temperance and middle-class domesticity had become synonymous.

The first wave of temperance converts came from the upper and middle classes. Businessmen welcomed temperance as a model of self-discipline in their efforts to regiment factory work. Young, upwardly mobile professionals and petty entrepreneurs learned in temperance how to be thrifty, self-controlled, respectable, and creditworthy.

Temperance made its first significant inroads among the working classes during the economic depression of 1839–1843. Joining together in what they called Washington Temperance Societies, small businessmen and artisans, many of them reformed drunkards, carried temperance into working-class districts. The Washingtonians insisted that workers could survive the depression only if they stopped drinking and adopted the temperance ethic of frugality and self-help. Their wives organized auxiliary societies and pledged to enforce sobriety and economic restraint at home. In a telling measure of the temperance movement's success, per capita alcohol consumption fell from an all-time high of 7.1 gallons per year in 1830 to less than 2 gallons per year by 1845.

Women's Role in Reform

The first phase of women's reform activities represented an extension of the domestic ideal promoted in the cult of domesticity. Assumptions about women's unique moral qualities permitted, and even encouraged, them to assume the role of "social mother" by organizing on behalf of the orphaned and the widowed. Founded in 1797, the Society for the Relief of Poor Widows with Small Children in New York typified these early approaches to reform. The women in the society came from socially prominent families. Motivated by religious charity and social duty, they visited poor women and children, dispensed funds, and set up work programs. However, they limited their benevolence to the "deserving poor," socially weak but morally strong people who had suffered personal misfortune, and screened out all who were thought to be unworthy.

The revivalist call in the 1820s for moral action inspired middle-class women to join voluntary female groups. They founded maternal associations, where they prayed and fasted for the moral strength to save the souls of their children. Other associations sponsored revivals, visited the poor, established Sunday schools, and distributed Bibles and religious tracts. These reformers widened the public role of women, but their efforts also reinforced cultural stereotypes of women as nurturing helpmates who deferred to males.

A second phase in the reform efforts by women developed in the 1830s. Unlike their benevolent counterparts, the reformers now began to challenge male prerogatives and move beyond moral suasion. The crusade against prostitution exemplified the new militancy. Women seized leadership of the movement in 1834 with the founding of the New York Female Moral Reform Society. In the pages of their journal, *Advocate for Moral Reform,* members identified male greed and licentiousness as the causes for the fallen state of women. Identified, too, were the male patrons of the city's brothels. The society blamed businessmen for the low wages that forced some women to resort to prostitution and denounced lustful men for engaging in "a regular crusade against [our] sex."

In 1839, this attack on the sexual double standard became a national movement with the establishment of the **American Female Moral Reform Society**. With 555 affiliates throughout the evangelical heartland of the North, female activists mounted a lobbying campaign that, unlike earlier efforts, bypassed prominent men and reached out to a mass audience. By the 1840s, such unprecedented political involvement enabled women to secure the first state laws criminalizing seduction and adultery.

Other women's groups developed a more radical critique of U.S. society and its male leadership. The Boston Seamen's Aid Society, founded in 1833 by Sarah Josepha Hale, a widow with five children, soon rejected the benevolent tradition of distinguishing between "respectable" and "unworthy" poor. Hale discovered that her efforts to guide poor women toward self-sufficiency flew in the face of the low wages and substandard housing that trapped her clients in poverty. Hale attacked male employers for exploiting the poor. "Combinations of selfish men are formed to beat down the price of female labor," she wrote in her 1836 annual report, "and then they call the diminished rate the market price."

American Female Moral Reform Society Organization founded in 1839 by female reformers that established homes of refuge for prostitutes and petitioned for state laws that would criminalize adultery and the seduction of women.

Backlash against Benevolence

Some of the benevolent empire's harshest critics came out of the populist revivals of the early 1800s. They considered the Protestant reformers' program a conspiracy of orthodox Calvinists from old-line denominations to impose social and moral control on behalf of a religious and economic elite. The goal of the "orthodox party," warned the Universalist *Christian Intelligencer,* was the power of "governing the nation."

These criticisms revealed a profound mistrust of the emerging market society. In contrast to the evangelical reformers, drawn from the well-educated business and middle classes who were benefiting from economic change, most evangelical members of the grassroots sects and followers of the itinerant preachers were unschooled, poor, and hurt by market fluctuations that they could not control. Socially uprooted and economically stranded, they found a sense of community in their local churches and resisted control by wealthier, better-educated outsiders. Above all, they clung to beliefs that shored up the threatened authority of the father over his household.

With the elevation of women to the status of moral guardians of the family and agents of benevolent reform outside the household, middle-class evangelicalism in the Northeast was becoming feminized. This new social role for women was especially threatening, indeed, galling, for men who were the casualties of the more competitive economy. Raised on farms where the father had been the unquestioned lawgiver and provider, these men attacked feminized evangelicalism for undermining their paternal authority. They found in Scripture an affirmation of patriarchal power for any man, no matter how poor or economically dependent.

The **Church of Jesus Christ of Latter-day Saints** (also known as the **Mormon Church**) represented the most enduring religious backlash of economically struggling men against the aggressive efforts of reforming middle-class evangelicals. Joseph Smith, who established the church in upstate New York in 1830, came from a New England farm family uprooted and impoverished by market speculations gone sour. He and his followers were alienated not only from the new market economy but also from what they saw as the religious and social anarchy around them. Based on Smith's divine revelations as set forth in the *Book of Mormon* (1830), their new faith offered converts both a sanctuary as a biblical people and a release from social and religious uncertainties.

Mormonism provided a defense of communal beliefs centered on male authority. It assigned complete spiritual and secular authority to men. Only through subordination and obedience to their husbands could women hope to gain salvation. To be a Mormon was to join a large extended family that was part of a shared enterprise. Men bonded their labor in a communal economy to benefit all the faithful. A law of tithing, instituted in 1841, required Mormons to give 10 percent of their property to the church upon conversion and 10 percent of their annual income thereafter. Driven by a strong sense of social obligation, the Mormons forged the most successful alternative vision in antebellum America to the individualistic Protestant republic of the benevolent reformers. (For the Mormons' role in the westward movement, see Chapter 13.)

Church of Jesus Christ of Latter-day Saints (Mormon Church) Church founded in 1830 by Joseph Smith and based on the revelations in a sacred book he called the *Book of Mormon.*

Institutions and Social Improvement

12.3 How did Enlightenment ideas shape the reform of institutions for the poor, criminals, and the mentally ill?

Although evangelical Protestantism was its mainspring, antebellum reform also had its roots in the European Enlightenment. Like the evangelicals inspired by religious optimism, reformers drawing on Enlightenment doctrines of progress had unbounded faith in social improvement. They saw in the United States an unlimited potential to fashion a model republic of virtuous, intelligent citizens.

School Reform

Before the 1820s, schooling in America was an informal, haphazard affair that nonetheless met the basic needs for reading, writing, and arithmetic skills of an overwhelmingly rural population. Private tutors and academies for the wealthy, a few charitable schools for the urban poor, and rural one-room schoolhouses open for a few months each year constituted formal education at the primary level.

The first political demands for free tax-supported schools originated with the **workingmen's movement** in eastern cities in the 1820s. In pushing for "equal republican education," workers sought to guarantee that all citizens, no matter how poor, could achieve meaningful liberty and equality. Their proposals, however, met stiff resistance from wealthier property holders, who refused to pay taxes to support the education of working-class children.

12.1

12.2

12.3

12.4

workingmen's movement Associations of urban workers who began campaigning in the 1820s for free public education and a 10-hour workday.

The breakthrough in public education came in New England, where the disruptive forces of industrialization and urbanization were felt the earliest. Increased economic inequality, growing numbers of impoverished Irish Catholic immigrants, and the emergence of a mass democracy based on nearly universal white male suffrage convinced reformers of the need for state-supported schools.

In 1837, the Massachusetts legislature established the nation's first state board of education. The head of the board for the next twelve years was Horace Mann, a former Whig politician and temperance advocate who now tirelessly championed educational reform. Mann demanded that the state government assume centralized control over Massachusetts schools.

Once this system was in place, Mann promised, the schools would become "the great equalizer of the conditions of men, the balance-wheel of the social machinery." Poverty would no longer threaten social disruption because the ignorant would have the knowledge to acquire property and wealth. Education, Mann stated, "does better than disarm the poor of their hostility against the rich; it prevents being poor." Trained in self-control and punctuality, youths would be able to take advantage of economic opportunities and become intelligent voters concerned with the rights of property.

Democrats in the Massachusetts legislature denounced Mann's program as "a system of centralization and of monopoly of power in a few hands, contrary in every respect, to the true spirit of our democratical institutions." The laboring poor, who depended for economic survival on the wages their children could earn, resisted compulsory-attendance laws and a longer school year. Farmers fought to maintain local control over schooling and to block the higher taxes needed for a more comprehensive and professionalized system. The Catholic Church protested the thinly veiled attempts of the reformers to indoctrinate all students in the moral strictures of middle-class Protestantism. Catholics began, at great expense, to build their own parochial schools.

Mann and his allies nonetheless prevailed in most of the industrializing states, with strong support from the professional and business constituencies of the Whig party. Manufacturers hoped that the schools would turn out a more obedient and punctual labor force, and the more skilled and prosperous workers saw in public education a key to upward mobility for their children.

Most important for its political success, school reform appealed to the growing northern middle class. Schools would instill the moral and economic discipline that the middle class deemed essential for a progressive and ordered society.

Out of the northern middle class also came the young female teachers who increasingly staffed elementary schools. Presumed by their nature to be more nurturing than men, women now had an entry into teaching, the first profession open to them. Besides, women could also be paid far less than men; school boards assumed that they would accept low wages while waiting to be married.

Just over 50 percent of the white children between 5 and 19 years of age in the United States were enrolled in school in 1850, the highest percentage in the world at the time. Working-class parents pulled their children out of school at an earlier age than higher-income, middle-class parents. Planters continued to rely on private tutors or academies, and southern farmers saw little need for public education. The slave states, especially in the Lower South, lagged behind the rest of the nation in public education.

Prisons, Workhouses, and Asylums

Up to this time, Americans had depended on voluntary efforts to cope with crime, poverty, and social deviance. Convinced that these efforts were inadequate, reformers turned to public authorities to establish a host of new institutions to deal with social problems.

The reformers held that people's environments shaped their character for good or evil. The Boston Children's Friend Society was devoted to the young, "whose plastic natures may be molded into images of perfect beauty, or . . . perfect repulsiveness." Samuel Gridley Howe, a prison reformer, proclaimed: "Thousands of convicts are made so in consequence of a faulty organization of society. . . ." In the properly ordered environment of new institutions, discipline and moral character would be instilled in criminals and other deviants who lacked the self-control to resist the society's corrupting vices and temptations.

Reformers had particularly high expectations for the penitentiary systems pioneered in Pennsylvania and New York in the 1820s. Unlike earlier prisons, the penitentiaries were huge, imposing structures that isolated the prisoners from each other and the outside world. No longer were criminals to be brutally punished or thrown together under inhumane conditions that perpetuated a cycle of moral depravity. Now, cut off from all corrupting influences, forced to learn that hard work teaches moral discipline, and uplifted by religious literature, criminals would be guided toward becoming law-abiding, productive citizens.

Workhouses. The same philosophy of reform provided the rationale for asylums to house the poor and the insane. The number of transient poor and the size of urban slums increased as commercial capitalism uprooted farmers from the land and undercut the security of craft trades. Believing that the poor, much like criminals, had only themselves to blame, public officials and their evangelical allies prescribed a therapeutic regimen of discipline and physical labor to cure the poor of their moral defects. The structured setting for the regimen was the workhouse.

The custodians of the workhouses banished drinking, gambling, and idleness. Their prime responsibility was to supervise the inmates in a tightly scheduled daily routine built around manual labor. Once purged of their laziness and filled with self-esteem as the result of work discipline, the poor would be released to become useful members of society.

Asylums for the Mentally Ill. Public insane asylums offered a similar order for the mentally ill. Reformers believed that too many choices in a highly mobile, materialistic, and competitive society drove some people insane. Following the lead of New York and Massachusetts in the 1830s, twenty-eight states had established mental hospitals by 1860. These facilities set rigid rules and work assignments to teach patients how to order their lives.

In the early 1840s, Dorothea Dix, a Massachusetts schoolteacher, discovered that the insane in her home state were dumped into jails and almshouses, where they suffered filthy, inhumane treatment. Horrified, Dix lobbied state legislatures across the nation for the next twenty years to improve treatment for the mentally ill.

While the reformers did provide social deviants with cleaner, safer living conditions, their penitentiaries and asylums succeeded more in classifying and segregating inmates than in reforming them. Submission to routine turned out not to be the best builder of character. Penitentiaries, reformatories, and workhouses failed to eliminate or noticeably check poverty, crime, and vice. Refusing to question their basic premise that repressive institutions could promote individual responsibility, reformers abandoned their environmental explanations for deviance. By mid-century, they were defining deviants and dependents as permanent misfits with ingrained character defects.

The asylums remained; but, stripped of their earlier optimism, they became little more than holding pens for the outcasts of society.

Utopian Alternatives

Unlike the reformers, who aimed to improve the existing order by guiding individuals to greater self-discipline, the utopians sought perfection by withdrawing from society and its confining institutions. A radically new social order, not an improved old one, was their goal.

Though following different religious and secular philosophies of communitarian living, all the utopians wanted to fashion a more rational and personally satisfying alternative to the competitive materialism of antebellum America. Nearly all the communities sought to transform the organization and rewards of work, thus challenging the prevailing dogmas about private property.

The most successful utopian communities were religious sects whose reordering of both sexual and economic relations departed sharply from middle-class norms. The **Shakers**, at their height in the 1830s, attracted some 6,000 followers. Organized around doctrines of celibate **communism**, Shaker communities held all property in common. The sexes worked and lived apart from each other. Dancing during religious worship brought men and women together and provided an emotional release from enforced sexual denial. In worldly as well as spiritual terms, women enjoyed an equality in Shaker life that the outside world denied them. For this reason, twice as many women as men joined the Shakers.

John Humphrey Noyes, a graduate of Dartmouth who studied for the ministry at Yale, established the **Oneida Community** in upstate New York in 1848. He attracted more than 200 followers with his perfectionist vision of plural marriage, community nurseries, group discipline, and common ownership of property. Charged with adultery, Noyes fled to Canada in 1879, but the Oneida Community, reorganized in 1881 as a joint-stock company in the United States and committed thereafter to conventional sexual mores, survived into the twentieth century.

Secular utopians aspired to perfect social relations through rationally designed planned communities. Bitter critics of the social evils of industrialization, they tried to construct models for a social order free from poverty, unemployment, and inequality. They envisioned cooperative communities that balanced agricultural and industrial pursuits in a mixed economy that recycled earnings to the laborers who actually produced the wealth.

Despite their high expectations, nearly all the planned communities ran into financial difficulties and soon collapsed. The pattern was set by the first of the controversial socialist experiments, **New Harmony** in Indiana, the brainchild of the wealthy Scottish industrialist and philanthropist Robert Owen. A proponent of utopian **socialism**, Owen promised to create a new order where "the degrading and pernicious practices in which we are now well trained, of buying cheap and selling dear, will be rendered unnecessary" and "union and co-operation will supersede individual interest." But within two years of its founding in 1825, New Harmony fell victim to inadequate financing and internal bickering.

About the only secular cooperative that gained lasting fame was **Brook Farm** in West Roxbury, Massachusetts (today part of Boston). Established in 1841, Brook Farm was a showcase for the transcendentalist philosophy of Ralph Waldo Emerson. A former Unitarian minister in Boston, Emerson taught that intuition and emotion could grasp a truer ("transcendent") reality than could the senses alone. Although disbanded after six years as an economic failure, Brook Farm inspired intellectuals such as Nathaniel Hawthorne, who briefly lived there. In turn, his writings and those of other writers influenced by **transcendentalism** flowed into the great renaissance of American literature in the mid-nineteenth century, an outpouring of work that grappled with Emersonian themes of individualism and the reshaping of the American character.

Shakers The followers of Mother Ann Lee, who preached a religion of strict celibacy and communal living.

communism A social structure based on the common ownership of property.

Oneida Community Utopian community established in upstate New York in 1848 by John Humphrey Noyes and his followers.

New Harmony Short-lived utopian community established in Indiana in 1825, based on the socialist ideas of Robert Owen, a wealthy Scottish manufacturer.

socialism A social order based on government ownership of industry and worker control over corporations as a way to prevent worker exploitation.

Brook Farm A utopian community and experimental farm established in 1841 near Boston.

transcendentalism A philosophical and literary movement centered on an idealistic belief in the divinity of individuals and nature.

A Distinctly National Literature.   In an 1837 address at Harvard titled "The American Scholar," Emerson called for a distinctly national literature devoted to the democratic possibilities of American life. Writers soon responded to Emerson's call.

Walt Whitman, whose *Leaves of Grass* (1855) foreshadowed modern poetry in its use of free verse, shared Emerson's faith in the possibilities of individual fulfillment, and his poems celebrated the democratic variety of the American people. Henry David Thoreau, Emerson's friend and neighbor, embodied the transcendentalist fascination with nature and self-discovery by living in relative isolation for 16 months at Walden Pond, near Concord, Massachusetts. His *Walden; or, Life in the Woods* (1854) became an American classic.

Nathaniel Hawthorne and Herman Melville, the greatest novelists of the American renaissance, focused on the existence of evil and the human need for community. In *The Scarlet Letter* (1850) and *The House of the Seven Gables* (1851), Hawthorne probed themes of egoism and pride to reveal the underside of the human soul. Melville's *Moby Dick* (1851) depicted the consequences of a competitive individualism unchecked by a social conscience. In his relentless pursuit of the great white whale, Captain Ahab destroys himself and his crew.

Much of the appeal of the utopian communities flowed from the same concern about the splintering and selfishness of antebellum society that animated Hawthorne and Melville. The works of these novelists have endured, but the utopian experiments quickly collapsed. Promising economic security and social harmony to buttress a threatened sense of community, the utopians failed to lure all but a few Americans from the acquisitiveness and competitive demands of the larger society.

Abolitionism and Women's Rights

12.4   What was the relationship between abolitionism and the women's rights movement?

Abolitionism emerged from the same religious impulse that energized reform throughout the North. Like other reformers, the abolitionists came predominantly from evangelical, middle-class families, particularly those of New England stock. What distinguished the abolitionists was their insistence that slavery was *the* great national sin, an evil that mocked American ideals of liberty and Christian morality.

Rejecting Colonization

In the early nineteenth century, when slavery was expanding westward, almost all white Americans regardless of class or region were convinced that emancipation would lead either to a race war or the debasement of their superior status through racial interbreeding. This paralyzing fear of general emancipation, rooted in pervasive racism, long shielded slavery from sustained attack.

In 1817, antislavery reformers from the North and the South founded the **American Colonization Society**. Slaveholding politicians from the Upper South, notably Henry Clay, James Madison, and President James Monroe, were the leading organizers of the society. Gradual emancipation accompanied by the removal of black people from America to Africa was the only solution these white reformers could imagine for ridding the nation of slavery and avoiding a racial bloodbath. Their goal was to make America all free *and* all white.

The American Colonization Society had no real chance of success. No form of emancipation, no matter how gradual, could appeal to slave owners who could profit from the labor of their slaves. Moreover, the society could never afford to purchase the freedom of any significant number of slaves. Almost all the African Americans it transported to Liberia, the West African colony it helped found, were already free. At

American Colonization Society
Organization, founded in 1817 by antislavery reformers, that called for gradual emancipation and the removal of freed blacks to Africa.

the height of its popularity in the 1820s, the society sent only 1,400 colonists to Africa. During that same decade, the U.S. slave population increased by more than 450,000.

Free African Americans bitterly attacked the colonizers' central assumption that free black people were unfit to live as citizens in America. Most free African Americans were native-born, and they considered themselves Americans with every right to enjoy the blessings of republican liberty. As a black petition in 1817 stated, banishment from America "would not only be cruel, but in direct violation of the principles, which have been the boast of this republic."

Organizing through their own churches in northern cities, free African Americans founded some fifty abolitionist societies, offered refuge to fugitive slaves, and launched the first African American newspaper in 1827, *Freedom's Journal*. David Walker, a free black man who had moved from North Carolina to Massachusetts, published his **Appeal to the Colored Citizens of the World** in 1829. In a searing indictment of white greed and hypocrisy, he rejected colonization and insisted that "America is more our country, than it is the whites', we have enriched it with our *blood and tears*." He warned white America that "wo, wo, will be to you if we have to obtain our freedom by fighting."

Appeal to the Colored Citizens of the World An abolitionist tract by a free black calling on the enslaved to overthrow their bondage.

As if in response to this call for revolutionary resistance by the enslaved, Nat Turner's Rebellion exploded in the summer of 1831 (see Chapter 11). Both alarmed and inspired by the increased tempo of black militancy, a small group of antislavery white people abandoned all illusions about colonization and embarked on a radically new approach for eradicating slavery (see Table 12.3 for the types of antislavery reform).

Abolitionism

William Lloyd Garrison, a Massachusetts printer and the leading figure in early abolitionism, became coeditor of an antislavery newspaper in Baltimore in 1829. Before the year was out, Garrison was arrested and convicted of criminal libel for his editorials against a Massachusetts merchant engaged in the domestic slave trade, and he spent seven weeks in jail before a New York City philanthropist paid his $100 fine. Recognizing that his lack of freedom in jail paled against that of the slave, Garrison emerged with an unquenchable hatred of slavery. Returning to Boston, he launched his own antislavery newspaper, the *Liberator,* in 1831. A year later, he was instrumental in founding the New England Anti-Slavery Society.

As militant as the free African Americans who comprised the bulk of the early subscribers to the *Liberator,* Garrison thundered, "If we would not see our land deluged in blood, we must instantly burst asunder the shackles of the slaves." He committed abolitionism to the twin goals of immediatism, an immediate moral commitment to end slavery, and racial equality. Only by striving toward these goals, he insisted, could white America ever hope to end slavery without massive violence.

The abolitionists' demand for the legal equality of black people was as unsettling to public opinion as their call for immediate, uncompensated emancipation. Denied the vote outside New England, segregated in all public facilities, prohibited from moving into several western states, and excluded from most jobs save menial labor, free black people everywhere were walled off as an inferior caste.

Garrison, harsh and uncompromising in denouncing slavery and advocating black rights, instilled the antislavery movement with moral urgency. But without the

TABLE 12.3 TYPES OF ANTISLAVERY REFORM

Type	Definition	Example
Gradualist	Accepts notions of black inferiority and attempts to end slavery gradually by purchasing the freedom of slaves and colonizing them in Africa	American Colonization Society
Immediatist	Calls for immediate steps to end slavery and denounces slavery and racial prejudice as moral sins	Abolitionists
Political antislavery	Recognizes slavery in states where it exists but insists on keeping slavery out of the territories	Free-Soilers

organizational and financial resources of a national society, the message of the early Garrisonians rarely extended beyond free black communities in the North.

The success of British abolitionists in 1833, when gradual, compensated emancipation was enacted for Britain's West Indian colonies, inspired white and black abolitionists to gather at Philadelphia in December 1833 and form the **American Anti-Slavery Society**. Arthur and Lewis Tappan, two wealthy merchants who dominated the abolitionist movement in New York City, provided financial backing for the Anti-Slavery Society.

The young evangelical minister Theodore Dwight Weld, fusing abolitionism with the moral passion of religious revivalism, brought the antislavery message of the eastern radicals to the West in 1834 with the revivals he preached at Lane Theological Seminary in Cincinnati. The "Lane rebels," students gathered by Weld, fanned out as itinerant agents to seek converts for abolitionism throughout the Yankee districts of the rural North.

The abolitionists spread their message through revivals, rallies, paid lecturers, children's games and toys, and the printed word. Drawing on the experience of reformers in Bible and tract societies, the abolitionists harnessed steam power to the cause of moral suasion. They distributed millions of antislavery tracts, and by the late 1830s, abolitionist sayings appeared on posters, emblems, song sheets, and even candy wrappers.

Women were essential in all of these activities. From the very beginning of the movement, they established their own antislavery societies as auxiliaries to the national organizations run and dominated by men. As Christian wives and mothers, they identified with the plight of the black family under slavery. Initially, their role was limited to raising funds, circulating petitions, and visiting homes to gain converts. Often operating out of local churches, women were grassroots organizers of a massive petition campaign launched in the mid-1830s. Women signed more than half of the antislavery memorials sent to Congress.

The abolitionists focused their energies on mass propaganda because they saw their role as social agitators who had to break through white apathy and change public opinion. By 1840 they had succeeded in enlisting nearly 200,000 northerners in 2,000

This ceramic plate, with the image of the kneeling slave holding a Bible, is one of the many ways in which the abolitionists used consumer goods to spread their message on the centrality of religion in ending slavery.

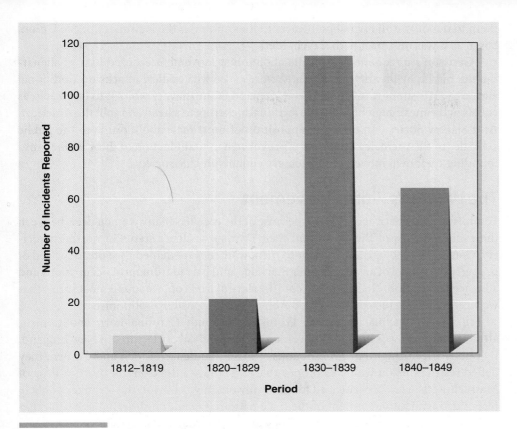

FIGURE 12.3 MOB VIOLENCE AND THE ABOLITIONISTS Civil disturbances resulting in attacks on individuals or property increased sharply in the 1830s. The abolitionist campaign to flood the country with antislavery literature triggered much of this surge. Nearly half of the mob activity in the 1830s was directed against abolitionists.

SOURCE: Leonard L. Richards, "Gentlemen of Property and Standing": *Anti-Abolitionist Mobs in Jacksonian America* (1970 Oxford University Press.)

local affiliates of the American Anti-Slavery Society. Most whites, however, remained unmoved, and some violently opposed the abolitionists.

Antiabolitionist mobs in the North went on a rampage in the mid-1830s (see Figure 12.3). White working men in Washington, DC, ransacked the popular restaurant of Beverly Snow, a free black whose success as a businessman upended racist assumptions that innately inferior African Americans could be useful to society only as slave laborers. Elsewhere, mobs disrupted antislavery meetings, beat and stoned speakers, destroyed printing presses, burned the homes of the wealthy benefactors of the movement, and vandalized free black neighborhoods in a wave of terror that drove many black people from several northern cities. Elijah P. Lovejoy, an abolitionist editor in Illinois, was killed by a mob in 1837. Local elites, especially those with profitable ties to the slave economy of the South, often incited the mobs, whose fury expressed the anxiety of semiskilled and common laborers that they might lose their jobs if freed slaves moved north.

In the South, the hostility to abolitionism took the form of burning and censoring antislavery literature, offering rewards for the capture of leading abolitionists to stand trial for allegedly inciting slave revolts, and tightening up slave codes and the surveillance of free black people. Meanwhile, Democrats in Congress yielded to slaveholding interests in 1836 by passing a gag rule that automatically tabled antislavery petitions with no debate.

The hostility and violence abolitionism provoked convinced Garrison and some of his followers that U.S. institutions and values were fundamentally flawed. In 1838, Garrison helped found the New England Non-Resistant Society, dedicated to the belief that a complete moral regeneration, based on renouncing force in all human relationships, was necessary if the United States were ever to live up to its Christian and republican ideals. The Garrisonian nonresistants rejected all coercive authority, whether expressed in capital punishment, human bondage, clerical support of slavery, male dominance in the patriarchal family, the racial oppression of back people, or the police power of government. The logic of their stand as Christian anarchists drove them to denounce all formal political activities and even the legitimacy of the Union, based as it was on a pact with slaveholders.

Garrison's opponents within the abolitionist movement accused him of alienating the public by identifying the antislavery cause with radical attacks on traditional authority. His support for the growing demand of antislavery women to be treated as equals in the movement brought the factional bickering to a head and split the American Anti-Slavery Society. In turn, the opposition of most male abolitionists to the public activities of their female counterparts provoked a militant faction of these women into founding their own movement to achieve equality in U.S. society.

The Women's Rights Movement

Feminism grew out of abolitionism because of the parallels many women drew between the exploited lives of the slaves and their own subordinate status in northern society. Considered biologically inferior to men, women were denied the vote, deprived of property or control of any wages after marriage, and barred from most occupations and advanced education. "In striving to cut [the slave's] irons off, we found most surely that we were manacled *ourselves*," argued Abby Kelley, a Quaker abolitionist.

In 1837, Angelina and Sarah Grimké, the South Carolina–born abolitionists, attracted large crowds of men and women to their antislavery lectures in New England. By publicly lecturing to a "promiscuous" (mixed) audience of men and women, they defied restrictions on women's proper role and enraged the Congregational clergy of Massachusetts. Harshly criticized for their unwomanly behavior, the Grimkés publicly responded with an indictment of the male patriarchy and the shocking assertion that "men and women are *created equal!* They are both moral and accountable beings and whatever is right for man to do is right for woman."

Now more sensitive than ever to the injustice of their assigned role as men's submissive followers, antislavery women demanded an equal voice in the abolitionist movement. Despite strong opposition from many of his fellow male abolitionists, Garrison helped Abby Kelley win a seat on the business committee of the American Anti-Slavery Society at its convention in 1840. The anti-Garrisonians walked out of the convention and formed a separate organization, the American and Foreign Anti-Slavery Society.

What was rapidly becoming known as the "woman question" also disrupted the 1840 World Anti-Slavery Convention in London. The refusal of the convention to seat the U.S. female delegates was the final indignity that transformed the discontent of women into a self-conscious movement for women's equality. Two of the excluded delegates, Lucretia Mott and Elizabeth Cady Stanton, vowed to build an organization to "speak out for *oppressed* women."

Their work went slowly. Early feminists were dependent on the abolitionists for most of their followers, and they were unable to do more than hold local meetings and sponsor occasional speaking tours. Many women sympathetic to the feminist movement hung back lest they be shunned in their communities. A minister's wife in Portsmouth, New Hampshire, wrote to a feminist friend, "There are but few here who think of women as anything more than slave or plaything, and they think I am different from most women."

In 1848, Stanton and Mott were finally able to call the first national convention ever devoted to women's rights at Seneca Falls, in upstate New York. The **Seneca Falls Convention** issued the **Declaration of Sentiments**, a call for full female equality. Modeled directly on the Declaration of Independence, it identified male patriarchy as the source of women's oppression and demanded the vote for women as a sacred and inalienable right of republican citizenship. This call for suffrage raised the prospect of women's self-determination as independent citizens. The Seneca Falls agenda defined the goals of the women's movement for the rest of the century.

The feminists' few successes before the Civil War came in economic rights. By 1860, fourteen states had granted women greater control over their property and wages, most significantly under New York's Married Women's Property Act of 1860. The act established women's legal right to control their own wage income and to sue fathers and husbands who tried to deprive them of their wages.

Seneca Falls Convention The first convention for women's equality in legal rights, held in upstate New York in 1848.

Declaration of Sentiments The resolutions passed at the Seneca Falls Convention of 1848 calling for full female equality, including the right to vote.

Shown here are seven leaders of the founding generation of American feminists. Clockwise from the top: Lucretia Mott, Elizabeth Cady Stanton, Mary A. Livermore, Lydia Maria Child, Susan B. Anthony, and Grace Greenwood. In the center is Anna E. Dickinson.

Despite such successes, the feminist movement did not attract broad support. Most women found in the doctrine of separate spheres a reassuring feminine identity that they could express either at home or in benevolent and reform societies. Within the reform movement as a whole, women's rights were always a minor concern. Abolitionists focused on emancipation.

Political Antislavery

Most of the abolitionists who had broken with Garrison in 1840 believed that emancipation could best be achieved by moving abolitionism into the mainstream of U.S. politics. Political abolitionism had its roots in the petition campaign of the late 1830s. Congressional efforts to suppress the discussion of slavery backfired when John Quincy Adams, the former president who had become a Massachusetts congressman, resorted to an unending series of parliamentary ploys to get around the gag rule (see Chapter 10). Adams became a champion of the constitutional right to petition Congress for redress of grievances. White northerners who had shown no interest in abolitionism as a moral crusade for black people now began to take a stand against slavery when the issue involved the civil liberties of whites and the dominant political power of the South. By the hundreds of thousands, they signed abolitionist petitions in 1837 and 1838 to protest the gag rule and the admission of Texas as a slave state.

In 1840, anti-Garrisonian abolitionists tried to turn this new antislavery constituency into an independent political party, the **Liberty Party**. This party opposed any expansion of slavery in the territories, condemned racial discrimination in the North as well as slavery in the South, and won the support of most black abolitionists. "To it," recalled Samuel Ward of New York, "I devoted my political activities; with it I lived my political life." In 1843, a national African American convention in Buffalo endorsed the Liberty Party.

Liberty Party The first antislavery political party, formed in 1840.

Read the Document National Convention of Colored People, "Report on Abolition"

Born a slave about 1797 in Ulster County, New York, with the name of Isabella Van Wagener, Sojourner Truth, as she called herself after 1843, is shown here in a print taken in 1864. She was one of the most powerful and charismatic speakers on behalf of abolitionism and women's rights. As she memorably proclaimed to one audience, "I could work as much . . . and bear the lash as well [as a man]—and aren't I a woman?"

This political activism was part of a concerted effort by African Americans to assert leadership in an antislavery movement that rarely treated them as equals. Frederick Douglass was their most dynamic spokesman. After escaping from slavery in 1838, Douglass became a spellbinding lecturer for abolitionism and in 1845 published his classic autobiography, *Narrative of the Life of Frederick Douglass, an American Slave.* Increasingly dissatisfied with Garrison's Christian pacifism and his stand against political action, Douglass broke with Garrison in 1847 and founded a black abolitionist newspaper, the *North Star.* The break became irreparable in 1851 when Douglass publicly denied the Garrisonian position that the Constitution was a pro-slavery document. If properly interpreted, Douglass insisted, "the Constitution is a *glorious liberty document,*" and he called for a political war against slavery.

Led by Joshua R. Giddings, a small but vocal bloc of antislavery politicians began to popularize the frightening concept of "the **Slave Power**," a vast conspiracy of planters and their northern lackeys that controlled the federal government and was plotting to spread slavery and subvert any free institutions that opposed it. As proof, they cited the gag rule, which had shut off debate on slavery, and the campaign of the Tyler administration to annex slaveholding Texas.

Slave Power A key concept in abolitionist and northern antislavery propaganda that depicted southern slaveholders as the driving force in a political conspiracy to promote slavery at the expense of white liberties.

The specter of the Slave Power made white liberties, and not black bondage, central to northern concerns about slavery. This shift redefined the evil of slavery to appeal to the self-interest of white northerners who had rejected the moral appeals of the Garrisonians. White people who had earlier been apathetic now began to view slavery as a threat to their rights of free speech and self-improvement.

The image of the Slave Power predisposed many northerners to see the expansionist program of the incoming Polk administration as part of a southern plot to secure more territory for slaveholders at the expense of northern farmers. Northern fears that free labor would be shut out of the new territories won in the Mexican War provided the rallying cry for the Free-Soil Party of 1848, which foreshadowed the more powerful Republican Party of the late 1850s.

Conclusion

With surprising speed after 1815, transportation improvements, technological innovations, and expanding markets drove the economy toward industrialization. Wealth inequality increased, old classes were reshaped, and new ones formed. These changes were most evident in the Northeast, where capital, labor, and growing urban markets spurred the acceleration of manufacturing. The reform impulse that both reflected and shaped these changes was also strongest in the Northeast. The new evangelical Protestantism promised that human perfectibility was possible if individuals strove to free themselves from sin. Influenced by this promise, the northern middle class embraced reform causes that sought to improve human character. Temperance changed U.S. drinking habits and established sobriety as the cultural standard for respectable male behavior. Middle-class reform also emphasized institutional solutions for what were now defined as the social problems of ignorance, crime, and poverty.

The most radical of the reform movements focused on women's equality and the elimination of slavery. The women's rights movement emerged out of women's involvement in reform, especially in abolitionism. Feminism and abolitionism triggered a backlash from the more conservative majority, a response that strengthened the resolve of reformers such as Angelina Grimké. This backlash prevented women from gaining legal and political equality, the major demand of the feminists, and convinced most abolitionists that they had to switch from moral agitation to political persuasion. The political abolitionists soon found that the most effective approach in widening the antislavery appeal was their charge that a Slave Power conspiracy threatened the freedoms of white northerners.

For Suggested Readings go to MyHistoryLab.

Chapter Review

Industrial Change and Urbanization

12.1 How did industrialization contribute to growing inequality and the creation of new social classes? p. 307

As the transportation revolution sharply lowered the cost and increased the speed of moving goods in the economy, manufacturing expanded to meet the growing domestic demand. Once employment was no longer tied directly to the land, new social classes emerged— a wealthy commercial elite, a middle class of retailers and salaried employees, and a working class of laborers all but impoverished by low wages and irregular employment.

Reform and Moral Order

12.2 What role did religion play in the reform movements that followed the War of 1812? p. 321

The series of revivals known as the Second Great Awakening stressed that all individuals had a free choice in determining their salvation. Once converted, the evangelical Christian had a moral responsibility to combat sin on both an individual and a social level. The result was a surge of religious benevolence expressed in a host of reform societies committed to the moral purification and betterment of society.

Institutions and Social Improvement

12.3 How did Enlightenment ideas shape the reform of institutions for the poor, criminals, and the mentally ill? p. 326

Confidence in the ability of human reason to promote social progress was at the core of the Enlightenment ideas that came out of eighteenth-century Europe. When linked to the Enlightenment belief that environmental factors shaped character, these ideas inspired reformers to believe that new institutions could reform the character of social deviants and mold them into responsible, productive citizens.

Abolitionism and Women's Rights

12.4 What was the relationship between abolitionism and the women's rights movement? p. 330

Involvement in abolitionism made women more aware that they, like slaves, lacked any legal individuality of their own and were assigned subordinate roles based on gender in their marriages and public life. Out of this awareness came a determination to launch a movement for women's rights and legal equality.

Timeline

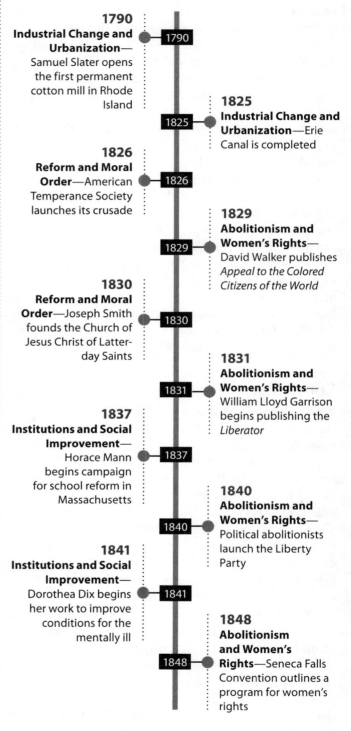

1790
Industrial Change and Urbanization—Samuel Slater opens the first permanent cotton mill in Rhode Island

1790

1825
Industrial Change and Urbanization—Erie Canal is completed

1825

1826
Reform and Moral Order—American Temperance Society launches its crusade

1826

1829
Abolitionism and Women's Rights—David Walker publishes *Appeal to the Colored Citizens of the World*

1829

1830
Reform and Moral Order—Joseph Smith founds the Church of Jesus Christ of Latter-day Saints

1830

1831
Abolitionism and Women's Rights—William Lloyd Garrison begins publishing the *Liberator*

1831

1837
Institutions and Social Improvement—Horace Mann begins campaign for school reform in Massachusetts

1837

1840
Abolitionism and Women's Rights—Political abolitionists launch the Liberty Party

1840

1841
Institutions and Social Improvement—Dorothea Dix begins her work to improve conditions for the mentally ill

1841

1848
Abolitionism and Women's Rights—Seneca Falls Convention outlines a program for women's rights

1848

13 The Way West
1815–1850

One American Journey

Journal Entry of an Artist on a Native American Critique of White Civilization

O**n an occasion when** I had interrogated a Sioux chief, on the upper Missouri, about their Government, their punishments and tortures of prisoners, for which I had freely condemned them for the cruelty of the practice, he took occasion, when I had got through, to ask *me* some questions relative to modes in the *civilized world,* which, with his comments upon them, were nearly as follows: and struck me, as I think they must every one, with great force.

He . . . told me he had often heard that white people hung their criminals by the neck, and choked them to death like dogs, and those their own people; to which I answered, "yes." He then told me he had learned that they shut each other up in prisons, where they keep them a great

LEARNING OBJECTIVES

13.1 ((·	13.2 ((·	13.3 ((·	13.4 ((·
How did economic and demographic pressures in the East spur migration to the West? p. 341	What strategies did the Sioux use to maintain their power on the Great Plains? p. 347	What forces contributed to the Americanization of Texas? p. 352	Why was James K. Polk so eager to provoke a war with Mexico? p. 359

((· Listen to Chapter 13 on MyHistoryLab

As depicted in this painting by George Catlin, Native Americans were still the dominant power on the Great Plains when this Comanche war party met up with a scouting expedition of the U.S. Army in the 1830s. Within a decade, a wave of white settlement challenged the power in a series of clashes for control of the Trans-Mississippi West.

Watch the Video Series on MyHistoryLab

Learn about some key topics related to this chapter with the *MyHistoryLab Video Series: Key Topics in U.S. History.*

1 **Manifest Destiny Marches West: 1832–1858** This video introduces the westward migration of the mid-nineteenth century as well as the ideals—and stark realities—behind it. The video includes a discussion of Manifest Destiny, which convinced Americans that the West was theirs to build, homestead, farm, mine, fence, and the like, as well as to exploit. The migrants who trekked from the East to the West remade the West in the process and faced challenges that often resulted in violence and tragedy.

 Watch on **MyHistoryLab**

The Oregon Trail Using the Oregon Trail as a primary example, this video describes the landward routes of migration during the nineteenth-century settlement of the American West. Whether traveling in wagon trains or individually, settlers typically experienced many ordeals, including resistance by Native Americans, harsh weather and terrain, and difficulties in finding sources of food and water. **2**

Watch on **MyHistoryLab**

3 **War with Mexico** Large-scale westward expansion was not possible until the United States had provoked its rival, Mexico, into going to war. This video reveals how the United States acquired Mexico's vast territorial claims that now comprise Texas, California, and the present-day American Southwest.

 Watch on **MyHistoryLab**

Treaty of Guadalupe Hidalgo This video discusses the peace treaty between the United States and Mexico that ended the Mexican-American War (1846–1848). In addition to providing the territory for many new states, the peace changed the culture of the region, with the arrival of ever-increasing numbers of Anglo settlers in formerly Mexican territories, and accelerated its development and exploitation. **4**

Watch on **MyHistoryLab**

part of their lives *because they can't pay money!* I replied in the affirmative to this, which occasioned great surprise and excessive laughter, even among the women. . . . He said . . . that he had been along the Frontier, and a good deal amongst the white people, and he had seen them whip their little children, a thing that is very cruel, he had heard also, from several white *medicine-men,* that the Great Spirit of the white people was the child of a white woman, and that he was at the last put to death by the white people! This seemed to be a thing that he had not been able to comprehend, and he concluded by saying, "the Indians' Great Spirit got no mother—the Indians no kill him, he never die." He put me a chapter of other questions as to the trespasses of the white people on their lands, their continual corruption of the morals of their women, and digging open the Indians' graves to get their bones, &c. To all of which I was compelled to reply in the affirmative, and quite glad to close my note-book, and quietly to escape from the throng that had collected around me, and saying (though to myself and silently), that these and an hundred other vices belong to the civilized world, and are practiced upon (but certainly, in no instance, reciprocated by) the "cruel and relentless savage."

George Catlin

Virgil J. Vogel, ed., *A Documentary History of the American Indian,* pp. 138–139. 1972 HarperCollins Publishers.

Personal Journeys Online

- Edward Harris, *Journal excerpt,* 1843. Account by a naturalist of the smallpox epidemic of 1837 on the Upper Missouri.
- Pierre Jean de Smet, S. J., *Letter from a Catholic priest,* 1841. Impressions of the character and intelligence of Indians in the Rocky Mountains.

George Catlin, one of the great illustrators of the American Indians, recorded these words in the 1830s when he traveled over the Trans-Mississippi West painting and sketching, in his words, "the looks and customs of the vanishing races of native man in America." Unlike most whites of his generation, he approached Indian cultures with respect, and he realized that native peoples had a valid critique of the culture and values of white America.

From his first contact with the tribes along the upper Missouri River in the early 1830s, Catlin sensed that he was witness to a way of life that was about to vanish. He worked at a feverish pace to create a pictorial record of what he saw in a collection of art he called "Catlin's Indian Gallery." The proceeds from exhibiting his work in Europe enabled him to live quite comfortably in the 1840s, but he suffered a severe setback in 1852 when a financial speculation went sour. A failure as an entrepreneur, he nonetheless succeeded brilliantly as an artist in depicting the Native American peoples of the Trans-Mississippi West just as they were about to be engulfed by a surging tide of white settlement.

Some 300,000 Americans traveled the **Oregon Trail** in the 1840s and 1850s in a trek that eventually made the United States a nation that spanned the continent. These overlanders, as they came to be known, were part of a restless tide of white migration that eventually saw more than 50,000 Americans a year migrate west of the Appalachians after the War of 1812. They were also part of a worldwide process fed by population growth on a global scale and improved, cheap forms of international travel. Migrants streamed into the frontier regions of the Southern Hemisphere as well as the North American West. As newcomers poured in, indigenous foraging and pastoral peoples were wiped out, displaced, herded onto reservations, or forced to fundamentally change their ways of life, the victims of disease and superior military force and technology.

The West became a meeting ground of people from diverse cultures as Anglo-Americans came into contact and conflict with the Indians of the Plains and the Mexicans of the Southwest. Convinced of the superiority of their political and cultural values, Anglo-Americans asserted a God-given right to spread across the continent and impose their notions of liberty and democracy on peoples whose land they coveted. In the process, they changed forever much in the Native American culture that Catlin had so respectfully painted.

Oregon Trail Overland trail of more than two thousand miles that carried American settlers from the Midwest to new settlements in Oregon, California, and Utah.

The Agricultural Frontier

13.1 How did economic and demographic pressures in the East spur migration to the West?

The U.S. population ballooned from 5.3 million in 1800 to more than 23 million by 1850. As the population expanded, it shifted westward. Fewer than one in ten Americans lived west of the Appalachians in 1800; by 1850, about half did (see Map 13.1).

The tremendous amount of land available for settlement accounted for both phenomena. Through purchase and conquest, the land area of the United States more than tripled in the first half of the nineteenth century. Here was space where Americans could raise the large families of a rural society in which, on average, six to eight children survived to adolescence.

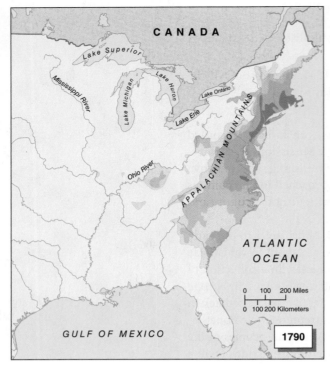

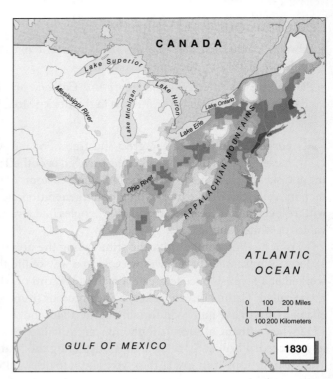

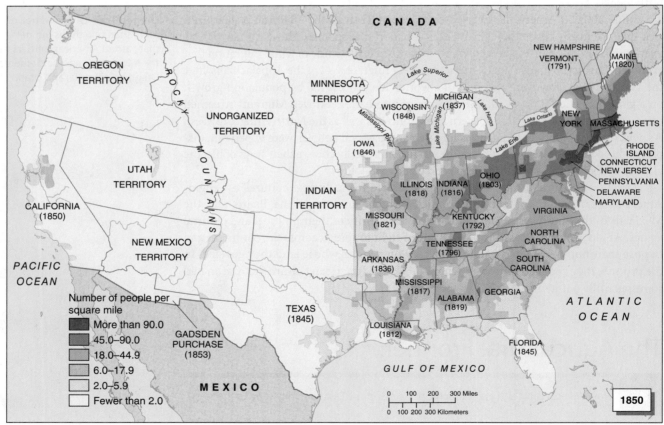

Number of people per square mile

More than 90.0
45.0–90.0
18.0–44.9
6.0–17.9
2.0–5.9
Fewer than 2.0

MAP 13.1 THE WESTWARD SHIFT OF THE U.S. POPULATION, 1790–1850 With a speed that was unimaginable in 1790, the United States quickly became a continental nation that stretched from the Atlantic to the Pacific by 1850. Particularly dramatic was the population growth in what became the Midwest.

Declining soil fertility and rising population pressure in the rural East propelled these migrations. A common desire for greater economic opportunity, however, resulted in two distinct western societies by the 1840s. North of the Ohio River, in the Old Northwest, free labor and family farms defined the social order. South of the Ohio was the Old Southwest, a society dominated by slave labor and the plantation.

The Crowded East

By the early nineteenth century, land was scarce in the East, especially in New England. After generations of population growth and subdivisions of landholdings to male heirs, most New England communities no longer had enough arable land to satisfy all the young men who wanted their own farms. Even such recently opened areas as Vermont felt the pressure of rural overpopulation.

Land was more productive and expensive farther south, in the mid-Atlantic states. Keyed to the major export crop of wheat, agriculture was more commercialized than in New England, and economic inequality was thus higher. Successful farmers became wealthy by specializing in wheat and hiring the rural poor to work their fields. One-third to one-half of the young men in the commercialized agricultural districts of New Jersey and Pennsylvania were landless by the end of the eighteenth century. These men and their families, many of whom were recently arrived Scots-Irish and German immigrants, led the western migration from Pennsylvania.

The pressure to move west was greatest in the slave states along the eastern seaboard. Although population density here was just two-thirds of that in New England, landholdings were more concentrated and the soil more exhausted than in the Northeast. Tenants who wanted their own land and small farmers tired of competing against slave labor were forced west across the mountains. They were joined by the sons of planters. Despite marriages arranged to keep land within the wealthy families, there was no longer enough good land left to carve out plantations for all the younger sons.

By the early 1800s, the young and the poor in the rural East had every incentive to head west, where fertile land was abundant, accessible, and, at $2 to $3 per acre, far cheaper than in the East. Land was the basis of wealth and social standing, and its ownership separated the independent from the dependent, the rooted from the rootless.

The western settler, observed a traveler on the Missouri frontier in the 1820s, wanted "to be a freeholder, to have plenty of rich land, and to be able to settle his children around him." Government policy under the Jeffersonian Republicans and Jacksonian Democrats attempted to promote these goals. Central to the land policy of the federal government after 1800 was the conviction that political liberties rested on the broadest possible base of land ownership. Thus, public policy and private aspirations merged in the belief that access to land was the key to preserving U.S. freedom.

When Jefferson took office in 1801, the minimum price for public land was $2 per acre, and a block of 320 acres had to be purchased at one time. By the 1830s, the price was down to $1.25 per acre, and the minimum purchase was only 80 acres. Congress also protected squatters, who had settled on public land before it was surveyed, from being outbid by speculators at land sales. The Preemption Act of 1841 guaranteed the right to purchase up to 160 acres at the minimum price of $1.25 when the public auction was held.

The Old Northwest

The number of Americans who settled in the heartland of the Old Northwest—Ohio, Indiana, and Illinois—rose tenfold from 1810 to 1840. The end of the War of 1812 and the abandonment by the British of their former Indian allies opened the region to a flood of migrants.

Travelers passing through the Ohio Valley just after the war were astonished by the number of Americans trekking west. Wagonloads of migrants bounced along turnpikes to disembark on the Ohio River at Pittsburgh and Wheeling, where they bought flatboats to carry them down to the interior river valleys. Moving north across the Ohio were families from the hill country of Virginia and Kentucky. These two streams of migrants, one predominantly northern and the other southern, met in the lower Midwest and viewed each other as strangers.

A Mosaic of Settlements. The Old Northwest was less a melting pot in which regional cultures merged than a mosaic of settlements in which the different values and folkways of regional cultures from throughout the East took root and expanded. Belts of migration generally ran along a line from east to west as settlers sought out soil types and ecological conditions similar to those they had left behind. Thus, the same North-South cultural differences that existed along the Atlantic seaboard in 1800 were to be found half a century later in the Mississippi Valley.

A transplanted Yankee culture from New England and upstate New York spread over the upper Midwest, northern Ohio, Indiana, and Illinois, as well as Michigan and Wisconsin. These westerners were Whiggish in their politics, tended to be anti-slavery, and valued a communal sense of responsibility that regulated moral behavior and promoted self-improvement. The highland southerners who settled the lower Midwest, southern Ohio, Indiana, and Illinois, as well as Kentucky, were Democrats: They fiercely distrusted any centralized authority, political or moral, and considered Yankees intolerant do-gooders. Holding the balance of cultural and political power were the migrants from Pennsylvania and New Jersey, who were accustomed to ethnic diversity and the politics of competing economic groups. They settled principally in central Ohio, Indiana, and Illinois. By emphasizing economic growth and downplaying the cultural politics that pitted Yankees against southerners, they built a consensus around community development.

It took about ten years of backbreaking labor to create an 80-acre farm in heavily wooded sections. The work of women was essential for the success of the farm and the production of any salable surplus. Wives and daughters helped to tend the field crops, milked cows, and churned butter, and they produced the homespun cloth that, along with their dairy goods, found a market in the first country stores on the frontier.

Because outside labor was scarce and expensive, communities pooled their efforts for such tasks as raising a cabin. Groups of settlers also acted as cooperative units at public land auctions. Local associations known as **claims clubs** enforced the extralegal right of squatters to enter noncompetitive bids on land they had settled and improved. Members of the clubs physically intimidated speculators and refused to step aside until local settlers had acquired the land they wanted. The high cost of hauling goods to outside markets kept the early frontier economy barely above self-sufficiency. Any surplus was sold to newcomers moving into the area or bartered with local storekeepers for such essentials as salt, sugar, and metalware. This initial economy, however, soon gave way to a more commercially oriented agriculture when steamboats, canals, and railroads opened up vast new markets (see Chapter 12).

The first large market was in the South, down the corridor of the Ohio and Mississippi rivers, and its major staples were corn and hogs. By the 1830s, the Erie Canal and its feeder waterways in the upper Midwest began to reorient much of the western farm trade to the Northeast. Wheat, because of its ready marketability for milling into flour, became the major cash crop for the northern market.

Although southern cotton was the raw material that fueled New England textile factories in the first stages of industrialization, the commercialization of agriculture in the West also contributed to the growth of eastern manufacturing. Western farms supplied eastern manufacturers with inexpensive raw materials for processing into finished goods. By flooding national markets with corn and wheat, western produce not only supplied eastern workers with cheap food but also forced noncompetitive eastern farmers either to move west or to work in factories in eastern cities. In turn, the West itself became an ever-growing market for eastern factory goods. For example, nearly half of the nation's iron production in the 1830s was fashioned into farm implements.

In the 1820s, the Old Northwest was just emerging from semisubsistence and depended on the southern trade. Thirty years later it had become part of a larger Midwest whose economy was increasingly integrated with that of the Northeast. Settlers continued to pour into the region, and three additional states, Michigan (1837), Iowa (1846), and Wisconsin (1848), joined the Union.

claims clubs Groups of local settlers on the nineteenth-century frontier who banded together to prevent the price of their land claims from being bid up by outsiders at public land auctions.

Cyrus McCormick pioneered the development of horse-drawn mechanical reapers, one of the labor-saving inventions that made possible far larger harvests of grain crops.

The combination of favorable farm prices and steadily decreasing transportation costs generated a rise in disposable income that was spent on outside goods or invested in internal economic development. A network of canals and railroads was laid down, and manufacturing cities grew from towns favorably situated by water or rail transport. There was still room for subsistence farming, but the West north of the Ohio was now economically specialized and socially diverse.

The Old Southwest

"The *Alabama Feaver* rages here with great violence and has carried off vast numbers of our Citizens," wrote a North Carolina planter in 1817 about the westward migration from his state. About as many people migrated from the old slave states in the East to the Old Southwest as those states gained by natural increase in the 1820s and 1830s. By 1850, more than 600,000 white settlers from Maryland, Virginia, and the Carolinas lived in slave states to the south and west, and many of them had brought their slaves with them. Indeed, from 1790 to 1860, more than 800,000 slaves were moved or sold from the South Atlantic region into the Old Southwest.

Soaring cotton prices after the War of 1812 and the smashing of Indian confederations during the war, which opened new lands to white settlement, propelled the first surge of migration into the Old Southwest (see Map 13.1 on page 342). Before cotton prices plunged in the Panic of 1819, planters flooded into western Tennessee and the Black Belt, a crescent-shaped band of rich, black loamy soil arcing westward from Georgia through central Alabama and Mississippi. Migration surged anew in the 1830s when cotton prices

TABLE 13.1 WESTWARD EXPANSION AND THE GROWTH OF THE UNION, 1815–1850

New Free States	New Slave States	Territories (1850)
Indiana, 1816	Mississippi, 1817	Minnesota
Illinois, 1818	Alabama, 1819	Oregon
Maine, 1820	Missouri, 1821	New Mexico
Michigan, 1837	Arkansas, 1836	Utah
Iowa, 1846	Florida, 1845	
Wisconsin, 1848	Texas, 1845	

were again high and the Chickasaws and Choctaws had been forced out of the incredibly fertile Delta country between the Yazoo and Mississippi rivers (see Chapter 10). The 1840s brought Texas fever to replace the Alabama fever of the 1810s, and a steady movement to the Southwest rounded out the contours of the cotton South. In less than thirty years, six new slave states—Mississippi (1817), Alabama (1819), Missouri (1821), Arkansas (1836), Florida (1845), and Texas (1845)—joined the Union (see Table 13.1, Westward Expansion and the Growth of the Union, 1815–1850).

The southwestern frontier attracted both slaveholding planters and small independent farmers. The planters, though a minority, had the capital or the credit to acquire the best lands and the slave labor to make those lands productive. The slaveholders were responding both to the need for fresh land and to the extraordinary demand for short-staple cotton. Led by the booming output of the new plantations in the Old Southwest, the South increased its share of world cotton production from 9 percent in 1800 to 68 percent in 1850.

The most typical settlers on the southern frontier were the small independent yeomen farmers who generally owned no slaves. Usually settling in the valleys, on the ridges, and in the hill country, they often soon sold out to neighboring planters and headed west again.

The yeomanry moved onto the frontier in two waves. The first consisted of stockmen-hunters, a restless, transient group that spread from the pine barrens in the Carolina backcountry to the coastal plain of eastern Texas. These pioneers prized unfettered independence and measured their wealth in the livestock left to roam and fatten on the sweet grasses of uncleared forests. They were quick to move on when farmers, the second wave, started to clear the land for crops.

The yeoman farmers practiced a diversified agriculture aimed at feeding their families. Corn and pork were the mainstays of their diet, and both could readily be produced as long as there was room for the open-range herding of swine and for patches of corn. The more ambitious farmers, usually those who owned one or two slaves, grew some cotton, but most preferred to avoid the economic risks of cotton production. The yeoman's chief source of labor was his immediate family, and to expand that labor force to produce cotton meant going into debt to purchase slaves. The debt could easily cost the yeoman his farm if the price of cotton fell.

Measured by per capita income, and as a direct result of the profits from slave-produced cotton on virgin soils, the Old Southwest was a wealthier society than the Old Northwest in 1850. In the short term, the settlement of the Old Southwest was also more significant for national economic development. Cotton accounted for more than half the value of all U.S. exports after the mid-1830s. More than any other commodity, cotton paid for U.S. imports and underpinned national credit. But southern prosperity was not accompanied by the same economic development and social change as in the Old Northwest. Compared to the slave West in 1860, the free-labor West was twice as urbanized, and far more of its workforce was engaged in nonagricultural pursuits.

The Southwest Ordinance, enacted by Congress in 1790, opened all territories south of the Ohio River to slavery. Slaves, land, and cotton were the keys to wealth on the southern frontier, and agricultural profits were continually plowed back into more land and slaves to produce more cotton. In contrast, prosperous farmers in the Old Northwest had no slaves to work additional acres. Hence, they were much more likely to invest their earnings in promotional schemes designed to attract settlers whose presence would raise land values and increase business for local merchants and entrepreneurs. As early as the 1840s, rural communities in the Old Northwest were supporting bustling towns that offered jobs in trade and manufacturing on a scale far surpassing anything in the slave West. By the 1850s, the Midwest was almost as urbanized as the Northeast had been in 1830, and nearly half its labor force no longer worked on farms.

The Old Southwest remained overwhelmingly agricultural. Once the land was settled, the children of the first generation of slaveholders and yeomen moved west to the next frontier rather than compete for the good land that was left. Relatively few newcomers took their place. By the 1850s, Kentucky, Tennessee, Alabama, and Mississippi, the core states of the Old Southwest, were all losing more migrants than they were gaining.

The Frontier of the Plains Indians

13.2 What strategies did the Sioux use to maintain their power on the Great Plains?

Few white Americans had ventured west of the Mississippi by 1840. Americans had no legal claim to much of the Trans-Mississippi West, or merely the paper title of the Louisiana Purchase, to which none of the native inhabitants had acquiesced. Beyond Texas and the boundary line drawn by the Trans-Continental Treaty of 1819 lay the northern possessions of Mexico. Horse-mounted Indian tribes dominated by the Sioux were a formidable power throughout the central Plains.

Before the 1840s, only fur trappers and traders, who worked with and not against the powerful Sioux, had pushed across the Great Plains and into the Rockies. The 1840s brought a sudden change, a large migration westward that radically altered the ecology of the Great Plains. Farm families trapped in an agricultural depression and enticed by Oregon's bounty turned the trails blazed by the fur traders into ruts on the Oregon Trail, the route that led to the first large settlement of Americans on the Pacific Coast.

Tribal Lands

At least 350,000 Native Americans lived in the plains and mountains of the Trans-Mississippi West in 1840. They were loosely organized into tribal groups, each with its own territory and way of life. Most inhabited the Great Plains region, which lay north and west of the Indian Territory reserved for eastern tribes in the present state of Oklahoma. The point where the prairies of the Midwest gave way to the higher, drier plains marked a rough division between predominantly agricultural tribes to the east and nomadic, hunting tribes to the west.

In the 1830s, the U.S. government set aside a broad stretch of country between the Platte River to the north and the Red River to the south (most of what is now Oklahoma and eastern Kansas) exclusively for tribes resettled from the East under the Indian Removal Act of 1830 and for village-living groups native to the area. Many government officials envisioned this territory as a permanent sanctuary that would separate Indians from white people and allow them to live in peace on allotments of land granted as compensation for the territory they had ceded to the federal government. However, even as Congress was debating the idea of a permanent Indian reserve, the pressure on native peoples in the Mississippi Valley both from raiding parties of Plains Indians and the incessant demands of white farmers and speculators for land was rendering a stable Indian-white boundary meaningless.

On the eve of Indian removal in the East, the Sauks, Foxes, Potawatomis, and other Indian peoples inhabited Iowa. The defeat of the Sauks and Foxes in what white Americans called Black Hawk's War in 1832 opened Iowa to white settlement and forced tribes to cede land (see Chapter 10). In 1838, Congress created the Territory of Iowa, which encompassed all the land between the Mississippi and Missouri rivers north of the state of Missouri. The remaining Indians were now on the verge of being pushed completely out of the region. Throughout the upper Mississippi Valley in the 1830s, other groups suffered a similar fate, and the number of displaced Indians swelled.

The first to be displaced were farming peoples whose villages straddled the woodlands to the east and the open plains to the west. These border tribes were caught in a vise between the loss of their land to advancing white people and the seizure of their horses and agricultural provisions by Indian raiders from the plains. The Pawnees were among the hardest hit.

By the 1830s, the Pawnees were primarily an agricultural people who embarked on seasonal hunts for game in the Platte River Valley. In 1833, they signed a treaty with the U.S. government in which they agreed to withdraw north of the Platte in

Shown here are Lakota shirts that were specially woven for Sioux warriors who had distinguished themselves in battle.

return for subsidies and military protection from the hostile Indians on the plains. Once the Pawnees moved north of the Platte, Sioux attacked them and seized control of the prime hunting grounds. Sioux raiders seeking provisions and horses also harassed Pawnee agricultural villages. When the Pawnees in desperation filtered back south of the Platte, in violation of the treaty of 1833, they encountered constant harassment from white settlers. In vain the Pawnee leaders cited the provisions of the treaty that promised them protection from the Sioux. Forced back north of the Platte by the U.S. government, the Pawnees were eventually driven out of their homeland by the Sioux.

The Sioux were the dominant power on the northern and central Great Plains, more than able to hold their own against white Americans in the first half of the nineteenth century. In the eighteenth century, these western Sioux had separated from their woodland kin (known as the Santee Sioux), left their homeland along the headwaters of the Mississippi River, and pushed onto the Minnesota prairies. Armed with guns they had acquired from the French, the western Sioux dominated the prairies east of the Missouri River by 1800.

The Sioux learned to use the horse from the Plains Indians. Introduced to the New World by the Spanish, horses had revolutionized the lives of native peoples on the Great Plains. As they acquired more horses through trading and raids, the Plains Indians evolved a distinctly new nomadic culture. The Sioux were the most successful of all the tribes in melding two facets of white culture, the gun and the horse, into an Indian culture of warrior-hunters.

When the United States acquired title to the Great Plains in the Louisiana Purchase of 1803, the western Sioux economy was based on two seasonally restricted systems of hunting. In summer, the Sioux hunted buffalo on horseback on the plains. In winter, on foot, they trapped beaver. In great spring trading fairs, the western Sioux exchanged their buffalo robes and beaver pelts for goods acquired by the Santee Sioux from European traders.

This painting by George Catlin captures the excitement of a buffalo hunt on the mixed-grass prairie.

As the supply of beaver dwindled and the demand for buffalo hides from American and European traders increased in the early 1800s, the Sioux extended their buffalo hunts. In a loose alliance with the Cheyennes and Arapahos, Sioux war parties pushed aside or subjugated weaker tribes to the south and west of the Missouri River basin. Reduced to a dependent status, these tribes were forced to rely on the Sioux for meat and trading goods.

Epidemic diseases brought to the plains by white traders helped Sioux expansion. Because they lived in small wandering bands, the Sioux were less susceptible to these epidemics than the more sedentary village peoples. The Sioux were also one of the first tribes to be vaccinated against smallpox by doctors sent up the Missouri River by the Bureau of Indian Affairs in the early 1830s. Smallpox reached the plains in the 1780s, and a major epidemic in 1837 probably halved the region's Indian population. Particularly hard hit were tribes attempting to resist the Sioux advance. Sioux losses were relatively light and, unlike the other tribes, their population grew.

By 1850, the Sioux had increased in power and numbers since they first encountered American officials during the Lewis and Clark Expedition in 1804 and 1805. Americans could vilify the Sioux, but they could not force them into dependence in the first half of the nineteenth century. The Sioux continued to extend their influence, and they were shrewd enough to align themselves with the Americans whenever their interests dictated conciliation.

The Fur Traders

The western fur trade originated in the rivalry between British and U.S. companies for profitable furs, especially beaver pelts. Until the early 1820s, the Hudson's Bay Company, a well-capitalized British concern, dominated the trans-Mississippi fur trade. A breakthrough for U.S. interests came in 1824 when two St. Louis businessmen, William Henry Ashley and Andrew Henry of the Rocky Mountain Fur Company, developed the rendezvous system, which eliminated the need for permanent and costly posts deep in Indian territory. In keeping with Indian traditions of periodic intertribal meetings, the rendezvous system brought together trappers, Indians, and traders in a grand annual fair at a designated site in the high mountain country of Wyoming. White trappers and Indians exchanged the animal skins they had gathered in the seasonal hunt for guns, traps, tobacco, whiskey, textiles, and other trading goods with agents of the fur companies in St. Louis.

Living conditions in the wilderness were primitive, even brutal. Mortality rates among trappers ran as high as 80 percent a year. Death could result from an accidental gunshot wound, an encounter with a grizzly, or an arrow from an Indian whose hunting grounds a trapper had transgressed.

For all its dangers, the life of a trapper appealed to unattached young men. They were fleeing the confinements, as well as the comforts, of white civilization and were as free as they could be. When on a hunt with the Indians, they were part of a spectacle unknown to other white Americans, one that was already passing into history.

Such spectacles were increasingly rare after 1840, the year of the last mountain men's rendezvous on the Green River in Wyoming. The most exploitative phase of the fur trade in the 1830s had ravaged the fur-bearing animals and accelerated the spread of smallpox among the tribes. Whiskey, the most profitable item among the white man's trading goods, had corrupted countless Indians and undermined the vitality of tribal cultures.

The mountain men were about to pass into legend, but before they did, they explored every trail and path from the front (or eastern) range of the Rockies to the Pacific. The main trading corridor of the fur trade—up the lower Missouri to the North Platte and across the plains to the South Pass, a wide plateau crossing the Continental

Divide, and into the Wyoming basin—became the main overland route to the West in the 1840s. The mountain men had removed the mystery of western geography, and in so doing they hastened the end of the frontier conditions that had made their unique way of life possible.

The Oregon Trail

Before the 1830s, few Americans had heard of Oregon, and practically none lived there. Under an agreement reached in 1818, the Oregon Country was still jointly administered by the United States and Great Britain. Furs, whether beaver pelts or the skins of the Pacific sea otter, had attracted a few U.S. trappers and merchants, but the British-controlled Hudson's Bay Company dominated the region. Protestant missionaries established the first permanent white settlements in the 1830s. Reports of Oregon's fertility that the missionaries sent east sparked the first popular interest in the region, especially among midwestern farmers stuck in the agricultural depression that followed the Panic of 1837 (see Figure 13.1).

The first large party of overlanders on the Oregon Trail left Independence, Missouri, for the Willamette Valley in 1842. Independence and St. Joseph in Missouri and, by the 1850s, Council Bluffs in Iowa were the jumping-off points for the Oregon Trail. Most overlanders were young farm families from the Midwest, who had moved at least once before in their restless search for the perfect farm that would keep them out of debt. The journey was long and dangerous. In the 1840s, some 5,000 of the 90,000 men, women, and children who set out on the Oregon Trail died along the way.

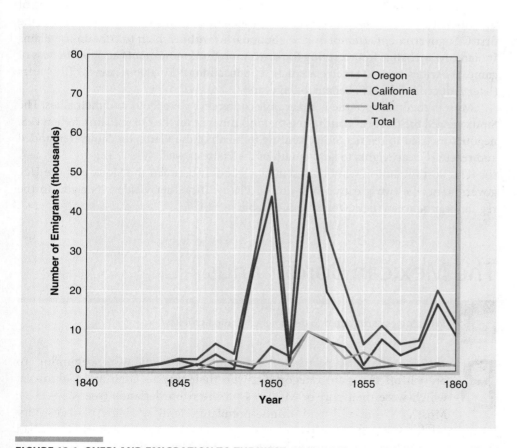

FIGURE 13.1 OVERLAND EMIGRATION TO THE WEST, 1840–1860 Immigration to the Trans-Mississippi West steadily increased in the 1840s as farm families moved to Oregon or Utah. After the discovery of gold in California in 1849, California attracted the bulk of the emigrants, many of whom were single men hopeful of striking it rich.

SOURCE: Based on Unruh, John D. (1993). *The Plains Across: The Overland Emigrants and the Trans-Mississippi West, 1840–60*. University of Illinois Press. Pages 119–120.

Although the overlanders were terrified of encountering Indians, who they assumed would be hostile, few died from Indian attacks. As long as the wagon trains were just passing through, the Plains Indians left the white people alone. At first they watched with bemused curiosity, and then, as the white migrants kept coming, they traded game for clothing and ammunition. Indians killed only 115 migrants in the 1840s, and trigger-happy white migrants provoked most of the clashes. Disease, especially cholera, was the great killer. Second to disease were accidents, especially drownings that resulted when drivers tried to force overloaded wagons across swollen rivers.

Cooperation between families was the key to a successful overland crossing. The men in a party often drew up a formal, written constitution at the start of a trip spelling out the assignments and work responsibilities of each wagon. Before the trail was well marked, former mountain men hired on as captains to lead wagon trains. Timing was crucial. A wagon train had to leave late enough in the spring to get good grass in Nebraska for the oxen and mules. Too early a departure, and the wagon train risked getting bogged down in spring mud; too late, and it risked being trapped in the snows of the Pacific coastal ranges.

Before "Oregon fever" had run its course, the flow of white settlers across the continent radically changed the economy and ecology of the Great Plains. Pressure mounted on plants and animals, reducing the land's ability to support all the tribes accustomed to living off it. Intertribal warfare intensified as the supply of buffalo and other game dwindled. Far from being separated from white people by a permanent line of division, the Plains Indians now stood astride the main path of white migration to the Pacific.

In response, officials in the Bureau of Indian Affairs organized a great gathering of the tribes in 1851. At this conference, they pushed through the Fort Laramie Treaty, the first U.S. government attempt to draw boundaries within which to contain the Plains Indians. In exchange for accepting limitations on their movements and for the loss of game, the tribes were to receive annual compensation of $50,000 a year for fifty years (later reduced by the U.S. Senate to ten years).

Most of the Indians at the Fort Laramie conference were Sioux and their allies. The Sioux viewed the treaty as confirming their dominance on the Great Plains. When U.S. negotiators tried to restrict Sioux hunting to north of the Platte, the Sioux demanded and received treaty rights to lands south of the Platte as well.

The Fort Laramie Treaty represented a standoff between the Sioux and the U.S. government, the two great powers on the Plains. If neither yielded its claim to the region, war between them would be inevitable.

The Mexican Borderlands

13.3   What forces contributed to the Americanization of Texas?

By the mid-1840s, parties of emigrant Americans were beginning to branch off the main Oregon Trail on their way to Utah and California, which were then part of Mexico's northern borderlands (see Map 13.2). Mostly a semiarid and thinly populated land of high plateaus, dry basins, and desert bisected north to south by mountain ranges, the borderlands had been part of the Spanish empire in North America. Mexico inherited this territory when it won independence from Spain in 1821. Mexico's hold on the region was always weak. It lost Texas in 1837, and, in the next decade, the U.S. penetration of Utah and California set the stage for the U.S. seizure of most of the rest in the Mexican War.

📖 Read the Document Elizabeth Dixon Smith Geer, Journal (1847, 1848)

MAP 13.2 WESTERN OVERLAND TRAILS The great overland trails to the West began at the Missouri River. The Oregon Trail crossed South Pass in Wyoming and then branched off to Oregon, California, or Utah. The Santa Fe Trail carried American goods and traders to the Mexican Southwest.

The Peoples of the Southwest

Diverse peoples lived in the Southwest. Imperial Spain had divided them into four main groupings: Indians, full-blooded Native Americans who retained their own languages and customs; *mestizos,* people of racially mixed ancestry, usually Spanish and Indian; *criollos,* U.S.-born whites of Spanish ancestry; and Spaniards. By far the smallest group was the Spaniards. Compared to the English, few Spaniards emigrated to the New World, and most who did were men. Consequently, Spanish males married or lived with native women, creating a large class of *mestizos.* Despite their small numbers, the Spanish, along with the *criollos,* monopolized economic and political power. This wealthy elite controlled the labor of the *mestizos* in the predominantly ranching economy of the borderlands.

The largest single group in the borderlands were the Indians, about half the population in the 1820s. Most had not come under direct Spanish or Mexican control. Those who had were part of the mission system. This instrument of Spanish imperial policy

353

forced Indians to live in a fixed area, convert to Catholicism, and work as agricultural laborers.

Spanish missions, most of them established by the Franciscan order, aimed both to Christianize and "civilize" the Indians, making them loyal imperial subjects. Mission Indians were forced to abandon their native economies and culture and settle in agricultural communities under the tight supervision of the friars (see Chapter 3). Spanish soldiers and royal officials, who lived in military garrisons known as *presidios,* accompanied the friars.

The largest concentration of Indians, some 300,000 when the Spanish friars arrived in the 1760s, was in California. Most of these, the Paiutes, Chumashes, Pomos, Shastas, and a host of smaller tribes, occupied their own distinct ecological zones where they gathered and processed what the rivers, forests, and grasslands provided. Fish and game were abundant, and wild plants and nuts, especially acorns, provided grain and flour.

The major farming Indians east of California were the Pueblo peoples of Arizona and New Mexico. Named after the adobe or stone communal dwellings in which they lived atop mesas or on terraces carved into cliffs, the Pueblo Indians were a peaceful people closely bound to small, tightly knit communities. (*Pueblo* is Spanish for "village.") Indeed, some of their dwellings, such as those of the Hopis in Arizona or the Acomas in New Mexico, have been continuously occupied for more than 500 years. Corn and beans were the staples of their irrigation-based agriculture. Formally a part of the Spanish mission system, they had incorporated the Catholic God and Catholic rituals into their own polytheistic religion, which stressed the harmony of all living things with the forces of nature. They continued to worship in their underground sanctuaries known as *kivas.*

Once the Pueblos made their peace with the Spaniards after their great revolt in 1680 (see Chapter 3), their major enemies were the nomadic tribes that lived by hunting and raiding. These tribes outnumbered the Pueblos four to one and controlled most of the Southwest until the 1850s. The horse, which many of the tribes acquired during Spain's temporary retreat from the region during the late seventeenth century in the wake of the Pueblo Revolt, was the basis of their way of life. As the horse frontier spread, the peoples of the southern Plains gained enormous mobility and the means of ranging far and wide for the economic resources that sustained their transformation into societies of mounted warriors.

West of the pueblos around Taos was the land of the Navajos, who herded sheep, raised some crops, and raided other tribes from their mountain fastnesses. Spilling over onto Navajo lands, the Southern Utes ranged up and down the canyon lands of Utah. The Gila Apaches were the dominant tribe south of Albuquerque and westward into Arizona. To the east in the Pecos River Valley roamed bands of Mescalero and Jicarillo Apaches. On the broad plains rolling northward from the Texas panhandle and southward into northern Mexico were war parties of Comanches and Kiowas.

The Comanches, a branch of the mountain Shoshonis who moved to the plains when horses became available, were the most feared of the nomadic peoples. Utterly fearless, confident, and masterful horsemen, they gained a reputation of mythic proportions for their prowess as mounted warriors. For food and clothing, they relied on the immense buffalo herds of the southern plains. For guns, horses, and other trading goods, they lived off their predatory raids. When the **Santa Fe Trail** opened in the early 1820s, their shrewdness as traders gave them a new source of firearms that strengthened their raiding prowess.

The three focal points of white settlement in the northern borderlands of Mexico, Texas, New Mexico, and Alta California (as distinguished from Lower, or Baja, California) were never linked by an effective network of communications or transportation. Each of these settlements was an isolated offshoot of Hispanic culture with a semiautonomous

Santa Fe Trail The 900-mile trail opened by American merchants for trading purposes following Mexico's liberalization of the formerly restrictive trading policies of Spain.

economy based on ranching and a mostly illegal trade with French, British, and U.S. merchants that brought in a trickle of needed goods.

Neither Spain, which tried to seal off its northern outposts from economic contact with foreigners, nor Mexico, which opened up the borderlands to outsiders, had integrated this vast region into a unified economic or political whole. Indeed, Mexico's most pressing problem in the 1820s was protecting its northern states from the Comanches. To serve as a buffer against the Comanches, the Mexican government in 1821 invited Americans into Texas, opening the way to the eventual U.S. takeover of the territory.

The Americanization of Texas

The Mexicans faced the same problems governing Texas that the Spanish had. Mexico City was about a thousand miles from San Antonio, the center of Hispanic settlement in Texas, and communications were slow and cumbersome. The ranching elite of *Tejanos* (Spanish-speaking Mexicans born in Texas) had closer economic ties to American Louisiana than they did to Coahuila, the Mexican state to which Texas was formally attached. The low agricultural productivity, combined with the low birthrate among mission Indians, outbreaks of disease, and the generally hostile frontier environment, sharply restricted population growth. Only some 5,000 Mexicans lived in Texas in the 1820s.

Tejanos A person of Spanish or Mexican descent born in Texas.

Sparsely populated and economically struggling, Mexican Texas shared a border with the United States along the Sabine River in Louisiana and the Red River in the Arkansas Territory (see Map 13.2). The threat that the nearby Americans posed to Mexico's security was obvious to Mexican officials. However, attempts to promote Mexican immigration into Texas failed. Reasoning that the Americans were going to come in any event and anxious to build up the population of Texas against Indian attacks, the Mexican government encouraged Americans to settle in Texas by offering huge grants of land in return for promises to accept Mexican citizenship, convert to Catholicism, and obey the authorities in Mexico City.

The first American *empresario,* the recipient of a large grant in return for a promise to bring in settlers, was Stephen F. Austin. After having the grant confirmed by the new Mexican government in 1821, Stephen Austin founded the first American colony in Texas. The Austin grant encompassed 18,000 square miles. Other grants were smaller but still lavish. The *empresarios* stood to grow wealthy by leasing out land, selling parcels to settlers, and organizing the rest into large-scale farms that produced cotton with slave labor in the bottomlands of the Sabine, Colorado, and Brazos rivers. As early as 1830, eastern and south-central Texas was becoming an extension of the plantation economy of the Gulf coastal plain. More than 25,000 white settlers, with around 1,000 slaves, had poured into the region.

empresario Agents who received a land grant from the Spanish or Mexican government in return for organizing settlements.

More Americans moved into Texas with slaves than the Mexicans had anticipated. Many settlers simply ignored Mexican laws, especially the Emancipation Proclamation of 1829, which forbade slavery in the Republic of Mexico. In 1830, the Mexican government attempted to assert its authority. It levied the first taxes on the Americans, prohibited the further importation of slaves, and closed the international border to additional immigration. Still, another 10,000 Americans spilled across the border in the early 1830s, and they continued to bring in slaves.

Unlike the *empresarios,* many of whom became Catholic and married into elite *Tejano* families, these newcomers lived apart from Mexicans and rejected Mexican citizenship. Cultural tensions escalated. Believing that they belonged to a superior race of liberty-loving white Anglo-Saxons, most of these new arrivals sneered at the Mexicans as a mongrelized race of black people, Indians, and Spaniards and resented having to submit to their rule. They considered Catholicism a despotic, superstitious religion and ignored legal requirements that they convert to it. A clash became inevitable in

Alamo Franciscan mission at San Antonio, Texas, that was the site in 1836 of a siege and massacre of Texans by Mexican troops.

1835 when General Santa Anna, elected president of Mexico in 1833, overturned the liberal Mexican constitution of 1824. He established himself as a dictator in 1834, and his centralist rule ended any hope of the American *empresarios* and their *Tejano* allies that Texas might become an autonomous state within a federated Mexico. Skirmishing between Mexican troops and rebellious Texans began in the fall of 1835.

At first, the Anglo-*Tejano* leadership sought to overthrow Santa Anna, restore the constitution of 1824, and win separate statehood for Texas within a liberal Mexican republic. Santa Anna, however, refused to compromise. When he raised a large army to crush the uprising, he radicalized the rebellion and pushed its leaders to declare complete independence on March 2, 1836. Four days later, a Mexican army of 4,000 annihilated the 187 defenders of the **Alamo**, an abandoned mission in San Antonio. A few weeks later at Goliad, another 300 Texans were killed after they had agreed to surrender (see Map 13.3).

"Remember the Alamo!" and "Remember Goliad!" were powerful rallying cries for the beleaguered Texans. Volunteers from the U.S. South rushed to the aid of the main Texan army, commanded by Sam Houston. Houston's victory in April 1836 at the Battle of San Jacinto established the independence of Texas. Captured while trying to flee, Santa Anna signed a treaty in May 1836, recognizing Texas as an independent republic with a boundary on the south and west at the Rio Grande. However, the Nueces River to the north of the Rio Grande had been the administrative border of Texas under Mexican rule. The Mexican Congress rejected the treaty, and the boundary remained in dispute.

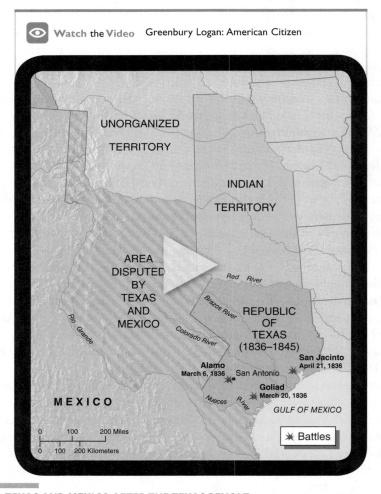

MAP 13.3 TEXAS AND MEXICO AFTER THE TEXAS REVOLT The Battle of San Jacinto was the decisive American victory that gained the independence of Texas, but the border dispute between Texas and Mexico would not be resolved until the Mexican War a decade later.

Soon forgotten during the ensuing eight years of Texas independence was the support that many *Tejanos* had given to the successful revolt against Mexican rule. In part because Mexico refused to recognize the Texas Republic, Anglos feared *Tejanos* as a subversive element. Pressure mounted on them to leave, especially after Santa Anna launched a major counterattack in 1842, capturing San Antonio. Those who stayed lost much of their land and economic power as Anglos used their knowledge of U.S. law or just plain chicanery to reduce the *Tejanos* to second-class citizens.

More difficult to subordinate were the Comanches. While he was president of Texas, Houston tried to fix a permanent boundary between the Comanches and white settlers, but Texas pride and ongoing white encroachments on Indian land undercut his efforts. By the early 1840s, Texans and Comanches were in a state of nearly permanent war. Only the force of the federal army after the Civil War ended the Comanches' long reign over the high, dry plains of northern and western Texas.

The Push into California and the Southwest

California. Mexican rule in California was always weak. The Sonoran desert and the resistance of the Yuman Indians in southeastern California cut off Mexico from any direct land contact with Alta California. Only irregular communications were maintained over a long sea route. For **Californios**, Californians of Spanish descent, Mexico was literally *la otra banda*, "the other shore." In trying to strengthen its hold on this remote and thinly populated region, the Mexican government relied on a program of economic development. As in Texas, however, Mexican policy had unintended consequences.

Californios Persons of Spanish descent living in California.

The centerpiece of the Mexican program was the secularization of the missions, opening up the landholdings of the Catholic Church to private ownership and releasing the mission Indians from paternalistic bondage. Small allotments of land were set aside for the Indians, but most returned to their homelands. Those who remained became a source of cheap labor for the *rancheros* who carved up the mission lands into huge cattle ranches. Thus, by the 1830s, California had entered what is called the *rancho* era. The main beneficiaries of this process, however, were not the Mexican authorities who had initiated it but the American traders who responded to the economic opportunities presented by the privatization of the California economy.

New England merchants had been trading in California since the 1780s. What first attracted them were the seal fisheries off the California coast, a source of otter pelts highly prized in the China trade. After the seals had been all but exterminated by the 1820s, Yankee merchants shipped out hides and tallow to New England for processing into shoes and candles. Ships from New England and New York sailed around Cape Horn to California ports, where they unloaded trading goods. Servicing this trade in California was a resident colony of American agents, some 300 strong by the mid-1840s.

Whereas Yankees dominated the American colonies in coastal California, it was mostly midwestern farm families who filtered into the inner valleys of California from the Oregon Trail in the 1830s and 1840s. Nearly a thousand Americans had arrived by 1846.

California belonged to Mexico in name only by the early 1840s. The program of economic development had strengthened California's ties to the outside world at the expense of Mexico. American merchants and California *rancheros* ran the economy, and both groups had joined separatist movements against Mexican rule. Unlike the *Californios,* who were ambivalent about their future political allegiance, the Americans wanted to be part of the United States and assumed that California would shortly be annexed. With the outbreak of the Mexican War in 1846, their wish became reality.

New Mexico. Except for Utah, the American push into the interior of the Mexican Southwest followed the California pattern of trade preceding settlement. When

Mexico liberalized the formerly restrictive trading policies of Spain, American merchants opened up the 900-mile-long Santa Fe Trail from Independence, Missouri, to Santa Fe, New Mexico. Starved for mercantile goods, the New Mexicans were a small but highly profitable market. They paid for their American imports with gold, silver, and furs.

Bent's Old Fort, an impregnable adobe structure built on the Arkansas River at the point where the Santa Fe Trail turned to the southwest, was the fulcrum for the growing economic influence of Americans over New Mexican affairs. Completed in 1832, the fort enabled the Bent brothers from Missouri to control a flourishing and almost monopolistic trade with Indians, trappers, caravans on the Santa Fe Trail, and the large landowners and merchants of New Mexico. This trade pulled New Mexico into the cultural and economic orbit of the United States and undermined what little sovereign power Mexico held in the region.

Although only a few hundred Americans were permanent residents of New Mexico in the 1840s, they had married into the Spanish-speaking landholding elite and were themselves beginning to receive large grants of land. Ties of blood and common economic interests linked this small group of American businessmen with the local elite. American merchants and New Mexican landlords were further united by their growing disdain for the instability of Mexican rule, Santa Anna's dictatorship, and sporadic attempts by Mexico to levy heavy taxes on the Santa Fe trade. Another bond was their concern over the aggressive efforts of the Texans to seize eastern New Mexico. After thwarting an 1841 Texan attempt to occupy Santa Fe, the leaders of New Mexico increasingly looked to the United States to protect their local autonomy. They quickly decided to cooperate with the U.S. army of invasion when the Mexican War got under way.

Utah.   At the extreme northern and inner reaches of the Mexican borderlands lay Utah. Dominated by an intermountain depression called the Great Basin, Utah was a starkly beautiful but dry region of alkaline flats, broken tablelands, cottonwood canyons, and mountain ranges. Here, and along the flat expanse of the Colorado Plateau to the southeast, lived the Bannocks, Utes, Navajos, Hopis, and small bands of other Indians. Aside from trade with the Utes, Spain and Mexico had largely ignored this remote region. Its isolation and lack of white settlers, however, were precisely what made Utah so appealing to the Mormons, the Church of Jesus Christ of Latter-day Saints. For the Mormons in the 1840s, Utah became the promised land in which to build a new Zion.

Founded by Joseph Smith in upstate New York in the 1820s, Mormonism grew rapidly within a communitarian framework that stressed hard work and economic cooperation under the leadership of patriarchal leaders (see Chapter 12). The economic success of close-knit Mormon communities, combined with the righteous zeal of their members, aroused the fears and hostility of non-Mormons. Harassed out of New York, Ohio, and Missouri, the Mormons thought they had found a permanent home by the late 1830s in Nauvoo, Illinois. But the murder of Joseph Smith and his brother by a mob in 1844 convinced the beleaguered Mormons that they had to leave the settled East for a refuge in the West. In 1846, a group of Mormons migrated to the Great Basin in Utah. Under the leadership of Brigham Young, they established a new community in 1847 at the Great Salt Lake on the western slopes of the Wasatch Mountains. An annual influx of about 2,000 converts enabled the initial settlement to grow rapidly.

The Mormons succeeded by concentrating their farms along the fertile and relatively well-watered Wasatch Front. They dispensed land and organized an irrigation system that coordinated water rights with the amount of land under production. To their dismay, however, they learned in 1848 that they had not left the United States after all. The Union acquired Utah, along with the rest of the northern borderlands of Mexico, as a result of the Mexican War.

Dominating Nauvoo, Illinois, by the early 1840s was this large temple built by the Mormons.

Politics, Expansion, and War

13.4 Why was James K. Polk so eager to provoke a war with Mexico?

The Democrats viewed their victory in the election of 1844 (see Chapter 10) as a popular mandate for expansion. James K. Polk, the new Democratic president, fully shared this expansionist vision. The greatest prize in his eyes was California. When he was stymied in his efforts to purchase California and New Mexico, he tried to force concessions from the Mexican government by ordering American troops to the mouth of the Rio Grande, far within the territory claimed by Mexico. When the virtually inevitable clash of arms occurred in late April 1846, war broke out between the United States and Mexico.

Victory resulted in the **Mexican Cession of 1848**, which added a half million square miles to the United States. Polk's administration also finalized the acquisition of Texas and reached a compromise with the British on the Oregon Territory that recognized U.S. sovereignty in the Pacific Northwest up to the 49th parallel. The United States was now a nation that spanned a continent.

Mexican Cession of 1848 The addition of half a million square miles to the United States as a result of victory in the 1846 war between the United States and Mexico.

Manifest Destiny

With a phrase that soon entered the nation's vocabulary, John L. O'Sullivan, editor and Democratic politician, proclaimed in 1845 America's "manifest destiny to overspread and to possess the whole of the continent which Providence has given us for

From Then to Now

Manifest Destiny and American Foreign Policy

From the birth of the nation in 1776 to the U.S. war on terrorism in the wake of the attacks on September 11, 2001, a sense of mission has often imbued U.S. foreign policy. Manifest Destiny was one expression of that sense of mission. According to its lofty rhetoric, the United States would fulfill its divinely ordained mission by absorbing all the peoples of North America, at least those deemed capable of self-government, into the republic. Manifest Destiny helped inspire the United States surge to the Pacific and justify the Mexican War. But the war also provoked a contrary fear: Was the United States guilty of an imperial conquest that threatened the liberty of others rather than promoting it?

Expansionists in the late nineteenth century invoked Manifest Destiny to justify U.S. acquisition of an overseas empire following the Spanish-American War, but the new empire did not really fit the model. The advocates of Manifest Destiny had envisioned neighboring peoples in North America voluntarily joining the republic, not being forced into it as dependent possessions. Critics of that war insisted that America's true mission must be to serve as the "model republic" for others to follow.

This is the theme that characterized at least the public face of U.S. diplomacy in the twentieth century. President Woodrow Wilson justified U.S. intervention in World War I as a moral duty to save democracy in Europe, and Wilsonian idealism infused the foreign policy of President Franklin D. Roosevelt during World War II. Throughout the Cold War, the United States identified itself as the protector of democratic freedoms from the threat of international communism. In the post–Cold War world, Presidents George H. W. Bush and Bill Clinton cited the need to uphold human rights as grounds for U.S. military intervention abroad. President George W. Bush went further by claiming that the United States has the right to use preemptive force against any "evil power" deemed a threat to world peace and the future security of the United States.

Question for Discussion

- What do you believe explains the long-held view of many Americans that the United States has been entrusted with a unique mission to redeem the rest of the world?

U.S. troops faced far more hazardous conditions in Iraq than had been predicted.

In this late-1872 evocation of the spirit of Manifest Destiny, Indians retreat westward as white settlers, guided by a diaphanously clad America, spread the benefits of American civilization.

Manifest Destiny Doctrine, first expressed in 1845, that the expansion of white Americans across the continent was inevitable and ordained by God.

the development of the great experiment of Liberty and federated self-government entrusted to us." Central to **Manifest Destiny** was the assumption that white Americans were a special people, a view that dated back to the Puritans' belief that God had appointed them to establish a New Israel cleansed of the corruption of the Old World.

What distinguished the special U.S. mission as enunciated by Manifest Destiny was its explicitly racial component. Between 1815 and 1850, the term "Anglo-Saxon," originally loosely applied to English-speaking peoples, acquired racial overtones. Caucasian Anglo-Saxon Americans, as the descendants of ancient Germanic tribes that had purportedly brought the seeds of free institutions to England, were now said to be the foremost race in the world. The superior racial pedigree they claimed for themselves gave white Americans the natural right to expand westward, a chosen people carrying the blessings of democracy and progress. Only they, it was argued, had the energy, industriousness, and innate love of liberty to establish a successful free government.

Manifest Destiny was closely associated with the Democratic Party. For Democrats, expansionism would counterbalance the debilitating effects of industrialization and urbanization. As good Jeffersonians, they stressed the need for more land to realize the ideal of a democratic republic rooted in the virtues and rough equality of independent farmers. For their working-class Irish constituency, the Democrats touted the broad expanses of the West as the surest means to escape the misery of wage slavery.

Manifest Destiny captured the popular imagination when the country was still mired in depression after the Panic of 1837. The way out of the depression, according to many Democrats, was to revive the export trade to soak up the agricultural surplus. Thomas Hart Benton, a Democratic senator from Missouri, was the leading spokesman for the vast potential of U.S. trade with India and China, a trade to be secured by U.S. possession of the harbors on the Pacific Coast.

The Mexican War

Once in office, Polk proved far more conciliatory with the British than with the Mexicans. Polk was willing to compromise on Oregon because he dreaded the possibility of a two-front war against both the Mexicans and the British. Mexico had severed diplomatic ties with the United States over the annexation of Texas (see Chapter 10), and a war could break out at any time.

((• 📖 **Read** the **Document** Thomas Corwin, Speech Against the Mexican War (1847)

This colorful kerchief depicts scenes from the battles of General Zachary Taylor during the Mexican War.

In the spring of 1846, after Polk had abrogated the agreement on the joint occupation of Oregon, the British offered a compromise that they had earlier rejected. They agreed to a boundary at the 49th parallel if they were allowed to retain Vancouver Island in Puget Sound. Polk sent the offer to the Senate, which quickly approved it in June 1846.

Unlike Oregon, where he backed off from extravagant territorial claims, Polk refused to budge on the U.S. claim (inherited from the Texans when the United States annexed Texas in 1845) that the Rio Grande was the border between Texas and Mexico. The Mexicans insisted that the Nueces River, 100 miles north of the Rio Grande, was the border, as it had been when Texas was part of Mexico. An immense territory was at stake, for the headwaters of the Rio Grande were in northern New Mexico, and a boundary on the Rio Grande would more than double the size of Texas.

Citing rumors of a Mexican invasion, Polk sent 3,500 troops under General Zachary Taylor to the Nueces River in the summer of 1845. Polk also stepped up his efforts to acquire California. He instructed Thomas Larkin, the U.S. consul in Monterey, California, to inform the *Californios* and Americans that the United States would support them if they revolted against Mexican rule. Polk also secretly ordered the U.S. Pacific naval squadron to seize California ports if war broke out with Mexico. Polk's final effort at peaceful expansion was the Slidell mission in November 1845. He sent John L. Slidell to Mexico City to offer $30 million to purchase California and New Mexico and to secure the Rio Grande boundary.

When Polk learned that the Mexican government had refused to receive Slidell, he set out to draw Mexico into a war that would result in the U.S. acquisition of California. In early 1846, he ordered General Taylor to advance to the Rio Grande, deep in the disputed border region. Taylor blockaded the mouth of the Rio Grande (an aggressive act even if the river had been an international boundary) and built a fort on the northern bank across from the Mexican town of Matamoros. The Mexicans attacked and were repulsed on April 24.

Even before the news reached Washington, Polk had decided on war, on the grounds that the Mexican government had unjustifiably refused to sell territory to the United States and had fallen behind on debt payments owed to American citizens. Informed of the clash between Mexican and American troops in early May (it took ten days for the news to reach Washington), he sent a redrafted war message to Congress on May 9 asserting that Mexico "has invaded our territory, and shed American blood on American soil." Congress declared war on May 13, 1846.

The war was a stunning military success for the United States (see Map 13.4 on page 364), in large measure because decade-long Comanche raids had so pillaged and demoralized settlements across northern Mexico that the local inhabitants were in no condition to resist any invader. The Mexicans fought bravely, but they lacked the leadership, modern artillery, and naval capacity to check the U.S. advances. By the end of 1846, Polk had gained his objectives in the Mexican borderlands. An army sent west under Colonel Stephen W. Kearny occupied New Mexico. The conquest was relatively bloodless, because most of the local elite cooperated with the U.S. forces. Sporadic resistance was largely confined to poorer Mexicans and the Pueblo Indians, who feared that their land would be confiscated.

Kearny's army then moved to Tucson and eventually linked up in southern California with pro-American rebels and U.S. forces sent ashore by the Pacific squadron. As in New Mexico, the stiffest resistance came from ordinary Mexicans and the Spanish-speaking Indians.

Despite the loss of its northern provinces, Mexico refused to concede defeat. After Taylor had established a secure defensive line in northeastern Mexico with a victory at Monterrey in September 1846 and repulsed a Mexican counterattack at Buena Vista in February 1847, Polk directed General Winfield Scott to invade central Mexico. Following an amphibious assault on Vera Cruz in March 1847, Scott captured Mexico City in September.

✴ Explore the War with Mexico on MyHistoryLab

WHAT DID THE TEXAS REVOLUTION AND MEXICAN-AMERICAN WAR MEAN FOR AMERICAN EXPANSION?

In the 1830s, the Mexican government faced problems in its northern state of Texas. The area was home to many Anglo-American settlers, and they were growing increasingly unhappy under Mexican governance. Texans successfully rebelled, forming the independent Republic of Texas in 1836. During the next decade, the United States annexed Texas as a new state, but disputed land claims quickly led to war between the United States and Mexico in 1846. The U.S. victory over the Mexican forces in 1848, after a series of consecutive U.S. battle successes, led to huge territorial losses for its southern neighbor as the United States acquired the territory that today is the modern Southwest.

When the United States annexed Texas, it triggered a territorial dispute that became the Mexican-American War (1846–1848)—the premise for President Polk to realize his policy of Manifest Destiny and expand the United States to California. This print depicts General Zachary Taylor, who repulsed a larger Mexican army, at the Battle of Buena Vista, February 22–23, 1847.

MAJOR BATTLES OF THE MEXICAN-AMERICAN WAR

Battle	Date	Victor
Battle of Palo Alto	May 8, 1846	U.S.
Battle of Resaca de la Palma	May 9, 1846	U.S.
Battle of Monterrey	Sept. 21–24, 1846	U.S.
Battle of San Pasqual	Dec. 6, 1846	Mexico
Battle of Rio San Gabriel	Jan. 8, 1847	U.S.
Battle of Buena Vista	Feb. 22–23, 1847	U.S.
Battle of Sacramento River	Feb. 27, 1847	U.S.
Battle of Veracruz	March 29, 1847	U.S.
Battle of Cerro Gordo	April 18, 1847	U.S.
Battle of Mexico City	Sept. 13–14, 1847	U.S.

KEY QUESTIONS Use **MyHistoryLab** *Explorer* to **answer** these **questions:**

Context ▶▶▶ *What was the political situation in Mexico leading up to its war with the United States?*

Map the nation's transformations between the 1820s and 1840s.

Response ▶▶▶ *How did the Texas Revolution unfold?*

Understand the progress, troop movements, and major battles.

Consequence ▶▶▶ *What did the acquisition of Mexican territory mean for the slavery in the United States?*

Consider the potential implications for the extension of slavery.

Read the Document   James K. Polk, First Inaugural Address (1845)

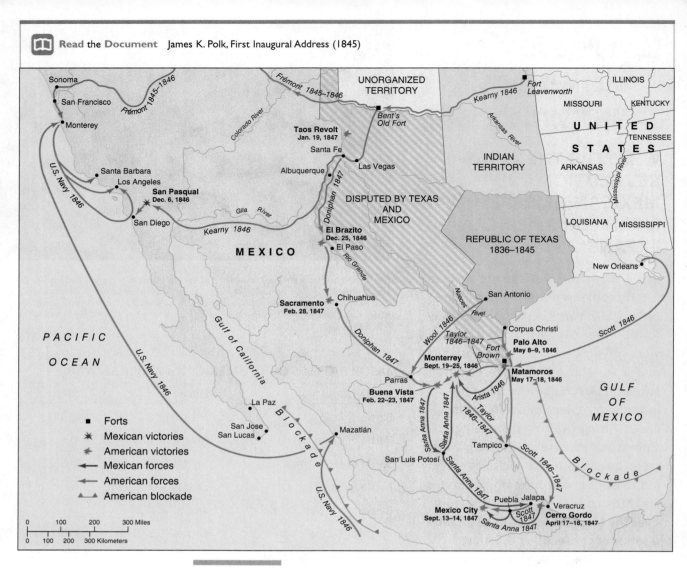

MAP 13.4 THE MEXICAN WAR Victories by General Zachary Taylor in northern Mexico secured the Rio Grande as the boundary between Texas and Mexico. Colonel Stephen Kearny's expedition won control of New Mexico, and reinforcements from Kearny ensured the success of American troops landed by the Pacific Squadron in gaining Alta California for the United States. The success of General Winfield Scott's amphibious invasion at Vera Cruz and his occupation of Mexico City brought the war to an end.

After a frustrating delay while Mexico reorganized its government, peace talks finally got under way and concluded in the Treaty of Guadalupe Hidalgo, signed on February 2, 1848. Mexico surrendered its claim to Texas north of the Rio Grande and ceded Alta California and New Mexico (including present-day Arizona, Utah, and Nevada). The United States paid $15 million, assumed over $3 million in claims of American citizens against Mexico, and agreed to grant U.S. citizenship to Mexican residents in its new territories.

Polk had gained his strategic goals, but the cost was 13,000 American lives (most from diseases such as measles and dysentery), 50,000 Mexican lives, and the poisoning of Mexican-American relations for generations. The war also, as will be seen in Chapter 14, heightened sectional tensions over slavery and weakened the political structure that was vital to preserving the Union.

Conclusion

Americans were an expansionist people. Their surge across the continent between 1815 and 1850 was fully in keeping with their restless desire for personal independence on a plot of land. Population pressure on overworked farms in the East impelled much of this westward migration, but by the 1840s, expansion had seemingly acquired a momentum all its own, one that increasingly rejected the claims of other peoples to the land.

Far from being a process of peaceful, evolutionary, and democratic change, expansion involved the spread of slavery, violent confrontations, and the uprooting and displacement of native peoples. As Catlin sensed in the 1830s, the coming of white settlement quickly had a devastating impact on the native peoples he visited and befriended. By 1850, the earlier notion of reserving the Trans-Mississippi West as a permanent Indian country had been abandoned. The Sioux and Comanches were still feared by white settlers, but their final subjugation was not far off. The derogatory stereotypes of Mexican Americans that were a staple of both popular thought and expansionist ideology showed clearly that U.S. control after the Mexican War would relegate Spanish-speaking people to second-class status.

However misleading and false much of it was, the rhetoric of Manifest Destiny did highlight a central truth. Broad, popular support existed for expanding across the continent. As the Mexican War made clear, the United States was now unquestionably the dominant power in North America. The only serious threat to its dominance in the near future would come from inside, not outside, its domain.

For Suggested Readings go to MyHistoryLab.

Chapter Review

The Agricultural Frontier

13.1 How did economic and demographic pressures in the East spur migration to the West? p. 341

The population in the East continued to grow as land became increasingly scarce and declined in fertility. The West provided an outlet for a surplus rural population no longer able to settle on their own family farms. Areas opened to white settlement after 1815 offered land that was far cheaper and more fertile than was available in the East.

The Frontier of the Plains Indians

13.2 What strategies did the Sioux use to maintain their power on the Great Plains? p. 347

As shown by their blending of the horse and the gun into a new culture of nomadic warrior-hunters, the Sioux were a resourceful and innovative people. They used their military dominance on the northern Plains to expand the range of their buffalo hunts and to force other tribes to rely on them for meat and trading goods. They sought an accommodation with the U.S. army as long as they considered it in their best interests.

The Mexican Borderlands

13.3 What forces contributed to the Americanization of Texas? p. 352

The Mexican province of Texas was very sparsely settled when large numbers of Americans began moving in after Mexico encouraged settlement in the 1820s. Within a decade, Americans easily outnumbered native-born Mexicans. Tensions over religion, slavery, and political rights exploded into conflict when Mexico attempted to tighten its control in the mid-1830s. By 1836, Texas was an independent republic anxious to join the United States.

Politics, Expansion, and War

13.4 Why was James K. Polk so eager to provoke a war with Mexico? p. 359

Polk was intent on acquiring the Mexican province of California for the United States. Unwilling to wait for a pro-American revolt to break out, and frustrated when Mexico refused to consider any of his offers to purchase California, Polk fell back on the option of acquiring California in a war he incited by ordering U.S. troops into disputed territory claimed by Mexico.

Timeline

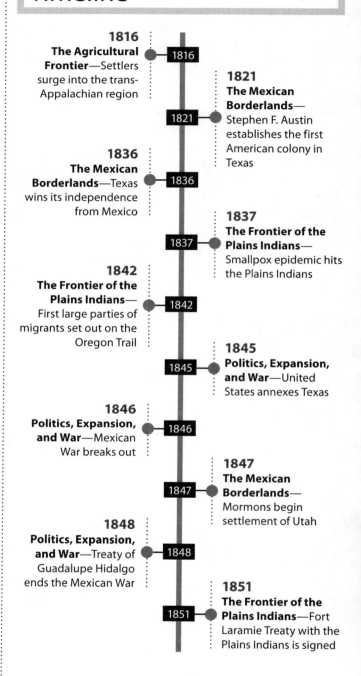

1816
The Agricultural Frontier—Settlers surge into the trans-Appalachian region
1816

1821
The Mexican Borderlands—Stephen F. Austin establishes the first American colony in Texas
1821

1836
The Mexican Borderlands—Texas wins its independence from Mexico
1836

1837
The Frontier of the Plains Indians—Smallpox epidemic hits the Plains Indians
1837

1842
The Frontier of the Plains Indians—First large parties of migrants set out on the Oregon Trail
1842

1845
Politics, Expansion, and War—United States annexes Texas
1845

1846
Politics, Expansion, and War—Mexican War breaks out
1846

1847
The Mexican Borderlands—Mormons begin settlement of Utah
1847

1848
Politics, Expansion, and War—Treaty of Guadalupe Hidalgo ends the Mexican War
1848

1851
The Frontier of the Plains Indians—Fort Laramie Treaty with the Plains Indians is signed
1851

14 The Politics of Sectionalism 1846–1861

One American Journey

Letter from Harriet Beecher Stowe

December 16, 1852

My Dear Madam,

So you want to know what sort of woman I am! Well, if this is any object, you shall have statistics free of charge. To begin, then, I am a little bit of a woman, somewhat more than forty, about as thin and dry as a pinch of snuff, never very much to look at in my best days and looking like a used up article now.

I was married when I was twenty-five years old to a man rich in Greek and Hebrew and Latin and Arabic, and alas, rich in nothing else. . . . But then I was abundantly furnished with wealth of another sort. I had two little curly headed twin daughters to begin with and my stock in this line has gradually increased, till I have been the mother of seven children, the most beautiful and the most loved of whom lies buried near my Cincinnati residence. It was at his dying bed and at his grave that I learned what a poor slave mother may feel when her child is torn away from her. In those depths of sorrow which seemed to me

Vivid illustrations accompanied the numerous editions of *Uncle Tom's Cabin* depicting the brutal realities of slavery and the unmerited suffering of the slave. These images sharpened the tragedy of Harriet Beecher Stowe's story. Here, Tom dies following a savage beating.

LEARNING OBJECTIVES

14.1 ((•
How did slavery transform from a political issue to a moral crusade? p. 370

14.2 ((•
How did the intrusion of religion into the political process contribute to the rise of the Republican Party? p. 379

14.3 ((•
How did the elevation of slavery to a moral issue polarize North and South during the 1850s? p. 390

((• **Listen to Chapter 14 on MyHistoryLab**

Watch the Video Series on MyHistoryLab

Learn about some key topics related to this chapter with the *MyHistoryLab Video Series: Key Topics in U.S. History.*

1 **Slavery at the Watershed: 1848–1860** This introductory video reveals the way slavery became the central and most divisive issue in the decade leading up to the Civil War. As a political, social, and economic issue, slavery dominated the national agenda of the "Antebellum" (before the war) period and served as a wedge that emphasized geographical differences as well as communal differences in both the North and South. It brought about the first direct and violent confrontations between pro and anti-slavery forces and, ultimately, war.

 Watch on MyHistoryLab

The Compromise of 1850 The Compromise of 1850 is a critical development in the path to civil war. This video discusses how the Compromise was the U.S. Congress's signature piece of legislation for the coming decade. It dealt with a host of issues, arising from the expansion of slavery into territories and new states, such as Texas and California, and the Fugitive Slave Act. The debates surrounding the compromise also witnessed the eclipse of such great legislators as Henry Clay, Daniel Webster, and John C. Calhoun, and the rise of Stephen A. Douglas. **2**

Watch on MyHistoryLab

3 **The *Dred Scott* Decision** The Supreme Court's *Dred Scott v. Sandford* decision of 1858 is featured in this video. Chief Justice Roger B. Taney's controversial explanation of the majority opinion in the case went beyond any previous legal position interpreting the rights of slaves and even free persons of color. The decision resulted from Scott's attempt to legally free himself and his family from their owner and, although he ultimately lost, contributed to the growing antislavery sentiment and further divided the United States during the final years before the Civil War.

 Watch on MyHistoryLab

The Lincoln–Douglas Debates In 1858, Senator Stephen A. Douglas of Illinois, a popular and established political figure, was challenged for his seat by a former one-term Congressman, Abraham Lincoln of the new Republican Party. During the course of the campaign, they held a series of debates that epitomized the national discussion over slavery and states' rights. For this reason, they were heavily covered in the nation's newspapers. Although he lost his bid for senator, this video explains how the debates helped Lincoln establish a national following that paved the way for his election to the presidency in 1860 defeating, among two other candidates, Stephen A. Douglas. **4**

Watch on MyHistoryLab

immeasurable, it was my only prayer to God that such anguish might not be suffered in vain. There were circumstances about his death of such peculiar bitterness, of what seemed almost cruel suffering that I felt that I could never be consoled for it unless this crushing of my own heart might enable me to work out some great good to others.

I allude to this here because I have often felt that much that is in that book had its root in the awful scenes and bitter sorrow of that summer. It has left now, I trust, no trace on my mind except a deep compassion for the sorrowful, especially for mothers who are separated from their children. . . .

This horror, this nightmare abomination! Can it be in my country! It lies like lead on my heart, it shadows my life with sorrow; the more so that I feel, as for my own brothers, for the South, and am pained by every horror I am obliged to write, as one who is forced by some awful oath to disclose in court some family disgrace. . . .

Yours affectionately,

H. B. Stowe

Harriet Beecher Stowe to Eliza Cabot Follen, December 16, 1852; from *The Limits of Sisterhood: The Beecher Sisters on Women's Rights and Woman's Sphere* by Jeanne Boydston, Mary Kelley, and Anne Margolis. (Copyright © 1988 by the University of North Carolina Press.) www.uncpress.unc.edu.

Personal Journeys Online

- Carl Schurz, *Reminiscences,* 1908. Account of his participation in Germany's failed Revolution of 1848 and his subsequent journey to freedom in the United States.

- Frederick Douglass, three excerpts: "What of the Night?" May 5, 1848; "A Letter to American Slaves," September 5, 1850; "Letter to James Redpath," June 29, 1860. These excerpts chart the famous black abolitionist's journey from a belief in moral suasion and political action as the best strategy to liberate the nation's slaves to an embrace of direct action and violence as the only remedy for bondage.

Harriet Beecher Stowe, in her letter to the poet and fellow abolitionist Eliza Cabot Follen in the year that *Uncle Tom's Cabin* became an international best seller, revealed how being a wife and a mother had influenced her perception of slavery and inspired her writing. Stowe's experience demonstrates how a personal journey can influence the course of a nation. Barely out of her teens, she left her comfortable New England home for the raw frontier town of Cincinnati in 1832. Stowe's father, Lyman Beecher, already a famous Protestant evangelical preacher, moved there with his family to save the West from Roman Catholicism. Stowe wrote a geography textbook, married a young scholar from her father's seminary, and settled into motherhood. The growing antislavery crusade prompted her to write a few articles on the subject. Not until the death of her beloved son, Charley, in a cholera epidemic in 1849, however, did she make the connection between her own tragedy and the national tragedy of human bondage.

Slavery was an abstract concept to most white northerners at the time. Stowe personalized it in a way that made them see it as an institution that did not just oppress black people but also destroyed families and debased well-meaning Christian masters. The deep piety expressed in the letter permeated the book and changed people's moral perceptions about slavery.

As slavery took on a personal and tragic meaning for Stowe, so it would move from being just another political issue to a moral crusade. Stowe's personal journey transformed it into a political passion; for the millions who read her book, the political became personal. Yet the anguish she expressed in her writing and the outrage it generated among her readers were hardly prefigured when a relatively obscure congressman from Pennsylvania stepped forward in 1846 with a modest proposal that not only placed slavery front and center as a national political issue, a position that only strengthened over the next fifteen years, but would shake the Union to its very core.

Slavery was not, of course, a new political issue. But after 1846, the clashes between northern and southern congressmen over issues relating to slavery became more frequent and more difficult to resolve. In the coming years, several developments, including white southerners' growing consciousness of themselves as a minority, the mixture of political issues with religious questions, and the rise of the Republican Party, would aggravate sectional antagonism. But the flash point that first brought it to the fore was the issue of slavery in the territories acquired from Mexico.

Slavery in the Territories

14.1 How did slavery transform from a political issue to a moral crusade?

Whatever its boundaries over the years, the West symbolized the hopes and dreams of white Americans. It was the region of fresh starts, of possibilities. The West also represented the fulfillment of God's destiny for America to conquer the continent from sea to shining sea. It was a region not only of promise, but also of prophecy. To exclude slavery from the western territories was to exclude white southerners from pursuing their vision of the American dream. Exclusion, an Alabamian declared, meant "that a free citizen of Massachusetts was a better man and entitled to more privileges than a free citizen of Alabama." Northern politicians disagreed. They argued that exclusion preserved equality, the equality of all white men and women to live and work without competition from slave labor or rule by despotic slaveholders. The issue of slavery in the territories became an issue of freedom for both sides. From the late 1840s until 1861, northern and southern leaders

📖 **Read the Document**   Horace Greeley, from *An Overland Journey* (1860)

Emanuel Leutze's "Westward the Course of Empire Takes Its Way" (1861) hangs in the west wing of the U.S. Capitol Building. The German-born American painter completed this composition in 1861 on the eve of the Civil War. It is the apotheosis of Manifest Destiny, depicting the westward advance of European Americans across the continent as a divinely inspired mission. Note Moses and the Israelites on the painting's borders and the cross on the rock in the middle of the canvas.

attempted to fashion a solution to the problem of slavery in the territories. Four proposals dominated the debate:

- Outright exclusion
- Extension of the Missouri Compromise line to the Pacific
- Popular sovereignty, allowing the residents of a territory to decide the issue
- Protection of the property of slaveholders (meaning their right to own slaves) even if few lived in the territory

The first major debate on these proposals occurred during the early days of the Mexican War and culminated in the **Compromise of 1850.**

The Wilmot Proviso

In August 1846, David Wilmot, a Pennsylvania Democrat, offered an amendment to an appropriations bill for the Mexican War. The language of the **Wilmot Proviso** stipulated that "as an express and fundamental condition to the acquisition of any territory from the Republic of Mexico . . . neither slavery nor involuntary servitude shall ever exist in any part of said territory."

Wilmot explained that he wanted only to preserve the territories for "the sons of toil, of my own race and own color." By thus linking the exclusion of slavery in the territories to freedom for white people, he hoped to generate support across the North, regardless of party, and even in some areas of the Upper South. Linking freedom for white people to the exclusion of slaves infuriated southerners. It implied that the mere proximity of slavery was degrading and that white southerners were therefore a degraded people, unfit to join other Americans in the territories.

Northern lawmakers, a majority in the House of Representatives (because the northern states had a larger population than the southern states), passed more than fifty versions of the proviso between 1846 and 1850. In the Senate, however, where each state had equal representation, the proviso was consistently rejected and never became law.

The proviso debate sowed distrust and suspicion between northerners and southerners. Congress had divided along sectional lines before, but seldom had the divisions become so personal.

Religious differences also sharpened the sectional conflict over the proviso. The leading evangelical Protestant denominations—Methodists, Baptists, and Presbyterians—split along sectional lines by the mid-1840s. Growing numbers of northern evangelicals advocated political action. During the debate on the Wilmot Proviso, a Boston minister wrote, "The great problem for the Christian world now to accomplish is to effect a closer union between religion and politics. . . . We must make men to do good and be good." Southern evangelicals recoiled from such mixing of church and state, charging northerners with abandoning the basic tenets of evangelical Christianity: the importance of individual salvation above all, and the Bible as the unerring word of God. The leaders of the Democratic and Whig parties, disturbed that the issue of slavery in the territories could so monopolize Congress and poison sectional relations, sought to defuse the issue as the presidential election of 1848 approached.

The Election of 1848

Both Democrats and Whigs wanted to avoid identification with either side of the Wilmot Proviso controversy, and they selected their 1848 presidential candidates accordingly. The Democrats nominated Michigan senator Lewis Cass, a party stalwart, whose public career stretched back to the War of 1812. Cass understood the destructive potential of the slavery issue. In 1847, he suggested that territorial residents, not Congress, should decide slavery's fate. This solution, **popular sovereignty,** had a do-it-yourself charm: Keep the politicians out of it, and let the people decide. Cass was deliberately ambiguous, however, on when the people should decide. The timing was important. If residents could decide only when applying for statehood, slavery would be legal up to that point. The ambiguity aroused more fears than it allayed.

Compromise of 1850 The four-step compromise that admitted California as a free state, allowed the residents of the New Mexico and Utah territories to decide the slavery issue for themselves, ended the slave trade in the District of Columbia, and passed a new fugitive slave law to enforce the constitutional provision stating that a slave escaping into a free state shall be delivered back to the owner.

Wilmot Proviso The amendment offered by Pennsylvania Democrat David Wilmot in 1846 which stipulated that "as an express and fundamental condition to the acquisition of any territory from the Republic of Mexico . . . neither slavery nor involuntary servitude shall ever exist in any part of said territory."

popular sovereignty A solution to the slavery crisis suggested by Michigan senator Lewis Cass by which territorial residents, not Congress, would decide slavery's fate.

The Whigs were silent on the slavery issue. Reverting to their winning 1840 formula of nominating a war hero, they selected General Zachary Taylor of Mexican War fame. Taylor belonged to no party and had never voted. If one had to guess his views, his background provided some clues. He owned a hundred-slave plantation in Louisiana.

Taylor's background disturbed many antislavery northern Whigs. These Conscience Whigs, along with remnants of the old Liberty Party and a scattering of northern Democrats, bolted their parties and formed the Free-Soil Party. The name reflected the party's vow to keep the territories free. Its slogan, "Free soil, free speech, free labor, free men," was a catalog of white liberties that the South had allegedly threatened over the previous decade.

The Free-Soilers' appeal centered on their opposition to slave labor in the territories. Free labor, they believed, could not compete with bonded labor. The party nominated former president Martin Van Buren. Chalking up one out of seven northern votes, Van Buren ran strongly enough in eleven of the fifteen northern states to deny the winning candidate in those states a majority of the votes cast. But he could not overcome Taylor's strength in the South. Taylor was elected, giving the nation its first president from the Lower South.

The Gold Rush

Events in distant California, recently acquired from Mexico, would leave Taylor little time to savor his victory. By the time he took office in March 1849, a gold rush was underway there.

Through 1849 and 1850, more than 100,000 hopefuls flooded into California. Though the trek to California took months, whether overland or by the sea route, and travelers battled disease, weather, and each other, the lure of gold, easy to get at with just simple tools, was a powerful motivator.

Huge fortunes accrued, not only from the gold, but from supplying the miners. Young Levi Strauss experimented with trousers made out of canvas that miners particularly favored; two brothers, Henry Wells and William Fargo, offered banking, transportation, and mail services for the newcomers. The rush also attracted migrants from around the world. California soon became a polyglot empire of Chinese, Chileans, Mexicans, Irish, Germans, and Turks. Blacks, mostly slaves brought by southern masters, also roamed the gold fields.

By 1853 gold-mining operations had undergone structural and technological changes that made many miners superfluous. The new hydraulic extraction techniques also severely damaged the pristine rivers of central California. Almost overnight, San Francisco was transformed from a modest port to a cosmopolitan metropolis. The image of California, and of the West in general, as wild or golden, dates from this era. But the romance of California and the wealth it generated loomed more troubling back east as the territory filled up with people in 1849; the western dream would soon become ensnared in the conflict over slavery.

The Compromise of 1850

When the California territory's new residents began asking for statehood and drafted a state constitution, the document contained no provision for slavery. The constitution reflected antiblack rather than antislavery sentiment. Keeping California white would shield residents against social and economic interaction with black people. In the context of territorial politics, "free" became a synonym for "whites only." If Congress accepted the residents' request for statehood, California would enter the Union as a free state. The Union at the time consisted of fifteen free states and fifteen slave states. The admission of California would tip the balance and give free states a majority in the Senate. New Mexico (which then included most of present-day New Mexico, Arizona, small parts of Nevada, and Colorado) appeared poised to follow suit and enter the Union as the seventeenth free state. Southerners saw their political power slipping away. Northern leaders saw an opportunity to stop the extension of slavery and reduce southern influence in the federal government.

When Congress confronted the issue of California statehood in December 1849, partisans on both sides began marshaling forces for what promised to be a long and bitter struggle. Because nine Free-Soil candidates had won seats in the House of Representatives, neither Whigs nor Democrats held a majority there. No one, at first, knew where Taylor stood.

He supported, it turned out, a version of popular sovereignty and favored allowing California and the other territories acquired from Mexico to decide the slavery issue for themselves. Under normal circumstances, the residents of a new territory organized a territorial government under the direction of Congress. When the territory's population approached 30,000 or so, residents could draft a constitution and petition Congress for statehood. California already easily exceeded the population threshold. Taylor proposed bypassing the territorial stage, and congressional involvement in it, and having California and New Mexico admitted as free states directly.

The president was a nationalist and a strong believer in Manifest Destiny. As a slaveholder, he did not oppose slavery, but he abhorred the slavery issue because it threatened his vision of a continental empire. Thus he was willing to forgo the extension of slavery into the territories. Southerners were certain to object strongly. But the president had a chilling message for them: "Whatever dangers may threaten [the Union] I shall stand by it and maintain it in its integrity."

Southerners resisted Taylor's plan, and Congress deadlocked on the territorial issue. Henry Clay then stepped forward with his last great compromise. To break the impasse, Clay urged that Congress should take five steps:

- Admit California as a free state, as its residents clearly preferred.
- Allow the residents of the New Mexico and Utah territories to decide the slavery issue for themselves.
- End the slave trade in the District of Columbia.
- Pass a new fugitive slave law to enforce the constitutional provision stating that a person "held to Service or Labor in one state . . . escaping into another . . . shall be delivered upon Claim of the party to whom such Service or Labor may be due."
- Set the boundary between Texas and New Mexico and pay Texas $10 million for the territory given up to New Mexico. (Texas, incidentally, would use this payment to retire its state debt and fund a public school system.)

Clay's proposal provoked a historic Senate debate that began in February 1850, featuring America's three most prominent statesmen, Clay, John C. Calhoun, and Daniel Webster, together for the last time. The emaciated Calhoun, who would be dead in two months, had to be carried into the Senate chamber. Too weak to read his remarks, he passed them to Virginia senator James M. Mason. Calhoun argued that the compromise did not resolve the slavery issue to the South's satisfaction, and he proposed to give southerners in Congress the right to veto legislation as a way to safeguard their minority rights. Webster stood up to support the compromise, at deep political peril to himself. His Massachusetts constituents detested the fugitive slave provision, which gave southern slaveholders the right to "invade" northern states to reclaim escaped slaves. Webster declared that he came to the debate "not as a Massachusetts man, nor as a Northern man, but as an American." He would swallow the fugitive slave law to save the Union.

After tumultuous deliberation that lasted into the summer of 1850, the Senate rejected the compromise. Calhoun had died at the end of March 1850, before the debate ended. The 73-year-old Clay, exhausted, left Washington to recover his health. He would die less than two years later. Webster, estranged from fellow northern Whigs, left the Senate and went to his grave a few months after Clay. President Taylor, who had vowed to veto any compromise, died unexpectedly of a stomach ailment after overindulging in cherries and milk in the hot sun at a July 4 celebration in Washington. Vice President Millard Fillmore, a pro-Clay New Yorker, assumed the presidency after Taylor's death. Fillmore let it be known that he favored Clay's package and would sign it if passed.

Although the Senate had rejected the compromise, Illinois senator Stephen A. Douglas kept it alive. A small man with a large head that gave him a mushroom-like appearance, Douglas epitomized the promise of American life for men of his generation. A native Vermonter, he migrated first to New York, then to Illinois as a teenager, became a lawyer, and developed a voracious appetite for politics. By the age of 28, he had already served as state legislator, chairman of the state Democratic Party, and judge of the state supreme court. He envisioned an urban, industrial West linked to the East by a vast railroad network eventually extending to the Pacific. Above all, Douglas professed an unbending nationalism. To him, according to a biographer, "the Union was sacred, the symbol of all human progress." After his election to Congress in 1842, the Little Giant, as his constituents affectionately called him, developed a reputation as an astute parliamentarian and a tenacious debater.

Like Webster, Douglas feared for the Union if the compromise failed. Realizing that it would never pass as a package, he proposed to break it up into its components and hold a separate vote on each. With a handful of senators voting for all parts, and with different sectional blocs supporting one provision or another, Douglas engineered a majority for the compromise, and Fillmore signed it.

The Compromise of 1850 (see Map 14.1) was not a compromise in the sense of each opposing side consenting to certain terms desired by the other. The North gained California but would have done so in any case. Southern leaders looked to the West and saw no slave territories awaiting statehood. Their future in the Union appeared to be one of numerical and economic decline, and the survival of their institutions seemed doubtful. They gained the **Fugitive Slave Act,** which reinforced their right to seize and return to bondage slaves who had fled to free territory, but it was slight consolation. One Lower South senator termed it "useless." Since most slaves who escaped to the North did so from neighboring slave states, the law affected mainly the states

Fugitive Slave Act Law, part of the Compromise of 1850, that required authorities in the North to assist southern slave catchers and return runaway slaves to their owners.

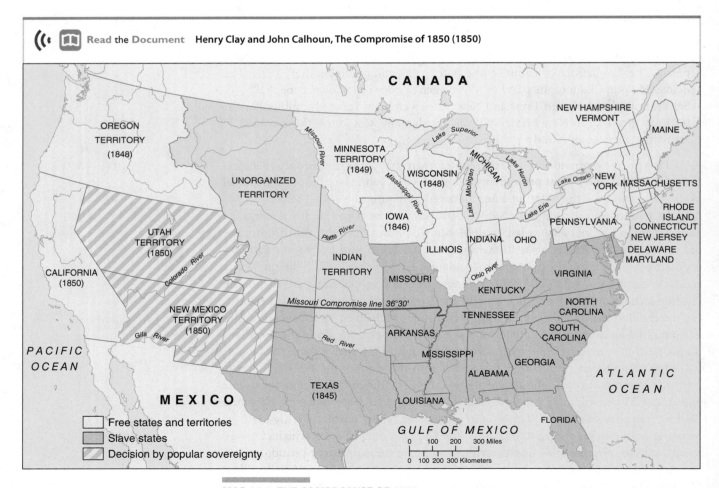

((• 🕮 Read the Document   Henry Clay and John Calhoun, The Compromise of 1850 (1850)

MAP 14.1 THE COMPROMISE OF 1850 Given the unlikely prospect that any of the western territories would opt for slavery, the compromise sealed the South's minority status in the Union.

of the Upper South. Few slave owners from the Lower South would bear the expense and uncertainty of chasing an escaped slave into free territory. And the North's hostile reception to the law made southerners doubt its commitment to the compromise.

Response to the Fugitive Slave Act

The Fugitive Slave Act was ready-made for abolitionist propaganda mills and heart-rending stories. A few months after Congress passed it, a Kentucky slaveholder visited Madison, Indiana, and snatched a black man from his wife and children, claiming that the man had escaped nineteen years earlier. Black people living in northern communities feared capture, and some fled across the Canadian border. Several northern cities and states vowed resistance, but except for a few publicized cases, northern authorities typically cooperated with southern slave owners to help them retrieve their runaway property. The effect of the act on public opinion, however, was to polarize North and South even further.

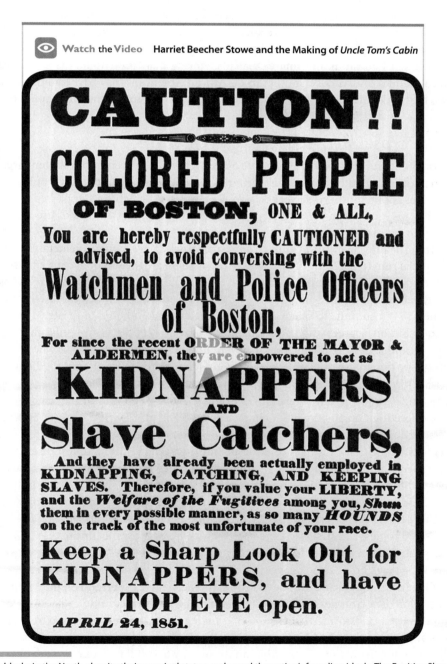

Watch the Video Harriet Beecher Stowe and the Making of *Uncle Tom's Cabin*

> CAUTION!!
>
> COLORED PEOPLE
> OF BOSTON, ONE & ALL,
> You are hereby respectfully CAUTIONED and advised, to avoid conversing with the
> Watchmen and Police Officers of Boston,
> For since the recent ORDER OF THE MAYOR & ALDERMEN, they are empowered to act as
> KIDNAPPERS
> AND
> Slave Catchers,
> And they have already been actually employed in KIDNAPPING, CATCHING, AND KEEPING SLAVES. Therefore, if you value your LIBERTY, and the *Welfare of the Fugitives* among you, *Shun* them in every possible manner, as so many *HOUNDS* on the track of the most unfortunate of your race.
> Keep a Sharp Look Out for KIDNAPPERS, and have TOP EYE open.
> *APRIL 24, 1851.*

Free blacks in the North, despite their marginal status, embraced the nation's founding ideals. The Fugitive Slave Act threatened to reverse and even end their journey toward equality. This notice, typical of warnings posted in northern cities, urged Boston's African American population to take precautions.

The strongest reaction to the act was in the black communities of the urban North. Previously, black abolitionists in the North had focused on freeing slaves in the South. The Fugitive Slave Act brought the danger of slavery much closer to home. No black person was safe under the new law. Mistaken identity, the support of federal courts for slaveholders' claims, and the presence of informants made reenslavement a real possibility. The lives that 400,000 black northerners had constructed, often with great difficulty, appeared suddenly uncertain.

Congress had, in effect, nationalized slavery. No black person was safe on American soil. Frederick Douglass, the great black abolitionist and an escaped slave himself, was invited to give the Fourth of July address at a meeting of the Rochester (New York) Ladies' Anti-Slavery Society in 1852. Douglass declined. Instead, he delivered his speech on July fifth because "I am not included within the pale of this glorious anniversary! The rich inheritance of justice, liberty, prosperity, and independence, bequeathed by your fathers, is shared by you, not by me."

Black northerners formed associations to protect each other and repel, violently if necessary, any attempt to capture and reenslave them. Frederick Douglass explained the need for such organizations: "We must be prepared . . . to see the streets . . . running with blood . . . should this law be put into operation." Some black people left the United States. In October 1850, 200 left Pittsburgh for Ontario, Canada, vowing that "they would die before being taken back into slavery." As many as 20,000 African Americans may have found their way across the border during the 1850s in response to fears over capture and reenslavement.

Uncle Tom's Cabin

Sectional controversy over the Fugitive Slave Act was relatively modest compared to the firestorm ignited by abolitionist writer Harriet Beecher Stowe with the publication of a novel about southern slavery. *Uncle Tom's Cabin,* which first appeared in serial form in 1851, moved many northern white people from the sidelines of the sectional conflict to more active participation.

At the beginning of *Uncle Tom's Cabin,* a Kentucky slave owner is reluctantly forced by financial ruin to sell some of his slaves. Among them are the son of two mulatto slaves, George and Eliza Harris, and an older slave, Tom. Eliza escapes across the ice-choked Ohio River, clutching her son to her breast as slave catchers and their bloodhounds pursue them. Tom submits to sale to a New Orleans master. When that master dies, Tom is sold to Simon Legree, who owns a plantation on the Red River in Louisiana. Legree is vicious and sadistic, the only major slaveholding character in the book whom Stowe portrays in this manner. Tom, a devout Christian, remains loyal and obedient until Legree asks him to whip another slave. When Tom refuses, Legree beats him to death. Legree, incidentally, is from Vermont. Aiming to evoke strong emotions in the reader, Stowe offered not abstractions but characters that seemed real. The broken family, the denial of freedom, and the Christian martyr were emotional themes. The presence of mulattoes in the book testified to widespread interracial and extramarital sex, which northerners, then in the midst of a religious revival, viewed as an abhorrent sin destructive to family life. And the depiction of southern masters struggling unsuccessfully with their consciences focused public attention on how slavery subverted Christianity.

Uncle Tom's Cabin created a sensation in the United States and abroad. The book sold 10,000 copies in its first week and 300,000 within a year. By the time of the Civil War, it had sold an unprecedented 3 million copies in the United States and tens of thousands more in Europe. Stowe's book gave slavery a face; it changed people's moral perceptions about the institution in an era of deep Protestant piety; it was a Sermon on the Mount for a generation of northerners seeking witness for their Christianity and a crusade on behalf of their faith. It transformed abolitionism, bringing the movement, whose extreme rhetoric many northerners had previously viewed with disapproval, to the edge of respectability, moving the nation a bit further on its journey to fulfill its founding ideals.

For southerners, *Uncle Tom's Cabin* was a damnable lie, a political tract disguised as literature. Some southerners retaliated with crude plays and books of their own. In these versions of slavery, no slave families were broken up, no slaves were killed, and all masters were models of Christian behavior.

Black northerners embraced *Uncle Tom's Cabin.* Frederick Douglass's National Black Convention resolved that the book was "a work plainly marked by the finger of God" on behalf of black people. Some black people hoped that the book's popularity would highlight the hypocrisy of white northerners who were quick to perceive evil in the South but were often blind to discrimination against African Americans in the North. Despite reactions to Stowe's book, however, black northerners continued to face voting restrictions, segregation, and official harassment.

The Election of 1852

While the nation was reading and reacting to *Uncle Tom's Cabin,* a presidential election campaign took place. The Compromise of 1850 had divided the Whigs deeply. Northern Whigs perceived it as a capitulation to southern slaveholding interests and refused to support the renomination of President Millard Fillmore. Many southern Whigs, angered by the suspicions and insults of their erstwhile northern colleagues, abandoned the party. Although the Whigs nominated Mexican War hero and Virginian Winfield Scott for president, few southern Whigs viewed the nonslaveholding general as a friend of their region.

The Democratic Party entered the campaign more united. Despite reservations, the northern and southern wings of the party both announced their support for the Compromise of 1850. Southern Democrats viewed the party's nominee, Franklin Pierce of New Hampshire, as safe on the slavery issue despite his New England heritage. Pierce satisfied northerners as a nationalist devoted to the idea of Manifest Destiny. He belonged to Young America, a mostly Democratic group that advocated extending American influence into Central and South America and the Caribbean with an aggressive foreign policy. His service in the Mexican War and his good looks and charm won over doubters from both sections.

Given the disarray of the Whigs and the relative unity of the Democrats, the election results were predictable. Pierce won overwhelmingly with 254 electoral votes to Scott's 42. But Pierce's landslide victory could not obscure the deep fissures in the American party system. The Whigs, although they would continue to run local candidates through the rest of the 1850s, were finished as a national party. And the Democrats, despite their electoral success, emerged frayed from the election. In the Lower South, conflicts within the party between supporters and opponents of the Compromise of 1850 had overshadowed the contests between Democrats and Whigs. Southern Democrats had wielded great influence at the party's nominating convention and dominated party policy, clouding its prospects in the North. During the election, much of the party's support in the North had come from the first-time votes of mainly Catholic immigrants. But the growing political influence of Catholics alarmed evangelical Protestants of both parties, thus adding religious bigotry to the divisive issues undermining the structure of the national parties.

Immigration and Revolution

Two events in Europe at this time had a profound effect on American politics and party realignment. In the heavily Catholic southern part of Ireland, absentee English landlords had been squeezing the land and the labor out of tenants for decades. Disease accompanied poverty: In 1840 less than one-fifth of the population lived beyond the age of 40.

Just when it seemed things could get no worse, they did. First came the potato blight that destroyed the country's staple crop, and then the British repealed the Corn Laws, which had protected Ireland's wheat farmers from foreign competition. The English landlords evicted their Irish tenants, throwing nearly a million people out of work and toward starvation. That these rural people typically settled in American cities is hardly surprising given the association between farming and poverty in their native land.

ONE OF THE PEOPLE'S SAINTS
for the Calendar of Liberty
1852.

"Fight for us"

"One of the People's Saints for the Calendar of Liberty," 1852. The failure of the European revolutions of 1848 deeply disappointed and concerned many Americans. Here, Hungarian patriot Lajos Kossuth attempts in vain to aid a fallen Liberty, vanquished by a three-headed monster representing the Vatican, Austria, and its ally, Russia.

America offered a better alternative. By the mid-1850s, Ireland had lost one quarter of its population to either famine or emigration. Poor, mostly illiterate, and Roman Catholic, the Irish arrivals faced a rocky reception. Irish neighborhoods became synonymous in the public mind with intemperance, prostitution, gambling, violence, and disease, just when Protestant reformers were embarking on crusades against these vices. Unremarked at the time was the fact that hardworking Irish immigrants were remitting millions of dollars annually to the folks back home, a remarkable feat given the circumstances and recency of their arrival. These impressive sums underscored how much Irish labor pushed the urban economy.

At the same time the Irish streamed across the Atlantic to America, newcomers from the German states arrived in great numbers as well. Many Germans had arrived in America to escape the oppressions of the petty German princes, especially Jews, whose civil liberties were progressively eroded during this era. Others arrived as failed revolutionaries or because of the same problems the Irish encountered: a potato blight in 1845, oppressive landlords, and a shortage of tillable land. Often traveling in groups, the Germans settled more diversely than the Irish, selecting midwestern farmland as well as cities from the Northeast to the Mississippi River. Nearly as numerous as the Irish, 1.3 million German immigrants had arrived in the United States by 1860.

The Germans were builders: factories, refineries, distilleries, musical instruments, professions, and associations of all kinds. Henry Steinway, chafing under production restrictions established by his guild in Germany, migrated to New York in 1851. Together with his four sons, he began to manufacture pianos. Within eight years, he employed 800 workers and turned out sixty pianos a week. Although most of the Germans were Protestants or Catholics, some 10,000 Bavarian Jews entered the migration stream in the 1840s. Mainly middle-class, they brought their mercantile skills and traditions of philanthropy and mutual assistance to American cities. One young Jewish German woman, Rebecca Gratz of Philadelphia, pioneered the profession of social work, and her good deeds so impressed Sir Walter Scott that he may have modeled the character of Rebecca in *Ivanhoe* after Miss Gratz.

The large Irish and German immigration of the late 1840s and early 1850s troubled many Americans. Never before or since has the proportion of immigrants coming to American shores been greater. Although the total number of immigrants arriving between 1845 and 1854—2.9 million—was considerably less than the 9.2 million who came between 1905 and 1914, they represented nearly 15 percent of the total population compared with the latter group, which comprised less than 11 percent of Americans living at that time.

Nativism, always present in American life, grew rapidly in reaction to the influx of immigrants, especially Roman Catholics who were perceived as threatening to the nation's democratic traditions. Nativists believed that Catholics owed their allegiance to the pope, not to the president, and that they would vote precisely as their priests told them.

The Order of the Star-Spangled Banner appeared in New York City in 1849 to promote nativist candidates for elective office. The organization favored lengthening the period of naturalization from five to twenty-one years, limiting the political rights of foreigners and their sons unless they were educated in American schools, and prohibiting foreigners from holding elective office. Immigration, like the slavery issue, drew religious concerns into the political process.

The concern over Catholic subversion coincided with the failure of republican revolutions throughout Europe in 1848. First in France, then in the German states, and spreading through the vast Austro-Hungarian Empire, the urban middle and working classes took to the streets to demand representative government. The events heartened Americans. The United States was the only modern nation that functioned on the basis of consent of the governed. Often, commentators would refer to our system as an "experiment." If, however, Europeans struck for the cause of democratic government, then the experiment might become the rule.

The revolutions failed, however. Authoritarian governments reasserted themselves across the continent. The collapse of the popular movements in Europe underscored the fragility of democratic institutions. Would the new immigrants undermine those institutions in America? Would the slavery controversy pull the world's foremost democracy apart? Would religious sensitivities, heightened by these developments, further fracture the body politic?

Political Realignment

14.2 How did the intrusion of religion into the political process contribute to the rise of the Republican Party?

The conflicts over slavery, immigration, and religion wrecked the Second American party system. The Whigs disintegrated, though remnants persisted in several states and localities, and the Democrats became more southern and more closely identified with immigrants, especially Roman Catholics. The Republicans, a new party, combined the growing antislavery and anti-southern sentiment in the North with religious nativism. Whether America would dissolve into warring factions over slavery or sectarian strife was anyone's guess in the mid-1850s. Eventually, the issue of slavery overwhelmed ethnic and religious concerns.

Franklin Pierce hoped to duck the slavery issue by focusing on Young America's dreams of empire. But his attempts to forge national sentiment around an aggressive foreign policy failed. And his administration's inept handling of a new territorial controversy in Kansas forced him to confront the slavery debate.

Young America's Foreign Misadventures

Pierce's first missteps occurred in pursuit of Young America's foreign ambitions. The administration turned a greedy eye toward Spanish-ruled Cuba, just 90 miles off the coast of Florida. Spanish authorities were harassing American merchants exporting sugar from Cuba and the American naval vessels protecting the merchants' ships. Southerners supported an aggressive Cuba policy, seeing the island as a possible new slave state. And nationalists saw great virtue in replacing what they perceived as a despotic colonial regime with a democratic government under the guidance of the United States.

In October 1854, three American diplomats met in Ostend, Belgium, to discuss Cuba. It is not clear whether Pierce approved or even knew of their meeting, but the diplomats believed that they had the administration's blessing. One of them, the American minister to Spain, Pierre Soulé of Louisiana, was especially eager for the United States to acquire Cuba. The group composed a document on Cuba called the **Ostend Manifesto** that claimed that the island belonged "naturally to the great family of states of which the Union is the Providential Nursery." The implication was that Spain's control of Cuba was unnatural. The United States would offer to buy Cuba from Spain, but if Spain refused to sell, the authors warned, "by every law, human and Divine, we shall be justified in wresting it from Spain."

The Ostend Manifesto caused an uproar and embarrassed the Pierce administration when it became public. In the polite world of nineteenth-century diplomacy, it was a significant breach of etiquette. Other nations quickly denounced it as a "buccaneering document" and a "highwayman's plea." It provoked a similar reaction in the United States, raising suspicions in the North that the South was willing to provoke a war with Spain to expand the number of slaveholding states.

While Pierce fumbled in the area of foreign policy, Senator Stephen A. Douglas of Illinois was developing a national project that also promised to draw the country together, the construction of a transcontinental railroad and the settling of the land it traversed. The result was worse conflict and the first outbreak of sustained sectional violence.

Ostend Manifesto Message sent by U.S. envoys to President Pierce from Ostend, Belgium, in 1854, stating that the United States had a "divine right" to wrest Cuba from Spain.

Stephen Douglas's Railroad Proposal

Douglas, like many westerners, wanted a transcontinental railroad. He himself had a personal stake in railroad building in that he owned some Chicago real estate and speculated in western lands. Railroads and the people and business they carried drove up property values. But beyond personal gain, Douglas, the supreme nationalist, understood that a transcontinental railroad would enhance the nation's journey toward a continental empire. Not only would it physically link East and West, it would also help spread American democracy.

Douglas had in mind a transcontinental route extending westward from Chicago through the Nebraska Territory. Unfortunately for his plans, Indians already occupied this region, many of them on land the U.S. government had set aside as Indian Territory and barred to white settlement. Removing the "Indian barrier" and establishing white government were "first steps," in the senator's view, toward a "tide of emigration and civilization."

Once again, and not for the last time, the federal government responded by reneging on earlier promises and forcing Indians to move. In 1853, President Pierce sent agents to convince the Indians in the northern part of the Indian Territory to cede land for the railroad.

With the Indian "obstacle" removed, Douglas sought congressional approval to establish a government for the Nebraska Territory. But southern senators defeated his proposal. They objected to it not only because it called for a northern rather than southern route for the transcontinental railroad but also because the new territory lay above the Missouri Compromise line and would enter the Union as yet another free state. Bowing to southern pressure, Douglas rewrote his bill and resubmitted it in January 1854. He predicted that the new bill would "raise a hell of a storm." He was right.

The Kansas-Nebraska Act

Douglas's Kansas-Nebraska Bill split the Nebraska Territory into two territories, Kansas and Nebraska, with the implicit understanding that Kansas would become a slave state and Nebraska a free state. Consistent with Douglas's belief in popular sovereignty, it left the actual decision on slavery to the residents of the territories. But because it allowed southerners to bring slaves into an area formerly closed to slavery, it repealed the Missouri Compromise (see Map 14.2).

Northerners of all parties were outraged. The Missouri Compromise had endured for thirty-four years as a basis for sectional accord on slavery. Now it was threatened, northern leaders charged, by the South's unquenchable desire to spread slavery and expand its political power. President Pierce, however, backed the bill, ensuring the support of enough northern Democrats to secure it a narrow victory. The **Kansas-Nebraska Act** was law.

Because of its fertile soil, favorable climate, and location adjacent to the slave state of Missouri, Kansas was the most likely of the new territories to support slavery. As a result, both southerners and antislavery northerners began an intensive drive to recruit settlers and establish a majority there.

As pro-slavery residents of Missouri poured into Kansas, antislavery organizations funded and armed their own migrants. In March 1855, pro-slavery forces, relying on the ineligible votes of Missouri residents, fraudulently elected a territorial legislature. This legislature promptly passed a series of harsh measures, including a law mandating the death penalty for aiding a fugitive slave and another making it a felony to question

> **Kansas-Nebraska Act** Law passed in 1854 creating the Kansas and Nebraska Territories but leaving the question of slavery open to residents, thereby repealing the Missouri Compromise.

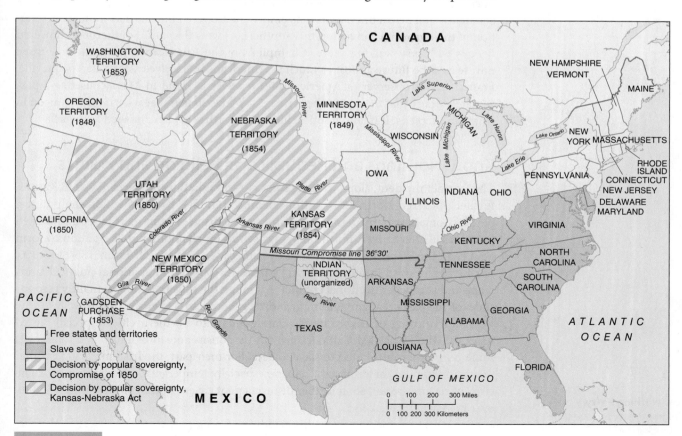

MAP 14.2 THE KANSAS-NEBRASKA ACT, 1854 The Kansas-Nebraska Act of 1854, which divided the Nebraska Territory in two and repealed the Missouri Compromise, reopened the incendiary issue of slavery in the territories.

slaveholding in Kansas. For good measure, the pro-slavery majority expelled the few free-staters elected to the assembly. In response, free-staters established their own government in Topeka and vowed to make Kansas white.

A sporadic civil war erupted in Kansas in November 1855 and reached a climax in the spring of 1856. Journalists dubbed the conflict "**Bleeding Kansas.**" On May 21, a group of pro-slavery officials attacked the free-state stronghold of Lawrence, subjecting it to a heavy artillery barrage. No one was killed, but the town suffered substantial damage. Eastern newspapers, exaggerating the incident, called it "the sack of Lawrence." Three days later, antislavery agitator John Brown, originally from Connecticut, went with several sympathizers to Pottawatomie Creek south of Lawrence in search of pro-slavery settlers. Armed with razor-sharp broadswords, they split the skulls and hacked the bodies of five men.

The memory of the failed revolutions in Europe remained fresh in the minds of Americans concerned about their own fragile democratic institutions. The disintegration of law and order on the Plains brought a foreboding recognition to many Americans. Indiana congressman Schuyler Colfax compared the Kansas territorial legislature's pro-slavery statutes, "dictated and enacted by usurpers and tyrants," to Louis Napoleon's wresting of democracy from the French people and confirming his office with a fraudulent plebiscite. The double outrage of a fraudulent election followed by severe legislation resembled more the despotism of restored regimes in Europe than the extension of American democracy.

Kansans were not the only Americans bleeding over slavery. Five days before the "sack of Lawrence," Massachusetts senator Charles Sumner delivered a long-winded diatribe, "The Crime Against Kansas," full of personal insults against several southerners, especially elderly South Carolina senator Andrew P. Butler. Two days after Sumner's outburst, and a day after the story of the sack of Lawrence appeared in the newspapers, Butler's cousin, South Carolina congressman Preston Brooks, entered the mostly vacant Senate chamber, where Sumner sat working on a speech. Seeking to defend his cousin's honor, Brooks raised his walking cane and beat Sumner over the head. Bloody and unconscious, the senator slumped to the floor. He recovered but did not return to the Senate for more than three years. His empty chair offered northerners' mute confirmation of their growing conviction that southerners were despotic. Southerners showered Brooks with new walking canes. Champions of the American experiment in Europe now feared the future almost as much as Americans themselves. Alexis de Tocqueville, France's sharp observer of American life, wrote to a friend in Massachusetts, "I passionately desire that the great experience of *self-government* that is currently going on in America succeeds. If it fails, political liberty on earth would be finished for ever."

Know-Nothings and Republicans: Religion and Politics

The Sumner incident, along with the Kansas-Nebraska Bill and the civil war in Kansas, further polarized North and South, widening sectional divisions within the political parties. Some northern Democrats distanced themselves from their party and looked for political alternatives; northern Whigs seized on changing public opinion to form new coalitions; and free-soil advocates gained new adherents. From 1854 to 1856, northerners moved into new political parties that altered the national political landscape and sharpened sectional conflict. Although the slavery issue was mainly responsible for the party realignment in the North, other factors played a role as well.

The crowding of Irish Catholic immigrants into northern cities especially irked nativists, who associated Catholicism with despotism and immorality, the same evils some northerners attributed to slaveholders. For their part, the Irish made it clear that they had little use for Protestant reform, especially temperance and abolitionism. The clash of cultures would soon further disturb a political environment increasingly in flux over the slavery issue.

New parties emerged from this cauldron of religious, ethnic, and sectional strife. Anti-immigrant, anti-Catholic sentiment gave rise to the **Know-Nothing Party,** which began as a secret organization in July 1854. Its name derived from the reply that members

Gangs of New York. Paramilitary political gangs were not an invention of the Reconstruction-era South. Throughout (mostly northern) cities, groups of street gangs, affiliated with rival political parties and divided by religious differences, clashed. On July 4, 1857, the "Bowery Bhoys" supporters of the Know-Nothings, fought a pitched battle with their Irish Catholic adversaries, the "Dead Rabbits," who favored the city's Democratic mayor, Fernando Wood. The frequency of political and sectarian violence in the nation's growing cities troubled many Americans in the 1850s.

gave when asked about the party: "I know nothing." Although strongest in the North, Know-Nothing chapters blossomed in several southern cities that had experienced some immigration since 1848, among them Richmond, Louisville, New Orleans, and Savannah. The party's members in both North and South were mostly former Whigs. In addition to their biases against Catholics and foreigners, the Know-Nothings shared a fear that the slavery issue could destroy the Union. But because attempts to solve the issue seemed only to increase sectional tensions, the Know-Nothings hoped to ignore it.

Know-Nothing candidates fared surprisingly well in local and congressional elections during the fall of 1854, carrying 63 percent of the statewide vote in Massachusetts and making strong showings in New York and Pennsylvania. In office, Know-Nothings achieved some notable reforms. In Massachusetts, where they pursued an agenda similar to that of the Whigs in earlier years, they secured administrative reforms and supported public health and public education programs.

The Know-Nothings' anti-Catholicism, however, overshadowed their reform agenda. In several states and cities, they passed legislation barring Catholics from public office and unsuccessfully sought to increase the time required for an immigrant to become a citizen from one year to twenty-one years. The Know-Nothings also fostered anti-Catholic violence, such as the bloody election day riot that erupted in Louisville, Kentucky, in 1855.

Ethnic and religious bigotry were weak links to hold together a national party. Southern and northern Know-Nothings fell to quarreling over slavery despite their vow to avoid it, and the party split. Many northern Know-Nothings soon found a congenial home in the new **Republican Party.** The Republican Party formed in the summer of 1854 from a coalition of antislavery Conscience Whigs and Democrats disgusted with the Pierce administration's Kansas policy. Like the Know-Nothings, the Republicans advocated strong state and federal governments to promote economic and social reforms. But the new party rarely openly espoused the Know-Nothings' anti-Catholic and anti-immigrant positions. The overriding bond among Republicans was their opposition to the extension of slavery in the territories.

Reflecting its opposition to slavery, the Republican Party was an anti-southern sectional party. Northern Whig merchants and entrepreneurs who joined the party were impatient with southern obstruction in Congress of federal programs for economic development, such as a transcontinental railroad, harbor and river improvements, and high tariffs to protect American industries (located mostly in the North) from foreign competition. In a bid to keep slavery out of the territories, the Republicans favored

Republican Party Party that emerged in the 1850s in the aftermath of the bitter controversy over the Kansas-Nebraska Act, consisting of former Whigs, some northern Democrats, and many Know-Nothings.

383

limiting homesteads in the West to 160 acres. Not incidentally, populating the territories with northern whites would ensure a western base for the new party.

Heightened sectional animosity laced with religious and ethnic prejudice fueled the emergence of new parties and the weakening of old political affiliations in the early 1850s. Accompanying the political realignment were diverging views on the proper role of government. As the nation prepared for the presidential election of 1856, the Democrats had become a party top-heavy with southerners; the Know-Nothings splintered along sectional lines; some Whigs remained active under the old party name, mainly on the state and local levels in North and South; and the Republican Party was becoming an important political force in the North and, to southerners, the embodiment of evil. (See From Then to Now, Religion, Politics, and Political Parties.)

The Election of 1856

The presidential election of 1856 proved to be one of the strangest in American history. The Know-Nothings and the Republicans faced a national electorate for the first time while the Democrats were deeply divided over the Kansas issue.

The upstart Republicans held their convention in Philadelphia in mid-July. The platform condemned the "twin relics of barbarism"—slavery and polygamy. There was no epidemic, current or pending, of men and women seeking multiple partners. But, as everyone understood at the time, the Mormons in Utah Territory espoused, though did not require, polygamy. Memories of Mormon settlements in the Midwest and the turmoil they generated remained fresh in the minds of residents in a region where Republicans hoped to pick up significant support. Although anti-southern sentiment varied, few voters were sympathetic to the Mormons.

The Republicans passed over their most likely candidate, the New York senator and former Whig William H. Seward. Instead, they followed a tried-and-true Whig precedent and nominated a military hero, John C. Frémont, a handsome, dark-haired soldier of medium height and medium intelligence. His wife, Jessie Benton, the daughter of Missouri senator Thomas Hart Benton, was his greatest asset. In effect, she ran the campaign and wisely encouraged her husband to remain silent. The Know-Nothings split into "South Americans" and "North Americans." The South Americans nominated Millard Fillmore, although he was not a Know-Nothing. The North Americans eventually and reluctantly embraced Frémont, despite the widespread but mistaken belief that he was a Roman Catholic.

The Democrats, facing a northern revolt and southern opposition to any candidate who did not support the extension of slavery, turned to Pennsylvania's James Buchanan whose greatest virtue was that he had been out of the country the previous four years as ambassador to Great Britain. Southerners accepted him as electable and sensitive to slavery. Northern Democrats hoped for the best. Tall and white-haired, he exuded the air of experience, though he looked like a "well-preserved mummy." Whether he would preside over the nation as a competent veteran or as a cadaver well beyond his time remained to be seen.

Democratic Party strategy in the North focused on shoring up their immigrant base by connecting the Republicans to the Know-Nothings and simultaneously appealing to evangelical Protestants by intimating that Frémont had received a Catholic education, had studied for the priesthood, or was himself a Roman Catholic secretly attending mass and "going through all the crosses and gyrations, and eating wafers," take your pick.

The importance of evangelical imagery in the political campaigns of the major parties was especially evident among the Republicans. A minister supporting the Republican ticket saw the election as "as a decisive struggle . . . between freedom and Slavery, truth and falsehood, justice and oppression, God and the devil."

Away from the pulpit, Republican campaigners sometimes found tough going in the North, indicating how much the slavery extension debate had overtaken sectarian issues. A portion of the northern electorate viewed the Republican Party as a gilded version of the radical antislavery parties of the 1840s, promoting racial equality and emancipation to the detriment of whites.

From Then to Now
Religion, Politics, and Political Parties

T he Republican Party presented a dilemma for Carl Schurz. Schurz and his family came to America in 1852 as part of the wave of German migration in the aftermath of the failed revolutions of 1852. Like many Germans, Schurz was adamantly antislavery: "Such a contradiction is that between liberty, founded upon the natural rights of man, and slavery, founded upon usurpation; between democracy, which is the life-element of our Federal Constitution, and privilege, which is the life-element of the slaveholding system and of Southern society."

Yet, the Republican Party included elements from the Know-Nothing movement that were openly hostile to immigrants. Although Schurz was a Protestant, he objected strongly to attacks on Roman Catholic immigrants. American political parties include people of diverse views. It is almost an art form to balance sometimes conflicting opinions in order to cast as broad a net as possible to win elections. Winning is more important than ideological purity. In its 1860 platform, the Republican Party barely mentioned immigration. Instead, it adopted a strong antislavery plank and promised an active government to enhance economic development. Schurz's political journey to the Republican Party was, he felt, a natural extension of his revolutionary activity in Germany on behalf of representative government. He went on to serve in the Civil War and in President Ulysses Grant's cabinet as secretary of the interior.

Sidestepping divisive issues is a common practice during election years. True, a party must energize its base, but it cannot win solely on that constituency. The Republican Party of the 1850s welcomed anti-immigrant and anti-Catholic voters from the defunct Know-Nothing Party, but they did not publicly promote their views. And, in fact, some party leaders, Lincoln in particular, abhorred the religious bigotry of some northern evangelicals.

The Republican welcome mat for evangelicals has persisted into the twenty-first century. Though not all evangelicals are Republican today, many evangelical activists support the party, as they support public policies that would codify their religious views into law. As in the 1850s, today's party leaders have welcomed these activists, though they have been reluctant to promote their views until recently for the same reasons that the original Republicans avoided alienating a portion of the northern electorate.

Evangelicals today face the same quandary between ideological purity and political pragmatism. Just as Carl Schurz swallowed his concerns about the Republicans' anti-immigrant policies, evangelicals have often supported candidates who have not professed open support for their programs. As late as 1972, the Republican Party platform did not contain a single reference to God.

But as challenges to traditional morality and authority mounted, culminating with the U.S. Supreme Court's decision in *Roe v. Wade* (1973) to legalize abortion, the balance between religion and politics within the Republican Party began to shift in favor of a merger, especially as evangelicals increased in strength, financing, and organization. The 2012 Republican Party platform contained ten references to God, nineteen references to faith, and the first reference ever to a "war on religion." The platform also accused "liberal elites" of trying to "drive religious beliefs—and religious believers—out of the public square." The outcome of the 2012 presidential election indicated that such candor likely narrowed rather than expanded the party's appeal.

Question for Discussion

- Although evangelicals have always found a welcome home in the Republican Party, why only recently have party officials openly embraced evangelical causes?

Activists display a representation of the Ten Commandments October 2003 during a rally at the West Lawn of the U.S. Capitol in Washington, DC. Christian activists gathered on Capitol Hill as the last stop of a five-state rally tour.

A nativist newspaper, 1852, with a front page along with a cartoon where immigrants wave placards declaring their allegiance to the pope and U.S. citizens counter with banners warning of "foreign influence." The nativist program outlined below the cartoon became the platform of the Know-Nothing Party.

James Buchanan emerged victorious. The only national party had won a national election. The Democrats did it by holding the lower North as Pennsylvania, New Jersey, Illinois, Indiana, and California voted for Buchanan, and sweeping the Lower South. But "Old Buck's" victory was narrow in these northern states; the Republicans performed remarkably well considering it was the first time they had fielded a presidential candidate. They had achieved a "victorious defeat," making Buchanan the first candidate to win without carrying the North since 1828. Republicans eagerly looked forward to the next presidential contest and the good prospects of prying at least Pennsylvania, Indiana, and Illinois from the Democratic column. For the first time ever, an avowedly antislavery party had carried eleven free states.

The South had not yet lapsed into one-party politics. Millard Fillmore garnered 40 percent of the popular vote in the South, but won only the state of Maryland. He fared poorly in the Lower South. The states that had the greatest stake in the slave economy voted solidly Democratic.

Buchanan, who brought more than a generation of political experience to the presidency, would need every bit and more. He had scarcely settled into office when two major crises confronted him: a Supreme Court decision that challenged the right of Congress to regulate slavery in the territories and renewed conflict over Kansas.

The *Dred Scott* Case

Dred Scott was a slave owned by an army surgeon based in Missouri. In the 1830s and early 1840s, he had traveled with his master to the state of Illinois and the Wisconsin Territory before returning to Missouri. In 1846, Scott sued his master's widow for freedom on the grounds that the laws of Illinois and the Wisconsin Territory barred slavery. After a series of appeals, the case reached the Supreme Court. Chief Justice Roger Taney of Maryland, joined by five other justices of the nine-member Supreme Court (five of whom came from slave states), dismissed Scott's suit two days after Buchanan's inauguration in March 1857.

Taney's opinion contained two bombshells. First, using dubious logic and failing to take into account the status of African Americans in several northern states, he argued that black people were not citizens of the United States. Because Scott was not a citizen, he could not sue. In reaching this conclusion, Taney noted that the framers of the Constitution had never intended citizenship for slaves. The framers, according to Taney, respected a long-standing view that slaves were "beings of an inferior order . . . so far inferior that they had no rights which the white man was bound to respect."

Second, Taney held that even if Scott had standing in Court, his residence in the Wisconsin Territory did not make him a free man. This was because the Missouri Compromise, which was still in effect in the 1840s, was, in Taney's view, unconstitutional. (The Wisconsin Territory lay above the compromise line.) The compromise, the chief justice explained, deprived citizens of their property (slaves) without the due process of law granted by the Fifth Amendment to the U.S. Constitution. In effect, Taney ruled that Congress could not bar slavery from the territories.

Dred Scott decision Supreme Court ruling, in a lawsuit brought by Dred Scott, a slave demanding his freedom based on his residence in a free state and a free territory with his master, that slaves could not be U.S. citizens and that Congress had no jurisdiction over slavery in the territories.

The **Dred Scott** decision was especially unsettling to the tens of thousands of free blacks throughout the country, particularly in the South. The Court, in stripping their citizenship, made them vulnerable to reenslavement or expulsion. The case also accelerated restrictions on the southern free black population as its legal recourse vanished with the decision. Several cities, including Charleston, experimented with requirements that free blacks purchase and wear badges identifying them as free.

For African Americans, the enemy was no longer the slaveholder, but the very government from which they had hoped for redress. The decision also shocked Republicans. The right of Congress to ban slavery from the territories, which Taney had apparently voided, was one of the party's central tenets. Republicans responded by ignoring the implications of the decision for the territories while promising to abide by it so far as it affected Dred Scott himself. Once in office, Republicans vowed they would seek a reversal. This position allowed them to attack the decision without appearing to defy the law.

Dred Scott and his wife, Harriet, are portrayed here with their children as an average middle-class family, an image that fueled northern opposition to the Supreme Court's 1857 decision that denied Scott's freedom and citizenship

The *Dred Scott* decision boosted Republican fortunes in the North even as it seemed to undercut the party. Fears of a southern Slave Power conspiracy now seemed ever more justified. If Congress could not ban slavery from the territories, Republicans asked, how secure was the right of states to ban slavery within their borders? A small group of slaveholders, they charged, was holding nonslaveholding white people hostage to the institution of slavery.

The Lecompton Constitution

Establishing a legitimate government in Kansas was the second major issue to bedevil the Buchanan administration. The president made a good start, sending his friend and fellow Pennsylvanian Robert Walker (then a resident of Mississippi) to Kansas as territorial governor to oversee the election of a constitutional convention in June 1857. Walker, though sickly, was a man of integrity.

The violence had subsided in Kansas, and prospects had grown for a peaceful settlement. But free-staters, fearing that the slavery forces planned to stuff the ballot box with fraudulent votes, announced a boycott of the June election. As a result, pro-slavery forces dominated the constitutional convention, which was held in Lecompton. And

Lecompton Constitution
Pro-slavery draft written in 1857 by Kansas territorial delegates elected under questionable circumstances; it was rejected by two governors, supported by President Buchanan, and decisively defeated by Congress.

Panic of 1857 Banking crisis that caused a credit crunch in the North; it was less severe in the South, where high cotton prices spurred a quick recovery.

Walker, although a slaveholder, let it be known that he thought Kansas would never be a slave state. He thus put himself at odds with pro-slavery residents from the outset.

Walker persuaded the free-staters to vote in October to elect a new territorial legislature. The returns gave the pro-slavery forces a narrow victory, but Walker discovered irregularities. In McGee, Kansas, twenty voters somehow had cast 1,200 votes for pro-slavery candidates. And in Oxford, a community of a mere six houses, 1,601 names appeared on the voting rolls, all in the same handwriting and all copied from the Cincinnati city directory. Walker threw out these returns, and the free-staters took control of the territorial legislature for the first time.

Undeterred, the pro-slavery forces drafted a pro-slavery constitution at the constitutional convention in Lecompton. Buchanan, who had promised southerners a pro-slavery government in Kansas, dismissed Walker before he could rule on the **Lecompton Constitution,** then ignored the recommendation of Walker's successor that he reject it. He submitted the Lecompton Constitution to the Senate for approval even though it clearly sidestepped the popular sovereignty requirement of the Kansas-Nebraska Act.

Like the Kansas-Nebraska Act, the Lecompton Constitution outraged many northerners. Northern Democrats facing reelection refused to support a president of their own party, and, though the constitution passed in the Senate, Democratic opposition killed it in the House. Among Lecompton's opponents was Stephen A. Douglas, who justified his vote with an impassioned defense of popular sovereignty, which the president and pro-slavery Kansans had openly defied. Congress would eventually admit Kansas to the Union as a free state in January 1861.

Douglas knew that the *Dred Scott* decision and Buchanan's support of the Lecompton Constitution would help the Republicans and hurt him and his fellow northern Democrats in the 1858 congressional elections. The **Panic of 1857,** a severe economic recession that lingered into 1858, also worked to the advantage of the Republicans.

The Democratic administration did nothing as unemployment rose; starvation stalked the streets of northern cities, and homeless women and children begged for food and shelter. Republicans claimed that government intervention, specifically, Republican-sponsored legislation to raise certain tariffs, give western land to homesteaders, and fund transportation projects, if passed by Congress, could have prevented the panic. The Democrats' inaction, they said, reflected the southern Slave Power's insensitivity to northern workers.

Southerners disagreed. The panic had scarcely touched them. Cotton prices were high, and few southern banks failed. Cotton seemed indeed to be king. The financial crisis in the North reinforced the southern belief that northern society was corrupt and greedy. The Republicans' proposed legislative remedies, in their view, would enrich the North and beggar the South.

The Religious Revival of 1857–1858

In the midst of economic depression and sectional controversy, a religious revival swept across the nation's cities in the winter of 1857–1858. Beginning with lunchtime prayer meetings among businessmen in New York City, the phenomenon spread throughout the country, though concentrating in the larger urban centers of the Northeast. The sectional crisis and the economic downturn had a part in bringing urban middle-class men into churches and meeting halls at the noon hour, but the gatherings emphasized prayer and personal reflection, avoiding political discussion and focusing on individual redemption. Sectional strife had diverted attention from personal salvation, and the financial panic served as a reminder that wealth and possessions could be fleeting, but the soul was everlasting. Ministers and lay leaders of the movement encouraged men to turn away from the reform "isms" of the era—feminism, abolitionism, and socialism among them. Men, they suggested, should not worship secular ideologies, but should make the Bible the foundation of their behavior and thought. And they should reestablish their leadership both in spiritual and family matters.

Religion provided not only solace but also explanations for a time beset by increasing uncertainty. The revival did not change society dramatically any more than it pulled the nation out of the economic doldrums. But now with each turn in the political arena many more people, not only the fervent evangelicals, came to understand that these mere events held transcendent meaning.

Some feared that the growing integration of religion and politics could harm the nation's religious life and burden the political process with sharper divisions than were necessary. But by 1858, it became increasingly difficult to distinguish the political from the spiritual. The Illinois senatorial contest between Democrat Stephen A. Douglas and Abraham Lincoln of the Republican Party proved a case in point. Their debates underscored the moral dimensions of political questions and the resulting difficulties of effecting compromises.

The Lincoln-Douglas Debates

Douglas faced a forceful opponent in his 1858 reelection campaign. The Republicans had nominated Abraham Lincoln, a 49-year-old lawyer and former Whig congressman. The Kentucky-born Lincoln had risen from modest circumstances to become a prosperous lawyer in the Illinois state capital of Springfield. His marriage to wealthy and well-connected Mary Todd helped both his law practice and his pocketbook. After one term in Congress from 1847 to 1849, he returned to his law practice but maintained his interest in politics. Strongly opposed to the extension of slavery into the territories, he considered joining the Republican Party after the passage of the Kansas-Nebraska Act. Lincoln had developed a reputation as an excellent stump speaker with a homespun sense of humor, a quick wit, and a self-deprecating style that fit well with the small-town residents and farmers who composed the majority of the Illinois electorate.

But substance counted more than style with Illinois voters. Most of them opposed the extension of slavery into the territories, although generally not out of concern for the slaves. Illinois residents, like most northerners, wanted to keep the territories free for white people. Few voters would support dissolving the Union over the slavery issue. Douglas, who knew his constituents well, branded Lincoln a dangerous radical for warning, in a biblical paraphrase, that the United States, like "a house divided against itself," could not "endure permanently half slave and half free."

Lincoln could not allow the charge of radicalism to go unanswered. Little known beyond the Springfield area, he had to find a way to gain greater exposure. So, in July 1858, he challenged Douglas to a series of debates across the state. Douglas was reluctant to provide exposure for his lesser-known opponent, but he could not reject Lincoln's offer outright, lest voters think he was dodging his challenger. He agreed to debates in seven of the state's nine congressional districts.

The **Lincoln-Douglas debates** were a defining event in American politics. Farmers rode into such market towns as Ottawa, Galesburg, Alton, and Freeport, bringing their families and picnic baskets. They settled in their wagons or on the ground under trees to hear the two great debaters confront each other on the most troubling issue of the day. What a sight it must have been, the stubby-legged, animated, barrel-chested Little Giant engaging the gangly, deliberate former rail-splitter, Abe Lincoln.

For Douglas, slavery was not a moral issue. What mattered was what white people wanted. If they wanted slavery, fine; if they did not, fine also. Lincoln and many Republicans had a very different view. For them, slavery was a moral issue. As such, it was independent of what the residents of a territory wanted.

Lincoln framed the debate as a contest between good and evil. Evangelical rhetoric had pervaded political discourse for nearly two decades. But coming on the heels of a national religious revival, Lincoln's assertion reinforced the perception that the nation was approaching a crossroads, not only a secular divide, but a battle that could determine the future of mankind for eternity: "As I view the contest, it is not less than a contest for the advancement of the kingdom of Heaven or the kingdom of Satan." The difficulty with raising the stakes of an election so high is that it threatened to polarize the electorate so that one side or the other could find the results of a democratic election totally unacceptable. For how do you compromise with the devil?

Lincoln tempered his moralism with practical politics. He took care to distance himself from the abolitionists, asserting that he abided by the Constitution and did not seek to

Lincoln-Douglas debates Series of debates in the 1858 Illinois senatorial campaign during which Democrat Stephen A. Douglas and Republican Abraham Lincoln staked out their differing opinions on the issue of slavery in the territories.

interfere in places where slavery existed. At Charleston, Illinois, the site of the fourth debate, Lincoln stated, "I am not, nor ever have been, in favor of bringing about in any way the social and political equality of the white and black race, that I am not nor ever have been in favor of making voters or jurors of negroes, nor of qualifying them to hold office, nor to intermarry with white people; and I will say in addition to this that there is a physical difference between the white and black races which I believe will forever forbid the two races living together on terms of social and political equality." Historians have pondered over the seeming contradictions between these remarks and the statements he made during other debates and would make in the coming years on slavery and African Americans generally.

Lincoln, like most Republicans, hated the institution of slavery, but held ambivalent views about African Americans. These views would change in time, sometimes prodded by events, other times by thought and prayer. About slavery, there was little ambiguity in his position, even if he tried to project a moderate image on the campaign trail. Privately, he hoped for its demise. To Lincoln, slavery was immoral, but inequality was not. The Republican Party was antislavery, but it did not advocate racial equality.

Illinois voters retained a narrow Democratic majority in the state legislature, which reelected Douglas to the U.S. Senate. (State legislatures elected senators until 1913, when the Seventeenth Amendment provided for direct election by the people.) But Douglas alienated southern Democrats with his strong defense of popular sovereignty and lost whatever hope he had of becoming the standard-bearer of a united Democratic Party in 1860. Lincoln lost the senatorial contest but won national respect and recognition.

Despite Lincoln's defeat in Illinois, the Republicans made a strong showing in the 1858 congressional elections across the North. The increased Republican presence and the sharpening sectional divisions among Democrats portended a bitter debate over slavery in the new Congress. Americans, more than ever before, were viewing issues and each other in sectional terms. *Northern* and *southern* took on meanings that expressed a great deal more than geography.

The Road to Disunion

14.3 How did the elevation of slavery to a moral issue polarize North and South during the 1850s?

The unsatisfying Compromise of 1850, "Bleeding Kansas" and "Bleeding Sumner," the *Dred Scott* case, and Lecompton convinced many northerners that southerners were conspiring with the federal government to restrict their political and economic liberties. Southerners saw these same events as evidence of a northern conspiracy to reduce the South's political and economic influence. There were no conspiracies, but with so little goodwill on either side, hostility predominated. Slavery, above all, accounted for the growing divide.

In 1859 abolitionist John Brown, who had avenged the "sack of Lawrence" in 1856, led a raid against a federal arsenal at Harpers Ferry, Virginia, in the vain hope of sparking a slave revolt. This event brought the frustrations of both sides of the sectional conflict to a head. The presidential election campaign of 1860 began before the uproar over the raid had subsided. In the course of that contest, one of the last nationally unifying institutions, the Democratic Party, broke apart. The election of Abraham Lincoln, a sectional candidate, triggered a crisis that defied peaceful resolution.

Although the crisis spiraled into a civil war, this outcome did not signal the triumph of sectionalism over nationalism. Ironically, in defending their stands, both sides appealed to time-honored nationalist and democratic sentiments. Southern secessionists believed they were the true keepers of the ideals that had inspired the American Revolution. They were merely re-creating a more perfect Union. It was not they, but the Republicans, who had sundered the old Union by subverting the Constitution's guarantee of liberty. Lincoln similarly appealed to nationalist themes, telling northerners that the United States was "the last best hope on earth."

Northerners and southerners both appealed to nationalism and democracy but applied different meanings to these concepts. The differences underscored how far apart the sections had grown. When southerners and northerners looked at each other, they no longer saw fellow Americans; they saw enemies. The reason was slavery.

Slavery and its corollary, white supremacy, lay at the core of the sectional crisis that prompted secession and the bloody civil war that followed. For many white southerners, the journey from the ideals of the American Revolution led naturally to a Slave Republic: Enslavement of blacks guaranteed the freedom and equality of whites. Many northerners believed that slavery represented a tragic detour from the nation's founding principles, especially as articulated in the Declaration of Independence. Contemporaries understood that these fundamentally different views of slavery led directly to the breakup of the Union.

North-South Differences

Slavery accounted for or played a role in creating distinctions between North and South that transcended their shared heritage.

Economic Differences. Behind the ideological divide that separated North and South lay real and growing social and economic differences (see Table 14.1). As the North became increasingly urban and industrial, the South remained primarily rural and agricultural. The urban population of the free states increased from 10 to 26 percent between 1820 and 1860. In the South, in the same period, it increased only from 5 to 10 percent. Likewise the proportion of the northern workforce in agriculture declined from 68 percent to 40 percent between 1800 and 1860, whereas in the South it increased from 82 percent to 84 percent. Northern farmers made up for the decline in farm workers by relying on machinery. In 1860, the free states had twice the value of farm machinery per worker as the slave states.

The demand for farm machinery in the North reflected the growing demand for manufactured products in general. The need of city dwellers for ready-to-wear shoes and clothing, household iron products, processed foods, homes, workplaces, and public amenities boosted industrial production in the North. In contrast, in the South, the slower rate of urbanization, the lower proportion of immigrants, and the region's labor-intensive agriculture kept industrial development modest. The proportion of U.S. manufacturing capital invested in the South declined from 31 to 16 percent between 1810 and 1860. In 1810, per capita investment in industrial enterprises was 2.5 times greater in the North than in the South; in 1860, it was 3.5 times greater.

The South and West had about the same levels of manufacturing investment and urban population in the 1850s, but the rate of growth was even greater in the West than in the North. What is more, a vast railroad network linked the West to the Northeast rather than to the South.

TABLE 14.1 SOUTH AND NORTH COMPARED IN 1860

	South	North
Population	Biracial; 35 percent African American	Overwhelmingly white; less than 2 percent African American
Economy	Growing, though relatively undiversified; 84 percent of workforce in agriculture	Developing through industrialization and urbanization; 40 percent of workforce in agriculture
Labor	Heavily dependent on slave labor, especially in the Lower South	Free wage labor
Factories	15 percent of national total	85 percent of national total; concentrated in the Northeast
Railroads	Approximately 10,000 miles of track; primarily shorter lines, with fewer links to trunk lines	Approximately 20,000 miles of track; more effectively linked in trunk lines connecting East and West
Literacy	17 percent illiteracy rate for free population	6 percent illiteracy rate

These economic developments generated communities of innovation in the North, especially in the rapidly expanding cities, where people traded ideas and technical information and skills. One of the most important innovations of the era was the telegraph, pioneered by Samuel F. B. Morse, who convinced the government to subsidize a line from Washington, DC, to Baltimore, Maryland, in 1843 and then electrified his patrons with instantaneous reports from the political party conventions of 1844. As information became a valuable currency for a new age, such improvements in communications and transportation tended to reinforce the economic dominance of the Northeast.

Social and Religious Differences. More subtle distinctions between North and South became evident as well by mid-century. The South had a high illiteracy rate, nearly three times greater than the North, eight times greater if black southerners are included. The "ideology of literacy," as one historian called it, was not as widespread in the South as in the North. Northerners, for example, supported far more public schools and libraries than southerners. In the South, education was barred by law to slaves and limited for most white people. Many white leaders viewed education more as a privilege for the well-to-do than a right for every citizen. A South Carolinian wrote in the 1850s that "it is better that a part should be fully and highly educated and the rest utterly ignorant."

Evangelical Protestantism attracted increasing numbers in both North and South, but its character differed in the two regions. In the North, evangelical Protestants viewed social reform as a prerequisite for the Second Coming of Christ. As a result, they were in the forefront of most reform movements. Southern evangelicals generally defended slavery.

The Effects of Slavery. Slavery permeated southern society. Investment in land and slaves limited investment in manufacturing and railroads. The availability of a large slave labor force reduced the need for farm machinery and limited the demand for manufactured products. Slaves were relatively immobile. They did not migrate to cities in massive numbers as did northern farmers. Nor could they quickly fill the labor demands of an expanding urban economy. Agriculture usually took precedence.

Slavery also divided northern from southern churches. And it accounted for the contrast between the inward, otherworldly emphasis of southern theology and the reformist theology of northern evangelicals. Southerners associated black slavery with white freedom; northerners associated it with white degradation.

Slavery contributed to the South's martial tradition and its lukewarm attitude toward public education. Fully 95 percent of the nation's black population lived in the South in 1860, and 90 percent of these were slaves. As a result, the South was often a region on edge. Fearful of revolt, especially in the 1850s, when rumors of slave discontent ran rampant, white people felt compelled to maintain patrols and militias in constant readiness. The South was also determined to keep slaves as ignorant as possible. Educated slaves would be susceptible to abolitionist propaganda and more inclined to revolt.

The South's defense of slavery and the North's attack on it fostered an array of stereotypes that exaggerated the real differences between the sections. Like all stereotypes, these reduced individuals to dehumanized categories. They encouraged the people of each section to view those of the other less as fellow Americans than as aliens in their midst.

Ironically, although slavery increasingly defined the character of the South in the 1850s, a growing majority of white southerners did not own slaves. Slavery nonetheless implicated nonslaveholders in ways that ensured their support for it. By satisfying the demand for labor on large plantations, it relieved many rural white southerners from serving as farmhands and enabled them to work their own land. Slaveholders also recruited nonslaveholders to suppress slave violence or rebellion. It was nonslaveholders, for example, who often manned patrols and militia companies. Some nonslaveholders hoped to purchase slaves someday. Many dreamed of migrating westward to the next cotton frontier where they might find greater opportunity to own land and slaves. This dream not only bound white southerners together on slavery but also prompted their strong support for southern access to the western territories. Finally, regardless of a white man's social or economic status, he shared an important feature

Explore the Sectional Crisis on MyHistoryLab

HOW DID THE NATION INCREASINGLY FRACTURE DURING THE SECTIONAL CRISIS?

Between 1790 and 1860, the ever-expanding United States saw dramatic changes in its population. The Missouri Compromise of 1820 evaded dealing with the explosive issue of slavery by allowing future southern states to permit slavery and banning its expansion in future northern states. As states were admitted across the South, slavery expanded westward. Enslaved African Americans came to make up significant portions of the total populations of states from the Atlantic coast to Texas. In the North, however, slavery had been gradually banned and industrialization boomed across the region. As the 1860 presidential election neared, the United States found itself ever more divided between North and South, a division centered on slavery.

ABOLITION FROWNED DOWN.

When abolitionists petitioned the House of Representatives to curtail and eliminate slavery, pro-slavery congressmen responded with a series of gag rules, such as the Pinckney Resolutions of 1836 and the Twenty-first Rule of 1840, to prevent anti-slavery petitions from being read.

SLAVES AS TOTAL POPULATION PERCENTAGE IN SLAVEHOLDING STATES

State	Percent
Alabama	45%
Arkansas	26%
Delaware	2%
Florida	44%
Georgia	44%
Kentucky	20%
Louisiana	47%
Maryland	13%
Mississippi	55%
Missouri	10%
North Carolina	33%
South Carolina	57%
Tennessee	25%
Texas	30%
Virginia	31%

SOURCE: The Civil War Home Page, http://www.civil-war.net/pages/1860_census.html. Created 1997.

KEY QUESTIONS Use **MyHistoryLab** *Explorer* to **answer** these **questions:**

Comparison ▶▶▶ *How did the demographics of the North differ from those of the South?*

Explore the populations of the two regions based on census results.

Consequence ▶▶▶ *What impact did slavery have on immigration to the South?*

Map the percentage of foreign-born immigrants in the United States.

Analysis ▶▶▶ *In what areas did more people live in towns and cities during this time?*

Theorize what effects differences in levels of urban population had on area economies.

with the largest slaveholder: As long as racial slavery existed, the color of his skin made him a member of a privileged class that could never be enslaved.

While white southerners were more united on slavery than on other issues, their defense of slavery presented them with a major dilemma. By the 1850s, most Western nations had condemned and abolished the institution. And because northerners controlled the flow of information through the popular newspapers and the national network of communications, credit, and commerce, southerners were likely to find themselves increasingly isolated. A minority in their own country and a lonely voice for a despised institution that was for them a significant source of wealth, southerners were understandably jittery.

John Brown's Raid

Shortly after he completed his mayhem at Pottawatomie Creek, John Brown left Kansas and approached several New England abolitionists for funds to continue his private war in the territory. By 1857, Brown had become a rustic celebrity in New England. He had dined at Ralph Waldo Emerson's home, had tea with Henry David Thoreau, and discussed theology with the abolitionist minister Theodore Dwight Weld. Brown's frontier dress, rigid posture, reticent manner, and piercing eyes gave him the appearance of a biblical prophet.

When Brown returned to Kansas in late 1857, he discovered that peace had settled over that troubled territory. Residents now cared more about making money than about making war. Leaving Kansas for the last time, he went east with a new plan. He proposed to attack and capture the federal arsenal at Harpers Ferry, Virginia, a small town near the Maryland border. The assault, Brown imagined, would spark a slave uprising that would eventually spread to the rest of the state. With funds from his New England friends, he equipped a few dozen men and hired an English army officer to train them.

Brown and his "army" moved to a Maryland farmhouse in the summer of 1859 to train and complete planning for the raid. On the night of October 16, 1859, he and

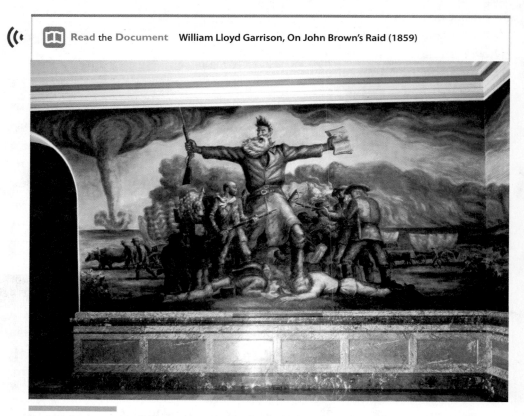

(((•   📖 Read the Document   William Lloyd Garrison, On John Brown's Raid (1859)

The John Brown mural in the Kansas State House demonstrates the connection between history and memory as much as artistic license. The artist depicts Brown as a crazed patriarch with a rifle in one hand and a Bible in the other while standing on slain corpses. In the background, Confederate and Union troops battle. In reality, the Kansas Brown was clean-shaven and the Civil War began more than a year after Brown's death. The artist makes the dubious claim that the civil war in Kansas led directly to the larger conflict.

twenty-two followers captured the federal arsenal at Harpers Ferry and waited for the slaves to rally to his banner. Meanwhile, the townspeople alerted outside authorities. The Virginia militia and a detachment of U.S. Marines under the command of Colonel Robert E. Lee arrived and put a quick end to **John Brown's Raid.** They wounded Brown and killed or captured most of his force.

Brown had launched the operation without provisions and at a site from which escape was impossible. Although the primary goal of the attack had been to inspire a slave insurrection, no one had bothered to inform the local slaves. And despite the secret nature of the expedition, Brown had left behind a mountain of documents at the Maryland farmhouse. Was he crazy? As the *Boston Post* editorialized after the raid, "John Brown may be a lunatic, [but if so] then one-fourth of the people of Massachusetts are madmen."

Although the *Post* may have exaggerated, the editorial reflected an article of faith among many abolitionists that, given the signal, slaves would immediately throw off their chains, slaughter their masters, and join a rebellion. But even those slaves in the area who knew of the raid understood the odds against Brown and had the good sense not to join him. As Abraham Lincoln observed, "It was not a slave insurrection. It was an attempt by white men to get up a revolt among slaves, in which the slaves refused to participate."

The raid, though foolish and unsuccessful, played on southerners' worst fears of slave rebellion, adding a new dimension: Here was an attack engineered not from within the South but from the North. Some southern white people may have dismissed the ability or even the desire of slaves to mount revolts on their own, but they less easily dismissed the potential impact of outside white agitators. The state of Virginia tried Brown on the charge of treason to the state. Brown, recovering from his wounds, attended most of the trial on a stretcher. The trial was swift but fair. The jury sentenced Brown to hang. Throughout his brief imprisonment and trial, Brown maintained a quiet dignity that impressed even his jailers. The governor of Virginia spoke admiringly of him as "a man of clear head, of courage, fortitude, and simple ingenuousness." Speaking to the court after his sentencing, Brown asserted that he was God's agent in a holy war: "I believe that to have interfered as I have done . . . in behalf of [God's] despised poor, is no wrong, but right. Now, if it is deemed necessary that I should forfeit my life for the furtherance of the ends of justice, and mingle my blood further with the blood of my children and with the blood of millions in this slave country whose rights are disregarded by wicked, cruel, and unjust enactments, I say, let it be done."

The outpouring of northern grief over Brown's death convinced white southerners that the threat to their security was not over. The discovery of Brown's correspondence at his Maryland farmhouse further fueled southern rancor, and southerners increasingly ceased to believe northern disclaimers about the raid. John Brown's Raid significantly changed southern public opinion. However much they defended slavery, most southerners were for the Union. The northern reaction to John Brown's trial and death, however, troubled them. The *Richmond Whig,* a newspaper that reflected moderate Upper South opinion, observed in early 1860, "recent events have wrought almost a complete revolution in the sentiments, the thoughts, the hopes, of the oldest and steadiest conservatives in all the southern states. . . . There are thousands upon . . . thousands of men in our midst who, a month ago, scoffed at the idea of a dissolution of the Union as a madman's dream, but who now hold the opinion that its days are numbered, its glory perished."

It was one thing to condemn slavery in the territories but another to attack it violently where it was long established. Southerners now saw in the Republican Party the embodiment of John Brown's ideals and actions. So, in their view, the election of a Republican president would be a death sentence for the South.

The Election of 1860

An atmosphere of mutual sectional distrust and animosity characterized the campaign for the presidential election of 1860. In April, the Democratic Party, the sole surviving national political organization, held its convention in Charleston, South Carolina. The location was not conducive to sectional reconciliation. The city had been a hotbed of nullification

John Brown's Raid New England abolitionist John Brown's ill-fated attempt to free Virginia's slaves with a raid on the federal arsenal at Harpers Ferry, Virginia, in 1859.

sentiment during the 1830s, and talk of disunion had surfaced periodically ever since. At the convention, Charlestonians packed the galleries and cheered for their favorite extremists.

Northern Democrats arrived in Charleston united behind Stephen A. Douglas. Although they constituted a majority of the delegates, they could not muster the two-thirds majority necessary to nominate their candidate. Other issues, however, were decided on a simple majority vote, permitting northern Democrats to defeat a platform proposal for a federal slave code in the territories.

Southern extremists who favored secession hoped to disrupt the convention and divide the party. They reasoned that the Republicans would then win the presidency, providing the South with the justification to secede. The platform vote gave them the opportunity they were seeking. Accompanied by spectators' cheers, delegates from five Lower South states, South Carolina, Florida, Mississippi, Louisiana, and Texas, walked out. The Arkansas and Georgia delegations joined them the following day.

Still without a nominee, the Democrats agreed to reconvene in Baltimore in June. This time, the Upper South delegations marched out when Douglas Democrats, in a commanding majority, refused to seat the Lower South delegations that had walked out in Charleston. The remaining delegates nominated Douglas for president. The bolters, who included almost all the southern delegates plus a few northerners loyal to President Buchanan, met in another hall and nominated John C. Breckinridge of Kentucky.

The disintegration of the national Democratic Party alarmed those southerners who understood that it would ensure the election of a Republican president in November. The *Memphis Appeal* warned that "the odium of the Black-Republican party has been that it is *Sectional.*" Should southerners now allow a group of "restless and reckless or misguided men to destroy the national Democratic party?" the *Appeal* asked. Its emphatic answer was "No!"

The *Appeal* reflected the sentiment of many former Whigs, mainly from the Upper South, who would not support Breckinridge and could not support Douglas. Together with Whig allies in the North who had not defected to the Republican Party, they met in Baltimore in May 1860 to form the **Constitutional Union Party** and nominated John Bell of Tennessee for president.

Sensing victory, the Republicans convened in Chicago. If they could hold the states won by Frémont in 1856, add Minnesota (a new Republican-leaning state), and win Pennsylvania and one of three other Lower North states, Illinois, Indiana, or New Jersey, their

Constitutional Union Party
National party formed in 1860, mainly by former Whigs, that emphasized allegiance to the Union and strict enforcement of all national legislation.

"Dividing the National Map": Reflecting the sectional nature of the campaign, three of the four candidates in the 1860 presidential election tear the fabric of national unity. Lincoln and Douglas yank at the North and West and Breckinridge pulls at the South, while the fourth candidate, John Bell of the Constitutional Union Party, makes a futile attempt to glue the pieces back together.

candidate would win. These calculations dictated a platform and a candidate who could appeal to the four Lower North swing states, where antislavery sentiment was not so strong.

In selecting an appropriate presidential nominee, the Republicans faced a dilemma. Senator William H. Seward came to Chicago as the leading candidate. But his immoderate condemnation of southerners and slavery worried moderate northern voters—precisely the voters the party needed for victory.

Reservations about Seward benefited Abraham Lincoln. Lincoln's lieutenants at the convention stressed their candidate's moderation and morality, distancing him from both the abolitionists and Seward. Moreover, Chicago was Lincoln's home turf, and he had many friends working for him at the convention. When Seward faltered, Lincoln rose and won the Republican nomination.

The presidential campaign of 1860 actually comprised two campaigns. In the South, the contest was between Breckinridge and Bell; in the North, it was Lincoln against Douglas. Breckinridge and Bell had scattered support in the North, as did Douglas in the South, but in the main this was a sectional election. Lincoln did not even appear on the ballot in most southern states.

Lincoln became the nation's sixteenth president, with 40 percent of the popular vote (see Map 14.3). Douglas, though second after Lincoln in the popular balloting, won the undivided electoral vote of only one state, Missouri.

Lincoln took most northern states by significant margins and won all the region's electoral votes except three in New Jersey. This gave him a substantial majority of 180 electoral votes. Breckinridge won eleven southern states but received a majority of the popular vote in just four. In the South as a whole, his opponents, Bell and Douglas, together reaped 55 percent of the popular vote, confirming Republicans' skepticism about southern determination to secede.

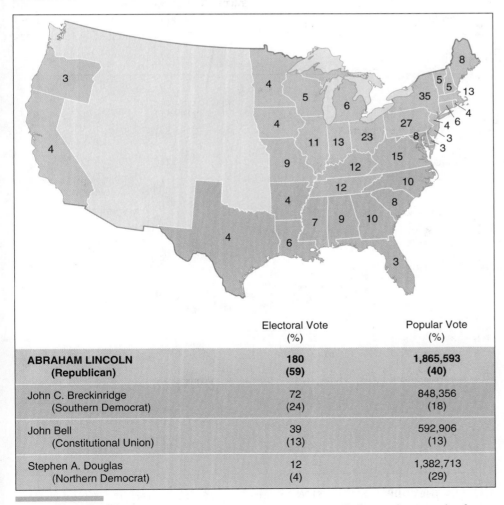

	Electoral Vote (%)	Popular Vote (%)
ABRAHAM LINCOLN (Republican)	**180** **(59)**	**1,865,593** **(40)**
John C. Breckinridge (Southern Democrat)	72 (24)	848,356 (18)
John Bell (Constitutional Union)	39 (13)	592,906 (13)
Stephen A. Douglas (Northern Democrat)	12 (4)	1,382,713 (29)

MAP 14.3 THE ELECTION OF 1860 The election returns from 1860 vividly illustrate the geography of sectionalism.

Confederate States of America
Nation proclaimed in Montgomery, Alabama, in February 1861 after the seven states of the Lower South seceded from the United States.

Secession and Slavery

The events following Lincoln's election demonstrated how wildly mistaken were those who dismissed southern threats of secession. Four days after Lincoln's victory, the South Carolina legislature called on the state's citizens to elect delegates to a convention to consider secession. Meeting on December 20, the delegates voted unanimously to leave the Union. By February 1, six other states had all held similar conventions and decided to leave the Union (see Map 14.4). Representatives from the seven seceding states met to form a separate country, the **Confederate States of America.** On February 18, Jefferson Davis was sworn in as its president.

The swiftness of secession in the Lower South obscured the divisions in most southern states over the issue. Secessionists barely secured a majority in the Georgia and Louisiana conventions. In Mississippi, Florida, and Alabama, the secessionist majority was more comfortable, but pro-Union candidates polled a significant minority of votes. With Lincoln headed for the White House, the greatest support for secession came from large landowners in counties in which slaves comprised a majority of the population. Support for secession was weakest among small, nonslaveholding farmers.

The secessionists mounted an effective propaganda campaign, deftly using the press to persuade voters to elect their delegates to the state conventions. Framing the issue as a personal challenge to every southern citizen, they argued that it would be cowardly to remain in the Union, a submission to despotism and enslavement. Most of all, secessionists focused on the threat to the institution of slavery as the primary cause for leaving the Union.

The delegates who voted to take Texas out of the Union, for example, issued a "declaration of causes" to explain their action. A Lincoln administration, the Texans charged, would result in "the abolition of negro slavery" and "the recognition of political equality between the white and negro races." South Carolina delegates justified secession by alleging that Northerners "have encouraged and assisted thousands of our slaves to leave their homes; and those who remain, have been incited by emissaries,

MAP 14.4 THE COURSE OF SECESSION Before the firing on Fort Sumter in April 1861, the Confederacy consisted primarily of states in the Lower South. After Sumter, and after President Lincoln called upon them for troops, the Upper South states of Virginia, North Carolina, Tennessee, and Arkansas seceded.

books and pictures to servile insurrection." Leaders in Georgia and Mississippi issued similar declarations. Just in case there was any doubt as to what the Confederate States of America stood for, Vice President Alexander Stephens proclaimed the "corner-stone" of the new government "rests upon the great truth that the negro is not equal to the white man; that slavery, subordination to the superior race, is his natural and moral condi-tion." Slavery thus defined the South, and any attempt to lure the errant slave states back into the Union required unprecedented negotiating skills and a willingness to compro-mise. Neither the outgoing nor incoming administrations would possess these attributes.

Presidential Inaction

Because Lincoln would not take office until March 4, 1861, the Buchanan administra-tion had to cope with the secession crisis during the critical months of December and January. The president's failure to work out a solution with Congress as secession fever swept the Lower South undermined Unionist forces in the seceding states.

When Buchanan lost the support of northern Democrats over the Lecompton Con-stitution, he turned to the South for support and filled his cabinet with southerners. Now, facing the secession crisis, he proposed holding a constitutional convention to amend the Constitution in ways that would satisfy the South's demands on slavery. This outright surrender to southern demands, however, had no chance of passing in Congress.

Buchanan's administration quickly fell apart. As the Lower South states left the Union, their representatives and senators left Washington, and with them went Buchan-an's closest advisers and key cabinet officials. Commenting on the emotionally charged atmosphere in the Senate as prominent southerners gave their farewells and departed, one observer wrote, "There was everywhere a feeling of suspense, as if, visibly, the pillars of the temple were being withdrawn and the great Government structure was tottering."

Buchanan, a lame duck, bereft of friends and advisers, did little more than con-demn secession. He was reluctant to take action that would limit the options of the incoming administration or, worse, tip the balance in the Upper South toward seces-sion. He hoped that waiting might bring an isolated Lower South to its senses and give efforts to mediate the sectional rift a chance to succeed.

Peace Proposals

Previous sectional conflicts, dating from the Missouri Compromise of 1820, had brought forth the ingenuity and goodwill of political leaders to effect compromise and draw the Union back from the brink of disintegration. Both ingenuity and goodwill were scarce commodities in the gray secession winter of 1860–1861. The two conflict-ing sides had little trust in each other, and the word "compromise" was viewed as more a synonym for capitulation than salvation.

Kentucky senator John J. Crittenden chaired a Senate committee that proposed a package of constitutional amendments in December 1860 designed to solve the sectional crisis. The central feature of the Crittenden Plan was the extension of the Missouri Compromise line through the territories all the way to California. The plan was of marginal interest to the South because it was unlikely to result in any new slave states. And Republicans opposed it because it contradicted one of their basic principles, the exclusion of slavery from the territories. Despite a flood of letters supporting the Crittenden Plan, including a petition from 38,000 citizens of New York City, Republi-cans bottled it up in Congress and prevented action on it.

Meanwhile, ex-president John Tyler emerged from retirement to lead an effort by the Border States, the Upper South, and the Lower North to forge a peace. Delegates from these states met in February 1861, but their plan differed little from Crittenden's, and it, too, got nowhere in Congress.

Lincoln counted on Unionist sentiment to keep the Upper South from seceding. Like Buchanan, he felt that the longer the Lower South states remained isolated, the more likely they would be to return to the fold. For a while, events seemed to bear him out. One by one, Upper South states registered their support for the Union. North Carolinians went to the polls in February and turned down the call for a secession convention. Also in February, Virginians elected Unionists to their convention by a five-to-one margin. In Missouri, not one secessionist won election to the state convention. In Kentucky, the legislature adjourned without taking action on a convention or a statewide referendum on secession. And the Maryland legislature, already out of session, showed no inclination to reconvene.

A closer look, however, reveals that there were limits to the Upper South's Unionism. Most voters in the region went to the polls assuming that Congress would eventually reach a compromise based on the Crittenden proposals, Tyler's peace conference, or some other remedy. Leaders in the Upper South saw themselves as peacemakers. But what if arbitration failed? Or what if the Lower South states precipitated a crisis that forced the Upper South to choose sides? It was unlikely that the Upper South would abide the use of federal force against its southern neighbors.

Lincoln believed that the slavery issue had to come to a crisis before the nation could solve it. Although he said in public that he would never interfere with slavery in the slave states, the deep moral revulsion he felt toward the institution left him more ambivalent in private. As he confided to a colleague in 1860, "The tug has to come, and better now, than any time hereafter."

Fort Sumter: The Tug Comes

In his inaugural address on March 4, 1861, Abraham Lincoln denounced secession and vowed to uphold federal law but tempered his firmness with a conciliatory conclusion. Addressing southerners specifically, he assured them, "We are not enemies but friends. . . . Though passion may have strained, it must not break our bonds of affection. The mystic chords of memory, stretching from every battlefield, and patriot grave, to every living heart and hearthstone, all over this broad land, will yet swell the chorus of the Union, when again touched, as surely they will be, by the better angels of our nature."

Southerners wanted concessions, not conciliation, however. The new president said nothing about slavery in the territories, nothing about the constitutional amendments proposed by Crittenden and Tyler, and nothing about the release of federal property in the South to the Confederacy. Even some northerners hoping for an olive branch were disappointed. But Lincoln was hoping for time—time to get the Lower South states quarreling with one another, time to allow Union sentiment to build in the Upper South, and time to convince northerners that the Union needed preserving. He did not get that time.

One day after Lincoln's inauguration, Major Robert Anderson (like Lincoln, a native Kentuckian), the commander of **Fort Sumter** in Charleston harbor, informed the administration that he had only four to six weeks' worth of provisions left. Anderson assumed that Lincoln would understand the hopeless arithmetic and order him to evacuate Fort Sumter. The commanding general of the army, Winfield Scott, advised the president accordingly, as did many members of his cabinet. Lincoln stalled.

The issue was simple, though the alternatives were difficult: Do not provision Fort Sumter and the garrison would fall to the Confederate government; provision the fort and risk a military confrontation as the Confederate authorities would perceive such action as an act of war. Lincoln had vowed in his inaugural address to uphold the Constitution and "to protect and defend" the country's interests; yet, he had also promised that he would not make any aggressive movements against the South.

News of Anderson's plight changed the mood in the North. The Slave Power, some said, was holding him and his men hostage. Frustration grew over Lincoln's silence and inaction. The Confederacy's bold resolve seemed to contrast sharply with the federal government's confusion and inertia.

Hoping to avoid a confrontation, the president did not send the troops that Anderson had requested. Instead, he ordered unarmed ships to proceed to the fort, deliver the provisions, and leave. Only if the Confederates fired on them were they to force their way into the fort with the help of armed reinforcements. Lincoln notified South Carolina authorities that he intended to do nothing more than "feed the hungry."

Fort Sumter Begun in the late 1820s to protect Charleston, South Carolina, it became the center of national attention in April 1861 when President Lincoln attempted to provision federal troops at the fort, triggering a hostile response from on-shore Confederate forces, opening the Civil War.

At Charleston, Confederate general P. G. T. Beauregard had standing orders to turn back any relief expedition. But President Davis wanted to take Sumter before the provisions arrived to avoid fighting Anderson and the reinforcements at the same time. He also realized that the outbreak of fighting could compel the Upper South to join the Confederacy. But his impatience to force the issue placed the Confederacy in the position of firing, unprovoked, on the American flag and at Major Anderson, who had become a hero to the North.

On April 10, Davis ordered Beauregard to demand the immediate evacuation of Fort Sumter. Anderson refused but wondered what the hurry was, considering that his provisions would run out in a few days. The remark gave Beauregard pause and prompted additional negotiations. Anderson did not yield, and before dawn on April 12, 1861, the first Confederate shell whistled down on the fort. After more than a day of shelling, during which more than 5,000 artillery rounds struck Fort Sumter, Anderson surrendered. Remarkably, neither side suffered any casualties, a deceptive beginning to an exceptionally bloody war.

When the verdict of Fort Sumter reached President Lincoln, he called on the southern states still in the Union to send troops to put down the rebellion. Refusing to make war on South Carolina, the Upper South states of Virginia, North Carolina, Tennessee, and Arkansas seceded, and the Confederacy expanded to eleven states.

Conclusion

When David Wilmot submitted his amendment to ban slavery from the territories gained from Mexico, he could not have foreseen that the debate he unleashed would end in civil war just fifteen years later. Northerners and southerners had lived together in one nation for nearly eighty years. During that time, they had reached accommodations on slavery at the Constitutional Convention of 1787, in the Compromises of 1820 and 1850, and on numerous lesser occasions. But by the 1850s the slavery issue had become weighted with so much moral and political freight that it defied easy resolution. Throughout the Western world, attitudes toward slavery were changing. Northern evangelical Protestants in the 1840s and 1850s branded slavery a sin and slaveholders sinners. The overwhelming popularity of *Uncle Tom's Cabin* both tapped and fed this sentiment. America could no longer continue its journey as a nation half slave and half free.

The political conflict over slavery coalesced around northern efforts to curtail southern expansion and power and southern attempts to maintain power and influence in the federal government by planting the institution in the western territories. This conflict eventually helped undo the Compromise of 1850 and turned Stephen A. Douglas's railroad bill into a battle royal over Kansas. Unable to resolve sectional differences over slavery, the Whigs disintegrated, and the Democrats divided into northern and southern factions. The Republican Party was formed from the political debris. Ethnic and religious conflicts further disturbed the political landscape and contributed to party realignment.

Northerners and southerners eventually interpreted any incident or piece of legislation as an attempt by one side to gain moral and political advantage at the other's expense. Northerners viewed the *Dred Scott* decision, the Lecompton Constitution, and the southern reaction to John Brown's Raid as evidence of a Slave Power conspiracy to deny white northerners their constitutional rights. Southerners interpreted the northern reaction to these same events as evidence of a conspiracy to rob them of security and equality within the Union.

Ironically, as Americans in both sections talked of freedom and self-determination, the black men and women in their midst had little of either. Their American journey generated scant recognition. Lincoln went to war to preserve the Union; Davis, to defend a new nation. Slavery was the spark that ignited the conflict, but white America seemed more comfortable embracing abstract ideals than real people. Northerners and southerners would confront this irony during the bloodiest war in American history, but they would not resolve it.

For Suggested Readings go to MyHistoryLab.

Chapter Review

Slavery in the Territories

14.1 How did slavery transform from a political issue to a moral crusade? p. 370

Settling the West would enable Americans to fulfill their destiny of a continental empire. Northerners interpreted this blessing as establishing a region for free labor. For southerners, it meant an opportunity to bring their property to new lands. In these similar economic, but divergent moral objectives lay the seeds of conflict.

Political Realignment

14.2 How did the intrusion of religion into the political process contribute to the rise of the Republican Party? p. 379

Religious bigotry and the controversy over slavery tore apart the Second American party system. The new party structure merged religion and politics, a toxic blend. Eventually, the slavery issue overwhelmed ethnic and religious conflicts to create a sectional antislavery party, the Republicans, leaving the Democrats as America's only national party.

The Road to Disunion

14.3 How did the elevation of slavery to a moral issue polarize North and South during the 1850s? p. 390

The political system could not resolve the controversy over slavery. As the political center eroded, the extremes rendered compromise less likely. North and South believed they each possessed the moral high ground and the nation's legacy of constitutional government, and that the other subverted both morality and democracy.

Timeline

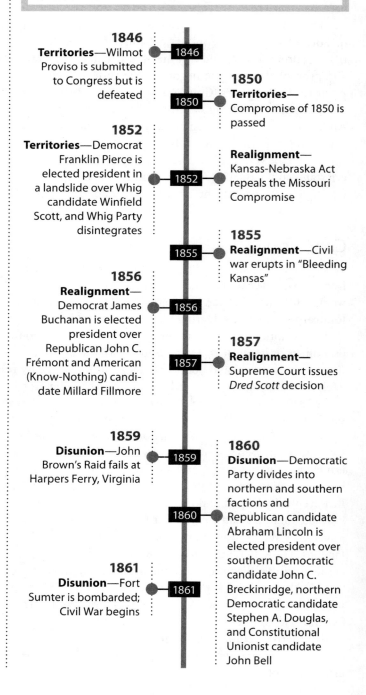

1846
Territories—Wilmot Proviso is submitted to Congress but is defeated
`1846`

1850
Territories—Compromise of 1850 is passed
`1850`

1852
Territories—Democrat Franklin Pierce is elected president in a landslide over Whig candidate Winfield Scott, and Whig Party disintegrates
`1852`

Realignment—Kansas-Nebraska Act repeals the Missouri Compromise

1855
Realignment—Civil war erupts in "Bleeding Kansas"
`1855`

1856
Realignment—Democrat James Buchanan is elected president over Republican John C. Frémont and American (Know-Nothing) candidate Millard Fillmore
`1856`

1857
Realignment—Supreme Court issues *Dred Scott* decision
`1857`

1859
Disunion—John Brown's Raid fails at Harpers Ferry, Virginia
`1859`

1860
Disunion—Democratic Party divides into northern and southern factions and Republican candidate Abraham Lincoln is elected president over southern Democratic candidate John C. Breckinridge, northern Democratic candidate Stephen A. Douglas, and Constitutional Unionist candidate John Bell
`1860`

1861
Disunion—Fort Sumter is bombarded; Civil War begins
`1861`

15 Battle Cries and Freedom Songs: The Civil War 1861–1865

One American Journey

A Soldier's Letter to His Wife Explaining Why He Must Fight

July 14, 1861
Camp Clark, Washington, DC

My very dear Sarah:

The indications are very strong that we shall move in a few days, perhaps tomorrow. And lest I should not be able to write you again I feel impelled to write a few lines that may fall under your eye when I am no more. Our movement may be one of a few days' duration and be full of pleasure. And it may be one of severe conflict and death to me. "Not my will but thine O God

Awaiting combat, 1861: Union soldiers from New York relax at camp awaiting orders to move to the front. The young men show great confidence and determination for their coming engagements, though one fellow to the left of the tent, perhaps a teenager far from home, seems to long for something as he stares beyond the camera. At this early stage of the war, a combination of romance and apprehension enveloped these hopeful recruits. Note the African American youth with a broom sitting apart from the soldiers. Before recruitment of African Americans following the Emancipation Proclamation in January 1863, blacks in the Union army performed menial tasks, as they did in the Confederate forces.

LEARNING OBJECTIVES

15.1	15.2	15.3	15.4	15.5	15.6	15.7
What were the North's key advantages at the outset of the war? p. 406	How did the two sides' objectives dictate their strategies in the early years of the war? p. 411	How did the Emancipation Proclamation change the nature of the war? p. 417	How did the changing nature of the war affect soldiers on both sides? p. 423	What impact did the war have on the North's economy? p. 431	How did the war affect civilian life in the South? p. 435	What was Grant's strategy for ending the war? p. 438

((• Listen to Chapter 15 on MyHistoryLab

15.1

15.2

15.3

15.4

15.5

15.6

15.7

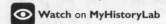 Watch the Video Series on MyHistoryLab

Learn about some key topics related to this chapter with the *MyHistoryLab Video Series: Key Topics in U.S. History.*

1 **The Civil War: 1861–1865** This video focuses on the roots, progress, and legacy of the American Civil War. The conflict between the North and South revolved around the question of slavery and its future in American society. The war was devastating, but ultimately provided a decisive answer to at least part of that debate.

 Watch on MyHistoryLab

The Emancipation Proclamation With the Civil War, abolitionists and their sympathizers began to urge President Lincoln to emancipate the slaves. This video looks at how emancipation had been attempted unofficially before the Emancipation Proclamation of 1863 as well as the story behind its conception and the historic document that freed the slaves in the Confederate states during the height of the Civil War. **2**

Watch on MyHistoryLab

3 **Gettysburg: A Turning Point** General Robert E. Lee, building on the momentum gained from the Confederate victory at Chancellorsville, led the Army of Northern Virginia into Pennsylvania in an attempt to decapitate the Union by outflanking Union forces and ultimately capturing Washington, DC. This video explains the importance of the crucial battle of Gettysburg, fought in early July 1863, a turning point in the Civil War.

 Watch on MyHistoryLab

The Surrender at Appomattox Court House The leadership of Generals Ulysses S. Grant and William T. Sherman, while costly in life and property, proved effective in breaking the resistance of the Confederate armies. This video surveys the last year and a half of the Civil War and General Robert E. Lee's surrender at Appomattox Court House in northern Virginia in April 1865. **4**

Watch on MyHistoryLab

be done." If it is necessary that I should fall on the battle-field for my Country I am ready. I have no misgivings about, or lack of confidence in the cause in which I am engaged, and my courage does not halt or falter. I know how American Civilization now leans upon the triumph of the government and how great a debt we owe to those who went before us through the blood and suffering of the Revolution. And I am willing, perfectly willing, to lay down all my joys in this life, to help maintain this government, and to pay that debt. But my dear wife, when I know that with my own joys I lay down nearly all of yours, . . . is it weak or dishonorable that while the banner of my purpose floats calmly and proudly in the breeze, underneath, my unbounded love for you my darling wife and children should struggle in fierce though useless contest with my love of country? . . .

Sarah, my love for you is deathless, it seems to bind me with mighty cables that nothing but omnipotence can break; and yet my love of Country comes over me like a strong wind and bears me irresistibly with all those chains to the battle-field.

The memories of the blissful moments I have enjoyed with you come crowding over me, and I feel most deeply grateful to God and you, that I have enjoyed them for so long. And how hard it is for me to give them up and burn to ashes the hopes and future years, when, God willing, we might still have lived and loved together, and see our boys grown up to honorable manhood around us. . . . If I do not [return], my dear Sarah, never forget how much I loved you, nor that when my last breath escapes me on the battle-field, it will whisper your name. Forgive my many faults, and the many pains I have caused you. How thoughtless, how foolish I have sometimes been! . . .

But, O Sarah, if the dead can come back to this earth and flit unseen around those they love, I shall be with you, in the gladdest days and the darkest nights . . . always, always, and if there be a soft breeze upon your cheek, it shall be my breath[;] as the cool air fans your throbbing temple, it shall be my spirit passing by. Sarah do not mourn me dead; think I am gone and wait for thee, for we shall meet again. . . .

Sullivan

Sullivan Ballou to Sarah Ballou, July 14, 1861. Geoffrey C. Ward et al.,
The Civil War: An Illustrated History, Alfred Knopf, 1990, pp. 82–83.

Personal Journeys Online

- Sam R. Watkins, Co. "Aytch": A Confederate Memoir of the Civil War, 1882. A Confederate soldier recounts the horrors of war he witnessed in a southern hospital and on the battlefield.
- Ambrose Bierce, "What I Saw of Shiloh," *Civil War Stories,* 1909. Account of a Union soldier's experiences at the Battle of Shiloh.

Sullivan Ballou's letter to his wife on the eve of the First Battle of Bull Run typified the sentiments of the civilian armies raised by both North and South: a clear purpose of the importance of their mission, a sense of foreboding, an appeal and acknowledgment of the guiding hand of God, and, most of all, words of love for family. Such romantic expressions were common in mid-nineteenth-century American correspondence between husband and wife, lover and loved.

Yet the Civil War lent urgency to such expressions. Most of the soldiers had no combat experience and, aside from some perfunctory training, knew little about military life before going into battle. Just a few months earlier, Major Sullivan Ballou of the Second Regiment, Rhode Island Volunteers, was a 32-year-old attorney. He led a quiet life in Providence with his wife and two young sons. But the events of the 1850s stoked Ballou's interest in politics, and he became a dedicated Republican and devoted supporter of Abraham Lincoln. When the war came, he volunteered and was sent to Washington, DC, to await further orders. He wrote this letter from his camp. A few days later, his company marched to Manassas, Virginia, where they engaged Confederate troops on July 21 at the First Battle of Bull Run. Sullivan Ballou was killed in the battle.

Sullivan Ballou took the ultimate journey for his beliefs and his love. The Civil War preserved the Union, abolished slavery, and killed at least 750,000 soldiers, more than in all the other wars the country fought from the Revolution to the Korean conflict combined. To come to terms with this is to try to reconcile the war's great accomplishments with its awful consequences. When the war began, only a small minority of northerners linked the preservation of the Union with the abolition of slavery. By 1863, Union and freedom had become inseparable Federal objectives. The Confederacy fought for independence and the preservation of slavery. The Confederate objectives dictated a defensive military strategy; the Union objectives dictated an offensive strategy.

During the war's early years, both sides faced similar problems, raising an army, financing the war effort, mobilizing the civilian population, and marshaling resources. The Confederates confronted the added burden of starting a government from scratch with relatively fewer resources than the Federals.

At the end of the war's first year, the Confederacy's strong military position east of the Appalachians belied its numerical and economic inferiority. By the end of 1862, Union officers had begun to expose southern military shortcomings, and federal officials had expanded the North's war aims to include the abolition of slavery. Within a year, the trans-Mississippi portion of the Confederacy capitulated. A slim victory at Gettysburg, Sherman's destructive and demoralizing march through Georgia, and

15.1

15.2

15.3

15.4

15.5

15.6

15.7

15.1

Emancipation Proclamation
Decree announced by President Abraham Lincoln in September 1862 and formally issued on January 1, 1863, freeing slaves in all Confederate states still in rebellion.

15.2

15.3

15.4

15.5

15.6

15.7

the relentless assaults of the new Union commander, Ulysses S. Grant, overwhelmed Confederate resistance. The North, too, suffered social and political disruption, but the marvelous elixir of battlefield victory did wonders to allay these ills.

Black southerners seized the initiative in the war against slavery, especially in the months after the **Emancipation Proclamation**, eventually joining Union forces in combat against their former masters. Soon, another war to secure the fruits of freedom would begin.

Mobilization, North and South

15.1 What were the North's key advantages at the outset of the war?

Neither side was prepared for a major war. The Confederacy lacked a national army. Each southern state had a militia, but by the 1850s, these companies had become more social clubs than fighting units. Aside from privately owned ships and some captured Federal vessels, the Confederacy also lacked a navy. The Union had a regular army of only 16,000 men, most of whom were stationed west of the Mississippi River. Their major responsibility had been to intervene between white settlers and Indians.

Each government augmented these meager military reserves with thousands of new recruits and developed a bureaucracy to mount a war effort. At the same time, the administrations of Presidents Lincoln and Davis secured the loyalty of their civilian populations and devised military strategies for a war of indeterminate duration. How North and South went about these tasks reflected both the different objectives of the two sides and the distinctive personalities of their leaders, Abraham Lincoln and Jefferson Davis.

War Fever

The day after Major Robert Anderson surrendered Fort Sumter, President Lincoln moved to enlarge his small, scattered army by mobilizing state militias for ninety days. Four states—Virginia, Arkansas, North Carolina, and Tennessee—refused the call and seceded from the Union. About one-third of the officer corps of the regular army, including some of the highest-ranking officers, resigned their commissions to join the Confederacy. Still, Lincoln seemed likely to meet his target of 75,000 troops.

Lincoln's modest ninety-day call-up reflected the general belief, North and South, that the war would end quickly. Not everyone thought the war would be brief. William T. Sherman, who had recently headed a Louisiana military academy and would become one of the Union's few great commanders, wrote in April 1861, "I think it is to be a long war, very long, much longer than any politician thinks."

Northerners closed ranks behind the president after the Confederacy's attack on Fort Sumter. Southerners were equally eager to support their new nation. Appeals to God were commonplace on both sides. The feeling that a holy war was unfolding energized recruits.

As war fever gripped North and South, volunteers on both sides rushed to join, quickly filling the quotas of both armies. By early spring of 1862, however, the Confederate government was compelled to order the first general draft in American history. It required three years' service for men between 18 and 35 (a range later expanded from 17 to 50). In 1864, the Confederate Congress added a compulsory reenlistment provision. At that point, the only way a recruit could get out of the army was to die or desert.

The Confederate draft law allowed several occupational exemptions. Among them was an infamous provision that allowed one white man on any plantation with more than twenty slaves to be excused from service. The reason for the exemption was to

15.1

15.2

15.3

15.4

15.5

15.6

15.7

ensure the security and productivity of large plantations, not to protect the privileged, but it led some southerners to conclude that the struggle had become "a rich man's war but a poor man's fight."

The initial flush of enthusiasm faded in the North as well. Responding to a call for additional troops, some northern states initiated a draft during the summer of 1862. In March 1863, Congress passed the Enrollment Act, a draft law that, like the Confederate draft, allowed for occupational exemptions. A provision that allowed a draftee to hire a substitute aroused resentment among working-class northerners. Anger at the draft, as well as poor working conditions, sparked several riots during 1863. But the North was less dependent on conscription than was the South. Only 8 percent of the Union's soldiers were drafted, compared to 20 percent for the Confederacy.

The complaints of many rank-and-file soldiers may give the impression that only people of lesser or modest means fought, but in fact the armies of both sides included men from all walks of life, from common laborers to clerks to bankers. An undetermined number of women, typically disguised as men, also served in both armies. Perhaps as many as 300 women joined the Union ranks, and about half that number enlisted in the Confederate army. They joined for the same reasons as men: adventure, patriotism, and glory.

The North's Advantage in Resources

The resources of the North, including its population, industrial and agricultural capacity, and transportation network, greatly exceeded those of the South (see Figure 15.1). The 2.1 million men who fought for the Union represented roughly half the men of military age in the North. The 900,000 men who fought for the Confederacy, by contrast, represented fully 90 percent of its eligible population. Irish and German immigrants continued to flow into the North during the war, although at a slower rate than before, and thousands of them enlisted, often as substitutes for native-born northerners. Nearly 200,000 African Americans, most of them ex-slaves from the South, took up arms for the Union. Not until the last month of the war did the Confederacy consider arming slaves.

At the beginning of the war, the North controlled 90 percent of the nation's industrial capacity. The North had dozens of facilities for producing war matériel; the South had only one munitions plant, the Tredegar Iron Works in Richmond. Northern farms, more mechanized than their southern counterparts, produced record harvests of meat, grain, and vegetables. Southern farms were also productive, but the South lacked the North's capacity to transport and distribute food efficiently. The railroad system in the North was more than twice the size of the South's.

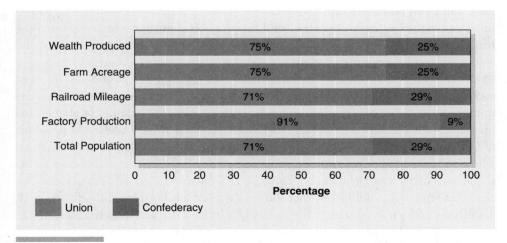

FIGURE 15.1 COMPARISON OF UNION AND CONFEDERATE CONTROL OF KEY RESOURCES AT THE OUTSET OF THE CIVIL WAR The resources of the North greatly exceeded those of the South at the beginning of the Civil War.

SOURCE: United States Government, Military Records for Civil War

15.1

15.2

15.3

15.4

15.5

15.6

15.7

Thanks to the North's abundance of resources, no soldier in any previous American army had ever been outfitted as well as the blue-uniformed Union trooper. The official color of the Confederate uniform was gray, although a dusty brown shade was more common. Most southern soldiers, however, did not wear distinguishable uniforms, especially toward the end of the war. They also often lacked proper shoes or any footwear at all. Still, the South never lost a battle because of insufficient supplies or inadequate weaponry. New foundries opened, and manufacturing enterprises in Augusta, Georgia; Selma, Alabama; and elsewhere joined the Tredegar Iron Works in keeping the Confederate armies equipped.

Unstable finances proved more of a handicap for the Confederacy than its relatively low industrial capacity. The Confederate economy, and its treasury, depended heavily on cotton exports. But a Union naval blockade and the ability of textile manufacturers in Europe to find new sources of supply restricted this crucial source of revenue. The imposition of taxes would have improved the Confederacy's finances, but southerners resisted taxation. The government sold interest-bearing bonds to raise money, but as Confederate fortunes declined, so did bond sales. With few other options, the Confederacy financed more than 60 percent of the $1.5 billion it spent on the war with printing-press money. Inflation spiraled out of control, demoralizing civilians.

The Union had more abundant financial resources than the Confederacy, and the federal government was more successful than the Confederate government at developing innovative ways to meet the great cost of the war. Its first recourse was to borrow money by selling long-term interest-bearing bonds and shorter-term interest-bearing treasury notes. Together these bonds accounted for 66 percent of the $4 billion that the Union raised to wage the war. Like the Confederacy, the federal government issued paper money, bills derisively known as "greenbacks," that was not backed by gold or silver. But the federal government also offset its expenses with the country's first income tax, which citizens could pay in greenbacks, a move that bolstered the value and credibility of the paper currency. These financial measures eliminated the need for wage and price controls and rationing, and warded off ruinous inflation in the North.

Leaders, Governments, and Strategies

Leadership ability, like resources, played an important role in the war. It was up to the leaders of the two sides to determine and administer civilian and military policy, to define war objectives, and to inspire a willingness to sacrifice in both citizens and soldiers.

Jefferson Davis and the South.   The Confederate president, Jefferson Davis, had to build a government from scratch during the war. Abraham Lincoln at least had the benefit of an established governmental structure, a standing army, healthy financial resources, and established diplomatic relations with the nations of Europe.

Davis and Lincoln were both born in Kentucky within a year and 100 miles of each other. Davis, like Lincoln, was born into modest circumstances. He attended the military academy at West Point, where he was a mediocre student. He abandoned his military career after seven years of service and married the 16-year-old daughter of General Zachary Taylor. Davis and his bride moved to a plantation in Mississippi, where she soon died of yellow fever. Immersing himself in books and cotton farming, Davis had emerged as a gentleman planter by the 1840s and married Varina Howell in 1845. He returned to military service during the Mexican War, fought well, and used his success to become a senator from Mississippi in 1847. He served as secretary of war under President Franklin Pierce and returned to the Senate in 1857.

Although Davis's career qualified him for the prodigious task of running the Confederacy, aspects of his character compromised his effectiveness. He had a sharp intellect but related awkwardly to people. Colleagues found him aloof. He was inclined to equate compromise with weakness and interpreted any opposition as a personal attack.

Abraham Lincoln and the North.   Northerners, like southerners, needed a convincing reason to endure the prolonged sacrifice of the Civil War. For them, the struggle was a distant one, fought mostly on southern soil. Lincoln and other northern leaders secured support by convincing their compatriots of the importance of preserving the Union. The president viewed the conflict in global terms, its results affecting the hopes for democratic government around the world. He concluded that the war "presents to the whole family of man, the question, whether a constitutional republic . . . can or cannot maintain its territorial integrity, against its own domestic foes."

Lincoln handled disagreement better than Davis did. He defused tense situations with folksy humor, and his simple eloquence captured the imagination of ordinary people, even if it did not persuade his political enemies. The president's occasional visit to the front generated both amusement and gratitude from the troops, owing to his ungainly appearance on a horse, and his easy way of conversing with the men. They serenaded "Old Abe," as they called him affectionately, with the popular tune "We Are Coming, Father Abraham." There is no record of Confederate tunesmiths composing similar ditties for their leaders.

Lincoln's Fight for the Border States.   The secession of Virginia, Arkansas, North Carolina, and Tennessee left four border slave states, Maryland, Delaware, Kentucky, and Missouri, hanging in the balance. Were Maryland and Delaware to secede, the Federal capital at Washington, DC, would be surrounded by Confederate territory. The loss of Kentucky and Missouri would threaten the borders of Iowa, Illinois, Indiana, and Ohio and remove the Deep South from the threat of imminent invasion. Kentucky's manpower, livestock, and waterways were important to both sides. The state also had special symbolic significance as the birthplace of the two rival presidents.

Lincoln adopted a "soft" strategy to secure the border states, stressing the restoration of the Union as the sole objective of federal military operations and assuring border residents that his government would not interfere with slavery. Union commanders barred fugitive slaves from their camps during the first year of the war, promising "to keep the war a lily-white crusade," as one officer put it. But early reports from the four states were troubling. The four governors displayed polite indifference or overt hostility to the federal government.

Maryland's strategic location north of Washington, DC, rendered its loyalty to the Union vital. Although a majority of its citizens opposed secession, a mob attack on Union troops passing through Baltimore in April 1861 indicated strong pro-southern sentiment. Lincoln dispatched troops to monitor the fall elections in the state, placed its legislature under military surveillance, and arrested officials who opposed the Union cause, including the mayor of Baltimore. This show of force guaranteed the pro-Union candidate for governor an overwhelming victory and saved Maryland for the Union. Delaware, although nominally a slave state, remained staunchly for the Union.

Missourians settled their indecision by combat. The fighting culminated with a Union victory in March 1862 at the Battle of Pea Ridge, Arkansas. The Union victory was notable for two reasons. First, the Confederate force included 3,500 mounted Indians led by Col. Stand Watie, a Cherokee, who achieved one of the rare Rebel victories during the two-day battle. The Cherokees joined the Confederate cause in the hopes of securing a better deal than they had received from Washington. The official Union report praised the bravery and skill of "the hordes of Indians . . . that were arrayed against us." Second, the decisive Union victory at Pea Ridge secured Missouri and northern Arkansas for Federal forces, further diminishing Confederate influence in the Upper South.

Kentucky never seceded but attempted to remain neutral at the outset of the war. The legislature was pro-Union, the governor pro-southern. Both sides actively recruited soldiers in the state. In September 1861, when Confederate forces invaded Kentucky and Union forces moved to expel them, the state became one of the war's battlegrounds.

15.1

15.2

15.3

15.4

15.5

15.6

15.7

15.1

15.2

15.3

15.4

15.5

15.6

15.7

Although Virginia went with the Confederacy, some counties in the western part of the state opposed secession and, as early as the summer of 1861, took steps to establish a pro-Union state. In June 1863, West Virginia became the nation's thirty-fifth state.

Strategies and Tactics. To a great extent, the political objectives of each side determined its military strategy. Southerners wanted independence and protection of their institutions; Northerners fought to preserve the Union. The North's goal required conquest. Federal forces had to invade the South, destroy its armies, and rout its government, a difficult assignment considering the vast geographic extent of the Confederacy. The Confederacy, for its part, did not need to conquer the North. Fighting a defensive battle in its own territory, the South had only to hang on until growing northern opposition to the war or some decisive northern military mistake convinced the Union to stop fighting.

But the South's strategy had two weaknesses. First, it demanded more patience than the South had shown in impulsively attacking Fort Sumter. Second, the South might not have sufficient resources to draw out the war long enough to swing northern public opinion behind peace. The question was: What would break first, northern support for the war or southern ability to wage it?

The Southern Landscape

The southern landscape played a significant strategic role in the Civil War. The South covered 800,000 square miles or about the size of Spain, Italy, France, Germany, and Poland combined. The region was mostly rural with a 3,500-mile coastline, impenetrable forests and swamps, numerous rivers, a mountain chain, and irregular terrain except on the coast. Union and Confederate officers who had attended West Point learned open field combat with two armies arrayed against each other in close formation, firing weapons with limited range and accuracy. The introduction of rifled muskets and light artillery increased the accuracy, range, and deadliness of weaponry. Attacking entrenched soldiers or troops with commanding geographical positions rarely proved successful and usually resulted in high casualties for the attacking army.

The dense forests of the South also hampered traditional battle tactics. Bullets and artillery shells often ignited the underbrush, creating an inferno that trapped troops as happened in the Wilderness campaign of May 1864. The dense smoke caused by fire and weapons restricted visibility. Some soldiers became victims of friendly fire as a result.

Then there was the cloying heat and humidity of the South. Most of the major engagements occurred in the late spring, summer, and fall. Wool uniforms exhausted troops, and unsanitary conditions, compounded by the absence of frost until the late fall, heightened the casualties from disease. The moisture and excessive heat also generated sustained and often violent thunderstorms. Downpours turned roads into mud and gentle streams into raging rivers. The condition of southern roads, never very good even in fine weather, played a role in delaying deployment of troops, the coordination of attacks, and the pursuit of a defeated foe.

The South's uneven terrain also hampered traditional battle tactics. At Antietam, for example, the numerous depressions, or valleys, between hills meant that soldiers disappeared from view every so often. In hilly terrain the artillery echoed off hills, making it difficult for troops to determine the direction of firing.

These environmental idiosyncrasies of the South should have given Confederate troops a significant advantage. They fought on their home turf and they maneuvered among friendly residents. The Confederates, however, like most of their Union counterparts, had rarely ventured beyond their neighborhoods growing up and often found themselves in unfamiliar terrain. The respective commanders adapted to the geography on the fly. The Union's superiority in railroads, steamships, and telegraphy, especially during the last eighteen months of the war, enabled commanders to transcend environmental barriers and the South's immense territory to move troops and information quickly.

The Early War, 1861–1862

15.2	How did the two sides' objectives dictate their strategies in the early years of the war?

The North's offensive strategy dictated the course of the war for the first two years. In the West (the area beyond the Appalachian Mountains), the Federal army's objectives were to hold Missouri, Kentucky, and Tennessee, to control the Mississippi River, and eventually to detach the area west of the Appalachians from the rest of the Confederacy. In the East, Union forces sought to capture Richmond, the Confederate capital. The U.S. Navy imposed a blockade along the Confederate coast and pushed into inland waterways to capture southern ports.

The Confederates defended strategic locations throughout their territory or abandoned them when prudence required. Occasionally, taking advantage of surprise or terrain, southern forces ventured out to engage Union armies. Between engagements, each side sniped at, bushwhacked, and trapped the other.

By the end of 1862, the result remained in the balance. Although Union forces had attained some success in the West, the southern armies there remained intact. In the East, where resourceful Confederate leaders several times stopped superior Union forces, the southerners clearly had the best of it.

First Bull Run

By July 1861, when the border states appeared more secure for the Union, President Lincoln shifted his attention southward and ordered General Irvin McDowell to move his forces into Virginia to take Richmond (see Map 15.1). Confronting McDowell 20 miles southwest of Washington at Manassas, an important junction on the railroad that supplied the Confederate capital, was a Confederate army under General P. G. T. Beauregard. The two armies clashed on July 21 at the First Battle of Bull Run (known to the Confederacy as the First Battle of Manassas). The Union troops seemed at first on the verge of winning. But Beauregard's forces, along with General Joseph E. Johnston's reinforcements, repulsed the assault, scattering not only the Union army but also hundreds of picnickers who had come out from Washington to watch the fight. At the height of the battle, General Barnard Bee of South Carolina called out to Colonel Thomas J. Jackson for assistance. Jackson, a Virginia college professor turned officer, either did not hear Bee or chose to ignore him. In exasperation, Bee shouted, "There stands Jackson, like a damned stone wall!" The rebuke became, in the curious alchemy of battlefield gossip, a shorthand for courage and steadfastness. Jackson's men henceforth called him "Stonewall."

Bull Run dispelled some illusions and reinforced others. It boosted southerners' confidence and seemed to confirm their boast that one Confederate could whip ten Yankees, even though the opposing armies were of relatively equal strength when the fighting began. The Union rout planted the suspicion in northern minds that perhaps the Confederates were invincible and destroyed the widespread belief in the North that the war would be over quickly.

The War in the West

Federal forces may have retreated in Virginia, but they advanced in the West. Two Confederate forts on the Tennessee-Kentucky border, Fort Henry on the Tennessee River and Fort Donelson on the Cumberland River, guarded the strategic waterways that linked Tennessee and Kentucky to the Mississippi Valley. The forts also defended Nashville, the Tennessee state capital (see Map 15.2). In February 1862, Union general Ulysses S. Grant coordinated a land and river campaign against the forts, with Flag Officer Andrew H. Foote commanding a force of ironclad Union gunboats.

15.1

15.2

15.3

15.4

15.5

15.6

15.7

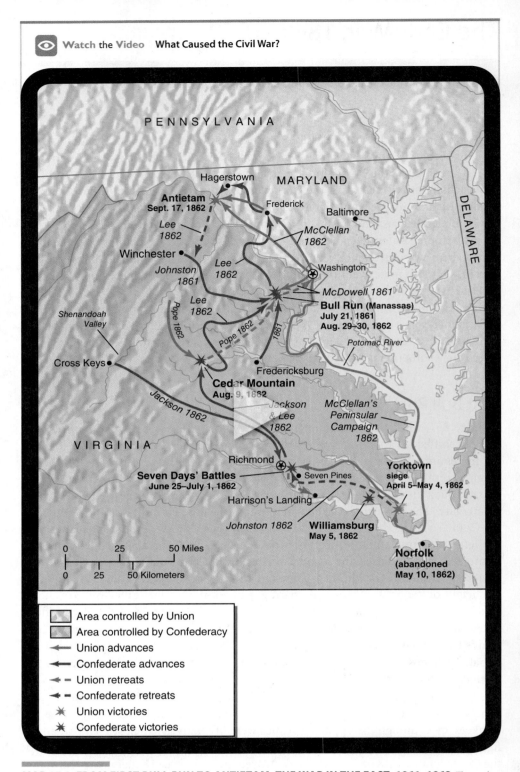

Watch the Video   **What Caused the Civil War?**

MAP 15.1 FROM FIRST BULL RUN TO ANTIETAM: THE WAR IN THE EAST, 1861–1862 The early stages of the war demonstrated the strategies of the Confederacy and the Union. Federal troops stormed into Virginia hoping to capture Richmond and bring a quick end to the war. Through a combination of poor generalship and Confederate tenacity, they failed. Confederate troops hoped to defend their territory, prolong the war, and eventually win their independence as northern patience evaporated. They proved successful initially, but, with the abandonment of the defensive strategy and the invasion of Maryland in the fall of 1862, the Confederates suffered a political and morale setback at Antietam.

Grant, recently promoted to brigadier general, had resigned from the army in the 1850s after a mediocre career marked by bouts of excessive drinking. Before rejoining the army, he had worked in his family's struggling leather business in Illinois. A plain-looking man, with dark-brown hair and a beard streaked with gray, he often looked as

15.1

15.2

15.3

15.4

15.5

15.6

15.7

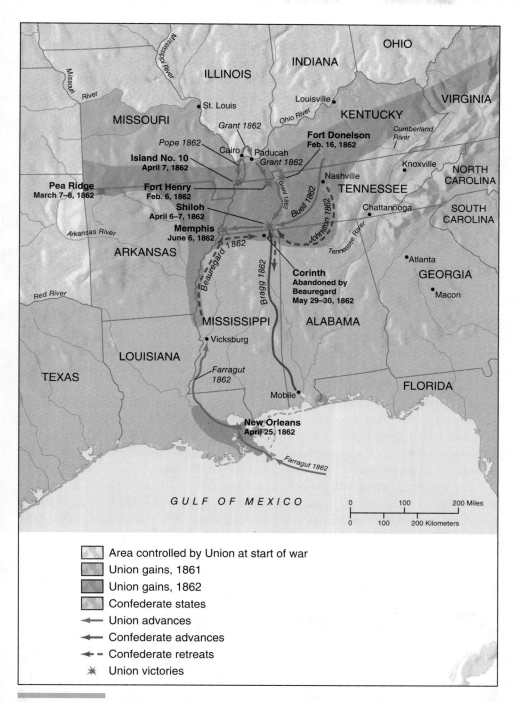

Area controlled by Union at start of war
Union gains, 1861
Union gains, 1862
Confederate states
← Union advances
← Confederate advances
← - Confederate retreats
✳ Union victories

MAP 15.2 THE WAR IN THE WEST, 1861–1862 Because of the early Union emphasis on capturing Richmond, the war in the West seemed less important to northerners. But from a strategic standpoint, the victories at Forts Henry and Donelson, which drove a wedge into southern territory and closed the Confederacy's quickest path to the West from Virginia and the Carolinas, and the capture of New Orleans and its Mississippi River port were crucial and set the stage for greater Federal success in the West in 1863.

if he had slept in his uniform. Behind the rumpled appearance lay a flexible military mind that would eventually grasp how the Civil War must be won.

Grant appreciated the strategic importance of river systems in the conquest of the western Confederacy. His combined river and land campaign caught the southerners unprepared and outflanked. By February 16, both forts had fallen. The Union victory drove a wedge into southern territory and closed the Confederacy's quickest path to the West from Virginia and the Carolinas. The Confederacy's only safe link across the Appalachians was now through Georgia. The Confederacy never recovered its strategic advantage in the West after the loss of Forts Henry and Donelson.

15.1

15.2

15.3

15.4

15.5

15.6

15.7

Grant next moved his main army south to Pittsburgh Landing on the Tennessee River, to prepare for an assault on the key Mississippi River port and rail center of Vicksburg. After blunting a surprise Confederate attack at Shiloh Church near Pittsburgh Landing, Grant pushed the southerners back to Corinth, Mississippi.

Federal forces complemented their victories at Shiloh and Corinth with another important success at New Orleans. Admiral David G. Farragut, who remained a Unionist even though born in Tennessee, blasted the Confederate river defenses protecting New Orleans and sailed a Federal fleet to the city in April 1862. The result was to open 200 miles of the Mississippi River, the nation's most vital commercial waterway, to Union traffic. With the fall of Memphis to Union forces in June, Vicksburg remained the only major river town still in Confederate hands. The western losses exposed a major problem in the Confederates' defensive strategy: Their military resources were stretched too thin to defend their vast territory.

The Real War.   The fierce fighting at Shiloh wrought unprecedented carnage. More American soldiers were lost at Shiloh than in all of the nation's wars combined up to that time. Each side suffered more than 10,000 casualties. By the time the smoke had cleared, the soldiers' initial enthusiasm and bravado were replaced by the sober realization that death or capture was a likely outcome, and that heroism, courage, and piety did not guarantee survival. "Too shocking, too horrible," a Confederate survivor of Shiloh wrote. "God grant that I may never be the partaker in such scenes again . . . when released from this I shall ever be an advocate of peace."

All wars are bloody, but none more so in American history than the Civil War. Old military tactics combined with modern weapons accounted for some of the gore, and primitive medical practice added to the toll. Death and physical wounds were not the only results of battle. The experience of combat and the scenes of human and natural destruction had a profound psychological impact on the soldiers.

Some soldiers coped with the gore by writing about it, thus distancing themselves from the awful reality. At the brutal battle of Spotsylvania in May 1864, only an earthen parapet separated the two armies firing at close range. A Union soldier wrote, "The dead and wounded were torn to pieces. . . . The mud was half-way to our knees, and

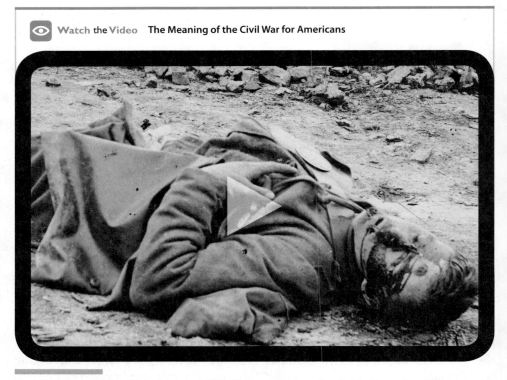

👁 **Watch the Video**   **The Meaning of the Civil War for Americans**

Dead Confederate soldier at Petersburg, April 1865. Modern weapons and ancient tactics produced great carnage. Those who survived came home with gruesome memories such as this.

15.1

15.2

15.3

15.4

15.5

15.6

15.7

by our constant movement the dead were almost buried at our feet." Many men were "nothing but a lump of meat or clot of gore." Sam Watkins, a Confederate private from Tennessee came upon a wounded comrade. "I asked him if he was badly wounded. He only pulled down the blanket. . . . The lower part of his body was hanging to the upper part by a shred, and all of his entrails were lying on the cot with him, the bile and other excrements exuding from them, and they full of maggots."

Other soldiers were consumed by the death and suffering. The war changed them forever. Union soldier and future U.S. Supreme Court Justice Oliver Wendell Holmes, Jr., wrote to his parents, "Before you get this you will know how immense the butcher's bill has been. [T]hese nearly two weeks have contained all of the fatigue & horror that war can furnish. . . . I am not the same man." The same feeling gripped a young man on the other side, Marion Hill Fitzpatrick of Georgia. "I have changed much in my feelings," he wrote to his parents. "The bombs and balls excite me but little and a battlefield strewed with dead and wounded is an every day consequence."

Hospitals, whether tents in the field or in commandeered buildings in towns and cities were less places to recover than morgues-in-waiting. The war also transformed noncombatants in these grisly surroundings. A Union surgeon cried out, "I am sick. Yes sick and tired of bloodshed. Weary and worn out with it. . . . [I]t has been almost one continued scene of *carnage*."

Yet, after the war many writers presented the conflict as a tableau of flying flags, heroic combatants, noble causes, and triumphal parades. The war was all of these things, but much more. Walt Whitman, who served as a nurse during the conflict, worried that "the real war will never get into the history books." Soldiers understood that once the war was over, memory would sanitize the conflict. The "real war" lives on in their letters and diaries. Daniel Bond of the 1st Minnesota began a diary: "Believing war to be a concentration of all that is wicked; and the most cruel invention of the worst enemy

Read the Document   **Clara Barton, Memoirs about Medical Life at the Battlefield (1862)**

A Federal field hospital, Savage Station, Virginia, June 1862, during the Seven Days' Battles. Mortality rates were high in hospitals on both sides, and here is one reason why. Makeshift field hospitals, overcrowded and providing only straw on the bare ground for comfort, offered little sanitation or care for wounded soldiers.

15.1

15.2

15.3

15.4

15.5

15.6

15.7

of the human race. And believing that were the real truth with regard to its extreme cruelty known, much would be done at least to soften its horrors . . . I have written this Journal with a view to telling some truths that will not be recorded in its histories."

The war became more brutal after Shiloh. Civilian populations became fair game, and when Confederate marksmen used severely wounded Union combatants for target practice as they lay below them at Fredericksburg that winter, it was clear that the war was entering a new, more brutal phase. Total war? As far back as the Peloponnesian War, officers had targeted civilians. But the Civil War was the first industrialized war and the impact on combat was devastating. Union General William T. Sherman understood the terrible nature of this war early on: "war is cruelty, and you cannot refine it." And Sherman did not attempt to refine it. The length of the war contributed to its brutality. It was time to dehumanize the enemy and rationalize the killing. The North became more desperate to end the struggle, and the South to prolong it in order to exhaust the patience of northerners. Both objectives were prescriptions for tragedy. The journey to war had been easy. The journey out of it would be very hard.

The War in the East

With Grant and Farragut squeezing the Confederacy in the West, Lincoln ordered a new offensive against Richmond in the East that he believed would end the war. Following the defeat at Bull Run, he had shaken up the Union high command and appointed General George B. McClellan to lead what was now called the Army of the Potomac. A West Point graduate, McClellan had served with distinction in the Mexican War. He was now called back into active duty to assume command of the Army of the Potomac, which was no more than a collection of raw recruits and disgruntled veterans. McClellan succeeded in transforming it into a disciplined fighting force. He was well liked by his soldiers, who referred to him affectionately as "Little Mac." McClellan returned their affection, perhaps too much. A superb organizer, he would prove overly cautious on the field of battle.

In March 1862, at the outset of the Peninsula Campaign, McClellan moved his 112,000-man army out of Washington and maneuvered his forces by boat down the Potomac River and Chesapeake Bay to the peninsula between the York and James rivers southeast of the Confederate capital (see Map 15.1). Union forces took Yorktown, Williamsburg, and Norfolk. Confederate general Joseph E. Johnston withdrew his forces up the peninsula toward Richmond, preparing for what most felt would be the decisive battle of the war. McClellan, moving ponderously up the peninsula, clashed with Johnston's army inconclusively at Seven Pines in late May 1862. Johnston was badly wounded in the clash, and President Davis replaced him with General Robert E. Lee, who renamed the forces under his command the Army of Northern Virginia.

Lee was from a prominent Virginia family long accustomed to command. His father, "Light-Horse Harry" Lee, had been a Revolutionary War hero. Lee attended West Point, served with distinction in the Mexican War, and commanded the Federal force that captured John Brown at Harpers Ferry in 1859. In 1831, he married Mary Custis, the daughter of George Washington's adopted son. Their gracious home in Arlington, Virginia, had a commanding view of the Potomac and Washington, DC. Before the war, it had seemed as if Lee would live out his days as a soldier-farmer, much like his wife's grandfather.

In 1860, the army posted Lee to Texas, where he watched the secession drama unfold. He opposed secession but was unwilling to take up arms against his native Virginia. Refusing an offer from Winfield Scott to take command of the Federal forces, he resigned from the U.S. Army and went with Virginia after it left the Union. Lee's reserved and aristocratic bearing masked a gambler's disposition. A fellow officer noted, "his name might be Audacity. He will take more chances, and take them quicker than any other general in this country." Under his daring leadership, the Confederacy's defensive strategy underwent an important shift.

Lee seized the initiative on June 25, 1862, attacking McClellan's right flank. Although inconclusive, the attack pushed the nervous McClellan into a defensive position. For a week, the armies sparred in a series of fierce engagements known collectively as the Seven Days' Battles. More than 30,000 men were killed or wounded on both sides, the deadliest week of the war so far. Although McClellan prevailed in these contests, the carnage so shocked him that he withdrew to Harrison's Landing on the James River. An exasperated Lincoln replaced McClellan with John Pope. Although Lee had saved Richmond, his troops had suffered frightfully. He had lost one-fourth of his 80,000-man army, but he remained convinced of the wisdom of his offensive-defensive strategy.

Lee went to work to vindicate these tactics. A series of inconclusive skirmishes brought Union and Confederate armies together once more near Manassas Junction. The Second Battle of Bull Run was as much a disaster for the Union as the first had been. Lee's generalship befuddled Pope and again saved Richmond. Lee and the Army of Northern Virginia were developing a reputation for invincibility. In a few weeks, an event far from the battlefield would set in motion forces that changed the purpose and the nature of the war, and changed America as well.

15.1

15.2

15.3

15.4

15.5

15.6

15.7

The Emancipation Proclamation

15.3 How did the Emancipation Proclamation change the nature of the war?

Origins

While slavery was the primary cause of the Civil War, it was not the objective of Union forces to liberate slaves. Saving the Union was the singular focus of the northern effort at the beginning of the war. President Abraham Lincoln was a strong advocate of free labor and he hated the institution of slavery. But he loved the Union more. He understood that adding the liberation of four million slaves to the war agenda could undermine both freedom and Union. The border slave states—Kentucky, Missouri, Delaware, and Maryland—would assuredly join the Confederacy. As Lincoln told a fellow Kentuckian, "I hope to have God on my side, but I must have Kentucky." A premature move toward emancipation could also affect military recruitment in the North. Abolitionists, even after the firing on Fort Sumter, remained a small minority. Most white northerners opposed outright emancipation, even if many opposed the extension of slavery into the territories.

Yet most northerners understood that the war would have some impact on slavery if Union forces emerged victorious. Whether the result would be liberation or a gradual demise of the institution, few could predict. Also, northerners understood that slaves aided the Rebel war effort by cultivating the cotton that the Confederacy could trade abroad in return for arms and growing the food to feed the Rebel armies. Slaves also helped more directly in the war effort as Union soldiers discovered when they moved into the South. Bondsmen dug ditches, cooked, hauled water, and engaged in other menial tasks that helped the Confederate cause.

Given the slaves' work at the front, it is not surprising that the first steps toward a general emancipation occurred within the Union military. In August 1861, Union General John C. Frémont, commanding federal troops in Missouri, issued an order emancipating all slaves in his jurisdiction. Missouri was still in the Union, but, as a slave state, it became a bloody battleground between Union and Confederate forces.

Frémont's edict exceeded the provisions of the **First Confiscation Act** passed by Congress a few weeks earlier. The act liberated only those slaves who had directly assisted the Rebel war effort or whose masters were openly disloyal to the Union. Lincoln was furious with the general and ordered him to comply with the Confiscation Act and rescind the order. When Frémont refused, the president cancelled the order himself, and the general resigned.

In April 1862, Major General David Hunter, from his headquarters at Hilton Head, South Carolina, declared martial law in the seceding states of Georgia, Florida, and South Carolina. Accompanying the declaration was an emancipation edict, though Union

First Confiscation Act Law passed by Congress in August 1861, it liberated only those slaves who had directly assisted the Confederate war effort or whose masters were openly disloyal to the Union.

15.1

15.2

15.3

15.4

15.5

15.6

15.7

Second Confiscation Act Law passed by Congress in July 1862 giving Union commanders the right to seize slave property as their armies marched through Confederate territory.

forces could hardly enforce it on the mainland in these seceded states. Still, Sea Island slaves flocked to Union lines. Again, President Lincoln voided the order.

Yet, three months later, on July 22, 1862, Lincoln presented a draft of the Emancipation Proclamation to his cabinet. What had happened in the interim? Lincoln's private position on emancipation had not changed. He still hoped to abolish the institution. He had already signed a compensated emancipation bill for the District of Columbia, passed by Congress in April 1862, and hoped the border slave states would agree to a similar plan. Their intransigence surprised and disappointed him. Gradual, compensated emancipation would not work.

Between April and July 1862, the northern military situation deteriorated. After much fanfare and expectation, General George B. McClellan's offensive against Richmond fizzled, despite a vastly superior force in numbers. Northern public opinion was turning against the war and, especially, against the Lincoln administration.

An increasingly impatient Congress, where Republicans dominated, pushed Lincoln on emancipation as military prospects dimmed. On July 16, 1862, Congress passed the **Second Confiscation Act** giving Union commanders the right to seize slave property as they marched into the Confederacy. The act resolved the quandary of what to do with slaves who fled to Union lines. Lincoln signed the bill, but appended a lengthy explanation questioning the authority of Congress to "free a slave within a state." The act, in fact, had little legal standing. Lincoln was still straddling the fence on the issue, but he realized he would need to do something soon.

When he presented an emancipation proposal to his cabinet, he found cautious support. Secretary of State William H. Seward counseled that the president should wait until the North achieved a military victory. Otherwise, the measure would look like desperation rather than inspiration. The order was tabled.

The pressure from leading Republicans mounted over the summer. Lincoln's response to an editorial in Horace Greeley's Republican newspaper, the *New York Tribune,* added to the frustration of those hoping for an emancipation proclamation. Greeley charged that the president was unduly influenced by "fossil politicians" in the border states to remain inactive on the issue of slavery. Lincoln responded: "My paramount object in this struggle is to save the Union, and is not either to save or destroy slavery. If I could save the Union without freeing any slave I would do it, and if I could save it by freeing all the slaves I would do it; and if I could save it by freeing some and leaving others alone I would also do that." It was a politic response steering a middle course between the pro- and anti-abolitionists. It was a clear articulation of the primary war aim—to save the Union, thus reassuring those opposed to abolition. Yet, it held out the possibility that emancipation could become a war objective.

The Document

The Union victory at Antietam (see page 424) on September 17, 1862, though narrow, provided Lincoln with the military success he needed. On September 22, he presented the preliminary Emancipation Proclamation to his cabinet. The document fell far short of Lincoln's best rhetorical or written efforts. It was basically a legal brief. This was purposeful. Lincoln wanted the proclamation to pass legal muster and he framed it within the "war powers" provision of the Constitution, which allowed an expansion of executive authority to defend the nation during time of war. Roger B. Taney, the author of the notorious *Dred Scott* decision, still presided over the U.S. Supreme Court, and Lincoln strove to give the document as firm a legal foundation as possible. He also wanted to ensure the continued loyalty of the border slave states by exempting them from the edict. In fact, most of the document consisted of exceptions and exemptions. The proclamation would take effect on January 1, 1863.

Critics rightfully pointed out that the Emancipation Proclamation actually freed no slaves. It applied only to those states still in rebellion, which meant they lay beyond federal jurisdiction anyway and slaves in these areas remained in bondage. Frederick Douglass admitted, "It was not a proclamation of 'liberty throughout the land, unto all the inhabitants thereof,' such as we had hoped it would be, but was one marked by discriminations and reservations." Nevertheless, he called it "a vast and glorious step in the right direction."

As news of the emancipation document reached the Federal forces in late September, the reaction was mixed. An Ohio private, Chauncey Welton, assured his father, "I can tell you we don't think mutch [sic] of [the Emancipation Proclamation] hear [sic] in the army for we did not enlist to fight for the negro and I can tell you that we [never] shall or many of us anyhow no never."

Lincoln was aware of these sentiments. As he later confided to a friend, "I was in great doubt about it [the proclamation] myself. I did not think that the people had been quite educated up to it, and I feared its effects upon the border states." Lincoln also worried that northern voters would punish the Republican Party for the proclamation in the November elections. He was right. Democrats scored huge gains in the House of Representatives and in the U.S. Senate. Republicans lost their majority in the House, though they formed a coalition with a minor party to give them a working majority. Emancipation was only part of the reason for the Republican debacle. The course of the war and growing impatience with it, inflation, and charges of corruption, convinced voters that perhaps the Democrats would provide more decisive leadership.

Yet, emancipation had increasingly broad support in the army and among the civilian population of the North, not because of a sudden outpouring of feeling on behalf of the slave, but for both the incongruity of slavery with the nation's ideals and the military advantage emancipation might provide. At last, a Union soldier sighed, the American flag "shall triumphantly wave over a free land, which it has never done yet."

Southerners responded with fury. They accused the Lincoln administration of inciting racial warfare. President Jefferson Davis warned that any blacks captured during Rebel forays into northern territory would be summarily sent south into slavery. He concluded with bravado, "The day is not distant when the old Union will be restored with slavery nationally declared to be the proper condition of all of African descent."

Lincoln's message to Congress on December 1, 1862, what we call today the State of the Union address (though all nineteenth-century presidents sent the text to the House clerk to be read rather than delivering an address themselves) more accurately reflected his feelings about emancipation than the legalistic proclamation. Defending the proclamation that would be the law of the land one month hence, he wrote, "In giving freedom to the slave, we assure freedom to the free—honorable alike in which we give, and what we preserve." Lincoln knew he had raised the stakes of the war considerably. It was now a war for the Union *and* for freedom. He concluded, "We shall nobly save, or meanly lose, the last best hope of earth." The final version of the Emancipation Proclamation, issued on January 1, 1863, included a recommendation that able-bodied freedmen be "received into the armed service."

The Thirteenth Amendment to the Constitution, passed by Congress on January 31, 1865, and ratified by the states on December 6, 1865, secured freedom for the slaves. The Emancipation Proclamation, as a war powers document, would be subject to legal challenges. Constitutional amendments are not. By January 1, 1863, tens of thousands of slaves had already stolen their freedom anyway. The Union armies, not the proclamation, liberated the slaves. As soon as a Union force appeared within the vicinity, slaves in the area left their farms, towns, and plantations for the Federal lines. Eventually, 185,000 of these former slaves took up arms against their erstwhile masters, literally fighting to preserve their freedom and the Union.

Despite its limited effectiveness and its formal prose, the Emancipation Proclamation is one of America's most important documents. For the first time in the nation's history, the force of federal authority crushed a domestic institution at glaring odds with our founding principles. It marked a significant advance in the journey to fulfill those principles.

The Proclamation also had the practical effect of reducing the likelihood of foreign involvement in the Civil War. Though some of Great Britain's leaders and

15.1
15.2
15.3
15.4
15.5
15.6
15.7

15.1

15.2

15.3

15.4

15.5

15.6

15.7

Read the Document   Abraham Lincoln, The Emancipation Proclamation (1863)

A Union soldier reads the Emancipation Proclamation to newly freed slaves. After Lincoln signed the Proclamation, celebrations took place throughout the country.

the press derided the preliminary Emancipation Proclamation as a cynical attempt to resolve a military stalemate, the British public rallied around the Union cause in the aftermath of emancipation. British workers, even those in the textile industry hurt by the Union's embargo of southern cotton, believed the cause of free labor transcended temporary economic woes. Today, a statue of Abraham Lincoln adorns a public square in Manchester, erected by that city's textile workers.

The French under Napoleon III also had designs on intervention, or at least officially recognizing the Confederate States of America as a sovereign nation. At the time of the promulgation of emancipation in January 1863, the French were bombarding the Mexican port of Vera Cruz, the beginning of a campaign to conquer the country over alleged nonpayment of debts. Despite Lincoln's protests at this obvious violation of the Monroe Doctrine, there was little his administration could do in the midst of the Civil War. The emancipation, however, blunted French interest in the Confederacy, especially when the British government drew back as well.

More immediately, the Emancipation Proclamation enabled the Lincoln administration to replenish a tired and poorly motivated army with fresh and eager black recruits. More than 80 percent of the roughly 185,000 black soldiers and 20,000 black sailors who fought for the Union were slaves and free black men from the South. For the typical black southerner who joined the army, the passage from bondage to freedom came quickly. Making his escape from his master, he perhaps "stole" his family as well. He typically experienced his first days of freedom behind Union lines, where he may have learned to read and write. Finally, he put on the Federal uniform, experiencing, as one black southern volunteer commented, "the biggest thing that ever happened in my life."

The Confederate government formally labeled white officers leading black troops as instigators of slave rebellion and punished them accordingly, presumably by hanging. Black soldiers, when captured, were returned to slavery. The Lincoln administration retaliated by suspending prisoner exchanges, which resulted in horrible conditions in Confederate and Union prisons. Roughly 56,000 prisoners died in captivity, a toll

15.1

15.2

15.3

15.4

15.5

15.6

15.7

that would have been much lower had Confederate authorities treated black prisoners of war the same as whites.

On some occasions, Confederate treatment of African American prisoners of war was worse than a return to bondage. In April 1864, General Nathan Bedford Forrest, a slave trader prior to the war and a founder of the Ku Klux Klan after the war, over-ran Federal positions at Fort Pillow, Tennessee. Although the black Union defenders surrendered, Forrest's men shouted, "Kill the damn niggers, shoot them down!" More than 100 surrendered black soldiers were murdered, along with some white officers. The same month, a Confederate regiment of Choctaw Indians scalped and mutilated an even larger number of surrendered black troops at Poison Spring, Arkansas.

But for black volunteers, the promise of freedom and redemption outweighed the dangers of combat. Black abolitionists campaigned tirelessly for the enlistment of free black men and fugitive slaves in the Union army. Frederick Douglass, whose son Lewis distinguished himself in the all-black 54th Massachusetts Volunteer Infantry Regiment, explained in early 1863, "Once let the black man get upon his person the brass letters, 'U.S.,' let him get an eagle on his buttons and a musket on his shoulder and bullets in his pockets, and there is no power on earth which can deny that he has earned the right to citizenship in the United States." Although black soldiers were eager to engage the enemy and fought as ably as their white comrades, they received lower pay and performed the most menial duties in camp. Abolitionists and black leaders pressured President Lincoln for more equitable treatment of African American recruits. When Frederick Douglass complained to Lincoln about the lower pay for black troops, the president defended the practice, noting that "their enlistment was a serious offense to popular prejudice" and the fact "that they were not to receive the same pay as white soldiers seemed a necessary concession to smooth the way to their employment at all as soldiers."

Despite discrimination, black soldiers fought valiantly at Port Hudson, Louisiana; near Charleston; and, late in the war, at the siege of Petersburg, Virginia. The most celebrated black encounter with Confederate troops occurred in July 1863, during a futile assault by the 54th Massachusetts Regiment on Fort Wagner outside Charleston. The northern press, previously lukewarm toward black troops, heaped praise on the effort. "Through the cannon smoke of that dark night," intoned a writer in the *Atlantic Monthly,* "the manhood of the colored race shines before many eyes that would not see."

Black Union troops—former slaves—repelling Confederates at New Bern, North Carolina, February 1864; African Americans, both free and slave, fought valiantly and often fiercely for their freedom; the alternative was sometimes execution on the spot or reenslavement.

15.1

15.2

15.3

15.4

15.5

15.6

15.7

The Legacy

For more than a century after the Civil War, African Americans celebrated January 1 as Emancipation Day. As racial lines hardened, and not only in the South, the memory of the Emancipation Proclamation continued to evoke a celebratory response from black communities across the nation in the late nineteenth century. But in 1888, the great black abolitionist, Frederick Douglass, speaking on the twenty-fifth anniversary of the document's release, denounced the "so-called Emancipation as a Stupendous Fraud." It is easy to understand Douglass's frustration. Most African Americans still toiled in near-slavery on southern farms. Restrictions were tightening on the right to vote and racial segregation by law was becoming commonplace across the nation. Freedom was secure, but the rights normally accompanying that freedom had proved elusive in subsequent years.

The fiftieth anniversary of the Emancipation Proclamation in 1913 occurred during what historians have called the "nadir" of race relations in the United States. Lynchings, disfranchisement, and segregation by law had crystallized the second-class citizenship of African Americans. A somber tone marked the anniversary for blacks.

Read the Document   James Weldon Johnson, "Fifty Years" (1922)

Freedman's Monument, Lincoln Park, Washington, DC. Thomas Ball, Sculptor. Dedicated in 1876 and funded solely by contributions from former slaves. Although criticized by later generations of African Americans as depicting the freedman in a subservient position, that criticism did not take account of the fact that Ball took the tableau from a 1787 abolitionist broadside or the fact that the former slave might be in the process of rising up and breaking his chains.

15.1

15.2

15.3

15.4

15.5

15.6

15.7

James Weldon Johnson, perhaps the most widely read black writer of the era, composed a poem for the occasion. The *New York Times* published the poem on its editorial page on January 1, 1913. Johnson's poem, "Fifty Years," expressed disappointment that the promise of the proclamation remained unfulfilled. Rather than accept defeat, Johnson urged his black readers to challenge the present circumstances to attain the full citizenship that was rightfully theirs.

The Emancipation Proclamation remained a powerful symbol for African Americans, more of a hope than a reality. The centennial observance occurred in quite different circumstances from the commemoration fifty years earlier. Many African Americans and their white allies viewed the civil rights movement as a second emancipation, a fulfillment of the initial document. In November 1963, Vice President Lyndon B. Johnson visited Gettysburg on the hundredth anniversary of Abraham Lincoln's famous speech there. Johnson's theme was less about the Gettysburg Address than about the unfulfilled promise of the Emancipation Proclamation: "Until justice is blind, until education is unaware of race, until opportunity is unconcerned with the color of men's skins, emancipation will be a proclamation but not a fact." Much as the Declaration of Independence had supplied the principled grounding for Lincoln's document, the Emancipation Proclamation, a century later, inspired actions to complete the journey to full citizenship.

On the one hundred and fiftieth anniversary of the Emancipation Proclamation, January 1, 2013, many of the aspirations of 1863 and the promises of 1963 had been achieved. In the Oval Office, occupied by Barack Obama, there was a signed copy of the proclamation above a bust of Martin Luther King, Jr. The physical journey of the document was not great, but its fulfillment traveled a long and often hard road for one hundred and fifty years. The proclamation marked the beginning of the journey to attain the objective embodied in our nation's founding document, "We hold these truths to be self-evident that all men are created equal."

Turning Points, 1862–1863

15.4 How did the changing nature of the war affect soldiers on both sides?

The impressive Confederate victories in the East masked the delicate condition of southern fortunes. Lee's offensive-defensive strategy seemed to be working, but it raised the possibility that the Confederacy could exhaust its men and resources before it sealed its independence.

The waning summer months of 1862 brought other concerns to the Davis administration in Richmond. The Union navy was choking the South's commercial link with Europe. Davis looked to the nations of Europe for diplomatic recognition as well as for trade.

Having stymied the Union war machine, Lee contemplated a bold move, a thrust into northern territory to bring the conflict to the North and stoke northerners' rising hostility to the war. The Lincoln administration hoped for any good news from the battlefield to revive waning support for the war and the government. As the fall of 1862 approached, the Union and Confederate governments both prepared for the most significant conflicts of the war to date.

The Naval War

The Union's naval strategy was to blockade the southern coast and capture its key seaports and river towns. The intention was to prevent arms, clothing, and food from reaching the Confederacy and keep cotton and tobacco from leaving. Destroying the South's ability to carry on trade would prevent the Confederacy from raising money to purchase the goods it needed to wage war. This vital trade brought the Confederacy into contact with European nations, a connection its leaders hoped to reinforce on the diplomatic front.

15.1

15.2

15.3

15.4

15.5

15.6

15.7

Neither side had much of a navy at the outset of the war. With more than 3,000 miles of Confederate coastline to cover, the Union blockade was weak at first. As time passed and the number of ships in the Union navy grew, the blockade tightened.

The Confederate naval strategy was to break the blockade and defend the South's vital rivers and seaports. The Confederacy built several warships to serve as blockade runners and as privateers to attack Union merchant ships, and they briefly disrupted Federal operations before Union vessels regained the advantage. Historians disagree about the effectiveness of the Union naval blockade, but with limited resources and capital, the Confederacy was heavily dependent on the flow of trade. Any restriction in the flow hurt the southern cause.

Antietam

The alarming arithmetic of the offensive-defensive strategy convinced Lee that the South could not sustain a prolonged conflict. He knew that his army must keep up the pressure on the Union forces and, if possible, destroy them quickly. Union success in the Mississippi Valley threatened to cut the Confederacy in two and deprive it of the resources of a vast chunk of territory. Within a year, the Confederacy might cease to exist west of the Appalachians. He desperately needed a dramatic victory.

In September 1862, Lee crossed the Potomac into Maryland (see Map 15.1). He was on his way to cut the Pennsylvania Railroad at Harrisburg. Lee established camp at Frederick, scattering his army at various sites, convinced that McClellan and the Army of the Potomac would not attack him.

Luck intervened for the North. At an abandoned Confederate encampment, a Union corporal found three wrapped cigars on the ground, evidently tossed away by a careless Confederate officer. To the corporal's amazement, the wrapping was a copy of Lee's orders for the disposition of his army. But even with this information, "Little Mac" moved so cautiously that Lee had time to retreat to defensive positions at Sharpsburg, Maryland, along Antietam Creek. There Lee's army of 39,000 men came to blows with McClellan's army of 75,000.

The Battle of Antietam saw the bloodiest single day of fighting in American history. About 2,100 Union soldiers and 2,700 Confederates died, and another 18,500, equally divided, were wounded. McClellan squandered his numerical superiority with uncoordinated and timid attacks. Although the armies had fought to a tactical draw, the battle was a strategic defeat for the Confederacy. In the battle's aftermath, Lee's troops limped back across the Potomac into Virginia and McClellan did not pursue them.

Antietam marked a major turning point in the war. It kept Lee from directly threatening northern industry and financial institutions. It prompted Britain and France to abandon plans to grant recognition to the Confederacy as an independent nation. And it provided Lincoln with the victory he needed to announce the abolition of slavery.

From Fredericksburg to Gettysburg

President Lincoln, angered by McClellan's failure to pursue Lee, replaced him with General Ambrose E. Burnside. The new chief of the Army of the Potomac, an imposing physical presence, sported bushy whiskers on his cheeks that came to be known as "sideburns," a transposition of the two parts of his name. Despite his commanding stature, Burnside was shy and insecure. Claiming incompetence, he had twice refused the command. His judgment proved better than Lincoln's.

Fredericksburg.   Moving swiftly against Lee's dispersed army in northern Virginia, Burnside reached the Rappahannock River opposite Fredericksburg in November 1862 (see Map 15.3). But the pontoon bridges to ford his 120,000 soldiers across the river arrived three weeks late, giving Lee an opportunity to gather his 78,000 men. On December 13, the Union forces launched a poorly coordinated and foolish frontal

15.1

15.2

15.3

15.4

15.5

15.6

15.7

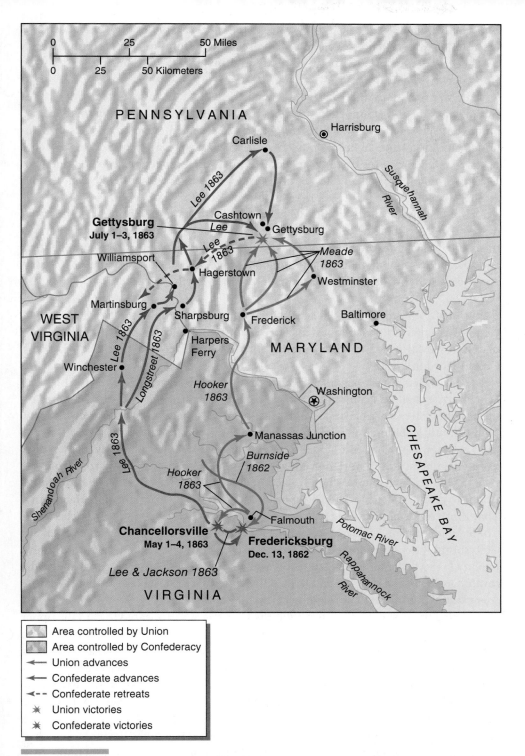

Area controlled by Union	
Area controlled by Confederacy	
Union advances	
Confederate advances	
Confederate retreats	
Union victories	
Confederate victories	

MAP 15.3 FROM FREDERICKSBURG TO GETTYSBURG: THE WAR IN THE EAST, DECEMBER 1862–JULY 1863 By all logic, the increasingly outgunned and outfinanced Confederacy should have been showing signs of faltering by 1863. But bungling by Union generals at Fredericksburg and Chancellorsville sustained southern fortunes and encouraged Robert E. Lee to attempt another invasion of the North.

assault that the Confederates repelled, inflicting heavy Federal casualties. Burnside, having performed to his own expectations, was relieved of command, and Lincoln installed Major General Joseph Hooker in his place.

Chancellorsville. The hard-drinking Hooker lacked Burnside's humility but not his incompetence. Resuming the offensive in the spring of 1863, Hooker hoped to outflank Lee. But the Confederate commander surprised Hooker by sending Stonewall Jackson to outflank the Union right. Between May 1 and May 4, Lee's

15.1

15.2

15.3

15.4

15.5

15.6

15.7

army delivered a series of crushing attacks on Hooker's forces at Chancellorsville. Outnumbered two to one, Lee had pulled off another stunning victory, but at a high cost. Lee lost some 13,000 men, fewer than Hooker's 17,000, but more than the Confederacy could afford.

Lee also lost Stonewall Jackson at Chancellorsville. Nervous Confederate sentries mistakenly shot and wounded him as he returned from a reconnoitering mission, and he died a week later. Known for his lightning strikes at the enemy and his brilliant understanding of the tactics of modern warfare, Jackson had helped Lee win some of the Confederacy's most stunning victories in 1862. Lee recognized the tragedy of Jackson's loss for himself and his country. "Any victory," the Confederate commander wrote, "would be dear at such a price. I know not how to replace him."

Still, Lee appeared invincible. Chancellorsville thrust Lincoln into another bout of despair. "My God!" he exclaimed in agony, "What will the country say! What will the country say!" Meanwhile, Lee, to take advantage of the Confederacy's momentum and the Union's gloom, planned another bold move. On June 3, 1863, the 75,000-man Army of Northern Virginia broke camp and headed north once again.

Gettysburg.   President Lincoln sent the Union Army of the Potomac after Lee. But General Hooker dallied, requested more troops, and allowed the Confederates to march from Maryland into Pennsylvania. An infuriated Lincoln replaced Hooker with George Gordon Meade.

Lee and Meade were personal friends, they had served together during the Mexican War, and the change in command worried the Confederate general. He had counted on the bungling Hooker as his opponent. "General Meade," he commented prophetically, "will commit no blunder in my front."

Lee's Army of Northern Virginia occupied a wide swath of Pennsylvania territory from Chambersburg to Wrightsville along the Susquehanna River, across from the state capital at Harrisburg. When Lee learned of Meade's movements, he ordered his troops to consolidate in a defensive position at Cashtown, 45 miles from Harrisburg. That the greatest battle of the war erupted at nearby Gettysburg was pure chance. A Confederate brigade left Cashtown to confiscate much-needed shoes from a factory in Gettysburg. Meeting Federal cavalry resistance near the town, the brigade withdrew. On July 1, 1863, a larger Confederate force advanced toward Gettysburg to disperse the cavalry and seize the shoes. What the Confederates did not realize was that the entire Army of the Potomac was coming up behind the cavalry.

During the first day of battle, July 1, the Confederates appeared to gain the upper hand, forcing Union forces back from the town to a new position on Cemetery Hill. On the second day, the entire Union army was in place, but the Confederates took several key locations along Cemetery Ridge before Federal forces pushed them back to the previous day's positions. Although the opposing sides had suffered heavy casualties, both armies were intact; and, if anything, Lee had the advantage. On July 3, the third day of the battle, Lee made a fateful error. Believing that the center of Meade's line was weak, he ordered an all-out assault against it. The night before, Meade had remarked to his colleague, Brigadier General John Gibbon, "If Lee attacks tomorrow, it will be in your front. He has made attacks on both our flanks and failed and if he concludes to try it again, it will be on our center." Thus Meade was prepared for Lee's assault.

The next morning, a bright, hot summer day, the Confederates launched an assault on Culp's Hill, only to fall back by noon. The key battle of the day occurred at three in the afternoon on the Union center at Cemetery Ridge, preceded by a fierce artillery duel. When the Union guns suddenly went silent, the Confederates, thinking they had knocked them out, began a charge led by General George E. Pickett. Pickett and his men marched out of the woods in a line extending a mile and a half. For a moment the Union infantry, now flat on their stomachs, watched in awe as Pickett's men moved forward in perfect formation, their bright red battle flags waving gently in the summer breeze, while the faint strains of "Dixie" wafted down from Seminary Ridge. Two hundred pieces of Union artillery boomed out, cutting huge holes in the Rebel lines, yet still Pickett's men advanced, filling in the gaps and holding their line. Union infantry, protected by a stone wall, one portion of which jutted out at an angle (henceforth known as the Bloody Angle), opened fire. Pickett's men continued forward, now on double-quick through the hail of bullets, balls, and shells, returning the fire.

Union soldiers, watching the destruction before them, cheered wildly and shouted, "Fredericksburg! Fredericksburg!" as if this slaughter could avenge the Union disaster the previous December. Some of Pickett's men got close enough to see the sooty faces of the Federal infantrymen, and a few breached the wall to engage the enemy in desperate hand-to-hand combat. Federal reserves, however, closed in on the insurgents and pushed them back into full retreat while Union artillery and infantry fire continued to pound the Confederates.

The charge cost Pickett two-thirds of his army, including every senior officer. Looking across the field of dead Confederate soldiers, Lee muttered, "All this has been my fault." The Battle of Gettysburg was over. Major Henry Abbott of the 20th Massachusetts summarized the feelings of his comrades: "By jove, it was worth all our defeats." On July 4, the remainder of Lee's Army of Northern Virginia filed down from Seminary Ridge and headed for the Potomac, unmolested by Meade's drained troops.

After the battle, Lee explained his disastrous frontal assault: "I believed my men were invincible." Gettysburg was the bloodiest battle of the war. The Union suffered 23,000 casualties; the Confederacy, 28,000. The battle's outcome boosted morale in the North and drained Lee's army of men and matériel. Yet Lincoln blasted Meade for failing to follow up on his victory. "I do not believe you appreciate the magnitude of the misfortune involved in Lee's escape," he wrote to his general. "He was within your easy grasp, and to have closed upon him would, in connection with our other late successes, have ended the war. As it is, the war will be prolonged indefinitely. . . . Your golden opportunity is gone, and I am distressed immeasurably because of it." Convinced by his aides that Meade would resign when he read the letter, Lincoln never sent it.

Despite Lincoln's perturbation, the Union victory at Gettysburg lifted the veil of gloom in the North. People exhaled collectively when Union troops foiled the Confederate invasion. President Lincoln, in his address dedicating the cemetery at Gettysburg in November of that year, used the evangelical metaphor of rebirth to comment on the importance of the sacrifice on that battlefield. On this consecrated ground, he declared, from the "honored dead," will come "a new birth of freedom."

While the battle changed the mood in the North, it did not mark the beginning of the end of the Confederacy. But coupled with the loss of Vicksburg on July 4 (see next section), it dealt a serious blow to Rebel fortunes. Many Confederate troops considered the Gettysburg campaign a draw or a temporary setback at worst; but there was no doubting the implications of the Vicksburg surrender on the nation's birthday.

Vicksburg, Chattanooga, and the West

As Union forces thwarted Confederate dreams in Pennsylvania, other Federal troops bore down on strategic Rebel strongholds in the western theater of the war (the area beyond the Appalachian mountains). Union military success in the West would seriously compromise the South's ability to move goods and men across rail lines and over waterways and leave vulnerable the ultimate western prize, the Confederate bread basket, Georgia.

Vicksburg. When Lincoln mentioned "our other late successes" in his letter to Meade, he was referring to another crucial Union victory. On July 4, one day after Pickett's charge at Gettysburg, the city of Vicksburg, the last major Confederate stronghold on the Mississippi, surrendered to Ulysses S. Grant.

15.1

15.2

15.3

15.4

15.5

15.6

15.7

15.1
15.2
15.3
15.4
15.5
15.6
15.7

✳ Explore the Civil War on MyHistoryLab

WHAT BROUGHT THE UNITED STATES TO THE CIVIL WAR?

By 1860, the United States was divided between North and South, a divergence centered on the issue of slavery. Other elements, however, also separated the two sides. The South was mostly agricultural and rural compared to the far more urbanized and industrialized North. By 1861, the two sides were in the Civil War as eleven southern states had seceded as the Confederacy. A bloody conflict ensued that lasted until 1865 and cost more American lives than any other U.S. war before or since. The Union eventually won, bolstered by its economic advantages, but only after the deaths of 752,000 men.

Union soldiers pose with a captured Confederate cannon.

RESOURCES OF THE UNION AND THE CONFEDERACY, 1861

	Industrial Workers	Factories	Railroad Tracks (miles)
Union	1,300,000	110,000	22,000
Confederacy	110,000	1,800	9,000

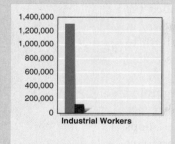

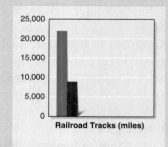

SOURCE: Multiple sources: Inter-University Consortium for Political and Social Research - http://www.icpsr.umich.edu/icpsrweb/ICPSR/studies/2896?archive=ICPSR&q=historical+economic+data+united+states]; Railroads and the Making of Modern America Digital History Project, University of Nebraska-Lincoln. [http://railroads.unl.edu/shared/resources/1861_Railroad.kml]; Inter-University Consortium for Political and Social Research - http://www.icpsr.umich.edu/icpsrweb/ICPSR/studies/2896?archive=ICPSR&q=historical+economic+data+united+states]

KEY QUESTIONS   Use **MyHistoryLab** *Explorer* to **answer** these **questions:**

Comparison ▶▶▶ *How did the South's population density contrast to that of the North?*

Map area data based on census information.

Response ▶▶▶ *Where were the major Civil War battles fought?*

Consider different regional strategies that affected military campaigns.

Analysis ▶▶▶ *How did the North win the Battle of Gettysburg?*

Examine the course of this decisive battle.

15.1

15.2

15.3

15.4

15.5

15.6

15.7

Grant had demonstrated an ability to use his forces creatively, swiftly, and with a minimum loss of life in his campaigns in the western Confederacy, but Vicksburg presented him with several strategic obstacles (see Map 15.4). In 1862, the formidable defenses on the city's western edge, which overlooked and controlled the Mississippi, had thwarted a Union naval assault, and the labyrinth of swamps, creeks, and woods protecting the city from the north had foiled General Sherman. The only feasible approaches appeared to be from the south and east.

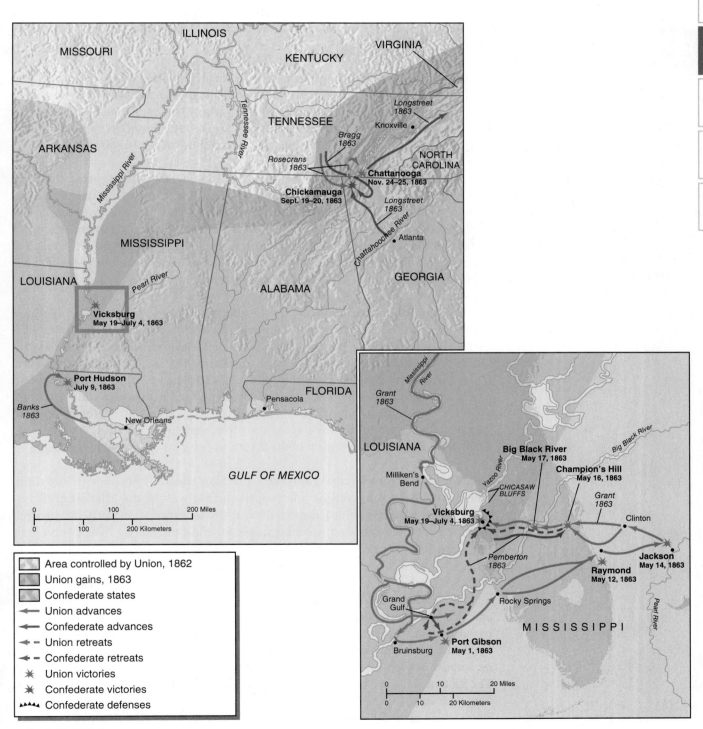

MAP 15.4 VICKSBURG AND CHATTANOOGA: THE WAR IN THE WEST, 1863 Devising a brilliant strategy, Union General Ulysses S. Grant took the last major Mississippi River stronghold from Confederate hands on July 4, 1863, dealing a significant economic and morale blow to the South. Coupled with the defeat at Gettysburg a day earlier, the fall of Vicksburg portended a bitter finale to hopes for southern independence. Grant completed his domination of the West by joining forces with several Union generals to capture Chattanooga and push Confederate forces into Georgia, setting the stage for the capture of that key southern state in 1864.

15.1

15.2

15.3

15.4

15.5

15.6

15.7

By March 1863, Grant had devised a brilliant plan to take Vicksburg that called for rapid maneuvering and expert coordination that worked with rather than against the area's geography. Grant had his 20,000 Union troops ferried across the Mississippi from the Louisiana side at a point south of Vicksburg. Then he marched them quickly into the interior of Mississippi. They moved northeastward, captured the Mississippi state capital at Jackson, and turned west toward Vicksburg. On May 22, 1863, Grant settled down in front of the city, less than 600 yards from Confederate positions. Grant's tight siege and the Union navy's bombardment from the river cut the city off completely. As food stores dwindled, residents were forced to eat mules and rats to survive. Their situation hopeless, General John Pemberton and his 30,000-man garrison surrendered on July 4.

Chattanooga. As Grant was besieging Vicksburg in June 1863, Union general William S. Rosecrans, commanding the Army of the Cumberland, advanced against Confederate general Braxton Bragg, whose Army of the Tennessee held Chattanooga, a "doorway" on the railroad that linked Richmond to the lower South. The capture of the city would complete the uncoupling of the West from the eastern Confederacy.

Bragg lacked confidence in his men and consistently overestimated the force and cunning of his enemy. At Rosecrans's approach, he abandoned Chattanooga and took up positions above nearby Chickamauga Creek. When the two armies clashed at Chickamauga on September 19, Bragg pushed Rosecrans back to Chattanooga. Bragg seized the railroad leading into Chattanooga and bottled up Rosecrans there, much as Grant had confined Pemberton at Vicksburg. Both sides had suffered heavily. Suddenly, the Union's careful strategy for the conquest of the western Confederacy seemed in jeopardy.

The Confederate position on the heights overlooking Chattanooga appeared impregnable. But the Confederate camp was plagued by dissension, with some officers openly questioning Bragg's ability. President Davis considered replacing him but had no one else available with Bragg's experience. Instead, Davis ordered General James Longstreet (along with one-third of Bragg's army) on a futile expedition against Union forces at Knoxville, Tennessee. Converging on Chattanooga with reinforcements, Union generals Grant, Sherman, and Hooker took advantage of the divided Confederate army to break the siege and force Bragg's army to retreat into Georgia. The Union now dominated most of the West and faced an open road to the East.

The War in the Trans-Mississippi West. The Confederacy's reverses at Vicksburg and Chattanooga mirrored its misfortunes farther west of the Mississippi River. Although a relatively minor theater of war, the territory west of the Mississippi provided supplies and strategic advantages for the Confederate West. Success in the Trans-Mississippi West could divert Federal troops and relieve the pressure on other parts of the Confederacy while allowing food and munitions to reach desperate southern armies.

Native American tribes in the Trans-Mississippi West, such as the Navajos, Dakotas, and Lakotas, spent a good deal of the Civil War battling Federal troops for territory and resources, quite apart from the sectional conflict. The Civil War drew soldiers from the frontier affording Indians an opportunity to press their concerns about tardy and incomplete delivery of food and supplies and the loss of lands granted to them by treaty. The Eastern Sioux in Minnesota confronted both starvation and the migration of whites onto their lands during the fall of 1862. With the white man's war raging in the East, the Sioux struck in the fall of 1862. About 200 Eastern Sioux attacked white settlements and killed between 350 and 800 men, women, and children. The Minnesota militia quelled the uprising. More than three hundred Sioux were tried and condemned to death, though President Lincoln pardoned all but thirty-eight. Federal authorities removed the remainder of the Eastern Sioux to a desolate area in the Dakota Territory and extinguished all of their remaining land rights in Minnesota.

15.1

15.2

15.3

15.4

15.5

15.6

15.7

Texas, however, was the focus of the trans-Mississippi campaign. The state was critical to Confederate fortunes, both as a source of supply for the East and as a base for the conquest of the Far West.

Texas was far from secure. It suffered from internal dissent and violence on its borders. Not all Texans supported secession. As early as 1862, areas of northern Texas rebelled against the state's Confederate government and were brutally suppressed. Germans in the Fredericksburg–San Antonio area openly defied the Confederacy from 1862 until the war's end. And the Mexican population in southern Texas supported the Union. On the state's western border, Comanches raided homesteaders at will until late 1864. In eastern Texas and along the southern frontier in the lower Rio Grande Valley, Union gunboats and troops disrupted Confederate supply lines. By 1864, with the Union in control of the Mississippi, and Federal troops along the Mexican border, Texas had lost its strategic importance.

The Confederacy's transcontinental aspirations died early in the war. In March 1862, a Confederate army seeking to conquer the Southwest was defeated by Union forces at the Battle of Glorieta Pass in New Mexico. The Southwest, from New Mexico to California, would remain firmly in Union hands.

War Transforms the North

15.5 What impact did the war have on the North's economy?

The Union successes in 1863 had a profound impact on both sides. For the North, hopes of victory and reunion increased. The federal government expanded its bureaucracy to wage war efficiently, and a Republican-dominated Congress passed legislation that broadened federal power and furthered the war effort. The Lincoln administration faced opposition on these measures and on its conduct of the war from Congress, from the Democratic Party, and from state leaders. But it successfully weathered dissent, thanks to the president's political skill, the desire of the Republicans to remain in power, and the Union's improving military fortunes. Boosted by federal economic legislation and wartime demand, the northern economy boomed. Women entered the workforce in growing numbers. But labor unrest and class and racial tensions suggested that prosperity had a price.

Wartime Legislation and Politics

Before the Civil War, the federal government rarely affected citizens' lives directly. But raising troops, protecting territory, and mobilizing the economy for war required a strong and active central government. With the departure of the South from the Union, Republicans dominated all branches of the federal administration. This left them in a position to test the constitutional limits of federal authority.

Suppressing Dissent.   President Lincoln began almost immediately to use executive authority to suppress opposition to the war effort in the North. In one of his most controversial actions, he issued a temporary suspension of the writ of habeas corpus, the constitutional protection against illegal imprisonment. Suspending it allowed the government to arrest suspected Confederate agents and hold them indefinitely, a procedure sanctioned by the Constitution "when in cases of rebellion or invasion the public safety may require it." The suspension became permanent in September 1862 and was used primarily in the border states to detain those suspected of trading with the enemy, defrauding the War Department, or evading the draft.

Executive sanctions fell particularly hard on the Democratic Party. "Disloyalty" was difficult to define in the midst of war. Although many Democrats opposed secession and supported the Union, they challenged the president on the conduct of the

Copperheads A term Republicans applied to northern war dissenters and those suspected of aiding the Confederate cause during the Civil War.

Radical Republicans A shifting group of Republican congressmen, usually a substantial minority, who favored the abolition of slavery from the beginning of the Civil War and later advocated harsh treatment of the defeated South.

Homestead Act Law passed by Congress in 1862 providing 160 acres of land free to anyone who would live on the plot and farm it for five years.

Land Grant College Act Law passed by Congress in July 1862 awarding proceeds from the sale of public lands to the states for the establishment of agricultural and mechanical (later engineering) colleges; also known as the Morrill Act, after its sponsor, Congressman Justin Morrill of Vermont.

war, on emancipation, and on his coolness toward peace initiatives. A few had ties with Confederate agents. Republicans called these dissenters "**Copperheads**," after the poisonous snake.

Despite the suspension of habeas corpus, Lincoln compiled a fairly good record for upholding basic American civil liberties. Although the authorities shut down a handful of newspapers temporarily, the administration made no attempt to control the news or subvert the electoral process. Two major elections were held during the war. In the first, the off-year election in 1862, Republicans retained control of Congress but lost several seats to Democrats. In the presidential election of 1864, Lincoln won reelection in a hard-fought contest.

While fellow Republicans sometimes chastised the president for violating civil liberties, mismanaging military command assignments, or moving too slowly on emancipation, they rarely threatened to disrupt the party. But there was dissent in the Republican Party, and it had an effect on national policy. **Radical Republicans** hounded Lincoln from early in his administration, establishing the Joint Committee on the Conduct of the War to examine and monitor military policy. Some of them accused Democratic generals, including McClellan, of deliberately subverting the war effort with their poor performance. They also pressed Lincoln for quicker action on emancipation, though they supported the president on most crucial matters.

Creating a National Economy. Lincoln likewise supported his party on an array of initiatives in Congress. Republicans used the federal government to enhance individual opportunities, especially in the West. The **Homestead Act**, passed in May 1862, granted 160 acres free to any settler in the territories who agreed to improve the land (by cultivating it and erecting a house) within five years of the grant. The act was also a boon for railroad companies.

Other legislation to boost the nation's economy and the fortunes of individual manufacturers and farmers included the **Land Grant College Act** of 1862, a protective tariff that same year, and the National Banking Act of 1863. The Land Grant Act awarded the proceeds from the sale of public lands to the states for the establishment of colleges offering instruction in "agriculture and mechanical arts." (President Buchanan had vetoed an earlier version of this act.) The tariff legislation protected northern industry from foreign competition while raising revenue for the Union. The National Banking Act of 1863 replaced the bank notes of individual states, which were often backed by flimsy reserves and subject to wild fluctuations in value, with a uniform national currency.

At the beginning of the war, American territory stretched from the Atlantic to the Pacific oceans, but loyalties were local and the federal government scarcely touched the lives of citizens. The Republican-dominated Congress forged a national economy that connected citizens to the fortunes of the national government. Construction began on a transcontinental railroad that, together with the Homestead Act, would help settle the West and bind the nation together in fact. A high protective tariff not only generated revenue for the government, but also bolstered northern manufacturing.

Through the sale of securities to the general public to help fund the war, hundreds of thousands of citizens now had a stake in the government's survival and success. A federal income tax bound Americans even closer to the government in Washington. A national currency fueled a national economy. Businesses, aided by government-subsidized efficiencies in transportation and communication, became national rather than regional enterprises. Farmers benefited from the Land Grant College Act that offered the latest labor-saving efficiencies for a scientific agriculture.

The Constitution of the United States did not explicitly sanction any of these measures. Operating under the broad mandate of the "war powers" allowed the Congress to support the government and protect the citizenry in times of insurrection. The results were a more powerful nation and a more centralized government. These measures helped sustain the Union war effort and enjoyed widespread support. The expansion of government into other areas, however, aroused opposition in some quarters, none more than the draft laws.

Conscription and the Draft Riots.   Congress passed the first national conscription law in 1863. Almost immediately, evasion, obstruction, and weak enforcement threatened to undermine it. As military authorities began arresting draft dodgers and deserters, secret societies formed to harbor draftees and instruct them on evasion.

Conflicts between citizens and federal officials over the draft sometimes erupted in violence. The worst draft riot occurred in New York City in July 1863. Neither the war nor the Republican administration was popular in New York City, especially among the Irish Catholic population. But that animosity paled before the hatred of the Irish for their African American neighbors. Competition for jobs, the use of blacks as strikebreakers, and the feeling that were it not for the Emancipation Proclamation, the war would be over made the Irish population adamant about avoiding fighting and dying for a cause they reviled. The fact that more affluent New Yorkers could buy their way out of the draft by hiring a substitute for $300 made this also a class issue for the mostly working-class and poor Irish residents of the city.

The racial and class issues were apparent in the **New York Draft Riot**. After a mostly Irish mob had destroyed the draft office, it launched an indiscriminate attack on the city's black population and institutions, including burning the Colored Orphan Asylum to the ground and hanging two black New Yorkers who wandered into their path. The rioters also sacked the mayor's house, tore up railroad tracks, looted the Brooks Brothers clothing store, and destroyed commercial and residential property on fashionable Fifth Avenue, crying, "Down with the rich!" City officials and the police stood by, unable or unwilling to stem the riot. Army units fresh from Gettysburg, along with militia and naval units, quelled the riot. Peace returned to the city at a cost of 105 lives and $5 million in property damage. The Democratic-controlled city council rewarded the rioters by appropriating funds to buy residents out of the draft.

New York Draft Riot A mostly Irish-immigrant protest against conscription in New York City in July 1863 that escalated into class and racial warfare that had to be quelled by federal troops.

15.1

15.2

15.3

15.4

15.5

15.6

15.7

NEW YORK—HANGING AND BURNING A NEGRO IN CLARKSON STREET.

The lynching of a black New Yorker during the Draft Riot in July 1863. The violence against black people during the riot reflected decades of racial tension, especially between Irish immigrants and black residents, over jobs and housing.

15.1

15.2

15.3

15.4

15.5

15.6

15.7

The Northern Economy

After an initial downturn during the uncertain months preceding the war, the northern economy picked up quickly. High tariffs and massive federal spending soon made up for the loss of southern markets and the closing of the Mississippi River. Profits skyrocketed for some businesses. The earnings of the Erie Railroad, for example, jumped from $5 million in 1860 to $10 million in 1863. New industries boomed, and new inventions increased manufacturing efficiency, as in the sewing machine industry, which was first commercialized in the 1850s. Technological advances there greatly increased the output of the North's garment factories. Production of petroleum, used as a lubricant, increased from 84,000 gallons to 128 million gallons during the war.

Despite the loss of manpower to the demands of industry and the military, the productivity of northern agriculture grew during the war. As machines replaced men on the farm, manufacturers of farm machinery became wealthy. Crop failures in Europe dramatically increased the demand for American grain. "Old King Cotton's dead and buried; brave young Corn is king," went a popular northern refrain.

Trade Unions and Strikebreakers.   Working people should have benefited from wartime prosperity. With men off to war and immigration down, labor was in short supply. Although wages increased, prices rose more. Declining real wages led to exploitation, especially of women in garment factories. The trade union movement, which suffered a serious setback in the depression of 1857, revived. Local unions of shoemakers, carpenters, and miners emerged in 1862 across the North, and so did a few national organizations. By 1865, more than 200,000 northern workers belonged to labor unions.

Employers struck back at union organizing by hiring strikebreakers, usually African Americans, who were available because until the war's midpoint, they were unwelcome for military service. Labor conflicts between striking white workers and black strikebreakers sparked riots in New York City and Cincinnati. The racial antagonism accounted in part for workers' opposition to Lincoln's Emancipation Proclamation and for the continued strength of the Democratic Party in northern cities.

Profiteers and Corruption.   The promise of enormous profits bred greed and corruption as well as exploitation. Illicit trade between North and South was inevitable when cotton could be bought at 20 cents a pound in New Orleans and sold for $1.90 a pound in Boston. Profiteers not only defied the government to trade with the enemy but also sometimes swindled the government outright. Some merchants reaped high profits supplying the army with shoddy goods at inflated prices. (The word *shoddy,* coined during the war, originally denoted poor-quality shoes.)

Some northerners viewed the spending spree uneasily. They were disturbed to see older men flaunting their wealth while young men were dying on the battlefield. Sentiments like these hinted at the deep social and ethical problems that were emerging in northern society and would become more pronounced in the decades after the Civil War. For the time being, the benefits of economic development for the Union cause outweighed its negative consequences. The thriving northern economy fed, clothed, and armed the Union's soldiers and kept most civilians employed and well fed. Prosperity and the demands of a wartime economy also provided northern women with unprecedented opportunities.

Northern Women and the War

More than 100,000 northern women took jobs in factories, sewing rooms, classrooms, hospitals, and arsenals during the Civil War. Stepping in for their absent husbands, fathers, and sons, they often performed tasks previously reserved for men but at lower pay. The expanding bureaucracy in Washington also offered opportunities for many women. The United States Treasury alone employed 447 women in the war years. And unlike private industry, the federal government paid women and men equally for the same work.

15.1

15.2

15.3

15.4

15.5

15.6

15.7

If the war created opportunities for many women, it also left tens of thousands widowed and devastated. In a society that expected women to be supported by men, the death of a husband could be a financial and psychological disaster. Many women were left to survive on meager pensions with few skills they could use to support themselves.

The new economic opportunities the war created for women left northern society more open to a broader view of women's roles. One indication of this change was the admission of women to eight previously all-male state universities after the war. Like the class and racial tensions that surfaced in northern cities, the shifting role of women during the Civil War hinted at the promises and problems of postwar life. The changing scale and nature of the American economy, the expanded role of government, and the shift in class, racial, and gender relations were all trends that signaled what historians call the "modernization" of American society. Many of these trends began before the war, but the war highlighted and accelerated them.

The Confederacy Disintegrates

15.6 How did the war affect civilian life in the South?

E ven under the best of conditions, the newly formed political and economic institutions of the Confederacy would have had difficulty maintaining control over the country's class and racial tensions. But as battlefield losses mounted, the Confederacy disintegrated.

After 1863, defeat infected Confederate politics, ruined the southern economy, and eventually invaded the hearts and minds of the southern people. What is remarkable is that such losses did not demoralize the Confederacy sooner. In fact, desertion rates did not exceed those of the Union forces, and Lee's Army of Northern Virginia included about as many men in the spring of 1865 as it had in the spring of 1863. True, civilians battled the policies of the Richmond government, but they protested less the sacrifices that war engendered than the unequal sharing of the burdens, including taxation, the military draft, food shortages, and inflation. Disillusionment against the Confederate government did not erode support for Lee and his army. The South pinned its waning hopes on its defensive military strategy. If it could prolong the conflict a little longer, perhaps a war-weary North would replace Lincoln and the Republicans in the 1864 elections with a Democratic president and Congress inclined to make peace.

Southern Politics

As the war turned against the Confederacy, southerners increasingly turned against each other. Some joined peace societies, which emerged as early as 1861. North Carolinians opposed to the war formed the Order of the Heroes of America, whose members not only demonstrated for peace but also took control of the Piedmont and mountain sections of the state. Other southerners preferred quieter dissent. They refused to join the army, pay taxes, or obey laws prohibiting trade with the enemy.

States' rights proved an obstacle to the Davis administration's efforts to exert central authority. The governors of Georgia and North Carolina gave the Richmond government particular difficulty, hoarding munitions, soldiers, supplies, food, and money. Even cooperative governors refused to allow state agents to collect taxes for the Confederacy.

Unlike Abraham Lincoln, Jefferson Davis could not appeal to party loyalty to control dissent because the Confederacy had no parties. Davis's frigid personality, his insistence on attending to minute details, and his inability to accept even constructive criticism gracefully, also set him apart from Lincoln and worsened political tensions within the Confederacy.

15.1

15.2

15.3

15.4

15.5

15.6

15.7

Several parts of the South began clamoring for peace during the fateful summer of 1863. By November 1864, the Confederacy was suffering as much from internal disaffection as from the attacks of Union armies. Confederate authorities could not suppress civilian unrest in Virginia, North Carolina, and Tennessee, and Union spies operated openly in Mobile, Wilmington, and Richmond.

Davis and other Confederate leaders might have averted some of these political problems had they succeeded in building a strong sense of Confederate nationalism among soldiers and civilians. They tried several strategies to do so. For example, Davis tried to identify the Confederacy's fight for independence with the American Revolution of 1776. But egalitarian revolutionary ideals quickly lost their appeal in the face of poverty, starvation, and defeat. Davis also tried to cast the Confederacy as a bastion of freedom standing up to Lincoln's despotic abuse of executive authority, but he, too, eventually invoked authority similar to Lincoln's. Confederate religious leaders sought to distinguish their new nation from the North by referring to southerners as God's "chosen people." But when Confederate military fortunes declined, religious leaders drew back from such visions of collective favor and stressed the need for individual salvation.

Southern Faith

In a devout society convinced it was fighting a holy war, some southerners sought to attribute their mounting losses to a moral failing. Some identified slavery as the culprit. But most Confederates held steadfast to the notion that God was on their side and that battlefield losses represented His temporary displeasure, not abandonment. They asked, as it is written in Judges 6:13, "If the Lord be with us, why then is all this befallen us?" They answered by drawing comfort from the Old Testament account of Job's suffering: "Though he slay me, yet will I trust him."

For black southerners, the Bible held other confirmations. The war was indeed becoming the fulfillment of a biblical prophecy. They turned to the Book of Daniel for its explicit explanation:

> For the king of the north shall return, and shall set forth a multitude greater than the former, and shall certainly come after certain years with a great army and with much riches.

> And in those times there shall many stand up against the king of the south: also the robbers of thy people shall exalt themselves to establish the vision; but they shall fall.

The Southern Economy

By 1863, the Confederacy was having a difficult time feeding itself. Destruction of farms by both sides and growing Union control of waterways and rail lines restricted the distribution of food. Speculators held certain commodities off the market to drive up prices, making shortages of food, cloth, and medicines worse. Bread riots erupted in Mobile, Atlanta, and Richmond. In Mobile, a group of women marched under banners reading "Bread or Blood" and "Bread and Peace." Armed with hatchets, they looted stores for food and clothing. In a show of grim humor, people in southern cities held "starvation parties" at which they served only water. "Deaths from starvation have absolutely occurred," a Confederate official informed President Davis in 1864.

Southern soldiers had marched off to war in neat uniforms with shiny buttons, many leaving behind self-sustaining families. But in August 1863, diarist Mary Chesnut, wife of a Confederate official in Richmond, watched 10,000 men marching near Richmond and commented, "Such rags and tags as we saw now. Most garments and arms were . . . taken from the enemy." The soldiers' families were threadbare as well. In the devastated areas near battle sites, civilians survived by selling fragments of dead soldiers' clothing stripped off their bodies and by collecting spent bullets and selling them for scrap.

Read the Document   Mary Boykin Chesnut, A Confederate Lady's Diary (1861)

15.1

15.2

15.3

15.4

15.5

15.6

15.7

Wartime food shortages, skyrocketing inflation, and rumors of hoarding and price-gouging drove women in several southern cities to protest violently. Demonstrations like the 1863 food riot shown here reflected a larger rending of southern society as Confederate losses and casualties mounted on the battlefield. Some southern women placed survival and providing for their families ahead of boosting morale and silently supporting a war effort that had taken their men away. Their defection hurt the Confederate cause.

The predations of both Union and Confederate soldiers further threatened civilians in the South. The women and children left alone on farms and plantations were vulnerable to stragglers and deserters from both armies who sometimes robbed, burned houses, raped, and murdered. Southerners also feared that slaves on isolated plantations would rise up against their masters. Most slaves, however, were more intent on escape than revenge.

As Confederate casualties mounted, more and more southern women and children, like their northern counterparts, faced the pain of grief. Funeral processions became commonplace in the cities and black the color of fashion. With little food, worthless money, and a husband, son, or father gone forever, the future looked bleak.

Southern Women and the War

In the early days of the Civil War, southern white women continued to live their lives according to antebellum conventions. Magazine articles urged them to preserve themselves as models of purity for men debased by the violence of war. The southern woman, by her moral example, "makes the Confederate soldier a gentleman of honor, courage, virtue and truth, instead of a cut-throat and vagabond," opined one magazine.

15.1

15.2

15.3

15.4

15.5

15.6

15.7

Women flooded newspapers and periodicals with patriotic verses and songs. A major theme of these works, illustrated by the following example from the *Richmond Record* in September 1863, was the need to suppress grief and fear for the good of the men at the front:

> *The maid who binds her warrior's sash*
> *And smiling, all her pain dissembles,*
> *The mother who conceals her grief*
> *[had] shed as sacred blood as e'er*
> *Was poured upon the plain of battle.*

A Virginia woman confided to her diary, "We must learn the lesson which so many have to endure, to struggle against our feelings."

By the time of the Civil War, such emotional concealment had become second nature to planters' wives. They had long had to endure their anguish over their husbands' nocturnal visits to the slave quarters. They were used to the condescension of men who assumed them to be intellectually inferior. And they accepted in bitter, self-sacrificing silence the contradiction between the myth of the pampered leisure they were presumed to enjoy and the hard demands their lives actually entailed. But some southern women chafed at their supporting role and, as Confederate manpower and matériel needs became acute, took on new productive responsibilities. Initially, they did so within the domestic context: Women formed clubs to sew flags and uniforms. To raise money for the war effort, they held benefits and auctions and collected jewelry and other valuables.

Soon, however, the needs of the Confederacy drew women outside the home to fill positions vacated by men. They managed plantations. They worked in the fields alongside slaves. They worked in factories to make uniforms and munitions. They worked in government offices as clerks and secretaries. They taught school. A few, like Belle Boyd and Rose O'Neal Greenhow, spied for the Confederacy. And many, like their northern counterparts, served as nurses. Eventually, battlefield reverses and economic collapse undermined all these roles, leaving women and men alike struggling simply to survive.

As the war dragged on and the southern economy and social order deteriorated, even the patriots suffered from resentment and doubt. By 1864, many women were helping their deserting husbands or relatives elude Confederate authorities. What had begun as a sacred cause had disintegrated into a nightmare of fear and deprivation. Uprooted from their homes, some women wandered through the war-ravaged South, exposed to violence, disease, and hunger and seeking shelter where they could find it. Those women fortunate enough to remain in their homes turned to work, others to protest, and many to religion. Some devoutly religious women concluded that it was God, not the Yankees, who had brought destruction on the South for its failure to live up to its responsibilities to women and children. Others blamed their men. After a series of reverses in the Confederate West, one woman confided to her diary that "If our soldiers continue to behave so disgracefully, we *women* had better take the field and send them home to raise chickens." However, despite hardship and privation, support for the Confederacy persisted among some women, stoked by fierce hatred of the enemy.

The Union Prevails, 1864–1865

15.7   What was Grant's strategy for ending the war?

Despite the Union's dominant military position after Vicksburg and Gettysburg and the Confederacy's mounting home front problems, three obstacles to Union victory remained. Federal troops under General William T. Sherman controlled Chattanooga and the gateway to Georgia, but the Confederate Army of Tennessee, now commanded by Joseph E. Johnston, was still intact, blocking

15.1
15.2
15.3
15.4
15.5
15.6
15.7

White family "refugeeing." In advance of Union armies, tens of thousands of southern families fled to safer locales, a bitter exodus that fulfilled the Federals' vow to bring the war to the South's civilian population.

Sherman's path to Atlanta. Robert E. Lee's formidable Army of Northern Virginia still protected Richmond. And the Confederacy still controlled the rich Shenandoah Valley, which fed Lee's armies and supplied his cavalry with horses. In March 1864, President Lincoln brought General Ulysses S. Grant to Washington and appointed him commander of all Union armies. Grant set about devising a strategy to overcome these obstacles.

Grant's Plan to End the War

Grant brought two innovations to the final campaign. First, he coordinated the Union war effort. Before, the Union's armies in Virginia and the West had operated independently, giving Confederate leaders the opportunity to direct troops and supplies to whichever arena most needed them. Now Grant proposed to deprive them of that option. The Union's armies in Virginia and the Lower South would attack at the same time, keeping steady pressure on all fronts. Second, Grant changed the tempo of the war. Before, long periods of rest had intervened between battles. Grant, with the advantage of superior numbers, proposed nonstop warfare.

Although Grant's strategy ultimately worked, several problems and miscalculations undermined its effectiveness. With Sherman advancing in Georgia, Grant's major focus was Lee's army in Virginia. But Grant underestimated Lee. The Confederate general thwarted him for almost a year and inflicted horrendous casualties on his army. Confederate forces under Jubal Early drove Union forces from the Shenandoah Valley in June 1864, depriving Grant of troops and allowing the Confederates to maintain their supply lines. And the incompetence of General Benjamin Butler, charged with advancing up the James River to Richmond in May 1864 to relieve Lee's pressure on Grant, further eroded Grant's plan. Finally, Grant had to contend with disaffection in his officer corps. Many of his officers felt enduring loyalty to General George B. McClellan, whom Lincoln had dismissed in 1862, and considered Grant a mediocrity who had triumphed in the West only because his opposition there had been third rate.

Lee's only hope was to make Grant's campaign so costly and time-consuming that the northern general would abandon it before the southerners ran out of supplies and troops. But despite problems and setbacks, Grant kept relentless pressure on Lee. Tied down in Virginia, the Confederate general was unable to send troops to help slow Sherman's advance in Georgia.

15.1

15.2

15.3

15.4

15.5

15.6

15.7

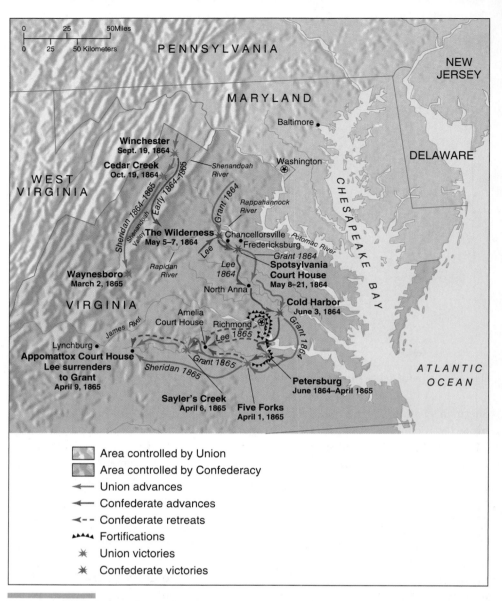

MAP 15.5 GRANT AND LEE IN VIRGINIA, 1864–1865 The engagements in Virginia from May 1864 to April 1865 between the two great generals proved decisive in ending the Civil War. Although Lee fared well enough in the Wilderness, Spotsylvania, and Cold Harbor campaigns, the sheer might and relentlessness of Grant and his army wore down the Confederate forces. When Petersburg fell after a prolonged siege on April 2, 1865, Richmond, Appomattox, and dreams of southern independence soon fell as well.

From the Wilderness to Cold Harbor. Grant and General George Meade began their campaign against Lee in May 1864, crossing the Rapidan River near Fredericksburg, Virginia, and marching toward an area known as the Wilderness (see Map 15.5). Lee attacked the Army of the Potomac, which outnumbered his forces 118,000 to 60,000, in the thickets of the Wilderness on May 5 and 6 before it could reach open ground. The densely wooded terrain reduced the Union army's advantage in numbers and artillery. Much of the fighting involved fierce hand-to-hand combat. Exchanges of gunfire at close range set the dry underbrush ablaze. Wounded soldiers, trapped in the fires, begged their comrades to shoot them before they burned to death. The toll was frightful, 18,000 casualties on the Union side, 10,000 for the Confederates. Other Union commanders would have pulled back and rested after such an encounter. But Grant, relentless in the pursuit of the enemy, startled Lee's army by pushing on, and Lee's offensive in the Battle of the Wilderness was his last. From then on, his army was on the defensive against Grant's relentless pursuit.

Marching and fighting, his casualties always higher than Lee's, Grant continued southward. Attacking the entrenched Confederate army at Spotsylvania, his army suffered

General Ulysses S. Grant had the pews from a local church moved to a grove of trees on May 21, 1864, where he and his officers planned the following day's assault on Confederate troops at Cold Harbor, Virginia. Grant appears at the left of the photograph, leaning over the shoulder of General George Meade and studying a map.

15.1

15.2

15.3

15.4

15.5

15.6

15.7

another 18,000 casualties to the Confederates' 11,000. Undeterred, Grant moved on toward Cold Harbor, where Lee's troops again awaited him in entrenched positions. Flinging his army against withering Confederate fire on June 3, he lost 7,000 men in eight minutes.

In less than a month of fighting, the Army of the Potomac had lost 55,000 men. The slaughter undermined Grant's support in northern public opinion and led peace advocates to renew their quest for a cease-fire. With antiwar sentiment growing in the North as the presidential elections approached in November, Lee's defensive strategy seemed to be working.

Grant decided to change his tactics. Abandoning his march on Richmond from the north, he shifted his army south of the James River to approach the Confederate capital from the rear. Wasting no time, he crossed his army over the James and, on June 17, 1864, surprised the Confederates with an attack on Petersburg, a critical rail junction 23 miles south of Richmond. It was a brilliant maneuver, but the hesitant actions of Union corps commanders gave Lee time to reinforce the town's defenders. Both armies dug in for a lengthy siege.

Atlanta.   While Grant engaged Lee in Virginia, Union forces under William T. Sherman in Georgia engaged in a deadly dance with the Army of Tennessee under the command of Joseph E. Johnston as they began the campaign to take Atlanta (see Map 15.6). Hoping to lure Sherman into a frontal assault, Johnston settled his forces early in May at Dalton, an important railroad junction in Georgia 25 miles south of Chattanooga and 75 miles north of Atlanta. The wily Union general declined to attack and instead made a wide swing around the Confederates, prompting Johnston to abandon Dalton, rush south, and dig in again at Resaca to prevent Sherman from cutting the railroad. Again Sherman swung around without an assault, and again Johnston rushed south to cut him off, this time at Cassville.

This waltz continued for two months, until Johnston had retreated to a strong defensive position on Kennesaw Mountain, barely 20 miles north of Atlanta. At this point,

15.1

15.2

15.3

15.4

15.5

15.6

15.7

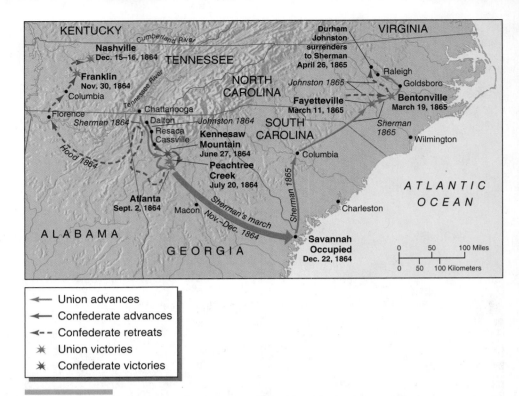

MAP 15.6 THE ATLANTA CAMPAIGN AND SHERMAN'S MARCH, 1864–1865 General William T. Sherman, a brilliant tactician who generally refused to be goaded into a frontal assault, "danced" with Confederate general Joseph E. Johnston until an impatient Jefferson Davis replaced Johnston with John Bell Hood, and soon Atlanta was in Federal hands. The fall of Atlanta opened the way to the rest of Georgia, a key supply state for the Confederacy. With orders not to harm the civilian population, Sherman's men took their wrath out on property as they made their way through Georgia and South Carolina.

early in July, Sherman decided to attack, with predictably disastrous consequences. The Union suffered 3,000 casualties, the Confederates only 600. Sherman would not make such a mistake again. He resumed his maneuvering and by mid-July had forced Johnston into defensive positions on Peachtree Creek just north of Atlanta. President Davis feared that Johnston would let Sherman take Atlanta without a fight and "dance" with the Union general until the sea stopped them both. Davis dismissed Johnston and installed John Bell Hood of Texas in his place. This was a grave error. Hood, in the opinion of those who fought for him, had a "lion's heart" but a "wooden head."

In late July, Hood began a series of attacks on Sherman, beginning at Peachtree Creek on July 20, and was thrown back each time with heavy losses. Sherman launched a series of flanking maneuvers around the city in late August that left Hood in danger of being surrounded. The Confederate general had no choice but to abandon Atlanta and save his army. On the night of September 1, Hood evacuated the city, burning everything of military value.

The loss of Atlanta was a severe blow to the Confederacy. Several of the South's major railroads converged at the city, and its industries helped arm and clothe the armies. Atlanta's fall also left Georgia's rich farmland at the mercy of Sherman's army. Most significant, the fall of Atlanta revived the morale of the war-weary North and helped ensure Lincoln's reelection in November. The last hope of the Confederacy, that a peace candidate would replace Lincoln and end the war, had faded.

The Election of 1864 and Sherman's March

Before Sherman's victory at Atlanta, northern dismay over Grant's enormous losses and his failure to take Richmond raised the prospect of a Democratic election victory. Nominating George B. McClellan, the former commander of the Union's armies, as their presidential candidate, the Democrats appealed to voters as the party of peace. They also appealed to the anti-emancipation sentiment that was strong in some parts of the North.

The fall of Atlanta and the Union's suddenly improved military fortunes undermined Democratic prospects. Another Union victory three weeks before the elections gave Lincoln a further boost and diminished McClellan's chances. Since September, Union forces, under General Philip H. Sheridan, had been on the offensive in the Shenandoah Valley (see Map 15.5). In lightning cavalry raids on farms and supply depots, they destroyed valuable Confederate food reserves. And, in a decisive battle on October 19, they overwhelmed the valley's Confederate defenders. Lee had now been deprived of a vital source of supply.

The Republican Victory.   In the voting on November 8, Lincoln captured 55 percent of the popular vote, losing only New Jersey, Delaware, and Kentucky. Republicans likewise swept the congressional elections, retaining control of both the Senate and the House of Representatives.

The Republican victory reinforced the Union commitment to emancipation. A proposed constitutional amendment outlawing slavery everywhere in the United States, not just those areas still in rebellion, passed Congress in January 1865 and was ratified as the **Thirteenth Amendment** to the U.S. Constitution. All the earlier amendments related to government powers and functions; this was the first to outlaw a domestic institution previously protected by the Constitution and state law.

Sherman's March to the Sea.   After Sherman took Atlanta, he proposed to break Confederate resistance once and for all by marching his army to the sea and destroying everything in its path (see Map 15.6). Sherman's March got underway on November 15. His force of 60,000 men, encountering little resistance, entered Savannah on December 22, 1864, and presented the city to Lincoln as a Christmas present. Just a few weeks earlier, Union forces in Tennessee had routed Hood's army at the Battle of Franklin and then crushed it entirely at the Battle of Nashville. Hood's defeat removed any threat to Sherman's rear.

Sherman resumed his march in February 1865, heading for South Carolina, the heart of the Confederacy and the state where the Civil War had begun. "The truth is," Sherman wrote a friend, "the whole army is burning with an insatiable desire to wreak vengeance on South Carolina." South Carolinians sent taunting messages promising stiff resistance, but these served only to further provoke Sherman's troops. They pushed aside the small force that assembled to oppose them, wreaked greater destruction in South Carolina than they had in Georgia, and burned the state capitol at Columbia. Sherman sent the colonel of a black regiment to receive the surrender of Charleston and ordered black troops to be the first to take possession of the city. The soldiers marched in singing "John Brown's Body," to the cheers of the city's black population.

Sherman ended his march in Goldsboro, North Carolina, in March 1865 after repelling a surprise Confederate attack at Bentonville led by the restored Joseph E. Johnston and the remnants of the Army of Tennessee. Behind the Union army lay a barren swath 425 miles long from Savannah to Goldsboro.

Lincoln's Second Inauguration.   When Abraham Lincoln took the oath of office for a second time on March 4, 1865, the result of the war was a foregone conclusion even if the precise date of its end was not. In a brief but inspirational address, the president provided the spiritual blueprint for reconciliation, though it disappointed some in the crowd who hoped for a declaration of victory, a promise of retribution against the rebel traitors, or at least an acknowledgment that God was clearly on the side of the Union. Instead, Lincoln declared that God had cursed both sides and had visited a destructive war on the nation because of the sin of slavery, a sin, he stressed, that was national, not regional.

Nor was the president prepared to proclaim victory, despite its inevitability. In fact, the war could continue for some indeterminate time: "Fondly do we hope—fervently do we pray—that this mighty scourge of war may speedily pass away. Yet, if God wills that it continue, until all the wealth piled by the bond-man's two hundred and fifty years of unrequited toil shall be sunk, and until every drop of blood drawn with the lash, shall be paid by another drawn with the sword, as was said three thousand years ago, so still it must be said 'the judgments of the Lord, are true and righteous altogether.'"

15.1

15.2

15.3

15.4

15.5

15.6

15.7

Thirteenth Amendment
Constitutional amendment ratified in 1865 that freed all slaves throughout the United States.

15.1

15.2

15.3

15.4

15.5

15.6

15.7

And once the bloody conflict ends, Lincoln intoned, let reconciliation rather than retribution inform the national policy: "With malice toward none; with charity for all; with firmness in the right, as God gives us to see the right, let us strive on to finish the work we are in; to bind up the nation's wounds; to care for him who shall have borne the battle, and for his widow, and his orphan—to do all which may achieve and cherish a just, and a lasting peace, among ourselves, and with all nations." In the meantime, the bitter struggle would continue.

Arming the Confederacy's Slaves.   In March 1865, in a move reflecting their desperation, Confederate leaders revived a proposal that they had previously rejected: to arm and free slaves. President Davis hoped this action would gain the Confederacy not only a military benefit but also diplomatic recognition from countries that had balked because of slavery.

The issue divided Confederate leaders. General Howell Cobb argued that "if slaves will make good soldiers, our whole theory of slavery is wrong." Others thought that it was preferable to abandon slavery than to lose independence.

Not surprisingly, slaves themselves greeted the proposal with little enthusiasm. They might have found service in the Confederate army an acceptable alternative to bondage earlier in the war, but not now, with Union victory imminent.

On March 13, 1865, a reluctant Confederate Congress passed a bill to enlist black soldiers, but without offering them freedom. Ten days later, President Davis and the War Office issued a general order that promised immediate freedom to slaves who enlisted. The war ended before the order could have any effect. The irony was that in the summer of 1864, a majority of northerners probably would have accepted reunion without emancipation had the Confederacy abandoned its fight.

The Road to Appomattox and the Death of Lincoln

With Sherman's triumph in Georgia and the Carolinas and Sheridan's rout of the Confederates in the Shenandoah Valley, Lee's army remained the last obstacle to Union victory. On April 1, Sheridan's cavalry seized a vital railroad junction on Lee's right flank, forcing Lee to abandon Petersburg and the defense of Richmond. Lee tried a daring run westward toward Lynchburg, hoping to secure much-needed supplies and to join Johnston's Army of Tennessee in North Carolina to continue the fight.

President Davis fled Richmond with his cabinet and headed toward North Carolina. Richard Gill Forrester, a 17-year-old black youth, awoke to find the evacuation under-way. He reached under his bed and pulled out an American flag. Maneuvering through the chaotic streets, young Forrester reached the state capitol building, climbed to the top, and affixed the banner to the flagpole. Union troops occupied the Confederate capital on April 3, and two days later, President Lincoln walked through its streets to the cheers of his army and an emotional reception from thousands of black people. "I know I am free," shouted one black spectator, "for I have seen Father Abraham and felt him."

The Surrender at Appomattox.   Grant's army of 60,000 outran Lee's diminishing force of 35,000 and cut off his escape at Appomattox Court House, Virginia, on April 7. Convinced that further resistance was futile, the Confederate commander met Grant on April 9, 1865, in the McLean house at Appomattox to sign the documents of surrender. The Union general offered generous terms, allowing Lee's men to go home unmolested and to take with them horses or mules "to put in a crop." Grant reported feeling "sad and depressed" at "the downfall of a foe who had fought so long and valiantly, and had suffered so much for a cause, though that cause was, I believe, one of the worst for which a people ever fought." Lee rode through the thinned ranks of his troops, who crowded around him in silent tribute, brushing the general's boots and the withers of his horse with their hats.

Though some southerners entertained fleetingly the idea of launching a guerrilla campaign against Union forces, most were sick of the war. One Confederate leader,

15.1
15.2
15.3
15.4
15.5
15.6
15.7

General Robert E. Lee at Appomattox after his surrender to Union General U. S. Grant on April 9, 1865. His men followed the defeated leader, poignantly brushing their hats against the withers of his horse, Traveler. Many wept openly. The war was over as the sun set on the dream of southern independence.

traveling through the stricken South in April 1865, reported that soldiers and civilians alike considered any continuation of the conflict "madness." Joseph E. Johnston surrendered to Sherman near Durham, North Carolina, on April 26. On May 10, Union cavalry captured President Davis in southern Georgia. On May 26, Texas general Kirby Smith surrendered his Trans-Mississippi army, and the Civil War came to an end.

The Death of Lincoln.   Washington greeted the Confederate surrender at Appomattox with raucous rejoicing, torchlight parades, cannon salutes, and crowds spontaneously bellowing "The Star-Spangled Banner." On April 11, President Lincoln addressed a large crowd from the White House balcony and spoke briefly of his plans to reconstruct the South with the help of persons loyal to the Union, including recently freed slaves. At least one listener found the speech disappointing. A sometime actor and full-time Confederate patriot, John Wilkes Booth, muttered to a friend in the throng, "That means nigger citizenship. Now, by God, I'll put him through. That is the last speech he will ever make."

On the evening of April 14, Good Friday, the president went to Ford's Theatre in Washington to view a comedy, *Our American Cousin.* During the performance, Booth shot the president, wounding him mortally, then jumped from Lincoln's box to the stage shouting "*Sic semper tyrannis*" ("Thus always to tyrants") and fled the theater. Union troops tracked him down to a barn in northern Virginia and killed him. Investigators arrested eight accomplices who had conspired with Booth to murder other high officials in addition to Lincoln. Four of the accomplices were hanged. Besides the

15.1

15.2

15.3

15.4

15.5

15.6

15.7

TABLE 15.1 MAJOR BATTLES OF THE CIVIL WAR, 1861–1865

Battle	Campaign Date	Outcome and Consequences
First Bull Run	July 21, 1861	Confederate victory; destroyed the widespread belief in the North that the war would end quickly, fueled Confederate sense of superiority
Forts Henry and Donelson	February 6–16, 1862	Union victory; gave the North control of strategic river systems in the western Confederacy and closed an important link between the eastern and western Confederacy
Shiloh Church	April 6–7, 1862	Union victory; high casualties transformed attitudes about the war on both sides
Seven Days' Battles	June 25–July 1, 1862	Standoff; halted McClellan's advance on Richmond in the Peninsula Campaign
Second Bull Run	August 29–30, 1862	Confederate victory; reinforced Robert E. Lee's reputation for invincibility
Antietam	September 17, 1862	Standoff; halted Lee's advance into the North, eliminated Confederacy's chance for diplomatic recognition, encouraged Lincoln to issue the Emancipation Proclamation
Fredericksburg	December 13, 1862	Confederate victory; revived morale of Lee's army
Chancellorsville	May 2–6, 1863	Confederate victory; Stonewall Jackson killed, encouraged Lee to again invade North
Gettysburg	July 1–3, 1863	Union victory; halted Confederate advance in the North, major psychological blow to Confederacy
Vicksburg	November 1862–July 1863	Union victory; closed the key Confederate port on the Mississippi, also dealt a severe blow to Confederate cause
Chattanooga	August–November 1863	Union victory; solidified Union dominance in the West
Wilderness and Cold Harbor	May and June 1864	Two Confederate victories; inflicted huge losses on Grant's army, turned public opinion against Grant but failed to force him to withdraw
Atlanta	May–September 1864	Union victory; Confederacy lost key rail depot and industrial center
Sherman's March	November 1864–March 1865	Nearly unopposed, Sherman's army cut a path of destruction through Georgia and South Carolina, breaking southern morale
Battles of Franklin and Nashville	November and December 1864	Union victories in Tennessee; effectively destroyed Army of Tennessee
Siege of Petersburg	June 1864–April 1865	Long stalemate ended in Union victory; led to fall of Richmond and surrender of Lee's army at Appomattox Court House

president, however, the only other official attacked was Secretary of State Seward, who received serious but not fatal knife wounds.

Southerners reacted to Lincoln's assassination with surprisingly mixed emotions. Many saw some slight hope of relief for the South's otherwise bleak prospects. But General Johnston and others like him were aware of Lincoln's moderating influence on the radical elements in the Republican Party that were pressing for harsh terms against the South. The president's death, Johnston wrote, was "the greatest possible calamity to the South."

Conclusion

Just before the war, William Sherman had warned a friend from Virginia, "You people of the South don't know what you are doing. This country will be drenched in blood. . . . [W]ar is a terrible thing." He was right. More than 400,000 Union soldiers died during the war, 140,000 in battle, and more than 350,000 Confederate soldiers, 100,000 in battle. Total casualties on both sides, including wounded, were more than 1 million.

The southern armies suffered disproportionately higher casualties than the northern armies. One in four Confederate soldiers died or endured debilitating wounds, compared to one in ten Federal soldiers. During the first year after the war, Mississippi allocated one-fifth of its budget to artificial limbs. Compounding the suffering of the individuals behind these gruesome statistics was the incalculable suffering—in terms of grief, fatherless children, women who never married, families never made whole—of the people close to them.

The war devastated the South. The region lost one-fourth of its white male population between the ages of 20 and 40. It also lost two-fifths of its livestock and half its farm machinery. Union armies destroyed many of the South's railroads and shattered its industry. Between 1860 and 1870, the wealth of the South declined by 60 percent, and its share of the nation's total wealth dropped from more than 30 percent to 12 percent. The wealth of the North, in contrast, increased by half in the same period. The Union victory solved the constitutional question about the right of secession and sealed the fate of slavery. The issue that dominated the prewar sectional debate had vanished. Now, when politicians intoned Independence Day orations or campaign speeches about the ideals of democracy and freedom, the glaring reality of human bondage would no longer mock their rhetoric.

The Civil War stimulated societal changes that grew more significant over time. It did not make the Union an industrial nation, but it taught the effectiveness of centralized management, new financial techniques, and the coordination of production, marketing, and distribution. Entrepreneurs would apply these lessons to create the expanding corporations of the postwar American economy. Likewise, the war did not revolutionize gender relations in American society, but by opening new opportunities to women in fields such as nursing and teaching, it helped lay the foundation for the woman's suffrage movement of the 1870s and 1880s.

For many Americans, especially black and white southerners, the war was the most important event in their lives, but it was not responsible for every postwar change in American society, and it left many features of American life intact. The experience of pulling together in a massive war effort, for example, did not soften class antagonisms. Capitalism, not labor, triumphed during the war. And it was industrialists and entrepreneurs, not working people, who most benefited from the war's bonanza. Lincoln brutally suppressed strikes at defense plants and threw labor leaders into military prisons.

For black southerners, emancipation was the war's most significant achievement. The war to end slavery changed some American racial attitudes, especially in the North. When Lincoln broadened the war's objectives to include the abolition of slavery, he connected the success of the Union to freedom for the slave. At the outset of the Civil War, only a small minority of northerners considered themselves abolitionists. After the Emancipation Proclamation, every northern soldier became a liberator.

Some white southerners were relieved by the end of slavery, but most greeted it with fear, anger, and regret. For them, the freed slaves would be living reminders of the South's defeat and the end of a way of life grounded in white supremacy.

If the Civil War resolved the sectional dispute of the 1850s by ending slavery and denying the right of the southern states to secede, it created two new equally troubling problems: how to reunite South and North and how to deal with the legacy of slavery. At his last cabinet meeting on April 14, Lincoln seemed inclined to be conciliatory, cautioning against reprisals on Confederate leaders and noting the courage of General Lee and his officers. The president said nothing about the rights of freedmen, although earlier statements indicated that he favored suffrage, but not social equality, for African Americans.

America's greatest crisis had closed. In its wake, former slaves tested their new freedom, and the nation groped for reconciliation. The struggle to preserve the Union and abolish slavery had renewed and vindicated the nation's ideals. It was time to savor the hard-fought victories before plunging into the uncertainties of Reconstruction.

In November 1863, President Lincoln was asked to say a few words at the dedication of the federal cemetery at Gettysburg. There, surrounded by a somber scene of fresh graves, Lincoln bound the cause of the Union to that of the country's founders: "Fourscore and seven years ago our fathers brought forth upon this continent a new nation, conceived in liberty and dedicated to the proposition that all men are created equal. Now we are engaged in a great civil war, testing whether that nation, or any nation so conceived and so dedicated can long endure." A Union victory, Lincoln hoped, would not only honor the past but also call forth a new nation, cleansed of its sins, to serve as an inspiration to oppressed peoples around the world. He called on the nation to resolve "that the nation shall, under God, have a new birth of freedom; and that government of the people, by the people, for the people, shall not perish from the earth." The two-minute Gettysburg Address captured what Union supporters were fighting for and connected their sacrifices to the noble causes of freedom and democratic government. That would be both the hope and the challenge of the peace that followed a hard war.

For Suggested Readings go to MyHistoryLab.

15.1

15.2

15.3

15.4

15.5

15.6

15.7

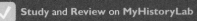

Chapter Review

Mobilization, North and South

15.1 What were the North's key advantages at the outset of the war? p. 406

Neither side was prepared for a major war. The Confederacy lacked a national army and the Union had a regular army of only 16,000 men. Mobilization required the recruitment of soldiers to fight and bureaucrats to manage the war effort. How both sides went about these efforts reflected both their different objectives and the distinctive personalities of their leaders.

The Early War, 1861–1862

15.2 How did the two sides' objectives dictate their strategies in the early years of the war? p. 411

The North's offensive strategy dictated the course of the first two years of the war in both the eastern and western theaters. The Confederates adopted a mostly defensive strategy, only occasionally mounting direct attacks on Union forces. By the end of 1862, the outcome of the war remained uncertain.

The Emancipation Proclamation

15.3 How did the Emancipation Proclamation change the nature of the war? p. 417

Military necessity and Lincoln's private moral objection to slavery propelled the president to abolish the institution. Although the proclamation had a limited practical impact, it joined freedom for the slaves to the salvation of the Union as dual objectives of the Federal war effort, thereby changing the nature of the war.

Turning Points, 1862–1863

15.4 How did the changing nature of the war affect soldiers on both sides? p. 423

Despite Confederate successes holding the Union armies at bay in the East, the protracted nature of the war drained precious resources and convinced southern strategists to undertake risky invasions of the North. The outcomes of these battles combined with Federal victories in the West tilted the course of the war in the Union's favor.

War Transforms the North

15.5 What impact did the war have on the North's economy? p. 431

Republican dominance in Congress and military victories in 1863 enabled the Lincoln administration to pass legislation expanding the federal government's role in economic development. The wartime economic boom allowed women to enter the workforce in record numbers, though it also produced labor and racial conflict.

The Confederacy Disintegrates

15.6 How did the war affect civilian life in the South? p. 435

Mounting battlefield losses after 1863 shredded the southern economy, creating increasing misery for the civilian population, and reduced support for the war.

Southern leaders hoped that their defensive strategy would ultimately encourage a war-weary North to call for an end to the conflict before the Confederacy ran out of resources to wage it.

The Union Prevails, 1864–1865

15.7 What was Grant's strategy for ending the war? p. 438

Despite Union successes, Confederate armies remained operative in both the West and the East in the spring of 1864. President Lincoln's appointment of General Ulysses S. Grant as commander of all the Union armies produced a coordinated military strategy designed to bring the long and bloody war to a swift end.

Timeline

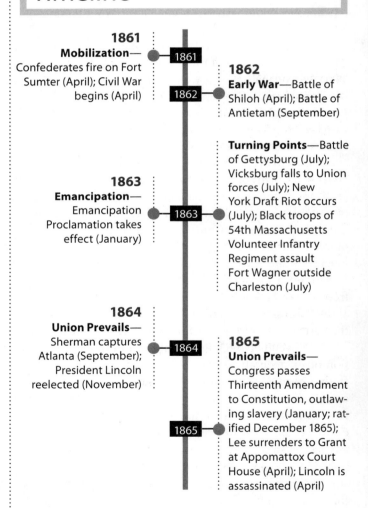

1861
Mobilization— Confederates fire on Fort Sumter (April); Civil War begins (April)

1861

1862
Early War—Battle of Shiloh (April); Battle of Antietam (September)

1862

Turning Points—Battle of Gettysburg (July); Vicksburg falls to Union forces (July); New York Draft Riot occurs (July); Black troops of 54th Massachusetts Volunteer Infantry Regiment assault Fort Wagner outside Charleston (July)

1863
Emancipation— Emancipation Proclamation takes effect (January)

1863

1864
Union Prevails— Sherman captures Atlanta (September); President Lincoln reelected (November)

1864

1865
Union Prevails— Congress passes Thirteenth Amendment to Constitution, outlawing slavery (January; ratified December 1865); Lee surrenders to Grant at Appomattox Court House (April); Lincoln is assassinated (April)

1865

16 Reconstruction
1865–1877

One American Journey

A Memoir

Marianna, Florida 1866

The white academy **opened** about the same time the church opened the school for the Negro children. As the colored children had to pass the academy to reach the church it was easy for the white children to annoy them with taunts and jeers. The war passed from words to stones which the white children began to hurl at the colored. Several colored children were hurt and, as they had not resented the rock-throwing in kind because they were timid about going that far, the white children became more aggressive and abusive.

One morning the colored children armed themselves with stones and determined to fight their way past the academy to their school. [They] approached the academy in formation whereas in the past they had been going in pairs or small groups. When they reached hailing distance, a half dozen white boys rushed out and hurled their missiles. Instead of scampering away, the colored children not

"A Hunger to Learn." This 1863 watercolor by Henry L. Stephens depicts an elderly African American, probably a former slave, learning to read. The newspaper's headline states, "Presidential Proclamation, Slavery." Learning transcended age among freed blacks in the South.

LEARNING OBJECTIVES

16.1 How did white southerners respond to defeat? p. 451

16.2 Why did black aspirations generate southern white violence? p. 453

16.3 How did Congressional Reconstruction change the status of the former slaves in the South? p. 459

16.4 How were white northerners and the federal government complicit in denying freed slaves the basic rights of American citizenship? p. 468

16.5 How and why did Reconstruction end? p. 473

((• Listen to **Chapter 16** on MyHistoryLab

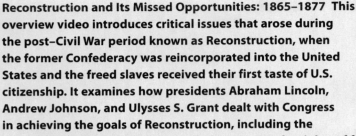

Watch the Video Series on MyHistoryLab

Learn about some key topics related to this chapter with the *MyHistoryLab Video Series: Key Topics in U.S. History.*

1 **Reconstruction and Its Missed Opportunities: 1865–1877** This overview video introduces critical issues that arose during the post–Civil War period known as Reconstruction, when the former Confederacy was reincorporated into the United States and the freed slaves received their first taste of U.S. citizenship. It examines how presidents Abraham Lincoln, Andrew Johnson, and Ulysses S. Grant dealt with Congress in achieving the goals of Reconstruction, including the constitutional amendments intended to protect the rights of freedmen and the policies to rebuild the South and reconcile it to a stronger federal government.

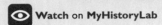 Watch on MyHistoryLab

The Amendments of Freedom Between 1865 and 1869, Congress passed the Thirteenth, Fourteenth, and Fifteenth Amendments to the Constitution, ending slavery, guaranteeing citizenship, and extending voting rights. This video reveals how these constitutional changes were enacted to protect the citizenship and rights of African Americans, including the formation of agencies such as the Freedman's Bureau. Despite the efforts of the federal government, however, southern states passed Black Codes and engaged in other repressive measures that lasted generations.

Watch on MyHistoryLab **2**

3 **Presidential Reconstruction** This video explains how Abraham Lincoln established the precedent of presidential Reconstruction through his legalistic interpretation of the Civil War as an armed rebellion within the United States, thereby enabling himself as commander in chief to control the definition and progress of Reconstruction. His successor, Andrew Johnson, met with stiff resistance from Radical Republicans in Congress who wanted Reconstruction to be a harsh process for the former Confederate states.

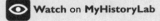 Watch on MyHistoryLab

The Compromise of 1877 The twelve years of federal occupation and Reconstruction came to an end in the South when its electoral delegates guaranteed Rutherford B. Hayes's victory in the 1876 election in exchange for the withdrawal of the remaining federal troops from the states of the former Confederacy, effectively ending southern Reconstruction. This video examines the Compromise of 1877, the political deal that made Hayes's victory possible.

Watch on MyHistoryLab **4**

only stood their ground and hurled their missiles but maintained a solemn silence. The white children, seeing there was no backing down as they expected, came rushing out of the academy and charged the colored children.

During some fifteen minutes it was a real tug of war. In the close fighting the colored children got the advantage gradually and began to shove the white children back. As they pressed the advantage the white children broke away and ran for the academy. The colored fighters did not follow them but made it hot for the laggards until they also took to their heels. There were many bruises on both sides, but it taught the white youngsters to leave the colored ones alone thereafter.

T. Thomas Fortune, "Norfolk Journal and Guide," August 20, 1927, reprinted in Dorothy Sterling, ed., *The Trouble They Seen: Black People Tell the Story of Reconstruction,* Doubleday, 1976, pp. 22–24.

Personal Journeys Online

- N. J. Bell, *Southern Railroad Man*, 1865. A railroad conductor recalls the aftermath of the Civil War and its impact on a white family in Wilmington, North Carolina.
- Adelbert Ames, *Letter from the Republican Governor of Mississippi*, 1875. Letter to his wife expressing frustration at the violence against black voters in his state and his hope for federal intervention.

Thomas Fortune felt that this incident encapsulated the dilemma of Reconstruction. In the journey from slavery to freedom, education emerged as an important element of full citizenship for African Americans. It was their "ticket" to economic independence, as it was for all Americans. When Thomas realized he could not obtain that ticket in the South, he journeyed north to New York City, where he obtained a job as a printer for the *New York Sun*. New York's gain was the South's loss, a process repeated many times over as talented young black men and women migrated north. It was a double tragedy for the South: losing people who could have rebuilt a shattered region and missing the opportunity to create a society based on racial equality.

Southern whites found the notion of black independence both ludicrous and frightening. Slavery may have ended, but subservience should not, whites believed. The eagerness with which black children (and adults) embraced education implied a pretense of equality, which whites could not accept. They resisted full black citizenship, often violently.

Reconstruction, though, was more than a story of white resistance against black aspirations. What is remarkable about the period is that African Americans continued to press for political, economic, and social rights in the face of withering and often violent white opposition. Most black resistance was futile, as Thomas would eventually discover. But if the failure of African Americans to attain the basic rights of the freedom they won during the Civil War cannot be attributed to their lack of effort and desire, it is also true that southern whites were not the only obstacles along the path of the African American journey from slavery to freedom. Not only did white northerners and the federal government ignore the violence, but they also often condoned or at least rationalized it. Reconstruction was not a southern failure; it was a national disgrace.

The position of African Americans in American society was one of the two great issues of the Reconstruction era. The other great issue was how and under what terms to readmit the former Confederate states. Between 1865 and 1867, under President Andrew Johnson's Reconstruction plan, white southerners pretty much had their way with the former slaves and with their own state governments. Congressional action between 1867 and 1870 attempted to balance black rights and home rule, with mixed results. After 1870, white southerners gradually regained control of their states and localities, often through violence and intimidation, denying black southerners their political gains while Republicans in Washington and white northerners lost interest in policing their former enemies.

By the time the last federal troops left the South in 1877, the white southerners had prevailed. The Confederate states had returned to the Union with all of their rights and many of their leaders restored. And the freed slaves remained in mostly subservient positions with few of the rights and privileges enjoyed by other Americans.

White Southerners and the Ghosts of the Confederacy, 1865

16.1 How did white southerners respond to defeat?

To understand how white southerners reacted to black aspirations after the Civil War, it is necessary to understand what whites saw, thought, and felt as they coped with the consequences of their defeat. Confederate soldiers, generals and troops alike, returned to devastated homes. General Braxton Bragg returned to his "once prosperous" Alabama home to find "all, all was lost, except my debts." Bragg and his wife found temporary shelter in a slave cabin. Yeomen farmers, the backbone of the Confederacy, found uprooted fences, farm animals dead or gone, and buildings destroyed. They and their families wandered about in a living nightmare, seeking shelter where they could. They lived in morbid fear of vengeful former slaves or the hated Yankee soldiers wreaking more damage.

Nathaniel Bell, a former Confederate soldier, was lucky enough to get a job on the North Carolina Railroad in 1865. Every two weeks, Bell enjoyed a two-day layover in the coastal city of Wilmington. "On one of these occasions," he wrote, "a small boy and little girl, both pretty children, came to me and asked me for something to eat. I gave them all the meat, bread, potatoes, and syrup that they could carry away. They were very proud of this. They said their father was killed in the war, and that their mother and grandmother were both sick. Some months afterwards I was passing by the same place where I saw the children, and a man got on my train. . . . I asked him about the two children. . . . He said the little boy and girl starved to death."

The casualties of war in the South continued long after the hostilities ceased. These were hardly the only cases of starvation that stalked the defeated region in the months after the surrender. Although soldiers of both sides would experience difficulty in reentering civilian life, the southerner's case was the more difficult because of the economic devastation, the psychological burdens of defeat, and the break-up of families through death, migration, or poverty. Cities such as Richmond, Atlanta, and Columbia lay in ruins; farmsteads were stripped of everything but the soil; infrastructure, especially railroads, was damaged or destroyed; factories and machinery were demolished; and at least 5 million bales of cotton, the major cash crop, had gone up in smoke. Add a worthless currency, and the loss was staggering, climbing into hundreds of billions of dollars in today's currency.

Their cause lost and their society destroyed, white southerners lived through the summer and fall of 1865 surrounded by ghosts, the ghosts of lost loved ones, joyful times, bountiful harvests, self-assurance, and slavery. Defeat shook the basic tenets of their religious beliefs. A North Carolinian cried, "Oh, our God! What sins we must have been guilty of that we should be so humiliated by Thee now!" Some praised God for delivering the South from the sin of slavery. A Virginia woman expressed thanks that "we white people are no longer permitted to go on in such wickedness, heaping up more and more wrath of God upon our devoted heads." But many other white southerners refused to accept their defeat as a divine judgment. How could they, as a devout people, believe that God had abandoned them? Instead, they insisted, God had spared the South for a greater purpose. They came to view the war as the **Lost Cause** and interpreted it, not as a lesson in humility, but as an episode in the South's journey to salvation. Robert E. Lee became the patron saint of this cause, his poignant nobility a contrast to the crassness of the Yankee warlords. White southerners transformed the bloody struggle into a symbol of courage against great odds and piety against sin. Eventually, they believed, redemption would come.

The southern white view of the Civil War (and of Reconstruction) was not a deliberate attempt to falsify history, but rather a need to justify and rationalize the devastation that accompanied defeat. This view, in which the war became the Lost Cause, and Reconstruction became the Redemption, also served to forge a community among white southerners at a time of great unrest. A common religion solidified the bond and sanctified it. The Lost Cause also enabled white southerners to move on with their lives and concentrate on rebuilding their shattered region. The Lost Cause was a historical rationalization that enabled believers to hope for a better future. The regrettable feature of elevating the Civil War to a noble, holy enterprise was that it implied a stainless Old South, a civilization worth fighting and dying for. This new history required the return of the freedmen, if not to the status of slaves, then at least to a lowly place in society. This new history also ignored the savagery of the war by romanticizing the conflict.

Lost Cause The phrase many white southerners applied to their Civil War defeat. They viewed the war as a noble cause and their defeat as only a temporary setback in the South's ultimate vindication.

The Lost Cause would exist not merely as a memory, but also as a three-dimensional depiction of southern history, in rituals and celebrations, and as the educational foundation for future generations. The statues of the Confederate common soldier erected typically on the most important site in a town, the courthouse square; the commemorations of Confederate Memorial Day, the birthdays of prominent Confederate leaders, and the reunions of veterans, all marked with flourishing oratory, brass bands, parades, and related spectacles; and the textbooks implanting the white history of the South in young minds and carrying the legacy down through the generations—all of these ensured that the Lost Cause would be not only an interpretation of the past, but also the basic reality of the present and the foundation for the future.

Most white southerners approached the great issues of freedom and reunification with unyielding views. They saw African Americans as adversaries whose attempts at self-improvement were a direct challenge to white people's belief in their own racial superiority, a belief endorsed by white southerners' view of the war and the Old South. A black boy like Thomas Fortune could not dream of success, for the very thought confounded the beliefs of southern whites. White southerners saw outside assistance to black southerners as another invasion. The Yankees might have destroyed their families, their farms, and their fortunes, but they would not destroy the racial order. The war may have ended slavery, but white southerners were determined to preserve strict racial boundaries.

More than Freedom: African American Aspirations in 1865

16.2   Why did black aspirations generate southern white violence?

Black southerners had a quite different perspective on the Civil War and Reconstruction, seeing the former as a great victory for freedom and the latter as a time of great possibility. But their view did not matter; it was invisible or, worse, distorted, in books, monuments, and official accounts. If, as the British writer George Orwell later argued, "who controls the present controls the past, and who controls the past controls the future," then the vanishing black perspective is not surprising. The ferocity with which white southerners attempted to take back their governments and their social structure was not only about nostalgia; it was also about power and the legitimacy that power conferred.

And, of course, the black perspective was decidedly different from that of whites. To black southerners the Civil War was a war of liberation, not a Lost Cause. The response of southern whites to black aspirations still stunned African Americans, who believed, naïvely perhaps, that what they sought—education, land, access to employment, and equality in law and politics—were basic rights and modest objectives. The former slaves did not initially even dream of social equality; far less did they plot murder and mayhem, as white people feared. They did harbor two potentially contradictory aspirations. The first was to be left alone, free of white supervision. But the former slaves also wanted land, voting and civil rights, and education. To secure these, they needed the intervention and support of the white power structure.

In 1865, African Americans had reason to hope that their dreams of full citizenship might be realized. They enjoyed a reservoir of support for their aspirations among some Republican leaders. The views of James A. Garfield, Union veteran, U.S. congressman, and future president, were typical of these Republicans. Commenting on the ratification of the Thirteenth Amendment, which abolished slavery, Garfield asked, "What is freedom? Is it the bare privilege of not being chained? . . . If this is all, then freedom is a bitter mockery, a cruel delusion."

Freedmen's Bureau Agency established by Congress in March 1865 to provide social, educational, and economic services, advice, and protection to former slaves and destitute whites; lasted seven years.

The first step Congress took beyond emancipation was to establish the Bureau of Refugees, Freedmen, and Abandoned Lands in March 1865. Congress envisioned the **Freedmen's Bureau**, as it came to be called, as a multipurpose agency to provide social, educational, and economic services, advice, and protection to former slaves and destitute white southerners. The bureau marked the federal government's first foray into social welfare legislation. Congress also authorized the bureau to rent confiscated and abandoned farmland to freedmen in 40-acre plots, with an option to buy. This auspicious beginning belied the great disappointments that lay ahead.

Education

The greatest success of the Freedmen's Bureau was in education. The bureau coordinated more than fifty northern philanthropic and religious groups, which, in turn, established 3,000 freedmen's schools in the South, serving 150,000 men, women, and children.

Initially, single young women from the Northeast comprised much of the teaching force. One of them, 26-year-old Martha Schofield, came to Aiken, South Carolina, from rural Pennsylvania in 1865. Like many of her colleagues, she had joined the abolitionist movement as a teenager and decided to make teaching her life's work. Her strong Quaker beliefs reflected the importance of Protestant Christianity in motivating the young missionaries. When her sponsoring agency, the Pennsylvania Freedmen's Relief Association, folded in 1871, her school closed. Undaunted, she opened another school on her own, and, despite chronic financial problems and the hostility of Aiken's white citizens, she and the school endured. (Since 1953, her school has been part of the Aiken public school system.)

By the time Schofield opened her school in 1871, black teachers outnumbered white teachers in the "colored" schools. The financial troubles of northern missionary societies and white northerners' declining interest in the freedmen's condition opened opportunities for black teachers. Support for them came from black churches, especially the African Methodist Episcopal (AME) Church.

The former slaves crowded into basements, shacks, and churches to attend school. "The children . . . hurry to school as soon as their work is over," wrote a teacher in Norfolk, Virginia, in 1867. "The plowmen hurry from the field at night to get their hour of study. Old men and women strain their dim sight with the book two and a half feet distant from the eye, to catch the shape of the letter. I call this heaven-inspired interest."

At the end of the Civil War, only about 10 percent of black southerners were literate, compared with more than 70 percent of white southerners. Within a decade, black literacy had risen above 30 percent. Joseph Wilson, a former slave, attributed the rise to "this longing of ours for freedom of the mind as well as the body."

Some black southerners went on to one of the thirteen colleges established by the American Missionary Association and black and white churches. Between 1860 and 1880, more than 1,000 black southerners earned college degrees at institutions still serving students today, such as Howard University in Washington, DC, Fisk University in Nashville, Hampton Institute (now University), Tuskegee Institute, and Biddle Institute (now Johnson C. Smith University) in Charlotte.

Pursuing freedom of the mind involved challenges beyond those of learning to read and write. Many white southerners condemned efforts at "Negro improvement." They viewed the time spent on education as wasted, forcing the former slaves to catch their lessons in bits and pieces between work, often by candlelight or on Sundays. White southerners also harassed white female teachers, questioning their morals and threatening people who rented rooms to them. After the Freedmen's Bureau folded in 1872 and many of the northern societies that supported freedmen's education collapsed or cut back their involvement, education for black southerners became more haphazard.

Watch the Video   The Schools That the Civil War and Reconstruction Created

The Freedmen's Bureau, northern churches, and missionary societies established more than 3,000 schools, attended by some 150,000 men, women, and children in the years after the Civil War. At first, mostly young white women from the Northeast staffed these schools, as at this one in Georgia. Note the wide age range, which indicates that the thirst for learning spanned generations.

"Forty Acres and a Mule"

Although education was important to the freed slaves in their quest for civic equality, land ownership offered them the promise of economic independence. For generations, black people had worked southern farms and had received nothing for their labor.

An overwhelmingly agricultural people, freedmen looked to farm ownership as a key element in their transition from slavery to freedom. "Gib us our own land and we take care of ourselves," a Charleston freedman asserted to a northern visitor in 1865. Even before the war's end, rumors circulated through black communities in the South that the government would provide each black family with 40 acres and a mule. These rumors were fueled by General William T. Sherman's **Field Order No. 15** in January 1865, which set aside a vast swath of abandoned land along the South Atlantic coast from the Charleston area to northern Florida for grants of up to 40 acres. The Freedmen's Bureau likewise raised expectations when it was initially authorized to rent 40-acre plots of confiscated or abandoned land to freedmen.

By June 1865, about 40,000 former slaves had settled on Sherman land along the southeastern coast. In 1866, Congress passed the **Southern Homestead Act**, giving black people preferential access to public lands in five southern states. Two years later, the Republican government of South Carolina initiated a land-redistribution program financed by the sale of state bonds. The state used proceeds from the bond sales to purchase farmland, which it then resold to freedmen, who paid for it with state-funded, long-term, low-interest loans. By the late 1870s, more than 14,000 African American families had taken advantage of this program.

Field Order No. 15 Order by General William T. Sherman in January 1865 to set aside abandoned land along the southern Atlantic coast for 40-acre grants to freedmen; rescinded by President Andrew Johnson later that year.

Southern Homestead Act Largely unsuccessful law passed in 1866 that gave black people preferential access to public lands in five southern states.

Land ownership did not ensure financial success. Most black-owned farms were small and on marginal land. The value of these farms in 1880 was roughly half that of white-owned farms. Black farmers also had trouble obtaining credit to purchase or expand their holdings. A lifetime of fieldwork left some freedmen without the managerial skills to operate a farm. The hostility of white neighbors also played a role in thwarting black aspirations. Black farmers often had the most success when groups of families settled together, as in the farm community of Promise Land in up-country South Carolina.

The vast majority of former slaves, however, especially those in the Lower South, never fulfilled their dreams of land ownership. Rumors to the contrary, the federal government never intended to implement a land-redistribution program in the South. General Sherman viewed his field order as a temporary measure to support freedmen for the remainder of the war. President Andrew Johnson nullified the order in September 1865, returning confiscated land to its former owners. Even Republican supporters of black land ownership questioned the constitutionality of seizing privately owned real estate. Most of the land-redistribution programs that emerged after the war, including government-sponsored programs, required black farmers to have capital. But in the impoverished postwar economy of the South, it was difficult for them to acquire it.

Republican Party rhetoric of the 1850s extolled the virtues and dignity of free labor over the degradation of slave labor. Free labor usually meant working for a wage or under some other contractual arrangement. But unlike slaves, according to the then prevailing view, free laborers could enjoy the fruits of their work and might someday become owners or entrepreneurs themselves. It was self-help, not government assistance, that guaranteed individual success. After the war, many white northerners envisioned former slaves assuming the status of free laborers, not necessarily of independent landowners.

Most of the officials of the Freedmen's Bureau shared these views and therefore saw reviving the southern economy as a higher priority than helping former slaves acquire farms. They wanted to both get the crop in the field and start the South on the road to a free labor system. Thus, they encouraged freedmen to work for their former masters under contract and to postpone their quest for land.

At first, agents of the Freedmen's Bureau supervised labor contracts between former slaves and masters. But after 1867, bureau surveillance declined. Agents assumed that both black laborers and white landowners had become accustomed to the mutual obligations of contracts. The bureau, however, underestimated the power of white landowners to coerce favorable terms or to ignore those they did not like. Contracts implied a mutuality that most planters could not accept in their relations with former slaves. As the northern journalist Whitelaw Reid noted in 1865, planters "have no sort of conception of free labor. They do not comprehend any law for controlling laborers, save the law of force."

By the late 1870s, most former slaves in the rural South had been drawn into a subservient position in a new labor system called **sharecropping**. The premise of this system was relatively simple: The landlord furnished the sharecroppers with a house, a plot of land to work, seed, some farm animals, and farm implements and advanced them credit at a store the landlord typically owned. In exchange, the sharecroppers promised the landlord a share of their crop, usually one-half. The croppers kept the proceeds from the sale of the other half to pay off their debts at the store and save or spend as they and their families saw fit. In theory, a sharecropper could save enough to secure economic independence.

But white landlords perceived black independence as both contradictory and subversive. With landlords keeping the accounts at the store, black sharecroppers found that the proceeds from their share of the crop never left them very far ahead. Not all white landlords cheated their tenants, but given the sharecroppers' innocence regarding accounting methods and crop pricing, the temptation to do so was great.

sharecropping Labor system that evolved during and after Reconstruction whereby landowners furnished laborers with a house, farm animals, and tools and advanced credit in exchange for a share of the laborers' crop.

Migration to Cities

Even before the hope of land ownership faded, African Americans looked for alternatives to secure their personal and economic independence. Before the war, the city had offered slaves and free black people a measure of freedom unknown in the rural South. After the war, African Americans moved to cities to find families, seek work, escape the tedium and supervision of farm life, or simply to test their right to move about.

For the same reasons, white people disapproved of black migration to the city. It reduced the labor pool for farms. It also gave black people more opportunities to associate with white people of similar social status, to compete for jobs, and to establish schools, churches, and social organizations, fueling their hopes for racial equality. Between 1860 and 1870, the African American population in every major southern city rose significantly. In Atlanta, for example, black people accounted for one in five residents in 1860 and nearly one in two by 1870. Some freedmen came to cities initially to reunite with their families. Every city newspaper after the war carried advertisements from former slaves seeking their mates and children. In 1865, the Nashville *Colored Tennessean* carried this poignant plea: "During the year 1849, Thomas Sample carried away from this city, as his slaves, our daughter, Polly, and son. . . . We will give $100 each for them to any person who will assist them. . . to get to Nashville, or get word to us of their whereabouts."

Once in the city, freedmen had to find a home and a job. They usually settled on the outskirts of town, where building codes did not apply. Rather than developing one large ghetto, as happened in many northern cities, black southerners lived in small concentrations in and around cities. Sometimes armed with a letter of reference from their former masters, black people went door to door to seek employment. Many found work serving white families, as guards, laundresses, or maids, for very low wages. Both skilled and unskilled laborers found work rebuilding war-torn cities like Atlanta. Frederick Ayer, a Freedmen's Bureau agent in Atlanta, reported to a colleague in 1866 that "many of the whites are making most vigorous efforts to retrieve their broken fortunes and . . . rebuild their dwellings and shops. . . . This furnished employment to a large number of colored people as Masons, Carpenters, Teamsters, and Common Workmen."

Most rural black southerners, however, worked as unskilled laborers. The paltry wages men earned, when they could find work, pushed black women into the workforce. They often had an easier time securing a job in cities as domestics and laundresses. Black men had hoped to assert their patriarchal prerogatives, like white men, by keeping wives and daughters out of the labor market, but necessity dictated otherwise. In both Atlanta and Nashville, black people comprised more than 75 percent of the unskilled workforce in 1870. Their wages were at or below subsistence level. A black laborer in Richmond admitted to a journalist in 1870 that he had difficulty making ends meet on $1.50 a day. "It's right hard," he reported. "I have to pay $15 a month rent, and only two little rooms." His family survived because his wife took in laundry, while her mother watched the children. Considering the laborer's struggle, the journalist wondered, "Were not your people better off in slavery?" The man replied, "Oh, no sir! We're a heap better off now. . . . We're men now, but when our masters had us we was only change in their pockets."

Faith and Freedom

Religious faith framed and inspired the efforts of African Americans to test their freedom on the farm and in the city. White southerners used religion to transform the Lost Cause from a shattering defeat to a premonition of a greater destiny. Black southerners, in contrast, saw emancipation in biblical terms as the beginning of an exodus from bondage to the Promised Land.

Some black churches in the postwar South had originated during the slavery era, but most split from white-dominated congregations after the war. White churchgoers

The black church was the center of African American life in the postwar urban South. Most black churches were founded after the Civil War, but some, such as the First African Baptist Church in Richmond, shown here in an 1874 engraving, traced their origins to before 1861.

deplored the expressive style of black worship, and black churchgoers were uncomfortable in congregations that treated them as inferiors. A separate church also reduced white surveillance.

The church became a primary focus of African American life. It gave black people the opportunity to hone skills in self-government and administration that white-dominated society denied them. Within the supportive confines of the congregation, they could assume leadership positions, render important decisions, deal with financial matters, and engage in politics. The church also operated as an educational institution. Local governments, especially in rural areas, rarely constructed public schools for black people; churches often served that function.

The desire to read the Bible inspired thousands of former slaves to attend the church school. The church also spawned other organizations that served the black community, such as burial societies, Masonic lodges, temperance groups, trade unions, and drama clubs. African Americans took great pride in their churches, which became visible measures of their progress. The church enforced family and religious values, punishing violators guilty of such infractions as adultery. Black churchwomen, both working class and middle class, were especially prominent in the family-oriented organizations.

The efforts of former slaves in the classroom, on the farm, in cities, and in the churches reflect the enthusiasm and expectations with which black southerners greeted freedom and raised the hopes of those who came to help them. But the majority of white southerners were unwilling to see those expectations fulfilled. For this reason, African Americans could not secure the fruits of their emancipation without the support and protection of the federal government. The issue of freedom was therefore inextricably linked to the other great issue of the era, the rejoining of the Confederacy to the Union, as expressed in federal Reconstruction policy.

Federal Reconstruction, 1865–1870

16.3	How did Congressional Reconstruction change the status of the former slaves in the South?

When the Civil War ended in 1865, no acceptable blueprint existed for reconstituting the Union. President Lincoln believed that a majority of white southerners were Unionists at heart, and that they could and should undertake the task of reconstruction. He favored a conciliatory policy toward the South in order, as he put it in one of his last letters, "to restore the Union, so as to make it . . . a Union of hearts and hands as well as of States." He counted on the loyalists to be fair with respect to the rights of the former slaves.

As early as 1863, Lincoln had proposed to readmit a seceding state if 10 percent of its prewar voters took an oath of loyalty to the Union, and it prohibited slavery in a new state constitution. But this Ten Percent Plan did not require states to grant equal civil and political rights to former slaves, and many Republicans in Congress thought it was not stringent enough. In 1864, a group of them responded with the Wade-Davis Bill, which required a majority of a state's prewar voters to pledge their loyalty to the Union and demanded guarantees of black equality before the law. The bill was passed at the end of a congressional session, but Lincoln kept it from becoming law by refusing to sign it (an action known as a "pocket veto").

Lincoln, of course, died before he could implement a Reconstruction plan. His views on reconstructing the Union during the war did not necessarily prefigure how his views would have unfolded after the war. Given his commitment in the Gettysburg Address to promote "a new birth of freedom," it is likely that had white southerners resisted black civil rights, Lincoln would have responded with harsher terms. Above all, Lincoln was a savvy politician: He would not have allowed a stalemate to develop between himself and the Congress, and, if necessary, he would have moved closer to the radical camp. On April 11, 1865, in one of his last pronouncements on Reconstruction, Lincoln stated that he favored a limited suffrage for the freedmen, though he admitted that each state had enough peculiarities that a blanket policy might not work. In a cabinet meeting on April 14, he dismissed an idea for military occupation, though he acknowledged that allowing the states to reconstruct themselves might not work either. In any case, his successor, Andrew Johnson, lacked his flexibility and political acumen.

The controversy over the plans introduced during the war reflected two obstacles to Reconstruction that would continue to plague the ruling Republicans after the war. First, neither the Constitution nor legal precedent offered any guidance on whether the president or Congress should take the lead on Reconstruction policy. Second, there was no agreement on what that policy should be. Proposals requiring various preconditions for readmitting a state, loyalty oaths, new constitutions with certain specific provisions, guarantees of freedmen's rights—all provoked vigorous debate.

President Andrew Johnson, some conservative Republicans, and most Democrats believed that because the Constitution made no mention of secession, the southern states had been in rebellion but had never left the Union, and therefore that there was no need for a formal process to readmit them. Moderate and radical Republicans disagreed, arguing that the defeated states had forfeited their rights. Moderates and radicals parted company, however, on the conditions necessary for readmission to the Union. The radicals wanted to treat the former Confederate states as territories, or "conquered provinces," subject to congressional legislation. Moderates wanted to grant the seceding states more autonomy and limit federal intervention in their affairs while they satisfied the conditions of readmission. Neither group held a majority in Congress, and legislators sometimes changed their positions (see Table 16.1).

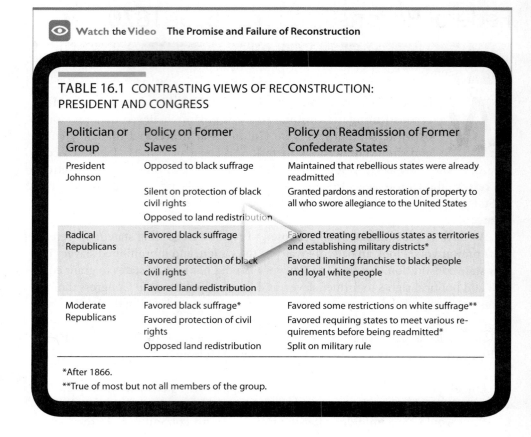

Watch the Video The Promise and Failure of Reconstruction

TABLE 16.1 CONTRASTING VIEWS OF RECONSTRUCTION: PRESIDENT AND CONGRESS

Politician or Group	Policy on Former Slaves	Policy on Readmission of Former Confederate States
President Johnson	Opposed to black suffrage	Maintained that rebellious states were already readmitted
	Silent on protection of black civil rights	Granted pardons and restoration of property to all who swore allegiance to the United States
	Opposed to land redistribution	
Radical Republicans	Favored black suffrage	Favored treating rebellious states as territories and establishing military districts*
	Favored protection of black civil rights	Favored limiting franchise to black people and loyal white people
	Favored land redistribution	
Moderate Republicans	Favored black suffrage*	Favored some restrictions on white suffrage**
	Favored protection of civil rights	Favored requiring states to meet various requirements before being readmitted*
	Opposed land redistribution	Split on military rule

*After 1866.

**True of most but not all members of the group.

Presidential Reconstruction, 1865–1867

When the Civil War ended in April 1865, Congress was not in session and would not reconvene until December. Thus, the responsibility for developing a Reconstruction policy initially fell on Andrew Johnson, who succeeded to the presidency upon Lincoln's assassination. Johnson seemed well suited to the difficult task. He was born in humble circumstances in North Carolina in 1808. He learned the tailoring trade and struck out for Tennessee as a teenager to open a tailor shop in the eastern Tennessee town of Greenville. Obtaining his education informally, he prospered modestly, purchased a few slaves, and began to pursue politics. He was elected alderman, mayor, state legislator, congressman, governor, and then, in 1856, U.S. senator. Johnson was the only southern senator to remain in the U.S. Senate after secession. This defiant Unionism won him acclaim in the North and credibility among Republican leaders, who welcomed him into their party. During the war, as military governor of Tennessee, he solidified his Republican credentials by advocating the abolition of slavery in Tennessee and severe punishment of Confederate leaders. His views landed him on the Republican ticket as the candidate for vice president in 1864. Indiana Republican congressman George W. Julian, who advocated harsh terms for the South and broad rights for black people, viewed Johnson's accession to the presidency in 1865 as "a godsend."

Most northerners, including many Republicans, approved Johnson's Reconstruction plan when he unveiled it in May 1865. Johnson extended pardons and restored property rights, except in slaves, to southerners who swore an oath of allegiance to the Union and the Constitution. Southerners who had held prominent posts in the Confederacy, however, and those with more than $20,000 in taxable property, had to petition the president directly for a pardon, a reflection of Johnson's disdain for wealthy whites. The plan said nothing about the voting rights or civil rights of former slaves. President Johnson, like many of his northern colleagues, was firm in his belief in the inferiority of African Americans, a status which would make them unfit to vote. As he explained, "it must be acknowledged that in the progress of nations Negroes have shown less capacity for government than any other race of people."

Northern Democrats applauded the plan's silence on these issues and its promise of a quick restoration of the southern states to the Union. They expected the southern states to favor their party and expand its political power. Republicans approved the plan because it restored property rights to white southerners, although some wanted it to provide for black suffrage. Republicans also hoped that Johnson's conciliatory terms might attract some white southerners to the Republican Party.

On the two great issues of freedom and reunion, white southerners quickly demonstrated their eagerness to reverse the results of the Civil War. Although most states accepted President Johnson's modest requirements, several objected to one or more of them. Mississippi and Texas refused to ratify the Thirteenth Amendment, which abolished slavery. Alabama accepted only parts of the amendment. South Carolina declined to nullify its secession ordinance. No southern state authorized black voting. When Johnson ordered special congressional elections in the South in the fall of 1865, the all-white electorate returned many prominent Confederate leaders to office.

In late 1865, the newly elected southern state legislatures revised their antebellum slave codes. The updated **black codes** allowed local officials to arrest black people who could not document employment and residence or who were "disorderly" and sentence them to forced labor on farms or road crews. The codes also restricted black people to certain occupations, barred them from jury duty, and forbade them to possess firearms. Apprenticeship laws permitted judges to take black children from parents who could not, in the judges' view, adequately support them. Given the widespread poverty in the South in 1865, the law could apply to almost any freed black family. Northerners looking for contrition in the South found no sign of it. Worse, President Johnson did not seem perturbed about this turn of events.

black codes Laws passed by states and municipalities denying many rights of citizenship to free blacks before the Civil War. Also, during the Reconstruction era, laws passed by newly elected southern state legislatures to control black labor, mobility, and employment.

The Republican-dominated Congress reconvened in December 1865 in a belligerent mood. When radicals, who comprised nearly half of the Republican Party's strength in Congress, could not unite behind a program, their moderate colleagues took the first step toward a congressional Reconstruction plan. The moderates shared the radicals' desire to protect the former slaves' civil rights. But they would not support land-redistribution schemes or punitive measures against prominent Confederates, and disagreed on extending voting rights to the freedmen. The moderates' first measure, passed in early 1866, extended the life of the Freedmen's Bureau and authorized it to punish state officials who failed to extend equal civil rights to black citizens. But President Johnson vetoed the legislation.

Undeterred, Congress passed the Civil Rights Act of 1866 in direct response to the black codes. The act specified the civil rights to which all U.S. citizens were entitled. In creating a category of national citizenship with rights that superseded state laws, the act changed federal-state relations (and in the process overturned the *Dred Scott* decision). President Johnson vetoed the act, but it became law when Congress mustered a two-thirds majority to override his veto, the first time in American history that Congress passed major legislation over a president's veto.

To keep freedmen's rights safe from presidential vetoes, state legislatures, and federal courts, the Republican-dominated Congress moved to incorporate some of the provisions of the 1866 Civil Rights Act into the Constitution. The **Fourteenth Amendment**, which Congress passed in June 1866, addressed the issues of civil and voting rights. It guaranteed every citizen equality before the law. The two key sections of the amendment prohibited states from violating the civil rights of their citizens, thus outlawing the black codes, and gave states the choice of enfranchising black people or losing representation in Congress. Some radical Republicans expressed disappointment that the amendment, in a reflection of northern ambivalence, failed to give the vote to black people outright.

The amendment also disappointed advocates of woman suffrage, for the first time using the word *male* in the Constitution to define who could vote. Wendell Phillips, a prominent abolitionist, counseled women, "One question at a time. This hour belongs to the Negro." Susan B. Anthony, who had campaigned for the abolition of slavery before the war and helped mount a petition drive that collected 400,000 signatures for the Thirteenth Amendment, founded the American Equal Rights Association in 1866 with her colleagues to push for woman suffrage at the state level.

Fourteenth Amendment Constitutional amendment passed by Congress in April 1866 incorporating some of the features of the Civil Rights Act of 1866. It prohibited states from violating the civil rights of their citizens and offered states the choice of allowing black people to vote or losing representation in Congress.

((Read the Document   Jourdon Anderson, Letter to His Former Master (1865)

"Selling a Freeman to Pay His Fine at Monticello, Florida." This 1867 engraving shows how the black codes of the early Reconstruction era reduced former slaves to virtually their pre–Civil War status. Scenes like this convinced northerners that the white South was unrepentant and prompted congressional Republicans to devise their own Reconstruction plans.

The Fourteenth Amendment had little immediate impact on the South. Although enforcement of black codes diminished, white violence against black people increased. In the 1870s, several decisions by the U.S. Supreme Court weakened the amendment's provisions. Eventually, however, it would play a major role in securing the civil rights of African Americans.

President Johnson encouraged southern white intransigence by openly denouncing the Fourteenth Amendment. In August 1866, at the start of the congressional election campaign, he undertook an unprecedented tour of key northern states to sell his message of sectional reconciliation to the public. Although listeners appreciated Johnson's desire for peace, they questioned his claims of southern white loyalty to the Union. The president's diatribes against the Republican Congress won him followers in those northern states with a reservoir of opposition to black suffrage. But the tone and manner of his campaign offended many as undignified. In the November elections, the Democrats suffered embarrassing defeats in the North as Republicans managed better than two-thirds majorities in both the House and Senate, sufficient to override presidential vetoes. Radical Republicans, joined by moderate colleagues buoyed by the election results and revolted by the president's and the South's intransigence, seized the initiative when Congress reconvened.

Congressional Reconstruction, 1867–1870

The radicals' first salvo in their attempt to take control of Reconstruction occurred with the passing over President Johnson's veto of the Military Reconstruction Acts. The measures, passed in March 1867, inaugurated a period known as **Congressional Reconstruction** or Radical Reconstruction. With the exception of Tennessee, the only southern state that had ratified the Fourteenth Amendment and been readmitted to the Union, Congress divided the former Confederate states into five military districts, each headed by a general. The commanders' first order of business was to conduct voter-registration campaigns to enroll black people and to bar white people who had held office before the Civil War and supported the Confederacy. The eligible voters would then elect delegates to a state convention to write a new constitution that guaranteed universal manhood suffrage. Once a majority of eligible voters ratified the new constitution and the Fourteenth Amendment, their state would be eligible for readmission to the Union.

The Reconstruction Acts fulfilled the radicals' three major objectives. First, they secured the freedmen's right to vote. Second, they made it likely that southern states would be run by Republican regimes that would enforce the new constitutions, protect former slaves' rights, and maintain the Republican majority in Congress. Finally, they set standards for readmission that required the South to accept the preeminence of the federal government and the end of slavery. These measures seemed appropriate in view of the war's outcome and the freedmen's status, but white southerners, especially those barred from participation, perceived the state and local governments constructed upon the new basis as illegitimate. Many southern whites would never acknowledge the right of these governments and their officials to rule over them.

To limit presidential interference with their policies, Republicans passed the **Tenure of Office Act**, prohibiting the president from removing certain officeholders without the Senate's consent. Johnson, angered at what he believed was an unconstitutional attack on presidential authority, deliberately violated the act by firing Secretary of War Edwin M. Stanton, a leading radical, in February 1868. The House responded by approving articles of impeachment against a president for the first time in American history. That set the stage for the next step prescribed by the Constitution: a Senate trial to determine whether the president should be removed from office.

Johnson had indeed violated the Tenure of Office Act, a measure of dubious constitutionality even to some Republicans, but enough Republicans felt that his actions fell short of the "high crimes and misdemeanors" standard set by the Constitution for dismissal from office. Seven Republicans deserted their party, and Johnson was acquitted. The seven Republicans who voted against their party did so not out of respect for Johnson but because they feared that a conviction would damage the office of the presidency and violate the constitutional separation of powers. The outcome weakened the radicals and eased the way for Ulysses S. Grant, a moderate Republican, to gain the party's nomination for president in 1868.

The Republicans viewed the 1868 presidential election as a referendum on Congressional Reconstruction. They supported black suffrage in the South but equivocated on allowing African Americans to vote in the North. Black northerners could vote in only eight of the twenty-two northern states, and between 1865 and 1869, white northerners rejected equal suffrage referendums in eight of eleven states. Republicans "waved the bloody shirt," reminding voters of Democratic disloyalty, the sacrifices of war, and the peace only Republicans could redeem. Democrats denounced Congressional Reconstruction as federal tyranny and, in openly racist appeals, warned white voters that a Republican victory would mean black rule. Grant won the election, but his margin of victory was uncomfortably narrow. Reflecting growing ambivalence in the North over

Congressional Reconstruction Name given to the period 1867–1870 when the Republican-dominated Congress controlled Reconstruction era policy. It is sometimes known as Radical Reconstruction, after the radical faction in the Republican Party.

Tenure of Office Act Passed by the Republican-controlled Congress in 1867 to limit presidential interference with its policies, the act prohibited the president from removing certain officeholders without the Senate's consent. President Andrew Johnson, angered at what he believed to be an unconstitutional attack on presidential authority, deliberately violated the act by firing Secretary of War Edwin M. Stanton. The House responded by approving articles of impeachment against a president for the first time in American history.

The Democratic Party ran an openly racist presidential campaign in 1868. This pro-Republican drawing by noted cartoonist Thomas Nast includes three Democratic constituencies: former Confederate soldiers (note the "CSA" on the belt buckle); the Irish or immigrant vote (note the almost simian depiction of the Irishman); and the well-dressed Democratic presidential candidate, Horatio Seymour, sporting a "5th Avenue" button and waving a wallet full of bills, a reference to the corrupt Democratic politics in New York City. The three have their feet on an African American soldier. In the background, note the "colored orphan asylum" and "southern school" ablaze, and the lynching of black children.

issues of race and federal authority, New York's Horatio Seymour, the Democratic presidential nominee, probably carried a majority of the nation's white vote. Black voters' overwhelming support for Grant probably provided his margin of victory.

The Republicans retained a strong majority in both houses of Congress and managed to pass another major piece of Reconstruction legislation, the **Fifteenth Amendment**, in February 1869. In response to growing concerns about voter fraud and violence against freedmen, the amendment guaranteed the right of American men to vote, regardless of race. Although the amendment provided a loophole allowing states to restrict the right to vote based on literacy or property qualifications, it was nonetheless a milestone. It made the right to vote perhaps the most distinguishing characteristic of U.S. citizenship.

The Fifteenth Amendment allowed states to keep the franchise a male prerogative, angering many in the woman suffrage movement more than had the Fourteenth Amendment. The resulting controversy severed the ties between the movement and Republican politics. Susan B. Anthony broke with her abolitionist colleagues and opposed the

Fifteenth Amendment Passed by Congress in 1869, guaranteed the right of American men to vote, regardless of race.

amendment. A fellow abolitionist and woman suffragist, Elizabeth Cady Stanton, charged that the amendment created an "aristocracy of sex." In an appeal brimming with ethnic and racial animosity, Stanton warned that "if you do not wish the lower orders of Chinese, African, Germans and Irish, with their low ideas of womanhood to make laws for you and your daughters . . . awake to the danger . . . and demand that woman, too, shall be represented in the government!" Such language created a major rift in the nascent women's movement.

Southern Republican Governments, 1867–1870

Away from Washington, the first order of business for the former Confederacy was to draft state constitutions. The documents embodied progressive principles new to the South. They mandated the election of numerous local and state offices. Self-perpetuating local elites could no longer appoint themselves or cronies to powerful positions. The constitutions committed southern states, many for the first time, to public education. Lawmakers enacted a variety of reforms, including social welfare, penal reform, legislative reapportionment, and universal manhood suffrage.

The Republican regimes that gained control in southern states promoted vigorous state government and the protection of civil and voting rights. Three Republican constituencies supported these governments: native whites, native blacks, and northern transplants. The small native white group was mostly made up of yeomen farmers. Residing mainly in the upland regions of the South and long ignored by lowland planters and merchants in state government, they were left devastated by the war. They struggled to keep their land and hoped for an easing of credit and for debt-stay laws to help them escape foreclosure. They wanted public schools for their children and good roads to get their crops to market. Some urban merchants and large planters also called themselves Republicans. They were attracted to the party's emphasis on economic development, especially railroad construction, and would become prominent in Republican leadership after 1867, forming a majority of the party's elected officials.

Collectively, opponents called these native white southerners **scalawags**. Although their opponents perceived them as a unified group, scalawags held a variety of views. Planters and merchants opposed easy debt and credit arrangements and the use of their taxes to support programs other than railroads or port improvements. Yeomen farmers desperately needed the debt and credit legislation to retain their land. And even though they supported public schools and road building, which would require increased state revenues, they opposed higher taxes.

Northern transplants, or **carpetbaggers**, as many southern whites called them, constituted a second and smaller group of southern Republicans. Thousands of northerners came south during and after the war. Many were Union soldiers who simply enjoyed the climate and perhaps married a local woman. Most were drawn by economic opportunity. Land was cheap and the price of cotton high. Although most carpetbaggers had supported the Republican Party before they moved south, few became politically active until the cotton economy nosedived in 1866. Financial concerns were not all that motivated carpetbaggers to enter politics; some hoped to aid the freedmen.

Carpetbaggers never comprised more than 2 percent of any state's population. Most white southerners viewed them as an alien presence, instruments of a hated occupying force. They estranged themselves from their neighbors by supporting and participating in the Republican state governments that most white people despised. In Alabama, local editors organized a boycott of northern-owned shops. Because many of them tended to support extending political and civil rights to black southerners, carpetbaggers were also often at odds with their fellow white Republicans, the scalawags.

African Americans constituted the Republican Party's largest southern constituency. In three states, South Carolina, Mississippi, and Louisiana, they also constituted the majority of eligible voters. They viewed the franchise as the key to civic equality and economic opportunity and demanded an active role in party and government affairs.

Black people began to take part in southern politics even before the end of the Civil War, especially in cities occupied by Union forces. In February 1865, black people in

scalawags Southern whites, mainly small landowning farmers and well-off merchants and planters, who supported the southern Republican Party during Reconstruction for diverse reasons; a disparaging term.

carpetbaggers Pejorative term to describe northern transplants to the South, many of whom were Union soldiers who stayed in the South after the war.

From Then to Now

African American Voting Rights in the South

R ight from the end of the Civil War, white southerners resisted African American voting rights. Black people, with equal determination, used the franchise to assert their equal right to participate in the political process. Black voting rights proved so contentious that Congress sought to secure them with the Fourteenth and Fifteenth Amendments to the U.S. Constitution. But U.S. Supreme Court decisions in *United States v. Cruikshank* (1876) and in the *Civil Rights Cases* (1883) undermined federal authority to protect the rights of freedmen, including voting rights. A combination of violence, intimidation, and legislation effectively disfranchised black southerners by the early twentieth century.

During the 1960s, Congress passed legislation designed to override state prohibitions and earlier court decisions limiting African American voting rights. The key measure, the 1965 Voting Rights Act, not only guaranteed black southerners (and later, other minorities) the right to register and vote but also protected them from procedural subterfuges. These protections proved necessary because of the extreme racial polarization of southern elections.

To ensure African American candidates

The Congressional Black Caucus of the 113th Congress (January 3, 2013–January 3, 2015)

Southern black men during Reconstruction went to great lengths to vote and to protect themselves on election day, as these voters fording a stream with rifles aloft attest.

an opportunity to win elections, the federal government after 1965 insisted that states and localities establish procedures to increase the likelihood of such a result. By the early 1990s, states were being directed to draw districts with majority-black voting populations to ensure African American representation in the U.S. Congress and in state legislatures. The federal government cited the South's history of racial discrimination and racially polarized voting to justify these districts. But white southerners

challenged such claims, as they had more than a century earlier, and their challenges proved partially successful in federal court.

As with the First Reconstruction, the U.S. Supreme Court has narrowed the scope of black voting rights in several decisions since the early 1990s. Despite the history of racial discrimination with respect to voting rights, the Court has often championed the standard of "color-blindness," which justices insist was codified in the Fourteenth Amendment. The principle of color-blindness, however wonderful in the abstract, ignores the history of black voting rights from the Reconstruction era to the present. The framers of the Reconstruction Amendments had the protection of the rights of the freedmen in mind (including and especially voting rights) when they wrote those measures.

The issue of African American voting rights in the South, and the degree to which the federal government may or may not intercede to protect those rights, remains as much at issue as it was more than a century ago. In the 2012 presidential election campaign, civil rights advocates charged that the attempts by more than a dozen states throughout the country to purge voter rolls or to require state-issued voter identification, allegedly to prevent voter fraud, weighed disproportionately against minorities, especially African Americans.

Question for Discussion

- There is considerable debate about whether the U.S. Constitution is color-blind with respect to voting rights. Should it be?

Norfolk, Virginia, gathered to demand a say in the new government that Union supporters were forming in that portion of the state. In April, they created the Colored Monitor Union Club, modeled after regular Republican Party organizations in northern cities, called **Union Leagues**. They demanded "the right of universal suffrage" for "all loyal men, without distinction of color." Black people in other southern cities held similar meetings, seeking inclusion in the democratic process to protect their freedom. Despite white threats, black southerners thronged to Union League meetings in 1867, even forging interracial alliances in states such as North Carolina and Alabama. Focusing on political education and recruitment, the leagues successfully mobilized black voters. In 1867, more than 90 percent of eligible black voters across the South turned out for elections. Black women, even though they could not vote, also played a role. During the 1868 presidential campaign, for example, black maids and cooks in the South wore buttons touting the candidacy of the Republican presidential nominee, Ulysses S. Grant.

Black southerners were not content just to vote; they also demanded political office. White Republican leaders in the South often took the black vote for granted. But on several occasions after 1867, black people threatened to run independent candidates, support rival Democrats, or simply stay home unless they were represented among Republican nominees. These demands brought them some success. The number of southern black congressmen in the U.S. House of Representatives increased from two in 1869 to seven in 1873, and more than 600 African Americans, most of them former slaves from plantation counties, were elected to southern state legislatures between 1867 and 1877.

White fears that black officeholders would enact vengeful legislation proved unfounded. African Americans generally did not promote race-specific legislation. Rather, they supported measures such as debt relief and state funding for education that benefited all poor and working-class people. Like all politicians, however, black officials in southern cities sought to enact measures beneficial to their constituents, such as roads and sidewalks.

During the first few years of Congressional Reconstruction, Republican governments walked a tightrope, attempting to lure moderate Democrats and unaffiliated white voters into the party without slighting the black vote. They used the lure of patronage power and the attractive salaries that accompanied public office. In 1868, for example, Louisiana's Republican governor, Henry C. Warmoth, appointed white conservatives to state and local offices, which he divided equally between Confederate veterans and black people, and repealed a constitutional provision disfranchising former Confederate officials.

Republicans also gained support by expanding the role of state government to a degree unprecedented in the South. Southern Republican administrations appealed to hard-pressed upland white constituents by prohibiting foreclosure and passing stay laws that allowed farm owners additional time to repay debts. They undertook building programs that benefited black and white citizens, erecting hospitals, schools, and orphanages. Stepping further into social policy than most northern states at the time, Republican governments in the South expanded women's property rights, enacted legislation against child abuse, and required child support from fathers of mulatto children. In South Carolina, the Republican government provided medical care for the poor; in Alabama, it provided free legal aid for needy defendants.

Despite these impressive policies, southern Republicans were unable to hold their diverse constituency together. Although the party had some success among white yeoman farmers, the liberal use of patronage failed to attract white conservatives. At the same time, it alienated the party's core supporters, who resented seeing their former enemies rewarded with lucrative offices.

The high costs of their activist policies further undermined the Republicans by forcing them to raise state taxes. In Mississippi, where the Republican government built a public school system for both black and white students, founded a black university, reorganized the state judiciary, built new courthouses and two state hospitals, and pushed through legislation giving black people equal access to public facilities, the state debt soared to $1.5 million between 1869 and 1873. This was in an era in which state budgets rarely exceeded $1 million. Unprecedented expenditures and the liberal

Union League A Republican Party organization in northern cities that became an important organizing device among freedmen in southern cities after 1865.

use of patronage sometimes resulted in waste and corruption. Problems like these were not limited to the South, but the perception of dishonesty was nonetheless damaging to governments struggling to build legitimacy among a skeptical white electorate.

The excesses of some state governments, high taxes, contests over patronage, and conflicts over the relative roles of white and black party members opened rifts in Republican ranks. Patronage triggered intraparty warfare. Every office secured by a Democrat created a disappointed Republican. Class tensions erupted in the party as economic development policies sometimes superseded relief and social service legislation supported by small farmers. There were differences among black voters too. In the Lower South, divisions that had developed in the prewar era between urban, lighter-skinned free black people and darker, rural slaves persisted into the Reconstruction era. In many southern states, black clergy, because of their independence from white support and their important spiritual and educational role, became leaders. But most preached salvation in the next world rather than equality in this one, conceding more to white people than to their rank-and-file constituents.

Counter-Reconstruction, 1870–1874

16.4 How were white northerners and the federal government complicit in denying freed slaves the basic rights of American citizenship?

Republicans might have survived battles over patronage, policy, expenditures, and taxes, but they could not overcome racism and the violence it generated. Racism killed Republican rule in the South because it deepened divisions within the party, encouraged white violence, and eroded support in the North. Southern Democrats discovered that they could use race baiting and racial violence to create solidarity among white people that overrode their economic and class differences. Unity translated into election victories.

Northerners responded to the persistent violence in the South, not with outrage, but with a growing sense of tedium. They came to accept the arguments of white southerners that it was folly to allow black people to vote and hold office, especially since most northern whites would not extend the franchise to African Americans in their own states. Racism became respectable. Noted intellectuals and journalists espoused "scientific" theories that claimed to demonstrate the natural superiority of white people over black people.

By 1874, Americans were concerned with an array of domestic problems that overshadowed Reconstruction. An economic depression left them more preoccupied with survival than racial justice. Corruption convinced many that politics was part of the nation's problems, not a solution to them. With the rest of the nation thus distracted and weary, white southerners reclaimed control of the South.

The Uses of Violence

Racial violence preceded Republican rule. As African Americans moved about, attempted to vote, haggled over labor contracts, and carried arms as part of the occupying Union forces, they tested the patience of white southerners, to whom any black assertion of equality seemed threatening. African Americans were the face of whites' defeat, of their world turned upside down. If the war was about slavery, then here was the visible proof of the Confederacy's defeat. Many white southerners viewed the term "free black" less as a status than as an oxymoron. The restoration of white supremacy meant the restoration of order and civilization, an objective southern whites would pursue with vengeance.

White paramilitary groups were responsible for much of the violence directed against African Americans. Probably the best-known of these groups was the **Ku Klux Klan**. Founded in Tennessee by six Confederate veterans in 1866, the Klan was initially a social club. Within a year, the Klan had spread throughout the South. In 1867, when black

Ku Klux Klan Perhaps the most prominent of the vigilante groups that terrorized black people in the South during Reconstruction Era, founded by Confederate veterans in 1866.

 Read the Document   Albion W. Tourgee, Letter on Ku Klux Klan Activities (1870)

16.1

16.2

16.3

16.4

16.5

The Klan directed violence at African Americans primarily for engaging in political activity. Here, a black man, John Campbell, vainly begs for mercy in Moore County, North Carolina, in August 1871.

people entered politics in large numbers, the Klan unleashed a wave of terror against them. Klan nightriders in ghostlike disguises intimidated black communities. The Klan directed much of its violence toward subverting the electoral process. One historian has estimated that roughly 10 percent of all black delegates to the 1867 state constitutional conventions in the South became victims of political violence during the next decade.

By 1868, white paramilitary organizations permeated the South. Violence was particularly severe in election years in Louisiana, which had a large and active black electorate. The most serious example of political violence in Louisiana occurred in Colfax in 1873 when a white Democratic mob attempted to wrest control of local government from Republicans. For three weeks, black defenders held the town against the white onslaught. When the white mob finally broke through, they massacred the remaining black defenders, including those who had surrendered and laid down their weapons. It was the bloodiest peacetime massacre in nineteenth-century America.

Racial violence and the combative reaction it provoked both among black people and Republican administrations energized white voters. Democrats regained power in North Carolina, for example, after the state's Republican governor enraged white voters by calling out the militia to counter white violence during the election of 1870. That same year, the Republican regime in Georgia fell as well. Some Republican governments countered the violence successfully for a time. Governor Edmund J. Davis of Texas, for example, organized a special force of 200 state policemen to round up Klan nightriders. Between 1870 and 1872, Davis's force arrested 6,000 and broke the Klan in

Texas. But other governors hesitated to enforce laws directed at the Klan, fearing that to do so would further alienate white people.

The federal government responded with a variety of legislation. One example was the Fifteenth Amendment. Another was the Enforcement Act of 1870, which authorized the federal government to appoint supervisors in states that failed to protect voting rights. When violence and intimidation persisted, Congress followed with a second, more sweeping measure, the Ku Klux Klan Act of 1871. This law permitted federal authorities, with military assistance, if necessary, to arrest and prosecute members of groups that denied a citizen's civil rights if state authorities failed to do so. The Klan Act was not successful in curbing racial violence, as the Colfax Massacre in 1873 made vividly clear. But with it, Congress, by claiming the right to override state authority to bring individuals to justice, established a new precedent in federal-state relations.

Northern Complicity

The success of political violence after 1871 reflected both a declining commitment on the part of northern Republicans to support southern Republican administrations and a growing hostility of white northerners to southern black aspirations. The erosion of northern support for Congressional Reconstruction began as early as 1867 when three states, Minnesota, Ohio, and Kansas, defeated black suffrage amendments. Could Congressional Republicans force whites in, say, Alabama, to accept African American voting, when their own constituents in the North opposed the franchise for blacks?

That northern base grew increasingly skeptical about Reconstruction policy in general and assistance to the freedmen in particular. Many Northern Republicans looked around their cities and saw the local political scene infested with unqualified immigrant voters and corruption. New York City's Democratic boss William M. Tweed and his associates bilked the city of an astounding $100 million dollars. When white southerners charged that unqualified blacks and grasping carpetbaggers corrupted the political process in the South, northerners recognized the argument.

Changing perceptions in the North also indicated a convergence of racial views with white southerners. As radical Republican congressman from Indiana George W. Julian admitted in 1865, white northerners "hate the negro." They expressed this hatred in their rejection of black suffrage, in racial segregation of their African American population, and in periodic violence against black residents, such as during the New York draft riots of 1863. Northerners' views were bolstered by prevailing scientific theories of race that "proved" blacks' limited capacities and, therefore, unfitness for either the ballot or skilled occupations.

Northerners also grew increasingly wary of federal power. The emerging scandals of the Grant administration, fueled, it seemed, by government subsidies to railroads and other private businesses, demanded a scaling back of federal power and discretion. When white southerners complained about federal meddling, again, they found resonance in the North.

The excesses and alleged abuses of federal power inspired a reform movement among a group of northern Republicans and some Democrats. In addition, business leaders decried the ability of wealthy lobbyists to influence economic decisions. An influential group of intellectuals and opinion makers lamented the inability of politicians to understand "natural" laws, particularly those related to race. And some Republicans joined the reform movement out of fear that Democrats would capitalize on the turmoil in the South and the political scandals in the North to reap huge electoral victories in 1872.

Liberal Republicans and the Election of 1872

Liberal Republicans, as the reformers called themselves, put forward an array of suggestions to improve government and save the Republican Party. They advocated civil service reform to reduce reliance on patronage and the abuses that accompanied office

THE IGNORANT VOTE—HONORS ARE EASY.

Thomas Nast, "The Ignorant Vote—Honors Are Easy," 1876. Many white northerners drew parallels between the corruption and inefficiency of their local and state governments, supported by immigrant and working-class votes, and similar problems in southern states where African Americans voted. Note the monkey-like portrayal of the Irish immigrant (labeled "white") and the stereotyped black figure.

seeking. To limit government and reduce artificial economic stimuli, the reformers called for tariff reduction and an end to federal land grants to railroads. For the South, they recommended a general amnesty for white people and a return to "local self-government" by men of "property and enterprise."

When the Liberals failed to convince other Republicans to adopt their program, they broke with the party. Taking advantage of this split, the Democrats forged an alliance with the Liberals. Together, they nominated journalist Horace Greeley to challenge Ulysses S. Grant for the presidency in the election of 1872. Grant won resoundingly, helped by high turnout among black voters in the South.

Economic Transformation

After 1873, the Republican Party in the South became a liability for the national party, especially as Americans fastened on economic issues. The major story of the decade would not be equal rights for African Americans—a long shot even in the heady days following freedom—but the changing nature of the American economy. An overextended banking and credit system generated the Panic of 1873 and caused extensive suffering, particularly among working-class Americans. But the depression masked a remarkable economic transformation as the nation moved toward a national industrial economy.

During the 1870s, the economy grew annually between 4.5 and 6 percent, among the fastest decadal growth rates on record. Consumption grew even faster; Americans purchased more food, more fuel, and more manufactured products than at any other

✳ Explore Reconstruction on MyHistoryLab

HOW DID RECONSTRUCTION AFFECT AFRICAN AMERICANS IN THE SOUTH?

In 1865, at the end of the Civil War, the United States was at a crossroads. The Thirteenth Amendment to the Constitution had freed the slaves of the rebellious eleven states, but questions remained on how to implement the rights of the newly liberated African Americans. Further, leaders were divided on how to reintegrate the war-torn southern states back into the Union. Many white Southerners tried to continue their ways of life while freed African Americans struggled in a society built on segregation. Though the subsequent Fourteenth and Fifteenth Amendments theoretically extended the realm of equality for blacks, in the end, whites in the North and South saw to it that the promises of Reconstruction for African Americans went unfulfilled.

Much hope was placed in the policies of Reconstruction as this allegorical lithograph shows. The reconciliation between the North and South, however, would have a mixed legacy, especially for African Americans.

RECONSTRUCTION AMENDMENTS TO THE CONSTITUTION

Amendment	Summary	Date
Thirteenth	Abolishes slavery	December 6, 1865
Fourteenth	Ensures equal rights and protections to every person born or naturalized in the United States	July 9, 1868
Fifteenth	Prohibits the denial of the right of vote based on race	February 3, 1870

SOURCE: United States Constitution

KEY QUESTIONS   Use **MyHistoryLab** *Explorer* to **answer** these **questions:**

Analysis ▶▶▶ *How did voting patterns for Republicans evolve during the Reconstruction period?*

Chart voting patterns to understand reasons behind voting trends.

Comparison ▶▶▶ *How did literacy rates differ between African Americans and Euro-Americans in the South?*

Theorize how this might affect black disenfranchisement.

Response ▶▶▶ *What was the landholding situation for African Americans at the end of the nineteenth century?*

Map land tenure to see discrepancies with whites.

previous time in the nation's history. Although unemployment was severe, overall, employment grew by 40 percent between 1870 and 1880, and productivity increased at least as fast. This seeming contradiction is explained by the rapid expansion of new industries such as oil refining and meatpacking, and the application of technology in iron and steel production. Technology also eliminated jobs, and those that remained were primarily low-skilled, low-paying positions—painful, to be sure, for those caught in the change, but liberating for those with education and ability who populated a burgeoning middle-management sector of the growing urban middle class.

The depression and the economic transformation occupied center stage in the American mentality of the mid-1870s, at least in the North. Most Americans had mentally forsaken Reconstruction long before the Compromise of 1877 made its abandonment a political fact. The sporadic violence against black and white Republicans in the South, and the cries of help from freedmen as their rights and persons were abused by white Democrats, became distant echoes from another era, the era of the Civil War, now commemorated and memorialized, but no longer an active part of the nation's present and future. Of course, for white southerners, the past was not yet past. There was still work to do.

Redemption, 1874–1877

16.5 How and why did Reconstruction end?

For southern Democrats, the Republican victory in 1872 underscored the importance of turning out larger numbers of white voters and restricting the black vote. They accomplished these goals over the next four years with a surge in political violence, secure in the knowledge that federal authorities would rarely intervene against them. Preoccupied with corruption and economic crisis, and increasingly indifferent, if not hostile, to African American aspirations, most Americans looked the other way. The elections of 1876 confirmed the triumph of white southerners.

In a religious metaphor that matched their view of the Civil War as a lost crusade, southern Democrats called their victory "Redemption" and depicted themselves as **Redeemers**, holy warriors who had saved the South from the hell of black Republican rule. Generations of American boys and girls would learn this interpretation of the Reconstruction era, and it would affect race relations for nearly a century.

Redeemers Southern Democrats who wrested control of governments in the former Confederacy from Republicans, often through electoral fraud and violence, beginning in 1870.

The Democrats' Violent Resurgence

The violence between 1874 and 1876 differed in several respects from earlier attempts to restore white government by force. Attackers operated more openly and more closely identified themselves with the Democratic Party. Mounted, gray-clad, ex-Confederate soldiers flanked Democratic candidates at campaign rallies and "visited" black neighborhoods afterward to discourage black men from voting. With black people intimidated and white people already prepared to vote, election days were typically quiet.

Democrats swept to victory across the South in the 1874 elections. "A perfect reign of terror" redeemed Alabama for the Democrats. The successful appeal to white supremacy inspired a massive white turnout to unseat Republicans in Virginia, Florida (legislature only), and Arkansas. Texas had fallen to the Democrats in 1873. Only South Carolina, Mississippi, and Louisiana, states with large black populations, survived the debacle. But the relentless tide of terror would soon overwhelm them as well.

Democratic leaders in those states announced a "white line" policy, inviting all white men, regardless of party affiliation, to "unite" and redeem the states. They all had the same objective: to eliminate African Americans as a political factor by any means. Black Republicans feared not only for their political future, but also for their lives.

A bold assault occurred in New Orleans in September 1874 when 8,500 White League troops, many of them leading citizens and Confederate veterans, attempted a coup to oust Republican Governor William P. Kellogg and members of his administration. The League's manifesto, promulgated in July 1874, offered a clear indication of its intentions: "Having solely in view the maintenance of our hereditary civilization and Christianity menaced by a stupid Africanization, we appeal to the men of our race . . . to unite with us against that supreme danger . . . in an earnest effort to re-establish a white man's government in this city and the State." These were no mincing words or veiled threats.

The New Orleans Leaguers overwhelmed the city's racially mixed Metropolitan Police Force under the command of former Confederate General James B. Longstreet. The timely arrival of federal troops, ordered to the scene by President Grant, prevented the takeover. The League was more successful in the Louisiana countryside in the weeks preceding the Democratic victory in November 1874. League troops overthrew or murdered Republican officials in eight parishes.

The Democratic victory in Louisiana encouraged a corresponding group, the White Liners, in Mississippi. Blacks dominated the Warren County government headquartered in Vicksburg. Liners demanded the resignations of all black officials including the sheriff, Peter Crosby, a black Union veteran. Republican Governor Adelbert Ames, a native of Maine, ordered the Liners to disperse and granted Crosby's request to raise a protective militia to respond to future threats.

Peter Crosby's efforts to gather a militia force were too successful. An army of several hundred armed African Americans marched in three columns from the surrounding countryside to Vicksburg. Whites responded to the challenge, firing on the militia and tracking down and terrorizing blacks in the city and county over the next ten days. Among the victims were a black Presbyterian minister and several of his congregants kneeling in prayer. Liners killed at least twenty-nine blacks and wounded countless more. Democrats gained control of the county government.

The Vicksburg incident was a rehearsal for Democratic victories in statewide elections in 1875. The *Birmingham News* cheered on the Mississippi White Liners, "We intend to beat the negro in the battle of life, and defeat means one thing—EXTERMINATION." The intimidation worked; the Democrats swept to victory in Mississippi. They would not allow Governor Ames to finish his term, threatening him with impeachment. Fearing for his safety, Ames resigned and fled the state. The South's second war of independence was reaching its climax.

On July 4, 1876, America's one-hundredth birthday, a modest celebration unfolded in Hamburg, South Carolina, a small town in Edgefield County across the Savannah River from Augusta, Georgia. Blacks comprised more than 75 percent of the town's population. They held most of the political offices. An altercation occurred concerning the right of way between the black militia parading in the street and a passing wagon carrying several prominent white residents. When the aggrieved parties met four days later, more than 1,000 armed whites were milling in front of the wooden "armory" where 100 black militiamen had taken refuge. A shot rang out and shattered a second-floor window, and soon a pitched battled was raging. The white attackers fired a cannon that turned most of the building into splinters. As blacks fled, whites tracked them down. The white men also burned homes and shops and robbed residents of the town.

The November election went off in relative calm. In Edgefield County, out of 7,000 potential voters, 9,200 ballots were cast. Similar frauds occurred throughout the state. Still, the result hung in the balance. Both Democrats and Republicans claimed victory and set up rival governments. The following April, after a deal was brokered in Washington between the parties, federal troops were withdrawn from South Carolina and a Democratic government installed in Columbia. The victorious Democrats expelled twenty-four Republicans from the state legislature and elected Matthew C. Butler to the U.S. Senate. Butler had led the white attackers at Hamburg.

The Weak Federal Response

When Governor Daniel H. Chamberlain could no longer contain the violence in South Carolina in 1876, he asked the president for help. Grant acknowledged the gravity of Chamberlain's situation but would offer him only the lame hope that South Carolinians would exercise "better judgment and cooperation" and assist the governor in bringing offenders to justice "without aid from the federal Government."

Congress responded to blacks' deteriorating status in the South with the Civil Rights Act of 1875 (see Table 16.2). The act, which had no provision for voting rights because Congress presumed the Fifteenth Amendment protected those, prohibited discrimination against black people in public accommodations, such as theaters, parks, and trains, and guaranteed freedmen's rights to serve on juries. Most judges, however, either interpreted the law narrowly or declared it unconstitutional. In 1883, the U.S. Supreme Court agreed and overturned the act, declaring that only the states, not Congress, could redress "a private wrong, or a crime of the individual."

The Election of 1876 and the Compromise of 1877

Reconstruction officially ended with the presidential election of 1876, in which the Democrat Samuel J. Tilden ran against the Republican Rutherford B. Hayes. When the ballots were counted, it appeared that Tilden, a conservative New Yorker respectable

📖 **Read the Document**   **Thirteenth, Fourteenth, and Fifteenth Amendments**

TABLE 16.2 CONSTITUTIONAL AMENDMENTS AND FEDERAL LEGISLATION OF THE RECONSTRUCTION ERA

Amendment or Legislation	Purpose	Significance
Thirteenth Amendment (passed and ratified in 1865)	Prevented southern states from reestablishing slavery after the war	Final step toward full emancipation of slaves
Freedmen's Bureau Act (1865)	Oversight of resettlement, labor for former slaves	Involved the federal government directly in relief, education, and assisting the transition from slavery to freedom; worked fitfully to achieve this objective during its seven-year career
Southern Homestead Act (1866)	Provided black people preferential access to public lands in five southern states	Lack of capital and poor quality of federal land thwarted the purpose of the act
Civil Rights Act of 1866	Defined rights of national citizenship	Marked an important change in federal-state relations, tilting balance of power to national government
Fourteenth Amendment (passed 1866; ratified 1868)	Prohibited states from violating the rights of their citizens	Strengthened the Civil Rights Act of 1866 and guaranteed all citizens equality before the law
Military Reconstruction Acts (1867)	Set new rules for the readmission of former Confederate states into the Union and secured black voting rights	Initiated Congressional Reconstruction
Tenure of Office Act (1867)	Required congressional approval for the removal of any official whose appointment had required Senate confirmation	A congressional challenge to the president's right to dismiss cabinet members; led to President Andrew Johnson's impeachment trial
Fifteenth Amendment (passed 1869; ratified 1870)	Guaranteed the right of all American male citizens to vote regardless of race	The basis for black voting rights
Civil Rights Act of 1875	Prohibited racial discrimination in jury selection, public transportation, and public accommodations	Rarely enforced; Supreme Court declared it unconstitutional in 1883

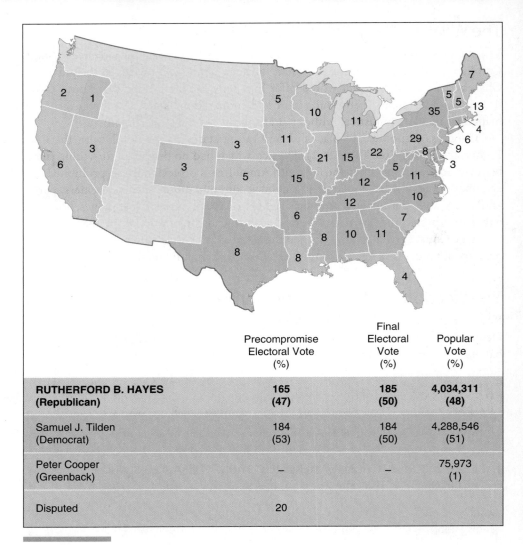

	Precompromise Electoral Vote (%)	Final Electoral Vote (%)	Popular Vote (%)
RUTHERFORD B. HAYES (Republican)	**165** **(47)**	**185** **(50)**	**4,034,311** **(48)**
Samuel J. Tilden (Democrat)	184 (53)	184 (50)	4,288,546 (51)
Peter Cooper (Greenback)	–	–	75,973 (1)
Disputed	20		

MAP 16.1 THE ELECTION OF 1876 The Democrat Samuel F. Tilden won a majority of the popular vote but eventually fell short of an electoral vote majority when the contested electoral votes of Florida, Louisiana, and South Carolina went to his Republican opponent, Rutherford B. Hayes. The map also indicates the Republicans' failure to build a base in the South after more than a decade of Reconstruction.

enough for northern voters and Democratic enough for white southerners, had won. But despite a majority in the popular vote, disputed returns in three southern states left him with only 184 of the 185 electoral votes needed to win (see Map 16.1). The three states—Florida, South Carolina, and Louisiana—were the last in the South still to have Republican administrations.

Both camps maneuvered intensively in the following months to claim the disputed votes. Congress appointed a fifteen-member commission to settle the issue. Because the Republicans controlled Congress, they held a one-vote majority on the commission.

Southern Democrats wanted Tilden to win, but they wanted control of their states more. They were willing to deal. Hayes intended to remove federal support from the remaining southern Republican governments anyway. It thus cost him nothing to promise to do so in exchange for the contested electoral votes. Republicans also made vague promises to invest in the southern economy and support a southern transcontinental railroad, but these were secondary. What the South wanted most was to be left alone, and that is what it got. The so-called **Compromise of 1877** installed Hayes in the White House and gave Democrats control of every state government in the South. Congress never carried through on the economic promises, and southern Democrats never pressed it to. Southern Democrats emerged the major winners from the Compromise of 1877. President Hayes and his successors into the next century left the South alone.

Compromise of 1877 The congressional settling of the 1876 election that installed Republican Rutherford B. Hayes in the White House and gave Democrats control of all state governments in the South.

In practical terms, the Compromise signaled the revocation of civil rights and voting rights for black southerners. The Fourteenth and Fifteenth Amendments would be dead letters in the South until well into the twentieth century. On the two great issues confronting the nation at the end of the Civil War, reunion and freedom, the white South had won. It reentered the Union largely on its own terms with the freedom to pursue a racial agenda consistent with its political, economic, and social interests.

The Memory of Reconstruction

Southern Democrats used the memory of Reconstruction to help them maintain power. Reconstruction joined the Lost Cause as part of the glorious fight to preserve the civilization of the Old South. As white southerners elevated Civil War heroes into saints and battles into holy struggles, they equated Reconstruction with Redemption. White Democrats had rescued the South from black rule and federal oppression. During the next century, whenever southern Democrats felt threatened, they reminded their white constituents of the sacrifices and heroism of the war, the "horrors of Reconstruction," the menace of black rule, and the cruelty of the Yankee occupiers. The southern view of Reconstruction permeated textbooks, films, and standard accounts of the period. By the early 1900s, professional historians at the nation's finest institutions concurred in this view, ignoring contrary evidence and rendering the story of African Americans invisible. By that time, therefore, most Americans believed that the policies of Reconstruction had been misguided and had brought great suffering to the white South. The widespread acceptance of this view allowed the South to maintain its system of racial segregation and exclusion without interference from the federal government.

Memorialists did not deny the Redeemers' use of terror and violence. To the contrary, they praised it as necessary. South Carolina Senator Benjamin R. Tillman, a participant in the Hamburg massacre, stood in front of his Senate colleagues in 1900 and asserted: "We were sorry we had the necessity forced upon us, but we could not help it, and as white men we are not sorry for it, and we do not propose to apologize for anything we have done in connection with it. We took the government away from them [African Americans] in 1876. We did take it. . . . We of the South have never recognized the right of the negro to govern white men, and we never will." The animosity of southern whites toward Republican governments had much less to do with alleged corruption and incompetence than the mere fact of African Americans casting ballots and making laws.

Not all memories of Reconstruction conformed to the theme of redemption. In 1913, John R. Lynch, a former black Republican congressman from Mississippi, published *The Facts of Reconstruction* to "present the other side." He hoped that his book would "bring to public notice those things that were commendable and meritorious, to prevent the publication of which seems to have been the primary purpose of nearly all who have thus far written upon that important subject." But most Americans ignored his book. Two decades later, a more forceful defense, W. E. B. Du Bois's *Black Reconstruction* (1935), met a similar fate. An angry Du Bois attacked the prevailing view of Reconstruction as "one of the most stupendous efforts the world ever saw to discredit human beings, an effort involving universities, history, science, social life and religion."

The national historical consensus grew out of a growing national reconciliation concerning the war, a mutual agreement that both sides had fought courageously and that it was time to move on. Hidden in all the goodwill was the tacit agreement between southern and northern whites that the South was now free to work out its own resolution to race relations. Reconstruction rested on a national consensus of African American inferiority.

There is much to be said in favor of sectional reconciliation as opposed to persistent animosity. There are enough examples in the world today of antagonists in the same country never forgetting or never forgiving their bloody histories. Ideally, Americans could have had *both* healing and justice, but instead they settled for the former.

Frederick Douglass, prescient as ever, worried about the peace that followed the Civil War and what it would mean for race relations: "If war among the whites brought peace and liberty to the blacks, what will peace among the whites bring?"

Modest Gains

If the overthrow of Reconstruction elicited a resounding indifference from most white Americans, black southerners greeted it with frustration. Their dreams of land ownership faded as a new labor system relegated them to a lowly position in southern agriculture. Redemption reversed their economic and political gains and deprived them of most of the civil rights they had enjoyed under Congressional Reconstruction. Although they continued to vote into the 1890s, they had by 1877 lost most of the voting strength and political offices they held. Rather than becoming part of southern society, they were increasingly set apart from it, valued only for their labor.

Still, the former slaves were better off in 1877 than in 1865. They were free, however limited their freedom. Some owned land; some held jobs in cities. They raised their families in relative peace and experienced the spiritual joys of a full religious life. They socialized freely with relatives and friends, and they moved about. The Reconstruction amendments to the Constitution guaranteed an array of civil and political rights, and eventually these guarantees would form the basis of the civil rights revolution after World War II. But that outcome was long, too long, in the future.

Black southerners experienced some advances in the decade after the Civil War, but these owed little to Reconstruction. Black families functioned as economic and psychological buffers against unemployment and prejudice. Black churches played crucial roles in their communities. Self-help and labor organizations offered mutual friendship and financial assistance. All of these institutions had existed in the slavery era, although on a smaller scale. And some of them, such as black labor groups, schools, and social welfare associations, endured because comparable white institutions excluded black people.

Black people also scored some modest economic successes during the Reconstruction era, mainly from their own pluck. In the Lower South, black per capita income increased 46 percent between 1857 and 1879, compared with a 35 percent decline in white per capita income. Sharecropping, oppressive as it was, represented an advance over forced and gang labor. Collectively, black people owned more than $68 million worth of property in 1870, a 240 percent increase over 1860, but the average worth of each was only $408.

The Fourteenth and Fifteenth Amendments to the Constitution are among the few bright spots in Reconstruction's otherwise dismal legacy. But the benefits of these two landmark amendments did not accrue to African Americans until well into the twentieth century. White southerners effectively nullified the Reconstruction amendments, and the U.S. Supreme Court virtually interpreted them, and other Reconstruction legislation, out of existence.

In the **Slaughterhouse cases** (1873), the Supreme Court contradicted the intent of the Fourteenth Amendment by decreeing that most citizenship rights remained under state, not federal, control. In **United States v. Cruikshank** (1876), the Court overturned the convictions of some of those responsible for the Colfax Massacre, ruling that the Enforcement Act applied only to violations of black rights by states, not individuals. Within the next two decades, the Supreme Court would uphold the legality of racial segregation and black disfranchisement, in effect declaring that the Fourteenth and Fifteenth Amendments did not apply to African Americans. The Civil War had killed secession forever, but states' rights enjoyed a remarkable revival.

As the historian John Hope Franklin accurately concluded, Reconstruction "had no significant or permanent effect on the status of the black in American life. . . . [Black people] made no meaningful steps toward economic independence or even stability."

Slaughterhouse cases Group of cases resulting in one sweeping decision by the U.S. Supreme Court in 1873 that contradicted the intent of the Fourteenth Amendment by decreeing that most citizenship rights remained under state, not federal, control.

United States v. Cruikshank Supreme Court ruling of 1876 that overturned the convictions of some of those responsible for the Colfax Massacre, ruling that the Enforcement Act applied only to violations of black rights by states, not individuals.

Conclusion

Formerly enslaved black southerners had entered freedom with many hopes, among the most prominent of which was to be left alone. White southerners, after four bloody years of unwanted attention from the federal government, also longed to be left alone. But they did not include their ex-slaves as equals in their vision of solitude. Northerners, too, began to seek escape from the issues and consequences of the war, abandoning their weak commitment to secure civil and voting rights for black southerners.

White southerners robbed black southerners of their gains and sought to reduce them again to servitude and dependence, if not to slavery. But in the process, the majority of white southerners lost as well. Yeoman farmers missed an opportunity to break cleanly from the Old South and establish a more equitable society. Instead, they allowed the old elites to regain power and gradually ignore their needs. They preserved the social benefit of a white skin at the cost of almost everything else. Many lost their farms and sank into tenancy. Few had a voice in state legislatures or the U.S. Congress. A new South, rid of slavery and sectional antagonism, had indeed emerged—redeemed, regenerated, and disenthralled. But the old South lingered on.

As federal troops left the South, an era of possibility for American society ended, and a new era began. "The southern question is dead," a Charleston newspaper proclaimed in 1877. "The question of labor and capital, work and wages" had moved to the forefront. The chance to redeem the sacrifice of a bloody civil war with a society that fulfilled the promise of the Declaration of Independence and the Constitution for all citizens slipped away. It would take a new generation of African Americans a long century later to revive it.

The journey toward equality after the Civil War had aborted. Reconstruction had not failed. It was overthrown. In the weeks and months after Appomattox, white southerners launched a war against the freedmen and their allies to return white Democrats to power and African Americans to a position of permanent subordination in southern society. The indifferent and often hostile attitudes of white northerners toward blacks played a role in limiting the federal response and ensuring the success of the white South in prosecuting this war. As with the Civil War, the overthrow of Reconstruction was a national tragedy. By 1877, the "golden moment," an unprecedented opportunity for the nation to live up to its ideals by extending equal rights to all its citizens, black and white alike, had passed. Thomas Fortune would leave the South the following year, giving up on fulfilling his dream of full citizenship in the region of his birth. Edward A. Pollard who, more than any other southern white articulated the Lost Cause, wrote in 1867 that, despite the surrender at Appomattox, victory was still possible. If white supremacy could be reestablished, he wrote, then the South "really triumphs in the true cause of the war with respect to all its fundamental and vital issues." And so it did.

For Suggested Readings go to MyHistoryLab.

Chapter Review

White Southerners and the Ghosts of the Confederacy, 1865

16.1 How did white southerners respond to defeat? p. 451

White southerners confronted a devastated homeland after the war. In order to cope with defeat and devastation, they rationalized their efforts during the war. The Lost Cause provided personal relief, affirmed their faith, and offered collective justification for their attitudes and policies toward former slaves and northerners.

More than Freedom: African American Aspirations in 1865

16.2 Why did black aspirations generate southern white violence? p. 453

Former slaves viewed the war's outcome very differently from their white neighbors. Freedom was just the beginning. They hoped to build productive and independent lives and exercise the rights of citizenship. Their hopes depended to a great extent on how much support they would receive from the federal government.

Federal Reconstruction, 1865–1870

16.3 How did Congressional Reconstruction change the status of the former slaves in the South? p. 459

White southerners reacted to President Andrew Johnson's mild Reconstruction program by oppressing the freed slaves and returning leading Confederates to power. Northern voters retaliated in 1866, sending strong Republican majorities to the Congress where members enacted a series of measures to guarantee freedmen's rights and limit the influence of former Rebels.

Counter-Reconstruction, 1870–1874

16.4 How were white northerners and the federal government complicit in denying freed slaves the basic rights of American citizenship? p. 468

White southerners responded violently to Congressional Reconstruction, engaging in acts of terror to limit African American participation in southern governments and in economic life. Northern whites grew increasingly indifferent to black aspirations and sympathized with southern white allegations of black fraud and incompetence.

Redemption, 1874–1877

16.5 How and why did Reconstruction end? p. 473

The Republican Party, fearing a backlash from their northern constituents, abandoned Reconstruction policy. Paramilitary groups roamed the South in support of white Democratic candidates, effectively suppressing black political power. The election of 1876 and the subsequent Compromise of 1877 restored white southerners and white supremacy to power in the South.

Timeline

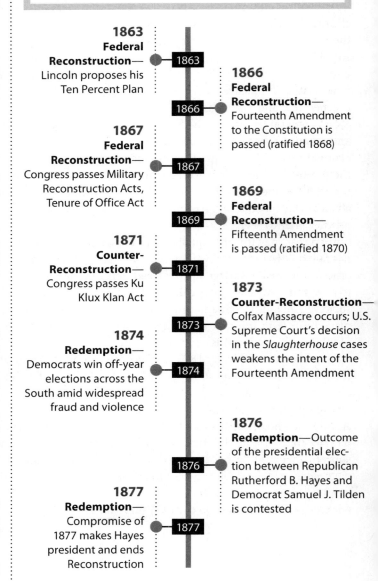

1863
Federal Reconstruction— Lincoln proposes his Ten Percent Plan

1866
Federal Reconstruction— Fourteenth Amendment to the Constitution is passed (ratified 1868)

1867
Federal Reconstruction— Congress passes Military Reconstruction Acts, Tenure of Office Act

1869
Federal Reconstruction— Fifteenth Amendment is passed (ratified 1870)

1871
Counter-Reconstruction— Congress passes Ku Klux Klan Act

1873
Counter-Reconstruction— Colfax Massacre occurs; U.S. Supreme Court's decision in the *Slaughterhouse* cases weakens the intent of the Fourteenth Amendment

1874
Redemption— Democrats win off-year elections across the South amid widespread fraud and violence

1876
Redemption— Outcome of the presidential election between Republican Rutherford B. Hayes and Democrat Samuel J. Tilden is contested

1877
Redemption— Compromise of 1877 makes Hayes president and ends Reconstruction

The Declaration of Independence

When in the course of human events it becomes necessary for one people to dissolve the political bands which have connected them with another and to assume, among the powers of the earth, the separate and equal station to which the laws of nature and of nature's God entitle them, a decent respect to the opinions of mankind requires that they should declare the causes which impel them to the separation.

We hold these truths to be self-evident, that all men are created equal; that they are endowed by their Creator with certain unalienable rights; that among these are life, liberty, and the pursuit of happiness. That, to secure these rights, governments are instituted among men, deriving their just powers from the consent of the governed; that, whenever any form of government becomes destructive of these ends, it is the right of the people to alter or to abolish it, and to institute a new government, laying its foundation on such principles, and organizing its powers in such form, as to them shall seem most likely to effect their safety and happiness. Prudence, indeed, will dictate that governments long established should not be changed for light and transient causes; and, accordingly, all experience hath shown that mankind are more disposed to suffer, while evils are sufferable, than to right themselves by abolishing the forms to which they are accustomed. But when a long train of abuses and usurpations, pursuing invariably the same object, evinces a design to reduce them under absolute despotism, it is their right, it is their duty, to throw off such government and to provide new guards for their future security. Such has been the patient sufferance of these colonies, and such is now the necessity which constrains them to alter their former systems of government. The history of the present King of Great Britain is a history of repeated injuries and usurpations, all having, in direct object, the establishment of an absolute tyranny over these States. To prove this, let facts be submitted to a candid world:

He has refused his assent to laws the most wholesome and necessary for the public good.

He has forbidden his governors to pass laws of immediate and pressing importance, unless suspended in their operation till his assent should be obtained; and, when so suspended, he has utterly neglected to attend to them.

He has refused to pass other laws for the accommodation of large districts of people, unless those people would relinquish the right of representation in the legislature, a right inestimable to them and formidable to tyrants only.

He has called together legislative bodies at places unusual, uncomfortable, and distant from the depository of their public records, for the sole purpose of fatiguing them into compliance with his measures.

He has dissolved representative houses, repeatedly for opposing, with manly firmness, his invasions on the rights of the people.

He has refused, for a long time after such dissolutions, to cause others to be elected; whereby the legislative powers, incapable of annihilation, have returned to the people at large for their exercise; the state remaining, in the meantime, exposed to all the danger of invasion from without and convulsions within.

He has endeavored to prevent the population of these States; for that purpose, obstructing the laws for naturalization of foreigners, refusing to pass others to encourage their migration hither, and raising the conditions of new appropriations of lands.

He has obstructed the administration of justice by refusing his assent to laws for establishing judiciary powers.

He has made judges dependent on his will alone for the tenure of their offices and the amount and payment of their salaries.

He has erected a multitude of new offices and sent hither swarms of officers to harass our people and eat out their substance.

He has kept among us, in time of peace, standing armies, without the consent of our legislatures.

He has affected to render the military independent of, and superior to, the civil power.

He has combined with others to subject us to a jurisdiction foreign to our Constitution and unacknowledged by our laws, giving his assent to their acts of pretended legislation—

For quartering large bodies of armed troops among us;

For protecting them by mock trial, from punishment for any murders which they should commit on the inhabitants of these States;

For cutting off our trade with all parts of the world;

For imposing taxes on us without our consent;

For depriving us, in many cases, of the benefit of trial by jury;

For transporting us beyond seas to be tried for pretended offences;

For abolishing the free system of English laws in a neighboring province, establishing therein an arbitrary government, and enlarging its boundaries, so as to render it at once an example and fit instrument for introducing the same absolute rule into these colonies;

For taking away our charters, abolishing our most valuable laws, and altering, fundamentally, the powers of our governments.

For suspending our own legislatures and declaring themselves invested with power to legislate for us in all cases whatsoever.

He has abdicated government here by declaring us out of his protection and waging war against us.

He has plundered our seas, ravaged our coasts, burnt our towns, and destroyed the lives of our people.

He is, at this time, transporting large armies of foreign mercenaries to complete the works of death, desolation, and tyranny already begun with circumstances of cruelty and perfidy scarcely paralleled in the most barbarous ages, and totally unworthy the head of a civilized nation.

He has constrained our fellow citizens, taken captive on the high seas, to bear arms against their country, to become the executioners of their friends and brethren, or to fall themselves by their hands.

He has excited domestic insurrections amongst us and has endeavored to bring on the inhabitants of our frontiers, the merciless Indian savages, whose known rule of warfare is an undistinguished destruction of all ages, sexes, and conditions.

In every stage of these oppressions, we have petitioned for redress in the most humble terms; our repeated petitions have been answered only by repeated injury. A prince whose character is thus marked by every act which may define a tyrant is unfit to be the ruler of a free people.

Nor have we been wanting in attention to our British brethren. We have warned them, from time to time, of attempts made by their legislature to extend an unwarrantable jurisdiction over us. We have reminded them of the circumstances of our emigration and settlement here. We have appealed to their native justice and magnanimity, and we have conjured them, by the ties of our common kindred, to disavow these usurpations, which would inevitably interrupt our connections and correspondence. They, too, have been deaf to the voice of justice and consanguinity. We must, therefore, acquiesce in the necessity which denounces our separation, and hold them, as we hold the rest of mankind, enemies in war, in peace, friends.

We, therefore, the representatives of the United States of America, in general Congress assembled, appealing to the Supreme Judge of the world for the rectitude of our intentions, do, in the name and by the authority of the good people of these colonies, solemnly publish and declare, that these united colonies are, and of right ought to be, free and independent states: that they are absolved from all allegiance to the British Crown, and that all political connection between them and the state of Great Britain is, and ought to be, totally dissolved; and that, as free and independent states, they have full power to levy war, conclude peace, contract alliances, establish commerce, and to do all other acts and things which independent states may of right do. And, for the support of this declaration, with a firm reliance on the protection of Divine Providence, we mutually pledge to each other our lives, our fortunes, and our sacred honor.

The Articles of Confederation and Perpetual Union*

Between the states of New Hampshire, Massachusetts-bay Rhode Island and Providence Plantations, Connecticut, New York, New Jersey, Pennsylvania, Delaware, Maryland, Virginia, North Carolina, South Carolina, and Georgia.

Article 1

The Stile of this Confederacy shall be "The United States of America."

Article 2

Each state retains its sovereignty, freedom, and independence, and every power, jurisdiction, and right, which is not by this Confederation expressly delegated to the United States, in Congress assembled.

---

*Agreed to in Congress November 15, 1777; ratified March 1781.

Article 3

The said States hereby severally enter into a firm league of friendship with each other, for their common defense, the security of their liberties, and their mutual and general welfare, binding themselves to assist each other, against all force offered to, or attacks made upon them, or any of them, on account of religion, sovereignty, trade, or any other pretense whatever.

Article 4

The better to secure and perpetuate mutual friendship and intercourse among the people of the different States in this Union, the free inhabitants of each of these States, paupers, vagabonds, and fugitives from justice excepted, shall be entitled to all privileges and immunities of free citizens in the several States; and the people of each State shall have free ingress and regress to and from any other State, and shall enjoy therein all the privileges of trade and commerce, subject to the same duties, impositions, and restrictions as the inhabitants thereof respectively, provided that such restrictions shall not extend so far as to prevent the removal of property imported into any State, to any other State of which the owner is an inhabitant; provided also that no imposition, duties or restriction shall be laid by any State, on the property of the United States, or either of them.

If any person guilty of, or charged with, treason, felony, or other high misdemeanor in any State, shall flee from justice, and be found in any of the United States, he shall, upon demand of the Governor or executive power of the State from which he fled, be delivered up and removed to the State having jurisdiction of his offense.

Full faith and credit shall be given in each of these States to the records, acts, and judicial proceedings of the courts and magistrates of every other State.

Article 5

For the most convenient management of the general interests of the United States, delegates shall be annually appointed in such manner as the legislatures of each State shall direct, to meet in Congress on the first Monday in November, in every year, with a power reserved to each State to recall its delegates, or any of them, at any time within the year, and to send others in their stead for the remainder of the year.

No State shall be represented in Congress by less than two, nor by more than seven members; and no person shall be capable of being a delegate for more than three years in any term of six years; nor shall any person, being a delegate, be capable of holding any office under the United States, for which he, or another for his benefit, receives any salary, fees or emolument of any kind.

Each State shall maintain its own delegates in a meeting of the States, and while they act as members of the committee of the States.

In determining questions in the United States in Congress assembled, each State shall have one vote.

Freedom of speech and debate in Congress shall not be impeached or questioned in any court or place out of Congress, and the members of Congress shall be protected in their persons from arrests or imprisonments, during the time of their going to and from, and attendence on Congress, except for treason, felony, or breach of the peace.

Article 6

No State, without the consent of the United States in Congress assembled, shall send any embassy to, or receive any embassy from, or enter into any conference, agreement, alliance or treaty with any King, Prince or State; nor shall any person holding any office of profit or trust under the United States, or any of them, accept any present, emolument, office or title of any kind whatever from any King, Prince or foreign State; nor shall the United States in Congress assembled, or any of them, grant any title of nobility.

No two or more States shall enter into any treaty, confederation or alliance whatever between them, without the consent of the United States in Congress assembled, specifying accurately the purposes for which the same is to be entered into, and how long it shall continue.

No State shall lay any imposts or duties, which may interfere with any stipulations in treaties, entered into by the United States in Congress assembled, with any King, Prince or State, in pursuance of any treaties already proposed by Congress, to the courts of France and Spain.

No vessel of war shall be kept up in time of peace by any State, except such number only, as shall be deemed necessary by the United States in Congress assembled, for the defense of such State, or its trade; nor shall any body of forces be kept up by any State in time of peace, except such number only, as in the judgement of the United States in Congress assembled, shall be deemed requisite to garrison the forts necessary for the defense of such State; but every State shall always keep up a well-regulated and disciplined militia, sufficiently armed and accoutered, and shall provide and constantly have ready for use, in public stores, a due number of filed pieces and tents, and a proper quantity of arms, ammunition and camp equipage.

No State shall engage in any war without the consent of the United States in Congress assembled, unless such State be actually invaded by enemies, or shall have received certain advice of a resolution being formed by some nation of Indians to invade such State, and the danger is so imminent as not to admit of a delay, till the United States in Congress assembled can be consulted; nor shall any State grant commissions to any ships or vessels of war, nor letters of marque or reprisal, except it be after a declaration of war by the United States in Congress assembled, and then only against the Kingdom or State and the subjects thereof, against which war has been so declared, and under such regulations as shall be established by the United States in Congress assembled, unless such State be infested by pirates, in which case vessels of war may be fitted out for that occasion, and kept so long as the danger shall continue, or until the United States in Congress assembled shall determine otherwise.

Article 7

When land forces are raised by any State for the common defense, all officers of or under the rank of colonel, shall be appointed by the legislature of each State respectively, by whom such forces shall be raised, or in such manner as such State shall direct, and all vacancies shall be filled up by the State which first made the appointment.

Article 8

All charges of war, and all other expenses that shall be incurred for the common defense or general welfare, and allowed by the United States in Congress assembled, shall be defrayed out of a common treasury, which shall be supplied by the several States in proportion to the value of all land within each State, granted to or surveyed for any person, as such land and the buildings and improvements thereon shall be estimated according to such mode as the United States in Congress assembled, shall from time to time direct and appoint.

The taxes for paying that proportion shall be laid and levied by the authority and direction of the legislatures of the several States within the time agreed upon by the United States in Congress assembled.

Article 9

The United States in Congress assembled, shall have the sole and exclusive right and power of determining on peace and war, except in the cases mentioned in the sixth article; of sending and receiving ambassadors; entering into treaties and alliances, provided that no treaty of commerce shall be made whereby the legislative power of the respective States shall be restrained from imposing such imposts and duties on foreigners, as their own people are subjected to, or from prohibiting the exportation or importation of any species of goods or commodities whatsoever; of establishing rules for deciding in all cases, what captures on land or water shall be legal, and in what manner prizes taken by land or naval forces in the service of the United States shall be divided or appropriated; of granting letters of marque and reprisal in times of peace; appointing courts for the trial of piracies and felonies committed on the high seas and establishing courts for receiving and determining finally appeals in all cases of captures, provided that no member of Congress shall be appointed a judge of any of the said courts.

The United States in Congress assembled shall also be the last resort on appeal in all disputes and differences now subsisting or that hereafter may arise between two or more States concerning boundary, jurisdiction or any other causes whatever; which authority shall always be exercised in the manner following. Whenever the legislative or executive authority or lawful agent of any State in controversy with another shall present a petition to Congress stating the matter in question and praying for a hearing, notice thereof shall be given by order of Congress to the legislative or executive authority of the other State in controversy, and a day assigned for the appearance of the parties by their lawful agents, who shall then be directed to appoint by joint consent, commissioners or judges to constitute a court for hearing and determining the matter in question: but if they cannot agree, Congress shall name three persons out of each of the United States, and from the list of such persons each party shall alternately strike out one, the petitioners beginning, until the number shall be reduced to thirteen; and from that number not less than seven, nor more than nine names as Congress shall direct, shall in the presence of Congress be drawn out by lot, and the persons whose names shall be so drawn or any five of them, shall be commissioners or judges, to hear and finally determine the controversy, so always as a major part of the judges who shall hear the cause shall agree in the determination: and if either party shall neglect to attend at the day appointed, without showing reasons, which Congress shall judge sufficient, or being present shall refuse to strike, the Congress shall proceed to nominate three persons out of each State, and the secretary of Congress shall strike in behalf of such party absent or refusing; and the judgement and sentence of the court to be appointed, in the manner before prescribed, shall be final and conclusive; and if any of the parties shall refuse to submit to the authority of such court, or to appear or defend their claim or cause, the court shall nevertheless proceed to pronounce sentence, or judgement, which shall in like manner be final and decisive, the judgement or sentence and other proceedings being in either case transmitted to Congress, and lodged among the acts of Congress for the security of the parties concerned: provided that every commissioner, before he sits in judgement, shall take an oath to be administered by one of the judges of the supreme or superior court of the State, where the cause shall be tried, "well and truly to hear and determine the matter in question, according to the best of his judgement, without favor, affection or hope of reward:" provided also, that no State shall be deprived of territory for the benefit of the United States.

All controversies concerning the private right of soil claimed under different grants of two or more States, whose jurisdictions as they may respect such lands, and the States which passed such grants are adjusted, the said grants or either of them being at the same time claimed to have originated antecedent to such settlement of jurisdiction, shall on the petition of either party to the Congress of the United States, be finally determined as near as may be in the same manner as is before prescribed for deciding disputes respecting territorial jurisdiction between different States.

The United States in Congress assembled shall also have the sole and exclusive right and power of regulating the alloy and value of coin struck by their own authority, or by that of the respective States; fixing the standards of weights and measures throughout the United States; regulating the trade and managing all affairs with the Indians not members of any of the States; provided that the legislative right of any State within its own limits be not infringed or violated; establishing or regulating post offices from one State to another, throughout all the United States, and exacting such postage on the papers passing through the same as may be requisite to defray the expenses of the said office; appointing all officers of the land forces in the service of the United States, excepting regimental officers; appointing all the officers of the naval forces, and commissioning all officers whatever in the service of the United States; making rules for the government and regulation of the said land and naval forces, and directing their operations.

The United States in Congress assembled shall have authority to appoint a committee, to sit in the recess of Congress, to be denominated "A Committee of the States," and to consist of one delegate from each State; and to appoint such other committees and civil officers as may be necessary for managing the general affairs of the United States under their direction; to appoint one of their members to preside, provided that no person be allowed to serve in the office of president more than one year in any term of three years; to ascertain the necessary sums of money to be raised for the service of the United States, and to appropriate and apply the same for defraying the public expenses; to borrow money, or emit bills on the credit of the United States, transmitting every half year to the respective States an account of the sums of money so borrowed or emitted; to build and equip a navy; to agree upon the number of land forces, and to make requisitions from each State for its quota, in proportion to the number of white inhabitants in such State; which requisition shall be binding, and thereupon the legislature of each State shall appoint the regimental officers, raise the men and cloath, arm and equip them in a soldierlike manner, at the expense of the United States; and the officers and men so cloathed, armed and equipped shall march to the place appointed, and within the time agreed on by the United States in Congress assembled; but if the United States in Congress assembled shall, on consideration of circumstances judge proper that any State should not raise men, or should raise a smaller number of men than the quota thereof, such extra number shall be raised, officered, cloathed, armed and equipped in the same manner as the quota of each State, unless the legislature of such State shall judge that such extra number cannot be safely spared out in the same, in which case they shall raise, officer, cloath, arm and equip as many of such extra number as they judge can be safely spared. And the officers and men so cloathed, armed, and equipped, shall march to the place appointed, and within the time agreed on by the United States in Congress assembled.

The United States in Congress assembled shall never engage in a war, nor grant letters of marque or reprisal in time of peace, nor enter into any treaties or alliances, nor coin money, nor regulate the value thereof, nor ascertain the sums and expenses necessary for the defense and welfare of the United States, or any of them, nor emit bills, nor borrow money on the credit of the United States, nor appropriate money, nor agree upon the number of vessels of war, to be built or purchased, or the number of land or sea forces to be raised, nor appoint a commander in chief of the army or navy, unless nine States assent to the same: nor shall a question on any other point, except for adjourning from day to day be determined, unless by the votes of the majority of the United States in Congress assembled.

The Congress of the United States shall have power to adjourn to any time within the year, and to any place within the United States, so that no period of adjournment be for a longer duration than the space of six months, and shall publish the journal of their proceedings monthly, except such parts thereof relating to treaties, alliances or military operations, as in their judgement require secrecy; and the yeas and nays of the delegates of each State on any question shall be entered on the journal, when it is desired by any delegates of a State, or any of them, at his or their request shall be furnished with a transcript of the said journal, except such parts as are above excepted, to lay before the legislatures of the several States.

Article 10

The Committee of the States, or any nine of them, shall be authorized to execute, in the recess of Congress, such of the powers of Congress as the United States in Congress assembled, by the consent of the nine States, shall from time to time think expedient to vest them with; provided that no power be delegated to the said Committee, for the exercise of which, by the Articles of Confederation, the voice of nine States in the Congress of the United States assembled is requisite.

Article 11

Canada acceding to this confederation, and adjoining in the measures of the United States, shall be admitted into, and entitled to all the advantages of this Union; but no other colony shall be admitted into the same, unless such admission be agreed to by nine States.

Article 12

All bills of credit emitted, monies borrowed, and debts contracted by, or under the authority of Congress, before the assembling of the United States, in pursuance of the present confederation, shall be deemed and considered as a charge against the United States, for payment and satisfaction whereof the said United States, and the public faith are hereby solemnly pledged.

Article 13

Every State shall abide by the determination of the United States in Congress assembled, on all questions which by this confederation are submitted to them. And the Articles of this Confederation shall be inviolably observed by every State, and the Union shall be perpetual; nor shall any alteration at any time hereafter be made in any of them; unless such alteration be agreed to in a Congress of the United States, and be afterwards confirmed by the legislatures of every State.

These articles shall be proposed to the legislatures of all the United States, to be considered, and if approved of by them, they are advised to authorize their delegates to ratify the same in the Congress of the United States; which being done, the same shall become conclusive.

The Constitution of the United States of America

We the people of the United States, in order to form a more perfect union, establish justice, insure domestic tranquillity, provide for the common defense, promote the general welfare, and secure the blessings of liberty to ourselves and our posterity, do ordain and establish this Constitution for the United States of America.

Article I

Section 1

All legislative powers herein granted shall be vested in a Congress of the United States, which shall consist of a Senate and House of Representatives.

Section 2

1 The House of Representatives shall be composed of members chosen every second year by the people of the several States, and the electors in each State shall have the qualifications requisite for electors of the most numerous branch of the State legislature.

2 No person shall be a representative who shall not have attained to the age of twenty-five years, and been seven years a citizen of the United States, and who shall not, when elected, be an inhabitant of that State in which he shall be chosen.

3 Representatives and direct taxes[1] shall be apportioned among the several States which may be included within this Union, according to their respective numbers, which shall be determined by adding to the whole number of free persons, including those bound to service for a term of years, and excluding Indians not taxed, three fifths of all other persons.[2] The actual enumeration shall be made within three years after the first meeting of the Congress of the United States, and within every subsequent term of ten years, in such manner as they shall by law direct. The number of representatives shall not exceed one for every thirty thousand, but each State shall have at least one representative; and until such enumeration shall be made, the State of New Hampshire shall be entitled to choose three, Massachusetts eight, Rhode Island and Providence Plantations one, Connecticut five, New York six, New Jersey four, Pennsylvania eight, Delaware one, Maryland six, Virginia ten, North Carolina five, South Carolina five, and Georgia three.

4 When vacancies happen in the representation from any State, the executive authority thereof shall issue writs of election to fill such vacancies.

5 The House of Representatives shall choose their speaker and other officers; and shall have the sole power of impeachment.

Section 3

1 The Senate of the United States shall be composed of two senators from each State, chosen by the legislature thereof,[3] for six years; and each senator shall have one vote.

2 Immediately after they shall be assembled in consequence of the first election, they shall be divided as equally as may be into three classes. The seats of the senators of the first class shall be vacated at the expiration of the second year, of the second class at the expiration of the fourth year, and of the third class at the expiration of the sixth year, so that one third may be chosen every second year; and if vacancies happen by resignation, or otherwise, during the recess of the legislature of any State, the executive thereof may make temporary appointments until the next meeting of the legislature, which shall then fill such vacancies.[4]

3 No person shall be a senator who shall not have attained to the age of thirty years, and been nine years a citizen of the United States, and who shall not, when elected, be an inhabitant of that State for which he shall be chosen.

4 The Vice President of the United States shall be President of the Senate, but shall have no vote, unless they be equally divided.

5 The Senate shall choose their other officers, and also a president pro tempore, in the absence of the Vice President, or when he shall exercise the office of the President of the United States.

6 The Senate shall have the sole power to try all impeachments. When sitting for that purpose, they shall be on oath or affirmation. When the President of the United States is tried, the chief justice shall preside: and no person shall be convicted without the concurrence of two thirds of the members present.

7 Judgment in cases of impeachment shall not extend further than to removal from office, and disqualification to hold and enjoy any office of honor, trust or profit under the United States: but the party convicted shall nevertheless be liable and subject to indictment, trial, judgment and punishment, according to law.

Section 4

1 The times, places, and manner of holding elections for senators and representatives, shall be prescribed in each State by the legislature thereof; but the Congress may at any time by law make or alter such regulations, except as to the places of choosing senators.

2 The Congress shall assemble at least once in every year, and such meeting shall be on the first Monday in December, unless they shall by law appoint a different day.

Section 5

1 Each House shall be the judge of the elections, returns and qualifications of its own members, and a majority of each shall constitute a quorum to do business; but a smaller number may adjourn from day to day, and may be authorized to compel the attendance of absent members, in such manner, and under such penalties as each House may provide.

---

[1]See the Sixteenth Amendment.
[2]See the Fourteenth Amendment.

[3]See the Seventeenth Amendment.
[4]See the Seventeenth Amendment.

2　Each House may determine the rules of its proceedings, punish its members for disorderly behavior, and, with the concurrence of two thirds, expel a member.

3　Each House shall keep a journal of its proceedings, and from time to time publish the same, excepting such parts as may in their judgment require secrecy; and the yeas and nays of the members of either House on any question shall, at the desire of one fifth of those present, be entered on the journal.

4　Neither House, during the session of Congress, shall, without the consent of the other, adjourn for more than three days, nor to any other place than that in which the two Houses shall be sitting.

Section 6

1　The senators and representatives shall receive a compensation for their services, to be ascertained by law, and paid out of the Treasury of the United States. They shall in all cases, except treason, felony, and breach of the peace, be privileged from arrest during their attendance at the session of their respective Houses, and in going to and returning from the same; and for any speech or debate in either House, they shall not be questioned in any other place.

2　No senator or representative shall, during the time for which he was elected, be appointed to any civil office under the authority of the United States, which shall have been created, or the emoluments whereof shall have been increased, during such time; and no person holding any office under the United States shall be a member of either House during his continuance in office.

Section 7

1　All bills for raising revenue shall originate in the House of Representatives; but the Senate may propose or concur with amendments as on other bills.

2　Every bill which shall have passed the House of Representatives and the Senate, shall, before it become a law, be presented to the President of the United States; If he approves he shall sign it, but if not he shall return it, with his objections, to that House in which it shall have originated, who shall enter the objections at large on their journal, and proceed to reconsider it. If after such reconsideration two thirds of that House shall agree to pass the bill, it shall be sent, together with the objections, to the other House, by which it shall likewise be reconsidered, and if approved by two thirds of that House, it shall become a law. But in all such cases the votes of both Houses shall be determined by yeas and nays, and the names of the persons voting for and against the bill shall be entered on the journal of each House respectively. If any bill shall not be returned by the President within ten days (Sundays excepted) after it shall have been presented to him, the same shall be a law, in like manner as if he had signed it, unless the Congress by their adjournment prevent its return, in which case it shall not be a law.

3　Every order, resolution, or vote to which the concurrence of the Senate and the House of Representatives may be necessary (except on a question of adjournment) shall be presented to the President of the United States; and before the same shall take effect, shall be approved by him, or being disapproved by him, shall be repassed by two thirds of the Senate and House of Representatives, according to the rules and limitations prescribed in the case of a bill.

Section 8

1　The Congress shall have the power.

1　To lay and collect taxes, duties, imposts, and excises, to pay the debts and provide for the common defense and general welfare of the United States; but all duties, imposts, and excises shall be uniform throughout the United States.

2　To borrow money on the credit of the United States;

3　To regulate commerce with foreign nations, and among the several States, and with the Indian tribes;

4　To establish a uniform rule of naturalization, and uniform laws on the subject of bankruptcies throughout the United States;

5　To coin money, regulate the value thereof, and of foreign coin, and fix the standard of weights and measures;

6　To provide for the punishment of counterfeiting the securities and current coin of the United States;

7　To establish post offices and post roads;

8　To promote the progress of science and useful arts, by securing for limited times to authors and inventors the exclusive right to their respective writings and discoveries;

9　To constitute tribunals inferior to the Supreme Court;

10　To define and punish piracies and felonies committed on the high seas, and offenses against the law of nations;

11　To declare war, grant letters of marque and reprisal, and make rules concerning captures on land and water;

12　To raise and support armies, but no appropriation of money to that use shall be for a longer term than two years;

13　To provide and maintain a navy;

14　To make rules for the government and regulation of the land and naval forces;

15　To provide for calling forth the militia to execute the laws of the Union, suppress insurrections and repel invasions;

16　To provide for organizing, arming, and disciplining the militia, and for governing such part of them as may be employed in the service of the United States, reserving to the States respectively, the appointment of the officers, and the authority of training the militia according to the discipline prescribed by Congress;

17　To exercise exclusive legislation in all cases whatsoever, over such district (not exceeding ten miles square) as may, by cession of particular States, and the acceptance of Congress, become the seat of the government of the United States, and to exercise like authority over all places purchased by the consent of the legislature of the State in which the same shall be, for the erection of forts, magazines, arsenals, dockyards, and other needful buildings; and

18　To make all laws which shall be necessary and proper for carrying into execution the foregoing powers, and all other powers vested by this Constitution in the government of the United States, or any department or officer thereof.

Section 9

1　The migration or importation of such persons as any of the States now existing shall think proper to admit, shall not be prohibited by the Congress prior to the year one thousand eight hundred and eight, but a tax or duty may be imposed on such importation, not exceeding ten dollars for each person.

2　The privilege of the writ of habeas corpus shall not be suspended, unless when in cases of rebellion or invasion the public safety may require it.

3 No bill of attainder or ex post facto law shall be passed.

4 No capitation, or other direct, tax shall be laid, unless in proportion to the census or enumeration herein-before directed to be taken.[5]

5 No tax or duty shall be laid on articles exported from any State.

6 No preference shall be given by any regulation of commerce or revenue to the ports of one State over those of another: nor shall vessels bound to, or from, one State be obliged to enter, clear, or pay duties in another.

7 No money shall be drawn from the treasury, but in consequence of appropriations made by law; and a regular statement and account of the receipts and expenditures of all public money shall be published from time to time.

8 No title of nobility shall be granted by the United States: and no person holding any office of profit or trust under them, shall, without the consent of the Congress, accept of any present, emolument, office, or title, of any kind whatever, from any king, prince, or foreign State.

Section 10

1 No State shall enter into any treaty, alliance, or confederation; grant letters of marque and reprisal; coin money; emit bills of credit; make any thing but gold and silver coin a tender in payment of debts; pass any bill of attainder, ex post facto law, or law impairing the obligation of contracts, or grant, any title of nobility.

2 No State shall, without the consent of the Congress, lay any imposts or duties on imports or exports, except what may be absolutely necessary for executing its inspection laws: and the net produce of all duties and imposts laid by any State on imports or exports, shall be for the use of the treasury of the United States; and all such laws shall be subject to the revision and control of the Congress.

3 No State shall, without the consent of the Congress, lay any duty of tonnage, keep troops, or ships of war in time of peace, enter into any agreement or compact with another State, or with a foreign power, or engage in war, unless actually invaded, or in such imminent danger as will not admit of delay.

Article II
Section 1

1 The executive power shall be vested in a President of the United States of America. He shall hold his office during the term of four years, and, together with the Vice President, chosen for the same term, be elected, as follows:

2 Each State shall appoint, in such manner as the legislature thereof may direct, a number of electors, equal to the whole number of senators and representatives to which the State may be entitled in the Congress: but no senator or representative, or person holding any office of trust or profit under the United States, shall be appointed an elector.

The electors shall meet in their respective States, and vote by ballot for two persons, of whom one at least shall not be an inhabitant of the same State with themselves. And they shall make a list of all the persons voted for, and of the number of votes for each; which list they shall sign and certify, and transmit sealed to the seat of the government of the United States, directed to the president of the Senate. The president of the Senate shall, in the presence of the Senate and House of Representatives, open all the certificates, and the votes shall then be counted. The person having the greatest number of votes shall be the President, if such number be a majority of the whole number of electors appointed; and if there be more than one who have such majority, and have an equal number of votes, then the House of Representatives shall immediately choose by ballot one of them for President; and if no person have a majority, then from the five highest on the list the said House shall in like manner choose the President. But in choosing the President, the votes shall be taken by States, the representation from each State having one vote; a quorum for this purpose shall consist of a member or members from two thirds of the States, and a majority of all the States shall be necessary to a choice. In every case after the choice of the President, the person having the greatest number of votes of the electors shall be the Vice President. But if there should remain two or more who have equal votes, the Senate shall choose from them by ballot the Vice President.[6]

3 The Congress may determine the time of choosing the electors, and the day on which they shall give their votes; which day shall be the same throughout the United States.

4 No person except a natural born citizen, or a citizen of the United States, at the time of the adoption of this Constitution, shall be eligible to the office of President; neither shall any person be eligible to the office who shall not have attained to the age of thirty-five years, and been fourteen years a resident within the United States.

5 In case of the removal of the President from office, or of his death, resignation, or inability to discharge the powers and duties of the said office, the same shall devolve on the Vice President, and the congress may by law provide for the case of removal, death, resignation or inability, both of the President and Vice President, declaring what officer shall then act as President, and such officer shall act accordingly until the disability be removed, or a President shall be elected.

6 The President shall, at stated times, receive for his services a compensation which shall neither be increased nor diminished during the period for which he shall have been elected, and he shall not receive within that period any other emolument from the United States, or any of them.

7 Before he enter on the execution of his office, he shall take the following oath or affirmation:—"I do solemnly swear (or affirm) that I will faithfully execute the office of President of the United States, and will to the best of my ability, preserve, protect and defend the Constitution of the United States."

Section 2

1 The President shall be commander in chief of the army and navy of the United States, and of the militia of the several States, when called into the actual service of the United States; he may require the opinion in writing, of the principal officer in each of the executive departments, upon any subject relating to the duties of their respective offices, and he shall have power to grant reprieves and pardons for offenses against the United States, except in cases of impeachment.

[5]See the Sixteenth Amendment.

[6]Superseded by the Twelfth Amendment.

2 He shall have power, by and with the advice and consent of the Senate, to make treaties, provided two thirds of the senators present concur; and he shall nominate, and by and with the advice and consent of the Senate, shall appoint ambassadors, other public ministers and consuls, judges of the Supreme Court, and all other officers of the United States, whose appointments are not herein otherwise provided for, and which shall be established by law; but the Congress may by law vest the appointment of such inferior officers, as they think proper, in the President alone, in the courts of laws, or in the heads of departments.

3 The President shall have power to fill up all vacancies that may happen during the recess of the Senate, by granting commissions which shall expire at the end of their next session.

Section 3

He shall from time to time give to the Congress information of the state of the Union, and recommend to their consideration such measures as he shall judge necessary and expedient; he may, on extraordinary occasions, convene both Houses, or either of them, and in case of disagreement between them with respect to the time of adjournment, he may adjourn them to such time as he shall think proper; he shall receive ambassadors and other public ministers; he shall take care that the laws be faithfully executed, and shall commission all the officers of the United States.

Section 4

The President, Vice President, and all civil officers of the United States, shall be removed from office on impeachment for, and conviction of, treason, bribery, or other high crimes and misdemeanors.

Article III
Section 1

The judicial power of the United States shall be vested in one Supreme Court, and in such inferior courts as the Congress may from time to time ordain and establish. The judges, both of the Supreme and inferior courts, shall hold their offices during good behavior, and shall, at stated times, receive for their services, a compensation, which shall not be diminished during their continuance in office.

Section 2

1 The judicial power shall extend to all cases, in law and equity, arising under this Constitution, the laws of the United States, and treaties made, or which shall be made, under their authority;—to all cases of admiralty and maritime jurisdiction;—to controversies to which the United States shall be a party;[7]—to controversies between two or more States;—between a State and citizens of another State;—between citizens of different States;—between citizens of the same State claiming lands under grants of different States, and between a State, or the citizens thereof, and foreign States, citizens or subjects.

2 In all cases affecting ambassadors, other public ministers and consuls, and those in which a State shall be party, the Supreme Court shall have original jurisdiction. In all the other cases before mentioned, the Supreme Court shall have appellate jurisdiction, both as to law and fact, with such exceptions, and under such regulations as the Congress shall make.

3 The trial of all crimes, except in cases of impeachment, shall be by jury; and such trial shall be held in the State where the said crimes shall have been committed; but when not committed within any State, the trial shall be such place or places as the congress may by law have directed.

Section 3

1 Treason against the United States shall consist only in levying war against them, or in adhering to their enemies, giving them aid and comfort. No person shall be convicted of treason unless on the testimony of two witnesses to the same overt act, or on confession in open court.

2 The Congress shall have power to declare the punishment of treason, but no attainder of treason shall work corruption of blood, or forfeiture except during the life of the person attained.

Article IV
Section 1

Full faith and credit shall be given in each State to the public acts, records, and judicial proceedings of every other State. And the Congress may by general laws prescribe the manner in which such acts, records and proceedings shall be proved, and the effect thereof.

Section 2

1 The citizens of each State shall be entitled to all privileges and immunities of citizens in the several States.[8]

2 A person charged in any State with treason, felony, or other crime, who shall flee from justice, and be found in another State, shall on demand of the executive authority of the State from which he fled, be delivered up to be removed to the State having jurisdiction of the crime.

3 No person held to service or labor in one State under the laws thereof, escaping into another, shall, in consequence of any law or regulation therein, be discharged from such service or labor, but shall be delivered up on claim of the party to whom such service or labor may be due.[9]

Section 3

1 New States may be admitted by the Congress into this Union; but no new State shall be formed or erected within the jurisdiction of any other State, nor any State be formed by the junction of two or more States, or parts of States, without the consent of the legislatures of the States concerned as well as of the Congress.

2 The Congress shall have power to dispose of and make all needful rules and regulations respecting the territory or other property belonging to the United States; and nothing in this Constitution shall be so construed as to prejudice any claims of the United States, or of any particular State.

---

[7]See the Eleventh Amendment.

[8]See the Fourteenth Amendment, Sec. 1.
[9]See the Thirteenth Amendment.

Section 4

The United States shall guarantee to every State in this Union a republican form of government, and shall protect each of them against invasion; and on application of the legislature, or of the executive (when the legislature cannot be convened) against domestic violence.

Article V

The Congress, whenever two thirds of both Houses shall deem it necessary, shall propose amendments to this Constitution, or, on the application of the legislatures of two thirds of the several States, shall call a convention for proposing amendments, which in either case shall be valid to all intents and purposes, as part of this Constitution, when ratified by the legislatures of three fourths of the several States, or by conventions in three fourths thereof, as the one or the other mode of ratification may be proposed by the Congress; Provided that no amendment which may be made prior to the year one thousand eight hundred and eight shall in any manner affect the first and fourth clauses in the ninth section of the first article; and that no State, without its consent, shall be deprived of its equal suffrage in the Senate.

Article VI

1 All debts contracted and engagements entered into, before the adoption of this Constitution, shall be as valid against the United States under this Constitution, as under the Confederation.[10]

2 This Constitution, and the laws of the United States which shall be made in pursuance thereof; and all treaties made, or which shall be made, under the authority of the United States, shall be the supreme law of the land; and the judges in every State shall be bound thereby, any thing in the Constitution or laws of any State to the contrary notwithstanding.

3 The senators and representatives before mentioned, and the members of the several State legislatures, and all executive and judicial officers, both of the United States and of the several States, shall be bound by oath or affirmation to support this Constitution; but no religious test shall ever be required as a qualification to any office or public trust under the United States.

Article VII

The ratification of the conventions of nine States shall be sufficient for the establishment of this Constitution between the States so ratifying the same.

Done in Convention by the unanimous consent of the States present the seventeenth day of September in the year of our Lord one thousand seven hundred and eighty-seven, and of the independence of the United States of America the twelfth. In witness whereof we have hereunto subscribed our names.

[Signatories' names omitted]

Articles in addition to, and amendment of, the Constitution of the United States of America, proposed by Congress, and ratified by the legislatures of the several States, pursuant to the fifth article of the original Constitution.

Amendment I

[First ten amendments ratified December 15, 1791]

Congress shall make no law respecting an establishment of religion, or prohibiting the free exercise thereof; or abridging the freedom of speech, or of the press; or the right of the people peaceably to assemble, and to petition the government for a redress of grievances.

Amendment II

A well regulated militia, being necessary to the security of a free State, the right of the people to keep and bear arms, shall not be infringed.

Amendment III

No soldier shall, in time of peace be quartered in any house, without the consent of the owner, nor in time of war, but in a manner to be prescribed by law.

Amendment IV

The right of the people to be secure in their persons, houses, papers, and effects, against unreasonable searches and seizures, shall not be violated, and no warrants shall issue, but upon probable cause, supported by oath or affirmation, and particularly describing the place to be searched, and the persons or things to be seized.

Amendment V

No person shall be held to answer for a capital or otherwise infamous crime, unless on a presentment or indictment of a grand jury, except in cases arising in the land or naval forces, or in the militia, when in actual service in time of war or public danger; nor shall any person be subject for the same offense to be twice put in jeopardy of life or limb; nor shall be compelled in any criminal case to be a witness against himself, nor be deprived of life, liberty, or property, without due process of law; nor shall private property be taken for public use, without just compensation.

Amendment VI

In all criminal prosecutions, the accused shall enjoy the right to a speedy and public trial, by an impartial jury of the State and district wherein the crime shall have been committed, which district shall have been previously ascertained by law, and to be informed of the nature and cause of the accusation; to be confronted with the witnesses against him; to have compulsory process for obtaining witnesses in his favor, and to have the assistance of counsel for his defense.

Amendment VII

In suits at common law, where the value in controversy shall exceed twenty dollars, the right of trial by jury shall be preserved, and no fact tried by a jury shall be otherwise reexamined in any court of the United States, than according to the rules of the common law.

Amendment VIII

Excessive bail shall not be required, nor excessive fines imposed, nor cruel and unusual punishments inflicted.

Amendment IX

The enumeration in the Constitution of certain rights shall not be construed to deny or disparage others retained by the people.

---

[10]See the Fourteenth Amendment, Sec. 4.

Amendment X

The powers not delegated to the United States by the Constitution, nor prohibited by it to the States, are reserved to the States respectively, or to the people.

Amendment XI [January 8, 1798]

The judicial power of the United States shall not be construed to extend to any suit in law or equity, commended or prosecuted against one of the United States by citizens of another State, or by citizens or subjects of any foreign State.

Amendment XII [September 25, 1804]

The electors shall meet in their respective States, and vote by ballot for President and Vice President, one of whom, at least, shall not be an inhabitant of the same State with themselves; they shall name in their ballots the person voted for as President, and in distinct ballots, the person voted for as Vice President, and they shall make distinct lists of all persons voted for as President and of all persons voted for as Vice President, and of the number of votes for each, which lists they shall sign and certify, and transmit sealed to the seat of the government of the United States, directed to the President of the Senate;—The President of the Senate shall, in the presence of the Senate and House of Representatives, open all the certificates and the votes shall then be counted;—The person having the greatest number of votes for President, shall be the President, if such number be a majority of the whole number of electors appointed; and if no person have such majority, then from the persons having the highest numbers not exceeding three on the list of those voted for as President, the House of Representatives shall choose immediately, by ballot, the President. But in choosing the President, the votes shall be taken by States, the representation from each State having one vote; a quorum for this purpose shall consist of a member or members from two thirds of the States, and a majority of all the States shall be necessary to a choice. And if the House of Representatives shall not choose a President whenever the right of choice shall devolve upon them, before the fourth day of March next following, then the Vice President shall act as President, as in the case of the death or other constitutional disability of the President. The person having the greatest number of votes as Vice President shall be the Vice President, if such number be a majority of the whole number of electors appointed, and if no person have a majority, then from the two highest numbers on the list, the Senate shall choose the Vice President; a quorum for the purpose shall consist of two thirds of the whole number of Senators, and a majority of the whole number shall be necessary to a choice. But no person constitutionally ineligible to the office of President shall be eligible to that of Vice President of the United States.

Amendment XIII [December 18, 1865]

Section 1

Neither slavery nor involuntary servitude, except as a punishment for crime whereof the party shall have been duly convicted, shall exist within the United States, or any place subject to their jurisdiction.

Section 2

Congress shall have power to enforce this article by appropriate legislation.

Amendment XIV [July 28, 1868]

Section 1

All persons born or naturalized in the United States, and subject to the jurisdiction thereof, are citizens of the United States and of the State wherein they reside. No State shall make or enforce any law which shall abridge the privileges or immunities of citizens of the United States; nor shall any State deprive any person of life, liberty, or property, without due process of law; nor deny to any person within its jurisdiction the equal protection of the laws.

Section 2

Representatives shall be apportioned among the several States according to their respective numbers, counting the whole number of persons in each State, excluding Indians not taxed. But when the right to vote at any election for the choice of electors for President and Vice President of the United States, representatives in Congress, the executive and judicial officers of a State, or the members of the legislature thereof, is denied to any of the male inhabitants of such State, being twenty-one years of age, and citizens of the United States, or in any way abridged, except for participating in rebellion, or other crime, the basis of representation there shall be reduced in the proportion which the number of such male citizens shall bear to the whole number of male citizens twenty-one years of age in such State.

Section 3

No person shall be a senator or representative in Congress, or elector of President and Vice President, or hold any office, civil or military, under the United States, or under any State, who having previously taken an oath, as a member of Congress, or as an officer of the United States, or as a member of any State legislature, or as an executive or judicial officer of any State, to support the Constitution of the United States, shall have engaged in insurrection or rebellion against the same, or given aid or comfort to the enemies thereof. But Congress may by a vote of two thirds of each House, remove such disability.

Section 4

The validity of the public debt of the United States, authorized by law, including debts incurred for payment of pensions and bounties for services in suppressing insurrection or rebellion; shall not be questioned. But neither the United States nor any State shall assume or pay any debt or obligation incurred in aid of insurrection or rebellion against the United States, or any claim for the loss or emancipation of any slave; but all such debts, obligations, and claims shall be held illegal and void.

Section 5

The Congress shall have the power to enforce, by appropriate legislation, the provisions of this article.

Amendment XV [March 30, 1870]

Section 1

The right of citizens of the United States to vote shall not be denied or abridged by the United States or by any State on account of race, color, or previous condition of servitude.

Section 2

The Congress shall have power to enforce this article by appropriate legislation.

Amendment XVI [February 25, 1913]

The Congress shall have power to lay and collect taxes on incomes, from whatever source derived, without apportionment among the several States, and without regard to any census or enumeration.

Amendment XVII [May 31, 1913]

The Senate of the United States shall be composed of two senators from each State, elected by the people thereof, for six years; and each senator shall have one vote. The electors in each State shall have the qualifications requisite for electors of the most numerous branch of the State legislature.

When vacancies happen in the representation of any State in the Senate, the executive authority of such State shall issue writs of election to fill such vacancies: Provided, That the legislature of any State may empower the executive thereof to make temporary appointments until the people fill the vacancies by election as the legislature may direct.

This amendment shall not be so construed as to affect the election or term of any senator chosen before it becomes valid as part of the Constitution.

Amendment XVIII[11] [January 29, 1919]

After one year from the ratification of this article, the manufacture, sale, or transportation of intoxicating liquors within, the importation thereof into, or the exportation thereof from the United States and all territory subject to the jurisdiction thereof for beverage purposes is thereby prohibited.

The Congress and the several States shall have concurrent power to enforce this article by appropriate legislation.

This article shall be inoperative unless it shall have been ratified as an amendment to the Constitution by the legislatures of the several States, as provided in the constitution, within seven years from the date of the submission hereof to the States by Congress.

Amendment XIX [August 26, 1920]

The right of citizens of the United States to vote shall not be denied or abridged by the United States or by any State on account of sex.

Congress shall have the power to enforce this article by appropriate legislation.

Amendment XX [January 23, 1933]

Section 1

The terms of the President and Vice President shall end at noon on the 20th day of January and the terms of Senators and Representatives at noon on the 3rd day of January, of the years in which such terms would have ended if this article had not been ratified; and the terms of their successors shall then begin.

Section 2

The Congress shall assemble at least once in every year, and such meeting shall begin at noon on the 3rd day of January, unless they shall by law appoint a different day.

---

[11]Repealed by the Twenty-first Amendment.

Section 3

If, at the time fixed for the beginning of the term of President, the President-elect shall have died, the Vice President-elect shall become President. If a President shall not have been chosen before the time fixed for the beginning of his term, or if the President-elect shall have failed to qualify, then the Vice President-elect shall act as President until a President shall have qualified; and the Congress may by law provide for the case wherein neither a President-elect nor a Vice President-elect shall have qualified, declaring who shall then act as President, or the manner in which one who is to act shall be selected, and such person shall act accordingly until a President or Vice President shall have qualified.

Section 4

The Congress may by law provide for the case of the death of any of the persons from whom, the House of Representatives may choose a President whenever the right of choice shall have devolved upon them, and for the case of the death of any of the persons from whom the Senate may choose a Vice President whenever the right of choice shall have devolved upon them.

Section 5

Sections 1 and 2 shall take effect on the 15th day of October following the ratification of this article.

Section 6

This article shall be inoperative unless it shall have been ratified as an amendment to the Constitution by the legislatures of three-fourths of the several States within seven years from the date of its submission.

Amendment XXI [December 5, 1933]

Section 1

The Eighteenth Article of amendment to the Constitution of the United States is hereby repealed.

Section 2

The transportation or importation into any State, Territory, or possession of the United States for delivery or use therein of intoxicating liquors in violation of the laws thereof, is hereby prohibited.

Section 3

This article shall be inoperative unless it shall have been ratified as an amendment to the Constitution by conventions in the several States, as provided in the Constitution, within seven years from the date of the submission thereof to the States by the Congress.

Amendment XXII [March 1, 1951]

No person shall be elected to the office of the President more than twice, and no person who has held the office of President, or acted as President, for more than two years of a term to which some other person was elected President shall be elected to the office of the President more than once.

But this article shall not apply to any person holding the office of President when this article was proposed by the Congress, and shall not prevent any person who may be holding the office of President, or acting as President, during the term within which this article becomes operative from holding the office of President or acting as President during the remainder of such term.

This article shall be inoperative unless it shall have been ratified as an amendment to the Constitution by the legislatures of three-fourths of the several States within seven years from the date of its submission to the States by the Congress.

Amendment XXIII [March 29, 1961]

Section 1

The District constituting the seat of Government of the United States shall appoint in such manner as the Congress may direct.

A number of electors of President and Vice President equal to the whole number of Senators and Representatives in Congress to which the District would be entitled if it were a State, but in no event more than the least populous State; they shall be in addition to those appointed by the States, but they shall be considered, for the purposes of the election of President and Vice President, to be electors appointed by a State; and they shall meet in the District and perform such duties as provided by the twelfth article of amendment.

Section 2

The Congress shall have power to enforce this article by appropriate legislation.

Amendment XXIV [January 23, 1964]

Section 1

The right of citizens of the United States to vote in any primary or other election for President or Vice President, for electors for President or Vice President, or for Senator or Representative in Congress, shall not be denied or abridged by the United States or any State by reason of failure to pay any poll tax or other tax.

Section 2

The Congress shall have power to enforce this article by appropriate legislation.

Amendment XXV [February 10, 1967]

Section 1

In case of the removal of the President from office or of his death or resignation, the Vice President shall become President.

Section 2

Whenever there is a vacancy in the office of the Vice President, the President shall nominate a Vice President who shall take office upon confirmation by a majority of both Houses of Congress.

Section 3

Whenever the President transmits to the President pro tempore of the Senate and the Speaker of the House of Representatives his written declaration that he is unable to discharge the powers and duties of his office, and until he transmits to them a written declaration to the contrary, such powers and duties shall be discharged by the Vice President as Acting President.

Section 4

Whenever the Vice President and a majority of either the principal officers of the executive departments or of such other body as Congress may by law provide, transmit to the President pro tempore of the Senate and the Speaker of the House of Representatives their written declaration that the President is unable to discharge the powers and duties of his office, the Vice President shall immediately assume the powers and duties of the office as Acting President.

Thereafter, when the President transmits to the President pro tempore of the Senate and the Speaker of the House of Representatives his written declaration that no inability exists, he shall resume the powers and duties of his office unless the Vice President and a majority of either the principal officers of the executive departments or of such other body as Congress may by law provide, transmit within four days to the President pro tempore of the Senate and the Speaker of the House of Representatives their written declaration that the President is unable to discharge the powers and duties of his office. Thereupon Congress shall decide the issue, assembling within forty-eight hours for that purpose if not in session. If the Congress, within twenty-one days after receipt of the latter written declaration, or, if Congress is not in session, within twenty-one days after Congress is required to assemble, determines by two-thirds vote of both Houses that the President is unable to discharge the powers and duties of his office, the Vice President shall continue to discharge the same as Acting President; otherwise, the President shall resume the powers and duties of his office.

Amendment XXVI [June 30, 1971]

Section 1

The right of citizens of the United States who are eighteen years of age or older to vote shall not be denied or abridged by the United States or by any State on account of age.

Section 2

The Congress shall have power to enforce this article by appropriate legislation.

Amendment XXVII[12] [May 7, 1992]

No law, varying the compensation for services of the Senators and Representatives, shall take effect until an election of Representatives shall have intervened.

---

[12]James Madison proposed this amendment in 1789 together with the ten amendments that were adopted as the Bill of Rights, but it failed to win ratification at the time. Congress, however, had set no deadline for its ratification, and over the years—particularly in the 1980s and 1990s—many states voted to add it to the Constitution. With the ratification of Michigan in 1992 it passed the threshold of three-fourths of the states required for adoption, but because the process took more than 200 years, its validity remains in doubt.

PRESIDENTIAL ELECTIONS

Year	Number of States	Candidates	Party	Popular Vote*	Electoral Vote†	Percentage of Popular Vote
1789	11	GEORGE WASHINGTON	No party designations		69	
		John Adams			34	
		Other Candidates			35	
1792	15	GEORGE WASHINGTON	No party designations		132	
		John Adams			77	
		George Clinton			50	
		Other Candidates			5	
1796	16	JOHN ADAMS	Federalist		71	
		Thomas Jefferson	Democratic-Republican		68	
		Thomas Pinckney	Federalist		59	
		Aaron Burr	Democratic-Republican		30	
		Other Candidates			48	
1800	16	THOMAS JEFFERSON	Democratic-Republican		73	
		Aaron Burr	Democratic-Republican		73	
		John Adams	Federalist		65	
		Charles C. Pinckney	Federalist		64	
		John Jay	Federalist		1	
1804	17	THOMAS JEFFERSON	Democratic-Republican		162	
		Charles C. Pinckney	Federalist		14	
1808	17	JAMES MADISON	Democratic-Republican		122	
		Charles C. Pinckney	Federalist		47	
		George Clinton	Democratic-Republican		6	
1812	18	JAMES MADISON	Democratic-Republican		128	
		DeWitt Clinton	Federalist		89	
1816	19	JAMES MONROE	Democratic-Republican		183	
		Rufus King	Federalist		34	
1820	24	JAMES MONROE	Democratic-Republican		231	
		John Quincy Adams	Independent-Republican		1	
1824	24	JOHN QUINCY ADAMS	Democratic-Republican	108,740	84	30.5
		Andrew Jackson	Democratic-Republican	153,544	99	43.1
		William H. Crawford	Democratic-Republican	46,618	41	13.1
		Henry Clay	Democratic-Republican	47,136	37	13.2
1828	24	ANDREW JACKSON	Democrat	647,286	178	56.0
		John Quincy Adams	National Republican	508,064	83	44.0
1832	24	ANDREW JACKSON	Democrat	687,502	219	55.0
		Henry Clay	National Republican	530,189	49	42.4
		William Wirt	Anti-Masonic	33,108	7	2.6
		John Floyd			11	
1836	26	MARTIN VAN BUREN	Democrat	765,483	170	50.9
		William H. Harrison	Whig		73	
		Hugh L. White	Whig		26	
		Daniel Webster	Whig	739,795	14	49.1
		W. P. Mangum	Whig		11	
1840	26	WILLIAM H. HARRISON	Whig	1,274,624	234	53.1
		Martin Van Buren	Democrat	1,127,781	60	46.9
1844	26	JAMES K. POLK	Democrat	1,338,464	170	49.6
		Henry Clay	Whig	1,300,097	105	48.1
		James G. Birney	Liberty	62,300		2.3

*Percentage of popular vote given for any election year may not total 100 percent because candidates receiving less than 1 percent of the popular vote have been omitted.

†Prior to the passage of the Twelfth Amendment in 1904, the electoral college voted for two presidential candidates; the runner-up became Vice-President. Data from Historical Statistics of the United States, Colonial Times to 1957 (1961), pp. 682–683, and The World Almanac.

Year	Number of States	Candidates	Party	Popular Vote*	Electoral Vote†	Percentage of Popular Vote
1848	30	ZACHARY TAYLOR	Whig	1,360,967	163	47.4
		Lewis Cass	Democrat	1,222,342	127	42.5
		Martin Van Buren	Free Soil	291,263		10.1
1852	31	FRANKLIN PIERCE	Democrat	1,601,117	254	50.9
		Winfield Scott	Whig	1,385,453	42	44.1
		John P. Hale	Free Soil	155,825		5.0
1856	31	JAMES BUCHANAN	Democrat	1,832,955	174	45.3
		John C. Frémont	Republican	1,339,932	114	33.1
		Millard Fillmore	American ("Know Nothing")	871,731	8	21.6
1860	33	ABRAHAM LINCOLN	Republican	1,865,593	180	39.8
		Stephen A. Douglas	Democrat	1,382,713	12	29.5
		John C. Breckinridge	Democrat	848,356	72	18.1
		John Bell	Constitutional Union	592,906	39	12.6
1864	36	ABRAHAM LINCOLN	Republican	2,206,938	212	55.0
		George B. McClellan	Democrat	1,803,787	21	45.0
1868	37	ULYSSES S. GRANT	Republican	3,013,421	214	52.7
		Horatio Seymour	Democrat	2,706,829	80	47.3
1872	37	ULYSSES S. GRANT	Republican	3,596,745	286	55.6
		Horace Greeley	Democrat	2,843,446	*	43.9
1876	38	RUTHERFORD B. HAYES	Republican	4,036,572	185	48.0
		Samuel J. Tilden	Democrat	4,284,020	184	51.0
1880	38	JAMES A. GARFIELD	Republican	4,453,295	214	48.5
		Winfield S. Hancock	Democrat	4,414,082	155	48.1
		James B. Weaver	Greenback-Labor	308,578		3.4
1884	38	GROVER CLEVELAND	Democrat	4,879,507	219	48.5
		James G. Blaine	Republican	4,850,293	182	48.2
		Benjamin F. Butler	Greenback-Labor	175,370		1.8
		John P. St. John	Prohibition	150,369		1.5
1888	38	BENJAMIN HARRISON	Republican	5,447,129	233	47.9
		Grover Cleveland	Democrat	5,537,857	168	48.6
		Clinton B. Fisk	Prohibition	249,506		2.2
		Anson J. Streeter	Union Labor	146,935		1.3
1892	44	GROVER CLEVELAND	Democrat	5,555,426	277	46.1
		Benjamin Harrison	Republican	5,182,690	145	43.0
		James B. Weaver	People's	1,029,846	22	8.5
		John Bidwell	Prohibition	264,133		2.2
1896	45	WILLIAM McKINLEY	Republican	7,102,246	271	51.1
		William J. Bryan	Democrat	6,492,559	176	47.7
1900	45	WILLIAM McKINLEY	Republican	7,218,491	292	51.7
		William J. Bryan	Democrat; Populist	6,356,734	155	45.5
		John C. Woolley	Prohibition	208,914		1.5
1904	45	THEODORE ROOSEVELT	Republican	7,628,461	336	57.4
		Alton B. Parker	Democrat	5,084,223	140	37.6
		Eugene V. Debs	Socialist	402,283		3.0
		Silas C. Swallow	Prohibition	258,536		1.9
1908	46	WILLIAM H. TAFT	Republican	7,675,320	321	51.6
		William J. Bryan	Democrat	6,412,294	162	43.1
		Eugene V. Debs	Socialist	420,793		2.8
		Eugene W. Chafin	Prohibition	253,840		1.7

*Because of the death of Greeley, Democratic electors scattered their votes.

Year	Number of States	Candidates	Party	Popular Vote*	Electoral Vote†	Percentage of Popular Vote
1912	48	WOODROW WILSON	Democrat	6,296,547	435	41.9
		Theodore Roosevelt	Progressive	4,118,571	88	27.4
		William H. Taft	Republican	3,486,720	8	23.2
		Eugene V. Debs	Socialist	900,672		6.0
		Eugene W. Chafin	Prohibition	206,275		1.4
1916	48	WOODROW WILSON	Democrat	9,127,695	277	49.4
		Charles E. Hughes	Republican	8,533,507	254	46.2
		A. L. Benson	Socialist	585,113		3.2
		J. Frank Hanly	Prohibition	220,506		1.2
1920	48	WARREN G. HARDING	Republican	16,143,407	404	60.4
		James M. Cox	Democrat	9,130,328	127	34.2
		Eugene V. Debs	Socialist	919,799		3.4
		P. P. Christensen	Farmer-Labor	265,411		1.0
1924	48	CALVIN COOLIDGE	Republican	15,718,211	382	54.0
		John W. Davis	Democrat	8,385,283	136	28.8
		Robert M. La Follette	Progressive	4,831,289	13	16.6
1928	48	HERBERT C. HOOVER	Republican	21,391,993	444	58.2
		Alfred E. Smith	Democrat	15,016,169	87	40.9
1932	48	FRANKLIN D. ROOSEVELT	Democrat	22,809,638	472	57.4
		Herbert C. Hoover	Republican	15,758,901	59	39.7
		Norman Thomas	Socialist	881,951		2.2
1936	48	FRANKLIN D. ROOSEVELT	Democrat	27,752,869	523	60.8
		Alfred M. Landon	Republican	16,674,665	8	36.5
		William Lemke	Union	882,479		1.9
1940	48	FRANKLIN D. ROOSEVELT	Democrat	27,307,819	449	54.8
		Wendell L. Willkie	Republican	22,321,018	82	44.8
1944	48	FRANKLIN D. ROOSEVELT	Democrat	25,606,585	432	53.5
		Thomas E. Dewey	Republican	22,014,745	99	46.0
1948	48	HARRY S. TRUMAN	Democrat	24,105,812	303	49.5
		Thomas E. Dewey	Republican	21,970,065	189	45.1
		J. Strom Thurmond	States' Rights	1,169,063	39	2.4
		Henry A. Wallace	Progressive	1,157,172		2.4
1952	48	DWIGHT D. EISENHOWER	Republican	33,936,234	442	55.1
		Adlai E. Stevenson	Democrat	27,314,992	89	44.4
1956	48	DWIGHT D. EISENHOWER	Republican	35,590,472	457*	57.6
		Adlai E. Stevenson	Democrat	26,022,752	73	42.1
1960	50	JOHN F. KENNEDY	Democrat	34,227,096	303†	49.9
		Richard M. Nixon	Republican	34,108,546	219	49.6
1964	50	LYNDON B. JOHNSON	Democrat	42,676,220	486	61.3
		Barry M. Goldwater	Republican	26,860,314	52	38.5
1968	50	RICHARD M. NIXON	Republican	31,785,480	301	43.4
		Hubert H. Humphrey	Democrat	31,275,165	191	42.7
		George C. Wallace	American Independent	9,906,473	46	13.5
1972	50	RICHARD M. NIXON‡	Republican	47,165,234	520**	60.6
		George S. McGovern	Democrat	29,168,110	17	37.5

*Walter B. Jones received 1 electoral vote.
†Harry F. Byrd received 15 electoral votes.
‡Resigned August 9, 1974: Vice President Gerald R. Ford became President.
**John Hospers received 1 electoral vote.

Year	Number of States	Candidates	Party	Popular Vote*	Electoral Vote†	Percentage of Popular Vote
1976	50	JIMMY CARTER	Democrat	40,828,929	297***	50.1
		Gerald R. Ford	Republican	39,148,940	240	47.9
		Eugene McCarthy	Independent	739,256		
1980	50	RONALD REAGAN	Republican	43,201,220	489	50.9
		Jimmy Carter	Democrat	34,913,332	49	41.2
		John B. Anderson	Independent	5,581,379		
1984	50	RONALD REAGAN	Republican	53,428,357	525	59.0
		Walter F. Mondale	Democrat	36,930,923	13	41.0
1988	50	GEORGE H. W. BUSH	Republican	48,901,046	426****	53.4
		Michael Dukakis	Democrat	41,809,030	111	45.6
1992	50	BILL CLINTON	Democrat	43,728,275	370	43.2
		George Bush	Republican	38,167,416	168	37.7
		H. Ross Perot	United We Stand, America	19,237,247		19.0
1996	50	BILL CLINTON	Democrat	45,590,703	379	49.0
		Robert Dole	Republican	37,816,307	159	41.0
		H. Ross Perot	Reform	7,866,284		8.0
2000	50	GEORGE W. BUSH	Republican	50,459,624	271	47.9
		Albert Gore, Jr.	Democrat	51,003,328	266	49.4
		Ralph Nader	Green	2,882,985		2.7
2004	50	GEORGE W. BUSH	Republican	62,040,610	286*****	50.7
		John F. Kerry	Democrat	59,028,444	251	48.3
2008	50	BARACK H. OBAMA	Democrat	69,456,897	365	52.9
		John McCain	Republican	59,934,814	173	45.7
2012	50	BARACK H. OBAMA	Democrat	65,446,032	332	51.0
		Mitt Romney	Republican	60,589,084	206	47.1

***Ronald Reagan received 1 electoral vote.
****Lloyd Bentsen received 1 electoral vote.
*****John Edwards received 1 electoral vote.

abolitionist movement   A radical antislavery crusade committed to the immediate end of slavery that emerged in the three decades before the Civil War.

Act for Religious Toleration   The first law in America to call for freedom of worship for all Christians. It was enacted in Maryland in 1649 to quell disputes between Catholics and Protestants, but it failed to bring peace.

actual representation   The practice whereby elected representatives normally reside in their districts and are directly responsive to local interests.

Age of Enlightenment   Major intellectual movement occurring in Western Europe in the late seventeenth and early eighteenth centuries.

Alamo   Franciscan mission at San Antonio, Texas, that was the site in 1836 of a siege and massacre of Texans by Mexican troops.

Albany Plan of Union   Plan put forward in 1754 calling for an intercolonial union to manage defense and Indian affairs. The plan was rejected by participants at the Albany Congress.

Albany Regency   Popular name after 1820 for the state political machine in New York headed by Martin Van Buren.

Alien and Sedition Acts   Collective name given to four acts passed by Congress in 1798 that curtailed freedom of speech and the liberty of foreigners resident in the United States.

American Anti-Slavery Society   The first national organization of abolitionists, founded in 1833.

American Colonization Society   Organization, founded in 1817 by antislavery reformers, that called for gradual emancipation and the removal of freed blacks to Africa.

American Female Moral Reform Society   Organization founded in 1839 by female reformers that established homes of refuge for prostitutes and petitioned for state laws that would criminalize adultery and the seduction of women.

American system of manufacturing   A technique of production pioneered in the United States in the first half of the nineteenth century that relied on precision manufacturing with the use of interchangeable parts.

American System   The program of government subsidies favored by Henry Clay and his followers to promote American economic growth and protect domestic manufacturers from foreign competition.

American Temperance Society   National organization established in 1826 by evangelical Protestants that campaigned for total abstinence from alcohol and was successful in sharply lowering per capita consumption of alcohol.

Anglican   Of or belonging to the Church of England, a Protestant denomination.

Anglo-American Accords   Series of agreements reached in the British-American Conventions of 1818 that fixed the western boundary between the United States and Canada, allowed for joint occupation of Oregon, and restored American fishing rights.

Annapolis Convention   Conference of state delegates at Annapolis, Maryland, that issued a call in September 1786 for a convention to meet at Philadelphia in May 1787 to consider fundamental changes to the Articles of Confederation.

Antifederalist   An opponent of the Constitution in the debate over its ratification.

Anti-Masons   Third party formed in 1827 in opposition to the presumed power and influence of the Masonic order.

Appeal to the Colored Citizens of the World   An abolitionist tract by a free black calling on the enslaved to overthrow their bondage.

Articles of Confederation   Written document setting up the loose confederation of states that comprised the first national government of the United States from 1781 to 1788.

Aztecs   A warrior people who dominated the Valley of Mexico from about 1100 until their conquest in 1519–1521 by Spanish soldiers led by Hernán Cortés.

Bacon's Rebellion   Violent conflict in Virginia (1675–1676), beginning with settler attacks on Indians but culminating in a rebellion led by Nathaniel Bacon against Virginia's government.

Bank War   The political struggle between President Andrew Jackson and the supporters of the Second Bank of the United States.

Battle of New Orleans   Decisive American War of 1812 victory over British troops in January 1815 that ended any British hopes of gaining control of the lower Mississippi River Valley.

Battle of Plattsburgh   Victory of Commodore Thomas McDonough over a British fleet in Lake Champlain, September 11, 1814.

Battle of Put-in-Bay   American naval victory on Lake Erie in September 1813 in the War of 1812 that denied the British strategic control over the Great Lakes.

Battles of Lexington and Concord   The first two battles of the American Revolution, which resulted in a total of 273 British soldiers dead, wounded, and missing and nearly 100 Americans dead, wounded, and missing.

Beaver Wars   Series of bloody conflicts, occurring between the 1640s and 1680s, during which the Iroquois fought the Hurons and French for control of the fur trade in the east and the Great Lakes region.

benevolent empire   Network of reform associations affiliated with Protestant churches in the early nineteenth century dedicated to the restoration of moral order.

bill of rights   A written summary of inalienable rights and liberties.

black codes   Laws passed by states and municipalities denying many rights of citizenship to free blacks before the Civil War. Also, during the Reconstruction era, laws passed by newly elected southern state legislatures to control black labor, mobility, and employment.

Black Hawk's War   Short 1832 war in which federal troops and Illinois militia units defeated the Sauk and Fox Indians led by Black Hawk.

"Bleeding Kansas"   Violence between pro- and antislavery forces in Kansas Territory after the passage of the Kansas-Nebraska Act in 1854.

Boston Massacre   After months of increasing friction between townspeople and the British troops stationed in the city, on March 5, 1770, British troops fired on American civilians in Boston.

Boston Tea Party   Incident that occurred on December 16, 1773, in which Bostonians, disguised as Indians, destroyed £9,000 worth of tea belonging to the British East India Company in order to prevent payment of the duty on it.

British Constitution   The principles, procedures, and precedents that governed the operation of the British government.

Brook Farm   A utopian community and experimental farm established in 1841 near Boston.

Cahokia   Located near modern St. Louis, this was one of the largest urban centers created by Mississippian peoples, containing perhaps 30,000 residents in 1250.

Californios   Persons of Spanish descent living in California.

carpetbaggers   Pejorative term to describe northern transplants to the South, many of whom were Union soldiers who stayed in the South after the war.

Charles River Bridge v. Warren Bridge Supreme Court decision of 1837 that promised economic competition by ruling that the broader rights of the community took precedence over any presumed right of monopoly granted in a corporate charter.

Cherokee War Conflict (1759–1761) on the southern frontier between the Cherokee Indians and colonists from Virginia southward.

Chesapeake Incident Attack in 1807 by the British ship *Leopard* on the American ship *Chesapeake* in American territorial waters.

Church of Jesus Christ of Latter-day Saints (Mormon Church) Church founded in 1830 by Joseph Smith and based on the revelations in a sacred book he called the *Book of Mormon*.

claims clubs Groups of local settlers on the nineteenth-century frontier who banded together to prevent the price of their land claims from being bid up by outsiders at public land auctions.

Coercive Acts Legislation passed by Parliament in 1774; included the Boston Port Act, the Massachusetts Government Act, the Administration of Justice Act, and the Quartering Act of 1774.

Columbian Exchange The transatlantic exchange of plants, animals, and diseases that occurred after the first European contact with the Americas.

Committee of Safety Any of the extralegal committees that directed the revolutionary movement and carried on the functions of government at the local level in the period between the breakdown of royal authority and the establishment of regular governments.

committees of correspondence Committees formed in the colonies to keep Americans informed about British measures that would affect them.

communism A social structure based on the common ownership of property.

Compromise of 1850 The four-step compromise that admitted California as a free state, allowed the residents of the New Mexico and Utah territories to decide the slavery issue for themselves, ended the slave trade in the District of Columbia, and passed a new fugitive slave law to enforce the constitutional provision stating that a slave escaping into a free state shall be delivered back to the owner.

Compromise of 1877 The congressional settling of the 1876 election that installed Republican Rutherford B. Hayes in the White House and gave Democrats control of all state governments in the South.

Conciliatory Proposition Plan whereby Parliament would "forbear" taxation of Americans in colonies whose assemblies imposed taxes considered satisfactory by the British government.

Confederate States of America Nation proclaimed in Montgomery, Alabama, in February 1861 after the seven states of the Lower South seceded from the United States.

Congressional Reconstruction Name given to the period 1867–1870 when the Republican-dominated Congress controlled Reconstruction era policy. It is sometimes known as Radical Reconstruction, after the radical faction in the Republican Party.

Constitutional Convention Convention that met in Philadelphia in 1787 and drafted the Constitution of the United States.

Constitutional Union Party National party formed in 1860, mainly by former Whigs, that emphasized allegiance to the Union and strict enforcement of all national legislation.

Constitution of the United States The written document providing for a new central government of the United States, drawn up at the Constitutional Convention in 1787 and ratified by the states in 1788.

Continental Army The regular or professional army authorized by the Second Continental Congress and commanded by General George Washington during the Revolutionary War.

Continental Association Agreement adopted by the First Continental Congress in 1774 in response to the Coercive Acts to cut off trade with Britain until the objectionable measures were repealed.

contract theory of government The belief that government is established by human beings to protect certain rights—such as life, liberty, and property—that are theirs by natural, divinely sanctioned law and that when government protects these rights, people are obligated to obey it.

Copperheads A term Republicans applied to northern war dissenters and those suspected of aiding the Confederate cause during the Civil War.

Country (Real Whig) ideology Strain of thought first appearing in England in the late seventeenth century in response to the growth of governmental power and a national debt. Main ideas stressed the threat to personal liberty posed by a standing army and high taxes and emphasized the need for property holders to retain the right to consent to taxation.

coureurs de bois French for "woods runners," independent fur traders in New France.

covenant A formal agreement or contract.

cult of domesticity The belief that women, by virtue of their sex, should stay home as the moral guardians of family life.

culture areas Geographical regions inhabited by peoples who share similar basic patterns of subsistence and social organization.

Dartmouth College v. Woodward Supreme Court decision of 1819 that prohibited states from interfering with the privileges granted to a private corporation.

Declaration of Independence The document by which the Second Continental Congress announced and justified its decision to renounce the colonies' allegiance to the British government.

Declaration of Rights and Grievances Asserted that the Stamp Act and other taxes imposed on the colonists without their consent were unconstitutional.

Declaration of Sentiments The resolutions passed at the Seneca Falls Convention of 1848 calling for full female equality, including the right to vote.

Declaration of the Causes and Necessity of Taking Up Arms Declaration of the Second Continental Congress that Americans were ready to fight for freedom and liberty.

Declaratory Act Law passed in 1766 to accompany repeal of the Stamp Act that stated that Parliament had the authority to legislate for the colonies "in all cases whatsoever."

deism Religious orientation that rejects divine revelation and holds that the workings of nature alone reveal God's design for the universe.

Democratic Party Political party formed in the 1820s under the leadership of Andrew Jackson; favored states' rights and a limited role for the federal government, especially in economic affairs.

Denmark Vesey's Conspiracy The most carefully devised slave revolt in which rebels planned to seize control of Charleston in 1822 and escape to freedom in Haiti, a free black republic, but they were betrayed by other slaves, and thirty-five conspirators were executed.

Dominion of New England James II's failed plan of 1686 to combine eight northern colonies into a single large province, to be governed by a royal appointee with no elective assembly.

Dred Scott decision Supreme Court ruling, in a lawsuit brought by Dred Scott, a slave demanding his freedom based on his residence in a free state and a free territory with his master, that slaves could not be U.S. citizens and that Congress had no jurisdiction over slavery in the territories.

Emancipation Proclamation Decree announced by President Abraham Lincoln in September 1862 and formally issued on January 1, 1863, freeing slaves in all Confederate states still in rebellion.

Embargo Act of 1807 Act passed by Congress in 1807 prohibiting American ships from leaving for any foreign port.

empresario Agents who received a land grant from the Spanish or Mexican government in return for organizing settlements.

encomienda In the Spanish colonies, the grant to a Spanish settler of a certain number of Indian subjects, who would pay him tribute in goods and labor.

enumerated products Items produced in the colonies and enumerated in acts of Parliament that could be legally shipped from the colony of origin only to specified locations.

Era of Good Feelings The period from 1817 to 1823 in which the disappearance of the Federalists enabled the Republicans to govern in a spirit of seemingly nonpartisan harmony.

federalism The sharing of powers between the national government and the states.

Federalist A supporter of the Constitution who favored its ratification.

Field Order No. 15 Order by General William T. Sherman in January 1865 to set aside abandoned land along the southern Atlantic coast for 40-acre grants to freedmen; rescinded by President Andrew Johnson later that year.

Fifteenth Amendment Passed by Congress in 1869, guaranteed the right of American men to vote, regardless of race.

First Confiscation Act Law passed by Congress in August 1861, it liberated only those slaves who had directly assisted the Confederate war effort or whose masters were openly disloyal to the Union.

First Continental Congress Meeting of delegates from most of the colonies held in 1774 in response to the Coercive Acts. The Congress endorsed the Suffolk Resolves, adopted the Declaration of Rights and Grievances, and agreed to establish the Continental Association.

Fletcher v. Peck Supreme Court decision of 1810 that overturned a state law by ruling that it violated a legal contract.

Fort Sumter Begun in the late 1820s to protect Charleston, South Carolina, it became the center of national attention in April 1861 when President Lincoln attempted to provision federal troops at the fort, triggering a hostile response from on-shore Confederate forces, opening the Civil War.

Fourteenth Amendment Constitutional amendment passed by Congress in April 1866 incorporating some of the features of the Civil Rights Act of 1866. It prohibited states from violating the civil rights of their citizens and offered states the choice of allowing black people to vote or losing representation in Congress.

Frame of Government William Penn's 1682 plan for the government of Pennsylvania, which created a relatively weak legislature and strong executive. It also contained a provision for religious freedom.

Franco-American Accord of 1800 Settlement reached with France that brought an end to the Quasi-War and released the United States from its 1778 alliance with France.

Freedmen's Bureau Agency established by Congress in March 1865 to provide social, educational, and economic services, advice, and protection to former slaves and destitute whites; lasted seven years.

French and Indian War The last of the Anglo-French colonial wars (1754–1763) and the first in which fighting began in North America. The war ended with France's defeat.

Fugitive Slave Act Law, part of the Compromise of 1850, that required authorities in the North to assist southern slave catchers and return runaway slaves to their owners.

Fundamental Constitutions of Carolina A complex plan for organizing the colony of Carolina, drafted in 1669 by Anthony Ashley Cooper and John Locke. Its provisions included a scheme for creating a hierarchy of nobles who would own vast amounts of land and wield political power; below them would be a class of freedmen and slaves. The provisions were never implemented by the Carolina colonists.

Gabriel Prosser's Rebellion Slave revolt that failed when Gabriel Prosser, a slave preacher and blacksmith, organized a thousand slaves for an attack on Richmond, Virginia, in 1800.

gag rule Procedural rule passed in the House of Representatives that prevented discussion of antislavery petitions from 1836 to 1844.

gang system The organization and supervision of slave field hands into working teams on southern plantations.

Gibbons v. Ogden Supreme Court decision of 1824 involving coastal commerce that overturned a steamboat monopoly granted by the state of New York on the grounds that only Congress had the authority to regulate interstate commerce.

Glorious Revolution Bloodless revolt that occurred in England in 1688 when parliamentary leaders invited William of Orange, a Protestant, to assume the English throne.

Grand Settlement of 1701 Separate peace treaties negotiated by Iroquois diplomats at Montreal and Albany that marked the beginning of Iroquois neutrality in conflicts between the French and the British in North America.

Great Awakening Tremendous religious revival in colonial America striking first in the Middle Colonies and New England in the 1740s and then spreading to the southern colonies.

Great Compromise Plan proposed by Roger Sherman of Connecticut at the 1787 Constitutional Convention for creating a national bicameral legislature in which all states would be equally represented in the Senate and proportionally represented in the House.

Great League of Peace and Power Confederation of five Iroquois nations— the Mohawks, Oneidas, Onondagas, Cayugas, and Senecas— formed in the fifteenth century to diminish internal conflict and increase collective strength against their enemies.

Halfway Covenant Plan adopted in 1662 by New England clergy to deal with problem of declining church membership, allowing children of baptized parents to be baptized whether or not their parents had experienced conversion.

headright system A system of land distribution during the early colonial era that granted settlers 50 acres for themselves and another 50 acres for each "head" (or person) they brought to the colony.

Homestead Act Law passed by Congress in 1862 providing 160 acres of land free to anyone who would live on the plot and farm it for five years.

House of Burgesses The legislature of colonial Virginia. First organized in 1619, it was the first institution of representative government in the English colonies.

impressment The coercion of American sailors into the British navy.

indentured servant An individual—usually male but occasionally female—who contracted to serve a master for a period of four to seven years in return for payment of the servant's passage to America. Indentured servitude was the primary labor system in the Chesapeake colonies for most of the seventeenth century.

Independent Treasury System Fiscal arrangement first instituted by President Martin Van Buren in which the federal government kept its money in regional vaults and transacted its business entirely in hard money.

Indian Removal Act Legislation passed by Congress in 1830 that provided funds for removing and resettling eastern Indians in the West. It granted the president the authority to use force if necessary.

Intolerable Acts American term for the Coercive Acts and the Quebec Act.

Jay's Treaty Treaty with Britain negotiated in 1794 in which the United States made major concessions to avert a war over the British seizure of American ships.

John Brown's Raid New England abolitionist John Brown's ill-fated attempt to free Virginia's slaves with a raid on the federal arsenal at Harpers Ferry, Virginia, in 1859.

joint-stock company Business enterprise in which a group of stockholders pooled their money to engage in trade or to fund colonizing expeditions. Joint-stock companies participated in the founding of the Virginia, Plymouth, and Massachusetts Bay colonies.

judicial review A power implied in the Constitution that gives federal courts the right to review and determine the constitutionality of acts passed by Congress and state legislatures.

Judiciary Act of 1789 Act of Congress that implemented the judiciary clause of the Constitution by establishing the Supreme Court and a system of lower federal courts.

Kansas-Nebraska Act Law passed in 1854 creating the Kansas and Nebraska Territories but leaving the question of slavery open to residents, thereby repealing the Missouri Compromise.

King George's War The third Anglo-French war in North America (1744–1748), part of the European conflict known as the War of the Austrian Succession.

King Philip's War Conflict in New England (1675–1676) between Wampanoags, Narragansetts, and other Indian peoples against English settlers; sparked by English encroachments on native lands.

King William's War The first Anglo-French conflict in North America (1689–1697), the American phase of Europe's War of the League of Augsburg.

Know-Nothing Party Anti-immigrant party formed from the wreckage of the Whig Party and some disaffected northern Democrats in 1854.

Ku Klux Klan Perhaps the most prominent of the vigilante groups that terrorized black people in the South during Reconstruction Era, founded by Confederate veterans in 1866.

Land Grant College Act Law passed by Congress in July 1862 awarding proceeds from the sale of public lands to the states for the establishment of agricultural and mechanical (later engineering) colleges; also known as the Morrill Act, after its sponsor, Congressman Justin Morrill of Vermont.

Land Ordinance of 1785 Act passed by Congress under the Articles of Confederation that created the grid system of surveys by which all subsequent public land was made available for sale.

Lecompton Constitution Pro-slavery draft written in 1857 by Kansas territorial delegates elected under questionable circumstances; it was rejected by two governors, supported by President Buchanan, and decisively defeated by Congress.

Liberty Party The first antislavery political party, formed in 1840.

Lincoln-Douglas debates Series of debates in the 1858 Illinois senatorial campaign during which Democrat Stephen A. Douglas and Republican Abraham Lincoln staked out their differing opinions on the issue of slavery in the territories.

Lost Cause The phrase many white southerners applied to their Civil War defeat. They viewed the war as a noble cause and their defeat as only a temporary setback in the South's ultimate vindication.

Manifest Destiny Doctrine, first expressed in 1845, that the expansion of white Americans across the continent was inevitable and ordained by God.

Marbury v. Madison Supreme Court decision of 1803 that created the precedent of judicial review by ruling as unconstitutional part of the Judiciary Act of 1789.

McCulloch v. Maryland Supreme Court decision of 1819 that upheld the constitutional authority of Congress to charter a national bank, and thereby to regulate the nation's currency and finances.

mercantilism Economic system whereby the government intervenes in the economy for the purpose of increasing national wealth.

Mexican Cession of 1848 The addition of half a million square miles to the United States as a result of victory in the 1846 war between the United States and Mexico.

Middle Passage The voyage between West Africa and the New World slave colonies.

Minute Men Special companies of militia formed in Massachusetts and elsewhere beginning in late 1774.

Missouri Compromise Sectional compromise in Congress in 1820 that admitted Missouri to the Union as a slave state and Maine as a free state and prohibited slavery in the northern Louisiana Purchase territory.

Monroe Doctrine In December 1823, Monroe declared to Congress that the Americas "are henceforth not to be considered as subjects for future colonization by any European power."

nationalists Group of leaders in the 1780s who spearheaded the drive to replace the Articles of Confederation with a stronger central government.

nativist/nativism Favoring the interests and culture of native-born inhabitants over those of immigrants.

Nat Turner's Rebellion Uprising of slaves led by Nat Turner in Southampton County, Virginia, in the summer of 1831 that resulted in the death of up to sixty white people.

natural rights Political philosophy that maintains that individuals have an inherent right, found in nature and preceding any government or written law, to life and liberty.

New Harmony Short-lived utopian community established in Indiana in 1825, based on the socialist ideas of Robert Owen, a wealthy Scottish manufacturer.

New Jersey Plan Proposal of the New Jersey delegation at the 1787 Constitutional Convention for a strengthened national government in which all states would have equal representation in a unicameral legislature.

New Lights People who experienced conversion during the revivals of the Great Awakening.

New York Draft Riot A mostly Irish-immigrant protest against conscription in New York City in July 1863 that escalated into class and racial warfare that had to be quelled by federal troops.

nonimportation movement A tactical means of putting economic pressure on Britain by refusing to buy its exports in the colonies.

Northwest Ordinance of 1787 Legislation passed by Congress under the Articles of Confederation that prohibited slavery in the Northwest Territories and provided the model for the incorporation of future territories into the Union as coequal states.

nullification A constitutional doctrine holding that a state has a legal right to declare a national law null and void within its borders.

nullification crisis Sectional crisis in the early 1830s in which a states' rights party in South Carolina attempted to nullify federal law.

Olive Branch Petition A last effort for peace that avowed America's loyalty to George III and requested that he protect them from further aggressions.

Oneida Community Utopian community established in upstate New York in 1848 by John Humphrey Noyes and his followers.

Oregon Trail Overland trail of more than two thousand miles that carried American settlers from the Midwest to new settlements in Oregon, California, and Utah.

Ostend Manifesto Message sent by U.S. envoys to President Pierce from Ostend, Belgium, in 1854, stating that the United States had a "divine right" to wrest Cuba from Spain.

Panic of 1857 Banking crisis that caused a credit crunch in the North; it was less severe in the South, where high cotton prices spurred a quick recovery.

pan-Indian resistance movement Movement calling for the political and cultural unification of Indian tribes in the late eighteenth and early nineteenth centuries.

Peace of Paris Treaties signed in 1783 by Great Britain, the United States, France, Spain, and the Netherlands that ended the Revolutionary War.

Pequot War Conflict between English settlers (who had Narragansett and Mohegan allies) and Pequot Indians over control of land and trade in eastern Connecticut. The Pequots were nearly destroyed in a set of bloody confrontations, including a deadly English attack on a Mystic River village in May 1637.

Pietists Protestants who stress a religion of the heart and the spirit of Christian living.

Pilgrims Settlers of Plymouth Colony, who viewed themselves as spiritual wanderers.

Pontiac's War Indian uprising (1763–1766) led by Pontiac of the Ottawas and Neolin of the Delawares.

popular sovereignty A solution to the slavery crisis suggested by Michigan senator Lewis Cass by which territorial residents, not Congress, would decide slavery's fate.

predestination The belief that God decided at the moment of Creation which humans would achieve salvation.

Proclamation of 1763 Royal proclamation setting the boundary known as the Proclamation Line that limited British settlements to the eastern side of the Appalachian Mountains.

proprietary colony A colony created when the English monarch granted a huge tract of land to an individual or group of individuals, who became "lords proprietor." Many lords proprietor had distinct social visions for their colonies, but these plans were hardly ever implemented. Examples of proprietary colonies are Maryland, Carolina, New York (after it was seized from the Dutch), and Pennsylvania.

Protestants Europeans who supported reform of the Catholic Church in the wake of Martin Luther's critique of church practices and doctrines.

Pueblo Revolt Rebellion in 1680 of Pueblo Indians in New Mexico against their Spanish overlords, sparked by religious conflict and excessive Spanish demands for tribute.

Puritans Individuals who believed that Queen Elizabeth's reforms of the Church of England had not gone far enough in improving the church, particularly in ensuring that church members were among the saved. Puritans led the settlement of Massachusetts Bay Colony.

putting-out system System of manufacturing in which merchants furnished households with raw materials for processing by family members.

Quakers Members of the Society of Friends, a radical religious group that arose in the mid-seventeenth century. Quakers rejected formal theology and an educated ministry, focusing instead on the importance of the "Inner Light," or Holy Spirit that dwelt within them. Quakers were important in the founding of Pennsylvania.

Quartering Acts Acts of Parliament requiring colonial legislatures to provide supplies and quarters for the troops stationed in America.

Quasi-War Undeclared naval war of 1797 to 1800 between the United States and France.

Quebec Act Law passed by Parliament in 1774 that provided an appointed government for Canada, enlarged the boundaries of Quebec, and confirmed the privileges of the Catholic Church.

Queen Anne's War   American phase (1702–1713) of Europe's War of the Spanish Succession.

Radical Republicans   A shifting group of Republican congressmen, usually a substantial minority, who favored the abolition of slavery from the beginning of the Civil War and later advocated harsh treatment of the defeated South.

reconquista   The long struggle (ending in 1492) during which Spanish Christians reconquered the Iberian Peninsula from Muslim occupiers, who first invaded in the eighth century.

Redeemers   Southern Democrats who wrested control of governments in the former Confederacy from Republicans, often through electoral fraud and violence, beginning in 1870.

redemptioner   Similar to an indentured servant, except that a redemptioner signed a labor contract in America rather than in Europe.

Reformation   Sixteenth-century movement to reform the Catholic Church that ultimately led to the founding of new Protestant Christian religious groups.

Regulators   Vigilante groups active in the 1760s and 1770s in the western parts of North and South Carolina. The South Carolina Regulators attempted to rid the area of outlaws; the North Carolina Regulators were more concerned with high taxes and court costs.

repartimiento   In the Spanish colonies, the assignment of Indian workers to labor on public works projects.

republicanism   The idea that governments must exercise power, but simultaneously cautioning that power could easily overwhelm liberty.

Republican   Party headed by Thomas Jefferson that formed in opposition to the financial and diplomatic policies of the Federalist Party; favored limiting the powers of the national government and placing the interests of farmers and planters over those of financial and commercial groups.

Republican Party   Party that emerged in the 1850s in the aftermath of the bitter controversy over the Kansas-Nebraska Act, consisting of former Whigs, some northern Democrats, and many Know-Nothings.

republican   Used to describe a theory derived from the political ideas of classical antiquity, Renaissance Europe, and early modern England. Republicanism held that self-government by the citizens of a country, or their representatives, provided a more reliable foundation for the good society and individual freedom than rule by kings. The character of republican government depended on the virtue of the people, but the nature of republican virtue and the conditions favorable to it became sources of debate that influenced the writing of the state and federal constitutions as well as the development of political parties.

Rhode Island system   During the industrialization of the early nineteenth century, the recruitment of entire families for employment in a factory.

Rush-Bagot Agreement   Treaty of 1817 between the United States and Britain that effectively demilitarized the Great Lakes by sharply limiting the number of ships each power could station on them.

Sabbatarian movement   Reform organization founded in 1828 by Congregationalist and Presbyterian ministers that lobbied for an end to the delivery of mail on Sundays and other Sabbath violations.

Santa Fe Trail   The 900-mile trail opened by American merchants for trading purposes following Mexico's liberalization of the formerly restrictive trading policies of Spain.

scalawags   Southern whites, mainly small landowning farmers and well-off merchants and planters, who supported the southern Republican Party during Reconstruction for diverse reasons; a disparaging term.

Second Bank of the United States   A national bank chartered by Congress in 1816 with extensive regulatory powers over currency and credit.

Second Confiscation Act   Law passed by Congress in July 1862 giving Union commanders the right to seize slave property as their armies marched through Confederate territory.

Second Continental Congress   Convened in Philadelphia on May 10, 1775, the Second Continental Congress called for the patchwork of local forces to be organized into the Continental Army, authorized the formation of a navy, established a post office, and printed paper continental dollars to meet its expenses.

Second Great Awakening   Series of religious revivals in the first half of the nineteenth century characterized by great emotionalism in large public meetings.

second party system   The national two-party competition between Democrats and Whigs from the 1830s through the early 1850s.

Seneca Falls Convention   The first convention for women's equality in legal rights, held in upstate New York in 1848.

separatists   Members of an offshoot branch of Puritanism. Separatists believed that the Church of England was too corrupt to be reformed and hence were convinced that they must "separate" from it to save their souls. Separatists helped found Plymouth Colony.

Shakers   The followers of Mother Ann Lee, who preached a religion of strict celibacy and communal living.

sharecropping   Labor system that evolved during and after Reconstruction whereby landowners furnished laborers with a house, farm animals, and tools and advanced credit in exchange for a share of the laborers' crop.

Shays's Rebellion   An armed movement of debt-ridden farmers in western Massachusetts in the winter of 1786–1787. The rebellion shut down courts and created a crisis atmosphere, strengthening the case of nationalists that a stronger central government was needed to maintain civil order in the states.

Slaughterhouse cases   Group of cases resulting in one sweeping decision by the U.S. Supreme Court in 1873 that contradicted the intent of the Fourteenth Amendment by decreeing that most citizenship rights remained under state, not federal, control.

slave codes   Sometimes known as "black codes." A series of laws passed mainly in the southern colonies in the late seventeenth and early eighteenth centuries to define the status of slaves and codify the denial of basic civil rights to them. Also, after American independence and before the Civil War, state laws in the South defining slaves as property and specifying the legal powers of masters over slaves.

Slave Power   A key concept in abolitionist and northern antislavery propaganda that depicted southern slaveholders as the driving force in a political conspiracy to promote slavery at the expense of white liberties.

socialism   A social order based on government ownership of industry and worker control over corporations as a way to prevent worker exploitation.

Songhai Empire   A powerful West African state that flourished between 1450 and 1591, when it fell to a Moroccan invasion.

Sons of Liberty   Secret organizations in the colonies formed to oppose the Stamp Act.

Southern Homestead Act   Largely unsuccessful law passed in 1866 that gave black people preferential access to public lands in five southern states.

Southwest Ordinance of 1790   Legislation passed by Congress that set up a government with no prohibition on slavery in U.S. territory south of the Ohio River.

sovereignty   The supreme authority of the state, including both the right to take life (as in the case of executions for capital crimes) and to tax.

Specie Circular   Proclamation issued by President Andrew Jackson in 1836 stipulating that only gold or silver could be used as payment for public land.

spoils system   The awarding of government jobs to party loyalists.

Stamp Act Congress   October 1765 meeting of delegates sent by nine colonies, which adopted the Declaration of Rights and Grievances and petitioned against the Stamp Act.

Stamp Act   Law passed by Parliament in 1765 to raise revenue in America by requiring taxed, stamped paper for legal documents, publications, and playing cards.

states' rights   Favoring the rights of individual states over rights claimed by the national government.

Stono Rebellion   Uprising in 1739 of South Carolina slaves against whites; inspired in part by Spanish officials' promise of freedom for American slaves who escaped to Florida.

Suffolk Resolves   Militant resolves adopted in 1774 in response to the Coercive Acts by representatives from the towns in Suffolk County, Massachusetts, including Boston.

suffrage   The right to vote in a political election.

Sugar Act   Law passed in 1764 to raise revenue in the American colonies. It lowered the duty from six pence to three pence per gallon on foreign molasses imported into the colonies and increased the restrictions on colonial commerce.

Tariff Act of 1789   The first national tariff was designed primarily to raise revenue and not to protect home industries.

Tea Act of 1773   Permitted the East India Company to sell through agents in America without paying the duty customarily collected in Britain, thus reducing the retail price.

Tejanos   A person of Spanish or Mexican descent born in Texas.

temperance   Reform movement originating in the 1820s that sought to eliminate the consumption of alcohol.

Tenure of Office Act   Passed by the Republican-controlled Congress in 1867 to limit presidential interference with its policies, the act prohibited the president from removing certain officeholders without the Senate's consent. President Andrew Johnson, angered at what he believed to be an unconstitutional attack on presidential authority, deliberately violated the act by firing Secretary of War Edwin M. Stanton. The House responded by approving articles of impeachment against a president for the first time in American history.

Thirteenth Amendment   Constitutional amendment ratified in 1865 that freed all slaves throughout the United States.

Tories   A derisive term applied to loyalists in America who supported the king and Parliament just before and during the American Revolution.

Townshend Duty Act of 1767   Imposed duties on colonial tea, lead, paint, paper, and glass.

Trail of Tears   The forced march in 1838 of the Cherokee Indians from their homelands in Georgia to the Indian Territory in the West; thousands of Cherokees died along the way.

transcendentalism   A philosophical and literary movement centered on an idealistic belief in the divinity of individuals and nature.

Trans-Continental Treaty of 1819   Treaty between the United States and Spain in which Spain ceded Florida to the United States, surrendered all claims to the Pacific Northwest, and agreed to a boundary between the Louisiana Purchase territory and the Spanish Southwest.

transportation revolution   Dramatic improvements in transportation that stimulated economic growth after 1815 by expanding the range of travel and reducing the time and cost of moving goods and people.

Treaty of Ghent   Treaty signed in December 1814 between the United States and Britain that ended the War of 1812.

Treaty of Greenville   Treaty of 1795 in which Native Americans in the Old Northwest were forced to cede most of the present state of Ohio to the United States.

Treaty of Lancaster   Negotiation in 1744 whereby Iroquois chiefs sold Virginia land speculators the right to trade at the Forks of the Ohio.

Treaty of Paris   The formal end to British hostilities against France and Spain in February 1763.

Treaty of San Lorenzo   Treaty with Spain in 1795 in which Spain recognized the 31st parallel as the boundary between the United States and Spanish Florida.

Treaty of Tordesillas   Treaty negotiated by the pope in 1494 to resolve the territorial claims of Spain and Portugal. It drew a north–south line approximately 1,100 miles west of the Cape Verde Islands, granting all lands west of the line to Spain and all lands east of the line to Portugal. This limited Portugal's New World empire to Brazil but confirmed its claims in Africa and Asia.

Underground Railroad   Support system set up by antislavery groups in the Upper South and the North to assist fugitive slaves in escaping the South.

Union League   A Republican Party organization in northern cities that became an important organizing device among freedmen in southern cities after 1865.

United States v. Cruikshank   Supreme Court ruling of 1876 that overturned the convictions of some of those responsible for the Colfax Massacre, ruling that the Enforcement Act applied only to violations of black rights by states, not individuals.

Valley Forge   Area of Pennsylvania approximately 20 miles northwest of Philadelphia where General George Washington's Continental troops were quartered from December 1777 to June 1778 while British forces occupied Philadelphia during the Revolutionary War.

Virginia Plan   Proposal of the Virginia delegation at the 1787 Constitutional Convention calling for a national legislature in which the states would be represented according to population. The national legislature would have the explicit power to veto or overrule laws passed by state legislatures.

virtual representation   The notion that parliamentary members represented the interests of the nation as a whole, not those of the particular district that elected them.

Waltham system   During the industrialization of the early nineteenth century, the recruitment of unmarried young women for employment in factories.

War Hawks   Members of Congress, predominantly from the South and West, who aggressively pushed for a war against Britain after their election in 1810.

War of 1812   War fought between the United States and Britain from June 1812 to January 1815 largely over British restrictions on American shipping.

Webster–Ashburton Treaty   Treaty signed by the United States and Britain in 1842 that settled a boundary dispute between Maine and Canada and provided for closer cooperation in suppressing the African slave trade.

Whig Party   Political party, formed in the mid-1830s in opposition to the Jacksonian Democrats, that favored a strong role for the national government in promoting economic growth.

Whigs   The name used by advocates of colonial resistance to British measures during the 1760s and 1770s.

Whiskey Rebellion   Armed uprising in 1794 by farmers in western Pennsylvania who attempted to prevent the collection of the excise tax on whiskey.

Wilmot Proviso   The amendment offered by Pennsylvania Democrat David Wilmot in 1846 which stipulated that "as an express and fundamental condition to the acquisition of any territory from the Republic of Mexico … neither slavery nor involuntary servitude shall ever exist in any part of said territory."

workingmen's movement   Associations of urban workers who began campaigning in the 1820s for free public education and a 10-hour workday.

XYZ Affair   Diplomatic incident in 1798 in which Americans were outraged by the demand of the French for a bribe as a condition for negotiating with American diplomats.

Credits

C-1

Index